Y0-CZQ-361

CONSUMERGUIDE®

COMPLETE GUIDE TO

USED CARS

2004 EDITION

CONTENTS

CONTENTS

CONTENTS

CONTENTS

CONTENTS

CONTENTS

CONTENTS

HOW TO USE THIS BOOK

Complete Guide to Used Cars is designed to help you select a suitable vehicle and buy it for the right price. Inside, you'll find reports on nearly 300 vehicles—from subcompact cars to full-size pickups.

The Buying Guide section covers used cars, minivans, pickup trucks, and sport-utility vehicles from 1990 to 2003. Vehicles are listed alphabetically according to make (Buick, Ford, etc.), then by model (Accord, Civic, etc.), and finally in ascending year order. The years are grouped so that the entire generation of a vehicle is listed in one report.

Because of space limitations, we are unable to list every vehicle available in this edition. We selected the most popular used cars and trucks, but if you can't find the vehicle you are looking for, we invite you to visit our Web site for a comprehensive listing. The Web address is the following: http://used.consumerguide.com.

At the top of each listing is a **Photo** of the covered vehicle. Though the picture may be of a 4-door body style, the report covers all models listed for those years.

Vehicle Details lists important facts about the car or truck. The *Class* will help you compare one vehicle with another. *Built in* lists the country of final assembly.

Best Buys As might be expected, not all used vehicles are created equal—some are better buys than others. A CG Best Buy is a solid used-car and one of the best values in its class. We base our Best Buy rating first and foremost on the vehicle itself and how well it does its job. We also consider factors like reliability, ownership cost, and utility.

Pro and Con points are not necessarily the only good or bad points of that particular vehicle; just the most pronounced.

The **Evaluation** section provides performance, fuel economy, and passenger/cargo space information. Our auto editors discuss how the vehicle accelerates, rides, and handles, and may warn of major service problems. In short, the Evaluation section lets you know what that vehicle would be like to live with on a daily basis.

Value for the Money gives you a quick overview of how the vehicle stacks up against others in the class and as a used-car purchase.

Trouble Spots lists the most common problems for each vehicle. We also list the manufacturer's solutions for these problems if one exists.

The **Average Replacement Costs** table lists the costs of likely repairs—things like air conditioning, brakes, and transmission repairs. The dollar amount listed includes the cost of the part(s) and labor for the average repair. Replacement costs can vary widely depending on region. These are ballpark figures and are most helpful in determining if one particular vehicle costs more to repair than another. It is quite possible that an actual repair will cost considerably more.

NHTSA Recall History lists major U.S. Government-mandated recalls for each vehicle. Not all recalls issued by NHTSA may be listed. Since manufacturers are not required to fix recall defects free of charge after an eight-year period, minor defects or problems that would be apparent immediately, have been omitted. To obtain a complete list of recalls for the vehicle you intend to buy visit them on the Web at http://www.nhtsa.gov.

Finally, our **Prices** detail a range of average prices in year-by-year listings, for vehicles in three condition levels: **Good**—a clean, low-mileage, solid-running vehicle that needs little or no repair. **Average**—a car with normal miles on the odometer, perhaps a few scrapes or dings; engine might need a minor repair or two, but runs acceptably well. **Poor**—might have potentially dangerous problems with the engine and/or body, or abnormally high mileage; definitely in need of mechanical attention. Valuations reflect wholesale prices paid by dealers at auction and retail prices on used-car lots. Each range covers all trim levels and engine types for a vehicle with a typical amount of equipment—usually an automatic transmission, air conditioning, stereo, etc. Fully loaded vehicles may cost more. Keep in mind that these are guidelines only.

Thank you for choosing Consumer Guide® as your automotive information source. We welcome your comments. Feel free to write us at:

Used Car & Truck Book, Consumer Guide, 7373 N. Cicero Avenue, Lincolnwood, IL 60712. You can also send an email to: info@consumerguide.com, Subject: Auto Editors.

1997-99 ACURA CL

CLASS: Near-luxury car
BUILT IN: USA
PROS: Acceleration (3.0CL)
• Ride • Steering/handling
CONS: Acceleration (4-cylinder w/automatic)
• Automatic-transmission performance

EVALUATION: Styling is unique; but inside, the CL coupe looks, feels, and behaves like a more robust, better-appointed Accord. Also like the Accord, handling is poised and sporty, while the ride is firm but comfortably absorbent. Because of its bigger tires, however, the CL does feel more athletic than an Accord. Both CL engines run smoothly, but the 4-cylinder version performs best with manual shift. With an automatic transmission, it loses energy. A 2.2CL with the 5-speed accelerated to 60 mph in 9.5 seconds—passable, but no powerhouse. Gas mileage was a bonus, however, averaging an impressive 22.2 mpg overall. The 2.3-liter engine installed in 1998 is about as quick and efficient as the initial 2.2-liter. With automatic, acceleration ranks only as adequate. In contrast, the 3.0-liter V6 delivers brisk acceleration. Unfortunately, with either engine the automatic transmission tends to shift with a bothersome jolt when pushing hard on the gas. In addition, the transmission sometimes seems almost confused about which gear to be in during stop-and-go driving. Four adults sit in reasonable comfort, which is a bonus for a sporty coupe. Of course, the interior is typical Acura/Honda, which means a comfortable driving position, unobstructed visibility, and simple, convenient instruments and controls. The power driver's seat in a 3.0CL automatically moves fore and aft to ease rear entry/exit, and it can sense obstructions and reverse direction as needed. Cargo space ranks as more than adequate, but there's only a pass-through opening to the trunk, not a folding rear seatback. Workmanship is top-notch, as expected from Honda's premium brand. This coupe feels robust even on rough roads and displays good detail finish.

VALUE FOR THE MONEY: All told, this is a competent, pleasant, and well-constructed coupe, marred only by unsatisfying operation of the automatic transmission. However, most of the CL's virtues are also available in the appealing but less-costly Honda Accord. That's no surprise, since the cars share a number of components.

TROUBLE SPOTS

Gauges: The tachometer needle fluctuates, and the "D4" light blinks due to a problem with the transmission control module (TCM) that is, in most cases, replaced under goodwill. (1997)

Mirrors: Fluttering or whistling noises come from the outside mirrors due to a faulty run channel that must be replaced. (1997)

Seat: The power seat may not move properly because the synchronizer cable comes loose from the seat. (1997)

Seat: The front passenger seat may not move forward when the access lever is pulled because the rear seat access cable comes loose. (1997)

Speedometer: The indicated speed (on the speedometer) and true speed may not jibe. Speedometers were being replaced under extended warranty. (1997)

Sunroof/moonroof: The moonroof seal may pop out when the roof is opened. (1997)

Windows: The windows rattle when partially open due to a problem with the guide pin and rear channel. (1997-98)

AVERAGE REPLACEMENT COSTS

A/C Compressor	$775	CV Joints	$855
Alternator	365	Exhaust System	360
Automatic Trans.	950	Radiator	515
Brakes	190	Shocks and/or Struts	430
Clutch	715	Timing Chain/Belt	235

NHTSA RECALL HISTORY

1997-98: Ball joints on certain cars could wear out prematurely and, in worst case, separate and cause front suspension to collapse. **1997-98:** Electrical contacts in the ignition switch can degrade due to the high electrical current that passes through the switch at startup. **1997-99:** Ignition-switch wear may lead to failure of interlock, making it possible to remove key without shifting into "Park." **1998:** Irregularity in transmission cover can limit movement of parking pawl actuation lever and prevent adequate engagement; car could roll down an incline while transmission is in "Park."

PRICES

	Good	Average	Poor
1997 2.2CL	$6,000-6,800	$5,200-5,900	$2,500-2,900
3.0CL	7,000-8,000	6,200-7,100	3,400-3,800
1998 2.3CL	8,000-9,000	7,200-8,100	4,100-4,600
3.0CL	9,000-10,000	8,100-9,000	4,700-5,200
1999 2.3CL	11,000-12,000	9,900-10,800	5,900-6,500
3.0CL	12,200-13,200	11,000-11,900	6,800-7,400

For detailed information on this vehicle visit
http://used.consumerguide.com and enter code **2254**

2001-03 ACURA CL

CLASS: Near-luxury car

BUILT IN: USA

PROS: Acceleration • Build quality • Steering/handling

CONS: Navigation-system controls • Rear-seat entry/exit • Rear-seat head room

EVALUATION: While the second-generation CL maintains solid near-luxury credentials, it's noticeably sportier than previous models. Each version is predictable, crisp, and responsive.

A Type-S with automatic ran 0-60 mph in just 6.7 seconds, and showed equally strong highway passing power. Add quick steering, fine grip and

ACURA

cornering balance, plus a stable high-speed ride, and the Type-S rivals most any competitor for dynamic ability—including the vaunted BMW 3-Series.

The base model is a shade tamer, but still boasts sure acceleration (0-60 in under 8 seconds) and confident road manners. Automatic transmissions in either model can be slightly indecisive in mountain driving, but otherwise smooth and alert, shifting promptly and without jolting. The six-speed's narrow gates can confuse gear selection in quick shifting.

Acura recommends premium fuel for both models. As for economy, new Type-S coupes averaged 19.5 to 23 mpg, while base models returned 19.3 to 24.5 mpg and a manual-shift Type-S scored 23.3 mpg.

Not an all-around athlete, the CL produces too much noseplow and tire scrubbing in aggressive cornering. A Type-S can suffer torque steer, too, under full-throttle bursts.

Either CL is taut but comfortable riding over broken surfaces, though lower-profile tires and a firmer suspension make the Type-S jiggle a bit on washboards and expansion joints. Tire roar intrudes on coarse pavement, and Type-S tire slap annoys on patchy surfaces. Wind noise is minimal, and refined engines emit a pleasant, muted snarl under hard throttle. Braking is swift, stable, confident, and easy to modulate, with little nosedive in panic stops.

Carefully assembled from classy materials, the CL cabin is rare among coupes for being airy and roomy (at least in front). Thin roof pillars and a low-cowl dashboard provide terrific visibility, though less so to the rear. Front bucket seats are well-shaped, comfortable and supportive, with plenty of leg and shoulder space; only tall folks may lack headroom.

In back is bucket-type seating for two, but only preteens will agree to ride there for long. Front entry/exit is no problem, but rear access is typical coupe crouch-and-crawl.

Because the CL uses the well-designed TL dashboard, standard climate controls are a stretch for drivers with shorter arms. The optional navigation system governs some climate and audio functions, but it's less distracting than some.

Interior storage is good, but cupholders are shallow. The roomy trunk features a knee-high liftover and a pass-through portal, but fold-down seatbacks are not available and sickle-shaped hinges steal cargo space.

VALUE FOR THE MONEY: Acura's prior CL seemed like little more than a restyled two-door Honda Accord. This one has a sportier personality that should satisfy demanding drivers. While lacking the agility of a BMW 3-Series, it appeals for brisk acceleration and adept ride/handling balance. Well-equipped when new, CLs make few concessions to pricier European coupes in performance, comfort, or quality.

TROUBLE SPOTS

Battery: The fan(s) for the radiator and/or air-conditioning condenser may run continuously and kill the battery. Both fan relays require replacement. (2001)

Clutch: The clutch master cylinder may leak into the passenger compartment and should be replaced. (2001)

Engine stalling: Vehicle may stall or be hard to start after sitting 15-20 minutes, especially during warm spells in colder weather where winter-blended fuel is sold. Replacing the fuel-pressure regulator and powertrain computer should fix it. (2001)

Oil leak: Oil leaks due to aluminum-engine porosity require patching and/or installation of special sealing bolts for the timing-belt adjuster pulley, motor-mount bracket, and transmission-mounting bolts. (2001-02)

Windshield washer: The tubing for the windshield washers deteriorates, causing wiper smearing. The tubing and wipers require replacement. (2001)

AVERAGE REPLACEMENT COSTS

A/C Compressor	$805	Exhaust System	$950
Alternator	355	Radiator	610
Automatic Trans.	2,350	Shocks and/or Struts	2,495
Brakes	495	Timing Chain/Belt	400
CV Joints	820		

NHTSA RECALL HISTORY

2003: Water pump timing-belt-tensioner pulley might be misaligned and could cause timing belt to fail, resulting in engine stalling. Dealers will inspect water pump and replace pump and timing belt if necessary.

PRICES	Good	Average	Poor
2001 3.2 CL	$17,000-18,000	$15,600-16,600	$10,900-11,500
3.2 CL Type-S	18,500-19,500	17,000-17,900	11,800-12,500
2002 3.2 CL	19,000-20,000	17,500-18,400	12,400-13,000
3.2 CL Type-S	20,500-22,000	18,900-20,200	13,300-14,300
2003 3.2 CL	22,000-23,500	20,200-21,600	14,300-15,300
3.2 CL Type-S	24,000-25,500	22,300-23,700	15,600-16,600

For detailed information on this vehicle visit
http://used.consumerguide.com and enter code **4486**

1994-01 ACURA INTEGRA

CG BEST BUY

CLASS: Sporty coupe

BUILT IN: Japan

PROS: Acceleration (5-speed models) • Antilock brakes (LS, GS-R) • Fuel economy • Roadholding • Steering/handling

CONS: Acceleration (w/automatic transmission) • No antilock brakes (RS) • Tire noise • Rear-seat room

EVALUATION: Integra engines rev like crazy, but lack enough low-end torque to perform with much zest with the automatic transmission. All Integras are swift with the 5-speed. When equipped with the automatic, progress slows considerably and the transmission constantly shifts between gears. Fuel economy is great. Our test LS averaged nearly 25 mpg in city/freeway driving, and a

ACURA

GS-R yielded an even more frugal 28.3 mpg. Both engines generate lots of noise at higher speeds, but cruise quietly. Tire hum is evident on all but mirror-smooth surfaces. Each Integra corners adeptly, with a bit less body lean than before and almost no front-drive "plowing," helped by sharp steering. The ride is slightly smoother than before, and the car's overall "feel" stouter. However, hatchbacks in particular still tend to bounce and jiggle on freeways, due in part to their shorter wheelbase. If you're fortunate enough to get your hands on a 1997 or '98 "Type-R" Integra, or the revived 2000 edition, you'll be in for the ride of your life. This limited-production model comes equipped with a highly modified 195-horsepower version of the 1.8-liter GS-R engine, sport-tuned suspension, and meaty 195/55VR/15 tires. Expect brisk acceleration, in the mid-6s. Built for performance, the Type-R omits some creature comforts (A/C for instance) and sound insulation to lose weight. Consequently, expect a noisier and bouncier ride than you get in other Integra models. Passenger space in the hatchback models isn't as good as in the Honda Civic hatchback. Medium-size people will fit fine up front, but only preteens are welcome in back. Because of its longer wheelbase, the sedan is roomier and more practical for buyers who often carry more than one passenger. Cargo room in the coupe is unexceptional. The glovebox offers scant space for anything other than the owner's manual. You can expect fine interior ergonomics and gauges in a typical Honda/Acura dashboard.

VALUE FOR THE MONEY: Any Integra should be reliable, but high resale value means they're not cheap secondhand. A Honda Civic actually offers many of the Integra's appealing features, at a considerably lower price.

TROUBLE SPOTS

Air conditioner: The air conditioner may stop working because the drive belt has come off the pulley. (1994-01)

Trunk latch: The rear hatch may be hard to close because the rubber stops are too tall. (1994-95)

AVERAGE REPLACEMENT COSTS

A/C Compressor	$530	CV Joints	$480
Alternator	420	Exhaust System	505
Automatic Trans.	895	Radiator	380
Brakes	195	Shocks and/or Struts	620
Clutch	580	Timing Chain/Belt	255

NHTSA RECALL HISTORY

1994: Retaining clip at automatic transmission can come off, so position of lever does not match actual transmission gear range. **2001:** Passenger-airbag module may not have been properly welded and may not deploy in a collision.

PRICES

	Good	Average	Poor
1994 Integra GS-R	$5,200-5,800	$4,400-4,900	$2,100-2,300
Integra RS, LS	4,000-5,200	3,300-4,300	1,300-1,700
1995 Integra GS-R	6,200-7,000	5,400-6,100	2,700-3,000
Integra LS, SE	5,100-6,200	4,300-5,300	2,000-2,500
Integra RS	4,600-5,400	3,800-4,500	1,700-2,000

1996 Integra GS-R	$7,200-8,000	$6,400-7,100	$3,500-3,900
Integra LS, SE	6,200-7,200	5,400-6,300	2,700-3,100
Integra RS	5,200-5,900	4,400-5,000	2,100-2,400
1997 Integra GS-R	8,200-9,000	7,400-8,100	4,200-4,600
Integra LS, GS	6,800-7,800	6,100-6,900	3,200-3,700
Integra RS	5,800-6,600	5,000-5,700	2,400-2,800
Type-R Coupe	10,000-11,000	9,000-9,900	5,200-5,700
1998 Integra GS-R	9,500-10,300	8,600-9,300	4,900-5,400
Integra LS, GS	8,200-9,500	7,400-8,600	4,200-4,800
Integra RS	7,000-7,800	6,200-6,900	3,400-3,700
Type-R Coupe	11,500-12,500	10,400-11,300	6,300-6,900
1999 Integra GS-R	10,800-11,800	9,700-10,600	5,800-6,400
Integra LS, GS	9,000-10,500	8,100-9,500	4,700-5,500
2000 Integra GS-R	12,500-13,500	11,300-12,200	7,100-7,700
Integra LS, GS	10,800-12,200	9,700-11,000	5,800-6,600
Type-R Coupe	15,000-16,000	13,700-14,600	9,500-10,100
2001 Integra GS-R	14,200-15,200	12,900-13,800	8,700-9,300
Integra LS, GS	12,500-14,000	11,300-12,600	7,100-8,000
Type-R Coupe	17,000-18,000	15,600-16,600	10,900-11,500

For detailed information on this vehicle visit
http://used.consumerguide.com and enter code **1996**

1991-95 ACURA LEGEND

CLASS: Near-luxury car
BUILT IN: Japan
PROS: Acceleration
• Antilock brakes
• Instruments/controls
• Passenger and cargo room
• Steering/handling
CONS: Automatic-trans-
mission performance • Fuel
economy • Rear-seat room (coupe) • Driver seating

EVALUATION: The higher-powered V6 engine in these Legends yields quick acceleration, but gas mileage is no bonus. Our tests ranged from 16-18 mpg in urban driving to the low 20s on the highway. Despite the momentary ignition-retard setup of the automatic transmission, midrange downshifts in earlier models still border on harsh and can get rough under hard acceleration. Performance also slips quite a bit with automatic.

Ride quality is smoother and more absorbent than before. The taut ride is never harsh, but falls short of the suppleness displayed by some European rivals. Though stable, it can get harsh and abrupt over rough surfaces. Handling earns high marks, nearly like that of a sports car. Quick turns bring some body lean, but grip, balance, and control are laudable. Standard antilocking makes the brakes feel strong and secure.

Though roomier in back than before, this is still essentially a spacious 4-seater. Front-seat occupants might lack head room with the sunroof, or find that the early nontilting, telescoping steering wheel crowds one's thighs. Leg room in the coupe's back seat is scant, and long doors hamper access. Trunks are hardly huge, but have a flat floor and handy bumper-height opening. Instruments and controls are logical, with a feather-touch feel.

VALUE FOR THE MONEY: Sporty manners, copious luxury (on LS), worthy workmanship, and stout construction help the Legend rival some more costly premium automobiles—including those from Infiniti and Lexus.

TROUBLE SPOTS

Audio system: If the remote volume control doesn't work, or there is static when the remote is used, the volume control motor inside the radio is bad. (1991-92)

Cruise control: The cruise control may not engage due to a faulty actuator. (1994)

Engine noise: Carbon buildup on the piston rings may cause piston slap. The fix is to clean the carbon using GM Top Engine Cleaner sucked in by way of a vacuum port on the throttle body. (1991-95)

Glovebox: The glovebox light stays on because the switch plunger is too short, requiring an extension cap over the plunger to prevent a dead battery. (1991-92)

Poor transmission shift: Debris collects on the screen in the engine's air intake causing poor acceleration (all models) or lack of upshift (automatic transmission) at full throttle. (1991-94)

Security alarm: The security alarm may not deactivate with the key in the driver's door, which sets off the alarm. Turning the key again may disarm it. (1991-95)

Steering noise: Telescopic steering columns may groan when the wheel is turned because there is not enough lubrication on the column. (1991-95)

Steering problems: Steering may be difficult during parking maneuvers due to a problem with the vehicle speed sensor in the power steering unit. (1991-94)

Steering problems: The vehicle speed sensor (VSS) tends to fail, but a repair kit has been released so that the whole power steering assembly need not be replaced. (1991-94)

AVERAGE REPLACEMENT COSTS

A/C Compressor	$715	CV Joints	$555
Alternator	360	Exhaust System	810
Automatic Trans.	1,005	Radiator	530
Brakes	200	Shocks and/or Struts	895
Clutch	965	Timing Chain/Belt	300

NHTSA RECALL HISTORY

1991 sedan: Transmission-shift-cable bracket can be damaged and shift lever may not correctly indicate gear position. **1991-92 w/Bose audio:** A transistor in the speaker amplifier could overheat, resulting in smoke or the possibility of a fire. **1992:** Passenger-side airbag assembly in small number of cars was produced without igniter material, which would cause nondeployment or slow deployment in case of collision.

PRICES

	Good	Average	Poor
1991 Legend coupe	$4,800-5,700	$4,100-4,800	$1,900-2,200
Legend sedan	3,600-4,400	2,900-3,500	1,000-1,200

1992 Legend coupe	$5,800-6,700	$5,000-5,800	$2,400-2,800
Legend sedan	4,300-5,200	3,500-4,300	1,500-1,800
1993 Legend coupe	7,000-8,000	6,200-7,100	3,400-3,800
Legend sedan	5,300-6,500	4,600-5,600	2,200-2,700
1994 Legend coupe	8,200-9,200	7,400-8,300	4,200-4,700
Legend sedan	6,500-7,500	5,700-6,600	2,900-3,400
1995 Legend coupe	10,000-11,200	9,000-10,100	5,200-5,800
Legend sedan	8,000-9,200	7,200-8,300	4,100-4,700

For detailed information on this vehicle visit
http://used.consumerguide.com and enter code **2017**

2001-03 ACURA MDX

CLASS: Luxury sport-utility vehicle

BUILT IN: Canada

PROS: Cargo room
• Passenger room
• Refinement

CONS: Climate controls
• Fuel economy
• Navigation-system controls

EVALUATION: Coming across as a highly competent and pleasing compromise, the MDX feels more nimble than a Lexus RX 300 and lighter on its feet than a Mercedes ML, if not quite as athletic as a V8 BMW X5. Road manners are carlike and even sporty, at reasonable cornering speeds.

The suspension is firm, but not jolting, over most large bumps, furnishing a nice balance between ride comfort and handling ability—though a Lexus RX or Toyota Highlander is better at ironing out lumpy freeways. Body lean isn't excessive, particularly by SUV standards. Brakes have good stopping power, with little nosedive.

Acura's 3.5-liter V6 pulls a lot of weight here, which makes it feel weaker than its power rating implies. Even so, acceleration is lively enough for most situations, aided by the transmission's smooth, prompt downshifts. A test Touring model accelerated to 60 mph in 8.7 seconds. Fuel economy ranks slightly above the six-cylinder midsize SUV norm, but premium fuel is needed. A test MDX averaged 17.8 mpg in city/freeway driving.

Tire hum and highway wind rush are noticeable, but tolerable for an SUV. The engine is quite hushed at idle, and refined under hard acceleration.

All but the very tallest front passengers have good head and leg room in comfortable, supportive seats. The driving position is efficient, except for an awkwardly shaped left-foot dead pedal. The cabin eschews opulence for a comfortably upscale, contemporary feel.

Passengers in the second-row seat have similarly generous head room, with knee space sufficient for six-footers. It's comfortable and wide enough for three-across adult seating, although shoulders will likely rub. The third-row seat is kid-sized, yet useful. Both back seats have reclining backrests, and second-row seats slide fore/aft. Step-in isn't carlike, but it's lower than many midsize SUVs.

Cargo room is modest with a full passenger load, but numerous seat-folding options help. Flush-folding second- and third-row seats have simple one-lever latches and are easy to stow for cargo hauling.

The dashboard layout is mostly clear, logical, and handy. Controls for the automatic climate system are high in the center and don't require an attention-diverting downward look, but they're a far reach for some drivers. Also, their indicator lights and temperature display wash out in bright sunlight. Though easier to use than some, an MDX's optional navigation system can still be distracting.

VALUE FOR THE MONEY: Although the MDX was a late arrival in the SUV market, Acura did its homework and the vehicle quickly became a hot seller. An MDX is competent, comfortable, and convenient—a must-see model for near-luxury SUV shoppers. Overall refinement and generous standard equipment make MDX a fine value, new or used, though the ride can be truck-lumpy at times.

TROUBLE SPOTS

Seat: The left seat in the second row fails to fold down or slide away for third-seat access because of a loose cable. (2001)

Water leak: Water may drip almost constantly for quite a while, especially after washing the vehicle. The mirrors should be removed and a drain slot cut into them at the base. (2001)

Wipers: The nut holding the rear wiper arm comes loose, allowing the wiper to become loose. A redesigned nut must be installed. (2001)

AVERAGE REPLACEMENT COSTS

A/C Compressor	$555	Exhaust System	$550
Alternator	310	Radiator	600
Automatic Trans.	955	Shocks and/or Struts	640
Brakes	290	Timing Chain/Belt	310
CV Joints	985		

NHTSA RECALL HISTORY

2002: Water pump timing-belt-tensioner pulley might be misaligned and could cause timing belt to fail, resulting in engine stalling. Dealers will inspect water pump and replace pump and timing belt if necessary.

PRICES

	Good	Average	Poor
2001 MDX	$27,500-29,000	$25,600-27,000	$18,400-19,400
MDX Touring	29,000-30,000	27,000-27,900	20,000-20,700
2002 MDX	30,000-31,500	27,900-29,300	21,000-22,100
MDX Touring	31,500-33,000	29,300-30,700	22,100-23,100
2003 MDX	32,500-34,000	30,200-31,600	22,800-23,800
MDX Touring	34,500-36,500	32,100-33,900	24,500-25,900

For detailed information on this vehicle visit
http://used.consumerguide.com and enter code **2475**

1996-98 ACURA TL

CLASS: Near-luxury car
BUILT IN: Japan
PROS: Acceleration (3.2TL)
• Antilock brakes
• Instruments/controls
• Steering/handling • Visibility
CONS: Automatic-transmission performance • Engine noise (2.5TL) • Rear-seat room • Road noise (3.2TL)

EVALUATION: Superior in road behavior, both versions of the TL handle well and inspire confidence, helped by precise, neatly assisted steering with ample feedback, plus fine high-speed braking. Front-drive cornering is predictable, with modest body lean and good grip. With less weight up front, the 2.5TL tends to corner with a crisper feel and slightly less understeer. Each model rides well, the fully independent suspension delivering solid comfort and taut control while smoothing out the rough spots with ease. Road noise is most prominent in the 3.2TL.

The automatic transmission is slow to kick down for passing. Also, its "Grade Logic" feature sometimes drops down a gear or two, whether you want it to or not. Though generally smooth, the 5-cylinder engine gets noisy when worked hard, emitting a coarse, throaty growl. Though not a slouch, it delivers only adequate pickup. Acceleration off-the-line is a bit lethargic, but the 2.5TL passes and merges quite quickly. Somewhat lumpy at idle, it's not as smooth as the silky, quiet V6 in the 3.2TL, which promises greater performance.

Gas mileage is close to average for this league. In a mix of city, suburban, and highway driving, we managed 19.2 mpg with a 2.5TL and 18.3 mpg from the 3.2TL. Both engines demand premium gasoline, however.

Interior space overall ranks as adequate rather than generous—unexceptional for the car's size, partly as a result of the typical Acura low profile. Head room is just adequate for 6-footers. The same is true of rear leg space, though it's five inches larger than in the prior Vigor. Not every driver and passenger might be delighted with seat comfort—especially the occupant of the center rear position, who must endure a hard seat and straddle a tall tunnel. Despite the low-slung styling, a glassy greenhouse with thin pillars produces easy viewing all around. Entry/exit is easy and the driving position is accommodating, facing fine instruments and controls.

VALUE FOR THE MONEY: Although these TL sedans are well-constructed, pleasant, and better than the previous Vigor in every way, they still fail to overshadow the competition in the midluxury league.

TROUBLE SPOTS

Audio system: The grille cloth pulls loose from the tweeter (speaker). (1996)
Audio system: Radio interference is caused by the ignition coils. (1996-97)
Steering problems: Power-steering pump leaks because the pump shaft was not machined properly causing the seal to wear. (1996)
Vehicle noise: Wind noise from the moonroof. (1996)

ACURA

AVERAGE REPLACEMENT COSTS

A/C Compressor	$725	CV Joints	$810
Alternator	395	Exhaust System	610
Automatic Trans.	1,270	Radiator	445
Brakes	215	Shocks and/or Struts	995
Clutch	1,010	Timing Chain/Belt	230

NHTSA RECALL HISTORY

1996-98 3.2: Bolt can loosen and fall out, allowing transmission to disengage from differential. Not only would the vehicle lose power to drive wheels without warning, but shifting into "Park" would not lock the wheels. **1996-98:** Ball joints on certain cars could wear out prematurely and, in worst case, separate and cause front suspension to collapse.

PRICES

	Good	Average	Poor
1996 2.5TL	$6,500-7,600	$5,700-6,700	$2,900-3,400
3.2TL	7,500-8,500	6,800-7,700	3,800-4,300
1997 2.5TL	8,000-9,500	7,200-8,600	4,100-4,800
3.2TL	9,000-10,500	8,100-9,500	4,700-5,500
1998 2.5TL	10,500-12,000	9,500-10,800	5,600-6,400
3.2TL	11,800-13,000	10,600-11,700	6,600-7,300

For detailed information on this vehicle visit
http://used.consumerguide.com and enter code **2150**

1999-03 ACURA TL

CG BEST BUY

CLASS: Near-luxury car

BUILT IN: USA

PROS: Acceleration • Build quality • Exterior finish • Interior materials • Refinement • Steering/handling

CONS: Climate controls • Navigation-system controls • Road noise (Type-S)

EVALUATION: Quick, quiet, and composed, the TL is a seriously polished performer with a smooth powertrain that takes an athletic approach to luxury. Acceleration is competitive, revealed by a 0-60 time of 8.2 seconds with an early model. Added sportiness stems from the exceptionally quick-shifting automatic/manual transmission. The five-speed automatic introduced for 2000 provides more relaxed cruising than many four-speed units, and also subtly improves acceleration. Impressive road manners include unerring high-speed stability, plus terrific grip and control in turns. The downside is a ride that's much firmer than such less-nimble competitors as the ES 300 and I30. Tire rumble and slap are more prominent than most rivals, but not objectionable. The Type-S, added in 2002, offers an even firmer ride than base models, but without sacrificing comfort. It's 260-hp edition of the base TL's V6 gives it slightly better acceleration and adds only minimally to otherwise low levels of engine noise. Braking is swift and stable, but with more nosedive than expected.

The driving position is low and sporty, but accommodating, in a cabin that feels roomier and more comfortable than before. Adults can stretch out in front. Back-seaters get good head room and ample toe clearance, but only adequate leg space. Seat cushions offer unexceptional thigh support, but the driving position is set-and-forget comfortable. Gauges are large and legible, visibility unobstructed. Climate controls are far from the driver and, with the optional navigation system, inadequately sized and illuminated in an otherwise thoughtful layout. The navigation system is useful, but covers only selected U.S. population centers, and the touch screen is susceptible to fingerprints. Storage space is generous, though the trunklid hinges intrude into the cargo area.

VALUE FOR THE MONEY: Solidly built and impeccably finished, the TL equals or exceeds anything in its class for quality and utility. Its sporty nature should please the most demanding driver, though at risk of turning away entry-luxury buyers who expect Lexus-like isolation. With so many features for the price, the value-packed TL ranked as a Best Buy when new.

TROUBLE SPOTS

Fuel gauge: Some higher-sulfur gasolines can damage the fuel-gauge sending unit causing the gauge to display inaccurate readings. (1999)

Keyless entry: Certain broadcast towers interfere with the keyless entry transmitter rendering it inoperative. (1999)

Wipers: The wipers streak/smear because washer fluid deteriorates the hoses. Replacement of the hoses and wiper blades is required. (1999-2001)

AVERAGE REPLACEMENT COSTS

A/C Compressor	$720	Exhaust System	$950
Alternator	355	Radiator	610
Automatic Trans.	1,350	Shocks and/or Struts	1,495
Brakes	450	Timing Chain/Belt	400
CV Joints	820		

NHTSA RECALL HISTORY

1999: Electrical contacts in the ignition switch can degrade due to the high electrical current that passes through the switch at startup. **1999:** Ignition-switch wear may lead to failure of interlock, making it possible to remove the key without shifting into Park. **2000:** Airbags may not deploy correctly, due to improper welding. **2000-02:** Damaged vehicle may not have been repaired with the correct seatbelt buckles. **2002:** Certain driver and passenger seatbelt buckles are improperly manufactured. **2002:** Driver-side power window with "Auto Up" feature may become inoperative, operate independently of switch activation, or the auto-reverse system may not operate.

PRICES	Good	Average	Poor
1999 TL	$14,500-15,500	$13,200-14,100	$9,000-9,600
2000 TL	16,500-17,500	15,000-15,900	10,600-11,200
2001 TL	18,500-19,500	17,000-17,900	11,800-12,500

2002 TL	$21,000-22,500	$19,300-20,700	$13,700-14,600
TL Type-S	22,500-24,000	20,700-22,100	14,600-15,600
2003 TL	24,500-26,500	22,800-24,600	15,900-17,200
TL Type-S	26,000-27,500	24,200-25,600	17,200-18,200

> For detailed information on this vehicle visit
> **http://used.consumerguide.com** and enter code **2362**

1993-98 AUDI 90/CABRIOLET

CLASS: Near-luxury car
BUILT IN: Germany
PROS: Antilock brakes
• Fuel economy • Wet-weather traction (Quattro)
• Steering/handling
CONS: Acceleration (w/automatic transmission)
• Automatic-transmission performance • Rear-seat room • Road noise

EVALUATION: Though a smooth runner, and a lot zippier than its predecessor when equipped with 5-speed manual shift, the V6 Audi lags in off-the-line acceleration with 4-speed automatic. Without a doubt, the engine runs smoothly and quietly, and power delivery is very linear. However, that automatic transmission drains the engine's ability to deliver quick bursts of speed in around-town driving. The automatic also shifts rather abruptly and tends to hold each gear too long. Audi's 5-speed gearbox, on the other hand, is smooth and precise. So is the car's clutch. The V6 engine demands premium fuel, though mileage is good.

Expect plenty of tire and suspension noise on any imperfect surfaces, plus a ride that's a bit too firm on harsh urban pavements. Tar strips and small bumps do not go unnoticed, though bigger obstacles are taken in stride. Stable handling from the taut suspension imparts a secure feeling at highway speeds, with good grip in hard corners.

The dashboard layout is businesslike, with clear audio and climate controls, plus a large round speedometer and tachometer. Interiors look a bit austere in the 90 S, but CS versions with their wood accents appear somewhat dressier. Either way, the materials that are used impart an impression of quality.

Most drivers are likely to feel comfortable behind the wheel. Seats are firm and supportive, with height adjustments for the shoulder belt and lower cushion. Despite the longer wheelbase, interior dimensions are virtually identical to the previous model, but trunk space grew from 10.2 to 14.0 cubic feet, increasing its utility. Front-seat space is ample, but the rear lacks leg room, giving the interior a rather cramped ambience.

Cabriolets look great but suffer from excessive body shake and flex on bumpy roads—out of character for the car's hefty price when new (and used, too). Performance is acceptable in day-to-day driving, but the lack of low-speed power and imperfect shift action makes it feel lethargic. Front seat space is adequate for average-size adults, and head room beats most convertibles. The rear seat is useful only for children. Controls are well-positioned, but the radio has too many small, poorly marked controls. Several competitors offer a glass rear window with electric defogger, in contrast to the Cabriolet's plastic pane.

Recent models have been well-assembled. The "Audi Advantage" plan covered most routine maintenance for three years or 50,000 miles.

VALUE FOR THE MONEY: Audi's 90 had some attractive features, including a sporty manner (at least with the 5-speed), available 4-wheel drive, and solid feel. Nevertheless, it did not sell strongly in the "near-luxury" market, which was dominated by such Japanese-brand models as the Acura Vigor, Infiniti J30, Lexus ES 300, and Nissan Maxima SE. When these cars were new, dealers offered big discounts to spur sales, so expect to find lower-than-average used-car prices for all except convertibles and high-performance models.

TROUBLE SPOTS

Climate control: Intermittent climate control operation can be caused by a loose wire on the control center. (1993-94)

Cruise control: The cruise control may not maintain speed due to a defective vacuum servo unit. (1995)

Oil leak: On any model with the V6 engine, the rear main seal may leak. (1993-94)

Steering noise: A clunk from the front when the steering wheel is turned is caused by a heat shield on the left motor mount that may be striking the bracket. (1993-94)

Wipers: The wiper blades skip or jerk across the windshield, which may damage the blades or scratch the windshield. (1993-96)

AVERAGE REPLACEMENT COSTS

A/C Compressor	$1,040	CV Joints	$680
Alternator	640	Exhaust System	450
Automatic Trans.	1,220	Exhaust System	550
Brakes	300	Shocks and/or Struts	1,410
Clutch	975	Timing Chain/Belt	240

NHTSA RECALL HISTORY

1993: Some airbag sensors do not comply with Audi's durability standards. **1993-95 w/V6 engine:** Internal seal of fuel injector can malfunction, allowing fuel leakage. **1994-96:** Defective ignition switch can cause some accessories (turn signals, lamps, wipers) to malfunction when engine is started. **1995-97:** Discharge of static electricity in low humidity conditions can activate driver's airbag when driver enters or exits car.

PRICES	Good	Average	Poor
1993 90 Quattro	$4,400-5,200	$3,700-4,300	$1,500-1,800
90 sedan	3,200-4,000	2,500-3,100	800-1,000
1994 90 Quattro	5,200-6,200	4,400-5,300	2,100-2,500
90 sedan	3,800-4,600	3,100-3,700	1,100-1,400
Cabriolet	7,000-8,000	6,200-7,100	3,400-3,800
1995 90 Quattro	6,000-7,000	5,200-6,100	2,500-2,900
90 sedan	4,800-6,000	4,000-5,000	1,800-2,300
Cabriolet	$8,200-9,200	$7,400-8,300	$4,200-4,700

AUDI

1996 Cabriolet	$9,500-10,500	$8,600-9,500	$4,900-5,500
1997 Cabriolet	11,000-12,500	9,900-11,300	5,900-6,800
1998 Cabriolet	12,500-14,000	11,300-12,600	7,100-8,000

For detailed information on this vehicle visit
http://used.consumerguide.com and enter code **2152**

1996-01 AUDI A4

CLASS: Near-luxury car
BUILT IN: Germany
PROS: Optional all-wheel drive • Automatic-transmission performance • Build quality • Handling • Ride
CONS: Rear-seat room • Steering feel

EVALUATION: Despite changing little for 1996, Audi's V6 felt like a new engine when installed in the A4—smoother, quieter, and a lot more responsive. Although it's not the most potent V6 in the "near-luxury" league, it feels energetic most of the time and gets the job done nicely. Performance with the more potent dual-cam V6, installed in 1997, isn't dramatically better. Gear changes with the new 5-speed automatic transmission are so smooth that they virtually set new standards for the entire industry. Downshifts occur promptly for passing, too. Tiptronic on the 1998 and beyond models makes an already-smooth transmission even better. Best bet for the turbocharged model is manual shift, though acceleration is adequate with automatic. With either engine, the manual gearbox is easy to operate.

As for economy, an A4 1.8T Quattro yielded nearly 24 mpg on a long highway trip. On the downside, the turbo engine growls at higher speeds. Audi's Quattro all-wheel-drive system works without any driver input to provide excellent traction in slippery conditions. Still, front-drive models offer better gas mileage and have sufficient traction for most drivers.

Road noise is generally pleasing in the A4, in contrast to the old 90. However, the car's aggressive high-performance tires generate considerable sound on rough pavement. Riding smoothly on rough roads, the A4's suspension easily soaks up dips and bumps. Body lean is well-controlled in hard cornering, with good tire grip and stable handling. An optional Sport Package, with a firmer suspension and higher-performance tires, sacrifices ride comfort for a small extra measure of cornering grip and handling agility. As for negative aspects, there are mainly two: over-assisted, somewhat numb power steering, and brakes that seem touchy at first.

Passenger space is generally good, with plenty of room for large occupants up front. But tall people still don't have an abundance of leg room in back. Furthermore, head room all around is only adequate with the optional sunroof installed. Gauges and most controls are easy to see and intuitive to use, with the exception of the climate-control panel, which is too small and low for easy reading. Cargo space is good, but not great. Detail finish is superior inside and out. Interior materials are also mostly excellent.

VALUE FOR THE MONEY: Audi's A4 has sufficient merits to withstand comparison with the BMW 3-Series, Lexus ES 300, and Mercedes-Benz C-Class, putting it in good company at the low end of the premium sedan market. As for build quality, there's no more solid small sedan on the market than an A4.

TROUBLE SPOTS

Brakes: Jump starting a dead battery, or charging the battery with more than 16 volts, may blow the fuse to the ABS system. (1996)

Cruise control: The cruise control may not hold the set speed requiring replacement of the vacuum servo. (1996)

Dashboard lights: Using cheap gas can cause carbon buildup on the valves, pistons, and combustion chamber, which will cause poor idling and illuminate the check-engine light. (1996)

Dashboard lights: The check-engine light may come on with less than three gallons in the fuel tank. This can lead to a lean misfire. (1996)

Engine misfire: If the battery is disconnected, the engine may idle rough or lack power requiring recalibration of the throttle valve control module. (1997)

Fuel gauge: The fuel gauge may not register full, due to a bad electrical ground connection. (1996)

Hard starting: The engine speed (crankshaft position) sensor can come loose causing the engine to crank, but not start. (1997-98)

AVERAGE REPLACEMENT COSTS

A/C Compressor	$1,065	CV Joints	$710
Alternator	615	Exhaust System	730
Automatic Trans.	1,540	Radiator	640
Brakes	280	Shocks and/or Struts	880
Clutch	910	Timing Chain/Belt	280

NHTSA RECALL HISTORY

1996: Horn may work only intermittently, due to insufficient electrical ground contact. **1996-97:** Discharge of static electricity in low-humidity conditions can activate driver's airbag when driver enters or exits car. **1996-97:** The plastic ignition switch housing can fracture causing the ignition key to stick and making certain electrical accessories (windshield wipers, headlights) inoperative. **1997:** Rear-seatbelt retractors may not lock properly, or may not remain locked. **1997-99 w/automatic transmission:** Control valve in vacuum hose may not open or close fully at temperatures below four degrees (F) under certain conditions; could cause insufficient vacuum to be provided to brake booster. **1998:** If engine backfires during cold-start, an air screen loosely seated in airflow meter can become damaged; screen pieces could enter intake system and prevent the throttle plate from returning to its full idle position. **1998-99:** Some tie-rod seals may not seal properly; if moisture and/or dust enters swivel mechanism, bearing could wear over time.

PRICES

	Good	Average	Poor
1996 A4 2.8 sedan	$6,000-7,500	$5,200-6,500	$2,500-3,200
1997 A4 1.8T sedan	7,200-9,000	6,400-8,000	3,500-4,300
A4 2.8 sedan	8,500-10,200	7,700-9,200	4,400-5,300

AUDI

1998 A4 1.8T sedan	$8,500-10,500	$7,700-9,500	$4,400-5,500
A4 2.8 Avant wgn	11,200-13,000	10,100-11,700	6,000-7,000
A4 2.8 sedan	10,200-12,200	9,200-11,000	5,300-6,300
1999 A4 2.8 Avant wgn	13,500-14,500	12,300-13,200	8,000-8,600
A4 1.8T sedan	10,500-12,500	9,500-11,300	5,600-6,600
A4 2.8 Avant wgn	15,000-16,500	13,700-15,000	9,500-10,400
A4 2.8 sedan	12,500-14,500	11,300-13,100	7,100-8,300
2000 A4 1.8T Avant wagon	16,000-17,500	14,600-15,900	10,200-11,200
A4 1.8T sedan	12,500-14,800	11,300-13,300	7,100-8,400
A4 2.8 Avant wgn	18,000-20,000	16,600-18,400	11,500-12,800
A4 2.8 sedan	15,000-17,500	13,700-15,900	9,500-11,000
S4 sedan	23,000-24,500	21,200-22,500	15,000-15,900
2001 A4 1.8T Avant wgn	18,500-20,000	17,000-18,400	11,800-12,800
A4 1.8T sedan	14,500-17,000	13,200-15,500	9,000-10,500
A4 2.8 Avant wgn	21,000-23,000	19,300-21,200	13,700-15,000
A4 2.8 sedan	17,500-20,000	16,100-18,400	11,200-12,800
S4 sedan	26,000-27,500	24,200-25,600	17,200-18,200
S4 wagon	27,000-28,500	25,100-26,500	18,100-19,100

For detailed information on this vehicle visit
http://used.consumerguide.com and enter code **2256**

1998-03 AUDI A6/ALLROAD QUATTRO

CG BEST BUY

CLASS: Luxury car
BUILT IN: Germany
PROS: Acceleration
• Standard antilock braking
• Side airbags • Build quali-
ty • Cargo room • Exterior
finish • Interior materials
• Passenger room
• Steering/handling

CONS: Climate controls • Rear visibility

EVALUATION: Thanks to throttle recalibrations and engine tuning, overall acceleration with the base engine is satisfying. Performance is swifter yet from the A6 2.7T and A6 4.2 sedans. The continuously variable automatic transmission (CVT), available in the 3.0, sharpens throttle response at high engine speeds vs. conventional automatic. Audi claimed 0-60 mph acceleration times below 7 seconds for each of the performance editions, and we wouldn't dispute those figures. They easily rank among the faster cars in the near-luxury class. Fuel economy is good for a near-luxury car. We averaged 22.4 mpg in a front-drive sedan. Heavier weight makes the Quattro editions somewhat less frugal.

Firm steering—especially in S6 models—communicates well in turns and helps the car head effortlessly down interstates and straightaways. Few front-wheel drive midsize sedans corner with more poise or grip than an A6. The penalty is a suspension that glides over rough pavement centers, but notices nearly every small bump and tar strip, making for a "busy" ride on many surfaces. On the plus side, the ride is generally supple and quiet. Brakes are strong, with neatly progressive pedal feel. Wind noise is very slight, but tires thump and whine. Limited-production RS6 is for the hard-core performance fan only. The ride is rough, noise levels much higher, and acceleration neck-snapping.

As for the interior, the A6 cabin is a breezy, sophisticated blend of color-matched surfaces and walnut trim, joined by touches of brightwork on the dashboard, doors, and console. The sedan is roomier than competitive BMW 5-Series or Mercedes-Benz E-Class models. Occupants enjoy an abundance of head, shoulder, and leg room. In back is a supportive bench seat that promises plenty of knee clearance, toe space, and head room. The wagon's 2-place rear seat is sized for preteens. Outside mirrors are small enough to hamper lane changes, but visibility otherwise is quite good. It's even better in the glassy wagon, which also boasts good load-carrying ability. Trunk space is cavernous and easily accessible. Interior storage is also plentiful, including map pockets on every door. Workmanship and materials are top-notch throughout. Panel gaps are precise, inside and out.

VALUE FOR THE MONEY: New or used, an A6 costs a lot less than a comparable BMW 528i or Mercedes-Benz E320, yet delivers a similar sense of Teutonic solidity and driving feel. Audi's allroad wagon brings the ride and comfort of an SUV into the mix without sacrificing sophisticated onroad capability. The A6 is a well-made machine that performs admirably on the road. All told, we recommend these great German machines highly, despite their relatively high prices.

TROUBLE SPOTS

Climate control: The heated steering wheel may not heat up or may not stay warm. (1998-99)
Fuel gauge: The fuel gauge is inaccurate. (1999)
Paint/body: The front bumper is low and several owners have complained of damage on parking curbs. (1998-99)
Power seats: The driver's power seat stops working because the electronic module loses its memory. (1998)
Windshield: The windshield may leak near the top edge. (1998)

AVERAGE REPLACEMENT COSTS

A/C Compressor	$780	CV Joints	$2,310
Alternator	465	Exhaust System	775
Automatic Trans.	1,100	Radiator	670
Brakes	745	Shocks and/or Struts	1,600
Clutch	800	Timing Chain/Belt	290

NHTSA RECALL HISTORY

1998: An incorrect filler neck that doesn't match the fuel cap was installed during assembly and could allow fuel to escape. **1998:** If engine backfires during cold start, an air screen loosely seated in airflow meter can become damaged; screen pieces could enter intake system and prevent throttle plate from returning to full idle position. **1998-01:** Sulfur in fuel could cause fuel gauge to read "full" when the tank is actually less than full. **1998-99 w/Quattro:** If car is refueled shortly after engine is started, and is kept running during refueling, fuel-vapor recovery system could produce sufficient pressure to expel fuel when nozzle is removed. **1998-99 w/automatic transmission:** Control valve in vacuum hose may not open or close fully at temperatures below four degrees (F) under certain conditions; could cause insufficient vacuum to be provided to brake booster. **1998-99:** Some tie-rod seals may not seal properly; if moisture and/or dust particles enter swivel bearing mechanism, bearing could wear over time, diminishing steering control. **2001 allroad:** Under heavy load conditions, the wiper blades could become entangled with each other and cease functioning. **2003:** Driver's airbag igniter may not have been assembled properly, making the air bag ineffective in the event of a crash. Dealer will inspect and replace affected parts.

PRICES

	Good	Average	Poor
1998 A6 Avant wagon	$11,000-12,000	$9,900-10,800	$5,900-6,500
A6 Quattro Avant	13,000-14,000	11,800-12,700	7,500-8,100
A6 Quattro sedan	12,500-13,500	11,300-12,200	7,100-7,700
A6 sedan	10,500-11,500	9,500-10,400	5,600-6,100
1999 A6 Avant wagon	15,500-16,800	14,100-15,300	9,900-10,800
A6 Quattro sedan	14,500-15,800	13,200-14,400	9,000-9,800
A6 sedan	12,500-13,700	11,300-12,300	7,100-7,800
2000 A6 2.7T Quattro sedan	21,000-22,500	19,300-20,700	13,700-14,600
A6 2.8 Quattro sedan	18,500-19,800	17,000-18,200	11,800-12,700
A6 2.8 sedan	16,000-17,200	14,600-15,700	10,200-11,000
A6 4.2 Quattro sedan	26,000-28,000	24,200-26,000	17,200-18,500
A6 Avant wagon	19,500-21,000	17,900-19,300	12,700-13,700
2001 A6 2.7T Quattro sedan	25,500-27,500	23,700-25,600	16,800-18,200
A6 2.8 Quattro sedan	23,000-24,500	21,200-22,500	15,000-15,900
A6 2.8 sedan	20,500-22,000	18,900-20,200	13,300-14,300
A6 4.2 Quattro sedan	30,500-32,500	28,400-30,200	21,400-22,800
A6 Avant wagon	24,000-25,500	22,300-23,700	15,600-16,600
allroad Quattro	29,000-30,500	27,000-28,400	20,000-21,000
2002 A6 2.7T Quattro sedan	29,500-31,500	27,400-29,300	20,400-21,700
A6 3.0 Quattro sedan	27,000-29,000	25,100-27,000	18,100-19,400
A6 3.0 sedan	24,500-26,000	22,800-24,200	15,900-16,900
A6 4.2 Quattro sedan	35,000-37,000	32,600-34,400	24,900-26,300
A6 Avant wagon	28,500-30,000	26,500-27,900	19,400-20,400
S6 Avant wagon	42,000-44,000	39,500-41,400	30,700-32,100
allroad Quattro	32,000-34,000	29,800-31,600	22,400-23,800
2003 A6 2.7T Quattro sedan	35,000-37,500	32,600-34,900	24,900-26,600
A6 3.0 Quattro sedan	32,000-34,000	29,800-31,600	22,400-23,800
A6 3.0 sedan	29,500-31,500	27,400-29,300	20,400-21,700
A6 4.2 Quattro sedan	40,500-43,000	37,700-40,000	29,200-31,000
A6 Avant wagon	33,000-35,000	30,700-32,600	23,400-24,900
S6 Avant wagon	48,000-51,000	45,100-47,900	35,500-37,700
allroad Quattro	35,500-37,500	33,000-34,900	25,200-26,600

For detailed information on this vehicle visit
http://used.consumerguide.com and enter code **2293**

2000-03 AUDI TT

CLASS:
Sports car

BUILT IN:
Hungary

PROS: Available AWD
• Acceleration • Build quality • Handling/roadholding
• Interior materials

CONS: Noise • Rear-seat entry/exit • Rear-seat room
• Ride • Visibility

CG BEST BUY

EVALUATION: Racy looks are the main attraction of the TT, whether fitted with a steel or fabric roof. The 180-bhp engine is not all that quick, though 0-60 mph acceleration in 7.4 seconds certainly isn't sluggish. However, the engine needs a lot of revs for quick takeoffs and brisk passing. Gas mileage is excellent, but premium fuel is required and Quattro models burn a little more gasoline than front drivers. With the 225-bhp engine, 0-60 time drops below 7 seconds, but that engine suffers annoying "turbo lag." Handling is sharp and balanced, but the steering wheel can wiggle as the optional 17-inch performance tires travel along deep-grooved pavement. On rough surfaces, the ride can grow harsh, and noise levels are on the high side. Civilized for a sports car, the TT offers cozy (but not cramped) seating up front, but the coupe's rear seat is for parcels rather than passengers. An imaginative cabin design makes use of top-notch materials. Visibility is poor to the sides, but not bad to the rear—certainly not as restricted as the low roof and virtual "bathtub" seat position might suggest. Cargo space is good with the coupe's rear seatbacks up, and terrific when they're folded down. Although the Roadster's trunk is small in capacity, it's usefully shaped.

VALUE FOR THE MONEY: A TT offers practical sports-car fun, with a style and personality all its own. It's a bit like the New Beetle in terms of differing smartly from the automotive pack, but despite a few drawbacks, the TT delivers a truly sporty experience along with its high style.

TROUBLE SPOTS

Audio system: If the CD player and rear defogger are operated at the same time, a whining noise may come from the audio speakers. This requires a filter on the wiring harness. (2000)

Paint/body: Hoists or floor jacks may damage early production models' sill panels. Later models are built with hoist lift pads that can be retrofitted. (2000)

AVERAGE REPLACEMENT COSTS

A/C Compressor	$801	Exhaust System	$950
Alternator	785	Radiator	615
Brakes	345	Shocks and/or Struts	1,795
Clutch	855	Timing Chain/Belt	345
CV Joints	2,635		

NHTSA RECALL HISTORY

2000: In high-speed turns or abrupt lane-change maneuvers at speeds substantially above posted limits, and depending upon road conditions, precise steering response may be demanded to retain directional stability. Dealers will replace front stabilizers in front-drive cars, and front/rear stabilizers in those equipped with all-wheel drive. A modified control arm will be installed, together with firmer front/rear shock absorbers and a rear spoiler. **2000:** Small section of fuel-line assembly on small number of cars could have been damaged during production; if so, fuel could leak. **2000-01 Quattro:** Rear track-control-arm mounting bushing and bolt could corrode leading to loss of vehicle control.

PRICES

	Good	Average	Poor
2000 TT Coupe	$16,000-18,500	$14,600-16,800	$10,200-11,800
2001 TT Coupe	19,000-21,000	17,500-19,300	12,400-13,700
TT Coupe Quattro	21,500-24,000	19,800-22,100	14,000-15,600
TT Roadster	22,000-24,000	20,200-22,100	14,300-15,600
TT Roadster Quattro	25,500-27,500	23,700-25,600	16,800-18,200
2002 TT Coupe	23,000-25,000	21,200-23,000	15,000-16,300
TT Coupe Quattro	25,500-28,500	23,700-26,500	16,800-18,800
TT Roadster	25,000-27,000	23,300-25,100	16,500-17,800
TT Roadster Quattro	29,000-31,000	27,000-28,800	20,000-21,400
2003 TT Coupe	27,500-30,000	25,600-27,900	18,400-20,100
TT Coupe Quattro	30,500-33,000	28,400-30,700	21,400-23,100
TT Roadster	29,500-32,000	27,400-29,800	20,400-22,100
TT Roadster Quattro	34,000-36,500	31,600-33,900	24,100-25,900

For detailed information on this vehicle visit
http://used.consumerguide.com and enter code **2361**

1999-03 BMW 3-SERIES

CG BEST BUY

CLASS: Near-luxury car

BUILT IN: Germany

PROS: Acceleration • Head-protection system • Build quality • Exterior finish • Steering/handling

CONS: Cargo room (convertible) • Rear-seat entry/exit (coupe/convertible) • Rear-seat room (coupe/convertible) • Ride (M3)

EVALUATION: Spirited performance, great handling, high refinement, and terrific workmanship mark BMW's compact models, which mimic the feel of the German automaker's larger 5-Series cars. All versions shine for silky engines; solid on-road feel; modest noise levels; and athletic, class-leading rear-drive handling. The 2.5-liter six is a model of smoothness and performs nearly as swiftly as the 328i—which is among the segment's best-accelerating cars. A 328i accelerated to 60 mph in 7.5 seconds, and BMW claimed that the later 330i could do it in 6.4 seconds with manual shift, or 7.0 with automatic. All engines demand premium fuel, but economy is laudable. A 328i averaged 23.5 mpg. Automatic transmissions provide quick, velvety gear changes in normal mode. The sequential manual transmission that became available on M3 models in 2002 offers lightning-quick shifts, but isn't as smooth as traditional automatic or manual transmissions. BMW's forte is ride control and comfort, along with handling balance. Sport suspensions (standard on coupes) and bigger tires produce noticeably sharper grip and steering response, but don't absorb bumps as well as the base tire/suspension setups. They also yield some jiggle on rough pavement and lack grip in snow—despite traction control and antiskid systems. Interiors are cozy, with a rather narrow cabin feel. Head room is plentiful in front and adequate in back. Rear knee and foot room are tight with front seats moved fully aft. Coupe front seats automatically slide forward to ease entry to the rear, but it's still tricky.

Large climate and audio panels are easy to use. Visibility is good, except in top-up convertibles—which are impressively solid, but suffer mild body shake on rough, broken pavement. Trunk volume is unexceptional, but space is usable and the opening is large.

VALUE FOR THE MONEY: Unchallenged in sporting character, these are the true "driver's cars" of the near-luxury class. Some rivals offer more interior room, but none are more refined or as sporty. Price is the main drawback, because resale values are strong.

TROUBLE SPOTS

Engine knock: The 3.2-L (S54) engine reportedly suffers connecting-rod-bearing failures at a higher than normal rate, perhaps because some car owners are not using the required 10W-60 synthetic oil which is not readily available in the aftermarket. BMW is extending the warranty to 6 years/100,000 miles, (2001-03)

Exhaust system: BMW issued a voluntary emissions recall to replace faulty crankshaft position sensors. (1999)

Steering noise: Steering wheel buzzes or vibrates due to poor isolation of the power steering pump. (1999)

Transmission leak: Manual transmissions' drain plugs may leak. BMW also suggests replacing the fill plug. (1999)

AVERAGE REPLACEMENT COSTS

A/C Compressor	$770	CV Joints	$1,235
Alternator	640	Exhaust System	895
Automatic Trans.	810	Radiator	650
Brakes	445	Shocks and/or Struts	1,320
Clutch	725	Timing Chain/Belt	415

NHTSA RECALL HISTORY

1999 323i/328i: Retaining clip that secures brake-booster pushrod to brake-pedal arm could detach from pin, allowing pushrod to disconnect, causing

BMW

brake failure. **1999:** Side airbag system is unduly sensitive to certain noncrash impacts, such as contacting large potholes or curbs at substantial speed; could deploy without an actual side crash. Battery Safety Terminal could also activate, disconnecting starter cable from battery, so engine could not be restarted after being shut off. **2000 323i/328i:** Brake-lamp switch could fail internally, remaining either in "off" or "on" position; brake lamps would then either not operate or be continuously illuminated. **2001 315i/335i:** On some vehicles, tires could lose air suddenly, affecting vehicle control. **2001 M3:** Screws could fall into the parking-brake drum, reducing effectiveness or making screeching noises. **2001:** Failure of engine-fan motor can cause electrical circuitry to overload and fail, causing fan to stop operating, with consequent engine overheating and possible engine damage. **2002 325Xi:** There may be a crack in the rear brake rotor(s) that could expand due to braking torque, separating the brake drum from the disc. **2002 325i, 330i:** The front strut could separate from the upper mount due to an improperly installed thrust bearing. **2003 M3/330i:** Antiwindow pinching devices are not functioning properly on some vehicles. Dealer will inspect and replace all affected parts.

PRICES

	Good	Average	Poor
1999 323i convertible	$20,000-21,500	$18,400-19,800	$13,000-14,000
323i coupe/sedan	16,000-17,000	14,600-15,500	10,200-10,900
328i convertible	22,500-24,500	20,700-22,500	14,600-15,900
328i coupe/sedan	19,000-20,500	17,500-18,900	12,400-13,300
M3 convertible	27,000-29,000	25,100-27,000	18,100-19,400
M3 coupe	23,000-24,500	21,200-22,500	15,000-15,900
2000 323i convertible	23,500-25,000	21,600-23,000	15,300-16,300
323i cpe/sdn/wgn	19,000-20,500	17,500-18,900	12,400-13,300
328i coupe/sedan	22,500-24,000	20,700-22,100	14,600-15,600
2001 325i convertible	28,000-29,500	26,000-27,400	19,000-20,100
325i cpe/sdn/wgn	22,000-24,000	20,200-22,100	14,300-15,600
330Ci convertible	32,000-34,000	29,800-31,600	22,400-23,800
330i coupe/sedan	25,500-27,500	23,700-25,600	16,800-18,200
M3 convertible	42,000-44,000	39,500-41,400	30,700-32,100
M3 coupe	36,000-38,000	33,500-35,300	25,600-27,000
2002 325Ci convertible	32,000-34,000	29,800-31,600	22,400-23,800
325i cpe/sdn/wgn	24,500-27,500	22,800-25,600	15,900-17,900
330Ci coupe/sedan	36,000-38,000	33,500-35,300	25,600-27,000
330i coupe/sedan	29,000-31,000	27,000-28,800	20,000-21,400
M3 convertible	46,000-48,000	43,200-45,100	34,000-35,500
M3 coupe	40,000-42,000	37,200-39,100	28,800-30,200
2003 325Ci convertible	33,000-35,000	30,700-32,600	23,400-24,900
325i cpe/sdn/wgn	27,000-30,000	25,100-27,900	18,100-20,100
330Ci convertible	40,500-42,500	37,700-39,500	29,200-30,600
330i coupe/sedan	31,500-34,000	29,300-31,600	22,100-23,800
M3 convertible	51,500-54,000	48,400-50,800	38,600-40,500
M3 coupe	45,000-47,000	42,300-44,200	32,900-34,300

For detailed information on this vehicle visit
http://used.consumerguide.com and enter code **2363**

1992-98 BMW 318i

CLASS: Near-luxury car
BUILT IN: Germany, USA
PROS: Antilock brakes
• Ride • Steering/handling
CONS: Wet-weather trac-
tion • Rear-seat room

EVALUATION: Four-cylinder BMWs target driving enthusiasts, who generally prefer manual shift. Because these engines come alive only at high rpm, they function better with manual shift than with automatic, which robs some of the engine's zest. Around town, though, you can expect to shift the 5-speed frequently.

Installation of the larger engine in 1996 did not boost performance appreciably. Fuel mileage has averaged more than 25 mpg with the manual shift.

All 3-Series BMWs shine brightest in their sporty handling characteristics. They devour twisting roads with ease, helped by sharply precise yet fluid steering. Quick turns produce more body lean than expected, but the cars feel lithe and sure-footed. Though the suspension is firm, ride quality beats many cars with softer suspensions, absorbing plenty of road flaws. Brakes are potent, too.

In wet or snowy weather, however, these rear drivers can get difficult to handle, as the tail slips easily sideways. Traction control is not all that effective.

Despite the increased size in this generation, interior space is not much larger than in previous BMWs. Rear space is acceptable only for two small adults, and rear head room is tight in the coupe due to its slightly lower roofline. Cabins are rather austere, with a lot of hard plastic surfaces that seem inappropriate for the car's price. Lack of a tilt feature means the steering wheel sits a bit high, but analog gauges are unobstructed and radio and climate controls are close at hand. Skimpy rear door openings hinder back seat entry into sedans. The trunk floor is flat, and its opening is large.

VALUE FOR THE MONEY: Despite high secondhand prices, 4-cylinder BMWs appeal to those who like spirited, high-revving driving enjoyment. For that purpose, they're hard to beat.

TROUBLE SPOTS

Air conditioner: Air conditioners that don't cool well enough may need to have some of the R-12 (Freon) removed if the system was overcharged. (1992-93)
Automatic transmission: The automatic transmission may suffer from delayed engagement after sitting overnight because the fluid drains out of the torque converter. (1992-95)
Climate control: Small flakes may come from the vents or a foul odor may be present when the A/C is operated. (1992-93)

Dashboard lights: The hazard flashers may begin flashing by themselves and the turn signals may flash at twice the normal speed due to condensation shorting out the circuit board. (1992-94)

Doors: If the central locking system unlocks itself after being locked or locks itself after being unlocked, the actuators could be defective or the trunk lock may need to be adjusted. (1992-93)

Starter: The starter may fail because it keeps running after the engine starts and eventually burns out. The root cause is a sticking ignition switch. The whole lock and switch must be replaced. (1992-94)

AVERAGE REPLACEMENT COSTS

A/C Compressor	$1,200	Exhaust System	$1,450
Alternator	420	Radiator	655
Automatic Trans.	1,150	Shocks and/or Struts	1,225
Brakes	260	Timing Chain/Belt	820
Clutch	570		

NHTSA RECALL HISTORY

1992: Airbag contact-ring locking tab can break without warning, eventually causing broken wiring; airbag would then not deploy in collision, and indicator would illuminate. **1992-93:** Fuel hoses can harden and "set" over time, allowing seepage that could result in fire. **1992-95:** Malfunction or failure of cooling system component can result in significantly increased coolant temperature and system pressure. **1992-97:** Plastic bushing for cruise-control and throttle cables could break, causing throttle valve to remain partially open; car might not decelerate as expected.

PRICES	Good	Average	Poor
1992 318i/is	$4,200-5,000	$3,400-4,100	$1,400-1,700
Convertible	5,500-6,500	4,700-5,600	2,300-2,700
1993 318i/is	5,200-6,000	4,400-5,100	2,100-2,400
1994 318i/is	6,300-7,100	5,500-6,200	2,800-3,200
Convertible	8,200-9,200	7,400-8,300	4,200-4,700
1995 318i/is	7,400-8,400	6,700-7,600	3,700-4,200
Convertible	10,000-11,000	9,000-9,900	5,200-5,700
1996 318i/is	8,500-9,500	7,700-8,600	4,400-4,900
Convertible	12,000-13,200	10,800-11,900	6,700-7,400
1997 318i/is	9,700-10,700	8,700-9,600	5,000-5,600
Convertible	14,000-15,500	12,700-14,100	8,500-9,500
1998 318i	11,000-12,000	9,900-10,800	5,900-6,500

For detailed information on this vehicle visit
http://used.consumerguide.com and enter code **2116**

1992-98 BMW 325i/328i/323i

CLASS: Near-luxury car
BUILT IN: Germany, USA
PROS: Acceleration • Standard antilock brakes and traction control (later models) • Ride • Steering/handling
CONS: Wet-weather traction • Control layout • Fuel economy • Rear-seat room

EVALUATION: Acceleration is swift and smooth at higher engine speeds, but early models suffered a shortage in low-end power, feeling somewhat lethargic until they revved past 3000 rpm or more. Performance in general is adequate with automatic, but these cars are best enjoyed with the highly inviting 5-speed manual gearbox. In town, though, that 5-speed needs to be shifted often. Fuel economy averaged 20.4 mpg in a test of a 1992 model with manual shift.

Swift turns with the base suspension bring more body roll than expected, but the 3-Series feels tight, lithe, and sure-footed. Antilock brakes deliver commendable stopping power and excellent sensitivity. Steering is sharp and precise, road manners nicely balanced. A firm, yet absorbent suspension soaks up road flaws while keeping the body stable.

Beware in wet weather, as rear-drivers can get twitchy in rain or snow. Even with the traction control, snow tires are a must in northern climates.

Space up front is adequate, but the rear is sufficient only for two on a narrow seat. Rear head room in coupes is tight, due to their slightly lower roofline, and the center rear occupant must straddle the driveline tunnel. Skimpy door openings on sedans hinder back-seat entry. The trunk floor is flat, with a large opening. Interiors are austere, with hard plastic surfaces. Radio and climate controls are close at hand but feature a confusing array of buttons.

VALUE FOR THE MONEY: Like their bigger brothers, 3-Series BMWs are far from cheap secondhand, but their many fans are willing to lay out the extra bucks for top-notch roadholding and high-quality materials.

TROUBLE SPOTS

Air conditioner: Air conditioners that don't cool well enough may need to have some of the R-12 (Freon) removed if the system was overcharged. (1992-93)

Automatic transmission: The automatic transmission may suffer from delayed engagement after sitting overnight because the fluid drains out of the torque converter. (1992-95)

Climate control: Small flakes may come from the vents or a foul odor may be present when the A/C is operated. (1992-93)

Dashboard lights: The hazard flashers may begin flashing by themselves and the turn signals may flash at twice the normal speed due to condensation shorting out the circuit board. (1992-94)

BMW

Doors: If the central locking system unlocks itself after being locked or locks itself after being unlocked, the actuators could be defective or the trunk lock may need to be adjusted. (1992-93)

Starter: The starter may fail because it keeps running after the engine starts and eventually burns out. The root cause is a sticking ignition switch. The whole lock and switch must be replaced. (1992-94)

AVERAGE REPLACEMENT COSTS

A/C Compressor	$970	Exhaust System	$670
Alternator	590	Exhaust System	790
Automatic Trans.	1,190	Shocks and/or Struts	980
Brakes	260	Timing Chain/Belt	1,265
Clutch	645		

NHTSA RECALL HISTORY

1992: Airbag contact-ring locking tab can break without warning, eventually causing broken wiring; airbag would not deploy in collision, and indicator would illuminate. **1992:** Failed to meet safety standard for driver chest injury in crash test. **1992-93:** Fuel hoses can harden and "set" over time. **1992-94 325i/iS:** Brake lights may fail to operate, or be on continuously. **1992-95 325i/325Ci:** Plastic bushing for cruise-control and throttle cables could break, causing throttle valve to remain partially open; car then might not decelerate as expected. **1992-95:** Malfunction or failure of cooling system component can result in significantly increased coolant temperature and system pressure. **1993-94 325i/iS:** Replace front transmission crossmember support. **1994 325iC:** Brake lights may fail to operate, or be on continuously. **1995 M3:** Brake lights may fail to operate, or be on continuously. **1995-97 M3:** Plastic bushing for cruise-control and throttle cables could break, causing throttle valve to remain partially open; car then might not decelerate as expected. **1997-98 M3:** Side airbag system is unduly sensitive to certain noncrash impacts, such as large potholes or curbs; could deploy without actual side crash. Battery Safety Terminal could also activate, so engine could not be restarted.

PRICES

	Good	Average	Poor
1992 325i/is	$5,500-6,300	$4,700-5,400	$2,300-2,600
Convertible	6,800-7,700	6,100-6,900	3,200-3,600
1993 325i/is	6,700-7,600	5,900-6,700	3,100-3,500
Convertible	8,200-9,200	7,400-8,300	4,200-4,700
1994 325i/is	8,000-9,000	7,200-8,100	4,100-4,600
Convertible	11,000-12,500	9,900-11,300	5,900-6,800
1995 325i/is	9,200-10,200	8,300-9,200	4,800-5,300
Convertible	13,000-14,500	11,800-13,200	7,500-8,400
M3 coupe	12,500-13,500	11,300-12,200	7,100-7,700
1996 328i/is	10,500-11,500	9,500-10,400	5,600-6,100
Convertible	15,500-17,000	14,100-15,500	9,900-10,900
M3 coupe	15,000-16,500	13,700-15,000	9,500-10,400
1997 328i/is	12,500-13,500	11,300-12,200	7,100-7,700
Convertible	17,500-19,000	16,100-17,500	11,200-12,200
M3 coupe/sedan	17,500-19,000	16,100-17,500	11,200-12,200

1998 323i convertible	$16,000-17,500	$14,600-15,900	$10,200-11,200
323is	12,700-13,700	11,400-12,300	7,200-7,800
328i convertible	19,500-21,500	17,900-19,800	12,700-14,000
328i/is	14,500-15,700	13,200-14,300	9,000-9,700
M3 convertible	24,500-26,500	22,800-24,600	15,900-17,200
M3 coupe/sedan	20,000-22,000	18,400-20,200	13,000-14,300

> For detailed information on this vehicle visit
> http://used.consumerguide.com and enter code **2117**

2000-03 BMW X5

CLASS: Luxury sport-utility vehicle

BUILT IN: USA

PROS: Acceleration • Build quality • Cargo room • Exterior finish • Interior materials

CONS: Fuel economy • Navigation-system controls

EVALUATION: Performance is a strong point. With its V8, the X5 4.4i can accelerate to 60 mph in 7 seconds, smoothly and quietly. A manual-shift 3.0i feels almost as strong. Even an automatic six-cylinder model hits 60 in 8.2 seconds and its transmission provides swift shifts. The manual gearbox yields smooth gear changes but requires a firm hand and careful clutch coordination.

Despite 2.5-ton heft, hard "panic" stops are short and fairly level. Though pleasantly calm overall, the V8's exhaust noise can become wearing.

With the absorbent base suspension, ride comfort and handling rank closer to the smaller, carlike Lexus RX 300 than to the trucklike Mercedes M-Class. An optional Sport Package tightens handling, but its low-profile 19-inch performance tires induce more jiggle and thump on rough surfaces. Some passengers won't like the Sport edition when it rolls through harsh urban pavement. Tight, fast turns produce some body lean and a 4.4i with the Sport Package has poor grip in snow.

Fuel economy is marginal. We averaged barely 14 mpg with a V8 model, not much more with an automatic six cylinder, and 17.6 mpg with a manual-shift 3.0i. All engines demand premium fuel.

The stylish, handsomely furnished cabin offers good room for four adults, with plenty of front head/leg room on firm, supportive seats. Rear head room is generous, but leg space tight if front seats are positioned fairly aft. A lofty floor height impedes entry/exit and cargo hauling. Load length is limited behind the back seat. Rear headrests slightly impede visibility.

Instruments and controls are pure BMW—handy and precise, except for a confusing audio/trip computer/phone setup.

VALUE FOR THE MONEY: All told, the X5 is the sporty "driving

BMW

machine" of SUVs, but not a serious off-roader. It's short on cargo space and costlier than rivals of similar size, power, and equipment. An RX 300 or MDX could be a better economic choice, partly because the BMW retains its value so well, making secondhand prices hefty.

TROUBLE SPOTS

Alarm system: Some hoods do not contact the alarm switch enough, causing false alarms. The company was replacing the switches on an as-needed basis. (2001)

Audio system: Alternator whine on certain radios after a cell phone is installed requires a filtering condenser; a weak battery causes a delay in the audio and display on vehicles that also have the navigation system; and lack of power to the antenna amp causes no AM reception and poor FM reception. (2000)

Dashboard lights: The CHECK OIL light may come on when the engine is turned off despite the dipstick reading full requiring the control module to be reprogrammed. (2000)

Fuel gauge: The fuel gauge may not read full despite a full tank on models built prior to Aug. 2000, requiring replacement of the sending unit. (2000-01)

Steering problems: Steering-wheel vibrations on early production models with automatic transmission and 3.0L engine can be corrected with a countermeasure vibration damper. (2001)

Transmission leak: The manual transmission may leak from the drain plug requiring installation of a countermeasure plug. (2000)

Vehicle noise: Early production models made a clicking noise when the windows were opened and closed while those built after May 2000 do not because a plastic coated regulator was used. It can be retrofitted into earlier models. (2000)

Windows: Water leaking into the A-pillar corrodes a connector for the power locks, windows, and mirrors rendering them inoperative, requiring replacement connectors and sealing the leak. (2000)

AVERAGE REPLACEMENT COSTS

A/C Compressor	$825	CV Joints	$670
Alternator	710	Exhaust System	1,100
Automatic Trans.	1,100	Radiator	720
Brakes	755	Shocks and/or Struts	860
Clutch	560	Timing Chain/Belt	1000

NHTSA RECALL HISTORY

2000: In rough road conditions, the collar on the steering rack may loosen and separate from the rack, causing loss of steering capability. **2000:** One of the steel-mesh oil lines may chafe a brake line, causing the brake line to rust through and leak. **2000-01:** Due to disruption in electrical current, the vehicle may switch from "Park" or "Neutral" to the emergency program and the ability to maintain speed in traffic will be diminished. **2000-01:** Some vehicles may have faulty safetybelt buckles. Dealer will inspect and replace affected parts. **2000-01:** The brake-pedal arm could detach from the bracket, rendering brakes ineffective. **2000-02:** Some vehicles may have faulty brake-line retaining clips, resulting in loss of brake fluid. Dealer will insect and replace affected parts. **2001:** A tie rod may disconnect from the steering gear box, causing noise from the steering linkage and misalignment. **2001:** Brake-pedal travel may be reduced due to relative movement between the pedal and booster, adversely affecting braking performance. **2001:** Front-seat seatbelt anchorages may not have been properly secured. **2001:** Loss of steering capability may result from a disconnected spindle. **2001:** The bolts that fasten the pulley to the pump could loosen and cause the pulley to throw off the drive belt. Power-steering assist, water pump, and alternator functions may be lost. **2001:** The cooling-fan motor may fail, overloading the circuitry of the fan-control unit and possibly overheating the engine. **2003:** On some vehicles, the distance between brake line and the steering shaft joint is too short, resulting in a reduction of front brake performance. Dealer will inspect and replace affected parts.

PRICES	Good	Average	Poor
2000 X5 4.4i	$32,000-33,500	$29,800-31,200	$22,400-23,500
2001 X5 3.0i	30,500-32,000	28,400-29,800	21,400-22,400
X5 4.4i	35,500-37,500	33,000-34,900	25,200-26,600
2002 X5 3.0i	34,000-36,000	31,600-33,500	24,100-25,600
X5 4.4i	39,500-41,500	36,700-38,600	28,400-29,900
X5 4.6is	51,000-54,000	47,900-50,800	38,300-40,500
2003 X5 3.0i	38,000-40,000	35,300-37,200	27,000-28,400
X5 4.4i	45,500-48,000	42,800-45,100	33,700-35,500
X5 4.6is	57,500-61,000	54,600-58,000	43,100-45,800

For detailed information on this vehicle visit
http://used.consumerguide.com and enter code **2445**

1996-02 BMW Z3

CLASS: Sports car
BUILT IN: USA
PROS: Acceleration (6-cylinder) • Steering/handling • Brake performance
CONS: Acceleration (4-cylinder/auto) • Noise • Passenger and cargo room

EVALUATION: Even though horsepower and torque are greater in a 4-cylinder Z3 than in Mazda's Miata, the BMW roadster does not feel any swifter—partly because it carries more pounds. Automatic is slower yet. Because the Z3's 4-cylinder engine does not develop much power below 3500 rpm, it cannot get an eager jump off the line when you push the gas pedal hard. Past 3500 rpm, acceleration becomes brisk. Performance is better with the 2.8-liter 6-cylinder engine. It doesn't set any records either, however. The 6-cylinder's extra torque is most beneficial because it reduces the amount of shifting when driving in town. A test manual-transmission 2.5i did 0-60 mph in a brisk 7.0 sec and had ample midrange passing punch. The 3.0i/manual hatchback felt more muscular—BMW lists 0-60 at 5.9 sec—but didn't present significantly more usable

BMW

acceleration on the street than the 2.5i. M-Series roadsters and hatchbacks have exhilarating performance—almost reminiscent of a Corvette.

Refinement is where BMW has the edge over the Miata. BMW's 4-cylinder engine is far smoother and quieter than Mazda's. It gets noisy only when working hard. The 6-cylinder engine is quieter yet.

Wind noise is intrusive at highway speeds, making it hard for the two occupants to converse in normal tones. Because these are sports cars, noises from the engine, road, and wind increase markedly with speed. Firm suspensions allow little lean in turns, and the Z3 corners as if it's on rails. For a car with such high cornering limits, the ride is supple—more comfortable than the Miata's. Still, it gets jiggly on anything other than glass-smooth surfaces. All told, the Z3 lags behind Mercedes' SLK in smothering bumps. Braking is straight and short. A "panic" stop from 60 mph took about 105 feet.

Space is adequate for medium-size adults, but large folks might feel cramped. Trunk space is meager by anything other than sports-car standards. The manual folding top is fairly easy to raise and lower, but the plastic back window is subject to easy wrinkling and scratches, especially if not cared for properly. Like most convertibles, the top's rear quarters are wide enough to restrict visibility over the driver's shoulders. Inside, you'll find a no-frills, Teutonic design—not inappropriate for a sports car. Standard "leatherette" upholstery on the 1.9, however, with its odd pebble-grain pattern, looks rather cheap for a car of this caliber.

VALUE FOR THE MONEY: Eye-catching appearance and BMW's reputation for handling prowess make the Z3 tempting. Still, based on performance or equipment, it's difficult to justify paying so much more for a Z3 than a Mazda Miata. M-Series models, on the other hand, perform as promised and just might be worth the extra dollars.

TROUBLE SPOTS

Vehicle noise: The fuel tank may rattle when it is full because the mounting strap is loose. Additional foam pads must be installed. (1996-97)

Vehicle noise: Incorrect installation or the wrong mount causes rattles from the rear shock mount. (1996)

Water leak: Water may leak between the convertible top and door windows due to a poor fitting seal. (1996)

Water leak: A leak may develop between the fabric top and the plastic seal that holds the rear window. (1996-99)

Windshield: The black tape on the windshield trim buckles and peels in hot weather. (1996-97)

AVERAGE REPLACEMENT COSTS

A/C Compressor	$1,250	CV Joints	$960
Alternator	410	Exhaust System	1,140
Automatic Trans.	1,150	Radiator	710
Brakes	295	Shocks and/or Struts	1,310
Clutch	570	Timing Chain/Belt	840

NHTSA RECALL HISTORY

1997: Plastic bushing for cruise-control and throttle cables could break, causing throttle valve to remain partially open; car then might not decelerate as expected. **1999:** Nut that secures positive cable to battery terminal clamp on some cars was not tightened properly, allowing cable to loosen over time; ultimately, engine could stop or lighting might be shut off. **1999:** Ring-gear bolts in differential on some cars were incorrectly torqued and could loosen, leading to noise; if a bolt worked loose fully, rear-axle lockup could occur.

PRICES

	Good	Average	Poor
1996 Z3 1.9	$10,500-11,500	$9,500-10,400	$5,600-6,100
1997 Z3 1.9	12,000-13,000	10,800-11,700	6,700-7,300
Z3 2.8	14,000-15,000	12,700-13,700	8,500-9,200
1998 M-Series	20,000-21,500	18,400-19,800	13,000-14,000
Z3 1.9	13,500-14,500	12,300-13,200	8,000-8,600
Z3 2.8	15,700-17,000	14,300-15,500	10,000-10,900
1999 M-Series Coupe	20,500-22,000	18,900-20,200	13,300-14,300
M-Series Roadster	22,500-24,000	20,700-22,100	14,600-15,600
Z3 2.3 Roadster	16,000-17,200	14,600-15,700	10,200-11,000
Z3 2.8 Coupe	16,200-17,500	14,700-15,900	10,400-11,200
Z3 2.8 Roadster	18,500-20,000	17,000-18,400	11,800-12,800
2000 M-Series Coupe	22,500-24,000	20,700-22,100	14,600-15,600
M-Series Roadster	25,000-26,500	23,300-24,600	16,500-17,500
Z3 2.3 Roadster	18,500-20,000	17,000-18,400	11,800-12,800
Z3 2.8 Coupe	18,500-20,000	17,000-18,400	11,800-12,800
Z3 2.8 Roadster	20,500-22,000	18,900-20,200	13,300-14,300
2001 M-Series Coupe	25,000-26,500	23,300-24,600	16,500-17,500
M-Series Roadster	27,500-29,500	25,600-27,400	18,400-19,800
Z3 2.5 Roadster	21,000-22,500	19,300-20,700	13,700-14,600
Z3 3.0 Coupe	21,200-23,000	19,500-21,200	13,800-15,000
Z3 3.0 Roadster	23,200-25,000	21,300-23,000	15,100-16,300
2002 M-Series Coupe	27,500-29,500	25,600-27,400	18,400-19,800
M-Series Roadster	30,000-32,000	27,900-29,800	21,000-22,400
Z3 2.5 Roadster	24,000-26,000	22,300-24,200	15,600-16,900
Z3 3.0 Coupe	24,000-25,500	22,300-23,700	15,600-16,600
Z3 3.0 Roadster	26,500-28,000	24,600-26,000	17,500-18,500

For detailed information on this vehicle visit
http://used.consumerguide.com and enter code **2257**

1990-96 BUICK CENTURY

CLASS: Midsize car

BUILT IN: USA

PROS: Acceleration (V6) • Antilock brakes (later models) • Passenger and cargo room • Quietness (V6) • Visibility

CONS: Acceleration (4-cylinder) • Handling (base suspension) • Ride

BUICK

EVALUATION: The rough 2.5-liter 4-cylinder engine is barely adequate for sedans, and weaker yet in the heavier station wagon. A smooth, responsive 3.3-liter V6 delivers ample power at low speeds and a surprisingly strong kick under heavy throttle for brisk highway passing. That engine also is fairly quiet, unlike the noisy standard four. Also, the 2.5-liter four did not prove to be trouble free, and fuel mileage wasn't much better than the V6. We averaged nearly 20 mpg with a 3.3-liter V6 in mixed city/suburban driving. A four gets only about two mpg more. The 2.2-liter four that replaced the 2.5-liter in 1993 isn't much improvement, lacking the power to move a car this size with any authority. Adding 10 horsepower to the four for '94 didn't make it a tempting choice, either. The 3.1-liter V6 installed in more recent models delivers ample power for passing and spirited takeoffs.

Century's Dynaride suspension delivers a soft and reasonably good ride, but handling won't win any awards. The base suspension and narrow standard tires are fine for gentle commuting, but spirited cornering causes the narrow tires to lose their grip. That suspension absorbs most bumps easily, but the front end bounces over wavy surfaces for a floaty, poorly controlled ride. An optional Gran Touring Suspension, with fatter tires, improves cornering ability but results in a harsh ride.

Six adults will fit inside, but four will be far more comfortable. Head and leg room are adequate all around, but three cannot fit across without squeezing. Luggage space is ample, with a deep, wide trunk that has a flat floor. Wagons have an optional rear-facing third seat, for 8-passenger capacity.

Front brakes tend to wear out quickly. Many early problems, including trouble with the rack-and-pinion power steering system, were eventually corrected on the later models.

VALUE FOR THE MONEY: Nothing flashy here, but Century can be a sensible choice for families on a budget. Forget the 4-cylinder models and look for a livelier, quieter V6. That shouldn't be difficult, as most late Centurys were sold with the V6 engine.

TROUBLE SPOTS

Automatic transmission: TH-125 or 440-T4 automatic transmissions may shift late or not upshift at all. The problem is a stuck throttle valve inside the transmission. (1990-94)

Automatic transmission: 4T60E transmissions may drop out of drive while cruising, shift erratically, or have no second, third, or fourth gear because of a bad ground connection for the shift solenoids. (1994)

Engine misfire: Cars with the 3.1-liter engine may stall, idle roughly, or suffer from tip-in hesitation after extended idling. Additionally, the defroster may not clear the windshield when the temperature is around 40-50 degrees F. The fix is to get a new PROM and a vacuum-hose elbow for the PCV system. (1994-95)

Engine noise: A tick or rattle when the engine is started cold may be due to too much wrist pin-to-piston clearance. (1994-95)

Engine noise: Bearing knock was common on many 3.3- and 3.8-liter engines due to too much clearance on the number one main bearing. (1992-93)

Engine noise: An intermittent rattling noise after starting is often caused by automatic transmission pump starvation or cavitation, or a sticking pressure-regulator valve. (1994-95)

Oil leak: The plastic valve covers on 3.1-liter engines were prone to leaks and should be replaced with redesigned aluminum valve covers. (1994-95)

Steering noise: The upper bearing mount in the steering column can get loose and cause a snapping or clicking, requiring a new bearing spring and turn-signal cancel cam. (1994-96)

Transmission leak: The right front-axle seal at the automatic transaxle is prone to leak and GM issued a revised seal to correct the problem. (1992-94)

AVERAGE REPLACEMENT COSTS

A/C Compressor	$555	Exhaust System	$450
Alternator	195	Radiator	430
Automatic Trans.	1,095	Shocks and/or Struts	825
Brakes	210	Timing Chain/Belt	350
CV Joints	535		

NHTSA RECALL HISTORY

1990-91 w/six-way power seats or power recliner: Short circuit could set seats on fire. **1990-96:** Rear-outboard seatbelt anchors may not withstand required load; in a collision, metal may tear and allow anchor to separate from body. **1992:** The reverse servo apply pin may bind causing the transmission to remain in reverse when shifted to neutral. **1993:** Right front brake hose on some cars is improperly manufactured and can cause reduced brake effectiveness. **1994:** Cruise control cable may separate from the conduit while engaged, resulting in loss of accelerator control. **1994:** Improperly tightened spindle nut can cause premature wheel bearing failure. **1994:** Secondary accelerator control may not return throttle to the fully closed position and could cause a collision. **1994:** Water can cause short circuit in power door-lock assembly.

PRICES	Good	Average	Poor
1990 Century	$1,200-1,700	$700-1,100	$100-200
1991 Century	1,500-2,100	1,000-1,400	200-300
1992 Century	1,800-2,400	1,200-1,600	300-400
1993 Century	2,100-2,700	1,500-1,900	400-500
1994 Century	2,400-3,100	1,800-2,300	500-600
1995 Century	2,700-3,400	2,000-2,600	600-700
1996 Century	3,000-3,800	2,300-2,900	700-900

For detailed information on this vehicle visit http://used.consumerguide.com and enter code **1995**

1997-03 BUICK CENTURY

CLASS: Midsize car
BUILT IN: Canada
PROS: Entry/exit
• Passenger and cargo room
CONS: Seat comfort
• Steering/handling

EVALUATION: Smooth and reasonably quiet, the V6 engine provides adequate acceleration, but it growls when asked to deliver sufficient action for passing. The automatic transmission shifts smoothly and promptly. Wind and road noise are low at highway speeds. A test Century averaged 28 mpg in mostly highway driving, and 18.5 mpg in urban conditions.

Only one suspension is used, and it's too soft for many drivers. Most bumps are absorbed well, but the body continues to bounce long after the initial impact. This limp suspension also allows too much body lean in turns, and makes the Century feel queasy over rough pavement surfaces. Retuning for '99 made the suspension deliver better control in turns, but body lean remains pronounced.

Century has a spacious interior that provides adult-size room, front and rear. Four occupants would be happier than five or six, however. Tall, wide doors ease entry and exit. As for luggage, the roomy trunk has a wide, flat floor, but you have to reach over a wide bumper-level shelf for loading and unloading.

Instruments are easy to read, but limited to a speedometer and fuel and coolant gauges. Most controls are clearly marked, easy for the driver to reach. Climate controls, however, are mounted low enough so they might interfere with a center passenger's knees. In addition, standard cloth seats are so softly padded that they might not suit everyone.

VALUE FOR THE MONEY: Though Century performs admirably, it won't satisfy an enthusiastic driver. Still, it's quiet, comfortable, and economical for a 6-passenger automobile. Modern and well thought out, it retains the no-surprises theme that made the prior Century popular with older buyers.

TROUBLE SPOTS

Engine noise: A ticking sound in the engine is caused by excessive clearance between the piston bores and wrist pins. Although this should not cause a problem, GM will replace all pistons under normal warranty. (1997-98)

Keyless entry: The remote keyless entry may not have much range, requiring a new receiver (with foil antenna) to be installed. (1997)

Suspension noise: A popping or groaning from the rear of the car is caused by the stabilizer shaft links. Redesigned links are available. (1997-98)

Vehicle shake: In warm weather the engine bounces in its mounts, causing a shaking sensation throughout the whole car. A new transmission mount should be installed under normal warranty. (1997-98)

AVERAGE REPLACEMENT COSTS

A/C Compressor	$380	Exhaust System	$400
Alternator	320	Radiator	380
Automatic Trans.	980	Shocks and/or Struts	720
Brakes	330	Timing Chain/Belt	315
CV Joints	1,100		

NHTSA RECALL HISTORY

1997: Windshield wipers may stop working, due to separation between drive pin and crescent in crank-arm assembly. **1998:** Vertical headlamp-adjusting device may not be calibrated properly. **1999:** ABS motor in some cars "shorts" to its case and grounds through brake fluid pipe; can cause extreme heating of brake pipe, which could melt nearby plastic fuel hose. **2000 w/rear drum brakes:** Bolt heads on rear spindle rod can separate and affected wheel can shift, causing loss of control. **2000:** Clamp that secures flexible fuel-fill hose to metal fill tube on a few cars may be loose and could separate, causing fuel leakage. **2000-01:** Some seatbelt assemblies were not properly heat treated and do not pass the load-bearing requirement. **2001:** Airbag labels on sunvisors are not standard size. **2001:** Driver's side airbag inflator separates from the airbag module during deployment, causing the airbag to deploy improperly.

PRICES	Good	Average	Poor
1997 Century	$4,000-5,000	$3,300-4,100	$1,300-1,600
1998 Century	4,800-6,000	4,100-5,100	1,800-2,300
1999 Century	5,800-7,000	5,000-6,100	2,400-2,900
2000 Century	7,000-8,400	6,200-7,500	3,400-4,000
2001 Century	8,500-10,200	7,700-9,200	4,400-5,300
2002 Century	10,000-12,000	9,000-10,800	5,200-6,200
2003 Century	12,000-14,500	10,800-13,100	6,700-8,100

For detailed information on this vehicle visit
http://used.consumerguide.com and enter code **2287**

1992-99 BUICK LESABRE

CG BEST BUY

CLASS: Full-size car

BUILT IN: USA

PROS: Acceleration • Antilock brakes • Automatic transmission performance • Passenger and cargo room

CONS: Radio and climate controls (early models) • Fuel economy • Steering feel

EVALUATION: Performance is brisk, from a standing start or on the highway. Transmission shifts go virtually unnoticed, and kickdowns come quickly. The 3800 Series II V6 found in the 1996 LeSabre is not only more powerful, it's also smoother and quieter than previous versions of this engine. It delivers ample acceleration, and it's mated to one of the smoothest transmissions available.

Power steering is over-assisted, deleting most of the road feel. Even so, handling and overall road manners best a number of rivals. With the base suspension, the LeSabre retains the smooth "big-car" ride that traditional Buick customers have come to expect. For those wanting less body lean and more precise steering feel, we recommend the optional Gran Touring Package. While the LeSabre's handling will never be mistaken for that of a European sport sedan, the optional handling package is a welcome improvement, making this full-size car much more manageable and athletic.

Adults can sit upright easily in back, in a spacious interior. Pre-1995 models have awkward reach to climate/radio controls. Roomy trunk has a wide, flat floor and bumper-height opening.

VALUE FOR THE MONEY: Pleasant to look at and to drive, LeSabre offers few surprises but carries on traditional Buick virtues. Buick's popular LeSabre is a roomy family sedan that offers most of the features found in the Park Avenue at a lower price. Along with its siblings at Oldsmobile and Pontiac, it ranks among the best choices in a full-size sedan.

TROUBLE SPOTS

Automatic transmission: 440-T4 automatic transmissions may shift late or not upshift at all. The problem is a stuck throttle valve inside the transmission. (All years)

Automatic transmission: 4T60E transmission may drop out of drive while cruising, shift erratically, or have no second, third, or fourth gear because of a bad ground connection for the shift solenoids. (1992-94)

Automatic transmission: The 4T60-E automatic transmission can suddenly go into neutral at highway speeds due to a problem with internal shift valves. (1995-96)

Cruise control: If the cruise control doesn't stay engaged, or drops out of cruise, the brake switch can usually be adjusted. (1992-95)

Engine knock: Bearing knock is caused by too much clearance on the number one main bearing. (1992-94)

Engine knock and oil leak: Models with the 3.8-liter engine are prone to excessive oil consumption often accompanied by spark knock due to failure of the valve-stem seals. (1993-95)

Engine noise: An intermittent rattling noise at start up is often caused by automatic-transmission pump starvation or cavitation, or a sticking pressure-regulator valve. (1992-95)

Steering noise: The upper bearing mount in the steering column can get loose and cause a snapping or clicking, requiring a new bearing spring and turn-signal cancel cam. (1994-95)

Transmission leak: The right front-axle seal at the automatic transaxle is prone to leak; GM issued a revised seal to correct the problem. (1992-94)

AVERAGE REPLACEMENT COSTS

A/C Compressor	$500	Exhaust System	$470
Alternator	195	Radiator	360
Automatic Trans.	1,045	Shocks and/or Struts	840

Brakes	$130	Timing Chain/Belt	$265
CV Joints	760		

NHTSA RECALL HISTORY

1992: Parking-brake lever assembly may release one or more teeth when applied, so parking brake might not hold the car. **1992-93:** Transmission-cooler line in cars with certain powertrains sold in specified states can separate at low temperature. **1995:** Driver-side headlamp lens has incorrect aim pad number. **1996:** "Key in the Ignition" warning chime, driver seatbelt-unbuckled warning, and other functions may fail to operate properly. **1996-97:** Backfire can break upper intake manifold, resulting in no-start condition and possible fire. **1997:** Seatbelt might not latch properly. **1999:** Clip that secures linkage of transmission detent lever can loosen and disconnect; indicated gear would then differ from actual state of the transmission.

PRICES	Good	Average	Poor
1992 LeSabre	$2,300-3,000	$1,700-2,200	$400-600
1993 LeSabre	2,700-3,500	2,000-2,600	600-800
1994 LeSabre	3,200-4,000	2,500-3,100	800-1,000
1995 LeSabre	3,800-4,700	3,100-3,800	1,100-1,400
1996 LeSabre	4,400-5,500	3,700-4,600	1,500-1,900
1997 LeSabre	5,100-6,200	4,300-5,300	2,000-2,500
1998 LeSabre	6,000-7,200	5,200-6,300	2,500-3,000
1999 LeSabre	7,500-9,200	6,800-8,300	3,800-4,600

For detailed information on this vehicle visit
http://used.consumerguide.com and enter code **2028**

2000-03 BUICK LESABRE

CG BEST BUY

CLASS: Full-size car
BUILT IN: USA
PROS: Acceleration • Automatic-transmission performance • Instruments/controls • Ride (base suspension)
CONS: Fuel economy • Rear-seat comfort • Ride (Gran Touring option)

EVALUATION: A generally capable performer, the LeSabre makes few demands on its driver. With a proven powertrain, it takes off smartly with ample passing power and smooth, fairly responsive gear changes. We averaged 17.9 mpg, and the engine takes regular-grade fuel. The base suspension's smooth ride is marred by some body float over big humps and dips. The Gran Touring suspension option does a poor job of absorbing most sharp bumps and rides. Worse, it compromises control by imparting a jittery feeling over all but blemish-free pavement. Directional stability is good with either suspension, but steering feels artificially heavy in directional changes. Handling is competent enough, with moderate body lean in turns and good grip in steady-state cornering. Brakes are easy to modulate, but stopping power fails to impress. Wind and road noise are well-muffled, but tires whine on grooved or pebbled pavement. Quiet while cruising, the engine emits a muted growl during hard acceleration. Thick front pillars and slightly narrowed rear side glass produce a somewhat closed-in sensation. Seats are not wide enough to fit three adults without squeezing. Bucket and bench front seats are both roomy for two, though some folks find the cushions too pillowlike. Rear-seat comfort is disappointing. The cushion is low to the floor and its soft foam provides little thigh or back support. Gauges and controls are large, simple, and generally well-positioned. Automatic climate controls on the Limited are hard to adjust while driving. Glossy plastic faces reflect light to obscure some readouts. The interior has a lot of hard plastic surfaces, along with budget-grade upholstery material.

VALUE FOR THE MONEY: For its core audience, the LeSabre imparts a feeling of size and substance, with a standard-equipment list that's well-planned. Still, subpar rear-seat accommodations and indifferent interior furnishings are letdowns.

TROUBLE SPOTS

Automatic transmission: Transmission may slip, shift harshly or erratically due to sediment in the pressure-control solenoid requiring replacement. (2000)

Brake noise: The original-equipment rear brake pads cause a humming or moaning noise, especially when the brakes are hot or warm. (2000)

Horn: If the horn becomes difficult to operate or sounds by itself in cold temperatures, the airbag module will have to be replaced. (2000)

Steering noise: A countermeasure high-pressure power-steering hose will reduce vibrations, shudders, or moans from the steering during slow-speed turns. (2000-01)

AVERAGE REPLACEMENT COSTS

A/C Compressor	$500	Exhaust System	$445
Alternator	380	Radiator	450
Automatic Trans.	1,090	Shocks and/or Struts	535
Brakes	470	Timing Chain/Belt	505
CV Joints	905		

NHTSA RECALL HISTORY

2000: Loose inner tie-rod nuts on certain cars can result in separation of tie rod, causing unexpected steering input. **2000:** Some cars have internal fluid leaks in brake hydraulic control unit; when rear-brake proportioning, antilock braking, traction control, or stability-control feature is activated in some driving situations, feature may not perform as designed. **2002:** Airbag inflator could fracture during deployment endangering passengers. **2002:** Gear-attachment bolts may be undertoqued or missing, causing uneven steering response or unusual noise during turns.

PRICES

	Good	Average	Poor
2000 LeSabre	$9,500-11,500	$8,600-10,400	$4,900-6,000
2001 LeSabre	11,500-14,200	10,400-12,800	6,300-7,800
2002 LeSabre	14,000-17,300	12,700-15,700	8,500-10,600
2003 LeSabre	17,000-21,000	15,600-19,300	10,900-13,400

For detailed information on this vehicle visit
http://used.consumerguide.com and enter code **2364**

1991-96 BUICK PARK AVENUE

CLASS: Near-luxury car
BUILT IN: USA
PROS: Acceleration
• Antilock brakes • Automatic-transmission performance
• Passenger and cargo room
CONS: Climate controls (early models) • Fuel economy • Steering/handling (base suspension)

EVALUATION: Although the initial engine in this heavyweight sounds harsh at full throttle, the sedan is fairly brisk and smooth, as the V6 responds quickly. Engine flaws are more noticeable because the transmission shifts so beautifully—and doesn't slip repeatedly into and out of overdrive like so many 4-speed automatics. The Ultra edition's supercharger does its job well, with a noticeable increase in passing ability. Step on the gas and you get a spirited, satisfying response—but in an understated manner with no hint of raucousness. Adding 35 horsepower to the base engine in 1994 gave it ample power for most situations. Neither engine is particularly economical, but they could be worse. A base Park Avenue registered an average of 21.4 mpg in a long trial. Mileage around town, however, was in the 15-18 mpg neighborhood. An Ultra averaged 19.7 mpg, and the supercharged engine demands premium fuel.

The Park Avenue's ride is comfortable, even cushy, with a soft feel from the base suspension. The car gets bouncy and floaty over wavy surfaces, and leans heavily in turns, which yield plenty of tire howling. The automatic ride control introduced in '93 reduces the floating sensation. Expect some firmness with the Gran Touring option, which got wide tires for better grip and handling, with only slight sacrifice in ride comfort. Steering in both the base and Ultra editions is too light, and doesn't center well after turns.

Four adults sit comfortably in pillowy seats, with generous head and leg room all around. Even six can ride without undue squeezing, helped by space under front seats for rear occupants' feet. Wide doors permit easy entry/exit. Automatic climate controls in the Ultra (optional on base model) are arranged in two rows of seven small buttons, mounted low and away on the dashboard, thus hard to reach. That situation improved in 1994.

BUICK

VALUE FOR THE MONEY: Park Avenue has sold well and is certainly worth a look. Take note, though: LeSabres offer many of the same features at a lower cost.

TROUBLE SPOTS

Automatic transmission: 4T60E transmissions may drop out of drive while cruising, shift erratically, or have no second, third, or fourth gear because of a bad ground connection for the shift solenoids. (1991-94)

Cruise control: If the cruise control doesn't stay engaged or drops out of cruise, the brake switch can usually be adjusted. (1991-95)

Cruise control: Cruise control doesn't stay engaged, or drops out of cruise. (1991-95)

Engine knock: Bearing knock was common on many 3.8-liter engines due to too much clearance on the number one main bearing. (1992-94)

Engine noise: An intermittent rattling noise at start up is often caused by automatic-transmission pump starvation or cavitation, or a sticking pressure-regulator valve. (1991-95)

Oil consumption and engine knock: Models with the 3.8-liter engine are prone to excessive oil consumption often accompanied by spark knock during normal driving conditions due to failure of the valve-stem seals. (1993-95)

Steering noise: The upper bearing mount in the steering column can get loose and cause a snapping or clicking, requiring a new bearing spring and turn-signal cancel cam. (1994-96)

Transmission leak: The right front-axle seal at the automatic transaxle is prone to leak and GM issued a revised seal to correct the problem. (1992-94)

AVERAGE REPLACEMENT COSTS

A/C Compressor	$725	CV Joints	$810
Alternator	395	Exhaust System	610
Automatic Trans.	1,270	Radiator	445
Brakes	215	Shocks and/or Struts	955
Clutch	1,010	Timing Chain/Belt	230

NHTSA RECALL HISTORY

1991: Parking-brake lever assembly may release one or more teeth when applied, reducing cable load to rear brakes; parking brake might not hold the vehicle, allowing it to roll. **1992-93:** Transmission-cooler line in cars with certain powertrains sold in specified states can separate at low temperature. **1995:** Driver-side headlamp lens has incorrect aim pad number; if headlamps are reaimed using those numbers, result would be out of specified range. **1996:** "Key in the Ignition" warning chime, driver seatbelt-unbuckled warning, and other functions may not operate properly. **1996:** Backfire can break upper intake manifold, resulting in possible fire. **1996:** Cars were assembled with one or more incorrect safetybelt and/or buckle ends, so belt may not latch properly.

PRICES

	Good	Average	Poor
1991 Park Avenue	$2,200-2,800	$1,600-2,000	$400-500
Park Avenue Ultra	2,500-3,100	1,800-2,300	500-700
1992 Park Avenue	2,700-3,400	2,000-2,600	600-700
Park Auenue Ultra	3,100-3,800	2,400-3,000	700-900

1993 Park Avenue	$3,200-3,900	$2,500-3,000	$800-900
Park Avenue Ultra	3,700-4,400	3,000-3,600	1,100-1,300
1994 Park Avenue	3,800-4,500	3,100-3,600	1,100-1,400
Park Avenue Ultra	4,300-5,000	3,500-4,100	1,500-1,700
1995 Park Avenue	4,400-5,200	3,700-4,300	1,500-1,800
Park Avenue Ultra	5,000-5,800	4,300-4,900	2,000-2,300
1996 Park Avenue	5,000-5,800	4,300-4,900	2,000-2,300
Park Avenue Ultra	5,800-6,800	5,000-5,900	2,400-2,900

For detailed information on this vehicle visit
http://used.consumerguide.com and enter code **1997**

1997-03 BUICK PARK AVENUE

CG BEST BUY

CLASS: Near-luxury car

BUILT IN: USA

PROS: Acceleration • Cargo room • Passenger room • Steering/handling (Ultra)

CONS: Fuel economy (supercharged V6) • Steering/handling (base suspension)

EVALUATION: Performance is satisfying in basic form—sufficient for most situations—but especially impressive when the engine is supercharged. Acceleration in an Ultra feels much like a small V8, so it makes a strong showing against the 6-cylinder competition. Helped by the automatic transmission's subtle and alert shifting, both models distribute ample, seamless power over a wide range of engine speeds. A base Park Avenue averaged 19.8 mpg using regular-grade fuel, helped by some highway time. Another base model averaged 19.5 mpg with a more even driving mix.

Standard steering and suspension settings favor low-effort comfort. Unfortunately, this produces steering that's too light at freeway speeds, as well as floaty body motions over undulating surfaces. The Ultra's suspension is markedly stiffer—possibly too much so for some luxury-car buyers. A Gran Touring suspension setup has been optional on both models. That unit does a fine job of soaking up bumps with little jarring, while maintaining a flat, stable ride. It also quells undue body lean and front-end plowing through corners. Part of that package is magnetic variable-effort steering, which responds quickly with good straightline stability, but feels a bit numb. Braking power feels strong. Simulated emergency stops can produce pronounced nosedive, but with no loss of stability or control. The Ultra, in particular, does a great job of muffling wind, road, and engine noises.

Roomy and comfortable, Park Avenue promises space for adults to relax. Head and leg room are abundant. Six-passenger capacity is a bonus, though everyone will be sitting shoulder-to-shoulder when the car is filled. Seats are

BUICK

comfortable, but not sufficiently contoured to give occupants good lateral support when the road turns twisty. Front lap and shoulder belts are anchored to the seat itself, so they move right along with the seats, fore and aft. Belts are handy to grab and always seem to fit just right. Gauges and switches are generous in size, easy to read and operate. A simple dashboard pull-knob operates the headlights. If a secondhand Park Avenue is equipped with OnStar, the buyer will have to pay a monthly service fee to make use of the system.

Park Avenues that were test driven when new demonstrated good fit and finish, inside and out. One Ultra driven in subfreezing weather, however, emitted creaks from its suspension when crossing speed bumps or entering driveways.

VALUE FOR THE MONEY: What do you get from a Park Avenue? Mainly, traditional American virtues— roominess, power, and amenities— at a sensible price. This domestic sedan is definitely worth a close look, though some of its virtues can be found in Buick's LeSabre for less money. In addition, it must be said that Buick's customer satisfaction ratings have not been as high as those of some foreign competitors.

TROUBLE SPOTS

Brake noise: The brakes make grinding, squealing, growling, and other noises, and new brake pads were issued; but new, heftier rotors are also needed. (1997-98)

Fuel odors: Fuel spurts out of the filler pipe as the tank reaches full. (1997)

Horn: The horn sounds by itself, especially in cold weather, requiring replacement of the horn pad assembly. (1997)

Keyless entry: The trunk pops open because the button on the remote is too sensitive and is easily activated while in a purse or pocket. (1997-98)

Oil consumption: The oil dipstick shows on overfilled level because the original dipstick tube is too short and must be replaced. (1997)

Seatbelts/safety: Some owners have complained of excessive shoulder belt slack. (1997-98)

AVERAGE REPLACEMENT COSTS

A/C Compressor	$500	Exhaust System	$475
Alternator	265	Radiator	450
Automatic Trans.	850	Shocks and/or Struts	900
Brakes	365	Timing Chain/Belt	325
CV Joints	750		

NHTSA RECALL HISTORY

1997: Electronic Brake Control or Brake/Traction-Control module can cause antilock brake system to cycle in non-ABS braking; could increase stopping distance. **1997-98:** Front shoulder belts might twist, becoming jammed in retractor. **1998-99:** Fuel-pressure regulator can leak, leading to vehicle backfire and, potentially, a fire. **1999:** A few cars may have been built with incorrect brake components, and could pull to one side during braking. **1999:** Brake booster to pedal assembly attachment nuts on some cars may be loose. **2000:** Due to internal fluid leakage in some cars, rear brake proportioning, ABS, traction control or stability control may not perform as designed. **2001:** Wiper-system processor is susceptible to voltage transients, which can cause a "latch-up" condition in the system controller rendering the low- and high-speed wiper modes inoperative.

PRICES	Good	Average	Poor
1997 Park Avenue	$6,000-6,800	$5,200-5,900	$2,500-2,900
Park Avenue Ultra	6,900-7,700	6,100-6,900	3,300-3,700
1998 Park Avenue	7,500-8,500	6,800-7,700	3,800-4,300
Park Avenue Ultra	8,700-9,700	7,800-8,700	4,500-5,000
1999 Park Avenue	9,500-10,500	8,600-9,500	4,900-5,500
Park Avenue Ultra	11,000-12,200	9,900-11,000	5,900-6,600
2000 Park Avenue	12,000-13,000	10,800-11,700	6,700-7,300
Park Avenue Ultra	14,000-15,300	12,700-13,900	8,500-9,300
2001 Park Avenue	15,000-16,200	13,700-14,700	9,500-10,200
Park Avenue Ultra	17,200-18,500	15,800-17,000	11,000-11,800
2002 Park Avenue	18,000-19,500	16,600-17,900	11,500-12,500
Park Avenue Ultra	21,000-23,000	19,300-21,200	13,700-15,000
2003 Park Avenue	22,500-24,000	20,700-22,100	14,600-15,600
Park Avenue Ultra	26,000-28,000	24,200-26,000	17,200-18,500

For detailed information on this vehicle visit
http://used.consumerguide.com and enter code 2296

1990-96 BUICK REGAL

CLASS: Midsize car

BUILT IN: Canada

PROS: Acceleration (3.8-liter V6) • Antilock brakes (optional until '94) • Passenger and cargo room • Ride

CONS: Engine noise (early models) • Fuel economy (3.8-liter V6) • Performance (early models) • Instruments/controls (early models) • Seat comfort • Steering feel

EVALUATION: Front-seat room is generous, and the rear is adequate for 6-footers. Both body styles are roomy, but leg and head room are better in the sedan, though the lower cushion feels puny for long-distance comfort. Front shoulder belts in the sedan were anchored to door pillars, so belts could ride on the neck of shorter passengers. Wide front pillars compromise visibility.

The initial Regal's lack of power was remedied by the arrival of the 3.8-liter engine in 1992. It gives the car sufficient oomph to accelerate smartly away from stoplights and pass safely. The early 3.1-liter, in contrast, sounds strained when a brisk getaway is called for, generating more noise than power. With the electronically controlled automatic installed in 1993, shifts grew swifter and smoother. Gas mileage is better with the 3.1-liter. We've averaged better than 20 mpg. The 3.8-liter yielded no more than 17-18 mpg.

Analog instrumentation in early Regals is not the greatest and some instruments are blocked by the steering wheel. The optional electronic

BUICK

cluster has poorly designed graphics and has to squeeze into the same tight space. Climate controls also are far to the right, but have big buttons. The new interior for 1995 cured many of these complaints.

Ride/handling aren't bad, even with the base suspension. It seems to strike a sensible compromise between soft ride and capable handling, though slanting toward the former. Steering is on the light side, and the car leans heavily in turns. The firmer Gran Sport suspension provides taut handling and a well-controlled ride, but gets a bit harsh when rolling through pavement irregularities. Antilock braking works well, but takes high pedal pressure for a quick stop.

VALUE FOR THE MONEY: A Regal might not be much to get excited about, but it's not a bad choice when prices are tempting. About 75 percent of Regals got the 3.8-liter V6, and that's the one that approaches Ford Taurus in appeal.

TROUBLE SPOTS

Automatic transmission: 4T60E transmissions may drop out of drive while cruising, shift erratically, or have no second, third, or fourth gear because of a bad ground connection for the shift solenoids. (1991-94)

Automatic transmission: 440-T4 automatic transmissions may shift late or not upshift at all. The problem is a stuck throttle valve inside the transmission. (1990-92)

Engine noise: An intermittent rattling noise at start up is often caused by automatic-transmission pump starvation or cavitation, or a sticking pressure-regulator valve. (1991-95)

Engine noise: An intermittent rattle at start up may be due to too much wrist pin-to-piston clearance. (1994-95)

Engine noise: Bearing knock was common on many 3.8-liter engines due to too much clearance on the number one main bearing. (1992-94)

Oil consumption: Models with the 3.8-liter engine are prone to excessive oil consumption often accompanied by spark knock during normal driving conditions due to failure of the valve-stem seals. (1993-95)

Steering noise: The upper bearing mount in the steering column can get loose and cause a snapping or clicking that can be both heard and felt. (1994-96)

Transaxle leak: The right front axle seal at the automatic transaxle is prone to leak and GM issued a revised seal to correct the problem. (1992-94)

Valve cover leaks: The plastic valve covers on 3.1-liter engines were prone to leaks and should be replaced with redesigned aluminum valve covers. (1994-95)

AVERAGE REPLACEMENT COSTS

A/C Compressor	$555	Exhaust System	$470
Alternator	215	Radiator	340
Automatic Trans.	1,075	Shocks and/or Struts	1,856
Brakes	200	Timing Chain/Belt	170
CV Joints	470		

NHTSA RECALL HISTORY

1990 w/Kelsey-Hayes steel wheels: Cracks may develop in wheel mounting surface; if severe, wheel could separate from car. **1990:** Brake lights may not illuminate, or will not stay lit all the time when brakes are applied, due to faulty switch. **1990:** Front shoulder belt may not properly restrain passenger in an accident. **1990-91:** Steering shaft could separate from steering gear. **1991 in 15 states:** Corrosion due to road salt could allow one or both front engine-cradle bolts to pull through their retainers; steering shaft could possibly separate from steering gear. **1991:** Front-door shoulder-belt guide loops may be cracked. **1992:** Reverse servo apply pin of 4-speed automatic transmission may bind, which could cause loss or slipping of reverse, poor performance, or transmission to remain in reverse while indicator shows neutral. **1993:** Manual recliner mechanisms on some front seats will not latch under certain conditions, causing seatback to recline without prior warning. **1993-95:** Replace clear front side-marker bulbs with amber. **1994-95:** Rear brake hoses can contact suspension components and wear through, resulting in loss of brake fluid. **1994-95:** Strained wire can cause intermittent or nonexistent wiper/washer operation. **1995:** Center-rear-seatbelt anchor plate could fracture in a crash. **1995:** On a few cars, steering-column support bolts could vibrate, loosen, or fall out. **1995:** Seatbelt anchor can fracture during crash. **1995-96:** The driver's airbag could deploy inadvertently and injure the driver. **1996 w/3.8-liter V6:** Backfire can break upper intake manifold, resulting in possible fire. **1996:** Left front brake line can contact transaxle mounting bracket or bolt, causing line to wear through, resulting in loss of fluid and eventual loss of half the brake system.

PRICES

	Good	Average	Poor
1990 Regal	$1,700-2,300	$1,100-1,500	$300
1991 Regal	2,100-2,800	1,500-2,000	400-500
1992 Regal	2,500-3,200	1,800-2,300	500-700
1993 Regal	2,800-3,600	2,100-2,700	600-800
1994 Regal	3,200-3,900	2,500-3,000	800-900
1995 Regal	3,600-4,400	2,900-3,500	1,000-1,200
1996 Regal	4,000-4,800	3,300-3,900	1,300-1,500

For detailed information on this vehicle visit http://used.consumerguide.com and enter code **1999**

1997-03 BUICK REGAL

CLASS: Midsize car

BUILT IN: Canada

PROS: Acceleration • Automatic-transmission performance • Passenger and cargo room • Ride

CONS: Fuel economy (supercharged engine)

EVALUATION: Well-known for smooth running, GM's 3.8-liter V6 engine feels great when installed in a Regal, furnishing good acceleration at low speeds, as well as plenty of passing power. Performance is better yet with the supercharged edition. Unfortunately, the GS suffers marked torque steer, in which the steering wheel is tugged in one direction during rapid takeoffs. Transmission behavior is absolutely sparkling and mannerly with either engine—just the way all automatic transmissions should function. We averaged between 16.9 and 20.1 mpg with a Regal GS. Gas mileage with an LS is about the same, but that model does not require premium fuel.

Although Buick has promoted the Regal as a sports sedan, the car leans more toward comfort than true handling prowess. Steering response is a little slow in quick changes of direction, and the body floats slightly over high-speed dips that European sport sedans would take in stride. Body lean is moderate, however, and the Regal's suspension soaks up large bumps with little intrusion toward occupants.

Pleasant inside, the Regal offers ample space in front and rear, though it's better for four adults than five. Comfortable front seats support the occupants nicely even during spirited driving. On the downside, the fold-down center armrest is too low to be of much value, yet its presence restricts outboard passenger space. Climate controls could be simpler, however. Having a trunklid release inside the car would be handy, too, but there's one only on the remote keyless entry fob. Not only does the lid to the big trunk open to 90 degrees, but its hinges do not intrude on luggage space.

VALUE FOR THE MONEY: Regal fails to match the overall refinement or proven reliability record of a Honda Accord or Toyota Camry, and prices are likely to be far higher than for a comparable Ford Taurus or Mercury Sable. Still, Regal's solidity, performance, and ample quantity of equipment make it worth a close look in the midsize family sedan league.

TROUBLE SPOTS

Engine misfire: An engine miss causes rough running and a check engine light. It is due to the spark-plug boots, cracking and allowing the voltage to jump to ground. (1997-98)

Engine noise: A ticking sound in the engine is caused by excessive clearance between the piston bores and wrist pins. GM will replace all pistons under normal warranty. (1997-98)

Keyless entry: The remote keyless entry may not have much range, requiring a new receiver (with foil antenna) to be installed. (1997)

Suspension noise: A popping or groaning noise from the rear of the car is caused by the stabilizer shaft links. Redesigned links are available. (1997-98)

Vehicle shake: In warm weather, the engine bounces in its mounts causing a shaking sensation throughout the whole car. A new transmission mount will be installed under normal warranty. (1997-98)

AVERAGE REPLACEMENT COSTS

A/C Compressor	$380	Exhaust System	$470
Alternator	240	Radiator	440
Automatic Trans.	980	Shocks and/or Struts	1,500
Brakes	520	Timing Chain/Belt	315
CV Joints	1,100		

NHTSA RECALL HISTORY

1997: Right front brake line can wear through; can result in fluid loss, and loss of half of braking system. **1997:** Windshield wipers may stop working, due to separation between drive pin and crescent in crank-arm assembly. **1998-99:** Vertical headlamp-adjusting device may not be calibrated properly. **1999:** Short in ABS motor can cause extreme heating of flexible brake pipe, where it can melt nearby plastic fuel hose. **2000 w/rear drum brakes:** Bolt heads on rear spindle rod can separate and affected wheel can shift, causing loss of control. **2000 w/rear drum brakes:** Bolt heads on rear spindle rod can separate and rear wheel can shift, causing rear steering of vehicle. **2000:** Clamp that secures flexible fuel-fill hose to metal fill tube on a few cars may be loose and could separate, causing fuel leakage. **2000:** Some seatbelt assemblies were not properly heat treated and do not pass the load-bearing requirement.

PRICES

	Good	Average	Poor
1997 Regal GS	$5,800-6,600	$5,000-5,700	$2,400-2,800
Regal LS	5,000-5,800	4,300-4,900	2,000-2,300
1998 Regal GS	7,000-8,000	6,200-7,100	3,400-3,800
Regal LS	6,000-6,900	5,200-6,000	2,500-2,900
1999 Regal GS	9,000-10,000	8,100-9,000	4,700-5,200
Regal LS	7,500-8,500	6,800-7,700	3,800-4,300
2000 Regal GS	10,700-11,700	9,600-10,500	5,700-6,200
Regal LS	9,000-10,000	8,100-9,000	4,700-5,200
2001 Regal GS	12,500-13,700	11,300-12,300	7,100-7,800
Regal LS	10,500-11,500	9,500-10,400	5,600-6,100
2002 Regal GS	14,700-16,000	13,400-14,600	9,100-9,900
Regal LS	12,500-13,500	11,300-12,200	7,100-7,700
2003 Regal GS	17,200-19,000	15,800-17,500	11,000-12,200
Regal LS	14,500-15,500	13,200-14,100	9,000-9,600

For detailed information on this vehicle visit
http://used.consumerguide.com and enter code **2288**

1992-97 BUICK SKYLARK

CLASS: Compact car

BUILT IN: USA

PROS: Acceleration (V6)
• Antilock brakes
• Automatic-transmission performance

CONS: Instrument cluster (early models) • Noise
• Rear-seat entry/exit

• Steering/handling (base suspension)

EVALUATION: Performance from the initial base engine isn't bad, but that 4-cylinder unit—though quiet enough at cruising speeds—grows noisy and coarse at higher rpm. Acceleration is adequate, but the snarling and growling can annoy. Either V6 is more responsive to the throttle at all speeds, yielding brisk passing power. Road noise gets to be a problem at highway speeds, and poor sound insulation just adds to the unpleasantness.

Unlike previous versions of GM's Quad 4 engine, the 150-horsepower variant for 1994 is smooth and quiet. Same with the slightly larger Twin Cam that arrived a year later. For that reason, a V6 isn't nearly as essential for comfortable cruising as it was in 1992-93 Skylarks.

Base suspensions do a poor job of absorbing rough pavement, and lose composure in tight turns. An optional firmer suspension and larger tires make a Skylark feel more agile and responsive, without a big penalty in ride quality. Standard antilock braking is a plus, activating quickly in panic stops; but lack of an airbag on early models is not.

Interior space isn't bad for four, even in the back seat. Rear leg room is adequate for adults, but there's not really enough space for stretching out. Access to the back seat isn't so easy, even in 4-doors.

Clearly marked analog gauges are spread out so far on early models that those at the ends are hidden by the steering wheel. The ample trunk has a bumper-height liftover, but the opening is too small for easy loading of large items.

VALUE FOR THE MONEY: Riding and handling better than prior Skylarks, this more modern Buick can still be a sensible choice, despite loud engines and poor insulation.

TROUBLE SPOTS

Automatic transmission: TH-125 automatic transmissions may shift late or not upshift at all. The problem is a stuck throttle valve inside the transmission. (1992-94)

Automatic transmission: 4T60E transmissions may drop out of drive while cruising, shift erratically, or have no second, third, or fourth gear, because of a bad ground connection for the shift solenoids. (1994)

Brake wear: The front brakes wear out prematurely because of the friction compound. GM, and several aftermarket companies, have brakes with lining that will last longer. (1991-95)

Coolant leak: Some cars mysteriously lose coolant because of a bad seal on the pressure cap of the surge tank. (1992-94)

Engine knock: Bearing knock was common on many 3.3-liter engines due to too much clearance on the number one main bearing. (1992-93)

Engine noise: An intermittent rattling noise at start up is often caused by automatic-transmission pump starvation or cavitation, or a sticking pressure-regulator valve. (1994-95)

Engine noise: An intermittent rattle at start up may be due to too much wrist-pin-to-piston clearance. (1994-95)

Ignition switch: The ignition switch may not return from the start to the run position or the accessories may not work because the screws that hold the switch in place were overtightened. (1992-94)

Traction control indicator light: The Enhanced Traction Control (ETC) warning light "ETC OFF" may glow and the cruise control stops working, but there is no problem with the system. If the computer failure memory is cleared, everything returns to normal. No current fix. (1996)

Transaxle leak: The right front axle seal at the automatic transaxle is prone to leak and GM issued a revised seal to correct the problem. (1992-94)

Valve cover leaks: The plastic valve covers on the 3.1-liter engine were prone to leaks and should be replaced with redesigned aluminum valve covers. (1994-95)

AVERAGE REPLACEMENT COSTS

A/C Compressor	$540	CV Joints	$565
Alternator	225	Exhaust System	450
Automatic Trans.	1,105	Shocks and/or Struts	450
Brakes	245	Timing Chain/Belt	350

NHTSA RECALL HISTORY

1992 coupe: Passenger's side easy-entry seat adjuster on some cars may fail to fully lock after seatback has been tilted forward and seat slid forward, then returned to original position; seat could slide forward in sudden stop. **1992 with column shift:** Misadjustment of "Park" lock cable on some cars makes it possible for steering column to lock while in motion and ignition switch is "off." **1992:** A small number of cars were assembled with incorrect right rear spring mount; in the event of a rear impact, the right rear wheelhouse flange could sever the fuel-tank filler pipe and spill fuel. **1993:** The neutral-start safety switch may have been fractured during installation which could cause the vehicle to move unexpectedly or not start at all. **1994:** On some cars, welds in rear assembly of fuel tank may be insufficient to prevent leakage in certain rear-impact collisions. **1995:** If the starter fails, and the key is held in the "start" position for an extended period, the high electrical current flowing through the ignition switch could cause a fire. **1996:** During deployment of the passenger airbag, the airbag can snag on a reinforcement inside the instrument panel. This might cause the airbag to not deploy properly. **1996:** If the key is held in the "start" position for an extended period, high currents flowing through the ignition switch can melt internal switch parts. **1996:** Interior lamps might come on unexpectedly while vehicle is being driven. **1996:** Steering-column lower pinch bolt was not properly tightened. This could cause loss of steering control. **1997:** In rear-end collision, sheetmetal in left rear quarter panel on some cars may damage fuel tank or lines. **1997:** Omitted protective cover for underhood fuse center could result in short circuit and possible fire.

PRICES	Good	Average	Poor
1992 Gran Sport	$1,600-2,200	$1,100-1,500	$200-300
Skylark	1,400-2,000	900-1,300	200
1993 Gran Sport	2,000-2,600	1,400-1,800	300-400
Skylark	1,700-2,300	1,100-1,500	300
1994 Gran Sport	2,400-3,000	1,800-2,200	500-600
Skylark	2,000-2,600	1,400-1,800	300-400
1995 Gran Sport	2,700-3,400	2,000-2,600	600-700
Skylark	2,300-3,000	1,700-2,200	400-600
1996 Gran Sport	3,100-3,800	2,400-3,000	700-900
Skylark	2,600-3,300	1,900-2,400	500-700
1997 Gran Sport	3,700-4,500	3,000-3,600	1,100-1,300
Skylark	3,200-4,000	2,500-3,100	800-1,000

For detailed information on this vehicle visit
http://used.consumerguide.com and enter code 2001

CADILLAC

2000-03 CADILLAC DEVILLE

CG BEST BUY

CLASS: Luxury car
BUILT IN: USA
PROS: Acceleration
• Build quality • Entry/exit
• Interior materials
• Passenger and cargo room
• Quietness
CONS: Fuel economy
• Navigation-system controls • Rear visibility

EVALUATION: Poised on the road, a DeVille DHS easily holds its own against imported luxury sedans, with a ride that's comfortable yet controlled. Acceleration is outstanding, as a DeVille is able to reach 60 mph in as little as 7 seconds. The refined powertrain features a smooth and responsive automatic transmission. As for gas mileage, a DTS sedan with the 300-bhp engine averaged 14.6 to 16.7 mpg. Cadillac recommends premium fuel, but regular is acceptable and does not affect performance by much. Few sedans are more spacious or comfortable than a DeVille. Front seats provide fine support and stretch-out room in outboard position, though the middle occupant of the front bench is likely to feel squeezed. Leg clearance in back ranks as limousinelike, with a firm, generous cushion that's wide enough for three adults. All doors open exceptionally wide for easy entry/exit. Whether digital or analog, gauges are unobstructed and legible. Though abundant, controls on the dashboard and steering wheel are large and clearly labeled. Outward visibility is generally good, but thick rear roof pillars hamper over-the-shoulder vision. The big trunk opens to bumper level. Cabin materials and workmanship are competitive with imported luxury cars, and notably better than other domestics. Two exceptions are the low-budget plastic in the dashboard center and crude movement of vent adjusters. Cadillac's Night Vision option is most useful in rural areas, displaying a moving image in the windshield that resembles a photographic negative. It does not interfere with normal forward vision, and can be switched off.

VALUE FOR THE MONEY: Spacious and powerful, the DeVille is loaded with jet-age gizmos. Priced below most V8 luxury rivals, it has a markedly different appearance than DeVilles of the past, which pleases some potential buyers but may distress others. Ride and handling are on a par with the world's most prestigious luxury sedans, accompanied by energetic performance.

TROUBLE SPOTS

Brakes: When warm, the front brake pads may cause the front end and steering wheel to vibrate and shake. Countermeasure pads are available. (2000)

Brakes: The original-equipment rear brake pads cause a humming or moaning noise, especially when the brakes are hot or warm. (2000)

Climate control: Due to insufficient tension on the pivots, the shut-off doors in the dashboard may close when the blower is set on high. (2000)

Horn: If the horn becomes difficult to operate or sounds by itself in cold temperatures, the airbag module will have to be replaced. (2000)

AVERAGE REPLACEMENT COSTS

A/C Compressor	$750	Exhaust System	$500
Alternator	550	Radiator	670
Automatic Trans.	1,190	Shocks and/or Struts	1,755
Brakes	575	Timing Chain/Belt	1,275
CV Joints	800		

NHTSA RECALL HISTORY

2000: Some cars have internal fluid leaks in brake hydraulic control unit; when rear-brake proportioning, antilock-braking, traction-control, or stability-control feature is activated in some driving situations, feature may not perform as designed. **2001:** Some seatbelt assemblies fail to comply with a 30-pound pushbutton release-effort requirement and may be difficult to unlatch in a crash. **2001:** Sunvisor center supports may be too small, increasing the possibility of injuries, such as lacerations, during a collision. **2001-02:** Lap- and shoulder-belt retractors may not remain locked. **2002:** Airbag inflator may fracture during deployment, endangering passengers. **2002:** Steering-gear attachment bolts may be undertorqued or missing, resulting in uneven steering response or unusual noise in turns. **2002-03 V8:** Faulty fuel-tank sensors may have been installed in certain vehicles, leading to fuel leakage. Dealer will inspect and replace all affected parts.

PRICES

	Good	Average	Poor
2000 DeVille	$18,000-19,500	$16,600-17,900	$11,500-12,500
DeVille DHS, DTS	20,500-22,500	18,900-20,700	13,300-14,600
2001 DeVille	21,000-22,500	19,300-20,700	13,700-14,600
DeVille DHS, DTS	24,000-26,000	22,300-24,200	15,600-16,900
2002 DeVille	24,500-26,000	22,800-24,200	15,900-16,900
DeVille DHS, DTS	28,000-30,500	26,000-28,400	19,000-20,700
2003 DeVille	28,500-30,500	26,500-28,400	19,400-20,700
DeVille DHS, DTS	33,000-35,500	30,700-33,000	23,400-25,200

> For detailed information on this vehicle visit
> http://used.consumerguide.com and enter code **2365**

1994-99 CADILLAC DEVILLE/CONCOURS

CLASS: Luxury car

BUILT IN: USA

PROS: Acceleration • Antilock brakes • Interior noise levels • Passenger and cargo room • Traction control

CONS: Climate control (base and d'Elegance) • Fuel economy • Rear visibility

CADILLAC

EVALUATION: Concours is the performance prince, but even a base DeVille boasts impressive acceleration, with brisk passing response. Power is plentiful with the 4.9-liter base engine—and even better with the later Northstar. With any of the Northstar V8s under the hood, you can expect surprisingly sizzling action, which belies the car's heft. A Concours, with the most potent V8 ready and waiting, actually rivals some sports sedans when pushing the pedal to the floor. Even better, Cadillac's 4-speed overdrive automatic transmission shifts with buttery smoothness.

Fuel economy is poor. Only on the highway did we average better than 20 mpg. Overall, a Concours averaged just 15.8 mpg in a long-term trial. Worse yet, all engines demand premium gasoline.

Because of a stiffer structure and better engine mounts, these two ride much more quietly than in previous years, with less noise and vibration. Both suspensions do a good job of isolating the cabin and keeping bouncing to a minimum. The Road Sensing Suspension does a commendable job of maintaining a stable, comfortable ride and minimizing body lean in turns. Agile may not be an appropriate word to describe either DeVille, but these sizable sedans handle reasonably well for cars in their category. Later models with StabiliTrak feel much more agile in hard driving, with no penalty in ride quality. Road and wind noise are minimal, though not necessarily nonexistent. Brakes are strong and fade-free. Steering is firm and responsive, but lacks true road feel and precision.

Inside, you get ample six-passenger seating in a spacious cabin, plus dual airbags. Basic dashboard design is borrowed from the Seville, so climate controls are just to the right of the steering wheel, where they're hard to see and reach. The trunk opens at bumper level and has a wide, flat floor that can hold loads of luggage.

VALUE FOR THE MONEY: Don't judge the latest DeVille and Concours just by their conservative styling, which continues to appeal mainly to older drivers. Both Cadillacs offer tempting performance and roomy accommodations, and represent good value for the money.

TROUBLE SPOTS

Blower motor: The blower motor fails if the spark plug wires are routed too close to the blower-motor housing. (1994-97)

Engine noise: A rattling noise from the engine at startup is often caused by automatic-transmission pump starvation or cavitation, or a sticking pressure-regulator valve. (1994-95)

Fuel odors: Leaks in the vapor recovery system, due to excessively short hoses coming loose, causes fuel odors inside the car. (1997)

Steering noise: The upper bearing mount in the steering column can get loose and cause a snapping or clicking, requiring a new bearing spring and turn-signal cancel cam. (1994-96)

AVERAGE REPLACEMENT COSTS

A/C Compressor	$475	CV Joints	$700
Alternator	350	Exhaust System	1,000
Automatic Trans.	1,160	Radiator	490
Brakes	210	Timing Chain/Belt	720

NHTSA RECALL HISTORY

1995: Inadvertent airbag deployment could occur, due to water intrusion. **1996:** Secondary hood latch may be improperly adjusted; if primary latch also is not engaged, hood could open unexpectedly. **1997:** Brake/traction-control module can cause antilock brake system to cycle in non ABS braking; could increase stopping distance. **1998:** Hood-hinge pivot bolts can break; could cause either the corner of the hood near the windshield to rise, or one side of hood to be unstable when opened. **1998:** Misrouted canister-purge evaporative-emissions harness could interfere with cruise control and throttle linkage, preventing return to close throttle position. **1999:** Some side-impact airbag-sensor modules have quality problems and may deploy inadvertently.

PRICES

	Good	Average	Poor
1994 Concours	$5,100-6,000	$4,300-5,100	$2,000-2,400
DeVille	4,500-5,300	3,700-4,400	1,600-1,900
1995 Concours	6,300-7,200	5,500-6,300	2,800-3,200
DeVille	5,500-6,300	4,700-5,400	2,300-2,600
1996 Concours	7,400-8,300	6,700-7,500	3,700-4,200
DeVille	6,500-7,400	5,700-6,500	2,900-3,300
1997 Concours	8,800-9,800	7,900-8,800	4,600-5,100
DeVille	7,700-8,700	6,900-7,800	3,900-4,400
1998 Concours	11,500-13,000	10,400-11,700	6,300-7,200
DeVille	9,500-11,000	8,600-9,900	4,900-5,700
1999 Concours	14,000-16,000	12,700-14,600	8,500-9,800
DeVille	12,000-14,000	10,800-12,600	6,700-7,800

For detailed information on this vehicle visit
http://used.consumerguide.com and enter code 2003

1992-02 CADILLAC ELDORADO

CLASS: Luxury car
BUILT IN: USA
PROS: Acceleration • Standard antilock brakes • Traction control (later models) • Steering/handling
CONS: Climate controls (early models) • Fuel economy • Rear visibility

EVALUATION: Despite the car's weight, Eldo acceleration is brisk with the original 4.9-liter engine. Dropping in one of the Northstar engines turns performance from brisk to nearly blistering—especially in Touring Coupe form. Cadillac claimed that both Northstar engines yielded 0-60 mph acceleration of 7.5 seconds, or nearly two seconds quicker than the base V8. No engine is economical. We averaged 16 mpg in a Touring

Coupe and 18 mpg in a Northstar-engined base coupe.

Computer Command Ride, which adjusts according to speed, delivers a secure road feel. Unlike prior Eldorados, this one does not bob or wallow over dips and around corners. Steering is precise, and the car is stable at speed and in curves. With a firmer suspension and new touring tires, the Touring Coupe is quieter and more supple than before.

Rear space is okay—generous for a coupe—but the rear seatback is too reclined for total comfort. Huge rear pillars impair the over-the-shoulder view. The large trunk has a usable shape. Buttons for heat and air conditioning are hidden behind the steering wheel. That flaw was corrected on 1996 Touring Coupes, but base coupes kept the former layout. Front bucket seats lack some lumbar bolstering, but are otherwise supportive.

VALUE FOR THE MONEY: In any guise, these are Cadillac's best premium coupes in a long while—excellent, expertly assembled, domestically built rivals to such imports as the Lexus SC 300/400, and competitive with Lincoln's Mark VIII. A solid structure completes this excellent package, giving the sizable coupe a unified feel, worthy of its price and status.

TROUBLE SPOTS

Automatic transmission: 440-T4 automatic transmissions may shift late or not upshift at all. The problem is a stuck throttle valve inside the transmission. (1992)

Automatic transmission: 4T60E transmissions may drop out of drive while cruising, shift erratically, or have no second, third, or fourth gear because of a bad ground connection for the shift solenoids. Poor grounds also allow wrong gear starts. (1992-93)

Engine noise: A rattling noise at startup is often caused by automatic-transmission pump starvation or cavitation, or a sticking pressure-regulator valve. (1992-93)

Steering noise: The upper bearing mount in the steering column can get loose and cause a snapping or clicking, requiring a new bearing spring and turn-signal cancel cam. (1994-96)

Transaxle leak: The right front axle seal at the automatic transaxle is prone to leak and GM issued a revised seal to correct the problem. (1992-93)

AVERAGE REPLACEMENT COSTS

A/C Compressor	$500	CV Joints	$800
Alternator	350	Exhaust System	1,135
Automatic Trans.	1,160	Shocks and/or Struts	1,225
Brakes	210	Timing Chain/Belt	820

NHTSA RECALL HISTORY

1992: Intermediate shaft to steering-rack lower-coupling pinch bolt may be missing on some cars; disengagement produces loss of steering control. **1993 w/4.6-liter engine:** Fuel feed and return lines to fuel-injection system could work loose, causing fuel leakage in engine compartment that could result in fire. **1993-94 w/4.6-liter V8:** If air conditioner compressor-clutch assembly contacts auxiliary engine oil-cooler hose, that hose may wear through, allowing leakage that could result in fire. **1994:** Throttle cable can disengage and interfere with cam mechanism. **1995:** Inadvertent airbag deployment could occur, due to water intrusion. **1996:** Analog instrument cluster on some cars could have internal short circuit disrupting Pass-Key system, causing failure of gauges and most telltale indicators, and possible no-start condition; panel could go black while driving. **1997:** Brake/traction-control module can cause antilock system to cycle in non-ABS braking; could increase stopping distance. **1998:** Misrouted canister purge evaporative emissions harness could interfere with cruise control and throttle linkage, preventing return to closed throttle position. **2000:** Inner tie-rod nuts on some cars are loose and can result in separation of tie rod, which can cause unexpected steering input.

PRICES

	Good	Average	Poor
1992 Eldorado	$4,000-4,700	$3,300-3,900	$1,300-1,500
Touring Coupe	4,500-5,300	3,700-4,400	1,600-1,900
1993 Eldorado	4,800-5,600	4,000-4,700	1,800-2,100
Touring Coupe	5,300-6,000	4,600-5,200	2,200-2,500
1994 Eldorado	5,800-6,600	5,000-5,700	2,400-2,800
Touring Coupe	6,400-7,300	5,600-6,400	2,800-3,200
1995 Eldorado	6,800-7,700	6,100-6,900	3,200-3,600
Touring Coupe	7,400-8,300	6,700-7,500	3,700-4,200
1996 Eldorado	8,000-9,000	7,200-8,100	4,100-4,600
Touring Coupe	8,800-9,800	7,900-8,800	4,600-5,100
1997 Eldorado	9,500-10,800	8,600-9,700	4,900-5,600
Touring Coupe	10,500-11,800	9,500-10,600	5,600-6,300
1998 Eldorado	11,500-13,000	10,400-11,700	6,300-7,200
Touring Coupe	12,700-14,000	11,400-12,600	7,200-8,000
1999 Eldorado	14,000-15,500	12,700-14,100	8,500-9,500
Touring Coupe	15,500-17,000	14,100-15,500	9,900-10,900
2000 Eldorado	17,500-19,000	16,100-17,500	11,200-12,200
Touring Coupe	19,200-20,500	17,700-18,900	12,500-13,300
2001 Eldorado	21,000-22,500	19,300-20,700	13,700-14,600
Touring Coupe	23,000-24,500	21,200-22,500	15,000-15,900
2002 Eldorado	25,000-27,000	23,300-25,100	16,500-17,800
Touring Coupe	27,200-29,000	25,300-27,000	18,200-19,400

For detailed information on this vehicle visit
http://used.consumerguide.com and enter code **2023**

1999-00 CADILLAC ESCALADE

CLASS: Luxury sport-utility vehicle

BUILT IN: USA

PROS: Passenger and cargo room • Trailer-towing capability

CONS: Entry/exit • Fuel economy • Ride/handling

CADILLAC

EVALUATION: In both performance and accommodations, the Escalade mirrored the closely related GMC Denali. Cadillac claimed that its SUV could accelerate to 60 mph in 10.5 seconds, which puts it around the midpoint in luxury models. Like GMC's Denali, though, the 5500-pound Escalade feels sluggish—especially when attempting to pass on the highway. Excess weight also hurts gas mileage. Our test Escalade averaged only 11.2 mpg.

Neither the Escalade nor the Denali is as quiet or comfortable as a luxury sedan—or as refined as the Chevrolet Tahoe/GMC Yukon, which were redesigned for 2000. Ride and handling are subpar by any measure, with mediocre suppression of harsh impacts and a ponderous feel through turns. Stopping power is satisfactory, but the brake pedal feels mushy.

Cadillac-grade leather upholstery imparts an impressively rich sensation, but front bucket seats are too soft and flat for optimum comfort. Lack of a powered backrest recliner and automatic climate control (on 1999 models) are telltale omissions for a vehicle in this price category.

The front cabin is spacious, with enough room in back for three adults without crowding. Lincoln's Navigator, on the other hand—and the 2000 Tahoe/Yukon duo—can seat as many as eight.

Tall interior step-in and surprisingly narrow rear-door bottoms make getting in and out of the back seat a problem. Cargo space is generous, even with the rear seatback in use. Plenty of storage bins and cubbyholes give space for miscellaneous items. Still, an abundance of hard plastic interior panels and parts-bin switchgear give the Escalade's cabin an ambiance that's closer to a GM truck than a luxury automobile.

VALUE FOR THE MONEY: Escalades came with plenty of standard features and conveniences, but on the whole this sport-utility vehicle feels more like a dashed-together collection of "luxury" SUV cues than an intelligent, cohesive design. For that reason alone, it does not rate a spot on our secondhand shopping list.

TROUBLE SPOTS

See the 1990-00 Chevrolet Blazer/Tahoe.

AVERAGE REPLACEMENT COSTS

See the 1990-00 Chevrolet Blazer/Tahoe.

NHTSA RECALL HISTORY

None to date.

PRICES

	Good	Average	Poor
1999 Escalade	$19,500-21,500	$17,900-19,800	$12,700-14,000
2000 Escalade	21,500-23,500	19,800-21,600	14,000-15,300

For detailed information on this vehicle visit
http://used.consumerguide.com and enter code **2446**

1993-96 CADILLAC FLEETWOOD

CLASS: Near-luxury car

BUILT IN: USA

PROS: Acceleration • Antilock brakes • Interior noise levels • Passenger and cargo room • Trailer-towing capability

CONS: Fuel economy • Size and weight • Rear visibility

EVALUATION: "Fleet" is definitely the word for the 1994-96 Fleetwood, with its Corvette-derived engine. With that powerplant on tap, you get swift takeoffs, as well as vigorous passing—which takes only a little more pressure on the gas pedal. Cadillac claimed that 0-60 mph acceleration took just 8.5 seconds—two seconds faster than the 1993 model. Fuel economy is no bargain; we averaged only 14.8 mpg.

Fleetwood suspensions are firmer than those in a Caprice or Roadmaster, so you don't get the pillowy-soft ride that characterized big Cadillacs of the more distant past. Sure, it filters out fewer bumps, but the massive sedan also wallows less and has better control in turns than its GM siblings. Even so, body lean is excessive and the undeniably soft suspension allows lots of bouncing on wavy roads. Steering is firmer too, for improved road feel. Traction control is a definite "plus." When actuated, it pushes back gently on the gas pedal, and an indicator light illuminates.

Inside, three can sit across, front or rear, but those in the middle won't have much leg room. Adults can stretch their legs at outboard positions. Front seats are "split-frame" design, in which the lower cushion adjusts independently of the backrest. Base-model seat cushions seem firmer and no less comfortable than the multi-adjustable seats in the costlier Brougham. Back seats are nothing short of cavernous, but the cushion lacks thigh support. Drivers face an uncluttered dashboard layout. A huge trunk holds several suitcases.

VALUE FOR THE MONEY: Quite a few traditional-type shoppers regret the fact that Cadillac stopped making these big rear-drive sedans. If you tow a trailer and travel cross-country, a Fleetwood just might be your best practical choice.

TROUBLE SPOTS

Automatic transmission: 700-R4 automatic transmissions may shift late or not upshift at all. The problem is a stuck throttle valve inside the transmission. (1993)

Steering noise: The upper bearing mount in the steering column can get loose and cause a snapping or clicking, requiring a new bearing spring and turn-signal cancel cam, which the manufacturer will warranty. (1994-96)

AVERAGE REPLACEMENT COSTS

A/C Compressor	$485	Radiator	$409
Alternator	225	Shocks and/or Struts	430

CADILLAC

Automatic Trans.	$780	Timing Chain/Belt	$220
Brakes	235	Universal Joints	270
Exhaust System	420		

NHTSA RECALL HISTORY

1993: Passenger-side airbag in a few cars could experience an inflator ignition delay in an accident; delayed deployment could increase risk of injury. **1994:** Fuel-tank strap fasteners can detach, eventually allowing tank to sag. **1994:** Oil-cooler inlet hose may be too close to steering gear, causing chafing; could result in leakage and fire. **1994:** On small number of cars, paint between wheel and brake rotor/drum can cause lug nut to loosen. **1994-95:** At low temperatures, throttle return spring could fail. **1994-95:** Lower ball joint on a few cars sent to Guam and Puerto Rico can separate. **1995:** Improperly adjusted transmission linkage may permit shifting from "Park" position with ignition key removed. **1995-96:** Wheel lug nuts were not tightened to the proper specification. This could result in wheel loss.

PRICES

	Good	Average	Poor
1993 Fleetwood	$4,500-5,300	$3,700-4,400	$1,600-1,900
1994 Fleetwood	5,500-6,400	4,700-5,500	2,300-2,600
1995 Fleetwood	6,700-7,600	5,900-6,700	3,100-3,500
1996 Fleetwood	7,500-8,500	6,800-7,700	3,800-4,300

For detailed information on this vehicle visit
http://used.consumerguide.com and enter code **2004**

1992-97 CADILLAC SEVILLE

CLASS: Luxury car

BUILT IN: USA

PROS: Acceleration
• Standard antilock brakes and traction control (later models) • Passenger and cargo room • Steering/handling

CONS: Climate controls (early models) • Fuel economy • Rear visibility • Ride (later STS)

EVALUATION: More than prior Sevilles, the 1992-96 edition displays fine road manners and a rock-solid feel, thanks to a stiffened chassis. Road noise was reduced, and improved engine-mounting better isolated the V8 from the passenger compartment. Despite the extra bulk, acceleration is brisk with the initial 4.9-liter engine, never lacking for strength whether in the city or on the highway. Shifts are almost imperceptible. The Northstar V8 added for 1993 is smoother and faster yet, but limits its most impressive acceleration to engine speeds above 3500 rpm. That gives the STS terrific performance on the open road.

Speed-dependent Computer Command Ride adds to the secure feel of early

Sevilles. Sure, the base-model ride is a bit soft at lower speeds (under 45 mph or so), but the bounce is nearly gone at highway velocities, and the sedan cruises with commendable stability and comfort. At low speeds, the 1993-up STS's Road Sensing Suspension floats less than the base setup. It's also more absorbent at higher speeds, and handles better on bumpy pavement. Steering is firm and precise, and the sedan remains stable through corners. Stiff tires give the later STS impressive handling, but a harsh, even jittery ride. Softer tires on the base (SLS) sedan transmit less impact and generate less noise. The '96 STS adopted softer tires, reducing the contrast between models.

Head room is ample, front and rear. Adult knees aren't likely to press into the front seatback. Wide rear doors make entry/exit a snap, but thick roof pillars hamper over-the-shoulder visibility. Dashboards are well laid out, but climate-control buttons are hidden to the right of the steering wheel. That flaw was corrected in the 1996 STS, but the SLS kept the prior layout. The roomy trunk has a flat floor that's wide at the rear and stretches well forward. Its lid opens nearly from bumper height for easy loading.

VALUE FOR THE MONEY: Especially in STS trim, the Seville is Cadillac's best premium sedan in ages, scoring strongly against such imported rivals as the BMW 740iL, Lexus LS 400, and Infiniti Q45.

TROUBLE SPOTS

Automatic transmission: 4T60E transmissions may drop out of drive while cruising, shift erratically, or have no second, third, or fourth gear because of a bad ground connection for the shift solenoids. Poor grounds also allow wrong gear starts. (1991-93)

Engine noise: A rattling noise at startup is often caused by automatic-transmission pump starvation or cavitation, or a sticking pressure-regulator valve. (1992-93)

Steering noise: The upper bearing mount in the steering column can get loose and cause a snapping or clicking, requiring a new bearing spring and turn-signal cancel cam. (1994-96)

Transaxle leak: 440-T4 automatic transmissions may shift late or not upshift at all. The problem is a stuck throttle valve inside the transmission. (1992)

Transaxle leak: The right front axle seal at the automatic transaxle is prone to leak and GM issued a revised seal to correct the problem. (1992-93)

AVERAGE REPLACEMENT COSTS

A/C Compressor	$465	Exhaust System	$998
Alternator	295	Radiator	375
Automatic Trans.	1,085	Shocks and/or Struts	1,360
Brakes	210	Timing Chain/Belt	265
CV Joints	810		

NHTSA RECALL HISTORY

1992: Intermediate shaft to steering rack lower-coupling pinch bolt may be missing on some cars; disengagement of shaft produces loss of steering control. **1993 w/4.6-liter V8:** Fuel feed and return lines to fuel injection system could work loose, causing fuel leakage in engine compartment. **1993-94 w/4.6-liter V8:** If air-conditioner compressor-clutch assembly contacts auxiliary engine-oil-cooler outlet hose, that hose may wear through. **1994:** Throttle cable can disengage and interfere with cam mechanism; car could accelerate unexpectedly. **1995:** Airbag could deploy inadvertently, due to water intrusion. **1996:** Analog instrument cluster on some cars could have internal short circuit disrupting Pass-Key system, causing failure of gauges and most telltale indicators, and possible no-start condition; panel could go black while driving. **1997:** Brake/traction-control module can cause antilock system to cycle in non-ABS braking; could increase stopping distance.

PRICES	Good	Average	Poor
1992 Seville	$4,000-4,700	$3,300-3,900	$1,300-1,500
Seville STS	4,300-5,000	3,600-4,200	1,500-1,700
1993 Seville	4,800-5,600	4,000-4,700	1,800-2,100
Seville STS	5,300-6,100	4,600-5,200	2,200-2,500
1994 Seville SLS	5,800-6,600	5,000-5,700	2,400-2,800
Seville STS	6,300-7,100	5,500-6,200	2,800-3,100
1995 Seville SLS	6,800-7,700	6,100-6,900	3,200-3,600
Seville STS	7,400-8,300	6,700-7,500	3,700-4,200
1996 Seville SLS	7,700-8,600	6,900-7,700	3,900-4,300
Seville STS	8,700-9,700	7,800-8,700	4,500-5,000
1997 Seville SLS	9,000-10,000	8,100-9,000	4,700-5,200
Seville STS	10,000-11,500	9,000-10,400	5,200-6,000

> For detailed information on this vehicle visit
> http://used.consumerguide.com and enter code **2005**

1998-03 CADILLAC SEVILLE

CLASS: Luxury car
BUILT IN: USA
PROS: Acceleration
• Automatic-transmission performance
• Handling/roadholding
• Interior materials • Interior storage space

CONS: Fuel economy • Rear visibility

EVALUATION: Seville again ranks among the class leaders in acceleration, courtesy of the unaltered Northstar V8 engines and little-changed curb weights. Behavior of the smooth 4-speed automatic transmission is beyond reproach—smooth and responsive. The SLS sedan focuses on low-speed acceleration, whereas the STS emphasizes high-speed responses. Both engines are on the thirsty side, achieving only 14.8 mpg in our tests. At least, the 2000 models manage on regular gasoline.

The SLS feels appropriately soft without being sloppy—nicely composed during directional changes. With its tauter suspension, aggressive tire tread, and lower ride height, an STS responds more quickly to steering inputs and corners with a greater degree of flatness. The STS also is prone to irritating steering-wheel tug in hard takeoffs, and its magnetic power steering can lag behind driver inputs. Cadillac has claimed that Seville was as quiet as a Lexus LS 400. That's almost true, but not quite.

Despite the 5-passenger claim, four adults is the comfortable limit inside a Seville. At that, back-seat riders must tuck their legs and swivel their ankles to negotiate narrow door bottoms. Front-seat space is generous. Rear-seat room ranks only as adequate. Tall riders' heads are likely to brush the headliner. Optional adaptive seats in the STS are comfortable, if not vastly more so than the regular seats. A new instrument panel, illuminated by fluorescent back-lighting and LED needles, gives the gauges outstanding definition. If desired, the driver can eliminate the illumination, leaving only a digital speed display. Switchgear is logically arranged, except that the climate controls sit low.

Wide rear roof pillars and a tall trunk limit the driver's view, both aft and over both shoulders. The trunk is spacious. Inside, the Seville boasts a class-leading array of 19 separate pockets, boxes, and a pouch.

VALUE FOR THE MONEY: Sevilles seem solid and well-assembled, and interior materials are top-notch. However, one test model suffered a wind leak around the driver's window, ill-fitting rear-door seals, and a wiring harness dangling beneath the driver's seat—not quite what's expected in this price league.

Were it not for such questionable details, Seville would be easy to recommend on the grounds of performance, features, and solidity. We give a higher rating to the SLS, which does a fine job balancing performance and comfort.

TROUBLE SPOTS

Audio system: The company is replacing radios that have poor AM reception or FM bleed into the AM band. (1998-99)

Brake noise: The front brakes make noises (squeals, grinding, groaning, etc.) requiring new brake pads and redesigned rotors. (1998)

Engine knock: The engine makes ticking noises and knocking noises that sound like main bearing knock, often due to cylinder carbon buildup. (1998-99)

Fuel gauge: The fuel gauge reads empty or swings between empty and full due to problem with the in-tank sending unit. (1998)

Paint/body: On white cars, the door handles turn yellow from the lock cylinder grease staining them. The company will replace the cylinders under warranty and there is a colorless grease available for service. (1998-99)

Poor transmission shift: Transmission is slow to engage between drive and reverse, often accompanied by a clunk requiring a transmission rebuild under warranty. (1998)

AVERAGE REPLACEMENT COSTS

A/C Compressor	$730	Exhaust System	$595
Alternator	735	Radiator	520
Automatic Trans.	1,350	Shocks and/or Struts	1,350
Brakes	570	Timing Chain/Belt	1,090
CV Joints	1,050		

NHTSA RECALL HISTORY

1998: Windshield wiper "Low" speed function can become inoperative if motor is switched from "High" to "Low." **1998-99:** Electrical short can develop in generator, even when engine is off. **2000:** Due to internal fluid leakage in some cars, rear-brake proportioning, ABS, traction control or stability control may not perform as designed. **2000:** Inner tie-rod nuts on some cars are loose and can result in separation of tie rod, which can cause unexpected steering input. **2001 w/235/55R17 tires:** These vehicles can have an incorrect tire-pressure label. **2002:** Steering-gear attachment bolts may be undertorqued or missing, resulting in uneven steering response or unusual noise during turns. **2002-03 V8:** Faulty fuel-tank sensors may have been installed in certain vehicles, leading to fuel leakage. Dealer will inspect and replace all affected parts.

PRICES	Good	Average	Poor
1998 Seville SLS	$12,000-13,500	$10,800-12,200	$6,700-7,600
Seville STS	13,500-15,000	12,300-13,700	8,000-8,900
1999 Seville SLS	14,500-16,000	13,200-14,600	9,000-9,900
Seville STS	16,200-17,800	14,700-16,200	10,400-11,400
2000 Seville SLS	17,000-18,500	15,600-17,000	10,900-11,800
Seville STS	19,500-21,000	17,900-19,300	12,700-13,700
2001 Seville SLS	20,000-21,500	18,400-19,800	13,000-14,000
Seville STS	23,000-24,500	21,200-22,500	15,000-15,900
2002 Seville SLS	24,000-25,500	22,300-23,700	15,600-16,600
Seville STS	27,500-30,000	25,600-27,900	18,400-20,100
2003 Seville SLS	28,500-31,000	26,500-28,800	19,400-21,100
Seville STS	33,000-36,000	30,700-33,500	23,400-25,600

For detailed information on this vehicle visit
http://used.consumerguide.com and enter code **2298**

1990-03 CHEVROLET ASTRO

CLASS: Minivan
BUILT IN: USA
PROS: Antilock brakes
• Optional AWD traction
• Passenger and cargo room
• Trailer-towing capability
CONS: Entry/exit • Fuel economy • Ride

EVALUATION: Spacious inside, Astro vans can be fitted to tow up to three tons and seat up to eight. The penalty that must be paid for its brawn is a rough, bouncy ride—definitely less carlike than front-drive minivans, which serve as replacements for the traditional old family station wagon. Clumsy handling also ranks as subpar. Even the least-potent V6 engine has plenty of torque for hauling heavy loads and towing, but that muscle does not translate into brisk acceleration. As for economy, we averaged just 14.5 mpg in an early

AWD, regular-length Astro. Expect around 15 mpg in urban driving, and not a whole lot more on the highway. Another demerit: Servicing isn't so easy.

Entry/exit to the front seats is hampered by doorways that are narrow at the bottom. There's also a tall step-up to get inside. Interiors offer loads of passenger and cargo room, though front-seat riders must deal with uncomfortably narrow footwells. The dashboard, as revised for 1996, has a convenient layout with plenty of built-in storage space. With eight seats, a regular-length Astro has little rear cargo room.

All-wheel drive offers better rain/snow traction, but with even more thirst for gas. It also makes the Astro an inch higher, adding to step-in height.

VALUE FOR THE MONEY: Like the now-extinct Ford Aerostar, the Astro and its GMC Safari cousin are truck-based vehicles, better suited to heavy-duty work than are front-drive minivans. Trucklike behavior could be a turnoff unless you need Astro's brand of brawniness for towing or other demanding applications.

TROUBLE SPOTS

Doors: Improper adjustment of the sliding door can make it hard to open or close. (1990-93)

Engine knock: A knocking sound may be due to three possible causes and may be fixed with either an oil filter having a built-in check valve, a revised PROM or replacement of the main bearings. (1990-95)

Engine misfire: The fuel injector wires tend to get pinched when the air filter is reinstalled. (1990-93)

Engine misfire: New valve-guide seals should eliminate the blue smoke from the tailpipe during cold starting. (1990-93)

Engine noise: An engine noise might be caused by the exhaust valves sticking in their guides. New valve-guide seals should correct the problem if the guides are not worn. (1996)

Transmission leak: The rear seal on the transmission (extension housing seal) may leak on vans with a one-piece drive shaft. (1990-94)

Transmission leak: Fluid may leak from the pump body on 4L60-E transmissions due to the pump bushing walking out of the valve body. (1995-96)

AVERAGE REPLACEMENT COSTS

A/C Compressor	$515	Exhaust System	$320
Alternator	245	Radiator	420
Automatic Trans.	770	Shocks and/or Struts	247
Brakes	225	Timing Chain/Belt	255
Clutch	555	Universal Joints	153

NHTSA RECALL HISTORY

1990-91: Bucket seat's knob-type recliner mechanism with foam or vinyl "soft joint" may loosen and cause bolt failure, allowing seatback to recline suddenly; could produce loss of control. **1992-94:** Front seatbacks do not conform to height requirements. **1994:** Airbag-advisory labels may be missing. **1995 w/L35 engine:** Fuel lines at tank were improperly tightened and could loosen, allowing leakage and possible fire. **1995:** On a few vans, left lower control-arm bolt could loosen, fatigue, and break. **1995-97:** The windshield-wiper motor may fail on certain vehicles. Dealer will inspect and replace affected parts. **1996-97:** Outboard-seatbelt webbing on right-rear bucket seat can separate during crash. **1996-98 w/integrated child seats:** Seatbelt-retractor clutch spring and/or pawl spring in child seat may be missing. **1998:** On certain vehicles, the outside rearview mirror switch may short circuit. Dealer will inspect and replace affected parts. **1999:** Audible fasten-seatbelt warning may not sound or may not sound as long as is required by the standard. **2003:** Poorly manufactured steering knuckles on some vehicles may allow for road contamination to enter and wear down the ball joint, resulting in difficulty controlling the vehicle

PRICES	Good	Average	Poor
1990 Astro 2WD	$1,600-2,400	$1,100-1,600	$200-300
Astro AWD	2,100-2,800	1,500-2,000	400-500
1991 Astro 2WD	1,900-2,800	1,300-1,900	300-400
Astro AWD	2,400-3,200	1,700-2,300	500-600
1992 Astro 2WD	2,300-3,500	1,700-2,500	400-700
Astro AWD	2,800-4,000	2,100-3,000	600-900
1993 Astro 2WD	2,500-3,800	1,800-2,800	500-800
Astro AWD	3,200-4,500	2,500-3,500	800-1,100
1994 Astro 2WD	3,000-4,500	2,300-3,500	700-1,000
Astro AWD	3,700-5,000	3,000-4,100	1,100-1,500
1995 Astro 2WD	3,600-5,000	2,900-4,000	1,000-1,400
Astro AWD	4,400-5,700	3,700-4,700	1,500-2,000
1996 Astro 2WD	4,500-5,500	3,700-4,600	1,600-2,000
Astro AWD	5,500-6,500	4,700-5,600	2,300-2,700
1997 Astro 2WD	5,200-6,500	4,400-5,500	2,100-2,600
Astro AWD	6,300-7,500	5,500-6,600	2,800-3,300
1998 Astro 2WD	6,000-7,500	5,200-6,500	2,500-3,200
Astro AWD	7,200-8,500	6,400-7,600	3,500-4,200
1999 Astro 2WD	7,500-9,200	6,800-8,300	3,800-4,600
Astro AWD	9,000-10,500	8,100-9,500	4,700-5,500
2000 Astro 2WD	9,200-11,000	8,300-9,900	4,800-5,700
Astro AWD	10,800-12,500	9,700-11,300	5,800-6,800
2001 Astro 2WD	11,000-12,800	9,900-11,500	5,900-6,900
Astro AWD	12,500-14,200	11,300-12,800	7,100-8,100
2002 Astro 2WD	13,000-14,800	11,800-13,500	7,500-8,600
Astro AWD	14,500-16,200	13,200-14,700	9,000-10,000
2003 Astro 2WD	15,000-17,000	13,700-15,500	9,500-10,700
Astro AWD	17,000-19,000	15,600-17,500	10,900-12,200

> For detailed information on this vehicle visit
> **http://used.consumerguide.com** and enter code **2121**

2002-03 CHEVROLET AVALANCHE

CLASS: Full-size pickup truck
BUILT IN: Mexico
PROS: Storage space
• Passenger and cargo room
• Trailer-towing capability
CONS: Fuel economy

EVALUATION: Uniqueness is the Avalanche's main attraction, though its driving qualities are more appealing than some might expect. Acceleration is much like the Suburban's. That's no surprise, since an Avalanche has similar weight and the same smooth, strong V8 with a silky, responsive automatic transmission and useful Tow/Haul mode.

Fuel economy earns no prizes. A test 4WD 1500 averaged just 12.9 mpg, though both engines use regular fuel.

Ride quality is comfortable even with the firm Z71 package. A long wheelbase helps the Avalanche ignore most small bumps, and it's less jarring than most true pickup trucks over big ruts and crests. Still, big bumps can induce some "float" or pitching.

Steering and handling are like the Suburban's, meaning it's a pleasant highway cruiser and agile for its size and weight, despite too-numb steering. Braking is strong and stable, but spongy pedal action on test models did not inspire confidence.

Although the engine roars at full throttle, an Avalanche is quite refined overall. Removing the rear window, or dropping the midgate, increases noise levels, but not unduly so.

Instruments/controls are identical to the Suburban's and mostly very good. So is the driving position. Inherited flaws include tight access to power controls on the side of front seat bases, and GM's typical low-budget plastic in too many places.

High tail trim hides any nearby object dead astern. Over-the-shoulder visibility is a bit obscured, but not bad. There's plenty of adult-size space up front, but also a fairly high step-in. The bench seat is nothing special, but optional buckets are comfortable.

Even with the midgate fully down, there's a tolerably mild inside breeze at highway speeds. Rear step-in is pretty lofty, and leg room isn't quite Suburban-ample, but space is adequate for three grownups, extravagant for two.

An Avalanche hauls what most big pickups can, though the back seat and midgate must be folded for bulky or long loads like 4x8 plywood sheets. Midgate/window removal is straightforward and quick. The hose-it-down cargo box has a tough composite-plastic liner, thick nonslip rubber mat, twin lamps that also light the lockable side storage boxes, eight tiedowns, water drains, and a gravel trap.

VALUE FOR THE MONEY: For the most part, an Avalanche weds big-SUV passenger room and comfort with big-pickup utility, in an imaginative and surprisingly solid package. Beware of seriously bad weather on really messy roads, though, if the midgate is fully open.

TROUBLE SPOTS

Engine knock: The engine (4.8L, 5.3L, or 6.0L) may knock for up to 30 seconds after a cold start. GM says this may be due to carbon buildup and is reportedly not harmful to the engine. (2002)

Engine noise: Some of the rocker-arm bearings may fail. The first indication may be needle bearings found in the oil when it is drained. All 16 rocker arms should be replaced. (2002)

Engine noise: Due to corrosion of the knock sensor on the rear bank, the 5.7-litre engine may suffer from spark knock (ping) that gets worse on hard acceleration, illuminating the "check engine" light. (2002)

Transmission slippage: The transmission may slip or there may be no 3rd or 4th gear (possibly accompanied by illumination of the "check engine" light) due to plugging of one of the shift solenoid valves. (2002)

Water leak: A water leak at the rear corner of the cargo box requires resealing of the catch cup. (2002)

AVERAGE REPLACEMENT COSTS

A/C Compressor	$390	Exhaust System	$455
Alternator	325	Radiator	555
Automatic Trans.	1,315	Shocks and/or Struts	665
Brakes	475	Timing Chain/Belt	610
CV Joints	890		

NHTSA RECALL HISTORY

2003: In certain extreme impacts frame cross member could tear fuel tank resulting in fuel leakage. Dealers will install a fuel-tank shield on affected vehicles.

PRICES

	Good	Average	Poor
2002 Avalanche 2WD	$22,000-23,500	$20,200-21,600	$14,300-15,300
Avalanche 4WD	24,000-25,500	22,300-23,700	15,600-16,600
2003 Avalanche 2WD	25,000-27,000	23,300-25,100	16,500-17,800
Avalanche 4WD	27,500-29,500	25,600-27,400	18,400-19,800

For detailed information on this vehicle visit
http://used.consumerguide.com and enter code **2474**

1995-03 CHEVROLET BLAZER

CLASS: Midsize sport-utility vehicle

BUILT IN: USA

PROS: Acceleration • Antilock brakes • 4WD traction • Passenger and cargo room • Ride

CONS: Fuel economy • Rear-seat comfort

EVALUATION: Acceleration is above average for a sport utility, livelier than a V6 Explorer from a standstill, with stronger passing power. Unfortunately, the automatic transmission pauses a moment before downshifting. Naturally, too, the Blazer's V6 cannot hope to match an Explorer's V8 when hitting the gas pedal hard.

Fuel economy wins no prizes. A long-term test of a 4-door 4WD Blazer averaged 15.2 mpg.

A variety of suspension choices have been offered, tailoring the ride from off-road firm to suburban-street soft. Of all the suspension packages available, we prefer the "premium ride" version, which absorbs most bumps easily and produces a comfortable, stable highway ride. In fact, that Blazer rides more like a car than a truck.

Blazers actually steer and handle much like a midsize sedan. Body lean is moderate in tight corners. Steering feels more precise than on the old S10 Blazer. Stopping power is adequate, though our test vehicle suffered a mushy brake-pedal feel, as well as substantial nosedive in quick stops. Things improved with the 4-wheel disc brakes on the '98 model.

Passenger space is about the same as before. That translates to good room for four adults in both body styles. In a pinch, five or even six can fit into the bigger 4-door. However, the rear seat has a short, hard backrest—bolt upright and uncomfortable. Cargo room is ample, improved in the 4-door by mounting the spare tire beneath the rear end. Visibility is fine in the 4-door, but obstructed by the 3-door's sloped roof pillars as well as the spare tire.

The modern-looking dashboard has clear gauges and easy-to-use controls. Power window and lock buttons are large and helpfully backlit. The climate system uses rotary switches for selecting mode and temperature.

Some engine roar remains in hard acceleration, but road and wind noise now are well-muffled, ranking as moderate.

VALUE FOR THE MONEY: Blazers are competitive with the Explorer and Jeep Grand Cherokee in most areas, and beat them on price when new. Good buys also can be found in the secondhand market.

TROUBLE SPOTS

Engine misfire: The powertrain control module may cause a lack of power, early upshifts, late shifting in the 4WD-Low range. (1996)

Engine noise: Engine knock at startup is usually eliminated by using an oil filter with a check valve. However, GM has revised PROMs and may even replace the main bearings if no other solution is found. (1995)

Engine noise: Exhaust valves may not get enough lubrication causing a variety of noises. Usually, the same engine consumes excess oil because the valve-guide seals on the exhaust valves are bad. (1996)

Transmission leak: Fluid may leak from the pump body on 4L60-E transmissions due to the pump bushing walking out of the valve body. (1995-96)

AVERAGE REPLACEMENT COSTS

A/C Compressor	$520	Exhaust System	$485
Alternator	225	Radiator	450
Automatic Trans.	850	Shocks and/or Struts	410

CHEVROLET

Brakes.............................	$220	Timing Chain/Belt.............	$230
Clutch..............................	800	Universal Joints................	270

NHTSA RECALL HISTORY

1995 w/4WD: A few upper ball-joint nuts were undertorqued; stud can loosen and fracture, resulting in loss of steering control. **1995 w/air conditioning:** Fan-blade rivets can break and allow blade to separate from hub. **1995:** Brake-pedal bolt on some vehicles might disengage, causing loss of braking. **1995-96 w/4WD and ABS:** Increased stopping distances can occur during ABS stops while in 2WD mode. **1995-96 w/4WD and ABS:** Under certain conditions, stopping distances in 2WD mode could be excessive. **1995-96 w/AWD/4WD:** During development testing, prop shaft contacted inboard side of fuel tank, rupturing the tank; fuel leakage was beyond permissible level. **1995-96:** Windshield wipers may work intermittently. **1996-97 2-door w/manual-locking recliner bucket seats:** Outboard seatbelt webbing can separate during frontal impact. **1996-97:** Failure of an upper and lower control-arm ball-joint assembly could occur due to corrosion, resulting in impaired steering or steering loss, or a partial or complete collapse of the front suspension. **1997:** On certain vehicles, the outside rearview mirror switch may short circuit. Dealer will inspect and replace affected parts. **1998 w/4WD or AWD:** On a few vehicles, one or both attaching nuts for lower control arm could separate from frame, resulting in loss of control. **1998:** Daytime running lights do not meet FMVSS No. 108 requirements. **1998:** Fatigue fracture of rear-axle brake pipe can occur, causing slow fluid leak and resulting in soft brake pedal; if pipe breaks, driver would face sudden loss of rear-brake performance. **2000 w/2WD:** On certain vehicles, right-hand ABS module feed pipe and/or brake crossover pipe tube nuts could have been tightened improperly; seal could have been broken, causing leakage and increasing stopping distance. **2000-01:** Some seatbelt assemblies were not properly heat treated and do not pass the load-bearing requirement. **2000-02:** Brake lights and rear hazard flashers may fail if the multifunction switch develops an open-circuit condition.

PRICES

	Good	Average	Poor
1995 Blazer 2-dr 2WD	$2,800-3,600	$2,100-2,700	$600-800
Blazer 2-dr 4WD	4,000-4,800	3,300-3,900	1,300-1,500
Blazer 4-dr 2WD	3,400-4,200	2,700-3,300	900-1,100
Blazer 4-dr 4WD	4,500-5,300	3,700-4,400	1,600-1,900
1996 Blazer 2-dr 2WD	3,200-4,000	2,500-3,100	800-1,000
Blazer 2-dr 4WD	4,400-5,400	3,700-4,500	1,500-1,900
Blazer 4-dr 2WD	3,800-4,800	3,100-3,900	1,100-1,400
Blazer 4-dr 4WD	5,000-6,000	4,300-5,100	2,000-2,400
1997 Blazer 2-dr 2WD	3,800-4,700	3,100-3,800	1,100-1,400
Blazer 2-dr 4WD	5,000-6,000	4,300-5,100	2,000-2,400
Blazer 4-dr 2WD	4,400-5,800	3,700-4,800	1,500-2,000
Blazer 4-dr 4WD	5,700-7,000	4,900-6,000	2,300-2,900
1998 Blazer 2-dr 2WD	4,500-5,500	3,700-4,600	1,600-2,000
Blazer 2-dr 4WD	5,800-6,700	5,000-5,800	2,400-2,800
Blazer 4-dr 2WD	5,300-6,500	4,600-5,600	2,200-2,700
Blazer 4-dr 4WD	6,700-7,700	5,900-6,800	3,100-3,500

1999 Blazer 2-dr 2WD	$5,800-7,000	$5,000-6,100	$2,400-2,900
Blazer 2-dr 4WD	7,300-8,500	6,600-7,700	3,600-4,200
Blazer 4-dr 2WD	6,800-8,300	6,100-7,400	3,200-3,900
Blazer 4-dr 4WD	8,300-9,500	7,500-8,600	4,300-4,900
2000 Blazer 2-dr 2WD	7,500-8,800	6,800-7,900	3,800-4,400
Blazer 2-dr 4WD	9,000-10,000	8,100-9,000	4,700-5,200
Blazer 4-dr 2WD	8,500-9,500	7,700-8,600	4,400-4,900
Blazer 4-dr 4WD	10,200-11,500	9,200-10,400	5,300-6,000
2001 Blazer 2-dr 2WD	9,500-10,800	8,600-9,700	4,900-5,600
Blazer 2-dr 4WD	11,000-12,000	9,900-10,800	5,900-6,500
Blazer 2-dr Xtreme	11,000-12,000	9,900-10,800	5,900-6,500
Blazer 4-dr 2WD	10,500-11,700	9,500-10,500	5,600-6,200
Blazer 4-dr 4WD	12,200-13,500	11,000-12,200	6,800-7,600
2002 Blazer 2-dr 2WD	11,500-13,000	10,400-11,700	6,300-7,200
Blazer 2-dr 4WD	13,200-14,500	12,000-13,200	7,700-8,400
Blazer 2-dr Xtreme	13,000-14,200	11,800-12,900	7,500-8,200
Blazer 4-dr 2WD	12,700-13,800	11,400-12,400	7,200-7,900
Blazer 4-dr 4WD	14,300-15,500	13,000-14,100	8,900-9,600
2003 Blazer 2-dr 2WD	14,000-15,500	12,700-14,100	8,500-9,500
Blazer 2-dr 4WD	16,000-17,500	14,600-15,900	10,200-11,200
Blazer 2-dr Xtreme	15,200-16,500	13,800-15,000	9,600-10,400
Blazer 4-dr 2WD	15,500-17,000	14,100-15,500	9,900-10,900
Blazer 4-dr 4WD	17,000-18,500	15,600-17,000	10,900-11,800

For detailed information on this vehicle visit
http://used.consumerguide.com and enter code **2124**

1992-00
CHEVROLET
BLAZER/TAHOE

CG BEST BUY

CLASS: Full-size sport-utility vehicle

BUILT IN: Mexico, USA

PROS: Acceleration (5.7-liter)
• Driver-side and dual airbags
(later models) • Passenger and
cargo room • Ride • Trailer-
towing capability

CONS: Entry/exit (2-door
and 4WD) • Fuel economy
• Ride (2-door)

EVALUATION: Blazers and their Tahoe successors are brawny but civilized,
both on-road and off. Acceleration with Blazer/Tahoe gasoline V8s ranks as
robust, and these models can pull a heavy trailer with ease. As for economy, an
early 2-door Tahoe averaged 12.5 mpg in mostly city driving. Vortec engines

CHEVROLET

of 1996-97 might be a bit more frugal. A 4-door 4WD returned 14.3 mpg.

Road behavior isn't bad, though body lean is still noticeable—but not as much as in earlier models. When loaded, at least, the big Blazer handles rough pavement with less bouncing and pitching than before. Unladen, the tail still tends to judder sideways over closely spaced bumps. Steering is a bit overassisted, but precise, and this version is quieter on the road than its predecessors.

Step-up into the interior isn't as high as before, and you get plenty of space for three abreast, with bountiful head and leg room. Dashboards have easy-to-read gauges and handy controls. Rear doors of the 4-door create unprecedented access to the back seat, but door openings are narrow at the bottom, and step-in height is tall. Cargo room in the 4-door benefits from the under-chassis location of the spare tire. Three-door models carry their spares inside.

VALUE FOR THE MONEY: Sure, a compact sport utility is more sensible and economical for everyday driving. But if you require real muscle, especially for towing, try the 4-door Tahoe and also Ford's Expedition.

TROUBLE SPOTS

Automatic transmission: Automatic transmissions may suffer harsh or shuddering shifts between first and second or may buzz or vibrate in park or neutral. (1992)

Climate control: The temperature-control lever may slide from hot to cold, usually when the blower is on high speed. (1992-94)

Dashboard lights: The oil-pressure gauge may read high, move erratically, or not work because the oil-pressure sensor is defective. (1990-93)

Transmission leak: Fluid may leak from the pump body on 4L60-E transmissions due to the pump bushing walking out of the valve body. (1995-96)

AVERAGE REPLACEMENT COSTS

A/C Compressor	$555	Exhaust System	$380
Alternator	220	Radiator	650
Automatic Trans.	750	Shocks and/or Struts	340
Brakes	260	Timing Chain/Belt	415
Clutch	730	Universal Joints	225

NHTSA RECALL HISTORY

1992 Blazer: Rotor sections may separate due to corrosion, resulting in loss of braking ability in the affected wheel. **1992-94 Blazer:** The ABS switch can malfunction causing increased stopping distances while in 2-wheel-drive mode. **1993 Blazer:** Vehicle may move unintentionally due to excessive wear to the low and reverse clutch. **1994 Blazer:** Tow-hitch attaching bolts were not tightened to standard and could allow the hitch and trailer to separate from the vehicle when towing. **1995 w/M30/MT1 automatic transmission:** When shift lever is placed in "Park" position, its indicator light may not illuminate. **1995-96 w/gasoline engine:** Throttle cable may contact dash mat and bind; engine speed might then not return to idle. **1997:** During a severe crash, seat belt buckles with an energy absorbing loop may malfunction, leading t full or partial ejection from the vehicle. Dealer will inspect and replace affected buckles. **1998 C10706:** Rear brake line can contact left front fender wheelhouse inner panel; a hole could be worn in brake line, allowing loss of fluid and reducing rear-brake effectiveness. **1998:** Lower steering pinch bolt may be "finger loose" or missing, resulting in off-center steering wheel or separation of shaft from steering gear. **1998:** On some vehicles, one or both front brake rotor/hubs may have out-of-spec gray iron that can fail during life of vehicle. **1999 Blazer:** Seatbelts may not meet locking requirements, leaving occupants improperly restrained in a crash. **1999-00 Tahoe:** In a crash, right front-passenger restraint systems may not meet neck extension requirements. **2000 Tahoe:** Airbag sensing module may have an anomaly that could keep the airbags from deploying in a collision. **2000 Tahoe:** Loose or missing rear wheelhouse plugs could allow noxious gases to enter the cabin.

PRICES

	Good	Average	Poor
1992 Blazer 4WD	$4,500-5,800	$3,700-4,800	$1,600-2,100
1993 Blazer 4WD	5,300-6,800	4,600-5,800	2,200-2,800
1994 Blazer 4WD	6,200-7,700	5,400-6,700	2,700-3,300
1995 Tahoe 2WD	6,000-6,800	5,200-5,900	2,500-2,900
Tahoe 4WD	7,300-8,200	6,600-7,400	3,600-4,000
Tahoe LS, LT 2WD	7,000-7,900	6,200-7,000	3,400-3,800
Tahoe LS, LT 4WD	7,900-8,900	7,100-8,000	4,000-4,500
1996 Tahoe 2WD	7,000-7,800	6,200-6,900	3,400-3,700
Tahoe 4WD	8,300-9,300	7,500-8,400	4,300-4,800
Tahoe LS, LT 2WD	7,600-8,800	6,800-7,900	3,800-4,400
Tahoe LS, LT 4WD	8,800-9,800	7,900-8,800	4,600-5,100
1997 Tahoe 2WD	7,800-8,700	7,000-7,800	4,000-4,400
Tahoe 4WD	9,200-10,200	8,300-9,200	4,800-5,300
Tahoe LS, LT 2WD	8,500-9,500	7,700-8,600	4,400-4,900
Tahoe LS, LT 4WD	9,800-10,800	8,800-9,700	5,100-5,600
1998 Tahoe 2WD	8,800-9,700	7,900-8,700	4,600-5,000
Tahoe 4WD	10,500-11,500	9,500-10,400	5,600-6,100
Tahoe LS, LT 2WD	9,800-11,200	8,800-10,100	5,100-5,800
Tahoe LS, LT 4WD	11,500-12,800	10,400-11,500	6,300-7,000
1999 Tahoe 2WD	10,000-11,000	9,000-9,900	5,200-5,700
Tahoe 4WD	12,000-13,000	10,800-11,700	6,700-7,300
Tahoe LS, LT 2WD	11,500-13,500	10,400-12,200	6,300-7,400
Tahoe LS, LT 4WD	13,500-15,000	12,300-13,700	8,000-8,900
2000 Tahoe Limited	15,500-17,000	14,100-15,500	9,900-10,900
Tahoe Z71	17,500-19,000	16,100-17,500	11,200-12,200

For detailed information on this vehicle visit
http://used.consumerguide.com and enter code **2123**

1990-98 CHEVROLET C/K PICKUP

CG BEST BUY

CLASS: Full-size pickup truck
BUILT IN: Canada, USA
PROS: Acceleration (V8) • Antilock brakes • Cargo room • Interior room • Cargo and towing ability • Visibility
CONS: Control layout • Fuel economy • Ride quality

EVALUATION: The V6 feels adequate with manual shift, but a 5.0- or 5.7-liter V8 would be wiser for any significant work, especially with automatic transmission. Short-bed Sportsides have a more sporty appearance and, with a larger V8, move impressively. A K2500 4x4 with 5.7-liter V8 and automatic averaged 13.3 mpg, and yielded strong low-end pulling power as well as good passing response. Braking can be a problem with rear antilocking, when the bed is unladen. Four-wheel ABS on later models is a better bet.

Acceleration in a 454 SS is actually neck-snapping, and its wide tires and sports suspension make it the best-handling full-size pickup you're likely to find.

Visibility is good from a wide, spacious cab that has ample room for even the largest occupants. Gauges are unobstructed but can be hard to read in sunlight, and electronic heat/vent controls are complicated. Gloveboxes are tiny. Ride quality is better than in prior pickups, but higher-capacity models don't take bumps so well when the box is unloaded. Only the short-wheelbase 4x4 with off-road suspension rides really harshly.

Engine improvements for '96 were impressive. The V6 still isn't ideal for heavy work, but the 5.0-liter V8 is now a smooth, capable choice (except for serious towing or hauling). The 5.7 V8 feels much livelier, furnishing robust acceleration and fine pulling power.

VALUE FOR THE MONEY: Chevrolet's C/K models are an excellent choice in the full-size pickup field. Trucks equipped with the 5.7-liter V8 are still our top choice.

TROUBLE SPOTS

Automatic transmission: Trucks with the 6.5L engine may have a transmission shudder when the torque-converter clutch applies and releases. (1991-94)

Automatic transmission: 700-R4 automatic transmissions may shift late or not upshift at all. The problem is a stuck throttle valve inside the transmission. (1990-92)

Clutch: A grinding noise during clutch engagement and difficulty shifting into first or reverse is caused by a clutch master cylinder pushrod that is too long. (1992-93)

Cruise control: The cruise control cuts out and won't reset unless the key is turned off because the cruise control module is too sensitive to vibrations at the brake pedal. (1994-95)

Engine knock: Engine knock at startup on 4.3-, 5.7-, or 7.4-liter engines is usually eliminated by using an oil filter with a check valve. If this does not fix it, GM has revised PROMs for the computers and will even replace the main bearings if all else fails. (1990-95)

Engine noise: The exhaust valves on 4.3-, 5.0-, or 5.7-liter engines may not get enough lubrication causing a variety of noises. Usually, the same engine consumes excess oil because the valve-guide seals on the exhaust valves are bad and have to be replaced. (1996)

AVERAGE REPLACEMENT COSTS

A/C Compressor	$560	Exhaust System	$420
Alternator	378	Radiator	350
Automatic Trans.	725	Shocks and/or Struts	335
Brakes	230	Timing Chain/Belt	210
Clutch	595		

NHTSA RECALL HISTORY

1990 diesel: Fuel lines can contact automatic-transmission linkage shaft and/or propshaft. **1990:** Brake-pedal pivot bolt could disengage. **1992 extended cab w/high-back bucket seats:** Seat recliner-to-frame bolts can loosen, fatigue, and fracture, allowing seatback to recline suddenly. **1992:** Brake-pedal pivot bolt could disengage. **1994:** Brake-pedal retainer may be missing, mispositioned, or poorly seated. **1994:** Reversed polarity of brake switch can cause contacts to wear prematurely; may result in loss of brake lights without warning. **1994:** Some drivers' seats could loosen. **1994-95 extended cab C10/15 w/high-back front bucket seats or 60/40 split bench seat:** Recliner-to-frame bolts could loosen, fatigue, and fracture, allowing seatback to recline suddenly. **1994-95 extended-cab C10/15 w/gas engine or 6.5-liter H.O. Turbodiesel:** If lap- and shoulder-belt energy-management loops on front seatbelt assemblies release at or near the same time, acceleration forces can cause release mechanism to activate and allow buckle to separate from latch. Also, a few trucks lack those loops. **1994-96 C10:** Solder joints can crack, causing windshield wipers to work intermittently. **1995:** Steering-column shaft nut could loosen and detach. **1995-96 Reg. andExtended Cab:** The windshield wiper motor may fail on certain vehicles. Dealer will inspect and replace affected parts. **1995-96 w/gasoline engine:** Throttle cable may contact dash mat, which could bind the throttle; engine speed might then not return to idle. **1995-97 Crew Cab:** The windshield wiper motor may fail on certain vehicles. Dealer will inspect and replace affected parts. **1995-97 extended cab w/Easy Entry:** Pinch point in recliner mechanism can trap and pinch a person's hand or fingers when Easy-Entry feature is activated. **1995-98 crew cab:** Front inner corner of fuel tank can contact body sill, wearing a hole in or cracking the tank; can result in fuel leakage. **1996 C10/15 w/7.4-liter engine:** Fuel-rail assemblies may have improperly crimped end retainer clip that results in leak. **1996:** Four U-bolts on either side of rear axle were under-torqued and could loosen and eventually fall off; could result in sudden loss of control. **1997 C10/20:** On some trucks, one or two front-seat mounting bolts were not installed. **1998 C10 extended cab and 4-door utility:** Steering-gear bolt can loosen and fall out, resulting in separation of shaft from gear. **1998 C10753 extended cab:** Rear brake line can contact left front-fender wheelhouse inner panel; a hole could be worn in brake line, allowing loss of fluid and reducing rear-brake effectiveness. **1998:** On certain vehicles, the outside rearview mirror switch may short circuit. Dealer will inspect and replace affected parts. **1998:** On some trucks, one or both front brake rotor/hubs may have out-of-spec gray iron that can fail during life of vehicle.

PRICES

	Good	Average	Poor
1990 C 1500 2WD	$2,100-3,600	$1,500-2,600	$400-600
C 2500 2WD	2,800-3,800	2,100-2,900	600-800
K 1500 4WD	2,800-4,000	2,100-3,000	600-900
K 2500 4WD	3,500-4,300	2,800-3,400	900-1,200
1991 C 1500 2WD	2,400-4,000	1,800-2,900	500-800
C 2500 2WD	3,500-4,500	2,800-3,600	900-1,200
K 1500 4WD	3,200-4,800	2,500-3,700	800-1,200
K 2500 4WD	4,200-5,100	3,400-4,200	1,400-1,700
1992 C 1500 2WD	2,800-4,800	2,100-3,600	600-1,100
C 2500 2WD	3,800-4,900	3,100-4,000	1,100-1,500
K 1500 4WD	3,600-5,500	2,900-4,400	1,000-1,500
K 2500 4WD	4,900-5,800	4,200-4,900	1,900-2,300
1993 C 1500 2WD	3,200-5,500	2,500-4,300	800-1,300
C 2500 2WD	4,500-6,300	3,700-5,000	1,600-2,200
K 1500 4WD	4,300-6,500	3,500-5,300	1,500-2,200
K 2500 4WD	5,800-7,000	5,000-6,100	2,400-2,900
1994 C 1500 2WD	3,600-6,200	2,900-5,000	1,000-1,700
C 2500 2WD	5,300-6,800	4,600-5,800	2,200-2,800
K 1500 4WD	4,800-7,800	4,000-6,600	1,800-3,000
K 2500 4WD	6,700-8,000	5,900-7,000	3,100-3,700
1995 C 1500 2WD	4,000-7,000	3,300-5,700	1,300-2,200
C 2500 2WD	5,700-7,500	4,900-6,500	2,300-3,100
K 1500 4WD	5,300-8,500	4,600-7,300	2,200-3,500
K 2500 4WD	7,200-9,500	6,400-8,500	3,500-4,700
1996 C 1500 2WD	4,500-8,000	3,700-6,600	1,600-2,900
C 2500 2WD	6,300-8,500	5,500-7,500	2,900-3,900
K 1500 4WD	6,100-10,000	5,300-8,700	2,600-4,300
K 2500 4WD	8,000-10,500	7,200-9,500	4,100-5,400
1997 C 1500 2WD	5,100-9,000	4,300-7,700	2,000-3,600
C 2500 2WD	7,300-10,000	6,600-9,000	3,700-5,100
K 1500 4WD	6,800-11,000	6,100-9,800	3,200-5,200
K 2500 4WD	9,200-11,500	8,300-10,400	4,800-6,000
1998 C 1500 2WD	6,000-10,200	5,200-8,900	2,500-4,300
C 2500 2WD	8,200-10,800	7,400-9,700	4,200-5,500
K 1500 4WD	7,600-12,000	6,800-10,800	3,800-6,000
K 2500 4WD	10,000-12,500	9,000-11,300	5,200-6,500

For detailed information on this vehicle visit
http://used.consumerguide.com and enter code **2024**

1993-02
CHEVROLET CAMARO

CG BEST BUY

CLASS: Sporty coupe

BUILT IN: Canada

PROS: Acceleration (Z28) • Airbags • Antilock brakes • Control layout • Handling

CONS: Fuel economy (Z28) • Wet-weather traction • Noise • Tire noise (Z28) • Rear-seat comfort • Ride (Z28) • Visibility

EVALUATION: This last Camaro generation beats its predecessor in two notable ways: ride quality and dashboard layout. Both the base model and the Z28 have softer suspensions, which reduces the harsh impacts commonly endured in prior models. Z28s are still quite harsh over rough pavement, but more easygoing than before, though optional high-performance tires generate too much noise at highway speeds. Both models retain their well-known handling prowess.

Gauges are easily visible through the steering wheel. Radio and climate controls are high-mounted, easy to reach and see.

Climbing inside can be a chore because of low seats. Wide rear roof pillars still obscure the view to sides and rear quarters. A hump in the right-front floorboard intrudes into passenger leg room. Rear head room is a tad better than before, but the cushion is narrow and knee space extremely limited. A deep cargo well doesn't hold much luggage. The low seating position hinders visibility.

Though somewhat gruff and noisy under acceleration, the 3.4-liter V6 performs nicely—especially with 5-speed manual shift. Acceleration in a Z28 is strong with either transmission, but the V8 demands premium fuel. We averaged only 13.2 mpg in mostly urban driving. Adding the 3.8-liter V6 narrowed the performance gap between the two modes. The 200-horsepower engine matches the 4.6-liter V8 in Ford Mustangs when the gas pedal hits the floor. Poor wet-weather traction remains a problem. Traction control wasn't optional until 1995.

VALUE FOR THE MONEY: This generation of Camaro is the best ever, but we feel that it forces too many compromises to be a daily driver for anyone but the performance enthusiast.

TROUBLE SPOTS

Automatic transmission: TH-200 or 700-R4 automatic transmissions may shift late or not upshift at all. The problem is a stuck throttle valve inside the transmission. (1993)

Cruise control: Because of oversensitivity, the cruise control cuts out and won't reset unless the key is turned off. GM will replace the cruise-control module. (1993-95)

CHEVROLET

Doors: Although the doors can be locked manually, the power door locks may not operate due to a rubber bumper falling off of the actuator arm. (1995-96)

Heater core: The seal on the heater core case gets loose and cold air enters, which reduces the heater performance. (1993-94)

Rear axle noise: Under warranty, the company will replace the entire rear axle (excluding brake rotors on cars with rear disc brakes) on a complete exchange basis. (1995)

Steering noise: The upper bearing mount in the steering column can get loose and cause a snapping or clicking, requiring a new bearing spring and turn-signal cancel cam. (1994-96)

Vehicle shake: Cars with the 5.7-liter engine may vibrate at highway speeds. Replacing the driveshaft fixes the problem, but usually results in axle noise becoming more apparent. (1993-96)

AVERAGE REPLACEMENT COSTS

A/C Compressor	$535	Exhaust System	$470
Alternator	290	Radiator	410
Automatic Trans.	775	Shocks and/or Struts	527
Brakes	255	Timing Chain/Belt	330
Clutch	775	Universal Joints	200

NHTSA RECALL HISTORY

1994: Misrouted V8 fuel line may contact "air" check valve; heat could damage line, which could leak fuel into engine compartment. **1995:** Lower coupling of steering intermediate shaft could loosen and rotate, resulting in loss of control. **1997:** Seatbelt retractors on some cars can lock-up on slopes. **1999 w/manual transmission:** Clutch master cylinder on a few cars may have incorrect retaining ring, preventing clutch from disengaging. **2002:** Welds near lower driver-side door hinge may not meet specifications, possibly causing severe injuries in a crash.

PRICES

	Good	Average	Poor
1993 Camaro Coupe	$3,000-3,600	$2,300-2,800	$700-800
Z28 Coupe	4,300-5,000	3,600-4,200	1,500-1,700
1994 Camaro Coupe	3,600-4,200	2,900-3,400	1,000-1,200
Conv., Z28 Coupe	4,700-5,600	3,900-4,700	1,800-2,100
Z28 Convertible	6,000-6,800	5,200-5,900	2,500-2,900
1995 Camaro Coupe	4,200-4,800	3,400-3,900	1,400-1,600
Conv., Z28 Coupe	5,300-6,200	4,600-5,300	2,200-2,500
Z28 Convertible	7,000-7,800	6,200-6,900	3,400-3,700
1996 Camaro Coupe	4,800-5,500	4,000-4,600	1,800-2,100
Conv., Z28 Coupe	6,000-7,000	5,200-6,100	2,500-2,900
Z28 Convertible	8,000-8,800	7,200-7,900	4,100-4,500
1997 Camaro Coupe	5,400-6,300	4,600-5,400	2,200-2,600
Conv., Z28 Coupe	6,500-7,700	5,700-6,800	2,900-3,500
Z28 Convertible	9,200-10,000	8,300-9,000	4,800-5,200
1998 Camaro Coupe	6,200-7,000	5,400-6,100	2,700-3,000
Conv., Z28 Coupe	7,500-9,000	6,800-8,100	3,800-4,500
Z28 Convertible	10,500-12,500	9,500-11,300	5,600-6,600

1999 Camaro Coupe	$7,500-8,300	$6,800-7,500	$3,800-4,200
Conv., Z28 Coupe	9,000-11,000	8,100-9,900	4,700-5,700
Z28 Convertible	12,500-13,500	11,300-12,200	7,100-7,700
2000 Camaro Coupe	9,200-10,000	8,300-9,000	4,800-5,200
Conv., Z28 Coupe	11,000-13,000	9,900-11,700	5,900-7,000
Z28 Convertible	15,000-16,000	13,700-14,600	9,500-10,100
2001 Camaro Coupe	11,000-12,000	9,900-10,800	5,900-6,500
Conv., Z28 Coupe	12,800-15,000	11,600-13,700	7,400-8,700
Z28 Convertible	17,300-18,800	15,900-17,300	11,100-12,000
2002 Camaro Coupe	13,000-14,000	11,800-12,700	7,500-8,100
Conv., Z28 Coupe	15,000-17,500	13,700-15,900	9,500-11,000
Z28 Convertible	19,500-21,000	17,900-19,300	12,700-13,700

For detailed information on this vehicle visit
http://used.consumerguide.com and enter code **2007**

1991-96 CHEVROLET CAPRICE/IMPALA SS

CLASS: Full-size car
BUILT IN: USA
PROS: Acceleration
• Antilock brakes
• Passenger and cargo room
• Trailer towing capability
CONS: Fuel economy
• Ride/handling/roadholding
(Caprice w/base suspension) • Steering feel (Caprice) • Wind noise

EVALUATION: Despite the new look for 1991, not much changed in this full-size sedan and wagon. Caprice's traditional soft ride is distressingly bouncy and floaty with the base suspension. Qualifying as virtually aquatic, the car leans way over in turns and wallows over wavy roads. Loose, vague steering impairs quick maneuvers. An optional F41 Ride/Handling suspension offers a slightly more assured feel, without much comfort loss. The sporty LTZ sedan option drew praise, and its stiffer suspension tightens handling considerably. The entertaining Impala SS of 1994-96 offers quite a secure feel on the road, leaning little in curves, its big tires grasping the pavement tenaciously. Wagon suspensions are firmer than those in sedans.

The 5.0-liter V8 is understressed and quiet, with good low-end torque for easy merging/passing as well as brisk getaways. Still, it doesn't respond quickly to sharp jabs at the gas pedal. Gas mileage is nothing to boast about, either: We averaged only 16 mpg in a '91 sedan. A 5.7-liter V8 is quicker without guzzling much more fuel. The Corvette-based V8 introduced in 1994 is swifter yet, and none of the V8s demand premium gasoline.

Mechanical noise while cruising is low, but wind roars constantly around the thick side pillars, detracting from the quiet ride. A Caprice is roomy, soft, and plush; though the bulky transmission tunnel robs leg room from center passengers, front and rear. The trunk is sizable. Controls are logical. Antilock braking is a welcome addition, but the nose dives too much in hard stops.

CHEVROLET

VALUE FOR THE MONEY: GM's front-drive full-size sedans (Buick LeSabre, Olds Eighty Eight, Pontiac Bonneville) handle better and consume less fuel, but can't match Caprice's towing ability.

TROUBLE SPOTS

Automatic transmission: TH-700-R4 automatic transmissions may shift late or not upshift at all. The problem is a stuck throttle valve inside the transmission. (1991-93)

Engine noise: The exhaust valves on the 4.3- or 5.7-liter engines may not get enough lubrication causing a variety of noises. Usually, the same engine consumes excess oil because the valve-guide seals on the exhaust valves are bad and have to be replaced. (1994-96)

Steering noise: The upper bearing mount in the steering column can get loose and cause a snapping or clicking, requiring a new bearing spring and turn-signal cancel cam. (1994-96)

AVERAGE REPLACEMENT COSTS

A/C Compressor	$465	Radiator	$480
Alternator	280	Shocks and/or Struts	250
Automatic Trans.	780	Timing Chain/Belt	305
Brakes	220	Universal Joints	260
Exhaust System	460		

NHTSA RECALL HISTORY

1991: Shoulder-belt guide-loop plastic covering may crack and expose the steel subplate; in a crash, seatbelt webbing can be cut. **1991-92:** Secondary hood-latch assembly can corrode. **1991-96 police/taxi:** Rear lower control arm can crack. **1992 w/special-order 4.3-liter engine:** Engine-mounted fuel-feed and return pipes on some cars may fracture. **1992:** Antilock brake-system modulator can corrode and leak fluid; may reduce brake effectiveness and increase stopping distance. **1994:** Fuel-tank strap fasteners can detach, eventually allowing tank to sag. **1994:** Oil-cooler inlet hose may be too close to steering gear, causing chafing that could result in leakage and fire. **1994:** On small number of cars, paint between wheel and brake rotor/drum can cause lug nut to loosen. **1994-95:** At low temperatures, throttle return spring could fail due to excess friction. **1994-95:** Lower ball joint on a few cars sent to Guam and Puerto Rico can separate (also applies to 1995-96 police/taxi/limo). **1995:** Improperly adjusted transmission linkage may permit shifting from "Park" position with ignition key removed. **1995-96 station wagon:** Airbag caution label and roof-rack caution label were incorrectly installed on same side of sunvisor. **1995-96:** Wheel lug nuts were not tightened to the proper specification. This could result in wheel loss.

PRICES

	Good	Average	Poor
1991 Caprice sedan	$2,000-2,600	$1,400-1,800	$300-400
Caprice wagon	2,300-3,000	1,700-2,200	400-600
1992 Caprice sedan	2,600-3,300	1,900-2,400	500-700
Caprice wagon	3,100-3,800	2,400-3,000	700-900
1993 Caprice sedan	3,200-4,000	2,500-3,100	800-1,000
Caprice wagon	3,900-4,600	3,200-3,700	1,200-1,400

1994 Caprice sedan	$3,800-4,600	$3,100-3,700	$1,100-1,400
Caprice wagon	4,500-5,200	3,700-4,300	1,600-1,900
Impala SS	8,500-9,500	7,700-8,600	4,400-4,900
1995 Caprice sedan	4,500-5,300	3,700-4,400	1,600-1,900
Caprice wagon	5,300-6,000	4,600-5,200	2,200-2,500
Impala SS	10,000-11,200	9,000-10,100	5,200-5,800
1996 Caprice sedan	5,200-6,000	4,400-5,100	2,100-2,400
Caprice wagon	6,200-7,000	5,400-6,100	2,700-3,000
Impala SS	11,500-13,000	10,400-11,700	6,300-7,200

For detailed information on this vehicle visit
http://used.consumerguide.com and enter code **2008**

1995-03 CHEVROLET CAVALIER

CLASS: Subcompact car
BUILT IN: USA
PROS: Acceleration (Twin Cam engine) • Airbags
• Standard antilock brakes
• Fuel economy
• Instruments/controls
• Visibility

CONS: Entry/exit (2-door models) • Rear-seat head room • Seat comfort

EVALUATION: An improved suspension, lengthened wheelbase, and stiffer structure combine to furnish a comfortable ride that absorbs most bumps easily, without floating or wallowing on wavy surfaces. Base and LS models lean considerably in turns, however, and respond lazily to quick steering changes. For tight control, look into the Z24, which also rides quite well on most pavement surfaces.

Early model base-engine acceleration is adequate with either transmission, but the engine feels coarse under hard throttle. Fortunately, that engine noise settles down to a peaceful level at cruising speed. The 2.4-liter Twin Cam unit is a better match to the automatic transmission than are some rival dual-cam engines because it produces slightly more torque over a broader range of engine speeds. Improved 2.2-liter 4-cylinder in '02 was smoother and most responsive engine yet. As for economy, we averaged 23.8 mpg with a base Cavalier sedan with the automatic transmission. We'd expect more than 30 mpg on the highway. The new 2.2-liter engine rates 1 mpg higher than the 2.4 in EPA fuel-economy estimates. Wind and road noise are moderate.

Gauges are clear and controls easy to reach and use, in a well-designed dashboard. Visibility is good to all angles. Six-footers have adequate room in front, though seats lack lower-back support. Rear leg room is okay, but head room suffices only for shorter folks. Getting in and out of the rear on 2-doors is tough. Trunk space is ample, but a small opening makes it difficult to load bulky items. A one-piece folding rear seatback is standard.

CHEVROLET

VALUE FOR THE MONEY: Compared with its most natural rival, the sportier-natured Dodge/Plymouth Neon, the refined Cavalier puts comfort and utility ahead of performance and style. All told, however, it doesn't match the refinement of the Toyota Corolla. For a reasonable sum, however, you get a car with dual airbags and antilock braking, even if it isn't quite as much fun to drive as a Neon.

TROUBLE SPOTS

Brake wear: The front brakes wear out prematurely because of the friction compound. GM and several aftermarket companies have brakes with lining that will last longer. (1995)

Traction control indicator light: The ETC warning light may glow and the cruise control stops working, but there is no problem with the systems. No current fix. (1996)

AVERAGE REPLACEMENT COSTS

A/C Compressor	$555	CV Joints	$480
Alternator	270	Exhaust System	320
Automatic Trans.	895	Radiator	347
Brakes	210	Shocks and/or Struts	640
Clutch	550	Timing Chain/Belt	315

NHTSA RECALL HISTORY

1995: Missing welds in lower front-suspension control-arm assemblies can result in separation of front bushing-sleeve subassembly from control arm, resulting in loss of vehicle control. **1995-96:** Front and/or rear hazard-warning lamps might not work. **1996:** Accelerator cable in a few cars could be kinked, causing high pedal effort, or sticking or broken cable. **1996:** If the key is held in the "start" position for an extended period, high current flowing through the ignition switch can melt internal switch parts. **1996:** Interior lamps might come on unexpectedly while vehicle is being driven. **1996:** Airbag could deploy inadvertently during low-speed crash or when an object strikes the floorpan. **1996-97:** Rear-suspension trailing-arm bolts can fatigue and break. **1996-98:** Faulty power steering bearings may have been installed on certain vehicles, resulting in difficulty turning the steering wheel. Dealers will inspect and replace all affected parts. **1997:** Driver's wiper blades on a few cars are 17 inches long instead of the required 22 inches. **1997:** Spare tire on small number of cars may have incorrect rim. **1999:** Instrument-panel backlighting on some cars may not function after driver adjusts interior-light intensity. **2000:** Instrument-panel lights have only one illumination level—not the two or more required—and could make it difficult to see objects outside the vehicle at night.

PRICES

	Good	Average	Poor
1995 Cavalier	$2,100-2,600	$1,500-1,800	$400-500
Cavalier Z24	2,700-3,400	2,000-2,600	600-700
LS Convertible	3,100-3,600	2,400-2,800	700-900
1996 Cavalier	2,500-3,000	1,800-2,200	500-600
Cavalier Z24	3,100-3,700	2,400-2,900	700-900
LS Convertible	3,500-4,100	2,800-3,300	900-1,100

1997 Cavalier	$2,900-3,500	$2,200-2,700	$700-800
Cavalier Z24	3,700-4,300	3,000-3,500	1,100-1,200
LS Convertible	4,200-4,800	3,400-3,900	1,400-1,600
1998 Cavalier	3,300-4,000	2,600-3,200	800-1,000
Cavalier Z24 coupe	4,400-5,100	3,700-4,200	1,500-1,800
Z24 Convertible	5,500-6,500	4,700-5,600	2,300-2,700
1999 Cavalier	3,900-4,600	3,200-3,800	1,200-1,400
Cavalier Z24 coupe	5,200-6,000	4,400-5,100	2,100-2,400
Z24 Convertible	6,500-7,500	5,700-6,600	2,900-3,400
2000 Cavalier	4,600-5,400	3,800-4,500	1,700-2,000
Cavalier Z24 coupe	6,200-7,000	5,400-6,100	2,700-3,000
Z24 Convertible	7,600-8,600	6,800-7,700	3,800-4,300
2001 Cavalier	5,500-6,700	4,700-5,800	2,300-2,700
Cavalier Z24	7,200-8,000	6,400-7,100	3,500-3,900
2002 Cavalier	6,800-8,800	6,100-7,800	3,200-4,100
2003 Cavalier	8,500-10,500	7,700-9,500	4,400-5,500

For detailed information on this vehicle visit
http://used.consumerguide.com and enter code 2010

1991-96 CHEVROLET CORVETTE

CLASS: Sports car
BUILT IN: USA
PROS: Acceleration • Antilock brakes • Steering/handling
CONS: Entry/exit • Fuel economy • Noise • Price • Ride

EVALUATION: Since the beginning, Corvettes have been cars for those who enjoy life in the fast lane—and are willing to sacrifice some comfort for the privilege. Improved assembly has greatly reduced the number of squeaks and rattles. The '90s suspension no longer jars your teeth while passing over bumps, but it's still quite firm. Corvettes offer great grip and ultraquick reflexes, though bumpy roads upset the composure of the stiff suspension. On the positive side, wide tires, a firm suspension, and a low center of gravity allow Corvettes to handle like a race car as long as the pavement is reasonably smooth.

Getting in and out of the deep bucket seats in the pitlike cabin tends to be a challenge. Luggage space and interior room are at a premium, and visibility could be better. Noise levels are high. A husky exhaust note is prominent at all times, accompanied by abundant tire noise at highway speeds.

Acceleration is sheer magnificence: lusty and bold, whether from the standard LT1 engine in 1992-96 models, the prior L98, or the super-powered

CHEVROLET

ZR-1. Each engine delivers a seamless rush of power from virtually any speed, causing the car to vault ahead under moderate to hard throttle. An LT1 pushes you back in your seat all the way to its 5500-rpm redline and feels discernably smoother than its predecessor. Fuel economy is nothing to boast about. There's an undeniable performance advantage in the ZR-1 package, but not enough to justify the huge prices that model still commands.

Acceleration Slip Regulation in 1992-96 models squelches the wheel spin that nearly incapacitated earlier Corvettes when accelerating on slippery surfaces.

VALUE FOR THE MONEY: Rivals such as a Nissan 300ZX Turbo and Toyota Supra are more refined, but simply cannot match a Corvette's all-American macho flavor. To those who love them, there's simply nothing like a Corvette.

TROUBLE SPOTS

Automatic transmission: Unless the shift-detent ball roller has been replaced, it may be hard to shift the manual 6-speed into reverse. (1995)
Climate control: The CD player may skip when driving on rough roads unless foam tape was applied to the top and bottom of the radio. (1991-94)
Engine misfire: The distributor-vacuum vent-wiring harness might rub the power-steering pulley. This can be fixed by tie-strapping the harness to the throttle body coolant hose. (1995)
Engine misfire: If the engines with a manual 6-speed transmission surge or sag at engine speeds below 2500 rpm, there is a revised PROM to correct it. (1995)
Transmission leak: Fluid may leak from the pump body on 4L60-E transmissions due to the pump bushing walking out of the valve body. (1995-96)

AVERAGE REPLACEMENT COSTS

A/C Compressor	$820	Exhaust System	$995
Alternator	280	Radiator	495
Automatic Trans.	890	Shocks and/or Struts	730
Brakes	365	Timing Chain/Belt	990
Clutch	785	Universal Joints	305

NHTSA RECALL HISTORY

1992-93 w/LT1 engine: Power-steering gear-inlet hose can fracture, causing flammable fluid to spray into engine compartment.

PRICES

	Good	Average	Poor
1991 Convertible	$10,500-12,000	$9,500-10,800	$5,600-6,400
Corvette	9,000-10,000	8,100-9,000	4,700-5,200
Corvette ZR-1	16,500-18,000	15,000-16,400	10,600-11,500
1992 Convertible	11,500-13,000	10,400-11,700	6,300-7,200
Corvette	10,000-11,000	9,000-9,900	5,200-5,700
Corvette ZR-1	18,500-20,500	17,000-18,900	11,800-13,100
1993 Convertible	13,000-14,500	11,800-13,200	7,500-8,400
Corvette	11,100-12,500	10,000-11,300	6,000-6,800
Corvette ZR-1	21,000-23,000	19,300-21,200	13,700-15,000

1994 Convertible	$14,500-16,000	$13,200-14,600	$9,000-9,900
Corvette	12,300-13,700	11,100-12,300	7,000-7,800
Corvette ZR-1	24,000-26,000	22,300-24,200	15,600-16,900
1995 Convertible	16,000-17,500	14,600-15,900	10,200-11,200
Corvette	13,500-15,000	12,300-13,700	8,000-8,900
Corvette ZR-1	27,000-29,000	25,100-27,000	18,100-19,400
1996 Convertible	17,500-19,000	16,100-17,500	11,200-12,200
Corvette	14,700-16,200	13,400-14,700	9,100-10,000

> For detailed information on this vehicle visit
> **http://used.consumerguide.com** and enter code **2126**

2000-03
CHEVROLET IMPALA

CG BEST BUY

CLASS: Midsize car
BUILT IN: Canada
PROS: Handling/road-holding • Instruments/controls • Passenger and cargo room
CONS: Rear-seat comfort • Road noise

EVALUATION: Even though the modern-day Impala is a far cry from the V8-powered Super Sport of the distant past, or the Impala SS of the early '90s, the sedan acquits itself nicely in most respects. Power is adequate with the base engine, while the 3.8-liter delivers usefully stronger takeoffs and passing response. An alert, smooth-shifting automatic transmission helps, but neither engine sounds smooth or refined when pushed hard. A 3.8-liter LS averaged 20.1 mpg, with a lot of highway mileage. In a more even mix of driving, a 3.4-liter Impala got 19.8 mpg. A good ride/handling balance makes this family four-door pleasing to drive. Even the Ride and Handling suspension that accompanies the bigger engine absorbs most bumps well, while tempering much of the float and wallow that plague the base suspension over high-speed dips. Any Impala furnishes good grip and balance, along with authoritative steering feel. Stopping power is good, though pedal feel could be firmer. Wind noise is low, but tire roar intrudes somewhat on coarse pavement. Space is sufficient for 6-footers to ride in tandem without cramping of legs. Still, there's not quite enough seat width for three large adults. The back-seat cushion is far too soft and short, lacking in contour for satisfying comfort. Head room is good all around, even with an optional moonroof. Entry/exit is big-car easy, but tall-tail styling impedes rearward vision. The ample flat-floor trunk has a long, wide opening, but the glovebox is puny.

VALUE FOR THE MONEY: A clear alternative to the Ford Taurus (as redesigned for 2000), the Impala promises comfort-oriented American

CHEVROLET

style as opposed to the Taurus's import-influenced approach. Impala beats Taurus in powertrain response, while Ford leads in safety features and back-seat comfort. Both offer more room and equipment for the price than an equivalent Accord or Camry, though Japanese-brand rivals are more polished all-around.

TROUBLE SPOTS

Automatic transmission: The column-mounted shift lever is hard to move out of park due to the interlock cable being too long. (2000)

Battery: A problem with the ground circuit of the trunk light causes the battery to go dead. (2000-01)

Brakes: The rear brakes make squealing or moaning noises. Countermeasure brake pads are available. (2000-01)

Vehicle noise: Banging, clunking, or popping noises from the front under acceleration or braking require shims between the engine cradle and frame. (2000)

Vehicle noise: Fuel makes banging and sloshing noises in the tank when less than half full. (2000)

AVERAGE REPLACEMENT COSTS

A/C Compressor	$525	Exhaust System	$565
Alternator	275	Radiator	450
Automatic Trans.	895	Shocks and/or Struts	975
Brakes	485	Timing Chain/Belt	325
CV Joints	750		

NHTSA RECALL HISTORY

2000 w/TRW seatbelt-buckle assemblies: Seatbelt-buckle assemblies fail to conform to federal requirements, because buckle base was not properly heat treated. **2001:** On certain cars, airbag sensing and diagnostic modules could experience a memory error, and airbags might not deploy during a crash. **2002:** Airbag inflator may fracture and cause injury.

PRICES

	Good	Average	Poor
2000 Impala	$8,000-9,000	$7,200-8,100	$4,100-4,600
Impala LS	10,000-11,200	9,000-10,100	5,200-5,800
2001 Impala	9,500-10,500	8,600-9,500	4,900-5,500
Impala LS	12,000-13,200	10,800-11,900	6,700-7,400
2002 Impala	11,000-12,500	9,900-11,300	5,900-6,800
Impala LS	14,200-15,500	12,900-14,100	8,700-9,500
2003 Impala	13,000-14,500	11,800-13,200	7,500-8,400
Impala LS	17,000-18,500	15,600-17,000	10,900-11,800

For detailed information on this vehicle visit
http://used.consumerguide.com and enter code **2369**

1990-96 CHEVROLET LUMINA APV/MINIVAN

CLASS: Minivan

BUILT IN: USA

PROS: Acceleration (3.8-liter V6) • Noise • Passenger and cargo room • Ride

CONS: Acceleration (3.1-liter) • Steering feel • Visibility

EVALUATION: The long sloping snout with steep windshield cuts into interior space and looks oddly daunting from the driver's seat—almost like you're steering from the back seat. Most people quickly get used to that, but it's still difficult to see the front end while maneuvering. Even after the snout was shortened for 1994, forward visibility could be a problem.

Don't be dissuaded by appearances, as the APV has several notable virtues. This minivan drives much like a passenger car, cornering with commendable control and absorbing most bumps without harshness or wallowing. Smooth and quiet on the road, the minivan leans modestly in turns and offers good rain/snow traction, but steering feels much too light.

Lack of power is a major drawback in early models, especially at passing speeds when fully loaded. The 3.1-liter V6 simply runs out of breath in a hurry. So, give yourself plenty of time and room to merge into traffic or overtake other vehicles. Once at highway speed, on the other hand, the minivan settles in for fine cruising. An optional 165-horsepower "3800" V6 with 4-speed automatic, offered since '92, moves more quickly and gives the Lumina performance to match or exceed its rivals from Ford and Chrysler. The 3.4-liter V6 installed in final Minivans feels stronger than the 3.1, but less lively than the 3.8-liter.

Undersized climate controls are the only serious flaw on the dashboard. Storage bins are everywhere, and there's no engine hump to hinder passage to the rear. Versatile interiors seat up to seven, using modular seats that weigh just 34 pounds each and remove in seconds. With all seats installed, there's little room for cargo, but each rear seatback folds down to create a 4x6-foot load space. The optional power sliding door is convenient.

VALUE FOR THE MONEY: If you need cargo space but demand the smooth ride and handling of a car, and don't like boxy vans, look no further. Dodge and Plymouth have long been the class leaders, but Luminas tend to be cheaper.

TROUBLE SPOTS

Automatic transmission: 4T60E transmissions may drop out of drive while cruising, shift erratically, or have no second, third, or fourth gear because of a bad ground connection for the shift solenoids. Poor grounds also allow wrong gear starts. (1992-94)

Automatic transmission: TH-125 automatic transmissions may shift late or not upshift at all. The problem is a stuck throttle valve inside the transmission. (1990-94)

CHEVROLET

Engine knock: Bearing knock on many 3.3- and 3.8-liter engines is due to too much clearance on the number one main bearing requiring it to be replaced with a 0.001-inch undersize bearing. (1992-94)

Engine noise: A rattling noise at startup is often caused by automatic-transmission pump starvation or cavitation, or a sticking pressure-regulator valve. (1992-95)

Oil consumption: The 3.8-liter engine is prone to excessive oil consumption often accompanied by spark knock due to failure of the valve-stem seals. (1993-95)

Steering noise: The upper bearing mount in the steering column can get loose and cause a snapping or clicking, requiring a new bearing spring and turn-signal cancel cam. (1994-96)

Transaxle leak: The right front axle seal at the automatic transaxle is prone to leak. GM issued a revised seal to correct the problem. (1992-94)

AVERAGE REPLACEMENT COSTS

A/C Compressor	$565	Exhaust System	$310
Alternator	280	Radiator	430
Automatic Trans.	1,095	Shocks and/or Struts	430
Brakes	230	Timing Chain/Belt	310
CV Joints	505		

NHTSA RECALL HISTORY

1990: Rear modular seat-frame hold-down hooks on some vans may not meet the required pull force at rear-seat anchorage. **1990-91:** Due to corrosion, steering shaft could separate from steering gear. **1992-93:** Seatbelt for left third-row seat of six-passenger van, or center second-row seat of seven-passenger van, may lock up. **1992-95:** Transmission-cooler line in cars with certain powertrains, sold in specified states, can separate at low temperature. **1993-94 w/optional power sliding door:** Second-row, right-hand shoulder belt can become pinched, unable to retract properly. **1994:** Pawl spring may be missing from retractors for rear-center lap belts. **1994:** Third-row seatbelt retractors may lock up when van is on a slope. **1995 w/3.1-liter engine:** Throttle cable support brackets could contact throttle-lever system and inhibit throttle return; engine speed would then decrease more slowly than anticipated. **1995:** On some vehicles, brake-pedal arm can fracture during braking.

PRICES

	Good	Average	Poor
1990 Lumina APV	$1,200-1,700	$700-1,100	$100-200
1991 Lumina APV	1,500-2,100	1,000-1,400	200-300
1992 Lumina APV	1,800-2,400	1,200-1,600	300-400
1993 Lumina APV	2,200-2,800	1,600-2,000	400-500
1994 Lumina Minivan	2,600-3,200	1,900-2,400	500-700
1995 Lumina Minivan	3,000-3,700	2,300-2,800	700-900
1996 Lumina Minivan	3,600-4,500	2,900-3,600	1,000-1,300

For detailed information on this vehicle visit
http://used.consumerguide.com and enter code **2012**

1995-01 CHEVROLET LUMINA/MONTE CARLO

CG BEST BUY

CLASS: Midsize car

BUILT IN: Canada

PROS: Antilock brakes • Automatic-transmission performance • Passenger and cargo room • Ride

CONS: Engine noise (3.4-liter) • Fuel economy (3.4-liter) • Rear-seat entry/exit (Monte Carlo) • Rear visibility (Monte Carlo) • Steering feel

EVALUATION: Performance is adequate from the 3.1-liter engine, though it feels a little slow initially. The 4-speed automatic transmission changes gears smoothly and downshifts promptly when passing power is needed. We've averaged 20.1 mpg in a Lumina with the base engine, with about half of the driving on expressways.

Expect a few mpg less with the stronger 3.4-liter engine. That one has more potent passing punch, but gets louder during hard acceleration. The smooth 3.8-liter on some later models is even more powerful—especially around town.

An absorbent suspension on the Lumina soaks up bumpy pavement without harshness or excessive bouncing. Steering in the Lumina is light and has little road feel.

As many as six people can fit in a Lumina—though everyone will be squeezed somewhat. There's ample room for four in the Monte Carlo, but a fifth might feel unwelcome.

The Monte Carlo requires plenty of room to fully open its wide doors, and climbing into the back seat demands some bending. Thick rear pillars hurt over-the-shoulder visibility in the Monte Carlo, whereas relatively narrow pillars and deep side windows in the Lumina help give a good view to all directions.

Dashboards have a clean, contemporary design. Simple controls are easy to see and reach while driving. Trunks in both models are roomy, with a flat floor that reaches well forward.

VALUE FOR THE MONEY: The Lumina is a pleasant, competent family sedan, which deserves consideration if you're shopping in the midsize field. Monte Carlo shares most of its pluses and minuses, in 2-door coupe form.

TROUBLE SPOTS

Engine temperature: The engine may overheat due to a problem with the heater hoses, which swell, then loosen from the heater core pipes and leak. (1996)

Fuel pump: Excess material in the plastic fuel tank can collect on the fuel pickup filter and restrict fuel flow. (1995-96)

Hard starting: There is a new Flash PROM available to correct hard starting and stalling under high-load, slow-speed operation. (1996)

CHEVROLET

Oil leak: Some cars have high oil consumption that is corrected by replacing the PCV harness as well as the valve cover, spark plugs and wires, and oil-fill cap. (1995)

Suspension noise: A popping noise from the front end is caused by a problem with the struts and can be corrected with an additional jounce bumper. (1995-96)

AVERAGE REPLACEMENT COSTS

A/C Compressor	$525	Exhaust System	$385
Alternator	200	Radiator	430
Automatic Trans.	1,180	Shocks and/or Struts	665
Brakes	270	Timing Chain/Belt	450
CV Joints	915		

NHTSA RECALL HISTORY

1995 Lumina: Steering-column bracket bolts on some cars may not be tightened. **1995:** Right lower control-arm ball-joint mounting hole was incorrectly positioned. **1995:** Seatbelt anchor can fracture in a crash. **1995:** Strained or separated windshield-wiper/washer switch wire can cause intermittent or nonexistent wash/wipe operation. **1996 Lumina:** Left front brake line can contact transaxle bracket or bolt and wear through. **1996:** Brake-booster tab is improperly located; if stopping distance is short, crash could occur. **1996:** Faulty power steering bearings may have been installed on certain vehicles, resulting in difficulty turning the steering wheel. Dealers will inspect and replace all affected parts. **2000 Lumina:** Clamp that secures flexible fuel-fill hose to metal fill tube on a few cars could be loose and might separate, causing fuel leakage. **2000 Lumina:** Passenger-airbag modules on a few cars have undersized inflator orifice, so module could explode during a crash. **2000 Lumina:** Right front brake hose on a few cars is incorrectly routed and could be cut or separated. **2000 Lumina w/rear drum brakes:** Bolt heads on rear spindle rod can separate and affected wheel can shift, causing loss of control. **2000-01:** Some seatbelt assemblies were not properly heat treated and do not pass the load-bearing requirement. **2001:** Airbag sensing diagnostic modules could experience a memory error prohibiting deployment in a collision.

PRICES

	Good	Average	Poor
1995 Lumina	$2,400-3,000	$1,700-2,200	$500-600
Monte Carlo	3,100-3,800	2,400-2,900	700-900
1996 Lumina	2,800-3,500	2,100-2,600	600-800
Monte Carlo	3,500-4,200	2,800-3,400	900-1,100
1997 Lumina	3,200-3,900	2,500-3,000	800-1,000
Monte Carlo	4,200-5,000	3,400-4,100	1,400-1,700
1998 Lumina	3,800-4,700	3,100-3,800	1,100-1,400
Monte Carlo	5,000-6,000	4,300-5,100	2,000-2,400
1999 Lumina	4,600-5,600	3,800-4,600	1,700-2,100
Monte Carlo	6,000-7,500	5,200-6,500	2,500-3,200
2000 Lumina	5,300-6,200	4,600-5,300	2,200-2,500
2001 Lumina	6,500-7,500	5,700-6,600	2,900-3,400

For detailed information on this vehicle visit
http://used.consumerguide.com and enter code **2249**

1997-03
CHEVROLET MALIBU

CG BEST BUY

CLASS: Midsize car

BUILT IN: USA

PROS: Standard antilock braking • Build quality • Cargo room • Fuel economy (4-cylinder) • Passenger room • Ride

CONS: Engine noise (4-cylinder) • Steering feel

EVALUATION: Acceleration is good with the 4-cylinder engine—more than sufficient for most owners. On the downside, the four gets loud when accelerating hard. A Malibu with the substantially smoother V6 is stronger off the line and around town, but does not feel markedly more energetic at highway speeds. The automatic transmission shifts without jarring, but does not always downshift promptly to furnish suitable passing power. A 4-cylinder Malibu averaged 22.5 mpg in a mix of city and expressway driving. A Malibu V6 returned about 19 mpg.

Malibu feels agile, maneuverable, and secure, but charging down a freeway off-ramp produces substantial body lean, as well as tire scrubbing. Malibu ride comfortably and stably on the highway. But there's a lot of suspension and tire thumping over ruts and potholes. Wind noise is tolerable, but the level of engine and tire noise yields less-than-serene cruising. Braking power is adequate, with good pedal modulation and moderate nosedive in hard braking.

Malibu is spacious for its size. Front head room is generous. Leg room is more than adequate all around. Rear head room is sufficient for folks under 6 feet tall. Front bucket seats are firm and nicely contoured, but the rear bench is harder and flatter than it should be. Malibu's dashboard is a gently curved model of efficiency.

A tasteful blend of fabrics, plastics, and padded surfaces gives Malibu the feel of a more-expensive automobile. Interior storage space ranks above average and trunk space is generous, helped by a flat floor, huge opening, and near-bumper-level sill to ease loading. Thin roof pillars and large outside mirrors offer good visibility. However, the rear parcel shelf is high enough to block the driver's view of the trunk while backing up.

VALUE FOR THE MONEY: Offering an admirable blend of utility, driving fun, and features, Malibu is an intermediate-sized sedan that warrants serious consideration.

TROUBLE SPOTS

Antenna: Because of the way it is routed, a passenger can accidentally disconnect the antenna so the cable must be rerouted. (1997-99)

Doors: The key reminder continues to sound after the key is removed from the ignition accompanied by power door locks not working due to a problem in the lock cylinder. (1997-99)

Doors: The power door locks fail, but still work manually, due to a rubber

CHEVROLET

part breaking on the actuator arm inside the door. (1997)

Paint/body: On white cars, the door handles turn yellow from the lock-cylinder grease staining them. The company will replace the cylinders under warranty and there is a colorless grease available for service. (1997-99)

Seat: The leather on the bucket seat back wears prematurely and the company will replace the seat cover and install extra padding under warranty. (1997-99)

Suspension noise: Noises from the front end (clunks, rattles, squeaks) may require replacement of the lower control arms or rack-and-pinion assembly or both. (1997-98)

AVERAGE REPLACEMENT COSTS

A/C Compressor	$500	Exhaust System	$475
Alternator	265	Radiator	450
Automatic Trans.	850	Shocks and/or Struts	900
Brakes	365	Timing Chain/Belt	325
CV Joints	750		

NHTSA RECALL HISTORY

1997: If airbag deploys, module could separate from instrument panel, striking and injuring occupant. **1997-98:** A buildup of snow or ice restricts the movement of the passenger-side windshield-wiper arm, the pivot housing can crack and the wipers will not operate. **2000:** Fuel-fill fitting is improperly secured to fuel tank and could leak an excessive amount of fuel, especially after refueling or when tank is more than half full. **2002:** Headlights may not meet light-intensity requirements.

PRICES

	Good	Average	Poor
1997 Malibu	$3,300-4,200	$2,600-3,300	$800-1,100
1998 Malibu	4,000-5,000	3,300-4,100	1,300-1,600
1999 Malibu	5,000-6,300	4,300-5,400	2,000-2,500
2000 Malibu	6,000-7,200	5,200-6,300	2,500-3,000
2001 Malibu	7,200-8,500	6,400-7,600	3,500-4,200
2002 Malibu	8,500-10,200	7,700-9,200	4,400-5,300
2003 Malibu	10,000-12,000	9,000-10,800	5,200-6,200

For detailed information on this vehicle visit
http://used.consumerguide.com and enter code **2299**

2000-03 CHEVROLET MONTE CARLO

CLASS: Midsize car

BUILT IN: Canada

PROS: Acceleration (SS)
• Instruments/controls
• Steering/handling (SS)

CONS: Engine noise
• Rear-seat entry/exit
• Road noise

EVALUATION: Modest handling skills are the rule for the LS version of this relatively large coupe, but it feels reasonably balanced and secure in corners. The SS edition shines on twisty roads, showing minimal body lean and great grip. Stable during highway cruising, both offer firm, accurate steering and a comfortable ride. A responsive automatic transmission works with the base V6 to furnish adequate acceleration. Although the SS is no muscle car, its bigger V6 provides brisk takeoffs and ready power for freeway merging and backroad passing. Both engines are loud and gruff in hard acceleration, and tire roar is prominent on coarse surfaces. Even the firm SS suspension is compliant enough on bumpy urban streets. Brakes feel strong and have good pedal modulation, but hard stops induce excessive nosedive. Midsize dimensions give the Monte a big advantage in interior space, compared to most coupes on the market. Two adults can stretch out in front, and rear leg room is adequate for average-size adults. Head room gets tight with an optional sunroof, but there's far more clearance than in, say, a Mercury Cougar or Dodge Stratus. The cabin feels roomier than an Accord or Solara. The trunk is tall, wide, and deep, with convenient bumper-height liftover. The driver gets a comfortable bucket seat with plenty of lateral bolstering, but thick rear roof pillars impede over-the-shoulder vision. Gauge groupings and graphics are excellent, controls handy, and front occupants have individual temperature controls.

VALUE FOR THE MONEY: Roomier than other sports coupes, the Monte trounces models like the Avenger in size, comfort, and performance. New or used, it also beats an Accord or Solara in features for the price. Though less poised than Japanese-brand rivals, it has its own American character. Resale value has not been strong, which can be a bonus for used-car shoppers.

TROUBLE SPOTS

Brakes: The rear brakes make squealing or moaning noises. Countermeasure brake pads are available. (2000-01)

Vehicle noise: Banging, clunking, or popping noises from the front under acceleration or braking require shims between the engine cradle and frame. (2000)

Vehicle noise: Fuel makes banging and sloshing noises in the tank when less than half full. (2000)

AVERAGE REPLACEMENT COSTS

A/C Compressor	$525	Exhaust System	$565
Alternator	275	Radiator	450
Automatic Trans.	895	Shocks and/or Struts	975
Brakes	485	Timing Chain/Belt	325
CV Joints	750		

NHTSA RECALL HISTORY

2000 w/TRW seatbelt-buckle assemblies: Seatbelt-buckle assemblies fail to conform to federal requirements because buckle base was not properly heat treated. **2001:** On certain cars, airbag sensing and diagnostic modules could experience a memory error, and airbags might not deploy during a crash. **2002:** Airbag inflator could fracture, possibly injuring passengers. **2003:**

CHEVROLET

Owner's manual doesn't adequately explain child-restraint anchorage system. Dealers will send vehicle owners a supplement to their manual.

PRICES

	Good	Average	Poor
2000 Monte Carlo LS	$9,000-10,000	$8,100-9,000	$4,700-5,200
Monte Carlo SS	11,500-12,700	10,400-11,400	6,300-7,000
2001 Monte Carlo LS	10,500-11,500	9,500-10,400	5,600-6,100
Monte Carlo SS	13,000-14,200	11,800-12,900	7,500-8,200
2002 Monte Carlo LS	12,000-13,200	10,800-11,900	6,700-7,400
Monte Carlo SS	15,000-16,500	13,700-15,000	9,500-10,400
2003 Monte Carlo LS	13,500-15,000	12,300-13,700	8,000-8,900
Monte Carlo SS	17,000-18,700	15,600-17,200	10,900-12,000

For detailed information on this vehicle visit
http://used.consumerguide.com and enter code 2368

1998-02
CHEVROLET PRIZM

CG BEST BUY

CLASS: Subcompact car

BUILT IN: USA

PROS: Optional antilock braking • Optional side airbags • Fuel economy • Ride

CONS: Automatic-transmission performance • Rear-seat room

EVALUATION: Anyone familiar with prior Prizms should feel right at home in this version. Though not exactly sparkling, acceleration is much better than most competitors. With 5-speed manual shift, a Prizm feels frisky and willing to move through traffic with authority. Performance with either automatic transmission, as expected, is less thrilling.

Prizm promises a controlled, but decidedly firm ride. You can expect to feel even small bumps, but the chassis generally does a good job of filtering out most of the harshness. With a standard suspension, the tires quickly run out of grip on twisty roads and allow moderate body lean. A Prizm LSi with the available Handling Package does a much better job of holding the road. Even better, it exacts little penalty in ride quality. Steering is direct and sharp. Brakes, while mushy in feel, do an adequate job in hauling the Prizm down from speed. Road noise is noticeable, but no louder than most of the competition. Visibility is excellent all around, helped by large outside mirrors that fight blind spots to the rear quarters.

Roomy and comfortable inside for average-size adults, the Prizm's fresh interior is also familiar. Head and leg room are ample. Two adults can sit comfortably in back, but only if the front seats are less than halfway back. Any farther, and rear leg room becomes tight and foot space is nearly nonexistent. Gauges are easy to see, and the dashboard hides no controls behind the steering wheel. Entry and exit to the rear seats is a bit tight through narrow door openings—a flaw found in most subcompact sedans. Cargo space is about average for Prizm's class, but you get a large trunk opening and handy bumper-height access.

VALUE FOR THE MONEY: Prizm is—to put it directly—among the best small cars on the market. New or used, Prizm basically comes across as a lower-cost Corolla, which has been outselling Chevrolet's subcompact by almost a 5-to-1 ratio. That's how it was before, and it's good news again, since the cars are so similar in structure. You can benefit from Toyota's reputation for durability, without paying quite the price that might be asked for a Corolla. Add capable road manners, and this is one small car that looks ready to stand up well to the punishment of daily driving. Don't finish up your subcompact shopping list without making sure Prizm—and Corolla—have prominent spots.

TROUBLE SPOTS

None: There are no trouble spots for this vehicle at this time.

AVERAGE REPLACEMENT COSTS

A/C Compressor	$405	CV Joints	$910
Alternator	535	Exhaust System	200
Automatic Trans.	690	Radiator	405
Brakes	220	Shocks and/or Struts	1,000
Clutch	390	Timing Chain/Belt	160

NHTSA RECALL HISTORY

None to date.

PRICES	Good	Average	Poor
1998 Prizm	$4,000-4,600	$3,300-3,800	$1,300-1,500
1999 Prizm	4,700-5,300	3,900-4,500	1,800-2,000
2000 Prizm	5,500-6,200	4,700-5,300	2,300-2,500
2001 Prizm	6,500-7,300	5,700-6,400	2,900-3,300
2002 Prizm	7,500-8,500	6,800-7,700	3,800-4,300

For detailed information on this vehicle visit
http://used.consumerguide.com and enter code **2300**

1994-03 CHEVROLET S-SERIES

CLASS: Compact pickup truck

BUILT IN: USA

PROS: Acceleration (V6)
• Optional third door (1996-later) • Handling
• Instruments/controls
• Passenger room • Ride (2WD models) **CONS:** Fuel economy • Rear-seat room (extended cab) • Ride (4WD models)

CHEVROLET

EVALUATION: Pleasant to drive, the S-Series is a solid-feeling truck. Cabins feel roomier than before, with more rearward seat travel and storage space. Extra glass area gives great visibility and an airy feel. Wind noise is reduced.

Acceleration is good with the V6. Automatic-transmission gear changes are smooth, though downshifts might be delayed for low-speed passing. An extended-cab V6 LS averaged 17.2 mpg in a long-term trial. When cold, however, that engine ran somewhat roughly, and its fan was intrusively loud. If you prefer a 4-cylinder pickup, your best bet is manual shift.

An extended-cab 2WD LS delivered ride quality as smooth as many cars. These pickups easily absorb most bumps, and take dips with minimal bouncing, but some optional tire/suspension setups are rougher. When the cargo bed is empty, the tail tends to hop over sharp bumps and ridges. Body lean is evident in turns, but the truck feels balanced and poised in directional changes. Standard antilock brakes prevent lock-up during simulated panic stops, but brake-pedal feel on early models is disturbingly spongy.

VALUE FOR THE MONEY: In their latest form, these compact pickups rank among the best in overall performance, ergonomics, and refinement. A Dodge Dakota has heftier hauling ability and an available V8 engine, but most buyers will be pleased with the Chevrolet. It outsells the Dakota and is a worthy contender to the sales-leading Ford Ranger.

TROUBLE SPOTS

Engine knock: Knock in the 4.3-liter engine is usually eliminated by using an oil filter with a check valve. If this does not fix it, GM has revised PROMs for the computers and will even replace the main bearings. (1994-95)

AVERAGE REPLACEMENT COSTS

A/C Compressor	$550	Exhaust System	$460
Alternator	255	Radiator	410
Automatic Trans.	750	Shocks and/or Struts	345
Brakes	210	Timing Chain/Belt	420
Clutch	545	Universal Joints	190

NHTSA RECALL HISTORY

1994 w/2.2-liter engine: Vacuum hose can detach from power-brake-booster check valve, as a result of engine backfire. **1994-95 Postal Vehicle:** Loose/worn steering shaft can result in separation from steering gear. **1994-96 w/4WD and ABS:** Increased stopping distances can occur during ABS stops while in 2WD mode. **1994-97:** Seatbelt webbing on certain models can separate during frontal impact. **1995 w/air conditioning and V6 engine:** Rivet can break and allow fan blade to separate from hub. **1996 2WD manual-shift w/2.2-liter engine:** Drive wheels could seize and lock while truck is moving. **1996:** Top coat of paint on a few trucks peels severely. **1996-97 w/V6 engine:** Front brake line can contact oil pan, causing wear that may result in fluid loss. **1997-98 electric:** Fuel-fired heater-pipe ground strap contacts rear brake pipe, leading to premature corrosion and eventual loss of brake-pipe integrity. **1998:** Daytime running lights do not meet FMVSS No. 108 requirements. **1998:** Fatigue fracture of rear-axle brake pipe can occur, causing slow fluid leak and resulting in soft brake pedal; if pipe breaks, driver would face sudden loss of rear-brake performance. **1998:** Wiring-harness clip can melt and drip onto exhaust manifold, possibly resulting in fire. **1999:** Safety-belt retractor may not meet the locking require-ments, leaving the occupant improperly restrained in a collision. **2000 w/2WD:** On certain vehicles, right-hand ABS module feed pipe and/or brake crossover pipe-tube nuts could have been tightened improperly; seal could have been broken, causing leakage and increasing stopping distance. **2000 w/all-disc brakes:** Out-of-spec spring clip in ABS motor could allow bearing to become misaligned; eventually, ABS and Dynamic Rear Proportioning system would become inoperative. **2000-01:** Some seatbelt assemblies were not properly heat treated and do not pass the load-bearing requirement.

PRICES	Good	Average	Poor
1994 S10 2WD	$2,100-3,800	$1,500-2,700	$400-700
S10 4WD	3,200-4,500	2,500-3,500	800-1,100
1995 S-Series 2WD	2,600-4,500	1,900-3,300	500-900
S-Series 4WD	4,000-5,700	3,300-4,700	1,300-1,800
1996 S-Series 2WD	3,100-5,200	2,400-4,100	700-1,200
S-Series 4WD	4,800-7,000	4,000-5,900	1,800-2,700
1997 S-Series 2WD	3,700-6,000	3,000-4,900	1,100-1,700
S-Series 4WD	5,600-8,000	4,800-6,900	2,300-3,300
1998 S-Series 2WD	4,400-7,000	3,700-5,800	1,500-2,500
S-Series 4WD	6,300-9,000	5,500-7,900	2,800-4,000
1999 S-Series 2WD	5,100-8,000	4,300-6,800	2,000-3,200
S-Series 4WD	7,100-10,200	6,300-9,100	3,400-4,900
2000 S-Series 2WD	5,800-9,000	5,000-7,800	2,400-3,800
S-Series 4WD	8,200-11,500	7,400-10,400	4,200-5,900
2001 S-Series 2WD	6,800-10,500	6,100-9,300	3,200-4,900
S-Series 4WD	9,500-13,500	8,600-12,200	4,900-7,000
2002 S-Series 2WD	8,000-12,000	7,200-10,800	4,100-6,100
S-Series 4WD	11,000-15,500	9,900-14,000	5,900-8,400
2003 S-Series 2WD	9,800-14,000	8,800-12,600	5,100-7,300
S-Series 4WD	13,000-17,500	11,800-15,900	7,500-10,200

For detailed information on this vehicle visit
http://used.consumerguide.com and enter code **2011**

1990-94 CHEVROLET S10 BLAZER

CLASS: Midsize sport-util-ity vehicle

BUILT IN: USA

PROS: Acceleration • Antilock brakes • 4WD traction • Passenger and cargo room • Ride (4-door)

CONS: Fuel economy • Noise • Rear-seat comfort • Ride (2-door models)

CHEVROLET

EVALUATION: The 4.3-liter engine develops considerable torque at low engine speeds, yielding strong acceleration around town, plus plenty of towing power. Sadly, it's also noisy.

Suspensions are among the least compliant in their class, but the 4-door's longer wheelbase improves ride quality. With a 2-door, you can expect to bounce and bang over bumpy roads.

Body lean in turns isn't bad, but Blazers don't match the smaller Jeep Cherokee in urban nimbleness. Interior room is good, but not as spacious as an Explorer or Grand Cherokee. Dashboard layout also is pleasing on the whole, but some controls are a long reach, and radio buttons are small. Interior noise gets bothersome on the highway.

Back seats are hard to get at in 2-doors. Four-door models, with their extra 6.5 inches of wheelbase, boast vastly improved access. Rear leg room is identical in each body style, but the 4-door's longer wheelbase allowed the back seat to be fitted ahead of rear wheelwells, for 15 inches more hip room than the 2-door.

Shift-on-the-fly 4WD and 4-wheel ABS are particularly appealing features.

VALUE FOR THE MONEY: By 1993, when Jeep launched its Grand Cherokee with a driver-side airbag and available V8, the Blazer was showing its age. Grand Cherokee and Explorers beat the Blazer in refinement, but the S10 Blazer still is a good choice in a smaller sport utility.

TROUBLE SPOTS

Automatic transmission: TH-700-R4 automatic transmissions may shift late or not upshift at all. The problem is a stuck throttle valve inside the transmission. (1990-94)

Engine knock: Knock in the 4.3-liter engine is usually eliminated by using an oil filter with a check valve. If this does not fix it, GM has revised PROMs for the computers and will even replace the main bearings. (1990-94)

AVERAGE REPLACEMENT COSTS

A/C Compressor	$365	Exhaust System	$405
Alternator	195	Radiator	415
Automatic Trans.	735	Shocks and/or Struts	275
Brakes	210	Timing Chain/Belt	205
Clutch	390	Universal Joints	160

NHTSA RECALL HISTORY

1990-91: Fuel-tank sender seal may be out of position, which could result in fuel leakage. **1990-92 w/2.5-liter engine and no air conditioning:** Fan blades could break off while engine is running. **1991:** Rear seatbelt-buckle release button can stick in unlatched position, under certain conditions. **1991-94 w/4WD and ABS:** Increased stopping distances can occur during ABS stops while in 2WD mode. **1993:** Rear seatbelts may not meet government requirements. **1994 w/weight-distribution trailer-hitch option:** Trailer-hitch attaching bolts were not tightened adequately.

PRICES	Good	Average	Poor
1990 S10 Blazer 2WD	$1,200-1,800	$700-1,100	$100-200
S10 Blazer 4WD	1,800-2,400	1,200-1,600	300-400

1991 S10 Blazer 2WD	$1,500-2,300	$1,000-1,500	$200-300
S10 Blazer 4WD	2,300-3,100	1,700-2,200	400-600
1992 S10 Blazer 2WD	1,800-3,000	1,200-2,000	300-500
S10 Blazer 4WD	2,700-3,800	2,000-2,900	600-800
1993 S10 Blazer 2WD	2,100-3,500	1,500-2,500	400-600
S10 Blazer 4WD	3,000-4,300	2,300-3,300	700-1,000
1994 S10 Blazer 2WD	2,400-4,000	1,700-2,900	500-800
S10 Blazer 4WD	3,400-5,000	2,700-4,000	900-1,300

For detailed information on this vehicle visit
http://used.consumerguide.com and enter code **2014**

1999-03 CHEVROLET SILVERADO

CG BEST BUY

CLASS: Full-size pick-up truck
BUILT IN: Mexico
PROS: Acceleration (V8) • Instruments/controls
CONS: Fuel economy • Rear-seat entry/exit (extended-cab) • Ride

EVALUATION: Silverado and GMC Sierra pickups perform better than their predecessors, though not always by a lot. New V8s are smooth and capable, but have slightly less torque than the previous engines, so acceleration and throttle response are similar. The Tow/Haul mode and optional adjustable suspension are welcome features, since most big pickups haul or tow at times. All-around performance easily matches Ford's F-150. Although the V6 struggles under heavy loads or up long grades, it's a smooth runner. The 5.3-liter V8 offers good power in all conditions, though it trails Ford's 5.4-liter in torque. Test Silverado SS did an impressive 7.2 sec 0-60 mph, and delivered strong passing punch. An alert, fuss-free automatic transmission helps get the most out of any engine. A 4WD extended cab with the 5.3 V8 averaged 13.7 mpg. Brakes offer good stopping power and firm, progressive pedal action, beating the previous model's mushy feel. Steering is more precise, but over-boosted. A stiffer structure helps improve ride quality, which is more compliant than Ford's, though the tail still stutters over bumps when the bed is empty. The Quadrasteer 4-wheel steering system, made available in 2002, is a revelation, giving this big pickup the close-quarters maneuverability of a small car as well as enhancing high-speed tracking and towing stability. Road, wind, and engine-noise levels are unobjectionable. The biggest improvements lie inside. In design, feel, and location, gauges and controls are best-in-class. GM was also the first to supplement the odometer with an engine-hour meter.

Front seats are roomy and supportive, with integrated seatbelts that move comfortably with the seats themselves. Some drivers might have trouble squeezing between the door panel and seat to reach some controls.

CHEVROLET

Both GM makes soundly trounce Ford and Dodge pickups in rear-seat accommodations, with more leg clearance. A contoured cushion and reclined backrest approach sedan levels of comfort. Doors open wider, too.

VALUE FOR THE MONEY: GM earns credit for refining its big pickups while introducing a host of worthy improvements. No extended cabs are more comfortable. Though a step behind Ford in innovation, GM pickups deliver high value for performance, comfort, and design, and beat Ford in 4WD convenience.

TROUBLE SPOTS

Automatic transmission: The front wheels slip while in 4WD requiring replacement of the clutch plates as well as the use of synthetic gear oil. (1999-2001)

Manual transmission: Manual transmissions tend to pop out of first gear because the transmissions were built without a detent ball and spring. These parts will be installed under warranty. (1999-2000)

Vehicle shake: Extended-cab, long-box models shudder when accelerating from a stop requiring replacement of the two-piece driveshaft with a one-piece driveshaft. (1999-2001)

AVERAGE REPLACEMENT COSTS

A/C Compressor	$390	CV Joints	$890
Alternator	325	Exhaust System	455
Automatic Trans.	1,115	Radiator	555
Brakes	375	Shocks and/or Struts	665
Clutch	455	Timing Chain/Belt	610

NHTSA RECALL HISTORY

1999-2000: Clearance between front right-hand brake pipe and body cross sill could decrease to the point of allowing contact, which could result in damage and loss of brake fluid and pressure. **2000 w/4-wheel disc brakes:** Out-of-spec spring clip in antilock brake system could allow motor bearing to become misaligned; eventually, ABS would be nonfunctional and Dynamic Rear-Proportioning system would become inoperative.

PRICES

	Good	Average	Poor
1999 Silverado 1500 2WD	$8,500-13,000	$7,700-11,700	$4,400-6,800
Silverado 1500 4WD	10,500-14,500	9,500-13,100	5,600-7,700
2000 Silverado 1500 2WD	9,500-14,000	8,600-12,600	4,900-7,300
Silverado 1500 4WD	12,000-16,500	10,800-14,900	6,700-9,200
2001 Silverado 1500 2WD	11,000-16,000	9,900-14,400	5,900-8,600
Silverado 1500 4WD	13,500-19,000	12,300-17,300	8,000-11,200
2002 Silverado 1500 2WD	12,500-19,000	11,300-17,100	7,100-10,800
Silverado 1500 4WD	15,200-21,500	13,800-19,600	9,600-13,500
2003 Silverado 1500 2WD	14,500-25,500	13,200-23,200	9,000-15,800
Silverado 1500 4WD	17,000-27,000	15,600-24,800	10,900-17,300

For detailed information on this vehicle visit
http://used.consumerguide.com and enter code **2367**

1992-99 CHEVROLET SUBURBAN

CLASS: Full-size sport-utility vehicle

BUILT IN: Mexico, USA

PROS: Acceleration (7.4-liter) • Antilock brakes • Passenger and cargo room • Highway ride • Trailer-towing capability • Visibility

CONS: Acceleration (early models) • Fuel economy • Handling • Maneuverability • Rear-seat entry/exit

EVALUATION: Evolved from GM pickup trucks, full-size Suburbans might be fitted to haul either cargo or passengers. Step-in height is a lot lower than in earlier Suburbans. Even so, it's tough to get in and out from the back because the opening between door pillar and seat is narrow, and step-in height of 4WD Suburbans is still quite tall. Access to the optional third seat demands some serious stooping.

Three can easily sit abreast, but there's not as much stretch-out leg room for adults in the back seats as the vehicle's size would suggest. Folding the 70/30 split middle bench is a two-step procedure, and a handy carpeted panel hinges down to create a flat load floor from front seatbacks to the front of the rear-most bench. Unfortunately, the rear bench's seatback does not fold flat. Though it's removable, that seat is heavy and cumbersome.

Visibility is fine, from a carlike seating position. Controls are within easy reach, though the climate and radio buttons suffer from a haphazard layout. Cargo space is cavernous and loading is easy, because the load floor is more than two feet off the ground.

Acceleration with the early 5.7-liter V8 is only adequate in town, and the transmission is reluctant to downshift. With its extra 50 horsepower, the Vortec gas V8 introduced for 1996 gives the Suburban a much-needed boost. That one is more lively off the line, and teams with an improved transmission to furnish better power for passing and climbing long grades. No longer is it necessary to push the pedal to the floor to induce a downshift.

Fuel economy is no bonus, with any engine. Don't expect much more than the miserable 10.7 mpg achieved in mixed driving with a K1500. The big 7.4-liter engine is the choice for truly heavy towing, but most shoppers will be satisfied with a 5.7-liter V8.

Suburbans are smooth and capable on the highway. Bumps are absorbed well, with only moderate floating over freeway dips—though turns at any speed are accompanied by noticeable body lean. Simulated panic stops induce pronounced nosedive, and occasionally a bit of rear-wheel lockup (despite the antilock braking system).

VALUE FOR THE MONEY: Through the early '90s, Suburbans were virtually unchallenged in the full-size wagon segment. GM's Tahoe/Yukon offers much of the Suburban's brawn in a more manageable size. Still, those two cannot match the Suburban's payload ratings and towing ability. Neither can they seat more than six—a feat that's possible, however, in a Ford Expedition with third-row seating, as well as in a full-size van.

Sales declined during 1996, for the first time in this generation. Some potential Suburban buyers evidently gravitated to the smaller Tahoe/Yukon.

No rival can match the Suburban's 149.5-cubic-foot cargo capacity. Also, no engine is as powerful as the muscular 7.4-liter V8.

TROUBLE SPOTS

Brake wear: Front brake linings wear rapidly. Replacing the proportioning valve and the rear shoes with a different friction material prolongs front brake life. (1992-99)

Clutch: The clutch may fail to engage or disengage, or become noisy due to overtravel of the clutch damper on trucks with the 6.5-liter diesel engine. Revised parts are available to prevent recurrence. (1992-99)

Dashboard lights: The oil-pressure gauge may read high, move erratically, or not work because the oil-pressure sensor is defective. (1992-93)

Doors: The rear cargo doors may be hard to open because the hinges corrode requiring the hinge pins and bushings to be replaced. (1992-97)

Fuel pump: The electronic injection pump on diesel engines is prone to failures and may be covered under an extended warranty up to 11 years or 120,000 miles.

Hard starting: No-starts, hard starting, or rough idle may be due to some gasolines dissolving compounds in the fuel-filler pipe that then clog the fuel injectors. (1997-99)

Oil leak: Oil loss and fouled spark plugs result from intake manifold gasket leaks. (1996-98)

Transmission leak: Fluid may leak from the pump body on 4L60-E transmissions due to the pump bushing walking out of the valve body. (1995-96)

AVERAGE REPLACEMENT COSTS

A/C Compressor	$520	Exhaust System	$485
Alternator	225	Radiator	450
Automatic Trans.	850	Shocks and/or Struts	410
Brakes	220	Timing Chain/Belt	230
Clutch	800	Universal Joints	270

NHTSA RECALL HISTORY

1992: Brake-pedal pivot bolt can disengage. **1994:** Reversed polarity of brake switch can cause contacts to wear prematurely; may result in loss of brake lights without warning. **1994-96:** Solder joints can crack, causing windshield wipers to work intermittently. **1994-97:** The windshield wiper motor may fail on certain vehicles. Dealer will inspect and replace affected parts. **1995 w/automatic transmission:** External transmission leak can occur. **1995 w/automatic transmission:** When shift lever is placed in "Park" position, its indicator light may not illuminate. **1995-96 w/gaso-**

line engine: Throttle cable may contact dash mat and bind. **1997-98:** On certain vehicles, the outside rearview mirror switch may short circuit. Dealer will inspect and replace affected parts. **1998:** On some vehicles, one or both front-brake rotor/hubs may have out-of-spec gray iron that can fail during life of vehicle. **1999:** In a crash, right front passenger-restraint systems may not meet neck extension requirements.

PRICES	Good	Average	Poor
1992 LS, LT 2WD	$5,400-6,200	$4,600-5,300	$2,200-2,500
LS, LT 4WD	6,300-7,000	5,500-6,200	2,800-3,100
Suburban 2WD	5,000-6,000	4,300-5,100	2,000-2,400
Suburban 4WD	5,800-6,800	5,000-5,900	2,400-2,900
1993 LS, LT 2WD	6,000-6,800	5,200-5,900	2,500-2,900
LS, LT 4WD	7,100-8,000	6,300-7,100	3,400-3,800
Suburban 2WD	5,500-6,500	4,700-5,600	2,300-2,700
Suburban 4WD	6,500-7,500	5,700-6,600	2,900-3,400
1994 LS, LT 2WD	6,500-7,300	5,700-6,400	2,900-3,300
LS, LT 4WD	7,700-8,500	6,900-7,700	3,900-4,300
Suburban 2WD	6,000-7,000	5,200-6,100	2,500-2,900
Suburban 4WD	7,100-8,200	6,300-7,300	3,400-3,900
1995 LS, LT 2WD	7,500-8,500	6,800-7,700	3,800-4,300
LS, LT 4WD	9,000-10,200	8,100-9,200	4,700-5,300
Suburban 2WD	6,700-7,700	5,900-6,800	3,100-3,500
Suburban 4WD	7,900-8,900	7,100-8,000	4,000-4,500
1996 LS, LT 2WD	8,400-9,400	7,600-8,500	4,400-4,900
LS, LT 4WD	9,700-11,000	8,700-9,900	5,000-5,700
Suburban 2WD	7,400-8,400	6,700-7,600	3,600-4,100
Suburban 4WD	8,600-9,600	7,700-8,600	4,500-5,000
1997 LS, LT 2WD	9,300-10,500	8,400-9,500	4,800-5,500
LS, LT 4WD	11,000-12,500	9,900-11,300	5,900-6,800
Suburban 2WD	8,200-9,200	7,400-8,300	4,200-4,700
Suburban 4WD	9,500-10,500	8,600-9,500	4,900-5,500
1998 LS, LT 2WD	10,500-11,500	9,500-10,400	5,600-6,100
LS, LT 4WD	12,000-13,500	10,800-12,200	6,700-7,600
Suburban 2WD	9,500-10,500	8,600-9,500	4,900-5,500
Suburban 4WD	10,800-11,800	9,700-10,600	5,800-6,400
1999 LS, LT 2WD	12,500-14,000	11,300-12,600	7,100-8,000
LS, LT 4WD	14,000-15,500	12,700-14,100	8,500-9,500
Suburban 2WD	11,000-12,200	9,900-11,000	5,900-6,600
Suburban 4WD	12,200-13,200	11,000-11,900	6,800-7,400

For detailed information on this vehicle visit
http://used.consumerguide.com and enter code **2127**

2000-03
CHEVROLET TAHOE
AND SUBURBAN

CG BEST BUY

CLASS: Full-size sport-utility vehicle

BUILT IN: USA

PROS: Passenger and cargo room • Trailer-towing capacity

CONS: Fuel economy • Rear-seat entry/exit

EVALUATION: Tahoe/Suburban advances were mainly evolutionary, but they yielded some noticeable improvements. New V8s feel slightly smoother than the engines they replaced, but not dramatically stronger. Acceleration is adequate, aided by the smooth automatic's astute shifting, but the 4.8-liter feels strained in towing or heavy hauling. Gas mileage is dismal. A Tahoe 4x4 with the 5.3-liter V8 averaged 12.9 mpg, while a similar Suburban got 11.5 mpg. These big SUVs don't corner like cars, but handling is better than their size might suggest. They feel balanced in directional changes, and are fairly easy to maneuver. Steering is reasonably precise, but road feel is only adequate. At lower speeds, the speed-variable assist makes steering too light for some tastes. Biggest improvements are in ride quality and brake feel. The suspension absorbs bumps well and is sure-footed on rough pavement. Stopping power is strong, with firm, progressive pedal action. Wind rush is noticeable but not intrusive. Tire noise is low for a full-size SUV, but audible at highway speeds. The dashboard layout is logical and handy, with clear gauges and easily accessed controls. Drivers get a commanding view, while moving the spare tire beneath the rear undercarriage improved visibility and cargo space. Suburbans have ample head, shoulder, and leg room for two grownups, but leg and head clearance in the Tahoe's third-row seat suggests children and occasional use. Entry/exit is somewhat hampered by modest back-door openings, especially on Tahoes. A Tahoe has only enough room for a single row of grocery bags behind the third row, but Suburbans are more sizable. Third-row seats fold easily, and have wheels for removal. The Suburban's heavy bench takes two people to remove, while the Tahoe's third row is in two sections.

VALUE FOR THE MONEY: GM's impressive new full-size SUVs are capable, comfortable, and easy to live with. Though too big for a lot of buyers, their size fits nicely into the gap between Ford's Expedition and Excursion. Don't buy a big SUV without trying a Chevrolet or GMC.

TROUBLE SPOTS

Climate control: Low output of the rear heater in very cold weather is due to a restrictor in the T-coupling. A revised coupling is offered. (2000-01)

Oil leak: An oil leak may be created by the front driveshaft hitting the oil filter on 4x4 models with the 7.4L engine. An adapter will relocate the filter. (2000)

AVERAGE REPLACEMENT COSTS

A/C Compressor	$390	Exhaust System	$455
Alternator	325	Radiator	555
Automatic Trans.	1,115	Shocks and/or Struts	665
Brakes	375	Timing Chain/Belt	610
CV Joints	890		

NHTSA RECALL HISTORY

2000: Clearance between front right-hand brake pipe and body cross sill could decrease to the point of allowing contact, which could result in damage and loss of brake fluid and pressure. **2000-01:** Rear wheelhouse plugs may be loose or missing, allowing exhaust gases to flow forward under certain conditions and accumulate in rear wheelhouse. **2001:** Outboard-seatbelt retractors for the 2nd and 3rd row of seats could be cracked. With repeated actuation of the locking mechanism, the crack could spread to the point such that the seatbelt would no longer lock. **2001-02 Tahoe:** Rearward folding head restraints may pinch and trap fingers if protective covers are not installed. **2003:** In certain extreme impacts frame cross member could tear fuel tank resulting in fuel leakage. Dealers will install a fuel-tank shield on affected vehicles.

PRICES

	Good	Average	Poor
2000 Suburban 1500 2WD	$15,500-19,500	$14,100-17,700	$9,900-12,500
Suburban 1500 4WD	17,300-21,500	15,900-19,800	11,100-13,800
Suburban 2500 2WD	16,300-20,500	14,800-18,700	10,400-13,100
Suburban 2500 4WD	17,500-22,500	16,100-20,700	11,200-14,400
Tahoe 1500 2WD	14,500-19,000	13,200-17,300	9,000-11,800
Tahoe 1500 4WD	16,000-21,000	14,600-19,100	10,200-13,400
2001 Suburban 1500 2WD	18,500-23,500	17,000-21,600	11,800-15,000
Suburban 1500 4WD	20,000-25,500	18,400-23,500	13,000-16,600
Suburban 2500 2WD	19,500-24,500	17,900-22,500	12,700-15,900
Suburban 2500 4WD	20,800-26,000	19,100-23,900	13,500-16,900
Tahoe 1500 2WD	17,500-22,500	16,100-20,700	11,200-14,400
Tahoe 1500 4WD	19,000-24,500	17,500-22,500	12,400-15,900
2002 Suburban 1500 2WD	23,000-26,500	21,200-24,400	15,000-17,200
Suburban 1500 4WD	25,000-28,500	23,300-26,500	16,500-18,800
Suburban 2500 2WD	24,000-27,000	22,300-25,100	15,600-17,600
Suburban 2500 4WD	26,000-29,000	24,200-27,000	17,200-19,100
Tahoe 1500 2WD	22,500-26,000	20,700-23,900	14,600-16,900
Tahoe 1500 4WD	24,500-28,000	22,800-26,000	15,900-18,200
2003 Suburban 1500 2WD	26,500-30,500	24,600-28,400	17,500-20,100
Suburban 1500 4WD	28,500-32,500	26,500-30,200	19,400-22,100
Suburban 2500 2WD	27,500-31,500	25,600-29,300	18,400-21,100
Suburban 2500 4WD	29,500-33,000	27,400-30,700	20,400-22,800
Tahoe 1500 2WD	26,000-30,000	24,200-27,900	17,200-19,800
Tahoe 1500 4WD	28,000-32,000	26,000-29,800	19,000-21,800

For detailed information on this vehicle visit
http://used.consumerguide.com and enter code **2366**

1999-03 CHEVROLET TRACKER

CLASS: Compact sport-utility vehicle

BUILT IN: Canada

PROS: Cargo room • Maneuverability

CONS: Acceleration • Rear seat entry/exit (2-dr) • Rear-seat room • Rear visibility • Steering/handling

EVALUATION: Both 4-cylinder engines feel weak and gruff when worked hard—which is necessary most of the time, even for ordinary driving. In the convertible, power is only passable; in the wagon, lethargic. No ball of fire itself, the V6 at least adds a welcome dose of oomph. Automatic transmissions are well-behaved, but the manual gearbox suffers vague shift action. Gas mileage is no bargain. A 4-cylinder 4x4 convertible with the 5-speed averaged 20.2 mpg. Ride and handling are nothing to shout about, either. Even on fairly smooth roads, Trackers are prone to fore-aft pitching, though they absorb most bumps without jarring. Cornering grip is only so-so. A CR-V or Forester is far more composed and comfortable. Tracker is the better off-road choice, however, thanks to its low-range gearing and truck-style construction. Rear space is tight, and rear entry/exit tricky. Up front, however, two occupants get more pleasing space and comfort. Relatively low seats mean drivers don't get so commanding a forward view. Tall rear headrests and an outside spare tire hamper rearward vision. Step-in height is moderate, but narrow rear doors make it hard to get into wagons. The convertible's back seat is cramped and park-bench hard.

Stereo and climate controls are too low for easy adjusting on the move, and the radio has annoyingly tiny buttons. Neither body style has much cargo space, and the tailgate swings to the right, which hampers curbside loading.

VALUE FOR THE MONEY: Despite some off-road prowess, Tracker is an also-ran among mini SUVs. A CR-V, RAV4, or Forester is more pleasant, spacious, and enjoyable for the kind of driving that most folks do. Because the Tracker's resale value is lower, it costs less secondhand.

TROUBLE SPOTS

Air conditioner: It the air conditioner loses refrigerant, the O-rings must be replaced at the compressor, evaporator, and condenser. (1999-2000)

Automatic transmission: Slow upshifts or downshifts while driving with the cruise control engaged are due to a faulty cruise-control servo. (1999-2000)

Engine noise: 2.0L or 2.5L engines make a ticking noise when cold started due to problems with the valve lifters. (1999-2001)

Manual transmission: 4WD transfer case shifter may be hard to move because the shift synchronizers have too much grab. New synchros, blocking rings, and front shift shaft are required. (1999-2000)

Pedals: The throttle valve cable (for the automatic transmission) corrodes inside the casing causing the accelerator pedal to become very stiff.

Water leak: Convertible tops leak from a gap between the retainer and hem, through a gap in the quarter trim panel, from the top joint trim molding, over the top of the trim, through the vent in the rear quarter panel, and through the rear quarter trim panel brace. (1999)

AVERAGE REPLACEMENT COSTS

A/C Compressor	$430	CV Joints	$430
Alternator	590	Exhaust System	210
Automatic Trans.	715	Radiator	400
Brakes	220	Shocks and/or Struts	525
Clutch	430	Timing Chain/Belt	275

NHTSA RECALL HISTORY

1999: Brake lights on some vehicles may be inoperative when brake pedal is depressed. On vehicles equipped with automatic transaxle, this failure may also prevent shifting out of "Park." **1999:** Steering shafts could separate, resulting in loss of steering control. **1999:** Windshield may have been improperly installed and may not be retained on front impact. **2001 4-dr :** Mislabeled seatbelts intended for 2-door models were installed in some 4-door vehicles, and do not work properly.

PRICES	Good	Average	Poor
1999 Tracker 2WD	$4,000-5,000	$3,300-4,100	$1,300-1,600
Tracker 4WD	5,200-6,300	4,400-5,400	2,100-2,500
2000 Tracker 2WD	5,200-6,300	4,400-5,400	2,100-2,500
Tracker 4WD	6,500-7,600	5,700-6,700	2,900-3,400
2001 Tracker 2WD	6,500-8,300	5,700-7,300	2,900-3,700
Tracker 4WD	8,000-10,000	7,200-9,000	4,100-5,100
2002 Tracker 2WD	8,000-10,500	7,200-9,500	4,100-5,400
Tracker 4WD	9,500-12,000	8,600-10,800	4,900-6,200
2003 Tracker 2WD	9,500-12,500	8,600-11,300	4,900-6,500
Tracker 4WD	11,000-15,200	9,900-13,700	5,900-8,200

> For detailed information on this vehicle visit
> http://used.consumerguide.com and enter code **2370**

1997-03 CHEVROLET VENTURE

CLASS: Minivan
BUILT IN: USA
PROS: Antilock brakes • Automatic-transmission performance • Passenger and cargo room • Ride
CONS: Fuel economy • Rear-seat comfort

CHEVROLET

EVALUATION: In terms of interior space utilization, General Motors designers did their job well. Even with the minivan's split-bench seats, they managed to retain the flexibility of the convenient modular seating concept. At the same time, they added innovative storage helpers throughout the interior, and the Venture's optional driver-side sliding door opens wide enough to permit access to the third row of seats.

Chevrolet's minivan feels somewhat sportier than those from Ford or Chrysler. Steering is precise and accurately communicates the action of the front tires. Body lean is moderate in turns, and the minivan's all-season tires grip securely. The suspension absorbs most bumps with ease and delivers a comfortable, stable highway ride. Test Ventures halted with good control and a progressive pedal feel. Wind noise around the mirrors has been prominent at highway speeds, but road and engine sounds tend to be well-muffled.

The 3.4-liter V6 engine produces sufficient acceleration for nearly every usage. On the other hand, both Ford and Chrysler have offered optional engines with higher torque ratings, which are better able to cope with full loads of cargo and/or passengers. The automatic transmission keeps unnecessary gear changes to a minimum. It also reacts quickly when a downshift is needed to pass or merge. As for economy, we averaged 15.3 mpg with an early Venture, in a blend of city/suburban commuting and freeway travel—just about average in the minivan league. A later test of an extended-length model averaged 17.6 mpg.

VALUE FOR THE MONEY: Critical shoppers are likely to find a lot to like about the GM trio of minivans, despite the discomfort endured by some backseat riders due to the low seats.

TROUBLE SPOTS

Air conditioner: If the air conditioning is insufficient, the engine cooling fan and the air-conditioning orifice tube may have to be replaced. (1997)

Brakes: The brake pedal may not return causing the brakes to drag, get hot and wear out prematurely. The cause may be misadjusted brake or cruise control switches of a defective brake-pedal assembly. (1997)

Climate control: The heater may not be adequate in cold weather requiring a revised heater core and possibly a new distribution duct. (1997)

Vehicle noise: A rattling noise from the rear on long wheelbase models equipped with electronic level control requires replacement shock absorbers. (1997-98)

Windows: If the "auto-down" feature of the power window quits, the integrated circuit that controls this function must be replaced. (1997)

Windshield: The windshield may crack in cold weather. (1997)

AVERAGE REPLACEMENT COSTS

A/C Compressor	$635	Exhaust System	$330
Alternator	380	Radiator	450
Automatic Trans.	1,160	Shocks and/or Struts	460
Brakes	240	Timing Chain/Belt	345
CV Joints	490		

NHTSA RECALL HISTORY

1997-01 w/passenger-side power doors: Door closes but may not be latched. If this happens, the sliding door can open while the vehicle is in motion. **1997-98 w/bucket seats or split bench seat in second or third row:** Seat-latch mechanism does not have protective covers; when activating release mechanism to roll a bucket seat forward, finger(s) could be severely injured or severed, if they are not kept clear. **1997-98:** Faulty power-steering bearings may have been installed on certain vehicles, resulting in difficulty turning the steering wheel. Dealers will inspect and replace all affected parts. **1997-98:** Windshield-wiper linkage arm can contact brake line connected to traction-control modulator valve; brake line can chafe, resulting in brake-fluid leakage. **1998:** Broken shift-cable fitting or loose shift linkage can occur; moving shift lever to "Park" position may not shift the transmission to "Park," and vehicle could roll. **1998-01 w/passenger-side sliding door:** Front passenger-side sliding doors may have inadequate welds. Actuator can jam in the unlatched position and, when the sliding door closes, it will not be latched. **1999:** Front lower insulator to cradle sleeve on small number of minivans may collapse, which could result in steering-shaft separation. **2000 w/extended wheelbase:** Small number of vehicles have inoperative fuel-tank rollover valves. **2000:** Some seatbelt assemblies were not properly heat treated and do not pass the load-bearing requirement. **2001:** Owner's manual doesn't adequately explain child-restraint anchorage system. Dealers will send vehicle owners a supplement to their manual. **2001:** Passenger-airbag inflator modules may have been built without the correct amount of explosive. Airbag explosion or failure could occur. **2001:** Seat-latch anchor wire diameter may be wider than 6.1 mm, potentially inhibiting the installation of child restraints. **2002:** Airbag-inflator could fracture and possibly injure passengers. **2003:** Owner's manual doesn't adequately explain child restraint anchorage system. Dealers will send vehicle owners a supplement to their manual.

PRICES

	Good	Average	Poor
1997 Venture extended	$5,000-5,800	$4,300-4,900	$2,000-2,300
Venture regular	4,200-5,000	3,400-4,100	1,400-1,700
1998 Venture extended	6,000-7,000	5,200-6,100	2,500-2,900
Venture regular	5,200-6,000	4,400-5,100	2,100-2,400
1999 Venture extended	7,800-8,800	7,000-7,900	3,900-4,400
Venture regular	6,500-7,400	5,700-6,500	2,900-3,300
2000 Venture extended	9,200-11,000	8,300-9,900	4,800-5,700
Venture regular	8,000-9,200	7,200-8,300	4,100-4,700
Warner Brothers	12,500-14,000	11,300-12,600	7,100-8,000
2001 Venture extended	11,500-13,200	10,400-11,900	6,300-7,300
Venture regular	10,000-11,500	9,000-10,400	5,200-6,000
Warner Brothers	15,000-16,500	13,700-15,000	9,500-10,400
2002 Venture extended	13,500-15,700	12,300-14,300	8,000-9,300
Venture regular	12,000-13,500	10,800-12,200	6,700-7,600
Warner Brothers	17,300-19,300	15,900-17,800	11,100-12,400

2003 Venture extended	$16,000-19,000	$14,600-17,300	$10,200-12,200
Venture regular	14,500-16,200	13,200-14,700	9,000-10,000
Warner Bros., Entertainer	20,000-22,500	18,400-20,700	13,000-14,600

> For detailed information on this vehicle visit
> http://used.consumerguide.com and enter code 2259

1999-03 CHRYSLER 300M/LHS

CG BEST BUY

CLASS: Near-luxury car
BUILT IN: Canada
PROS: Acceleration
• Passenger and cargo room
• Ride/handling
CONS: Trunk liftover
• Rear visibility

EVALUATION: Because LHS and 300M sedans have more horsepower than any 6-cylinder near-luxury rivals, acceleration and throttle response are a match for any direct competitor—and a clear step ahead of a Concorde or Intrepid. In overall refinement, however, both fall short of such import-brand models as the Lexus GS 300 and Acura TL.

Chrysler's engine isn't quite as smooth. Road and wind noise, while not objectionable, aren't as well-isolated. Fuel economy is no bargain, either. A test LHS averaged 17.7 mpg when new and 21.6 mpg in long-term testing, whereas a 300M averaged 18.6 mpg in mostly highway driving. Road manners are impressive. The LHS offers competent handling and a well-controlled ride. A 300M steers and turns with genuine assertiveness, yet the base suspension absorbs bumps well. Brakes on both are strong, with fine pedal feel. On rough pavement, the ride can get jarring in a 300M with the Performance Handling Group. The 300M Special's stiffer suspension and 18-inch tires make for an unforgiving ride on flawed pavement.

No near-luxury rival equals their generous interior volume, though the 300M's slight rear leg-room deficiency, compared to the LHS, is apparent. Rear-seat entry on both is hampered by elongated doors. Instruments are tastefully designed and imaginatively illuminated, but nighttime readability could be better. Controls are well-positioned and have good tactile feel. The driving position is easily tailored. Models with light-colored dashboard tops suffer annoying reflections in the windshield, and narrow back windows mean poor rearward visibility. The trunk is large on the LHS, with a wide opening. Cargo volume and opening are both smaller on the 300M.

VALUE FOR THE MONEY: Although these two give up a measure of refinement to their top competitors, and cabin decor is less sophisticated, they deliver more interior space and comparable performance at hard-to-match prices. Neither has established a track record for reliability and customer service. Still, Chrysler's flagships show promise.

TROUBLE SPOTS

Electrical problem: The interior lights may not work (or may stay on) and/or the overhead courtesy lights may flicker due to damaged wiring near the trunk light or bad terminal in the courtesy-light connector. (1999)

Keyless entry: The range of the optional automatic garage door opener is poor. A replacement antenna is available. (2000)

Steering noise: Pinhole leaks in the rubber bellows of the steering gear may cause a rattle from the front end. (1999-2000)

Steering problems: Loose or sloppy steering feel may be due to bad inner tie-rod bushings. (1999-2001)

Vehicle noise: Front end makes a squeaking noise when going over speed bumps, etc. due to problem with MacPherson struts' striker caps.

AVERAGE REPLACEMENT COSTS

A/C Compressor	$530	Exhaust System	$480
Alternator	425	Radiator	555
Automatic Trans.	1,670	Shocks and/or Struts	1,390
Brakes	360	Timing Chain/Belt	250
CV Joints	950		

NHTSA RECALL HISTORY

1998-02 300M/LHS: Some vehicles may have faulty seat recliner bolts, allowing the seat to unexpectedly recline. Dealer will inspect and replace affected parts. **1999 LHS:** Front seatbelt retractor on certain vehicles does not work properly. **1999-00:** Inadequately manufactured seatbelt shoulder height-adjustable turning loop top mounting bolt may not withstand sufficient force to function properly in certain impacts. **2000 300M:** Passenger-airbag inflator assembly in small number of cars contains incorrect inflator charge amount, which could increase risk of passenger injury under certain crash conditions. **2000:** Manufacturing molding error can prevent operation of G-lock and tilt lock functions on some driver's-side seatbelt retractors. **2000-01:** In the event of a crash, there is a potential for injury if the occupant's head were to contact the B-pillar. Owners will be sent a storage-bin accessory unit that can be attached to the B-pillar along with installation instructions. **2000-01:** Some owner's manuals are missing full instructions for properly attaching a child-restraint system's tether strap.

PRICES

	Good	Average	Poor
1999 300M	$10,500-11,500	$9,500-10,400	$5,600-6,100
LHS	9,300-10,200	8,400-9,200	4,800-5,300
2000 300M	12,500-13,700	11,300-12,300	7,100-7,800
LHS	11,000-12,000	9,900-10,800	5,900-6,500
2001 300M	15,000-16,500	13,700-15,000	9,500-10,400
LHS	13,200-14,500	12,000-13,200	7,700-8,400
2002 300M	18,000-19,500	16,600-17,900	11,500-12,500
2003 300M	21,500-23,500	19,800-21,600	14,000-15,300

For detailed information on this vehicle visit
http://used.consumerguide.com and enter code **2371**

1995-00 CHRYSLER CIRRUS

CLASS: Midsize car
BUILT IN: USA
PROS: Antilock brakes
• Instruments/controls
• Passenger and cargo room
• Ride • Steering/handling
CONS: Rear visibility
• Road noise

EVALUATION: Cirrus offers a lot to like, starting with spaciousness. Shorter than some compacts, its long wheelbase and roomy five-passenger interior move it into the mid-size class. Front passengers have generous space, and ample rear leg room allows some people to ride with legs crossed—though the seat isn't wide enough for three adults to fit comfortably. The modern, thoughtfully arranged dashboard has clear gauges, smooth-working wiper/light stalks, and simple climate controls. However, rearward visibility is severely restricted by a narrow back window and high rear ledge.

Six-cylinder acceleration is fairly brisk, but the engine does not generate much torque below 3000 rpm or so. For that reason, the engine initially feels flat in highway passing, or whenever you need a quick burst of power. The automatic transmission shifts smoothly and downshifts quickly for passing, though it occasionally lags just a bit, as if waiting for permission. Acceleration in the 4-cylinder Cirrus ranks as adequate, and that engine delivers better gas mileage. You're likely to notice a lot of road noise on most surfaces. Both engines are loud under hard throttle, too.

The nimble Cirrus maneuvers easily and corners with athletic agility, good grip, and little body lean—less than a Honda Accord, for instance. Power steering is quick and precise, centering well after turns. Tires on the softer-suspended LX model can squeal a little in tight corners. Suspensions produce a stable, comfortable ride on most surfaces, rebounding instantly to most bumps and holes, though they don't absorb pock-marked surfaces well. The sporty LXi has a well-controlled but firm ride, while the softer-sprung LX allows more bouncing.

VALUE FOR THE MONEY: This highly capable family 4-door equals its Japanese competition in many areas, and beats them soundly for passenger and cargo space.

TROUBLE SPOTS

Air conditioner: Air conditioning may be intermittent or stop completely due to failed pressure transducer. (1995)

Air conditioner: AC compressor fails on cars with 2.5-liter engine, especially if car is driven mostly in heavy traffic in hot weather. (1995-96)

Automatic transmission: Transmission may shudder when accelerating from a stop, thump when coasting down to a stop, or slip when shifting. (1995)

Headlights: Poor illumination from headlights corrected by replacing both headlamp modules. (1996-97)

Tail/brake lights: Moisture builds up in taillamps. (1995)

Water leak: Water leaks in between the door and interior door trim or from the cowl/plenum/floor/A-pillar seams. (1995-96)

AVERAGE REPLACEMENT COSTS

A/C Compressor	$450	CV Joints	$375
Alternator	315	Exhaust System	380
Automatic Trans.	1,015	Radiator	440
Brakes	320	Shocks and/or Struts	375
Clutch	560	Timing Chain/Belt	255

NHTSA RECALL HISTORY

1995: Rear-seatbelt anchors will not withstand loading required by Federal standard. **1995-96 w/2.4-liter:** Oil leakage could cause engine-compartment fire. **1995-96:** Brake master cylinder can leak fluid, due to damaged seal; warning light will signal impairment prior to partial brake-system loss. **1995-96:** Corrosion of ABS hydraulic control unit can cause solenoid valves to stick open, so car tends to pull from a straight stop when brakes are applied. **1995-97:** Lower ball joint can separate due to loss of lubrication; could cause loss of control. **1995-98 w/automatic transmission:** If operator presses button to shift out of "Park" with key in locked position, pin can break; "ignition-park" interlock would then be nonfunctional. **1996-97:** Secondary hood latch spring can disengage if hood is slammed. **1998-99:** Right rear-brake tube can contact exhaust system clamp and wear a hole in it; tube could then leak, reducing braking effectiveness. **2000:** Incorrect child lock instruction labels could cause confusion as to whether the childproof safety lock was activated. **2000:** Some of the owner's manuals for these vehicles are missing instructions for properly attaching a child restraint system's tether strap to the tether anchorage. **2000:** The right front-brake tube may get damaged.

PRICES	Good	Average	Poor
1995 Cirrus	$2,500-3,200	$1,800-2,300	$500-700
1996 Cirrus	2,900-3,700	2,200-2,800	700-900
1997 Cirrus	3,600-4,500	2,900-3,600	1,000-1,300
1998 Cirrus	4,800-5,600	4,000-4,700	1,800-2,100
1999 Cirrus	5,600-6,400	4,800-5,500	2,300-2,600
2000 Cirrus	6,300-7,500	5,500-6,600	2,800-3,300

For detailed information on this vehicle visit
http://used.consumerguide.com and enter code **2128**

1998-03 CHRYSLER CONCORDE

CG BEST BUY

CLASS: Full-size car

BUILT IN: Canada

PROS: Traction control (optional) • Cargo room • Fuel economy (2.7-liter) • Passenger room • Ride • Steering/handling

CONS: Trunk liftover • Rear visibility

EVALUATION: The 3.2-liter produces a stronger pull at low speeds, a deeper exhaust note, and more-impressive passing ability. The 3.5 is decidedly stronger, resulting in acceleration on par with the best in this class. Acceleration with the 2.7-liter is adequate, but that V6 has to work harder to deliver the same level of performance. On the plus side, the 2.7-liter gives this large sedan impressive fuel economy. We've averaged 26.2 mpg in a test that included plenty of highway driving. A 3.2-liter V6 averages about 21 mpg.

Both models offer impressive handling ability. Not only do they carve tight turns with good grip and minimal body lean, they respond instantly to changes in steering-wheel input. Concorde steers and changes direction with responsive confidence, though test models have not displayed topnotch braking performance or feel. Ride quality also is impressive. The Concorde's suspension soaks up rough pavement and provides a stable, comfortable highway experience. Road noise is markedly less than in the prior Concorde, but it's still not in the Lexus league for overall quietness.

Clear gauges and large, well-marked controls for the climate and audio systems highlight the Concorde's dashboard. Wide pillars, a sloping roof, and narrow rear window constrict the driver's rearward view, though it's a bit wider than in an Intrepid. Occupants can enjoy a generously sized interior, as before. Wide, tall doorways make it easy to get in and out of the front or rear compartment, and there's ample room for five adults. The cabin is wide enough to hold three grownups in the rear without uncomfortable squeezing, and a taller roof profile gives slightly more rear head room than in Dodge's Intrepid. Doorways are large, but the rear-door shape hampers entry. Concorde offers ample cargo room and a trunk opening wider than Intrepid's, but liftover is on the high side. Most interior materials are good quality, though door panels look plain and roof pillars are trimmed with hard plastic that looks cut-rate.

VALUE FOR THE MONEY: Stunning styling, loads of room, and exceptional handling are the foremost attributes of the current Concordes. Acceleration is ordinary, however, and long-term mechanical reliability remains a bit uncertain compared to such rivals as the Buick LeSabre and Toyota Avalon.

TROUBLE SPOTS

See the 1998-03 Dodge Intrepid.

AVERAGE REPLACEMENT COSTS

See the 1998-03 Dodge Intrepid.

NHTSA RECALL HISTORY

1998-02: Some vehicles may have faulty seat-recliner bolts, allowing the seat to unexpectedly recline. Dealer will inspect and replace affected parts. **1999:** The front-seatbelt retractor does not comply with the requirements of the standard. If the retractor does not work properly, it will not adequately protect occupants in the event of a crash. **1999-00:** Inadequately manufactured mounting bolt for seatbelt shoulder height-adjustable turning loop may not withstand sufficient force to function properly in certain impact situations. **2000 w/o ABS:** Brake master-cylinder piston-retainer snap ring may be bent inward, which could result in brake-drag condition. **2000:** Molding flash on primary lever may prevent operation of G-lock and tilt-lock functions on some driver's-side retractors, which could reduce driver protection during a frontal crash **2000:** Passenger-airbag inflator assembly on some cars contains incorrect inflator charge amount. **2000-01:** In the event of a crash, there is a potential for injury if the occupant's head were to contact the B-pillar. Owners will be sent a storage-bin accessory unit that can be attached to the B-pillar along with installation instructions. **2000-01:** Some of the owner's manuals for these vehicles are missing instructions for properly attaching a child-restraint system's tether strap to the tether anchorage.

PRICES	Good	Average	Poor
1998 Concorde	$5,700-6,800	$4,900-5,800	$2,300-2,800
1999 Concorde	6,700-8,200	5,900-7,200	3,100-3,800
2000 Concorde	8,000-10,000	7,200-9,000	4,100-5,100
2001 Concorde	9,500-12,000	8,600-10,800	4,900-6,200
2002 Concorde	11,500-15,500	10,400-14,000	6,300-8,500
2003 Concorde	14,000-19,000	12,700-17,300	8,500-11,600

For detailed information on this vehicle visit
http://used.consumerguide.com and enter code **2302**

1993-97 CHRYSLER CONCORDE/NEW YORKER/LHS

CLASS: Near-luxury car
BUILT IN: Canada
PROS: Acceleration (3.5-liter) • Antilock brakes • Passenger and cargo room • Ride • Steering/handling
CONS: Acceleration (3.3-liter) • Climate controls • Rear visibility (LHS/New Yorker)

CHRYSLER

EVALUATION: The unusually long wheelbase translates to ample leg room front and rear, while the sleek "cab-forward" profile pushes wheels out to the corners for exceptional backseat width. Three large adults can ride in the rear without crowding, and cargo space is ample. A low waistline and large windows add to the impression of spaciousness. Wide door openings ease entry/exit. New Yorker/LHS sedans offer all the space in the Concorde, and more yet for rear occupants.

With the Touring Package, the all-independent suspension delivers crisp, assured handling and a comfortable, controlled ride. The base '93 suspension isn't bad, but permits more body and wheel motion over large humps and dips.

Performance ranks only as adequate with the smaller engine. The bigger 24-valve V6 is a bit gruff under load, but offers more pulling power. Acceleration is definitely quick, but won't slam anyone into the seat. Reaching 60 mph took just 8.2 seconds with the 3.5-liter engine. The 3.3-liter takes about two seconds longer. Either way, the automatic transmissions shift smoothly. Fuel economy is about right for this league, even if it won't win any awards with either engine.

A well-arranged dashboard contains clear gauges and logical controls, though some interior trim is on the plasticky side. Climate controls, mounted low and in the center, are difficult to adjust while driving. Interior noise levels are low, but road noise can be noticeable in all LH sedans. Visibility to the rear is restricted by a narrow back window in the LHS/New Yorker.

VALUE FOR THE MONEY: Chrysler introduced the LH sedans to great fanfare and each version is well worth a test drive, including the New Yorker and LHS with their even more abundant backseats.

TROUBLE SPOTS

See the 1993-97 Dodge Intrepid.

AVERAGE REPLACEMENT COSTS

See the 1993-97 Dodge Intrepid.

NHTSA RECALL HISTORY

1993 w/3.3-liter engine: Deterioration of O-rings at fuel-injector tubes can cause fuel leakage, with potential for fire. **1993-95 Concorde, LHS:** Lower control-arm attaching brackets on some cars can crack due to fatigue and separate from engine cradle; transmission halfshaft could then pull out of transaxle. **1993-97 w/3.5-liter engine:** Fuel-injection system can leak from O-rings or hairline cracks in fuel-injection rail. **1994:** Right steering tie rod can rub through automatic-transmission wiring harness, causing short circuit; may result in stalling, or allow engine to start when selector is not in "Park" position.

PRICES

	Good	Average	Poor
1993 Concorde	$2,200-2,800	$1,600-2,000	$400-500
1994 Concorde	2,600-3,300	1,900-2,400	500-700
LHS	3,200-3,800	2,500-3,000	800-1,000
New Yorker	2,800-3,500	2,100-2,600	600-800

1995 Concorde	$3,000-3,800	$2,300-2,900	$700-900
LHS	3,700-4,300	3,000-3,500	1,100-1,200
New Yorker	3,300-4,000	2,600-3,200	800-1,000
1996 Concorde	3,400-4,400	2,700-3,500	900-1,100
LHS	4,200-4,900	3,400-4,000	1,400-1,700
New Yorker	3,500-4,200	2,800-3,400	900-1,100
1997 Concorde	4,000-5,200	3,300-4,300	1,300-1,700
LHS	5,100-6,000	4,300-5,100	2,000-2,400

> For detailed information on this vehicle visit
> **http://used.consumerguide.com** and enter code **2016**

1990-95 CHRYSLER LEBARON COUPE/CONVERTIBLE

CLASS: Midsize car
BUILT IN: USA
PROS: Acceleration (V6 and turbo) • Antilock brakes • Instruments/controls
CONS: Automatic-transmission performance • Cargo room • Engine noise (4-cylinder) • Rear-seat room • Road noise (convertible)

EVALUATION: With a Mitsubishi V6 beneath the hood, the shapely LeBarons gained refined power to match their sharp looks. Both the base 4-cylinder engine and its turbocharged counterparts are gruff and noisy, while the Mitsubishi-built V6 provides smoother performance. Sure, it has less power and torque than either of the turbocharged fours, but it's much quieter and delivers its strength in a far more linear manner. If you simply must have a turbocharged engine, note that the 2.5-liter turbo is less raucous than the earlier 2.2, which disappeared after 1990. We averaged 22.9 mpg with a V6 convertible in city/highway driving. Regardless of engine choice, automatic transmissions shift sloppily.

Convertibles lag somewhat in solidity. Even minor bumps cause the body to twist and flex more than most open cars. For anything beyond merely competent handling and roadholding, look for a GTC with its performance suspension and tires. But be prepared for a choppy ride over rough pavement. Abundant road noise can make it difficult to talk in normal tones at highway speeds.

The new, modern interior installed for 1990 is a vast improvement over prior dashboards, positioning controls closer to the driver. Gauges are easy to see, controls easy to use. Climate and radio controls are readily accessible. Six-footers are likely to be comfortable in front. Backseats are bigger than in most coupes, but insufficient for adults on long drives. Trunks are small.

VALUE FOR THE MONEY: Though not devoid of flaws, LeBarons still look sharp and perform reasonably well—at least with the smooth V6 engine.

TROUBLE SPOTS

Air conditioner: If the air conditioner gradually stops cooling and/or the airflow from the vents decreases, the computer (PCM) may not be sending a signal to the compressor clutch relay to cycle off, which causes the AC evaporator to freeze up. (1991-95)

Alternator belt: Unless a shield is installed under the engine on the right side, deep snow could knock the serpentine belt off the pulleys of a 3.0-liter engine. (1991-95)

Automatic transmission: Bad seals in the transmission lead to premature friction component wear, which causes shudder when starting from a stop, a bump when coasting to a stop, and slipping between gears. (1993-95)

Automatic transmission: 41TE or 42LE automatic transaxles could take several seconds to engage at startup because of a problem with the valve body. (1993-95)

Automatic transmission: Transmission shudder under light to moderate acceleration could be due to a worn bushing, which requires replacement of the pump as well as the torque converter. (1990-95)

Cold-starting problems: 2.2- or 2.5-liter engines may idle rough or stumble when first started below freezing temperatures unless a revised intake manifold (with an "X" cast into the number 1 runner) was installed (1992), a revised computer (PCM) was installed (1992-93), or the computer was reprogrammed. (1994)

Engine noise: The motor mount on the left side of the engine tends to break. (1992-93)

Oil consumption: High oil consumption and smoke from the exhaust at idle and deceleration on 3.0-liter engines is caused by exhaust valve guides that slide out of the heads. (1990-93)

AVERAGE REPLACEMENT COSTS

A/C Compressor	$450	CV Joints	$375
Alternator	315	Exhaust System	325
Automatic Trans.	905	Radiator	315
Brakes	240	Shocks and/or Struts	340
Clutch	515	Timing Chain/Belt	345

NHTSA RECALL HISTORY

1990: Engine valve cover gasket may dislocate and allow oil leak, which could cause a fire. **1991:** Front disc brake caliper guide pin bolts may not be adequately tightened and could loosen. **1991:** On small number of cars, mismatched parking brake cable to rear wheels may reduce braking capability to one wheel, possibly allowing inadvertent roll-away. **1992:** Hood-latch assembly may not have been properly installed and secondary latch may be prevented from engaging when hood is closed. **1992:** Zinc plating of some upper steering column shaft coupling bolts caused hydrogen embrittlement and breakage of the bolt.

PRICES	Good	Average	Poor
1990 Convertible	$1,500-2,200	$1,000-1,400	$200-300
LeBaron Coupe	1,000-1,600	600-1,000	100-200
1991 Convertible	1,800-2,500	1,200-1,700	300-400
LeBaron Coupe	1,300-1,900	800-1,200	200
1992 Convertible	2,200-3,000	1,600-2,100	400-600
LeBaron Coupe	1,600-2,300	1,100-1,500	200-300
1993 Convertible	2,600-3,300	1,900-2,400	500-700
LeBaron Coupe	2,100-2,800	1,500-2,000	400-500
1994 Convertible	3,200-3,900	2,500-3,000	800-1,000
1995 Convertible	3,700-4,400	3,000-3,600	1,100-1,300

For detailed information on this vehicle visit
http://used.consumerguide.com and enter code **2019**

2001-03 CHRYSLER PT CRUISER

CG BEST BUY

CLASS: Compact car
BUILT IN: Mexico
PROS: Entry/exit
• Handling/roadholding
• Passenger and cargo room
CONS: Acceleration
(w/automatic transmission)

EVALUATION: Not only does the PT Cruiser look great, it feels solid and stable, with no top-heavy tippiness. Pleasant and fairly refined, with predictable front-drive handling, it's adaptable and fun to drive. Steering is responsive, with just the right amount of power assistance. The firmer Touring/Limited suspension delivers surprisingly flat cornering and a comfortably controlled ride—except on washboard surfaces, where it tends to jiggle. Turbo models have slightly better road holding, but offer a stiffer ride. Noise levels are generally low, but coarse pavement induces some road roar from the Touring/Limited tires. Wind noise starts to intrude at 65 mph or so, and the engine note rises above 4000 rpm.

Though smooth, the base engine is not very muscular, especially when trudging up a long grade or passing with more than two aboard. Performance is fine in around-town cruising. Turbo models move out with much more authority, but suffer slightly from "turbo lag." The automatic transmission is responsive, though it sometimes shifts with a lurch. Chrysler's manual gearbox has a light but positive shift action. Braking feels strong with good pedal modulation, especially with the available ABS.

Chrysler claimed 26 seating/cargo configurations with the available fold-flat front passenger seat, but the rear bench must be folded or removed to get much cargo space. Tall and fairly wide back doors ease access. Interior storage is plentiful. The load floor is low and flat, and rear wheel arches don't steal much space. The cabin is roomy enough for four adults on chair-height seats. A high body gives all riders abundant head clearance. Even 6-footers have good leg space. Rear head restraints are a minor obstruction.

VALUE FOR THE MONEY: It's hard to beat this affordable vehicle's impressive combination of room, comfort, versatility, and driving pleasure. Mediocre acceleration is the only real flaw, though performance is actually on par with other small wagons. High demand has outstripped supply since the Cruiser went on sale, and they're not cheap secondhand.

TROUBLE SPOTS

Cruise control: An annoying surge at cruising speeds between 45-60 mph during warm weather can only be corrected by reprogramming the powertrain control module; look for modification decal under the hood. (2001-02)

Fuel gauge: The fuel gauge may not read full despite the tank being full on early production models and a countermeasure fuel pump module is available to correct this. (2001)

Hard starting: Difficulty starting may also require replacement of the fuel pump module with one that has a screen to prevent contamination of the integral pressure regulator. (2001)

Seat: The rear seats may not unlatch due to a problem with the cable and its attachments. (2001)

Sunroof/moonroof: If the sunroof deflector vibrates (usually above 40 mph), there is a deflector mounting kit that relocates the mounting attachments. (2001)

AVERAGE REPLACEMENT COSTS

A/C Compressor	$485	CV Joints	$770
Alternator	360	Exhaust System	310
Automatic Trans.	1,110	Radiator	450
Brakes	360	Shocks and/or Struts	590
Clutch	570	Timing Chain/Belt	280

NHTSA RECALL HISTORY

2001: Fuel supply line could contact the air-conditioning tube service port, causing a fuel leak which would increase the risk of fire. **2001:** Some of the owner's manuals for these vehicles are missing instructions for properly attaching a child-restraint system's tether strap to the tether anchorage. **2001:** The right rear seat center lower anchor was manufactured with a wire diameter greater than the maximum specified. If child-seat connectors are not properly secured, the occupant will not be fully restrained. **2001-02:** The fuel-pump-module mounting flange could leak fuel in a rollover crash, increasing the risk of vehicle fire. **2002:** A software error in the instrument-cluster microprocessor may render gauges, illumination, and warning lights inoperative. **2003 manual transmission:** Faulty flywheel and clutch assemblies were installed in some vehicles with manual transmissions, possibly leading to a disengaged clutch. Dealer will inspect and replace affected part.

PRICES	Good	Average	Poor
2001 PT Cruiser	$10,000-12,200	$9,000-11,000	$5,200-6,300
2002 PT Cruiser	11,500-14,000	10,400-12,600	6,300-7,700
2003 PT Cruiser	13,500-16,000	12,300-14,600	8,000-9,400
PT Cruiser GT	17,500-20,000	16,100-18,400	11,400-13,000

For detailed information on this vehicle visit
http://used.consumerguide.com and enter code 2447

1995-00 CHRYSLER SEBRING

CLASS: Sporty coupe

BUILT IN: Mexico, USA

PROS: Acceleration (4-cylinder manual, V6)
• Antilock brakes (optional on some) • Passenger and cargo room • Steering/handling

CONS: Acceleration (2.0-liter automatic) • Noise • Radio controls • Rear visibility

EVALUATION: Coupes have plenty of performance when equipped with the 4-cylinder and 5-speed manual transmission, but things slow down considerably with the automatic. Acceleration is decent with the V6, but it lacks low-speed torque and the automatic transmission is slow to downshift for passing. All told, though, it's a better choice than the 4-cylinder. Both engines promise excellent gas mileage, especially on the highway.

Handling limits are good, and the coupe's ride is firm but not harsh, apart from some lumpiness over coarse pavement. While wind noise is hushed, road and engine noise are high on the highway, which tends to make long drives more tiring.

The coupe's interior is just as roomy as Chrysler claims, with ample room for four adults to stretch out, in front and rear. The trunk is quite large, too.

Coupe controls are easy to reach while driving, but the stereo is too low in the center of the dashboard to adjust without a long look away from the road. Coupes also have poor rear visibility, because of wide rear pillars and a high parcel shelf.

Convertible acceleration is more than adequate with the V6 engine, though it can run low on vigor during a corner. Like the coupe, its ride is controlled and devoid of coarseness, if a tad jittery over washboard surfaces. Interiors are roomy, with impressive space for two adults in the backseat. Side windows drop as the power top is actuated, which happens without a hitch. With the top down, occupants can talk in normal tones at highway speeds.

Unfortunately, the convertible does not feel as solid as some rivals. In addition, despite large rear-quarter glass, the fabric top has wide rear "pillars" and a narrow back window, causing an over-the-shoulder blind spot that's big enough to hide another car. Convertibles have a different dashboard than coupes, with more convenient controls. Their front seats have integrated seatbelts, so you don't have to grope for a buckle.

VALUE FOR THE MONEY: All told, this stylish open car is also practical for all seasons, offering the expected virtues of the ragtop breed and only a few of the familiar vices. For an appealing combination of sport and practicality, these well-designed automobiles deserve a close look—despite a few drawbacks.

TROUBLE SPOTS

Alarm system: The theft alarm may go off randomly, most often in high winds, and is often due to a misaligned hood. (1995-96)

Automatic transmission: Transmission tends to default to second gear only for no apparent reason requiring the transmission control computer to be reprogrammed. (1996)

Engine misfire: Rough idle, hesitation, and hard restarts during cold weather are due to a defective engine control computer. (1995)

Hard starting: Intermittent no-starts may be due to a damaged wire near the transaxle shift lever. (1995)

Hard starting: A corroded connector behind the left headlight may cause hard starting, intermittently flashing "Check Engine" light, and radiator/condenser fan that will not run. (1995)

Sunroof/moonroof: The pivot pin in the power sunroof may come out, or the plastic tabs on the control unit may cause interference, preventing the sunroof from closing completely. (1995) The sunroof may open by itself if water shorts the control unit. (1995-96)

AVERAGE REPLACEMENT COSTS

A/C Compressor	$730	CV Joints	$375
Alternator	230	Exhaust System	285
Automatic Trans.	905	Radiator	570
Brakes	255	Shocks and/or Struts	490
Clutch	575	Timing Chain/Belt	220

NHTSA RECALL HISTORY

1995-97: Lower ball joint can separate due to loss of lubrication; could cause loss of control. **1996 JX w/2.5-liter engine:** Disconnected vacuum hose may cause increase in engine idle speed and loss of braking power assist. **1996 convertible:** Electrical contacts of power mirror switch can accumulate road salt, which may result in fire. **1996-98 w/automatic transmission:** If operator presses button to shift out of Park with key in locked position, pin can break; "ignition-park" interlock would then be nonfunctional. **1997 coupe:** On small number of cars, improperly welded head restraint support bracket on passenger side can break. **1998:** Dash panel pad can shift, interfering with throttle cable control. **1999-00:** Lower lateral ball joints may have been damaged during assembly, leaking moisture that could corrode the ball stud.

PRICES

	Good	Average	Poor
1995 Sebring coupe	$3,000-3,800	$2,300-2,900	$700-900

1996 Convertible	$4,400-5,500	$3,700-4,600	$1,500-1,900
Sebring coupe	3,500-4,500	2,800-3,600	900-1,200
1997 Convertible	5,200-6,300	4,400-5,400	2,100-2,500
Sebring coupe	4,200-5,300	3,400-4,300	1,400-1,800
1998 Convertible	6,300-7,800	5,500-6,900	2,800-3,400
Sebring coupe	5,100-6,300	4,300-5,400	2,000-2,500
1999 Convertible	8,000-9,700	7,200-8,700	4,100-4,900
Sebring coupe	6,200-7,500	5,400-6,500	2,700-3,200
2000 Convertible	10,000-12,000	9,000-10,800	5,200-6,200
Sebring coupe	7,800-9,400	7,000-8,500	4,000-4,800

For detailed information on this vehicle visit
http://used.consumerguide.com and enter code 2131

2001-03 CHRYSLER SEBRING

CLASS: Sporty coupe
BUILT IN: USA
PROS: Steering/handling
CONS: Acceleration (4-cyl)
• Rear-seat comfort (coupe)
• Rear-seat entry/exit (coupe, convertible)

EVALUATION: Each new V6 engine used in Sebrings (and their Stratus counterparts) is a clear step forward in both power and refinement. The Chrysler-made 2.7-liter in sedans and convertibles feels smoother than the coupe's Mitsubishi 3.0. Though slower than domestic and import rivals with larger V6s, any six-cylinder Sebring offers acceleration that's easily adequate for most needs. Four-cylinder owners are still relegated to the slow and noisy lane, even though both 2.4-liters are an improvement over their predecessors.

Regardless of engine, automatic transmission performance is improved, with smoother upshifts and fairly prompt downshifts. Optional Autostick is a welcome addition to coupe models, improving throttle response somewhat. As for economy, a manual-shift V6 Sebring coupe averaged 23.3 mpg, a V6 sedan with automatic managed 18.3 mpg, and an LXi convertible averaged 18.5 mpg.

Uplevel models handle noticeably better than base cars, with little penalty in ride quality. All feel competent on twisty roads, with better grip and less body lean than a Camry. Sebring coupes are slightly more nimble than the sedans, but their suspensions don't filter out bad pavement as well. Sedans and convertibles suffer some float over dips and swells.

The Sebring convertible feels stable and solid, despite some cowl shake and flex on undulating pavement. Steering feedback is good, though we'd prefer less around-town power assistance on the four-cylinder versions. Stopping power with ABS is a strong point, feeling sure and stable, with good pedal modulation.

Overall refinement falls short of Japanese-brand rivals, but noise levels are fairly quiet and drivetrain vibration is greatly reduced from the previous generation. Suppression of wind noise is admirable.

Sebring sedans have uncommonly roomy interiors for their exterior size, despite a slight loss of rear head clearance compared to prior models. Convertible front seating is spacious, while in the coupes, taller front-seat occupants might want a touch more head room.

With only a little squeezing, three adults can fit in the sedan's back seat. Leg and foot room are generous, but head space is a bit snug. The convertible has rear seating for two adults, and it's surprisingly comfortable. Coupes have three rear seat belts, but even two grown-ups will feel crowded, and the seat cushion is uncomfortably low and seatbacks are overly reclined. Entry/exit to the back seat isn't so easy, either.

Sedan and convertible gauges are clear and readable. Coupe instruments until 2003 mirror the gimmicky design in Mitsubishi two-doors. Coupe drivers sit low to the floor, whereas the sedan and convertible have airy-feeling cockpits. Convertibles suffer blind spots at the rear quarters.

Getting in or out of sedans is easy, but a low roofline hampers entry/exit to coupe front seats, and limits head room for taller folks. In addition, interference from the front seatbelts worsens the already cumbersome entry into the back. Convertibles mount their front shoulder belts to the seats, so they don't impair rear access. Cargo space is average for the class (good for a convertible), though coupe trunklid hinges dip into the luggage bay.

VALUE FOR THE MONEY: Despite improvements in driveline smoothness and overall refinement, the new Sebring sedans and coupes lack the polished feel of import-brand rivals. Each fulfills its purpose, and sedans are sporty-feeling family cars. While all three body styles offer competitive value, the real prize is the Sebring convertible, which is roomier than rivals and quite the pleasant cruiser.

TROUBLE SPOTS

Audio system: If the radio, instrument, or trip-computer lights flicker when the turn signals or high beams are switched on, the multifunction (turn-signal stalk) switch may be bad. (2001-02)

Automatic transmission: Some sedan owners received a non safety-related notice, advising them to replace a relay for the automatic transmission that does not work properly when cold. (2001)

Brake noise: The brakes may squeak on coupes with the 3.0-litre engine and 15-inch brakes. It can be repaired with revised brake-caliper mounting brackets. (2001-03)

Dashboard lights: The powertrain computer may mistakenly notice misfires and illuminate the check-engine light. Either have the computer reprogrammed (2001) or install hotter heat-range spark plugs. (2002)

Electrical problem: An intermittent short in the dome-light switch blows fuses that protect the radio, dome light, courtesy light, vanity mirrors, remote keyless entry, compass, and clock. (2001-02)

Suspension noise: The rear suspension makes a popping and squawking noise on the sedan or convertible that is corrected by replacing the upper control arms with revised ones. (2001)

AVERAGE REPLACEMENT COSTS

A/C Compressor	$775	Exhaust System	$675
Alternator	410	Radiator	715
Automatic Trans.	1,900	Shocks and/or Struts	1,445
Brakes	740	Timing Chain/Belt	655
CV Joints	1,290		

NHTSA RECALL HISTORY

2001 w/automatic transmission: Defective transaxle cooler hoses could lead to transmission fluid leak. Smoke and drivability problems could result. Dealers will replace the cooler hoses. **2001:** Crankshaft position sensor harness could ground with a protective shield causing engine to stall. Dealers will reroute the harness. **2001:** Defective passenger airbags could separate in an accident. Dealers will replace the passenger airbag. **2001:** Fuel return hose does not contain the desired ozone protection. Dealers will replace the fuel return hose. **2001:** Incorrect driver-seat mounting bolts may cause result in driver injury in an accident. Dealers will inspect and replace affected parts. **2001:** Smoke or burning smell might come from map lights due to contact with insulation material. Dealers will remove insulation material in affected vehicles. **2001:** Some owner's manuals are missing instructions for installing child seats. Owners will be provided with an addendum to the owners manual.

PRICES

	Good	Average	Poor
2001 Sebring Ltd. convertible	$15,000-16,500	$13,700-15,000	$9,500-10,400
Sebring convertible	12,000-14,000	10,800-12,600	6,700-7,800
Sebring coupe	9,000-11,000	8,100-9,900	4,700-5,700
Sebring sedan	8,200-10,500	7,400-9,500	4,200-5,400
2002 Sebring Ltd. convertible	18,000-19,500	16,600-17,900	11,500-12,500
Sebring convertible	14,200-16,500	12,900-15,000	8,700-10,100
Sebring coupe	10,500-12,500	9,500-11,300	5,600-6,600
Sebring sedan	9,300-11,300	8,400-10,200	4,800-5,900
2003 Sebring Ltd. convertible	22,000-23,500	20,200-21,600	14,300-15,300
Sebring convertible	16,500-19,000	15,000-17,300	10,600-12,200
Sebring coupe	12,500-15,000	11,300-13,500	7,100-8,600
Sebring sedan	11,000-13,500	9,900-12,200	5,900-7,300

For detailed information on this vehicle visit
http://used.consumerguide.com and enter code **4479**

1991-95 CHRYSLER TOWN & COUNTRY

CLASS: Minivan
BUILT IN: USA
PROS: Acceleration (3.8-liter V6) • Antilock brakes • Entry/exit • Passenger and cargo room • Ride/handling
CONS: Fuel economy

CHRYSLER

EVALUATION: Rearward visibility was improved with the '91 overhaul, and seats are more contoured and comfortable than before. Radio and climate controls are easy to reach, which they weren't in earlier versions. Other controls also are logically positioned. Cargo space is abundant behind the backseat.

Acceleration is adequate with the 3.3-liter V6, but nothing to boast about—especially if the Town & Country is filled with passengers and luggage. If you do a lot of heavy hauling, look for 1994-95 models with the 3.8-liter V6. With that engine under the hood, a Town & Country does not feel overburdened. Gas mileage is likely to be around 15-17 mpg in town, and the low 20s on the highway (a little less with all-wheel drive).

A recalibrated suspension reduced body roll in turns. Ride and handling both are excellent—soft but well controlled—much like a Grand Caravan or Voyager LE. Wind and road noise are minimal.

Unlike Caravan/Voyager, the Town & Country was not available with integrated child safety seats until 1994. Adjustable front shoulder belts in 1993-up models are pleasant to use, and an airbag (dual airbags for '94) and ABS are safety bonuses.

VALUE FOR THE MONEY: All three of these updated Chrysler Corporation minivans—Town & Country, Dodge Caravan, and Plymouth Voyager—belong at the top of their class. The Town & Country wraps all of their minivan virtues into an envelope of high luxury, packed with comforts and conveniences.

TROUBLE SPOTS

See the 1991-95 Dodge Caravan.

AVERAGE REPLACEMENT COSTS

See the 1991-95 Dodge Caravan.

NHTSA RECALL HISTORY

1991 w/ABS: High-pressure hose in antilock braking system may leak or detach at crimped end fitting, resulting in discharge of hydraulic fluid. **1991:** Liftgate support attaching bolts can break, resulting in liftgate falling unexpectedly. **1991-92:** The steering-wheel mounting armature can develop cracks and separate from the center hub attachment to the steering column. This can result in loss of vehicle control. **1991-93 w/ABS:** ABS hydraulic control unit can experience excessive actuator piston seal wear, causing pump-motor deterioration; ABS could fail, and power assist might be reduced. **1991-93:** Left windshield-wiper pivot-drive arm was not mechanically staked to shaft; arm could disengage, causing loss of wiper function. **1991-93:** Seatbelt-release button can stick inside cover, so buckle is only partly latched; also, center rear belt anchor clip can disconnect. **1992:** Improperly bent fuel-tank flanges may not allow specified clearance for mounting straps and fuel lines, both of which could be damaged; a broken strap would cause tank to drop, while damaged fuel line may leak fuel. **1992:** Zinc plating of some upper steering-column-shaft coupling bolts caused hydrogen embrittlement and breakage of the bolt. **1993-94:** 15-inch stamped steel wheels in some vans have malformed lug-nut seat configuration, which causes poor nut-to-wheel contact and centering of wheel during installation; could lead to possible loss of wheel and loss of vehicle control. **1993-94:** Liftgate

support attaching bolts can break, resulting in liftgate falling unexpectedly.
1993-95: Electrical short could cause airbags to deploy inadvertently.

PRICES

	Good	Average	Poor
1991 Town & Country	$2,300-2,900	$1,700-2,100	$400-600
1992 Town & Country	2,700-3,400	2,000-2,600	600-700
1993 Town & Country	3,000-3,900	2,300-3,000	700-900
1994 Town & Country	3,400-4,300	2,700-3,400	900-1,100
1995 Town & Country	3,800-4,800	3,100-3,900	1,100-1,400

For detailed information on this vehicle visit
http://used.consumerguide.com and enter code **2020**

1996-00 CHRYSLER TOWN & COUNTRY

CLASS: Minivan

BUILT IN: USA

PROS: Acceleration (3.8-liter) • Antilock brakes • Passenger and cargo room • Ride

CONS: Fuel economy • Wind noise

EVALUATION: The latest Town & Country is more spacious and practical than its predecessor. Door sills were lowered by 1.4 inches to improve entry and exit, which is easy all around—especially with the available driver-side sliding door. Step-in height is actually among the lowest in the minivan class. The dashboard is lower and side windows deeper, so visibility is improved. Choosing a long-wheelbase minivan means everyone has plenty of room. You get ample cargo space at the rear in long wheelbase models, and adequate space in the standard-size version. Cupholders and storage bins are sprinkled throughout the interior, with plenty of space for stashing small items.

Steering is precise, and hard cornering produces only modest body lean. The ride is supple, yet well-controlled at highway speeds. The shorter wheelbase Voyager gives a jumpier, less-forgiving ride, but offers good steering feel and adequate brakes. Voyager buyers should steer clear of the 4-cyl, as it lacks power for a vehicle this size. Acceleration is adequate with the 3.3-liter V6, even in the heavier long-wheelbase models, but the bigger engine has enough extra muscle to make a noticeable difference when merging onto the expressway and running uphill. Fuel economy is gloomy with any engine: Expect an average of 15-17 mpg in urban driving, or into the low 20s on the highway. Base Voyager's overworked 4-cyl likely will offer only slightly better economy. Tire noise is low, but wind noise grows prominent at highway speeds. All seats are comfortable for long treks.

CHRYSLER

VALUE FOR THE MONEY: On the road, Chrysler's minivans feel like big cars. Ford's Windstar and the latest GM minivans also are tempting, but Chrysler deserves to hang on to its title of best all-around buy. All of the Town & Country's extras are appealing, but of course a Dodge Caravan or Plymouth Voyager offers most of the same features, for fewer dollars.

TROUBLE SPOTS

See the 1996-00 Dodge Caravan.

AVERAGE REPLACEMENT COSTS

See the 1996-00 Dodge Caravan.

NHTSA RECALL HISTORY

1996: Fuel-tank rollover valve can allow fuel to enter vapor canister, creating potential for leakage and fire. **1996:** On a few minivans, bolts holding integrated child seat modules to seat frame can break. **1996:** On certain minivans, fuel can leak from tank at interface of fuel pump module attachment. **1996:** Static charge could cause spark as tank is filled; vapors could ignite. **1996-97 w/integrated child seats:** Shoulder-harness restraint on child seat can be difficult to release when latch plate becomes contaminated. **1996-98:** The clockspring may have been wound incorrectly, resulting in illumination of airbag warning light and possibly causing the driver's side airbag to not function. Dealer will insect and replace affected parts on vehicles with 70,000 miles or less. **1997:** Certain master-cylinder seals will not seal adequately, allowing hydraulic fluid to be drawn into power-assist vacuum reservoir; brake warning lamp will then illuminate. **1997:** The D-pillar mastic sound barrier patch could loosen and drop into the seatbelt assembly, rendering it inoperative. **1998 w/integrated child seats:** Shoulder-harness webbing was incorrectly routed around reinforcement bar; can fail to restrain child properly. **1999:** Front-seatbelt retractor does not work properly and will not adequately protect occupant in a crash. **1999-00 w/3.3-liter and 3.8-liter engines:** Fuel could leak from the underhood fuel-injection fuel rail, increasing risk of vehicle fire.

PRICES	Good	Average	Poor
1996 Town & Country	$4,300-5,000	$3,600-4,200	$1,500-1,700
Town & Country LXi	5,700-6,700	4,900-5,800	2,300-2,700
1997 Town & Country	5,200-6,500	4,400-5,500	2,100-2,600
Town & Country LXi	6,500-8,000	5,700-7,000	2,900-3,600
1998 Town & Country	6,500-8,000	5,700-7,000	2,900-3,600
Town & Country LXi	8,200-9,800	7,400-8,800	4,200-5,000
1999 LXi, Limited	10,200-12,200	9,200-11,000	5,300-6,300
Town & Country	8,200-9,700	7,400-8,700	4,200-4,900
2000 LXi, Limited	12,000-14,500	10,800-13,100	6,700-8,100
Town & Country	10,000-11,500	9,000-10,400	5,200-6,000

For detailed information on this vehicle visit
http://used.consumerguide.com and enter code **2132**

2001-03 CHRYSLER TOWN & COUNTRY

CLASS: Minivan
BUILT IN: Canada, USA
PROS: All-wheel drive • Entry/exit • Interior storage space • Passenger and cargo room
CONS: Fuel economy

EVALUATION: SUV-intenders would do well to consider an AWD Town & Country as a sensible, comfortable alternative. Riding about as comfortably as a full-size car, a spacious Town & Country absorbs bumps better than any SUV, and beats most minivans (Voyager included).

Bigger wheels and tires give the Town & Country an edge over Voyager in handling and roadholding, too, though both are carlike and friendly to drive. The Town & Country brakes with more authority than a Voyager, thanks to its standard antilock four-wheel discs.

A Town & Country requires the muscle of the 3.8-liter V6 to get off the line smartly and hold its own in highway passing and merging. Fuel economy hasn't changed much from the prior generation. A test minivan with 3.8-liter engine averaged 15 mpg.

Abundant sound insulation makes the Town & Country one of the quietest minivans, with fine suppression of wind, road, and engine noise. Playing its luxury role to the hilt, the Town & Country features comfortably supportive and generously sized seating at all positions, and may have been fitted with leather upholstery. Driver positioning is excellent, and entry/exit easy.

Split third-row seats remove easily, but unlike stowable alternatives, you must decide whether to take them out before you begin a trip. The power side doors' manual-override function is convenient, while the power liftgate (shared with Grand Caravan) is a useful innovation. Both systems stop and reverse direction quickly when encountering an obstruction, the liftgate's sensors proving particularly sensitive.

The available movable, lighted center console, if installed, enhances versatility. So does the multiposition rear parcel shelf, though we question the durability of its plastic pop-up dividers. The revamped dashboard moved controls closer to the driver, but front cupholders block access to the in-dash CD changer.

With no provision for an integrated navigation system, the add-on screen mounts atop the dashboard. A unique "three-zone" climate-system option allows for independent control of driver, front-passenger, and rear-seating settings.

VALUE FOR THE MONEY: DaimlerChrysler's lineup dominates the "shoulders" of the minivan market. By 2002, their minivans accounted for 62 percent of sales under $20,000 and 37 percent of those over $30,000. Such figures demonstrate the appeal of both the entry-level Voyager and the luxury Town & Country, which, bolstered by the 2001 redesign, are now stronger values than ever.

TROUBLE SPOTS

See the 1991-03 Dodge Caravan.

AVERAGE REPLACEMENT COSTS

See the 1991-03 Dodge Caravan.

NHTSA RECALL HISTORY

2001: Lower control-arm bolt could fracture and lead to a loss of vehicle control. Dealers will replace affected parts. **2001:** Sliding door latches could release in severe accidents. Dealers will replace both sliding door yet cylinder links free of charge. **2002:** Fuel-tank-control valve weld joint could separate resulting in a fuel leak or fire. Dealers will inspect and replace affected parts. **2002:** Some owner's manuals are missing instructions for installing child seats. Owners will be provided with an addendum to the owners manual.

PRICES

	Good	Average	Poor
2001 LXi, Limited	$16,000-18,500	$14,600-16,800	$10,200-11,800
Town & Country	12,000-14,500	10,800-13,100	6,700-8,100
2002 LXi, Limited	19,000-23,000	17,500-21,200	12,400-15,000
Town & Country	14,000-17,000	12,700-15,500	8,500-10,400
2003 LXi, Limited	23,000-28,000	21,200-25,800	15,000-18,200
Town & Country	17,500-21,000	16,100-19,300	11,200-13,400

For detailed information on this vehicle visit
http://used.consumerguide.com and enter code **4490**

1995-00 DODGE AVENGER

CLASS: Sporty coupe

BUILT IN: USA

PROS: Acceleration (V6)
• Available antilock brakes
• Passenger and cargo room
• Steering/handling

CONS: Acceleration (4-cylinder automatic) • Radio controls • Rear visibility
• Road noise

EVALUATION: Front bucket seats offer plenty of head and leg space for two adults. Rear seats are equally pleasing, with space for two adults. However, large people may not want to spend long periods in back, and getting in and out can be a chore. Avenger's trunk has a wide, flat floor, plus split-folding rear seatbacks. Although you sit relatively low, visibility is generally good in all directions. However, a narrow back window, tall parcel shelf, and wide roof pillars make it difficult to see what's directly behind the car. Instruments are easy to read, though auxiliary gauges are small. Most controls are easy to reach while driving. However, the radio is mounted too low and has too many small buttons.

Both engines provide adequate acceleration from a stop, but the 4-cylinder is noisy and slowed by the automatic transmission. Four-cylinder pickup is acceptable with manual shift. The V6 is smooth and more powerful, and fairly lively, but it doesn't produce much torque at low speeds. Step on the gas, and there might be a rather long pause before the automatic transmission downshifts.

Each model handles adeptly, zipping around corners and through curves with good grip and only moderate body lean. Roadholding is good overall, and the car responds well to steering inputs. Ride quality from the firm suspension is on the choppy side, and when encountering certain pavement separators. Road, engine, and wind noise might all become intrusive at high speeds.

VALUE FOR THE MONEY: Attractively styled and capable on the road, the Avenger has a lot going for it: proven mechanical elements, reasonable prices, and wholly adequate room for four.

TROUBLE SPOTS

See the 1995-00 Chrysler Sebring.

AVERAGE REPLACEMENT COSTS

See the 1995-00 Chrysler Sebring.

NHTSA RECALL HISTORY

1995-00: Rubber boots on lower ball joint can become damaged, allowing dirt and water intrusion, which can cause excessive wear and possible separation. **1997:** On a small number of cars, improperly welded head-restraint support bracket on passenger side can break. **1998:** Dash panel pad can shift, interfering with throttle-cable control.

PRICES

	Good	Average	Poor
1995 Avenger	$2,600-3,300	$1,900-2,400	$500-700
Avenger ES	3,000-3,700	2,300-2,800	700-900
1996 Avenger	3,200-3,900	2,500-3,000	800-1,000
Avenger ES	3,600-4,300	2,900-3,400	1,000-1,200
1997 Avenger	4,100-4,800	3,400-3,900	1,400-1,600
Avenger ES	4,600-5,300	3,800-4,400	1,700-2,000
1998 Avenger	5,000-5,800	4,300-4,900	2,000-2,300
Avenger ES	5,600-6,300	4,800-5,400	2,300-2,600
1999 Avenger	6,100-7,000	5,300-6,100	2,600-3,000
Avenger ES	6,800-7,600	6,100-6,800	3,200-3,600
2000 Avenger	7,500-8,500	6,800-7,700	3,800-4,300
Avenger ES	8,500-9,300	7,700-8,400	4,400-4,800

For detailed information on this vehicle visit
http://used.consumerguide.com and enter code **2133**

1991-95 DODGE CARAVAN

CLASS: Minivan
BUILT IN: Canada, USA
PROS: Passenger and cargo room • Ride
CONS: Acceleration (4-cylinder) • Fuel economy

EVALUATION: With the Caravan, avoid the weak 4-cylinder engine and balky 5-speed manual transmission. They are more trouble than the initial savings you might make in a lower purchase price. The 3.0- and 3.3-liter V6 engines provide adequate acceleration, but the 3.8-liter V6 delivers the best action in all situations. It's also the quietest. With any of the V6 engines, don't expect to get more than 20 mpg.

The standard front-wheel drive provides sufficient traction for most situations; however, the effective AWD system is a boon in the snow belt. But beware: AWD makes the ride rougher, hurts acceleration, and lessens fuel economy. The Caravan's ride is carlike and secure, but there's too much body lean and not enough traction for these vehicles to score as anything other than minivans when it comes to handling.

Though the regular-length versions can seat seven people, it gets crowded if everyone is an adult. In addition, cargo room is only adequate with all the seats in place. Grand Caravans have more space for everyone and ample cargo room. Though the middle and rear seats can be removed, they are quite heavy. The dashboard has a convenient design, and climate and radio controls are easy to use. However, front-seat occupants might find themselves craving more leg room.

VALUE FOR THE MONEY: The Caravan's initial basic design lasted more than a decade, and most of the bugs were worked out in the first generation. With so much versatility, these vans are an exceptional secondhand value. If you're shopping for a minivan, Caravan and its twins should be first on your list.

TROUBLE SPOTS

Air conditioner: If the air conditioner gradually stops cooling and/or the airflow from the vents decreases, the computer (PCM) may not be sending a signal to the compressor clutch relay to cycle off, which causes the AC evaporator to freeze up. (1991-95)

Alternator belt: Deep snow could knock the serpentine belt off the pulleys of a 3.0-liter engine. Installation of a shield fixes the problem. (1991-95)

Automatic transmission: 41TE or 42LE automatic transaxles could take several seconds to engage at startup because of a problem with the valve body. (1993-95)

Automatic transmission: If the transmission shudders under light to moderate acceleration, the transmission front pump could be leaking due to a worn bushing. (1991-95)

Automatic transmission: Any minivan with the 3.3-liter engine may have late, harsh, or erratic automatic transmission shifts that are not transmission related, but caused by a defective throttle position sensor. (1994)

Automatic transmission: Bad seals in the transmission lead to premature friction component wear, which causes shudder when starting from a stop, a bump when coasting to a stop, and slipping between gears. (1993-95)

Cold-starting problems: 2.2- or 2.5-liter engines idle rough or stumble when first started below freezing temperatures unless a revised intake manifold (with an "X" cast into the number 1 runner) was installed (1992), or a revised computer (PCM) was installed (1992-93), or the computer was reprogrammed. (1994)

Engine noise: The motor mount on the left side of the engine tends to break. (1992-93)

Oil consumption: Oil consumption and smoke from the exhaust at idle and deceleration on 3.0-liter engines is caused by exhaust valve guides that slide out of the heads. (1991-93)

AVERAGE REPLACEMENT COSTS

A/C Compressor	$455	Exhaust System	$400
Alternator	310	Radiator	325
Automatic Trans.	1,040	Shocks and/or Struts	230
Brakes	275	Timing Chain/Belt	265
CV Joints	385		

NHTSA RECALL HISTORY

1991 w/ABS: High-pressure hose in antilock braking system may leak or detach, which increases likelihood of brake lockup. **1991 w/ABS:** High-pressure pump of antilock braking system may be porous, resulting in increased stopping distances. **1991-92:** Steering-wheel mounting armature can develop cracks and separate from the center hub attachment to the steering column. This can result in loss of vehicle control. **1991-93 w/ABS:** Piston seal in control unit can wear excessively; ABS could fail, and power assist might be reduced. **1991-93:** Left windshield-wiper pivot-drive arm was not mechanically staked to shaft; arm could disengage, causing loss of wiper function. **1991-93:** Seatbelt-release button can stick inside cover, so buckle is only partly latched; also, center rear belt anchor clip can disconnect. **1991-95:** Liftgate-support attaching bolts can break, resulting in liftgate falling unexpectedly. **1992:** Brake-pedal pad-attachment to pedal arm may not have adequate strength. **1992:** Fuel tank may drop or lines may rupture near fuel tank, leading to possible fire. **1992:** Zinc plating of some upper steering-column shaft coupling bolts caused hydrogen embrittlement and breakage. **1993-94:** Lug nuts on optional 15-inch stamped steel wheels may have been improperly installed, which could lead to wheel separation. **1993-95:** Electrical short could cause airbags to deploy inadvertently.

PRICES

	Good	Average	Poor
1991 Caravan	$1,200-2,000	$700-1,200	$100-200
Grand Caravan	1,600-2,300	1,100-1,500	200-300
Grand LE, ES	2,100-2,800	1,500-2,000	400-500

DODGE

1992 Caravan	$1,400-2,400	$900-1,500	$200-300
Grand Caravan	1,800-2,700	1,200-1,800	300-400
Grand LE, ES	2,600-3,300	1,900-2,400	500-700
1993 Caravan	1,700-2,900	1,100-1,900	300-400
Grand Caravan	2,200-3,200	1,600-2,300	400-600
Grand LE, ES	3,100-4,000	2,400-3,100	700-1,000
1994 Caravan	2,000-3,300	1,400-2,300	300-600
Grand Caravan	2,500-3,500	1,800-2,600	500-700
Grand LE, ES	3,400-4,400	2,700-3,500	900-1,100
1995 Caravan	2,400-3,900	1,700-2,800	500-800
Grand Caravan	3,000-4,300	2,300-3,300	700-1,000
Grand LE, ES	4,200-5,300	3,400-4,300	1,400-1,800

For detailed information on this vehicle visit
http://used.consumerguide.com and enter code 2021

1996-00 DODGE CARAVAN

CG BEST BUY

CLASS: Minivan

BUILT IN: Canada, USA

PROS: Acceleration (3.8-liter) • Antilock brakes • Passenger and cargo room • Ride

CONS: Fuel economy • Road noise • Wind noise

EVALUATION: These highly impressive second-generation Caravans are a clear step ahead of the hugely popular 1984-95 minivans. Among other bonuses, you get more space in all seating positions. Design features included a lower dashboard and larger windows for improved visibility, and a 1.4-inch lower step-in height for easier entry and exit. A driver-side sliding door also helps on that latter score. The new dashboard has a more user-friendly layout, putting most controls within easy reach of the driver. Illuminated markers for the power window switches and other controls make them easier to find in the dark.

The innovative removable seats are handy, but each seat weighs about 90 pounds, so it might take two people to lift one in and out. You also get an assortment of storage bins, nooks, and crannies for stashing miscellaneous items. Performance with the 3.3-liter engine is adequate in daily driving, but the 3.8-liter is better yet, giving the Caravan enough power to pass and merge easily. Gas mileage should run 15-17 mpg in the city, and just above 20 on the highway. The 4-cylinder engine has nearly as much power as the 3.0-liter V6, but both are taxed by a full load of passengers.

Quieter and even more carlike than before, these minivans handle more like large sedans than vans, rolling along with a stable, comfortable attitude. Caravans hold the road well and lean moderately in tight turns. Road and wind noise grow obtrusive at higher speeds, but otherwise these minivans are great for long-distance cruising.

VALUE FOR THE MONEY: This assessment is simple: Caravans and their Chrysler-Plymouth cousins rank at the head of their class, just as their predecessors did.

TROUBLE SPOTS

Automatic transmission: Transmission may shudder when accelerating from a stop, thump when coasting down to a stop, or slip when shifting. (1996)

Blower motor: Blower motors make a whine in low and second speed. (1996)

Brakes: The antilock brakes may activate at speeds under 10 mph due to one or more faulty wheel speed sensors. (1996)

Dashboard lights: The instrument cluster, minitrip computer, and/or compass may show incorrect information or go completely blank due to a bad relay for the heated backlight. (1997)

Doors: Sliding door and/or liftgate power locks fail to lock or unlock both manually or electrically. (1996)

Radiator: The radiator fan may run after the key is turned off, or may not run, leading to engine overheating because the fan relay attaching screws break and the relay overheats. (1996-97)

Vehicle noise: A thud or thump, which comes from the rear when accelerating or stopping, is caused by fuel sloshing in the tank. A foam pad and strap kit does not always fix the problem. (1996-97)

Wipers: Windshield wipers come on by themselves or fail to stop when the switch is turned off due to a problem with the multifunction switch. (1996)

AVERAGE REPLACEMENT COSTS

A/C Compressor	$490	CV Joints	$385
Alternator	310	Exhaust System	330
Automatic Trans.	1,040	Radiator	480
Brakes	390	Shocks and/or Struts	330
Clutch	605	Timing Chain/Belt	230

NHTSA RECALL HISTORY

1996 w/bench seats, built at Windsor plant ("R" in 11th position of VIN): Rear-seat bolts can fracture; in an accident, seat could break away. **1996:** Fuel-tank rollover valve can allow fuel to pass into vapor canister, resulting in potential for leakage and fire. **1996:** On a few minivans, bolts holding integrated child seat modules to seat frame can break. **1996:** On certain minivans, fuel can leak from tank at interface of fuel pump module attachment. **1996:** Static charge could cause spark as tank is being filled; vapors could ignite. **1996-97 w/integrated child seats:** Shoulder-harness restraint on child seat can be difficult to release when latch plate becomes contaminated. **1996-98:** The clockspring may have been wound incorrectly, resulting in illumination of airbag warning light and possibly causing the driver's side airbag to not function. Dealer will insect and replace affected parts on vehicles with 70,000 miles or less. **1997 w/Goodyear tires and steel**

wheels: Tires were damaged, and may lose pressure suddenly. **1997:** Certain master-cylinder seals will not seal adequately, allowing hydraulic fluid to be drawn into power-assist vacuum reservoir; brake-warning lamp will then illuminate. **1997:** The D-pillar mastic sound-barrier patch could loosen and drop into the seatbelt assembly, rendering it inoperative. **1997:** Wheels on small number of minivans were damaged by equipment used for mounting. **1998 w/integrated child seats:** Shoulder-harness webbing was incorrectly routed around reinforcement bar; can fail to restrain child properly. **1999:** The front-seatbelt retractor does not comply with the requirements of the standard. If the retractor does not work properly, it will not adequately protect occupants in the event of a crash. **2000 w/3.3-liter and 3.8-liter engines:** Seals on fuel rails can degrade, allowing an under-hood fuel leak, which would increase likelihood of vehicle fire.

PRICES	Good	Average	Poor
1996 Caravan	$2,600-4,400	$1,900-3,300	$500-900
Grand Caravan	3,300-4,200	2,600-3,300	800-1,100
Grand LE, ES	5,000-5,800	4,300-4,900	2,000-2,300
1997 Caravan	3,200-5,500	2,500-4,300	800-1,400
Grand Caravan	4,000-6,000	3,300-4,900	1,300-1,900
Grand LE, ES	6,000-7,300	5,200-6,400	2,500-3,100
1998 Caravan	3,800-6,500	3,100-5,300	1,100-2,000
Grand Caravan	5,000-7,200	4,300-6,100	2,000-2,900
Grand LE, ES	7,000-8,500	6,200-7,600	3,400-4,100
1999 Caravan	4,700-7,800	3,900-6,600	1,800-3,000
Grand Caravan	6,700-9,000	5,900-7,900	3,100-4,100
Grand LE, ES	8,800-10,500	7,900-9,500	4,600-5,500
2000 Caravan	6,200-9,000	5,400-7,800	2,700-3,900
Grand Caravan	8,300-11,000	7,500-9,900	4,300-5,700
Grand LE, ES	10,800-13,000	9,700-11,700	5,800-7,000

For detailed information on this vehicle visit http://used.consumerguide.com and enter code **2134**

2001-03 DODGE CARAVAN

CLASS: Minivan

BUILT IN: Canada, USA

PROS: All-wheel drive • Cargo room (Grand) • Entry/exit • Interior storage space • Passenger room

CONS: Acceleration (4-cyl) • Fuel economy

BEST BUY CG

EVALUATION: New convenience features account for the most obvious improvements in the 2001 redesign, leaving Caravan's performance upgraded incrementally. That's fine because this was already among the most capable minivans on the road.

Acceleration is good—with the right engine, that is. In a vehicle this heavy, the four-cylinder is acceptable only for light-duty, low-speed chores. The 3.3-liter V6 provides good power off-the-line and on the highway, in a regular-length model, but it feels overburdened in a Grand Caravan loaded for a family vacation. That's makes the smooth, strong 3.8 the safest bet in Grands, where it supplies substantial muscle in all conditions.

It's the smoothest of these engines as well. While all work nicely with the four-speed automatic, the AutoStick (available with the 3.8) furnishes a sporty dimension that's absent in other minivans. Caravans (and Town & Country) are the only non truck-based minivans with the all-weather security of available AWD. In long-term testing, a 3.8 AWD Grand Caravan averaged 17.1 mpg. A four-cylinder SE returned 19.8 mpg.

Grand Caravans smooth out bumps better than the shorter-wheelbase models, but all Dodge minivans ride comfortably. Still, you'll feel most pavement imperfections if the Sport Touring suspension is installed.

Steering is nicely weighted, and straight-ahead stability is admirable. Caravans with 15-inch tires are modest but predictable handlers, whereas the 16- and 17-inch setups provide noticeably more grip and sharper response in turns. Stopping power is adequate, but pedal feel and confidence improve with the four-wheel disc brakes on ES and AWD Grands.

Heavy crosswinds and 70-mph cruising elevate wind rush. Certain road surfaces bring out marked tire noise.

As before, Caravans are roomier and more user-friendly than most minivans. Low step-in height and wide doorways ease entry, and front-seat occupants enjoy plenty of head, leg, and shoulder room. All seats are comfortably padded, and Caravans still offer integrated middle-row child safety seats.

Grands have generous knee and foot clearance in the second- and third-row seats, making them spacious where regular-length versions can be cramped. The same goes for cargo space behind the third-row seat.

The split third-row seats are invitingly simple to fold and remove, but not quite as convenient as a foldaway design. Middle-row bucket seats tip forward, with little effort to provide access to the rear.

The ability to easily stop or speed up the power side door by hand is genuinely useful, as is the power liftgate. Both systems respond quickly to obstructions. Movable center consoles with interior lighting and power outlets are a nice innovation. The rear parcel shelf also is handy, though its pop-up dividers seem flimsy.

Rear headrests obstruct outward vision slightly. Caravan gauges are unobstructed. Controls are easy to decipher and close to the driver, but cupholders block the in-dash CD changer.

VALUE FOR THE MONEY: Caravan's hold on the minivan sales title can only be strengthened by the 2001 redesign, which added desirable innovations to a vehicle that's hard to beat for refinement, utility, and carlike road manners. Don't buy a minivan without checking out Dodge's latest.

DODGE

TROUBLE SPOTS

Air conditioner: The A/C compressor may fail, causing a squealing or missing drive belt. The compressor fails from not turning on the rear A/C controls, but running only the front. After the A/C parts are replaced, the body control computer requires reprogramming. (2001)

Doors: Loose weather strip tricks the power sliding door into thinking there is an obstruction making it misbehave during opening or closing. The weather strip must be replaced.

Engine stalling: The engine may lose power or stall, especially when the temperature is below freezing, requiring replacement of if the throttle position sensor. (2001-02)

Fuel gauge: The fuel gauge may drop below the actual level while driving, but may return to the correct reading after sitting for about 10 minutes due to a kinked hose at the leak-detection-pump filter. (2001-02)

Suspension noise: Knocking or squawking sounds from the front suspension are corrected by replacing the sway-bar links. (2001)

Water leak: A wet passenger-side carpet is often due to condensation from the A/C drain tube blowing back into the passenger compartment and replacing the tube with a longer one corrects the problem. (2001-02)

Water leak: Some early production (prior to April 2001) vehicles may have a serpentine belt that squeals of jumps off (in cold weather) the pulley caused by water leaking from the wiper module drain tube. In cold weather, ice forms on the pulley. (2001)

AVERAGE REPLACEMENT COSTS

A/C Compressor	$415	Exhaust System	$415
Alternator	535	Radiator	395
Automatic Trans.	1,620	Shocks and/or Struts	1,500
Brakes	440	Timing Chain/Belt	180
CV Joints	990		

NHTSA RECALL HISTORY

2001 w/o keyless entry: Sliding door latches could release in severe accidents. Dealers will replace both sliding door cylinder links free of charge. **2001:** Lower control-arm bolt could fracture and lead to a loss of vehicle-control. Dealers will replace affected parts. **2002 Grand:** Fuel tank control valve weld joint could separate resulting in a fuel leak or fire. Dealers will inspect and replace affected parts. **2002:** Some owner's manuals are missing instructions for installing child seats. Owners will be provided with an addendum to the owners manual.

PRICES

	Good	Average	Poor
2001 Caravan	$9,000-10,500	$8,100-9,500	$4,700-5,500
Grand Caravan	11,000-14,000	9,900-12,600	5,900-7,600
Grand Caravan ES	14,500-16,000	13,200-14,600	9,000-9,900
2002 Caravan	10,500-13,000	9,500-11,700	5,600-6,900
Grand Caravan	13,500-17,500	12,300-15,900	8,000-10,300
Grand Caravan ES	18,000-20,500	16,600-18,900	11,500-13,100

2003 Caravan	$13,500-16,500	$12,300-15,000	$8,000-9,700
Grand Caravan	16,000-19,500	14,600-17,700	10,200-12,500
Grand Caravan ES	23,000-26,000	21,200-23,900	15,000-16,900
Grand Caravan Sport	17,500-19,000	16,100-17,500	11,200-12,200

> For detailed information on this vehicle visit
> http://used.consumerguide.com and enter code **4494**

1990-96 DODGE DAKOTA

CLASS: Compact pickup truck

BUILT IN: USA

PROS: Acceleration (V6, V8) • Passenger room

CONS: Acceleration (4-cylinder) • Interior storage space

EVALUATION: Regular cabs have ample space for three adults, but neither the bench seat nor the available buckets are particularly comfortable (1993 and later buckets are better). Not much storage space is available behind the seat, unless you opt for the Club Cab. But it's hard to get into the rear seat, which isn't sufficient for three and has limited knee room. The floor-mounted 4WD lever is low and sits well forward, so you have to reach under the dash to shift from 2WD to 4WD High. Other controls are easy to reach.

The base 4-cylinder engine is adequate, but not a wise choice unless you rarely carry cargo. Relaxed at highway speeds, the husky early V6 develops enough low-speed torque to haul heavy loads, but it's still no fireball when pushing hard. The "Magnum" V6 introduced for 1992 yields better acceleration (Dodge claimed a 0-60 mph time of 8.3 seconds), but engine and exhaust noise are more noticeable under hard throttle. Acceleration is more robust yet with the V8, which is the choice for towing. Dakotas handle competently and ride well considering their size, though the ride gets bouncy when the cargo box is empty. Despite ABS, rear wheels tend to lock prematurely in hard stops. We'd prefer a later model with the optional 4-wheel antilock braking.

VALUE FOR THE MONEY: Solid and robust, a Dakota makes a good practical choice. A long-wheelbase version with the 8-foot bed might serve nearly as well as a full-size pickup.

TROUBLE SPOTS

Air conditioner: If the air conditioner gradually stops cooling and/or the airflow from the vents decreases, the computer (PCM) may not be sending a signal to the compressor clutch relay to cycle off, which causes the AC evaporator to freeze up. (1991-95)

Automatic transmission: If the transmission will not engage when first started, chances are the torque converter is draining down. Chrysler will correct the problem by installing a check valve. (1993)

DODGE

Automatic transmission: If the transmission won't upshift in cool weather, it is probably due to defective cast iron seal rings in the governor drive. (1992-94)

Engine fan noise: In warm weather, the fan makes a roaring sound. Dodge will replace the fan, the fan clutch, and, on max cooling systems, the radiator cap. (All)

Exhaust backfire: Exhaust backfire and/or a popping noise in the exhaust may be caused by a defective Powertrain Control Module. (1994-95)

Oil leak: Rear main seals on 2.5- and 4.0-liter engines are prone to leakage. To prevent future failures, Chrysler has a rubber plug available that goes in a hole above the starter that protects the rear main seal. (1996)

Oil leak: Oil leak at the filter on 3.9-, 5.2-, and 5.9-liter engines is likely due to a warped adapter plate. (1995)

Oil pump: Oil pump gear wear results in bucking and surging when the engine is warm and lack of lubrication when the engine is cold. (1992-93)

Rough idle: Because of a problem with the idle air control motor, the engine idles rough, stalls at low speeds or when decelerating, especially in warm weather. (1992-94)

Transaxle leak: Automatic transmission fluid leaks from the speed sensor in the transmission. (1994)

Water leak: The roof seams leak water that seeps down behind the dashboard onto the floor. (1993-95)

AVERAGE REPLACEMENT COSTS

A/C Compressor	$415	Exhaust System	$310
Alternator	295	Radiator	405
Automatic Trans.	790	Shocks and/or Struts	190
Brakes	315	Timing Chain/Belt	190
Clutch	525	Universal Joints	130

NHTSA RECALL HISTORY

1990 light-duty 4x2 and club-cab w/V8: Frame can crack at steering-gear attachment and/or mounting bolts can fracture, allowing steering gear to separate. **1990:** Valve cover gasket may allow oil leakage. **1991 2WD:** Right front-brake hose may rub against tire during full-left turn. **1991 w/4-speed automatic:** Fuel hose may contact wiring harness, resulting in leakage. **1991:** Premium steering wheel could crack and separate from hub. **1991-92 w/A500 automatic transmission:** Inadvertent placement of shift lever in "Reverse" can occur when driver believes it has been placed in "Park." **1993:** ABS could become inoperative when hard pedal effort is applied. **1994:** Control-arm attaching bolts were not properly heat treated. If they break, steering control could be lost. **1994:** Dealers will install a redesigned steering-wheel back cover to keep extra keys from getting caught behind the wheel when the key is in the ignition. **1994:** Fuel-tank support straps could separate resulting in fuel leak and increased risk of fire. **1996 w/2.5-liter engine:** Power-brake-vacuum hose in some trucks could be improperly installed; disconnected hose can cause increase in idle speed and loss of power assist.

PRICES	Good	Average	Poor
1990 Dakota 2WD	$1,100-2,400	$700-1,500	$100-300
Dakota 4WD	1,600-2,600	1,100-1,700	200-400
1991 Dakota 2WD	1,300-2,600	800-1,600	200-300
Dakota 4WD	2,100-3,300	1,500-2,300	400-600
1992 Dakota 2WD	1,500-2,900	1,000-1,900	200-400
Dakota 4WD	2,500-3,800	1,800-2,800	500-800
1993 Dakota 2WD	1,800-3,400	1,200-2,300	300-500
Dakota 4WD	2,800-4,300	2,100-3,200	600-900
1994 Dakota 2WD	2,100-4,000	1,500-2,800	400-700
Dakota 4WD	3,300-5,100	2,600-4,000	800-1,300
1995 Dakota 2WD	2,400-4,500	1,700-3,200	500-900
Dakota 4WD	3,700-5,700	3,000-4,600	1,100-1,700
1996 Dakota 2WD	2,700-5,300	2,000-4,000	600-1,200
Dakota 4WD	4,100-6,800	3,400-5,600	1,400-2,200

> For detailed information on this vehicle visit
> **http://used.consumerguide.com** and enter code **2022**

1997-03 DODGE DAKOTA

CG BEST BUY

CLASS: Compact pickup truck

BUILT IN: USA

PROS: Acceleration (V8) • Quietness • Ride (2WD)

CONS: Acceleration (4-cylinder) • Fuel economy (V8) • Rear-seat room/comfort (ext. cab)

EVALUATION: The stiffer frame on this generation of Dakota evidently made a noticeable difference, as a 2WD Club Cab model proved to be impressively solid on rough roads. Ride quality was also pleasing. The suspension provided a comfortable and stable ride, with only a little bouncing on wavy surfaces. A 4-wheel-drive model, on the other hand, does not feel as stable or comfortable, jiggling more over bumps.

The 5.2-liter V8 is smoother and quieter than before, delivering strong acceleration and passing power. Gas mileage is another story. We averaged only 13.3 mpg with the V8, though that included mainly urban commuting. The overhead-cam 4.7-liter V8 that replaced the 5.2 in 2000 also furnishes strong acceleration. The base 4-cylinder engine is simply too weak for a vehicle of this size and weight. The V6 makes a sensible compromise. The Dakota R/T delivers impressive acceleration, but is hampered by a rough ride and lack of 4-wheel drive.

Although the Dakota is roomier than rival compact pickups, the rear bench seat in Club Cab models lacks sufficient leg room for adults. Getting into the rear seat is a squeeze, too. As a bonus, the rear-seat cushion folds up to reveal a couple of handy, flat-topped storage compartments. Rear doors on the Quad Cab are not technically full-size, but they open independently of the front doors and make entry/exit a lot more convenient. The Quad Cab also has more rear leg room than any rival's extended cab, though long-legged adults still will find their knees pressed into the front seatback.

This Dakota's dashboard looks more modern, but it's covered with flimsy plastic. Inside door panels are made of cheap-looking molded plastic that does not look or feel durable. In general, though, materials are comparable to those in most rival trucks. Visibility is good all around. Radio and climate controls are easy to reach. Two cupholders are molded into the center console.

VALUE FOR THE MONEY: Dakota offers a bit more interior space and towing capacity than compact pickup rivals, and a significant advantage in payload capacity. If you like the styling, the rest of the truck probably won't be disappointing.

TROUBLE SPOTS

Dashboard lights: The gauges and overhead console quit working because of a blown fuse. (1997)

Engine misfire: Engine bucking at about 5300 rpm may occur when many electrical devices are in use. Noise from the generator affects the transmission-governor pressure sensor delaying upshifts. (1997-98)

Engine noise: The timing chain makes a rattling noise, which requires a replacement chain, sprockets, and tensioner. (1997)

Exhaust system: The exhaust manifold studs on the 2.5-liter engine tend to break. (1997-98)

Keyless entry: If the remote keyless entry transmitter batteries die in less than two months, there is a problem with the transmitter and it will be replaced under warranty. (1997-98)

Paint/body: "Radiant Red Metallic" paint suffers chipping problems because antichip primer was not applied during production. (1997)

Vehicle noise: A popping noise can come from the rear of the cab because the sleeves in the cab isolators are too long and must be ground down. (1997-98)

AVERAGE REPLACEMENT COSTS

A/C Compressor	$525	Exhaust System	$510
Alternator	355	Radiator	400
Automatic Trans.	990	Shocks and/or Struts	330
Brakes	305	Timing Chain/Belt	205
Clutch	610	Universal Joints	180

NHTSA RECALL HISTORY

1997 w/131-inch wheelbase: Some vehicles may have inadequate clearance between fuel line and cab underbody. **1997:** Airbag could deploy inadvertently when ignition is shut off. **1997-00 w/2.5-liter engine:** Some vehicles may have inadequate clearance between left front brake tube and power-steering hose. **1997-00:** Some vehicles may have inadequate clearance between rear-axle vent hose and brake hose. **1997-00:** Sound-deadening material inside the steering wheel could become detached from the cover and housing causing the driver-airbag system to become disabled. The airbag-warning lamp will illuminate on the instrument panel. **1998 2WD:** Front-brake hoses or antilock brake-system sensor wire may be abraded at front wheels by contact with wheelhouse splash shield; prolonged contact with hose can cause partial braking loss. **1998:** Bolts used to attach cab and core support to frame may have been improperly hardened; can allow cab to separate from frame. **1999:** The front-seatbelt retractor does not comply with the requirements of the standard. If the retractor does not work properly, it will not adequately protect occupants in the event of a crash. **2000 w/4.7-liter engine and automatic:** Automatic transmission may expel fluid from fill tube during normal temperature operation. **2000-01:** Some of the owner's manuals for these vehicles are missing instructions for properly attaching a child-restraint system's tether strap to the tether anchorage. **2001 Quad Cab:** Front-outboard lower-seatbelt anchor bolts may not be tightened correctly. An improperly tightened seatbelt anchor may not provide the anticipated level of occupant restraint in a crash. **2001 w/4WD:** Electric shift-transfer case may not fully engage into gear, causing the transfer case to end up in the neutral position.

PRICES

	Good	Average	Poor
1997 Dakota 2WD	$3,500-6,000	$2,800-4,800	$900-1,600
Dakota 4WD	5,000-7,300	4,300-6,200	2,000-2,900
1998 Dakota 2WD	4,000-6,800	3,300-5,600	1,300-2,200
Dakota 4WD	6,000-9,000	5,200-7,800	2,500-3,800
1999 Dakota 2WD	4,700-8,000	3,900-6,700	1,800-3,000
Dakota 4WD	7,000-10,500	6,200-9,300	3,400-5,000
Dakota R/T	8,000-10,000	7,200-9,000	4,100-5,100
2000 Dakota 2WD	5,700-11,000	4,900-9,500	2,300-4,500
Dakota 4WD	8,200-13,500	7,400-12,200	4,200-6,900
Dakota R/T	9,500-11,500	8,600-10,400	4,900-6,000
2001 Dakota 2WD	7,000-13,200	6,200-11,700	3,400-6,300
Dakota 4WD	9,500-15,500	8,600-14,000	4,900-8,100
Dakota R/T	11,000-13,500	9,900-12,200	5,900-7,300
2002 Dakota 2WD	8,300-15,000	7,500-13,500	4,300-7,800
Dakota 4WD	11,000-17,500	9,900-15,800	5,900-9,500
Dakota R/T	12,500-15,000	11,300-13,500	7,100-8,600
2003 Dakota 2WD	11,000-17,500	9,900-15,800	5,900-9,500
Dakota 4WD	13,500-20,000	12,300-18,200	8,000-11,800
Dakota R/T	15,500-18,500	14,100-16,800	9,900-11,800

For detailed information on this vehicle visit
http://used.consumerguide.com and enter code **2260**

1998-03 DODGE DURANGO

CLASS: Midsize sport-utility vehicle

BUILT IN: USA

PROS: Acceleration (5.9-liter V8) • Optional antilock braking • Cargo room • Passenger room

CONS: Acceleration (V6) • Fuel economy • Rear-seat comfort

EVALUATION: Durango feels more like a large car than a truck, delivering a ride that's absorbent and composed even on bumpy roads, with little bouncing. Despite the usual SUV body lean and nose-plowing in quick turns, Durango does not feel ponderous. Directional stability is generally good, though steering is vague around center and a lot of correction may be needed to stay on course at highway speeds.

V8 engines are smooth and quiet. Vigor is adequate with the 4.7- and 5.2-liter, but they lack a strong punch at low speeds for quick getaways. The 5.9-liter V8 has a huskier tone and feels stronger off the line and in passing situations. In city/highway driving, we got a modest 12.4 mpg from a Durango with the 5.2-liter V8. A Durango with the 5.9-liter V8 managed only 11.2 mpg.

Durango uses its size well, providing generous shoulder width and head room. Squeezing eight seats into a vehicle the size of a midsize car is no small feat, but Dodge managed it in the Durango. Be warned, though: The third seat is better for children than adults. Second-row seats have thin padding that is less supportive than the more-substantial cushions used by many rivals. Cargo space behind the third seat, measuring 18.8 cubic feet, is adequate for a few small suitcases or a week's worth of groceries. Center and rear seats fold flat in seconds, for a handy alternative to removable seats that opens up ample cargo room.

All 4WD models have a floor-mounted transfer case lever, which is something of a stretch for the driver. The dashboard is simple and convenient, but thick side pillars and rear headrests impede rear vision. Also on the negative side, the climate-control system will not feed air to floor and face vents simultaneously. Workmanship is solid and thorough, but black plastic trim over the gauge cluster and main dashboard controls feels cheap and flimsy, and the inside door panels look plain.

VALUE FOR THE MONEY: Despite a few demerits, Durango is a well-designed truck that approaches full-size models for brawn and space, and therefore deserves strong consideration as a late-model, secondhand SUV.

TROUBLE SPOTS

Air conditioner: The air conditioner gradually becomes less effective, which may require a new evaporator. (1998-99)

Engine misfire: If the spark plug wires are misrouted, the engine may knock, the cylinders may misfire, and the vehicle surges (which may feel like a transmission problem) around 45 mph. (1998-99)

Keyless entry: The remote keyless entry system doesn't work due to a problem with the transmitter case. (1999)

Steering noise: The steering column makes popping noises and feels rough during parking maneuvers. (1998-00)

Vehicle noise: Squeaks from the front wheels may be caused by a loose spindle retaining nut. (1999)

AVERAGE REPLACEMENT COSTS

A/C Compressor	$415	Exhaust System	$385
Alternator	400	Radiator	560
Automatic Trans.	615	Shocks and/or Struts	490
Brakes	450	Timing Chain/Belt	615
Clutch	610	Universal Joints	215

NHTSA RECALL HISTORY

1998: Fastener that secures generator cable has insufficient clamp load, resulting in a loose connection and electrical arcing; could result in fire. **1998:** Rear-brake tube can contact underbody crossmember, eventually wearing a hole in the tube that could reduce braking from rear wheels. **1998-00:** Sound-deadening material inside the steering wheel could become detached from the cover and housing causing the the driver-airbag system to become disabled. The airbag-warning lamp will illuminate on the instrument panel. **1998-99:** Fuel-tank strap can separate due to fatigue during vehicle operation, causing tank to be unsupported. **1999:** The front-seatbelt retractor does not comply with the requirements of the standard. If the retractor does not work properly, it will not adequately protect occupants in the event of a crash. **2000-01:** Some of the owner's manuals for these vehicles are missing instructions for properly attaching a child restraint system's tether strap to the tether anchorage. **2001 w/4WD:** Electric shift-transfer case may not fully engage into gear, causing the transfer case to end up in the neutral position.

PRICES

	Good	Average	Poor
1998 Durango 4WD	$9,500-10,500	$8,600-9,500	$4,900-5,500
1999 Durango 2WD	10,000-11,200	9,000-10,100	5,200-5,800
Durango 4WD	11,500-12,800	10,400-11,500	6,300-7,000
2000 Durango 2WD	11,500-13,000	10,400-11,700	6,300-7,200
Durango 4WD	13,000-14,500	11,800-13,200	7,500-8,400
Durango R/T	15,500-17,000	14,100-15,500	9,900-10,900
2001 Durango 2WD	13,500-15,500	12,300-14,100	8,000-9,100
Durango 4WD	15,200-17,500	13,800-15,900	9,600-11,000
Durango R/T	18,000-19,500	16,600-17,900	11,500-12,500
2002 Durango 2WD	15,500-18,500	14,100-16,800	9,900-11,800
Durango 4WD	17,300-20,500	15,900-18,900	11,100-13,100
Durango R/T	21,500-23,500	19,800-21,600	14,000-15,300

2003 Durango 2WD	$17,500-21,200	$16,100-19,500	$11,200-13,600
Durango 4WD	19,300-23,000	17,800-21,200	12,500-15,000
Durango R/T	25,000-27,500	23,300-25,600	16,500-18,200

For detailed information on this vehicle visit
http://used.consumerguide.com and enter code 2303

1993-97 DODGE INTREPID

CG BEST BUY

CLASS: Full-size car

BUILT IN: Canada

PROS: Acceleration (3.5-liter) • Antilock brakes • Passenger and cargo room • Ride (base suspension) • Steering/handling

CONS: Acceleration (3.3-liter) • Climate controls • Rear visibility • Ride (Performance Handling Group) • Road noise

EVALUATION: Acceleration is adequate with the 3.3-liter V6, but it's not too snappy for quick passing. For that reason, an early ES is the better choice with the larger V6 engine and touring suspension employing 16-inch tires. This combination offers fine overall performance, including precise handling and cornering. But watch out for an ES with the optional Performance Handling Group, which yields a stiff ride.

By 1994, all Intrepids had the touring suspension as standard, delivering a satisfying level of handling precision without much loss in comfort. Even base Intrepids with that suspension handle as well as some smaller sports sedans, zipping through tight turns with little body lean and commendable grip. The ride is firm, but not harsh. Gas mileage with an ES sedan averaged 22 mpg in a long-term trial, including considerable highway mileage—not quite a miser, but better than some all-out full-size automobiles. Even stop-and-go commuting usually resulted in 16-18 mpg economy.

Three adults fit in back without crowding. Head room is good in front and adequate in back. Ergonomics are great. Instruments and controls are logically arranged and convenient, except for climate controls that are mounted too low for easy access. Lightweight plastic on the dashboard and door panels does not feel too durable. Cargo space is fine and the trunk opens at bumper level for easier loading of luggage. Road noise is prominent at highway speeds, even with the sound insulation added for 1996. Wind noise is low.

Workmanship is generally tight and solid, but some cars have suffered minor creaks, rattles, or assembly flaws—even when new.

VALUE FOR THE MONEY: Intrepid is an impressive and worthy family sedan with a healthy helping of flair, offering good value for the money. However, full-size General Motors cars, such as the Oldsmobile Eighty-Eight and Pontiac Bonneville, may have the edge in terms of overall quality.

TROUBLE SPOTS

Air conditioner: If the air conditioner is intermittent or quits altogether, but the refrigerant charge is OK, the pressure transducer is probably malfunctioning. (All)

Air conditioner: The air conditioner lines are prone to leak at the compressor because of nicks and sharp edges on the A/C line grooves for the O-rings, making it necessary to replace the lines. (1993-94)

Automatic transmission: 41TE or 42LE automatic transaxle could take several seconds to engage at startup because of a problem with the valve body. (1993-95)

Automatic transmission: Bad seals in the transmission lead to premature friction component wear, which causes a shudder when starting from a stop, a bump when coasting to a stop, and slipping between gears. (1993-95)

Automatic transmission: A defective throttle positions sensor could be the cause of late, erratic, or harsh shifting. (1994)

Automatic transmission: Transmission front pump could be leaking due to a worn bushing, which requires replacement of the pump as well as the torque converter. (1993-96)

Cold-starting problems: Hard starting and a miss at idle can be traced to defective fuel rails. (1993-94)

Engine noise: The motor mount on the left side of the engine tends to break. (1993)

AVERAGE REPLACEMENT COSTS

A/C Compressor	$365	Exhaust System	$418
Alternator	190	Radiator	350
Automatic Trans.	1,089	Shocks and/or Struts	480
Brakes	250	Timing Chain/Belt	230
CV Joints	310		

NHTSA RECALL HISTORY

1993 w/3.3-liter engine: O-rings used to seal interface of fuel-injector tubes are insufficiently durable; deterioration can cause fuel leakage, with potential for fire. **1993:** Lower control-arm washers in front suspension of some cars can crack and fall off due to hydrogen embrittlement; will cause clunking sound during braking and eventually result in loss of steering control. **1993-95:** Lower control-arm attaching brackets on some cars can crack due to fatigue and separate from engine cradle; transmission half-shaft could then pull out of transaxle. **1993-97 w/3.5-liter engine:** Fuel-injection system can leak from O-rings or hairline cracks in fuel-injection rail. **1994:** Right steering tie rod can rub through automatic-transmission wiring harness, causing short circuit; may result in stalling, or allow engine to start when selector is not in "Park" position.

PRICES	Good	Average	Poor
1993 Intrepid	$1,800-2,400	$1,200-1,600	$300-400
1994 Intrepid	2,100-2,800	1,500-2,000	400-500
1995 Intrepid	2,500-3,300	1,800-2,400	500-700

1996 Intrepid	$2,900-3,600	$2,200-2,700	$700-800
1997 Intrepid	3,500-4,500	2,800-3,600	900-1,200

For detailed information on this vehicle visit
http://used.consumerguide.com and enter code 2025

1998-03 DODGE INTREPID

CG BEST BUY

CLASS: Full-size car

BUILT IN: Canada

PROS: Cargo room • Passenger room • Ride • Steering/handling

CONS: Trunk liftover • Rear visibility

EVALUATION: The Intrepid's suspension is firm and stable at highway speeds, without growing harsh on rough pavement. Suspensions of the two models are tuned identically, but the wider tires on the ES provide slightly sharper feel in directional changes. Brakes provide short, straight stops from high speeds, with fine pedal modulation.

Although the 2.7-liter engine moves this full-size sedan with adequate swiftness, acceleration is hardly neck-snapping. Though it's no powerhouse, the stronger 3.2-liter V6 can chirp the tires during rapid takeoffs, and delivers a quicker burst of power for passing and merging. Autostick helps the ES scoot through traffic, and produce more confident passing and merging. Both engines are smooth and quiet, and road noise is less noticeable than in earlier Intrepids. Wind noise is noticeable but not excessive. As for economy, a test ES averaged 20.7 mpg.

Head room is generous in front, though the Intrepid's sloping roofline puts the heads of taller back-seaters right up to the headliner. Leg space is sufficient for 6-footers to be comfortable in all seats.

Most gauges and controls, including those for the climate system, are easy to see and reach. Radio controls are more difficult to reach, and demand some study to decipher. Intrepid has a much larger rear window than the Concorde, allowing the driver to see the trunk for parking and enjoy a better view of surrounding traffic. A high rear parcel shelf does impair visibility, however. Cargo space is ample, and split folding rear seats increases that total capacity.

VALUE FOR THE MONEY: When first seen as 1998 models, both the Intrepid and the Chrysler Concorde made other full-size automobiles look—and feel—dated. Roomy, athletic, and eye-catching, handling much like European sport sedans, Intrepids also offer plenty of interior space. Long-term mechanical reliability is still a question mark, but these stylish sedans can be good value, whether new or used.

TROUBLE SPOTS

Electrical problem: The interior lights will not go out or will not come on because of a blown fuse due to a damaged wiring harness in the roof area. (1998-99)

Electrical problem: Moisture getting inside the car behind the kick panels makes the windows, door locks, and power mirrors operate by themselves. (1998)

Oil leak: The oil filter adapter may come out of the engine block when the filter is removed on 3.2L and 3.5L engines. When this happens the adapter must be replaced, not reinstalled. (1998-99)

Steering problems: Drivability problems occur when the speed sensor wires pull out of the transmission. (1999)

AVERAGE REPLACEMENT COSTS

A/C Compressor	$440	Exhaust System	$425
Alternator	360	Radiator	430
Automatic Trans.	775	Shocks and/or Struts	1,505
Brakes	615	Timing Chain/Belt	360
CV Joints	1,300		

NHTSA RECALL HISTORY

1998: A few passenger-airbag module assemblies are missing some required components, so airbag would not deploy during a crash. **1998-02:** Some vehicles may have faulty seat-recliner bolts, allowing the seat to unexpectedly recline. Dealer will inspect and replace affected parts. **1999:** The front-seatbelt retractor does not comply with the requirements of the standard. If the retractor does not work properly, it will not adequately protect occupants in the event of a crash. **1999-00:** Inadequately manufactured mounting bolt for seatbelt shoulder height-adjustable turning loop may not withstand sufficient force to function properly in certain impact situations. **2000:** Brake master-cylinder piston-retainer snap ring may be bent inward, which could result in brake-drag condition. **2000:** Molding flash on primary lever may prevent operation of G-lock and tilt lock functions on some driver-side retractors, which could reduce driver protection during a frontal crash. **2000:** Passenger-airbag inflator assembly on some cars contains incorrect inflator charge amount. **2000-01:** In the event of a crash, there is a potential for injury if the occupant's head were to contact the B-pillar. Owners will be sent a storage-bin accessory unit that can be attached to the B-pillar along with installation instructions. **2000-01:** Some of the owner's manuals for these vehicles are missing instructions for properly attaching a child restraint-system's tether strap to the tether anchorage.

PRICES	Good	Average	Poor
1998 Intrepid	$4,800-6,000	$4,000-5,000	$1,800-2,300
1999 Intrepid	5,700-7,000	4,900-6,000	2,300-2,900
2000 Intrepid	7,200-8,600	6,400-7,700	3,500-4,200
Intrepid R/T	10,000-11,000	9,000-9,900	5,200-5,700
2001 Intrepid	8,500-10,000	7,700-9,000	4,400-5,200
Intrepid R/T	11,500-13,000	10,400-11,700	6,300-7,200

2002 Intrepid	$10,000-12,300	$9,000-11,100	$5,200-6,400
Intrepid R/T	13,500-15,000	12,300-13,700	8,000-8,900
2003 Intrepid	12,000-15,000	10,800-13,500	6,700-8,400

For detailed information on this vehicle visit
http://used.consumerguide.com and enter code **2304**

1995-99 DODGE NEON

CG BEST BUY

CLASS: Subcompact car

BUILT IN: Mexico, USA

PROS: Antilock brakes (optional) • Fuel economy • Instruments/controls • Passenger and cargo room • Ride • Steering/handling

CONS: Automatic-transmission performance • Engine noise

EVALUATION: The base engine is quick off the line with either transmission, but it growls loudly under hard throttle. Even so, it transmits little vibration to the car's interior and cruises quietly. The automatic transmission shifts abruptly during brisk acceleration, and tends to be oversensitive to the throttle. It also downshifts unexpectedly. Although the available dual-cam four is livelier than the base engine, the difference isn't big enough to make it a priority, and it's no quieter, either.

Fuel economy is commendable. We averaged 31 mpg with a 5-speed base engine model in a mix of city and highway driving. A Sport Neon with the base engine and automatic averaged 24.2 mpg, with most driving in and around urban areas.

Neons feel solid and well-planted on the road. The firm suspension soaks up bumps with little harshness, and neither floats nor bottoms out, though bad pavement can deliver a few jolts. Handling is sporty, even with the base model. Steering is firm, feels natural, and centers quickly, producing agile response on winding roads. Brakes have strong stopping power, too.

Passenger space is impressive for such a small vehicle. There's enough head and leg room to seat four 6-footers without squeezing, though rear doors are too small to allow easy entry and exit. The modern dashboard layout offers simple, convenient controls. The Neon's trunk opens at bumper level to a wide, flat cargo floor that reaches well forward to yield good luggage space.

VALUE FOR THE MONEY: In all, Neon offers a solid domestic alternative to the imports. Whether to pick a Dodge or Plymouth is a matter of individual choice; except for the insignia on the body, they're exactly the same car.

TROUBLE SPOTS

Air conditioner: A lack of cooling caused by the A/C evaporator freezing up because the compressor does not cycle off. (1995)

Battery: Batteries that go dead may be the result of one or more of the following: a glove box without a raised pad that closes the light switch, misaligned doors, a faulty trunklid switch and lamp assembly, or a missing door-ajar bumper pad. (1995)

Brakes: The front brakes wear abnormally fast on cars with four wheel studs, so heavy-duty linings should be used to replace them. (All)

Brakes: If the ABS warning light stays on, which disables the ABS, the ABS controller needs to be replaced. (1995)

Climate control: In cold weather, ice may form in the blower motor housing, which prevents the blower from moving and blows the fuse. The drain tube must be rerouted, the blower motor replaced, and a new fuse installed. (1995-97)

Rough idle: Faulty valve springs on the 2.0-liter DOHC engine cause rough idle, misfires. (1997-99)

Steering noise: Unless the power steering fluid is replaced with a revised fluid, the steering system makes noise for the first few minutes when started in cold weather. (1995-98)

AVERAGE REPLACEMENT COSTS

A/C Compressor	$400	CV Joints	$345
Alternator	300	Exhaust System	290
Automatic Trans.	555	Radiator	375
Brakes	295	Shocks and/or Struts	450
Clutch	535	Timing Chain/Belt	190

NHTSA RECALL HISTORY

1995: Fuel and rear-brake tubes can experience accelerated corrosion between metallic tubes and rubber isolator; may lead to brake fluid or fuel leakage. **1995:** Steering-column coupler can become disconnected when vehicle sustains underbody impact. **1995-96 w/ACR competition package:** Brake master cylinder can leak fluid due to damaged seal; warning light will signal impairment prior to partial brake-system loss. **1996 built in Mexico:** Wiring harness could short circuit, causing various malfunctions, including stalling. **1997:** Airbag could deploy inadvertently when ignition is shut off. **1998:** Rear suspension crossmember on some cars may be missing spot welds; can result in structural cracks in body, and reduced rear-impact crash protection. **1999:** Inadequate welding on some cars could allow pivot tube to separate from lower control arm in front suspension.

PRICES	Good	Average	Poor
1995 Neon	$1,700-2,300	$1,100-1,500	$300
Neon Sport	1,900-2,500	1,300-1,700	300-400
1996 Neon	2,000-2,600	1,400-1,800	300-400
Neon Sport	2,300-2,900	1,700-2,100	400-600
1997 Neon	2,400-3,000	1,700-2,200	500-600
1998 Neon	3,100-3,800	2,400-2,900	700-900
1999 Neon	3,800-4,600	3,100-3,700	1,100-1,400

For detailed information on this vehicle visit
http://used.consumerguide.com and enter code **2140**

2000-03 DODGE NEON

CLASS: Subcompact car
BUILT IN: USA
PROS: Fuel economy
• Steering/handling
CONS: Automatic-transmission performance
• Noise

EVALUATION: Compared to the 1995-99 generation, this Neon is an improvement, but modest acceleration remains a weak point. Though lively enough with manual shift, highway passing typically demands a downshift from fifth gear to third. Standing-start pickup is a lot duller with the automatic transmission. Most rival models have 4-speed automatics, which quicken takeoffs. SRT-4 model is jackrabbit quick and passes with authority. Gas mileage is a bonus. A test Neon with automatic transmission averaged 24 mpg in mostly highway driving, and 25.3 with manual shift in a mix of city/highway travel. Neon suspensions absorb most bumps well. Sporty steering and handling carry on the car's basic fun-to-drive character. Wind and road noise are noticeable, but the real sound culprit is the engine, which groans loudly under hard throttle. SRT-4 model has more wind, road, and engine noise than others, but also corners, stops, and steers better than base models.

For a subcompact, the Neon is roomy and reasonably comfortable. The driver sits in an alert, upright position. Both front buckets are comfortable, with plenty of head room. Leg room is sufficient in the back, where seat comfort is adequate, but head clearance is tight for anyone over 5-foot-8 or so. Generously sized gauges look dressy, but they lose contrast in dim light when the headlights are on. A high parcel shelf restricts the driver's view directly to the rear. Seat fabrics feel rich, and despite a surplus of hard plastic on doors and dashboard, nothing looks or feels cheap. Doorways are fairly large, but the rear-door shape hinders entry/exit. Trunk volume is good for this class, but liftover is high and the lid's hinges cut into load space. Acceleration is good with the R/T and ACR editions that were added for 2001, but fewer of those are on sale.

VALUE FOR THE MONEY: Tepid acceleration aside, the regular Neon is a capable, fairly refined, and well-equipped subcompact at an appealing price—perhaps even more tempting when secondhand than as a new car. Sales have been sluggish in new-car showrooms, which helps to keep prices down.

TROUBLE SPOTS

Air conditioner: A clunk or hooting sound from the A/C compressor can be corrected with a new expansion valve. (2000-01)

Antenna: The threads for the antenna get stripped when someone tries to tighten it because there is a gap between the antenna and base. (2000-01)

Climate control: Leaves, etc. getting inside the plenum and rubbing on the blower squirrel cage causes noises when the blower is running. Installing seals near the hood hinges and screens in the cowl will keep debris out. (2000)

Steering problems: Power steering moan or groan is caused by low fluid levels in the system. A revised cap/dipstick was also released to increase the fluid level in the reservoir. (2000-01)

Vehicle noise: Snapping noises from the front suspension, particularly on rough roads, is often due to loose front crossmember mounting bolts. (2000)

Vehicle shake: A countermeasure motor mount on the right side eliminates a shake in the steering wheel or seat. (2000)

AVERAGE REPLACEMENT COSTS

A/C Compressor	$495	CV Joints	$770
Alternator	360	Exhaust System	370
Automatic Trans.	1,110	Radiator	450
Brakes	360	Shocks and/or Struts	490
Clutch	570	Timing Chain/Belt	280

NHTSA RECALL HISTORY

2000 Neon: Vapors from PCV system on certain cars can condense and freeze inside throttle body, when operated in cold ambient temperatures; throttle might not return fully to idle. **2000:** Some front (passenger-side) airbags may not inflate properly in a crash. **2000-01:** Brake-booster-vacuum hose could swell and loosen from intake manifold, causing loss of power brake assist and increased engine idle speed. **2000-01:** Some owner's manuals are missing full instructions for properly attaching a child restraint system's tether strap. **2001 w/R/T pkg. And 16-inch wheels:** Certain vehicles have an incorrect tire placard, indicating that 14- and 15-inch tires are recommended.

PRICES	Good	Average	Poor
2000 Neon	$5,000-5,800	$4,300-4,900	$2,000-2,300
2001 Neon	5,800-7,000	5,000-6,100	2,400-2,900
2002 Neon	7,000-8,300	6,200-7,400	3,400-4,000
Neon R/T	9,000-10,000	8,100-9,000	4,700-5,200
2003 Neon	8,500-10,000	7,700-9,000	4,400-5,200
Neon R/T	11,000-12,500	9,900-11,300	5,900-6,800
SRT-4	14,000-15,500	12,700-14,100	8,500-9,500

For detailed information on this vehicle visit
http://used.consumerguide.com and enter code **2372**

2002-03 DODGE RAM 1500 PICKUP

CLASS: Full-size pickup truck
BUILT IN: Mexico, USA
PROS: Instruments/controls
• Trailer-towing capability
CONS: Fuel economy
• Ride (w/20-inch wheels)

EVALUATION: A V6 engine in the half-ton Ram feels labored under heavy load, particularly when passing or climbing hills. The 4.7 V8 has ample power; a 2WD regular-cab Ram with manual shift accelerated to 60 mph in 8.8 seconds. Still, only the 5.9 V8 feels really strong in these heavy trucks.

A test SLT Plus Quad Cab 4WD with the biggest engine averaged just 11.9 mpg. With 4WD and automatic, a Quad Cab with the 4.7 V8 averaged 12.6 mpg, and the overworked V6 should return no more than 15-16 mpg in daily driving. A slightly lighter 2WD version will do a little better. All engines use regular-grade fuel.

No full-size pickup rides really smoothly, but a Ram with 17-inch wheels is among the best in class despite mild bounding over big dips and crests, and some vertical jiggle on bumpy pavement. Available 20-inch wheels turn the ride uncomfortably busy, with abrupt vertical motions over even slightly rippled surfaces. Try before you buy.

Steering/handling is good for a full-size pickup. Body lean is fairly well-controlled, and grip adequate. New rack-and-pinion steering pays dividends in precise road feel. Standard all-disc brakes furnish more than ample stopping power in routine use, though pedal modulation isn't the best.

Cabins are impressively hushed for a truck, with some wind rush at highway speed but only modest tire noise. The V6 is raucous when worked hard, which it often needs to be. The V8s emit a muted rumble while cruising, a pleasing roar under hard acceleration.

Instruments and controls are clear and mostly handy in a simple layout, though climate and audio controls are a reach for the driver. New 4WD dashboard controls are similarly distant, but more convenient than the standard floor lever. Dash-top vents cast distracting windshield reflections.

Spacious up front even for very tall adults, the Ram has a center floor hump that protrudes into passenger foot space. Seats are fairly comfortable, but too flat for ideal support. Power-adjustable pedals improve comfort and help shorter drivers position themselves a safe distance from the steering-wheel airbag. Doors are heavy, and 4x4s have an extremely high step-up.

Quad Cab models offer good rear head room but won't feel roomy unless front seats are more than halfway forward. Otherwise, taller adults' knees press against seatbacks. The rear cabin is wide enough for three, though the floor hump limits a center rider's foot clearance.

Generous storage is provided between regular-cab seats. Quad Cabs' rear seat cushions fold up to expose storage bins or a handy available fold-out steel load floor.

VALUE FOR THE MONEY: The previous Ram was a sound design, made popular by attention-grabbing "big-rig" styling. The current model is better in every way—performance, comfort, solidity—and merits attention from every full-size pickup shopper.

TROUBLE SPOTS

Hood/trunk: The hood may have dents, or low spots, from how it was glued down at the factory. Melting the glue with a heat gun generally relieves the dents. (2002)

Rough idle: The 4.7L Hemi engine may idle too slowly when coming to a stop in gear requiring an update to the powertrain computer software. (2002)

Seat: The power seats may be loose and rock or chuggle when accelerating or braking, requiring replacement of the seat track(s). (2002)

Water leak: A water leak at the grab handle on the A-pillar (the section between the windshield and door) is likely due to a leak in the roof seam or the retainer that holds the door seal in place, while a leak at the rear window requires resealing from the inside. (2002)

AVERAGE REPLACEMENT COSTS

A/C Compressor	$1,035	CV Joints	$845
Alternator	455	Exhaust System	390
Automatic Trans.	1,615	Radiator	575
Brakes	395	Shocks and/or Struts	1,065
Clutch	455	Timing Chain/Belt	515

NHTSA RECALL HISTORY

2002 w/4WD: Rear axle flange weld could fatigue and allow brake caliper assembly to rotate resulting in loss of braking ability. Dealers will install rear brake caliper reinforcements on the rear axle assemblies. **2002:** Detent on exterior mirror may lose functionality resulting in restricted rearward vision. Dealers will install a kit to correct this condition. **2002:** Incorrect terminal for HVAC blower motor circuit could cause the blower motor to become inoperative. Dealers will install a wiring harness overlay to correct this condition.

PRICES

	Good	Average	Poor
2002 Quad Cab 2WD	$15,500-18,500	$14,100-16,800	$9,900-11,800
Quad Cab 4WD	18,000-21,000	16,600-19,300	11,500-13,400
Regular-cab 2WD	11,200-14,500	10,100-13,100	6,000-7,800
Regular-cab 4WD	13,500-16,000	12,300-14,600	8,000-9,400
2003 Quad Cab 2WD	17,500-21,500	16,100-19,800	11,200-13,800
Quad Cab 4WD	20,500-25,500	18,900-23,500	13,300-16,600
Regular-cab 2WD	13,000-18,000	11,800-16,400	7,500-10,400
Regular-cab 4WD	16,000-21,000	14,600-19,100	10,200-13,400

For detailed information on this vehicle visit
http://used.consumerguide.com and enter code **4502**

1994-01 DODGE RAM PICKUP

CLASS: Full-size pickup truck

BUILT IN: Mexico, USA

PROS: Acceleration (V8, V10) • Optional 4-wheel antilock brakes • Interior room • Cargo and towing ability

CONS: Acceleration (V6) • Fuel economy • Noise • Ride

EVALUATION: Acceleration is more than adequate with the 5.2-liter V8, which delivered average fuel economy of 14.4 mpg. We don't recommend a V6 for heavy-duty work. A burly Cummins turbodiesel is also available, but not too many folks really need that much pull. You don't get neck-snapping pickup with the V10, but it does propel the Ram with more authority than any V8, and generates less noise than expected. Gas mileage is dismal, however: just 10 mpg in mostly city travel. A turbodiesel delivered 14.6 mpg, but is slower in standing-start acceleration than a gas engine, and idles as roughly as a big rig.

Even with a base suspension, a Ram 1500 can get bouncy over dips and bumps when the bed is empty. Turns may be taken with good grip and balance, and gusty crosswinds have little effect on directional stability. Ride quality in a 2500-series is undeniably stiff. Four-wheel antilock braking brings this pickup to a halt with fine control. Engine and road noise are modest for a truck, but wind roar around front roof pillars is a problem.

Space is ample for three-across seating. The cab has plenty of space behind the seat, making it possible to recline seatbacks—a rarity in full-size pickups. The seatback center folds into an armrest that doubles as a compartmented console. Opening the large padded lid to gain access to the compartments, however, is not so easy while driving. Three can sit abreast in the back of a Club Cab, but the seat cushion is too short to offer real thigh support, and rear leg room is no better than in a compact car.

Gauges are plainly marked; controls near at hand and logical. Three simple knobs operate the climate control. Most controls are lit at night. A slide-out holder is big enough to carry two 16-ounce beverage containers, but it obstructs the radio controls when in use.

VALUE FOR THE MONEY: All told, the impressive Ram is as accommodating and refined as any Ford or General Motors rival. Even if you're leaning toward another brand, it's a good idea to test-drive a Ram before buying any full-size pickup.

TROUBLE SPOTS

Air conditioner: If the air conditioner gradually stops cooling and/or the airflow from the vents decreases, the computer (PCM) may not be sending a signal to the compressor clutch relay to cycle off, which causes the A/C evaporator to freeze up. (1994-95)

Automatic transmission: If the transmission will not engage when first started, chances are the torque converter is draining down. A check valve in the fluid line leading to the transmission cooler will fix the problem. (1994)

Automatic transmission: If the transmission won't upshift in cool weather, it is probably due to defective cast iron seal rings in the governor drive. (1994)

Suspension noise: A rattle or clunk from the front can often be traced to the sway bar links where they attach to the sway bar. (1994-95)

Transmission leak: Automatic transmission fluid leaks from the speed sensor in the transmission. (1994)

AVERAGE REPLACEMENT COSTS

A/C Compressor	$380	Exhaust System	$260
Alternator	295	Radiator	325
Automatic Trans.	795	Shocks and/or Struts	230
Brakes	295	Timing Chain/Belt	235
Clutch	610	Universal Joints	225

NHTSA RECALL HISTORY

1994 4WD: Front suspension attachment to axle may not be adequately tightened; can cause axle vibration. **1994 BR1500/2500 w/no rear bumpers:** Does not meet rear-impact test requirements, and increases the risk of fuel spill. **1994:** Component within passenger-side seatbelt-buckle assembly shatters, causing belt to release. **1994:** Seatback-release-latch lever might remain in released position. **1994-95 2500/3500:** Front spring/shock towers on certain trucks can crack and eventually separate from vehicle frame. **1994-95:** Lower steering shaft can separate from upper shaft if the retaining plastic pins and metal clip break; can result in loss of vehicle control. **1994-95:** While making a turn, extra keys in keyring can lodge in holes in back of steering wheel. **1994-96 w/diesel:** The throttle cable could unravel (fray) or break, resulting in a loss of throttle control. **1994-96 w/gasoline engine:** Valve on fuel tank can allow fuel to leak onto ground; could result in fire. **1994-96:** Ignition switch and wiring on certain trucks could overheat. **1994-97:** Under certain high-load conditions, fluid line could separate from transmission; fluid may then spray onto exhaust manifold. **1994-99 w/V10 engine, manual transmission, 4WD:** Under sustained maximum load, while driving up steep grade in 4WD low range in hot ambient conditions, hydraulic clutch line temperature can become excessive and possibly rupture. **1994-99:** Secondary hood-latch rod can bind and prevent engagement. **1995-96 w/diesel engine:** Vacuum hose may deteriorate and partially collapse, possibly reducing power-brake assist. **1996 w/6800- or 9000-pound GVW rating:** Tire/wheel specification information on certification label indicates smaller tire than is required. **1997 w/diesel engine:** Exhaust pipe may contact, or be too near, dash-panel silencer pad, causing smoldering and igniting of adjacent materials. **1997-01:** Sound-deadening material inside the steering wheel could become detached from the cover and housing causing the the driver-airbag system to become disabled. The airbag-warning lamp will illuminate on the instrument panel. **1998 w/5.9-liter diesel engine:** Intermittent high engine-idle condition can occur, due to malfunction of vehicle speed sensor. **1998 w/5.9-liter diesel engine:** Low-pressure supply tube between filter and high-pressure pump can fracture, allowing fuel to leak. **1998 w/V10 or heavy-duty 5.9-liter gas V8:** Exhaust-system heat-shield attaching screw is too close to fuel line, which can rub against the screw, possibly causing fuel leakage. **1998:** Bolts used to attach cab and core support to frame may have been improperly hardened; can allow cab to separate from frame. **1998:** Brake-rotor material strength on some trucks is not sufficient, causing hub fatigue fracture that can result in crack propagation and, ultimately, in wheel separation. **1998:** Front-seatbelt buckles were not properly riveted to support strap. **1998-00 w/optional trailer hitch:** Trailer-hitch side brackets may lack sufficient strength, and could fatigue and fracture in area where hitch mounts to frame. **1999:** The front-seatbelt retractor does not comply with the requirements of the standard. If the retractor does not work properly, it will not adequately protect occupants in the event of a crash. **1999:** Underbody hydraulic clutch line heat shield on some trucks is too short, allowing line material to be directly exposed to exhaust temperatures. **2000:** During full-lock turns, it is possible for the tire or wheel to contact the brake hose/ABS sensor wire assembly. Continued contact can result in wire damage and/or a hole in the brake line and reduced braking effectiveness. **2000:** Welds at right lower control-arm bracket to axle-tube attachment on a few trucks may have inadequate fatigue life; could result in separation. **2000-01:** Some of the owner's manuals for these vehicles are missing instructions for properly attaching a child restraint system's tether strap to the tether anchorage. **2001 Quad Cab w/camper:** Spacer plate could lead to deformation of the upper spring plate during assembly of the axle to the vehicle, resulting in a soft joint and possible loss of vehicle control.

PRICES

	Good	Average	Poor
1994 Ram 1500 pickup	$3,200-5,500	$2,500-4,300	$800-1,300
Ram 2500 pickup	5,000-7,300	4,300-6,200	2,000-2,900
1995 Ram 1500 pickup	3,700-7,000	3,000-5,700	1,100-2,000
Ram 2500 pickup	5,700-8,000	4,900-6,900	2,300-3,300
1996 Ram 1500 pickup	4,300-8,500	3,500-7,000	1,500-2,900
Ram 2500 pickup	6,500-9,500	5,700-8,400	2,900-4,300
1997 Ram 1500 pickup	4,900-9,500	4,200-8,100	1,900-3,700
Ram 2500 pickup	7,200-11,500	6,400-10,200	3,500-5,600
1998 Ram 1500 pickup	5,600-11,500	4,800-9,900	2,300-4,700
Ram 2500 pickup	8,000-13,200	7,200-11,900	4,100-6,700
1999 Ram 1500 pickup	6,400-13,000	5,600-11,400	2,800-5,700
Ram 2500 pickup	9,000-14,500	8,100-13,100	4,700-7,500
2000 Ram 1500 pickup	7,200-14,500	6,400-12,900	3,500-7,100
Ram 2500 pickup	10,000-16,300	9,000-14,700	5,200-8,500
2001 Ram 1500 pickup	8,000-15,500	7,200-14,000	4,100-7,900
Ram 2500 pickup	11,200-17,500	10,100-15,800	6,000-9,500

For detailed information on this vehicle visit
http://used.consumerguide.com and enter code **2026**

1990-94 DODGE SHADOW

CLASS: Subcompact car

BUILT IN: USA

PROS: Acceleration (V6, Turbo) • Antilock brakes • Cargo room • Ride/handling

CONS: Engine noise (4-cylinder) • Rear-seat room

EVALUATION: Performance is listless with the basic 2.2-liter engine, which is on the noisy side. Action is somewhat better—and smoother—with the 2.5-liter four, which doesn't consume much more fuel, either. It's a better choice with automatic, in particular, but by no means devoid of noise. Either turbo engine delivers swift acceleration, but it's accompanied by plenty of raucous behavior beneath the hood. The V6 engine is smooth and flexible, making a Shadow downright frisky when coupled to manual shift. Lacking an overdrive gear, the 3-speed automatic isn't the best choice for highway gas mileage and quiet cruising.

The standard suspension is firm for a domestic car. Handling beats most small cars, even in base form, and Shadows produce a stable highway ride. An ES version is tauter, but not harsh over most pavement surfaces. Quick-ratio power steering has good feel and centers well.

Interiors are nicely packaged, with reclining front bucket seats, tachometer, and gauges. Rear-seat room could be better but folding the seatbacks creates a generous cargo hold. Convertibles displayed some cowl shake and body flex even when new, but not to a troubling degree.

VALUE FOR THE MONEY: Assembly quality doesn't match that of Japanese competitors, and Shadows aren't the most refined small cars around. Some might call even them mechanically crude. Still, Dodge's subcompact is a solid vehicle that looks good, performs well, and costs considerably less.

TROUBLE SPOTS

Air conditioner: If the air conditioner gradually stops cooling and/or the airflow from the vents decreases, the computer (PCM) may not be sending a signal to the compressor clutch relay to cycle off, which causes the A/C evaporator to freeze up. (1991-94)

Alternator belt: Deep snow could knock the serpentine belt off the pulleys of a 3.0-liter engine. Installing a shield will solve the problem. (1991-94)

Automatic transmission: Bad seals in the transmission lead to premature friction component wear. (1993-94)

Automatic transmission: 41TE or 42LE automatic transaxles could take several seconds to engage at startup because of a problem with the valve body. (1993-94)

Automatic transmission: Transmission shudder under light to moderate acceleration could be caused by a leaking front trans pump due to a worn bushing. (1990-94)

DODGE

Cold-starting problems: 2.2- or 2.5-liter engines may idle rough or stumble when first started unless a revised intake manifold (with an "X" cast into the number 1 runner) was installed (1992) or a revised computer (PCM) was installed (1992-93) or the computer was reprogrammed. (1994)

Engine noise: The motor mount on the left side of the engine tends to break. (1992-93)

Oil consumption: Oil consumption and smoke from the exhaust at idle and deceleration on 3.0-liter engines is caused by exhaust valve guides that slide out of the heads. (1992-93)

AVERAGE REPLACEMENT COSTS

A/C Compressor	$450	CV Joints	$445
Alternator	280	Exhaust System	260
Automatic Trans.	675	Radiator	325
Brakes	250	Shocks and/or Struts	330
Clutch	625	Timing Chain/Belt	150

NHTSA RECALL HISTORY

1990: The engine valve cover gasket may become dislocated and allow an engine oil leak. **1991:** Both airbag system front impact sensors may not be secured to mounting brackets, so airbag would not deploy. **1991:** Front disc brake caliper guide pin bolts may not be adequately tightened and could loosen, which could cause reduced braking effectiveness that might result in an accident. **1991-92:** Lower driver's seatback attaching bolt can fail and separate. **1991-92:** Steering wheel mounting armature can develop cracks and separate from the center hub attachment to the steering column; can result in loss of vehicle control. **1991-94 2-door:** Bolt that attaches recliner mechanism to driver's seatback on certain cars could break; may result in seatback suddenly reclining. **1992:** Zinc plating of some upper steering column shaft coupling bolts caused hydrogen embrittlement and breakage of the bolt.

PRICES

	Good	Average	Poor
1990 Shadow	$1,000-1,400	$600-800	$100
1991 Shadow	1,100-1,600	700-1,000	100-200
Shadow Convertible	1,700-2,300	1,100-1,500	300
1992 Shadow	1,300-2,000	800-1,300	200
Shadow Convertible	2,100-2,700	1,500-1,900	400-500
1993 Shadow	1,500-2,100	1,000-1,400	200-300
Shadow Convertible	2,400-3,000	1,700-2,200	500-600
1994 Shadow	1,800-2,500	1,200-1,700	300-400

For detailed information on this vehicle visit
http://used.consumerguide.com and enter code **2027**

1990-95 DODGE SPIRIT

CLASS: Compact car

BUILT IN: Mexico, USA

PROS: Acceleration (V6, Turbo) • Antilock brakes (optional later models) • Passenger and cargo room

CONS: Engine noise (4-cylinder) • Rear-seat comfort • Ride • Road noise • Wind noise

EVALUATION: Acceleration with the base four is barely adequate and particularly meager when passing/merging. But gas mileage is impressive—a 4-cylinder Spirit averaged 22.3 mpg in mixed expressway/highway driving. The V6 is smooth and responsive, but its 4-speed automatic transmission shifts too quickly into higher gears, and also holds backs on downshifts when trying to pass. A 3-speed automatic is less frugal, but operates more dependably. Some turbos suffer lag that detracts from initial acceleration, but they're strong and swift after that opening period. Revisions for 1991 improved low-speed response, but the engine is noisy and coarse. Takeoffs are smooth and vigorous with the Spirit R/T, which suffers minimal turbo lag and offers balanced performance.

Firmer shock absorbers than those used on base and midlevel Acclaims yield a tauter ride and sharper steering/handling. The suspension does a good job of controlling bouncing on wavy roads, but bangs and clunks on rough surfaces. Road and wind noise intrude at highway speeds, too.

Roomy interiors for a car this size offer top-notch visibility. Getting in and out is a snap, and the big trunk with a flat floor is easy to load. Gauges are readable on a dashboard that's nicely laid out. Front seats feel fine, and rear head/knee room is adequate; but rear cushions are too low and short for comfort.

VALUE FOR THE MONEY: Solid, spacious, and competent, a Spirit might fail to stimulate anyone's spirit—unless it happens to be the wheel-twisting R/T, that is. Even in tamer form, Dodge's practical domestic sedan is worth a look.

TROUBLE SPOTS

Air conditioner: If the air conditioner gradually stops cooling and/or the airflow from the vents decreases, the computer (PCM) may not be sending a signal to the compressor clutch relay to cycle off, which causes the AC evaporator to freeze up. (1991-95)

Alternator belt: Deep snow could knock the serpentine belt off the pulleys of the 3.0-liter engine. Installing a shield will solve the problem. (1991-95)

Automatic transmission: Bad seals in the transmission lead to premature friction component wear. (1993-95)

Automatic transmission: Transmission shudder under light to moderate acceleration could be caused by a leaking front trans pump due to a worn bushing. (1990-95)

DODGE

Automatic transmission: 41TE or 42LE automatic transaxles could take several seconds to engage at startup because of a problem with the valve body. (1993-95)

Cold-starting problems: 2.2- or 2.5-liter engines may idle rough or stumble unless a revised intake manifold (with an "X" cast into the number 1 runner) was installed (1992), or a revised computer (PCM) was installed (1992-93), or the computer was reprogrammed. (1994)

Engine noise: The motor mount on the left side of the engine tends to break. (1992-93)

Oil consumption and exhaust smoke: Oil consumption and smoke from the exhaust at idle and deceleration on 3.0-liter engines is caused by exhaust valve guides that slide out of the heads. (1990-93)

AVERAGE REPLACEMENT COSTS

A/C Compressor	$415	Exhaust System	$320
Alternator	315	Radiator	335
Automatic Trans.	905	Shocks and/or Struts	340
Brakes	250	Timing Chain/Belt	290
CV Joints	660		

NHTSA RECALL HISTORY

1990: The engine valve cover gasket may become dislocated and allow an engine oil leak. **1991:** Both airbag system front impact sensors may not be secured to mounting brackets, so airbag would not deploy. **1991:** Front disc brake caliper guide pin bolts may not be adequately tightened and could loosen. **1992:** Zinc plating of some upper steering column shaft coupling bolts caused hydrogen embrittlement and breakage of the bolt. **1994:** Seatbelt assembly on small number of cars may fail in accident, increasing risk of injury.

PRICES	Good	Average	Poor
1990 Spirit	$1,000-1,500	$600-900	$100-200
1991 Spirit	1,200-1,700	700-1,100	100-200
Spirit R/T	1,700-2,300	1,100-1,500	300
1992 Spirit	1,400-2,000	900-1,300	200
Spirit R/T	2,100-2,700	1,500-1,900	400-500
1993 Spirit	1,700-2,300	1,100-1,500	300
1994 Spirit	2,000-2,600	1,400-1,800	300-400
1995 Spirit	2,400-3,100	1,700-2,200	500-600

For detailed information on this vehicle visit
http://used.consumerguide.com and enter code **2029**

1995-00 DODGE STRATUS

CG BEST BUY

CLASS: Midsize car

BUILT IN: USA

PROS: Acceleration
• Antilock brakes (ES)
• Passenger and cargo room
• Ride • Steering/handling

CONS: Noise • Rear visibility

EVALUATION: Although Stratus has the exterior dimensions of a compact car, it offers the interior room of a midsize model. In fact, there's plenty of leg space fore and aft, and sufficient rear-seat width for three medium-size adults to travel without feeling like sardines.

Visibility is great to all angles except the rear. The high rear parcel shelf makes it hard to see out the back window. A large trunk with a flat floor and low liftover gives the Stratus good cargo-carrying ability. The driving position is comfortable, and the dashboard layout logical. The sedan's abundant, airy interior is well-designed; however, some trim pieces on the dashboard and door panels look and feel cheap.

Of the several engine choices, we recommend the V6s for their smoother running and livelier acceleration. It's not the quietest engine around, but the 2.5-liter V6 takes off from a standstill with spirit. However, you're likely to experience a long pause before the automatic transmission downshifts for passing. Despite being shy two cylinders, the 2.4-liter 4-cylinder offers nearly as much punch as the V6, though at the expense of some refinement. The 2.0-liter four is noisier and a trifle slower, but gets great mileage with the 5-speed manual.

Stratus rides and handles more like a sports sedan than a typical American car. That means more interior noise and road vibrations than people may be used to. You benefit from agile handling with little body lean and good grip, making it easy to thread along twisting roads. An ES, in particular, takes corners and curves adeptly. Ride comfort is generally good on both models, despite the firmer suspension on the ES, and the Stratus does feel smoother than a Ford Contour.

VALUE FOR THE MONEY: Overall, the large, comfortable interior; moderate price; and attractive styling make the well-equipped Stratus a good buy. Our only reservation might be Chrysler's past reputation for poor build quality.

TROUBLE SPOTS

See the 1990-95 Chrysler Cirrus.

AVERAGE REPLACEMENT COSTS

See the 1990-95 Chrysler Cirrus.

NHTSA RECALL HISTORY

1995: Rear-seatbelt anchors will not withstand loading required by federal standard. **1995-96 w/2.4-liter:** Oil leakage could cause engine-compartment fire. **1995-96 w/ABS:** Corrosion of ABS hydraulic control unit can cause solenoid valves to stick open, so car tends to pull from a straight stop when brakes are applied. **1995-96:** Brake master cylinder can leak fluid, due to damaged seal; warning light will signal impairment prior to partial brake-system loss. **1995-97:** Lower ball joint can separate due to loss of lubrication; could cause loss of control. **1995-98 w/automatic transmission:** If operator presses button to shift out of Park with key in locked position, pin can break; "ignition-park" interlock would then be nonfunctional. **1996-97:** Secondary hood latch spring can disengage if hood is slammed. **1998-99:** Right rear brake tube can contact exhaust system clamp and wear a hole in it; tube could then leak, reducing braking effectiveness. **2000:** Incorrect child lock instruction label could cause confusion as to whether the childproof safety lock was activated. **2000:** Some of the owner's manuals for these vehicles are missing instructions for properly attaching a child restraint system's tether strap to the tether anchorage. **2000:** The right front-brake tube may get damaged.

PRICES

	Good	Average	Poor
1995 Stratus	$2,000-2,600	$1,400-1,800	$300-400
Stratus ES	2,300-2,900	1,700-2,100	400-600
1996 Stratus	2,400-3,000	1,700-2,200	500-600
Stratus ES	2,700-3,400	2,000-2,600	600-700
1997 Stratus	2,900-3,500	2,200-2,700	700-800
Stratus ES	3,300-4,000	2,600-3,200	800-1,000
1998 Stratus	3,400-4,000	2,700-3,200	900-1,000
Stratus ES	3,800-4,500	3,100-3,600	1,100-1,400
1999 Stratus	4,300-5,000	3,600-4,200	1,500-1,700
Stratus ES	5,000-5,700	4,300-4,800	2,000-2,300
2000 Stratus ES	6,500-7,500	5,700-6,600	2,900-3,400
Stratus SE	5,500-6,300	4,700-5,400	2,300-2,600

For detailed information on this vehicle visit
http://used.consumerguide.com and enter code **2144**

2001-03 DODGE STRATUS

CLASS: Midsize car
BUILT IN: USA
PROS: Steering/handling
CONS: Acceleration (4-cyl)
• Rear-seat comfort (coupe)
• Rear-seat entry/exit (coupe)

EVALUATION: The new V6 engines used in Stratus and its Sebring cousins took a clear step forward in both power and refinement. The Chrysler-made 2.7-liter in sedans feels markedly smoother than the coupe's Mitsubishi 3.0—though not quite as quick. Compared to domestic and import rivals with larger V6s, any V6 Stratus has acceleration that's easily adequate for most needs. Quickest of the lot, the R/T with manual shift could reach 60 mph in 7.5 seconds. Four-cylinder models are noisier and slower, even though both 2.4-liters are an improvement over their predecessors.

Regardless of engine, automatic transmission performance is improved, with smoother upshifts and reasonably prompt downshifts. Optional Autostick is a welcome addition to coupe models, and the Stratus ES, somewhat improving throttle responses. Sedans with V6 engines have averaged 17.5 to 18.3 mpg, while an R/T coupe with stick shift averaged 19.2 mpg. Manual gearboxes, though, fail to match the imports for mechanical smoothness.

Uplevel models handle noticeably better than base cars, with little penalty in ride quality. All feel competent on twisty roads, with better grip and less body lean than a Camry, and comfortably absorb most bumps. Coupes are slightly more nimble than the sedans, but don't filter out bad pavement as well. Low-profile 17-inch tires and a firmer suspension make the R/T feel agitated on all but smooth pavement.

Steering feedback is good, but four-cylinder versions have excessive power assistance. Stopping power with ABS is a high point, feeling sure and stable, with good pedal modulation. No Stratus suppresses tire noise completely.

Overall refinement still isn't up to that of Japanese-brand rivals, but these cars are fairly quiet. Drivetrain vibration is greatly reduced from the previous generation. Suppression of wind noise is admirable.

Stratus sedans have airy, uncommonly roomy interiors for their exterior size, despite a slight loss of rear head clearance compared to prior models. With only a little squeezing, three adults can fit in the sedan's back seat. They'll enjoy generous leg room, but head space is a tad snug. Coupes have three rear seatbelts, but even two adults will feel crowded, the seat cushion is uncomfortably low, and seatbacks recline too much.

Sedan gauges are clear and readable, but until 2003, coupe instruments echo the gimmicky design in Mitsubishi two-doors and coupe drivers sit low to the floor.

Getting in or out of the sedans is easy, but a low roofline hampers entry/exit to the coupes' front seat and limits head room for taller folks. Interference from the front seatbelts worsens getting into the back. Cargo space is average for the class, though coupe trunklid hinges dip into the luggage bay. Interior storage is adequate in two-door models.

VALUE FOR THE MONEY: Despite improvements in driveline smoothness and overall refinement, the latest Stratus sedans and coupes lack the polished feel of some import-brand rivals. Still, both body styles offer competitive value and sedans rank as sporty-feeling family carriers. Each model fulfills its mission, and the R/T appeals for its performance image.

DODGE

TROUBLE SPOTS

Audio system: If the radio, instrument or trip computer lights flicker when the turn signals or high beams are switched on, the multifunction (turn-signal stalk) switch may be bad. (2001-02)

Brake noise: The brakes may squeak on coupes with 3.0L engine and 15-inch brakes and is repaired with revised brake-caliper mounting brackets. (2001-03)

Dashboard lights: The powertrain computer may mistakenly detect engine misfires and illuminate the check-engine light. The compute should be reprogrammed. (2001) Sedans should get spark plugs with a hotter heat range installed as well. (2002)

Electrical problem: An intermittent short in the dome light switch blows fuses that protect the radio, dome light, courtesy light, vanity mirrors, remote keyless entry and the compass and clock on the coupe. (2001-02)

Suspension noise: The rear suspension makes a popping and squawking noise on the sedan that is corrected by replacing the upper control arms with revised ones. (2001)

AVERAGE REPLACEMENT COSTS

A/C Compressor	$475	CV Joints	$770
Alternator	360	Exhaust System	310
Automatic Trans.	1,110	Radiator	450
Brakes	360	Shocks and/or Struts	590
Clutch	570	Timing Chain/Belt	280

NHTSA RECALL HISTORY

2001 w/automatic transmission: Defective transaxle cooler hoses could lead to transmission-fluid leak. Smoke and drivability problems could result. Dealers will replace the cooler hoses. **2001:** Crankshaft position-sensor harness could ground with a protective shield causing engine to stall. Dealers will reroute the harness. **2001:** Defective passenger airbags could separate in an accident. Dealers will replace the passenger airbag. **2001:** Fuel return hose does not contain the desired ozone protection. Dealers will replace the fuel return hose. **2001:** Incorrect driver-seat mounting bolts may cause result in driver injury in an accident. Dealers will inspect and replace affected parts. **2001:** Smoke or burning smell might come from map lights due to contact with insulation material. Dealers will remove insulation material in affected vehicles. **2001:** Some owner's manuals are missing instructions for installing child seats. Owners will be provided with an addendum to the owners manual. **2001:** Steering-gear assembly nut may not be properly tightened causing loss of steering control. Dealers will inspect and replace affected parts.

PRICES

	Good	Average	Poor
2001 Stratus R/T coupe	$11,000-12,000	$9,900-10,800	$5,900-6,500
Stratus coupe	8,300-9,000	7,500-8,100	4,300-4,700
Stratus sedan	7,500-9,700	6,800-8,700	3,800-4,900
2002 Stratus R/T	12,200-13,500	11,000-12,200	6,800-7,600
Stratus coupe	9,700-10,700	8,700-9,600	5,000-5,600
Stratus sedan	8,600-11,000	7,700-9,900	4,500-5,700

2003 Stratus R/T	$14,000-15,500	$12,700-14,100	$8,500-9,500
Stratus coupe	11,500-12,800	10,400-11,500	6,300-7,000
Stratus sedan	10,000-13,000	9,000-11,700	5,200-6,800

For detailed information on this vehicle visit
http://used.consumerguide.com and enter code **4478**

1992-96 EAGLE SUMMIT WAGON

CLASS: Minivan

BUILT IN: Japan

PROS: Antilock brakes (optional) • All-wheel-drive traction (AWD) • Passenger and cargo room

CONS: Acceleration (w/automatic transmission) • Noise

EVALUATION: Compact size, great visibility, and good maneuverability at low speeds make the Summit Wagon a good urban vehicle. On the downside, you get lots of body lean in quick turns because of the vehicle's tall body and narrow track. Grip is poor with the base model's skinny tires, but improves with the LX wagon's wider rubber, and with the AWD version. Even if tight corners produce marked body roll and tire squealing, the Summit Wagon's ride is pliant—good over all surfaces. Braking feels strong and balanced, even without antilocking.

Acceleration is adequate—but no more—with the base engine and manual shift, but that engine lacks sufficient torque to keep the automatic transmission from frequent gear-hunting. It feels particularly underpowered with automatic when the wagon is loaded with passengers and cargo. The stronger 2.4-liter engine is a better all-around choice, with more torque for better throttle response and pulling power. The standard 5-speed manual gearbox shifts smoothly, and has a light clutch. The wagon's automatic transmission downshifts quickly to maintain speed on hills or to pass, but its gear changes are rather harsh.

Noise levels are high, which makes highway driving more tiring. Wind noise and road rumble are problems. Base models, in particular, are not well insulated against engine and wind sounds.

Entry and exit are eased by the wagon's low step-in height. The minivan-style sliding right-rear passenger door opens and closes via a unique inner-rail mechanism, which eliminates the bodyside channel that's necessary with traditional sliding doors. Passenger room is plentiful. Cargo space behind the backseat is tight, but the rear bench folds flat and tumbles forward to create a flat load floor ahead of the tailgate.

Seating positions are comfortably chairlike for great visibility out of an expansive greenhouse. However, the driver's seat might be too high for some shorter drivers. Gauges and controls are simple and logically laid out.

EAGLE

VALUE FOR THE MONEY: This versatile "mini-minivan" is worth a look if you need more practical utility than a small station wagon can provide, but don't want a regular compact van.

TROUBLE SPOTS

Automatic transmission: Delayed shifts from second to third, or third to fourth when the transmission fluid is cold, may appear to be a malfunction, but it is not. (1993-94)

Doors: The sliding doors may be hard to open due to a variety of problems including a faulty latch connecting rod clip, rear door lock holder, or striker that is out of adjustment. (1992-95)

Doors: The sliding door goes out of adjustment causing it to hit the rear of the front door. Installing shims will fix the problem. (1992)

Information stickers/paperwork: Replacement Vehicle Emission Control Information decals were sent to original owners because the original 1.8-liter engine valve clearance specs were wrong on vehicles built before mid-December 1992. (1993)

Suspension noise: The front stabilizer ball joint is prone to premature wear causing a rattling or popping noise while driving. (1992-93)

AVERAGE REPLACEMENT COSTS

A/C Compressor	$915	CV Joints	$710
Alternator	770	Exhaust System	500
Automatic Trans.	960	Radiator	390
Brakes	260	Shocks and/or Struts	700
Clutch	475	Timing Chain/Belt	165

NHTSA RECALL HISTORY

1992-93: Over time, abrading force on the lower edges of the chamber for the moving cable that controls driver's shoulder belt may be sufficient to allow cable to drop; could cause shoulder-belt anchorage to become stuck. **1992-96 w/AWD:** Lockup of transfer case can occur, due to insufficient lubrication.

PRICES

	Good	Average	Poor
1992 AWD Wagon	$2,000-2,500	$1,400-1,800	$300-400
Summit Wagon	1,800-2,300	1,200-1,600	100-300
1993 AWD Wagon	2,400-3,000	1,700-2,200	500-600
Summit Wagon	2,100-2,700	1,500-1,900	400-500
1994 AWD Wagon	2,800-3,400	2,100-2,600	600-700
Summit Wagon	2,400-3,000	1,700-2,200	500-600
1995 AWD Wagon	3,200-3,800	2,500-3,000	800-1,000
Summit Wagon	2,700-3,300	2,000-2,500	600-700
1996 AWD Wagon	3,500-4,200	2,800-3,400	900-1,100
Summit Wagon	3,000-3,600	2,300-2,800	700-800

For detailed information on this vehicle visit
http://used.consumerguide.com and enter code **2146**

CONSUMER GUIDE®

1995-98 EAGLE TALON

CLASS: Sporty coupe

BUILT IN: USA

PROS: Acceleration (TSi, TSi AWD) • Antilock brakes (optional) • AWD traction (AWD models) • Steering/handling

CONS: Acceleration (base/ESi auto) • Rear-seat room • Road noise

EVALUATION: A stiffer body structure makes this Talon feel more solid than before, and also provides better isolation from mechanical vibrations. The longer wheelbase and wider stance of this generation impart a more secure feel on the road. Especially in performance-oriented trim, Talons hug the pavement smartly and stay flat through curves, maneuvering with agility and nimbleness.

These Talons aren't too much heavier than their predecessors, but since horsepower grew little, performance isn't noticeably better. An ESi performs reasonably well with the manual gearbox; but below 3500 rpm, the base 4-cylinder engine feels weak. Lack of power is even more obvious with the automatic transmission, when you need to pass or merge into fast-moving traffic.

The turbocharged engine feels strong with either transmission but suffers some "turbo lag," in which power arrives a moment or two after the throttle is floored. Even so, acceleration with manual shift is super from a standstill, if a bit less invigorating at higher speeds, when needed for passing and merging.

Smooth-shifting in general, the 5-speed manual gearbox can get clanky at times, and resist entry into the lower gears. The Talon's clutch engages neatly, in a sporty manner. Ride quality diminishes greatly over bad pavement in stiffly sprung turbo models, which become bouncy and choppy when rolling through rough spots. Even on the highway, the ride can get a bit rough. Road noise is prominent on all Talons, but engine noise isn't bad. Braking prowess is excellent with the available antilocking setup.

Despite slightly greater shoulder room, there's no abundance of front-seat space, though six-footers have adequate room. The optional sunroof cuts into front headroom, however. The small rear seat is best suited for pre-schoolers—though most sport-coupe rivals are little better. The hatchback layout makes the most of available cargo space, but items stored in the rear are not as secure as in cars with a regular trunk.

Over-the-shoulder visibility could be better. The turbo model's monstrous rear spoiler blocks part of the rearward view, but most drivers can see just about everything, peering either above or below that obstacle. Despite tiny auxiliary gauges, the control and instrument layout in a driver-oriented cockpit is good.

VALUE FOR THE MONEY: Talons can be fun to drive, but so can many rivals. Apart from the TSi's all-wheel-drive capability, nearly all of Talon's virtues can be found in several similarly priced sports coupes, such as the Ford Probe, Mazda MX-6, and Acura Integra.

EAGLE

TROUBLE SPOTS
See the 1995-99 Mitsubishi Eclipse.

AVERAGE REPLACEMENT COSTS
See the 1995-99 Mitsubishi Eclipse.

NHTSA RECALL HISTORY
1995-96: Rubber boots on lower ball joint may be damaged, allowing dirt and water intrusion, which can cause excessive wear and possible separation. **1995-96:** Tank gaskets for fuel pump and/or gauge unit could have been incorrectly installed, allowing fuel or fumes to escape. **1995-98 w/AWD:** Lockup of transfer case can occur, due to insufficient lubrication. **1997:** On small number of cars, improperly welded head restraint support bracket on passenger side can break. **1998:** Dash panel pad can shift, interfering with throttle cable control.

PRICES	Good	Average	Poor
1995 Talon ESi	$3,200-3,800	$2,500-3,000	$800-1,000
Talon TSi	3,800-4,400	3,100-3,600	1,100-1,300
1996 Talon TSi	4,500-5,200	3,700-4,300	1,600-1,900
Talon/ESi	3,500-4,300	2,800-3,400	900-1,200
1997 Talon TSi	5,500-6,500	4,700-5,600	2,300-2,700
Talon/ESi	4,000-4,800	3,300-3,900	1,300-1,500
1998 Talon TSi	6,800-8,000	6,100-7,100	3,200-3,800
Talon/ESi	5,100-6,000	4,300-5,100	2,000-2,400

For detailed information on this vehicle visit
http://used.consumerguide.com and enter code **2145**

1993-97 EAGLE VISION

CLASS: Full-size car

BUILT IN: Canada

PROS: Acceleration (3.5-liter)
• Antilock brakes (optional)
• Passenger and cargo room
• Steering/handling

CONS: Acceleration (3.3-liter) • Climate controls
• Rear visibility

EVALUATION: Acceleration with the 3.3-liter engine is adequate but somewhat sluggish, though the eight horsepower added for '94 helps a bit. With a 3.5-liter engine providing the power, and a Touring Suspension underneath, you can easily forget you're in a large sedan. In that step-up guise, a Vision feels more like a Eurosedan. You get plenty of snap off the line, and highway passing power is excellent. Road noise can intrude and the upgraded suspension pounds a bit over rough pavement, but provides the grip of some sports cars. Taut handling and roadholding are top-notch, especially in that more costly TSi, but its stiff suspension and performance tires make the ride harsh. Some Visions have a Performance suspension that rides even more firmly. The ride in an ESi is a lot more compliant over bumps.

Variable-assist power steering, added for 1994, yields greater road feel at higher speeds. The electronically controlled 4-speed automatic transmission shifts smoothly. Autostick—on some 1996 models—is an innovative unit, fun to operate, but most drivers probably won't bother to use it much.

Major controls, for instance—and even seatbelt buckles—are lit at night for convenience. Rear-seat air ducts have a separate airflow control, and the climate-control system pumps out plenty of hot or cool air. Controls for that system are a stretch, however, mounted at the base of the dashboard. Other controls are high, easy to see and reach.

Vision occupants enjoy generous passenger space, with outstanding rear leg room, plus a roomy trunk. Rear visibility is impaired by a narrow back window, however. Hard plastic interior trim looks cheap and does not feel durable, and several test Visions have suffered minor interior creaks and rattles.

VALUE FOR THE MONEY: Despite a flaw or two, this well-designed member of the "LH" group is worthy of strong consideration, and belongs near the top of the shopping list for a mid- or full-size sedan.

TROUBLE SPOTS
See the 1993-97 Dodge Intrepid.

AVERAGE REPLACEMENT COSTS
See the 1993-97 Dodge Intrepid.

NHTSA RECALL HISTORY

1993 w/3.3-liter engine: O-rings used to seal interface of fuel-injector tubes are insufficiently durable; deterioration can cause fuel leakage, with potential for fire. **1993:** Lower control arm washers in front suspension of some cars can crack and fall off; will cause clunking sound during braking, and eventually result in loss of steering control. **1993-95:** Lower control arm attaching brackets on some cars can crack due to fatigue and separate from engine cradle; transmission halfshaft could then pull out of transaxle. **1993-97 w/3.5-liter engine:** Fuel injection system can leak from O-rings or hairline cracks in fuel-injection rail. **1994:** Right tie rod can rub through automatic-transmission wiring harness, causing short circuit; may result in stalling, or allow engine to start when selector is not in "Park" position.

PRICES

	Good	Average	Poor
1993 Vision ESi	$1,900-2,400	$1,300-1,700	$300-400
Vision TSi	2,100-2,700	1,500-1,900	400-500
1994 Vision ESi	2,200-2,700	1,600-1,900	400-500
Vision TSi	2,500-3,200	1,800-2,300	500-700
1995 Vision ESi	2,600-3,300	1,900-2,400	500-700
Vision TSi	2,900-3,600	2,200-2,700	700-800
1996 Vision ESi	2,900-3,600	2,200-2,700	700-800
Vision TSi	3,400-4,100	2,700-3,200	900-1,100
1997 Vision ESi	3,400-4,100	2,700-3,200	900-1,100
Vision TSi	4,000-4,800	3,300-3,900	1,300-1,500

For detailed information on this vehicle visit
http://used.consumerguide.com and enter code **2031**

1990-97 FORD AEROSTAR

CLASS: Minivan

BUILT IN: USA

PROS: Cargo room (extended-length)
• Optional AWD traction
• Passenger room • Trailer-towing capability

CONS: Entry/exit • Fuel economy • Ride

EVALUATION: The 3.0-liter engine produces adequate muscle, but the extra grunt of a 4.0-liter V6 is welcome, helping to haul around the hardware of the available 4-wheel-drive system. Don't expect great gas mileage with either engine: around 15 mpg in city/suburban driving, or low 20s on the highway.

Poor traction can be a problem in rain or snow with the rear-drive Aerostar. Ride quality is another drawback, even with the Aerostar's long wheelbase. Suspensions are not very compliant, producing a rather harsh experience over bumps, though an Aerostar is stable and well-controlled.

Cabins are roomy. Seven people can sit without squeezing, and the XLT and Eddie Bauer models contain plush and comfortable interior furnishings. Getting into the front seats requires a high step up. Cargo space is unimpressive in standard-size models, when all seats are in place.

VALUE FOR THE MONEY: Aerostar and the Chevrolet Astro/GMC Safari are better suited to heavy-duty work, such as hauling hefty payloads or towing trailers (up to 4800 pounds), than the league-leading front-drive Chrysler minivans.

TROUBLE SPOTS

Air conditioner: Air conditioner compressors are prone to failure if there is not enough A/C oil in the system. (1994-97)

Audio system: Whining noises in the radio speakers is caused by the gas tank fuel pump. An electronic noise filter must be installed on the fuel pump. (1990-96)

Engine noise: The dash panel rattles or buzzes due to interference between the trim on the front pillar and the side quarter glass. (1992-96)

Engine noise: A hammering noise and erratic temperature gauge reading is caused by a weak water pump. A revised pump is available. (1994-97)

Steering noise: A clanging noise comes from the power steering cooler. A replacement will eliminate the noise. (1990-96)

AVERAGE REPLACEMENT COSTS

A/C Compressor	$410	Exhaust System	$445
Alternator	315	Radiator	360
Automatic Trans.	775	Shocks and/or Struts	255
Brakes	305	Timing Chain/Belt	400
Clutch	450	Universal Joints	160

NHTSA RECALL HISTORY

1990 registered in specified states: Upper portion of fuel tank can develop cracks due to extended exposure to high ambient temperatures; fuel vapor or leakage could occur. **1990:** Inability to maintain pressure in master cylinder could increase brake-pedal travel. **1990:** With quad captain's chairs, tilt-forward latch of right-hand seat in second row may release under severe frontal impact. **1990-91:** Ignition switch could short-circuit, causing smoke and possible fire. **1990-91:** When automatic transmission is in Park position, pawl does not always engage park gear. **1992 w/AWD:** Powertrain bending resonance or transfer case output shaft bushing displacement can result in structural failure leading to fluid expulsion, driveshaft separation, or loss of vehicle drive. **1992-97 w/AWD:** Structural failure of transmission and/or transfer case can occur, resulting in fluid expulsion, driveshaft separation, or loss of drive. **1992-97:** During start-up, arcing could potentially cause pitting, which, over time, might create short circuit that leads to overheating and potential fire. **1994-95:** Heat generation in wiring harness to fuel pump assembly can cause electrical short; vehicle could experience loss of power and become immobilized, fuel gauge may be erratic, and possible heat damage could lead to fire. **1995:** Underbody spare tire can contact brake lines, resulting in fracture of line. **1996:** Certification label shows incorrect rear tire inflation pressure. **1996:** When in secondary latched position, driver's door may not sustain specified load. **1997 w/3.0-liter engine:** Accelerator cable may be kinked during installation, causing the core wires to eventually fray with wire strands breaking one at a time.

PRICES	Good	Average	Poor
1990 Aerostar extended	$1,400-2,100	$900-1,300	$200-300
Aerostar regular	1,100-1,800	700-1,100	100-200
1991 Aerostar extended	1,600-2,400	1,100-1,600	200-300
Aerostar regular	1,300-2,100	800-1,300	200-300
1992 Aerostar extended	2,000-2,800	1,400-2,000	300-500
Aerostar regular	1,600-2,400	1,100-1,600	200-300
1993 Aerostar extended	2,300-3,200	1,700-2,300	400-600
Aerostar regular	1,900-2,700	1,300-1,900	300-400
1994 Aerostar extended	2,800-3,700	2,100-2,800	600-800
Aerostar regular	2,200-3,100	1,600-2,200	400-600
1995 Aerostar extended	3,200-4,200	2,500-3,300	800-1,000
Aerostar regular	2,600-3,600	1,900-2,700	500-800
1996 Aerostar extended	4,100-5,300	3,400-4,300	1,400-1,700
Aerostar regular	3,300-4,500	2,600-3,600	800-1,100
1997 Aerostar extended	5,000-6,200	4,300-5,300	2,000-2,500
Aerostar regular	4,000-5,300	3,300-4,300	1,300-1,700

For detailed information on this vehicle visit
http://used.consumerguide.com and enter code **2156**

1995-00 FORD CONTOUR

CLASS: Compact car

BUILT IN: Mexico, USA

PROS: Acceleration (V6)
• Optional antilock brakes
and traction control
• Automatic-transmission
performance
• Steering/handling

CONS: Engine noise (4-cylinder) • Radio controls • Rear-seat room

EVALUATION: Smooth, responsive, and lively in acceleration, the 170-horsepower V6 is more than adequate for all ordinary driving situations. During testing, a V6 Contour accelerated to 60 mph in 9.3 seconds. The 190-horsepower SVT engine is even more powerful, but you really have to work the transmission to get the extra power. By contrast, the noisy 4-cylinder engine feels sluggish when going uphill and requires a heavy throttle foot for brisk acceleration. A V6 Contour with automatic averaged 21.7 mpg. Under similar conditions, the 4-cylinder with automatic did only a little better: 23 mpg, to be exact. Road noise has been prominent on all models.

Precise steering, sporty handling, and a firm ride make a Contour feel more German than American. Most road-testers praised the sporty SE, in particular, for its fun-to-drive qualities, though a few were less enthusiastic about its ride quality.

Front leg room is ample, but back-seat space for adults is barely adequate in 1995 Contours. That shortage of space was slightly improved in '96 models, but remains a drawback. Head room is generous in front and adequate in back.

The modern, attractive dashboard is well-designed, but the stereo has too many small buttons that are difficult to decipher. Large gauges are easy to read. The climate system is controlled by three rotary dials that are clearly labeled and easy to use.

VALUE FOR THE MONEY: Ford took a huge step forward in performance, refinement, and overall execution with its compact sedan. All told, Contour is a formidable rival to Japanese compacts and to the Chrysler Cirrus and Dodge Stratus.

TROUBLE SPOTS

Automatic transmission: The transmission may go into limp-in mode due to a faulty manual lever position sensor. (1995)

Brakes: Ice in the parking brake cables will not allow the parking brake to release or release fully. (1995-97)

Dashboard lights: A slipping drive belt causes a lack of power steering and the charge warning light to glow. A new belt, idler pulley, and a splash kit are needed. (1995-97)

Engine misfire: Lack of acceleration in below 32 degrees Fahrenheit on the 2.5-liter engine is often due to ice on the throttle plate. A revised engine computer prevents the problem. (1995)

Steering problems: If the steering wheel vibrates while idling with the transmission engaged and the A/C running, the steering mass damper, airbag module, and radiator mounts must be replaced. (1995-97)

Transmission noise: Gear clash going into third on the manual transmission can be remedied by a rebuilt input gear shaft and a new shift fork. (1995-97)

AVERAGE REPLACEMENT COSTS

A/C Compressor	$360	CV Joints	$465
Alternator	455	Radiator	345
Automatic Trans.	800	Shocks and/or Struts	345
Brakes	290	Shocks and/or Struts	700
Clutch	750	Timing Chain/Belt	175

NHTSA RECALL HISTORY

1995: Front-seatbelt anchor tabs may be cracked. **1995:** Fuel-tank filler reinforcement can leak. **1995:** If right rear-door window breaks, glass fragments will exceed allowable size. **1995:** Metal shield on plastic fuel-filler pipe can develop static charge during refueling; could serve as ignition source. **1995:** Passenger-airbag's inflator body is cracked and may not inflate properly. **1995-96 w/V6:** Tightening of the engine-cooling fan-motor bearings can result in increased motor torque and higher than normal motor current and accompanying high motor temperatures. **1995-96 w/traction control:** Throttle cables were damaged during assembly, leading to fraying or separation; could prevent engine from returning to idle. **1995-98:** Automatic-transmission control can be damaged if subjected to certain interior cleaning products; gear indicator can deteriorate and incorrectly indicate actual gear position. **1996:** Fuel-filler-pipe vent hose may have less than intended level of ozone resistance, which could result in brittleness and cracking. **1996-97 w/bi-fuel engine:** If natural-gas fuel line is damaged in a collision, gas leakage could occur. **1996-98 w/o ABS:** Pressure reducing valve in rear brakes may be subject to corrosion, which could result in malfunction when operated in areas that use salt compounds for deicing or dust control. **1996-98:** An open circuit in the wiring harness could lead to electrical arcing that could melt the connector housing material, increasing the potential for a fire. **1996-98:** Overheating at headlamp and wiring-harness terminals could result in open circuit for instrument lights, parking lamps, and taillamps. **1998:** Accelerator cable may have burr that could fray the core wire; cable could stick, bind, or cause high engine rpm. **1998:** Airbag-sensor wiring insulation can become brittle and crack over time; could cause airbag warning light to illuminate and disable airbag system. **1998:** Front coil springs may fracture as a result of corrosion in high corrosion environments. **1998:** Text and/or graphics for headlamp aiming instructions, provided in owner guides, are not sufficiently clear. **1999 w/automatic transmission:** Ignition key can be rotated to "Lock" position and removed, without shift lever being in "Park" position. **2000 w/ABS:** A pressure-conscious reducing valve in the rear brakes may corrode and malfunction, locking rear

FORD

wheels and adversely affecting handling. **2000:** Brake performance may be reduced due to incorrect power brake booster and master-cylinder assembly. **2000:** Fuel leak could result from a damaged fuel-tank-filler pipe grommet. **2000:** Improper label was installed on some cars, with incorrect instructions for activation of childproof safety locks. **2000:** Seatbelt-buckle assemblies were not properly heat treated and do not pass the load-bearing requirement.

PRICES

	Good	Average	Poor
1995 Contour	$2,000-2,600	$1,400-1,800	$300-400
Contour SE	2,400-3,000	1,800-2,200	500-600
1996 Contour	2,300-2,900	1,700-2,100	400-600
Contour SE	2,800-3,500	2,100-2,600	600-800
1997 Contour	2,600-3,300	1,900-2,400	500-700
Contour SE	3,200-3,900	2,500-3,000	800-900
1998 Contour	3,100-3,800	2,400-3,000	700-900
Contour SE	3,700-4,500	3,000-3,600	1,100-1,300
Contour SVT	7,000-8,200	6,200-7,300	3,400-3,900
1999 Contour	3,900-4,600	3,200-3,700	1,200-1,400
Contour SE	4,600-5,300	3,800-4,400	1,700-2,000
Contour SVT	8,200-9,500	7,400-8,600	4,200-4,800
2000 Contour	5,100-6,000	4,300-5,100	2,000-2,400
Contour SVT	9,500-11,000	8,600-9,900	4,900-5,700

For detailed information on this vehicle visit http://used.consumerguide.com and enter code **2159**

1992-03 FORD CROWN VICTORIA

CG BEST BUY

CLASS: Full-size car

BUILT IN: Canada

PROS: Acceleration
• Optional antilock brakes
• Passenger and cargo room
• Trailer-towing capability

CONS: Fuel economy
• Radio controls (early models) • Steering feel

EVALUATION: The Crown Vic's extra-smooth V8 sets the heavy sedan into motion swiftly enough, and past highway traffic without delay. Midrange response is more sluggish, however, worsened by the fact that the transmission seems reluctant to downshift. Gas mileage is nothing to boast about. One early test LX Crown Victoria averaged an impressive 19.9 mpg. Later, an LX yielded only 15.3 mpg.

Handling and stability are fine for a big sedan—improved in '03. The base suspension absorbs bumps nicely, yet doesn't wallow or float past pavement swells. The handling/performance option delivers a jittery ride, aggravated by too-light, numb power steering that easily turns twitchy. Traction can be a problem in the snow belt.

You're likely to hear virtually no road, wind, or engine noise. Expansive seating for six is marred only by a lack of lateral support in the driver's seat. Controls are grouped logically and work smoothly, though tiny horn buttons are an annoyance. Visibility is fine and the trunk ranks as close to cavernous, but a large well in the center of the floor could induce a little back strain when loading heavy objects.

VALUE FOR THE MONEY: Vastly more impressive than the prior generation, this Crown Vic mixes traditional values with contemporary virtues—a good choice if you like rear drive in a body-on-frame vehicle. Crown Vic and Mercury's Grand Marquis are the last of their kind.

TROUBLE SPOTS

Air springs: Air springs are prone to leaks caused by the bag rubbing against the axle or control arm. (1992-96)

Automatic transmission: The automatic transmission is notorious for shuddering or vibrating under light acceleration or when shifting between third and fourth gear. It requires that the transmission fluid (including fluid in the torque converter) be changed. (1992-94)

Automatic transmission: The transmission may slip and the engine may flare when the transmission shifts into fourth gear, which can be traced to a bad TR/MLP sensor. (1992-95)

Engine noise: The drive belt tensioner pulley or idler pulley bearings are apt to make a squealing noise when the engine is started in cold weather. (1993-96)

Hard starting: If the engine does not start or cranks for a long time then stalls, the idle air-control valve may be sticking. (1996)

Hard starting: The connector at the starter solenoid tends to corrode resulting in a "no crank" condition. (1992-94)

Oil leak: The oil filter balloons and leaks because the oil pump relief valve sticks. Higher than recommended viscosity oils cause wear to the valve bore. (1992-94)

Vehicle noise: A chattering noise that can be felt, and sometimes heard, coming from the rear during tight turns after highway driving is caused by a lack of friction modifier or over-shimming of the clutch packs in the Traction-Lok (limited-slip) differential. (1992-96)

Vehicle noise: A broken gusset or weld separation at the frame cross-member causes a rattle from the rear of the car. (1992)

AVERAGE REPLACEMENT COSTS

A/C Compressor	$380	Radiator	$380
Alternator	375	Shocks and/or Struts	505
Automatic Trans.	870	Timing Chain/Belt	330
Brakes	275	Universal Joints	125
Exhaust System	353		

NHTSA RECALL HISTORY

1992: "Antilock" brake warning lights in small number of cars will not actuate. **1992-93:** Speed-control deactivation switch can develop a short, which could potentially result in fire even if engine is not running. **1992-99 police/fleet/natural gas:** Bearing within lower ball joint can weaken slowly during use and eventually crack; could result in separation, allowing control arm to drop to the ground. **1993-94 w/police option:** Upper-control-arm bolts can loosen and fracture, causing substantial negative camber and steering pull; fracture at both holes could result in loss of control. **1994:** Nuts and bolts that attach rear brake adapter to axle flange can loosen and eventually separate. **1995:** In the event of short-circuit or overload, both headlamps can go out without warning. **1995:** On some cars, passenger-airbag's inflator body is cracked and may not inflate properly; also, igniter end cap can separate. **1995:** Rivet heads holding rear outboard seatbelt D-rings may fracture under load, reducing belt's restraining capability. **1995:** Seal material between fuel-filler pipe and tank may not have been fully cured, which could allow fuel to leak. **1995-96 fleet cars only:** Corrosion of inadequately lubricated Pitman arms can cause abnormal wear of joint, resulting in separation. **1996:** Driver's door, when closed only to secondary latched position, may not sustain specified load. **1996-00:** Replacement seatbelts made by TRW and sold by Ford may not restrain occupant in a collision. **1996-03 CNG vehicles:** Vehicle fire could lead to NG tank explosion. **1998-00:** Incorrect jacking instructions may cause personal injury. **2000:** During high-load conditions (ice, snow, or other debris), windshield wipers could become inoperative with no advance warning. **2000:** Left-rear seatbelt-retractor bolts were incorrectly tightened on a few cars. **2000:** Loose module on a few cars could result in delayed airbag deployment. **2001:** A restraint control module (RCM) or a side or front crash sensor may have been assembled with one or more of the screws that mount the circuit board in the housing missing. **2001:** Driver- and/or outboard front-passenger's seatbelt buckle may not fully latch. In the event of a crash, the restraint system may not provide adequate occupant protection. **2002:** A T-fitting that connects two of the fuel tanks can develop a leak when the ignition switch is on or during refueling, increasing the risk of fire.

PRICES

	Good	Average	Poor
1992 Crown Victoria	$2,100-2,900	$1,500-2,100	$400-500
1993 Crown Victoria	2,500-3,300	1,800-2,400	500-700
1994 Crown Victoria	3,000-3,800	2,300-2,900	700-900
1995 Crown Victoria	3,500-4,300	2,800-3,400	900-1,200
1996 Crown Victoria	4,000-4,800	3,300-3,900	1,300-1,500
1997 Crown Victoria	4,800-5,600	4,000-4,700	1,800-2,100
1998 Crown Victoria	6,000-7,200	5,200-6,300	2,500-3,000
1999 Crown Victoria	7,200-8,500	6,400-7,600	3,500-4,200
2000 Crown Victoria	8,500-10,000	7,700-9,000	4,400-5,200
2001 Crown Victoria	10,300-12,000	9,300-10,800	5,500-6,400
2002 Crown Victoria	12,500-14,500	11,300-13,100	7,100-8,300
2003 Crown Victoria	15,000-18,500	13,700-16,800	9,500-11,700

For detailed information on this vehicle visit
http://used.consumerguide.com and enter code **2032**

2001-03 FORD ESCAPE

CLASS: Compact sport-utility vehicle

BUILT IN: USA

PROS: Cargo room
• Maneuverability
• Visibility

CONS: Control layout (early automatic) • Noise

EVALUATION: Ford's Escape and its Mazda Tribute counterpart are today's most capable all-around compact SUVs, and the most refined. With V6 power, they're also among the quickest compacts, capable of reaching 60 mph in under 9 seconds. Available V6 power and locked-in 50/50 4WD give them a power and traction advantage over the similarly sized but four-cylinder Honda CR-V and Toyota RAV4. Those qualities, plus ample ground clearance and roominess, put them ahead of the Subaru Forester.

Most Escapes and Tributes have the V6, and are likely to have 4WD. The 4WD V6 models summon more power throughout the speed range than any of their four-cylinder rivals. Around-town acceleration, highway merging and two-lane passing are stress-free. An extended-test V6 model with AWD averaged 19.5 mpg with considerable highway driving, while others have managed 17.5 to 19.2 mpg.

Automatic transmissions shift smoothly and promptly, but feel some-what indecisive on lengthy uphill grades. The 4WD system provides suffi-cient traction to climb steep, gravelly hillsides; but absence of low-range gearing, or even all-terrain tires, rules out serious off-roading.

Steering/handling beats most rivals, but these SUV's certainly don't approach sport sedans. Fast, tight turns can trigger front-end plowing. Still, their steering is exceptionally direct (with Tribute the firmer of the pair), and stability at highway speeds is terrific. Balance and grip are quite good in rapid cornering, with less body lean than other SUVs of similar build.

Suspensions on Escape and Tribute, while different in tuning, feel markedly taut. Models tested did not wallow or float over dips and swells, though some sharp bumps register abruptly. Braking is controlled and sat-isfactorily strong, though some drivers might find pronounced nosedive in panic stops. Noise levels are not objectionable, but wind roar is prominent at speed and the tires whine on coarse pavement.

An airy, comfortable cabin belies Escape/Tribute's compact exterior dimen-sions. Taller riders will wish for more head room in sunroof equipped models, but clearance is otherwise generous. The rear seat deserves special praise, with leg room exceeding that of most midsize SUVs, enhanced by outstanding foot room beneath the front seats. Doorways are wide, but step-in is higher than on most compact SUVs. Visibility is unimpeded to the sides and rear.

Gauges and controls are legible and well-placed, but the long automat-ic-transmission shift lever on early models can be awkward to operate and it interferes with the driver's reach to the radio.

FORD

The climate system doesn't allow independent control of air recirculation or air conditioning. The driver gets an elevated view of the road ahead, and unimpeded vision to the sides and rear.

Interior furnishings are slightly less upscale than those of the Tribute, but both cabins feel solidly assembled with durable materials. No other compact SUV has more usable cargo room. Rear seatbacks easily fold flat once the headrests are removed, and seat bottoms tilt forward. The standard separate-opening rear glass is an added convenience.

VALUE FOR THE MONEY: Substantial feeling, roomy, comfortable, and even fun to drive, Escape and Tribute earn a slot on the compact SUV all-star team. They're also eminently sensible alternatives to any number of midsize SUVs, especially truck-based wagons, that are less efficient in their use of space and fuel. No wonder the Escape soon became America's top-selling compact SUV.

TROUBLE SPOTS

Door handles: If the door handle is pulled while trying to unlock the door with the keyless entry, the doors will not open. New door latches should be installed. (2001-02)

Heater core: Heater cores have reportedly suffered recurring failures and the most likely cause is electrolysis (the cooling system creates a current much like a battery) requiring a coolant flush and fill and possibly additional ground connections to the engine. (2001-02)

Poor transmission shift: Harsh or late upshifts may occur after transmission repairs due to a problem with the turbine-shaft speed sensor. (2001-02)

Steering problems: In areas where the temperature drops below zero (F), the power steering return hose may leak and a revised hose is available for retrofit. (2001-02)

AVERAGE REPLACEMENT COSTS

A/C Compressor	$650	CV Joints	$1,850
Alternator	410	Exhaust System	450
Automatic Trans.	2,200	Radiator	475
Brakes	455	Shocks and/or Struts	1,125
Clutch	410	Timing Chain/Belt	550

NHTSA RECALL HISTORY

2001 2WD w/o antilock brakes: Improper rear hubs may cause rear wheels to separate from vehicle. Dealers will inspect and replace if necessary. **2001 w/cruise control:** The speed-control cable can have a cracked or missing servo cap. Over time, corrosion could interfere with the function of the speed control. Dealers will inspect and replace affected caps. **2001:** Incorrect steering-wheel nut can lead to steering wheel separating from steering column. Dealers will inspect and replace affected steering-wheel assemblies. **2001:** O-ring seats in the fuel line might be damaged, causing an odor or fire. Dealers will inspect and replace affected fuel lines. **2001:** Windshield-wiper linkage can disengage, resulting in possible loss of wiper function. Dealers will inspect and replaced affected wiper linkages.

PRICES	Good	Average	Poor
2001 Escape 2WD	$11,000-12,800	$9,900-11,500	$5,900-6,900
Escape 4WD	12,500-14,300	11,300-12,900	7,100-8,200
2002 Escape 2WD	12,500-14,800	11,300-13,300	7,100-8,400
Escape 4WD	14,200-16,200	12,900-14,700	8,700-9,900
2003 Escape 2WD	14,700-18,500	13,400-16,800	9,300-11,700
Escape 4WD	16,500-20,000	15,000-18,200	10,600-12,800

For detailed information on this vehicle visit
http://used.consumerguide.com and enter code **4497**

1991-96 FORD ESCORT

CLASS: Subcompact car

BUILT IN: Mexico, USA

PROS: Acceleration (GT, LX-E) • Antilock brakes (optional) • Fuel economy • Ride

CONS: Engine noise • Rear-seat room • Road noise

EVALUATION: In hard acceleration, either engine causes the automatic transmission to jolt between gears. With automatic, there's just not enough low-end power for quick getaways. Acceleration to 60 mph took a leisurely 12.5 seconds. Though more powerful, the GT's engine gets lazy below 3500 rpm; but it runs smoother than the 1.9-liter. Both engines vibrate at idle, and are noisy while cruising. Gas mileage is great. An early automatic LX averaged 25.9 mpg. A later edition did better yet, averaging 26.8 mpg even while commuting.

Stable and well-controlled at highway speeds, the Escort's suspension is surprisingly absorbent on harsher pavement. A GT handles crisply, courtesy of its sport suspension and 15-inch tires. The same cannot be said of Pony and LX hatchbacks, whose 13-inch rubber easily loses grip in brisk cornering. Standard 4-wheel disc brakes on the GT bring the Escort to a swift, sure stop. Wind and road noise are noticeable, especially at highway speeds.

Visibility is good from the Escort's airy cabin. Head room isn't bad for a subcompact, unless it has the optional sunroof. Leg room is adequate, but three in back is a squeeze. The cargo area of hatchbacks and wagons is quite narrow between wheelwells, but wider at the rear. Controls are logically positioned, simply marked, operating with smooth precision that belies the car's modest roots.

VALUE FOR THE MONEY: With Escort you get plenty of practical value. Though the Escort can't match a Honda Civic or Toyota Corolla for refinement, it does give the impression of true quality in the subcompact field.

TROUBLE SPOTS

Blower motor: Squeaking or chirping blower motors are the result of defective brush holders. (1993-94)

FORD

Brake noise: Wear spots and ridges on the front brake caliper sleeves cause a knocking noise when gently applying the brakes. (1991-96)

Brakes: There is a redesigned brake master cylinder and brake booster available that provides better pedal feel and travel. (1993-95)

Engine knock: Carbon build-up on the pistons causes a knocking noise. Sometimes solved by cleaning the carbon from the pistons using carburetor cleaner, often pistons must be replaced with redesigned ones. (1991-93)

Fuel pump: Under general campaign number 94B55, Ford will install a fused jumper harness in the fuel pump electrical circuit to prevent erratic fuel gauge readings, stalling, or wiring damage. (1991-94)

Hard starting: If the engine does not start or cranks for a long time then stalls, the idle air control valve may be sticking. (1995-96)

Horn: Sometimes the horn will not work due to a poor ground circuit in the steering column. (1995-96)

Transmission noise: If a whine comes from the transmission during coast-down, it is probably because the idler gear teeth were not machined properly. (1995-96)

Vehicle noise: A grinding noise while turning is most likely due to dirt accumulating in the top strut mount bushing. (1991-92)

AVERAGE REPLACEMENT COSTS

A/C Compressor	$470	CV Joints	$585
Alternator	370	Exhaust System	375
Automatic Trans.	1,160	Radiator	382
Brakes	260	Shocks and/or Struts	620
Clutch	275	Timing Chain/Belt	145

NHTSA RECALL HISTORY

1991: Interference may occur between bolt that secures fuel line shield to lower dash and gas pedal, causing pedal to stick wide open. **1991:** Pins securing ignition lock can separate or move out of position; cylinder may disengage, causing steering column to lock up. **1991-92:** On some cars, fatigue crack can develop in solder joint between fuel return tube and fuel pump sending unit; fuel vapor could escape when tank is full, and small amount may leak. **1991-93:** On small number of front suspension units made by Dana Corp., the off-set-toe adjusting pin may fracture under certain conditions, resulting in loss of control. **1993:** Driver's seat in some cars may not engage fully in its track in positions near midpoint; could move in event of crash. **1994-95:** On a few cars, driver-side airbag may deploy improperly and expel hot gases. **1995 cars in certain states:** Cracks can develop in plastic fuel tank, resulting in leakage. **1995:** Two bolts that attach passenger-side airbag may be missing; in frontal impact, the airbag could fail to restrain the passenger.

PRICES

	Good	Average	Poor
1991 Escort	$1,000-1,400	$600-800	$100
Escort GT	1,200-1,800	700-1,100	100-200
1992 Escort	1,100-1,600	700-1,000	100-200
Escort GT	1,500-2,100	1,000-1,400	200-300

1993 Escort	$1,300-1,800	$800-1,100	$200
Escort GT	1,800-2,400	1,200-1,600	300-400
1994 Escort	1,500-2,000	1,000-1,300	200-300
Escort GT	2,000-2,600	1,400-1,800	300-400
1995 Escort	1,700-2,200	1,100-1,500	300
Escort GT	2,200-2,800	1,600-2,000	400-500
1996 Escort	1,900-2,500	1,300-1,700	300-400
Escort GT	2,500-3,200	1,800-2,300	500-700

> For detailed information on this vehicle visit
> **http://used.consumerguide.com** and enter code **2033**

1997-03 FORD ESCORT/ZX2

CG BEST BUY

CLASS:
Subcompact car

BUILT IN: Mexico, USA

PROS: Optional antilock brakes • Fuel economy • Price

CONS: Rear-seat room • Road noise (ZX2) • Wind noise (ZX2)

EVALUATION: Because the new Escort weighs about 120 pounds more than its predecessor, the increase of 22 horsepower does not result in inspiring performance. Acceleration is merely adequate, as before, but the new engine is smoother and quieter. The automatic transmission feels smoother with the new engine, and also downshifts faster for passing and merging. We averaged 23.9 mpg in an LX sedan with automatic, but most of that trial consisted of urban driving. On the highway, we'd expect well over 30 mpg. Manual-transmission Escorts feel livelier, as expected, and also get better gas mileage than cars with automatic.

A well-tuned suspension helps the Escort absorb bumps better than most subcompacts. Handling on sedans and wagons is competent rather than sporting, though steering feels natural in turns and its on-center sense contributes to stable cruising. Visibility is generally good, but the sedan's rear roof pillars are thick enough to block the driver's over-the-shoulder view. Road and wind noise are noticeable on the highway, but sedans and wagons aren't much noisier than a Honda Civic. The ZX2 coupe suffers from a lot more road and wind sound—enough to cause annoyance.

Partly due to the extra punch of its stronger engine, the ZX2 drives in a sporty manner. Here too, manual shift is quicker, but the 5-speed gets the engine turning at a buzzy 3000 rpm when traveling at 65 mph. We averaged an impressive 29 mpg with an automatic ZX2, which is at home on twisting roads, where grip and stability have proved to be good. Body roll in the ZX2 is well-controlled, too. Harder driving in a manual-shift ZX2 averaged 24.5 mpg.

FORD

Front head room is generous, even for tall occupants. Leg space is adequate for adults. Rear knee room is tight, as is head room in the coupe. The new dashboard puts gauges directly ahead of the driver. Audio and climate controls sit in an oval "integrated control panel." Interior storage is adequate, consisting of small door map pockets, a console with cupholders, and a small glovebox. Cargo space also ranks as adequate, and the wagon qualifies as a versatile hauler. The rear seatback folds for additional space, but does not lie totally flat.

VALUE FOR THE MONEY: Sensible design, competent road manners, and reasonable prices put both Escort and Tracer high on our list of desirable subcompacts, but we're less impressed by the noisier ZX2 coupe.

TROUBLE SPOTS

Audio system: Electrical noise caused by the electric fuel pump in the tank can cause a buzzing noise when the AM band of the radio is selected. (1997-98)

Automatic transmission: The transmission may not engage right away when the car has been parked overnight because the torque converter drains down. (1997)

Doors: The dome light may come on while driving or fail to come on when the door is opened. (1997-98)

Fuel gauge: The gas gauge may have an error of about 1/8 tank, may drop from full too fast, and the tank may take fuel slowly due to a problem with the fuel sending unit or slosh module. (1998)

Hard starting: If the engine will not start or the cooling fan does not shut off in cold weather, the integrated relay control module needs to be replaced. (1997-98)

Oil leak: In cold weather, moisture can freeze in the PCV system. When the engine is started, the dipstick pops out of its tube and oil leaks out. (1997-98)

Vehicle noise: The blower motor may chirp or squeak at low speeds. This can be corrected with a replacement motor. (1997)

AVERAGE REPLACEMENT COSTS

A/C Compressor	$665	CV Joints	$540
Alternator	475	Exhaust System	430
Automatic Trans.	1,175	Radiator	430
Brakes	320	Shocks and/or Struts	770
Clutch	665	Timing Chain/Belt	805

NHTSA RECALL HISTORY

1999 w/S/R option: Manual-transmission shift pattern for some cars is not displayed. **2000:** Seatbelt-buckle assemblies were not properly heat treated and do not pass the load-bearing requirement.

PRICES

	Good	Average	Poor
1997 Escort sedan	$2,300-2,900	$1,700-2,100	$400-600
Escort wagon	2,600-3,200	1,900-2,400	500-700
1998 Escort ZX2	2,900-3,400	2,200-2,600	700-800
Escort sedan	2,800-3,400	2,100-2,600	600-700
Escort wagon	3,200-3,800	2,500-3,000	800-900
1999 Escort ZX2	3,800-4,400	3,100-3,600	1,100-1,300
Escort sedan	3,600-4,200	2,900-3,400	1,000-1,200
Escort wagon	4,100-4,700	3,400-3,900	1,400-1,600

2000 Escort ZX2	$4,700-5,300	$3,900-4,500	$1,700-2,000
Escort sedan	4,500-5,200	3,700-4,300	1,600-1,900
2001 Escort ZX2	5,800-6,400	5,000-5,600	2,400-2,700
Escort sedan	5,500-6,200	4,700-5,300	2,300-2,500
2002 Escort ZX2	6,700-7,300	5,900-6,400	3,100-3,400
Escort sedan	6,500-7,200	5,700-6,300	2,900-3,200
2003 Escort ZX2	8,000-9,200	7,200-8,300	4,100-4,700

For detailed information on this vehicle visit
http://used.consumerguide.com and enter code **2261**

1997-02 FORD EXPEDITION

CG BEST BUY

CLASS: Full-size sport-utility vehicle

BUILT IN: USA

PROS: Acceleration (5.4-liter) • Passenger and cargo room • Trailer-towing capability • Visibility

CONS: Entry/exit (4WD) • Fuel economy

EVALUATION: On the road Expedition does not seem as large as the rival Tahoe and Yukon, partly because Expedition's deep side and rear windows—and sloping hood—provide good visibility to all directions. Not really agile, but easy enough to drive for a vehicle of this size, it corners with moderate body lean so long as speeds are modest. With 2WD, the ride is stable, well-controlled and relatively soft—less trucklike than some rival SUVs. Most bumps are easily absorbed, and the Expedition delivers an impressively solid feel. Ride quality is a little stiffer and more jiggly in a 4WD model, but not jarring.

Any model with the 5.4-liter V8 will accelerate smartly from a standstill, passing quickly and safely at highway speeds. A 2WD version with the smaller engine performs nearly as well off-the-line, but passing power falls short of snappy. The additional weight of 4WD puts a noticeable burden on the 4.6-liter V8. Both engines are smooth and fairly quiet, but the 5.4-liter V8 is the better choice for towing. As for economy, a 2WD Eddie Bauer edition got only 14.3 mpg in a mix of urban commuting and highway cruising. A 4WD Expedition with the 5.4-liter engine managed a measly 12 mpg.

In the cavernous, well-designed interior, space is ample for front and middle rows, which have reclining seatbacks. Front shoulder room is expansive, and three adults can ride in back in genuine comfort. A nearly flat floor means no one has to straddle a hump. The optional third seat is more for children than adults, however. Behind the third seat (if so equipped), the cargo area amounts to little more than a foot-long trench. Without that seat, cargo space is long and wide. Entry/exit is easy on 2WD models, with wide doorways and a moderate step up to the interior. 4WD versions sit much higher off the ground, so you have to hoist yourself up with the aid of an inside grab handle.

VALUE FOR THE MONEY: Competitively priced when new, the impressive Expedition has also been a popular model on the used-vehicle market. All told, it's a good alternative to GM's SUVs—more modern and refined, and well worth a close look. In fact, Expedition ranks as a trend-setter.

TROUBLE SPOTS

Audio system: Electrical noise caused by the electric fuel pump in the tank can cause a buzzing noise when the AM band of the radio is selected. (1997-98)

Automatic transmission: If water gets into the transfer case, the mode switch can be shorted out making it impossible to select a different range. (1997)

Automatic transmission: Transmission fluid can leak from the transmission into the transfer case. The low transmission fluid level causes shifting and engagement problems. (1997)

Climate control: Cold air may come out of the heater vents at the floor due to a door in the duct not sealing properly. (1997)

Dashboard lights: Water in the spark plug wells may cause the ignition spark to jump to ground causing a misfire and illuminating the check engine light. (1997)

Engine misfire: The engine may run rough or idle roughly if condensation from the air conditioning drips onto the oxygen sensor. (1997-98)

Seat: The front leather seats may wear out quickly because the foam sticks to the leather. New seat covers should be installed. (1997-98)

AVERAGE REPLACEMENT COSTS

A/C Compressor	$545	Radiator	$430
Alternator	515	Shocks and/or Struts	445
Automatic Trans.	930	Timing Chain/Belt	380
Brakes	320	Universal Joints	260
Exhaust System	485		

NHTSA RECALL HISTORY

1997: It is possible that the intermediate steering shaft yoke may break, causing a loss of steering control. Dealer will inspect and replace affected parts. **1997:** Rear-axle track-bar bracket can separate from frame due to missing welds or inadequate weld penetration; axle can move laterally until tires contact frame or wheelhouse. **1997-00:** Bolts that attach trailer-hitch assembly to frame could lose their clamp load; hitch could then separate from vehicle. **1997-98:** Certain off-lease vehicles, Canadian in origin but sold in the U.S., have daytime running lights that do not meet U.S. Specifications. **1997-98:** Due to insufficient clamp load, lug nuts could loosen and studs could fatigue and fail, creating potential for wheel to separate. **1997-98:** Main battery cable could short circuit, causing loss of electrical supply, or fire. **1999 w/4WD and 17-inch chrome steel wheels:** Due to insufficient wheel contact area with hub, loss of lug nut torque can cause vibration or separation of wheel. **1999:** Contact area between wheel and hug can deform, resulting in loss of lug nut torque that can cause vibration or separation of wheel/tire from vehicle. **1999:** Fuel-line assemblies on some vehicles may have been damaged by supplier during manufacture, and could leak. **1999:** Retainer clip that holds master cylinder pushrod to brake-pedal arm may be missing or partially installed, causing increased stopping distances. **2000-01:** A switch located in the plastic cover of the wiper-motor gear case could malfunction and overheat, potentially resulting in loss of wiper function or fire. **2000-01:** Some of the owner's manuals for these vehicles are missing instructions for properly attaching a child restraint system. **2001:** Driver- and/or front passenger-outboard seatbelt buckle may not fully latch. In the event of a crash, the restraint system may not provide adequate occupant protection. **2002 w/2WD:** Certification labels incorrectly state rear tire pressure.

PRICES

	Good	Average	Poor
1997 Eddie Bauer	$9,300-11,500	$8,400-10,400	$4,800-6,000
Expedition XLT	8,500-10,500	7,700-9,500	4,400-5,500
1998 Eddie Bauer	11,000-13,500	9,900-12,200	5,900-7,300
Expedition XLT	10,000-12,200	9,000-11,000	5,200-6,300
1999 Eddie Bauer	14,200-16,000	12,900-14,600	8,700-9,800
Expedition XLT	12,500-14,800	11,300-13,300	7,100-8,400
2000 Eddie Bauer	17,500-19,500	16,100-17,900	11,200-12,500
Expedition XLT	15,000-17,500	13,700-15,900	9,500-11,000
2001 Eddie Bauer	20,200-22,500	18,600-20,700	13,100-14,600
Expedition XLT	17,500-20,000	16,100-18,400	11,200-12,800
2002 Eddie Bauer	23,200-25,700	21,300-23,600	15,100-16,700
Expedition XLT	20,000-22,500	18,400-20,700	13,000-14,600

For detailed information on this vehicle visit
http://used.consumerguide.com and enter code 2262

1991-03 FORD EXPLORER/SPORT TRAC/SPORT

CLASS: Midsize sport-utility vehicle

BUILT IN: USA

PROS: Acceleration (V8) • Antilock brakes (optional later models) • 4WD traction • Passenger and cargo room • Visibility

CONS: Engine noise (ohv V6) • Fuel economy • Wind noise

EVALUATION: Explorers are easy to enter and depart from, due to a relatively low step-in height. Head room is generous all around. Rear leg

FORD

space is adequate. There's plenty of space for three abreast in the back of a 4-door. Split front seat backs fold flat to create a long load floor that suffers little intrusion from the rear wheels. There's no spare tire in the way of cargo, either. Controls are simple, analog gauges clearly legible; visibility fine through deep side and rear windows.

Acceleration is adequate from the ohv V6 engine, but it is sluggish and rough when first stomping the pedal and averaged a low 15.9 mpg. Eight-cylinder engines provide outstanding acceleration, and equally depressing fuel economy. The ohc V6 is probably the best option. It offers ample acceleration and averaged 20.4 mpg. Though smoother and quieter than the ohv unit, the ohc V6 engine feels a little rough and sounds gruff at low speeds. The automatic transmission responds neatly, and shifts nearly flawlessly—quick and unobtrusive.

The relatively long, wide stance gives either Explorer reasonable stability in turns, though you get a choppy ride from the shorter-wheelbase 3-door. Steering precisely, cornering confidently, an Explorer suffers less body lean than Chevrolet's Blazer.

VALUE FOR THE MONEY: Not cheap, an Explorer offers the utility of a minivan and the hauling power of a truck. If you're a likely prospect for a smaller sport utility, best not to buy until you've test-driven Ford's compact. But try a Chevy Blazer and Jeep Grand Cherokee, too. We do like the added versatility of the Sport Trac's crew cab design.

TROUBLE SPOTS

Air conditioner: Water may drip onto the floor when the air conditioner is operated because the evaporator strip seals were not properly positioned. (1995-96)

Hard starting: If the engine does not start or cranks for a long time then stalls, the idle air-control valve may be sticking. (1996)

Radiator: The radiator may leak in cold weather because of a bad seal between the tank and core. (1995-96)

Vehicle noise: Loose frame rivets should be replaced with bolts (welding is not approved). (1991-96)

Vehicle noise: A chattering noise that can be felt coming from the rear during tight turns after highway driving is caused by a lack of friction modifier or over-shimming of the clutch packs in the Traction-Lok differential. (1991-96)

Vehicle noise: Synthetic-rubber radius-arm bushings separate internally, causing noise and degraded steering control. (All)

AVERAGE REPLACEMENT COSTS

A/C Compressor	$505	Exhaust System	$295
Alternator	280	Radiator	440
Automatic Trans.	840	Shocks and/or Struts	175
Brakes	265	Timing Chain/Belt	400
Clutch	435	Universal Joints	105

NHTSA RECALL HISTORY

1991 w/A4LD automatic transmission: Vehicle may appear to be in "Park" position, when gear is not truly engaged. **1991:** Front heat shield may contact plastic fuel tank, causing damage to the extent of penetration. **1991:** Hot weld that attaches vapor vent-valve carrier to plastic fuel tank may partially fracture, allowing escape of fuel vapor. **1991:** Seatbelts may be defective, resulting in insufficiently latched or unlatched belt. **1991-93 w/factory sunroof:** Sunroof glass-panel assembly can separate while vehicle is moving. **1991-94:** On cars sold or registered in specified southern California counties, studs that attach master cylinder to power-brake-booster assembly can develop stress corrosion cracking after extended period; fractures could cause separation of master cylinder when brakes are applied. **1992-93:** Bracket welds for liftgate's hydraulic lift cylinders can fracture. **1992-94:** Short circuit can occur in remote power mirror switch's circuit board; overheated board and other plastic and elastomeric components can result in smoke or fire. **1993-94 w/manual shift:** Parking-brake self-adjust pawl does not line up properly and can slip. **1993-95:** Some hydraulic-lift-cylinder bracket welds could fracture, resulting in potential for liftgate bracket to gradually bend, allowing ball stud to disengage. **1995 2-door:** Brake tubes in some models were misrouted, resulting in excessive stopping distance. **1995:** Inner tie-rod assemblies can fracture, resulting in shaking or shimmy at low speeds. **1995:** Passenger-side airbag's inflator body may be cracked and not inflate properly; also, igniter end cap can separate, causing hot gases to be released. **1995-97:** Front-stabilizer-bar link stud can fracture from bending fatigue. **1996:** Certification label shows incorrect rear-tire-inflation pressure. **1996:** Driver's door, when closed only to secondary latched position, may not sustain specified load. **1996:** Gas-cylinder bracket may not properly support rear liftgate. **1996-97 in 15 northern states:** After operation at highway speeds, at below 20 degrees (F), engine may not return to idle. **1997-98 w/4.0-liter engine:** A gap between the plate and bore of throttle body was too narrow, causing the throttle pedal to stick. **1997-98 w/SOHC 4.0-liter engine:** Fuel lines can be damaged and fire could result if vehicle is jump-started and ground cable is attached to fuel-line bracket near battery. **1997-98:** Certain off-lease vehicles, Canadian in origin but sold in the U.S., have daytime running lights that do not meet U.S. Specifications. **1997-99:** Speed-control cable on certain vehicles can interfere with servo pulley, preventing throttle from returning to idle when disengaging the speed control. **1998 Eddie Bauer and Limited:** Key-in-ignition/door-open warning chime may not function properly. **1998-99:** Secondary hood latch on certain vehicles may corrode and stick in open position. **1999:** Right front-brake line to hydraulic control unit connection could separate, causing leakage when brake pedal is applied. **1999-00 w/3.27 or 3.55 rear axle:** Powertrain-control module could allow the vehicle to exceed the design intent top speed. **1999-00 w/4.0-liter engine and AWD:** Generic electronic module could "lock-up," so various functions (front wipers, interior lights, 4x4 system, etc.) could not be turned on or off. **2000 w/side airbags:** Side airbags could deploy if ignition key is in "run" position and seatbelt webbing is extracted from locked retractor with jerking motion. **2000-01 Sport and Sport Trac:** Hood striker could fracture causing the hood to fly open while the vehicle is being driven. **2002 Explorer:** Right-side tires may have horizontal cuts in the tread that could have occurred during assembly.

FORD

PRICES

	Good	Average	Poor
1991 Explorer 2WD	$1,500-2,300	$1,000-1,500	$200-300
Explorer 4WD	2,200-3,200	1,600-2,300	400-600
1992 Explorer 2WD	1,800-2,800	1,200-1,900	300-400
Explorer 4WD	2,500-3,600	1,800-2,600	500-800
1993 Explorer 2WD	2,200-3,500	1,600-2,500	400-700
Explorer 4WD	2,900-4,300	2,200-3,300	700-1,000
1994 Explorer 2WD	2,600-4,000	1,900-3,000	500-800
Explorer 4WD	3,400-4,800	2,700-3,800	900-1,200
1995 Explorer 2WD	3,000-4,500	2,300-3,500	700-1,000
Explorer 4WD	4,100-5,500	3,400-4,500	1,400-1,800
1996 Explorer 2WD	3,500-5,400	2,800-4,300	900-1,500
Explorer 4WD	4,700-6,500	3,900-5,500	1,700-2,400
1997 Explorer 2WD	4,300-6,400	3,500-5,200	1,500-2,200
Explorer 4WD	5,500-7,500	4,700-6,500	2,300-3,100
1998 Explorer 2WD	5,500-8,000	4,700-6,900	2,300-3,300
Explorer 4WD	7,000-9,200	6,200-8,200	3,400-4,400
1999 Explorer 2WD	7,000-10,000	6,200-8,900	3,400-4,800
Explorer 4WD	8,500-11,300	7,700-10,200	4,400-5,900
2000 Explorer 2WD	8,500-12,500	7,700-11,300	4,400-6,500
Explorer 4WD	10,500-14,000	9,500-12,600	5,600-7,400
Explorer Sport	8,000-10,000	7,200-9,000	4,100-5,100
2001 Explorer 2WD	11,000-15,500	10,000-14,100	7,000-9,900
Explorer 4WD	12,500-16,500	11,300-14,900	7,100-9,400
Explorer Sport	10,000-12,000	9,000-10,800	5,200-6,200
Explorer Sport Trac	14,500-16,500	13,200-15,000	9,000-10,200
2002 Explorer Sport	12,200-14,500	11,000-13,100	6,800-8,100
Explorer Sport Trac	17,000-19,500	15,600-17,900	10,900-12,500
2003 Explorer Sport	14,500-17,500	13,200-15,900	9,000-10,900
Explorer Sport Trac	19,500-22,500	17,900-20,700	12,700-14,600

For detailed information on this vehicle visit
http://used.consumerguide.com and enter code **2034**

1997-03
FORD F-150

CLASS: Full-size pickup truck

BUILT IN: Canada, USA

PROS: Cargo room • Passenger room • Trailer-towing capability

CONS: Acceleration (V6) • Engine noise (V6) • Fuel economy • Rear-seat comfort

EVALUATION: Ford's base V6 engine is noisy at idle, and grows raucous under hard throttle. Acceleration is adequate only in lighter-weight models with little cargo aboard. Both V8 engines are smoother and more powerful, but don't offer quite as much low-speed muscle as the bigger overhead-valve V8 from GM and Dodge. For most applications, a V8 is the wiser choice—and the bigger, the better. For most light-duty work, however, the 4.6-liter would suffice. It feels lively when accelerating from a standstill (at least with an empty cargo bed), but is a little short of power when you punch the gas quickly in the 25-40 mph range—especially in a heavier model. Passing response is ample at highway speeds, however. An F-150 SuperCab 4x4 averaged only 12.5 mpg in a mix of city and highway driving, and managed 16.2 mpg on a highway journey.

On the highway, an F-150 delivers a stable and comfortable ride, with little of the bounciness or pitching that's common to most pickups. When going through bumpy pavement, the suspension absorbs the worst of the rough stuff. In addition, the rear axle resists juddering even when the cargo bed is empty. Wind and road noise are moderate for a pickup truck. Depending on the model and option package—and there's a vast selection available—interior furnishings range from stark to utterly luxurious. All F-150s have a modern, convenient dashboard with handy controls. Cupholders pop out from the dashboard, and large map pockets are mounted on doors.

Head, leg, and shoulder room up front are generous. Because 4WD models sit high off the ground, entry and exit demand more effort than in the 2WD versions. The SuperCab's passenger-side rear door makes life easier. You get plenty of head room but marginal leg space in the rear seat. Getting into the back is definitely easier with the 1999 SuperCab's rear half-doors. And the 2001 SuperCrew is plenty roomy and comfortable for three adults, with a high step in but large crew-cab door openings.

VALUE FOR THE MONEY: All told, we rate the latest F-150 tops in its class, even with the arrival of new challengers for 1999: the redesigned Chevrolet Silverado and GMC Sierra.

TROUBLE SPOTS

Audio system: Electrical noise caused by the electric fuel pump in the tank can cause a buzzing noise when the AM band of the radio is selected. (1997)

Automatic transmission: Transmission fluid can leak from the transmission into the transfer case. The low transmission-fluid level causes shifting and engagement problems. (1997)

Automatic transmission: If water gets into the transfer case, the mode switch can be shorted out making it impossible to select a different range. (1997)

Climate control: Cold air may come out of the heater vents at the floor due to a door in the duct not sealing properly. (1997)

Dashboard lights: Water in the spark-plug wells may cause the ignition spark to jump to ground causing a misfire and illuminating the check-engine light. (1997)

Engine misfire: The engine may run rough or idle roughly if condensation from the air conditioning drips onto the oxygen sensor. (1997-98)

Engine noise: Piston slap on cold startup due to faulty pistons in 5.4-liter engine. (1998)

FORD

AVERAGE REPLACEMENT COSTS

A/C Compressor	$300	Exhaust System	$515
Alternator	315	Radiator	510
Automatic Trans.	930	Shocks and/or Struts	575
Brakes	320	Timing Chain/Belt	380
Clutch	620	Universal Joints	260

NHTSA RECALL HISTORY

1997 F150/F250: It is possible that the intermediate steering shaft yoke may break, causing a loss of steering control. Dealer will inspect and replace affected parts. **1997 in 10 northern states:** Operation at highway speeds in winter conditions can cause PVC fitting to freeze; throttle plate could then remain in cruising position after pedal is released. **1997:** Certification label shows incorrect rear-tire-inflation pressure. **1997:** Retainer clip that holds master-cylinder pushrod to brake-pedal arm could be missing, causing loss of braking. **1997:** Seatbelt-anchorage attachments are missing or misinstalled. **1997:** Separation of transmission bracket fitting from cable can result in inability to shift into "Park." **1997-98 w/4WD:** If vehicle is overloaded, rear leaf springs can fracture. **1997-98 w/V6, in any of 23 states:** Throttle is unable to return to idle due to ice forming in throttle body. **1997-98:** Certain off-lease vehicles, Canadian in origin but sold in the U.S., have daytime running lights that do not meet U.S. Specifications. **1997-98:** Lug nuts may loosen and studs may experience fatigue failure, with potential for wheel separation. **1997-98:** Main battery cable can contact body panel in trunk, resulting short circuit. **1999 4x4 w/Off Road package and 4x2 w/Sport package:** Tire and rim identification information is incorrect on certification labels. **1999:** Fuel-pressure regulator O-ring may have been damaged, allowing fuel-vapor leakage. **1999:** Speed-control cable on certain vehicles can interfere with pulley, preventing throttle from returning to idle when disengaging the speed control. **1999-00 Super Duty w/5.4-liter V8 and manual transmission:** Accelerator-cable core wire on certain trucks can wear the conduit end fitting; could lead to separation of strands, which could prevent throttle from returning to idle. **2000-01:** A switch located in the plastic cover of the wiper-motor gear case could malfunction and overheat, potentially resulting in loss of wiper function or fire. **2000-01:** Some of the owner's manuals for these vehicles are missing instructions for properly attaching a child-restraint system. **2001:** Driver's-and/or front passenger-outboard seatbelt buckle may not fully latch. In the event of a crash, the restraint system may not provide adequate occupant protection.

PRICES

	Good	Average	Poor
1997 F-150 2WD	$4,500-9,000	$3,700-7,500	$1,600-3,200
F-150 4WD	6,200-11,000	5,400-9,600	2,700-4,700
1998 F-150 2WD	5,500-10,500	4,700-9,000	2,300-4,300
F-150 4WD	7,500-12,500	6,800-11,300	3,800-6,300
1999 F-150 2WD	6,100-10,000	5,300-8,700	2,600-4,300
F-150 4WD	8,200-12,500	7,400-11,300	4,200-6,400
Lightning	16,500-18,500	15,000-16,800	10,600-11,800
SuperCab 2WD	8,500-13,000	7,700-11,700	4,400-6,800
SuperCab 4WD	10,500-15,000	9,500-13,500	5,600-8,000

CONSUMER GUIDE®

2000 F-150 2WD	$7,300-10,500	$6,600-9,500	$3,600-5,100
F-150 4WD	9,500-13,000	8,600-11,700	4,900-6,800
Harley-Davidson	18,000-20,000	16,600-18,400	11,500-12,800
Lightning	18,500-20,500	17,000-18,900	11,800-13,100
SuperCab 2WD	10,000-14,000	9,000-12,600	5,200-7,300
SuperCab 4WD	12,500-16,000	11,300-14,400	7,100-9,100
2001 F-150 2WD	9,000-12,500	8,100-11,300	4,700-6,500
F-150 4WD	11,500-14,800	10,400-13,300	6,300-8,100
Harley-Davidson	21,000-23,000	19,300-21,200	13,700-15,000
Lightning	21,000-23,000	19,300-21,200	13,700-15,000
SuperCab 2WD	12,000-15,800	10,800-14,200	6,700-8,800
SuperCab 4WD	14,200-18,000	12,900-16,400	8,700-11,000
SuperCrew 2WD	16,500-19,000	15,000-17,300	10,600-12,200
SuperCrew 4WD	19,000-21,500	17,500-19,800	12,400-14,000
2002 F-150 2WD	10,500-14,000	9,500-12,600	5,600-7,400
F-150 4WD	13,000-16,500	11,800-15,000	7,500-9,600
Harley-Davidson	25,000-27,500	23,300-25,600	16,500-18,200
Lightning	23,000-25,000	21,200-23,000	15,000-16,300
SuperCab 2WD	13,500-18,500	12,300-16,800	8,000-10,900
SuperCab 4WD	15,800-21,500	14,400-19,600	10,100-13,800
SuperCrew 2WD	19,000-22,000	17,500-20,200	12,400-14,300
SuperCrew 4WD	21,500-24,500	19,800-22,500	14,000-15,900
2003 F-150 2WD	13,200-17,000	12,000-15,500	7,700-9,900
F-150 4WD	15,500-19,000	14,100-17,300	9,900-12,200
Harley-Davidson	28,500-31,000	26,500-28,800	19,400-21,100
Lightning	26,000-28,500	24,200-26,500	17,200-18,800
SuperCab 2WD	16,000-20,500	14,600-18,700	10,200-13,100
SuperCab 4WD	18,200-23,500	16,700-21,600	11,600-15,000
SuperCrew 2WD	21,000-25,000	19,300-23,000	13,700-16,300
SuperCrew 4WD	24,000-27,500	22,300-25,600	15,600-17,900

For detailed information on this vehicle visit
http://used.consumerguide.com and enter code **2263**

1990-96 FORD F-150/250 PICKUP

CG BEST BUY

CLASS: Full-size pickup truck

BUILT IN: Canada, Mexico, USA

PROS: Acceleration (V8)
• Passenger and cargo room
• Trailer-towing capability

CONS: Fuel economy
• Handling • Interior storage space • Noise

FORD

EVALUATION: Even though the 6-cylinder engine nearly matches torque output of a 5.0-liter V8, we prefer gasoline V8 models on the basis of their impressive acceleration and passing ability. That was our appraisal of an F-150 XLT with the 5.0 and 4-speed automatic. The 5.0 was just about as responsive as a 5.8-liter, in fact, but both returned horrid gas mileage: around 12.5 mpg in a city/highway mix. Some 4-speed automatics have demonstrated slurred, lurching gear changes, plus sluggish downshifting for passing.

Tall and square, Ford trucks can be blown around in heavy crosswinds, but otherwise hold the road well—even with an empty cargo box. Steering feels looser than in a GM or Dodge pickup, and requires a bit more correction on the highway. An unloaded short-wheelbase 4x4 rides harshly over city streets, but longer-wheelbase models cope much better with bumps. Engine noise and tire rumble can annoy, though wind noise is modest.

Regular-cab models easily hold three adults, though the center rider straddles the transmission tunnel. Dashboards are better after 1991, with an easy-to-use climate system and audio controls grouped near the driver. All trucks have plenty of head room. The steering wheel sits near the driver's chest, and pedals are close to the chair-height seat cushion. SuperCab rear seats are a convenience, but have minimal knee and foot space.

VALUE FOR THE MONEY: If you're in the market for a pickup in this league, also look at the Chevrolet C/K and Dodge Ram. But we put the F-Series at the top of our list in terms of room, power, payload, and trailer-towing ability.

TROUBLE SPOTS

Alternator belt: If the accessory drive belt on 4.9-liter engines chirps, the pulley for the power steering may be misaligned on the pump or the A/C compressor may have to be repositioned. If the belt squeals, the automatic tensioner must be replaced. (1990-94)

Automatic transmission: If the transmission does not shift from second to third, the valve body separator plate may be distorted. (1990-94)

Automatic transmission: The transmission may slip and the engine may flare when the transmission shifts into fourth gear, which can often be traced to a bad TR/MLP sensor. (1994-95)

Ball joints: If water gets into the ball joints, they will wear out early and have to be replaced. (1990-96)

Hard starting: Hesitation, miss, stumble, no-start, or stalling could be due to a short in the wiring harness for the powertrain control module (PCM). (1993-95)

Hard starting: If the engine does not start or cranks for a long time then stalls, the idle air control valve may be sticking. (1995-96)

Manual transmission: On trucks with a diesel engine, the clutch may not release due to a leaking slave cylinder. (1993-95)

Suspension problems: The front leaf springs are prone to sag over time and must be replaced. (1991-94)

Suspension problems: Front tire cupping is common with Twin Axle suspension. Often new springs will help, but sometimes other suspension parts must also be replaced. Regular alignment is crucial. (All)

Vehicle noise: A chattering noise that can be felt coming from the rear during tight turns after highway driving is caused by a lack of friction modifier or over-shimming of the clutch packs in the Traction-Lok differential. (1990-96)

Vehicle noise: Loose frame rivets should be replaced with bolts (welding is not approved). (1990-96)

AVERAGE REPLACEMENT COSTS

A/C Compressor	$395	Exhaust System	$375
Alternator	290	Radiator	425
Automatic Trans.	560	Shocks and/or Struts	160
Brakes	295	Timing Chain/Belt	200
Clutch	515	Universal Joints	175

NHTSA RECALL HISTORY

1990 4x2 w/one-piece driveshaft and E40D transmission: Under certain conditions, snap ring may fracture and park gear would not engage. **1990 w/dual fuel tanks:** Supply and return fuel lines may be crossed on some trucks. **1990-91 F-250/350 w/7.3/.5 liter engine, and 4x4 w/5.8-liter:** Brake fluid may overheat, diminishing braking effectiveness. **1990-91:** Ignition switch could short-circuit and overheat, causing smoke and possible fire. **1990-93 w/dual fuel tanks:** Portion of unused fuel from one tank may be returned to the second, causing spillage. **1992 F-250/350 diesel:** Sound insulation can contact exhaust manifold. **1992:** Door latch may malfunction in below-freezing temperatures. **1992-94 w/manual shift:** Parking-brake pawl can slip; brake might not hold. **1993 F-150 w/Touch Drive:** Transfer case can slip out of 4x4 high gear during coasting or with power applied in reverse. **1993 w/dual fuel tanks:** Fuel-pressure regulator in the fuel system can wear out during the life of the vehicle, causing high-fuel system pressure. **1994 F-150/250:** Airbag and its warning light might not function; or, airbag might deploy when passenger door is slammed while key is turned to start position. **1994-95 Super Cab w/40/20/40 power driver's seat:** Wiring harness for power lumbar support could overheat, leading to melting, smoke, or possible ignition of surrounding materials. **1996 F-250:** Certification label shows incorrect rear-tire-inflation pressure. **1996 F-250/F-350/Super Duty:** Undersized fasteners on a few trucks can separate, causing fuel-tank strap to become disconnected.

PRICES

	Good	Average	Poor
1990 F-150	$1,600-2,800	$1,100-1,800	$200-400
F-150 SuperCab	2,500-3,500	1,800-2,600	500-700
F-250	2,300-3,500	1,700-2,500	400-700
F-250 SuperCab	3,100-4,000	2,400-3,100	700-1,000
1991 F-150	2,000-3,800	1,400-2,700	300-600
F-150 SuperCab	3,000-4,600	2,300-3,500	700-1,100
F-250	2,700-4,300	2,000-3,200	600-900
F-250 SuperCab	3,600-5,200	2,900-4,200	1,000-1,500

FORD

1992 F-150	$2,400-4,000	$1,800-2,900	$500-800
F-150 SuperCab	3,400-5,000	2,700-4,000	900-1,300
F-250	3,400-4,800	2,700-3,800	900-1,200
F-250 SuperCab	4,400-5,800	3,700-4,800	1,500-2,000
1993 F-150	2,800-5,000	2,100-3,800	600-1,100
F-150 SuperCab	4,500-6,200	3,700-5,100	1,600-2,200
F-250	4,000-5,500	3,300-4,500	1,300-1,800
F-250 SuperCab	5,300-6,700	4,600-5,800	2,200-2,700
1994 F-150	3,200-6,000	2,500-4,700	800-1,400
F-150 SuperCab	4,700-7,000	3,900-5,900	1,700-2,600
F-250	4,700-7,100	3,900-6,000	1,700-2,600
F-250 SuperCab	5,500-8,500	4,700-7,300	2,300-3,500
1995 F-150	3,600-6,900	2,900-5,500	1,000-1,900
F-150 SuperCab	5,500-8,500	4,700-7,300	2,300-3,500
F-250	5,300-7,200	4,600-6,200	2,200-3,000
F-250 SuperCab	6,500-9,200	5,700-8,100	2,900-4,100
1996 F-150	4,100-7,500	3,400-6,200	1,400-2,500
F-150 SuperCab	6,200-9,500	5,400-8,300	2,700-4,100
F-250	6,000-8,500	5,200-7,400	2,500-3,600
F-250 SuperCab/Crew	7,200-11,200	6,400-10,000	3,500-5,500

For detailed information on this vehicle visit
http://used.consumerguide.com and enter code 2035

2000-03
FORD FOCUS

CG BEST BUY

CLASS: Subcompact car
BUILT IN: Mexico
PROS: Cargo room (wagon) • Control layout • Fuel economy • Handling/roadholding
CONS: Acceleration • Engine noise • Rear-seat entry/exit (hatchback)

EVALUATION: Terrific road manners are tempered by mediocre engine performance. A Focus tackles twisty roads with linear, communicative steering, well-controlled body lean, and outstanding grip from the 15-inch tires that are standard on most models. Firm suspensions yield a flat, wallow-free highway ride, but bumps register with a thump. Honda's Civic rides softer and is quieter. Antilock braking feels strong and stable, with only moderate nosedive in simulated "panic" stops. Delivering slightly better acceleration, the twincam engine is a better choice than the tepid base 4-cylinder. Even with manual shift, though, both are merely adequate at merging with fast-moving traffic or pulling steadily up long grades. Automatic dulls off-the-line punch, but provides fuss-free gear changes. A 5-speed ZTS reached 60 mph in a so-so 9.5 seconds, and averaged 26.2 mpg. A ZTS with automatic averaged 23.2 mpg. Wind rush is noticeable, but noise is acceptable otherwise and engines are tolerably smooth.

Few subcompacts are roomier than a Focus. Occupants sit comfortably upright on chairlike cushions, enjoying bountiful head clearance and plenty of rear leg space, though rear head room is less generous. Controls are conspicuous and smooth-operating, and the air conditioner operates in all vent modes. No gauge is unobstructed, but the tachometer in the ZX3 and ZTS lacks a redline. Large front-door frames ease entry/exit, but rear doors don't open all that far. Cargo holds are generous, and rear seats flip/fold flat. Liftovers are low, and the sedan's trunklid hinges don't intrude into luggage space. Some test models have had poor-fitting interior panels.

VALUE FOR THE MONEY: Less refined than a class-leading Honda Civic and not as polished as the more conservative Toyota Corolla, the Focus offers more room, style, and body types than any competitor. Despite timid engines, it's also fun to drive. Word of advice: Don't buy a small car without checking out the Focus.

TROUBLE SPOTS

Climate control: The ventilation system may make fluttering noises when using the panel/defrost setting due to a problem with the linkage or whistle when the blower is running due to a gap on the resistor mounting. (2000)
Fuel pump: The fuel hose between the filler neck and tank may flake and clog. In-tank fuel filter and hoses are being replaced under a recall. (2000)
Vehicle noise: The right motor mount could break due to defective hardware resulting in noise, vibration, and possible driveshaft damage. Redesigned mounts were being installed under a recall. (2000)

AVERAGE REPLACEMENT COSTS

A/C Compressor	$650	CV Joints	$850
Alternator	410	Exhaust System	650
Automatic Trans.	1,200	Radiator	475
Brakes	455	Shocks and/or Struts	130
Clutch	410	Timing Chain/Belt	350

NHTSA RECALL HISTORY

2000 w/speed control: Control-cable core wire could catch on sleeve at cable end during wide-open throttle acceleration, preventing throttle from returning to idle. **2000:** Decklid wire harness on certain cars can fatigue and develop broken wires, resulting in loss of individual lamp functions or electrical short. **2000:** Hub retaining nuts can loosen, allowing left rear wheel and brake-drum assembly to separate. **2000-01 wagon and hatchback:** In certain vehicles with folding 60/40 second seat, when the 60-percent portion is folded down and load is applied to front edge of load floor, outboard-hinge pivot could disengage. **2000-01:** A switch located in the plastic cover of the wiper-motor gear case could malfunction and overheat, potentially resulting in loss of wiper function or fire. **2000-01:** Cars equipped with Zetec engines may have faulty battery cables, causing a short to occur, and possibly resulting in the illumination of the check-engine light and fire. Dealer will inspect and replace affected part. **2000-01:** On certain cars, bolts in the steering knuckle may become loose, resulting in vibration and eventual decrease in steering control. Dealer will inspect and tighten all loose bolts. **2000-01:** Contamination of fuel-filter delivery module can block fuel flow to the engine, causing stalling. **2001:** Seatback recliner handle spring on some vehicles could be damaged, causing seatback to be loose or to recline unexpectedly. **2002 SVT:** Throttle may not return to the closed position when the accelerator is released. It may be necessary to depress the clutch and apply the brake to stop the vehicle.

PRICES

	Good	Average	Poor
2000 Focus SE, ZTS	$5,600-6,400	$4,800-5,500	$2,300-2,600
Focus ZX3, LX	5,200-5,900	4,400-5,000	2,100-2,400
2001 Focus SE, ZTS	6,800-7,800	6,100-6,900	3,200-3,700
Focus ZX3, LX	6,200-6,900	5,400-6,900	2,700-3,000
2002 Focus SE, ZTS, ZX5, ZTW	8,000-10,000	7,200-9,000	4,100-5,100
Focus SVT	11,700-13,000	10,500-11,700	6,400-7,200
Focus ZX3, LX	7,200-8,000	6,400-7,100	3,500-3,900
2003 Focus SE, ZTS, ZX5, ZTW	9,500-11,500	8,600-10,400	4,900-6,000
Focus SVT	14,000-15,500	12,700-14,100	8,500-9,500
Focus ZX3, LX	8,500-9,500	7,700-8,600	4,400-4,900

For detailed information on this vehicle visit
http://used.consumerguide.com and enter code **2373**

1994-03 FORD MUSTANG

CG BEST BUY

CLASS: Sporty coupe
BUILT IN: USA
PROS: Acceleration (V8) • Antilock brakes (optional) • Handling/roadholding
CONS: Fuel economy (V8) • Rear-seat room • Ride (GT)

EVALUATION: All Mustangs take quick corners smartly, but because of a softened suspension, base cars ride with only modest jarring—considerably less shocking than in the past. A more stiffly suspended GT, on the other hand, grows harsh, actually crashing and banging over broken surfaces. Cobras and Mach 1s are stiffer-suspended yet, as expected, but their ride quality isn't noticeably worse.

Acceleration is adequate with the V6 and either transmission, though automatic downshifts tend to be delayed when dashing uphill. Obviously, the V8 is the choice for performance, though increased weight in this generation makes that engine seem a little less peppy than before. Fuel economy is good with a V6, but not with V8 power. The 4.6-liter V8 in later models yields little acceleration improvement, but it's smoother and more refined. Thrilling is the operative word for a session behind the wheel of a Cobra or Mach 1, both are true high-performance machines.

Wet-weather traction continues to be a problem on all Mustangs, especially V8s. All-disc brakes are fine, but we'd look for a Mustang with the optional antilocking brakes.

Entry/exit is easy enough, courtesy of the Mustang's relatively upright stance (compared to Camaro, at any rate). Backseat space is truly tight, but the cockpit has an open, airy feel. Instruments are unobstructed, controls near at hand, and the dual airbags are a safety bonus.

VALUE FOR THE MONEY: Cobras can be pricey, and don't expect discounts on the limited-production Bullitt. Overall, though, Mustang delivers sporty performance at a reasonable price—especially in base and GT form. A major improvement over its predecessor, and more user-friendly for everyday driving than Chevy's Camaro, the current Mustang is well worth a test drive.

TROUBLE SPOTS

Alternator belt: The drive-belt tensioner pulley or idler-pulley bearings are apt to make a squealing noise when the engine is started in cold weather. (1994-96)

Automatic transmission: The transmission may slip and the engine may flare when the transmission shifts into fourth gear, which can often be traced to a bad TR/MLP sensor. (1994-95)

Automatic transmission: The automatic transmission is notorious for shuddering or vibrating under light acceleration or when shifting between third and fourth gear above 35 mph. It requires that the transmission fluid be changed and that only Mercon fluid be used. (1994)

Blower motor: Squeaking or chirping blower motors are the result of defective brush holders. (1994)

Hard starting: If the engine does not want to start or cranks for a long time then stalls, the idle air-control valve may be sticking. (1995-96)

Vehicle noise: A chattering noise that can be felt coming from the rear during tight turns after highway driving is caused by a lack of friction modifier or over-shimming of the clutch packs in the Traction-Lok differential. (1994-96)

AVERAGE REPLACEMENT COSTS

A/C Compressor	$410	Exhaust System	$830
Alternator	535	Radiator	480
Automatic Trans.	675	Shocks and/or Struts	435
Brakes	245	Timing Chain/Belt	215
Clutch	435	Universal Joints	95

NHTSA RECALL HISTORY

1994 GT w/power lumbar adjustment: Electrical short can result in overheating, melting, smoke, and ignition of surrounding materials. **1994-96:** Tearing of bond between inner and outer hood panels during minor front-end collision can result in gap at leading edge of hood; could result in separation of outer panel. **1994-97:** Replacement driver-side airbag modules might not properly deploy in a crash. **1995 w/3.8-liter or 5.0-liter engines:** The engine-cooling-fan bearing can seize. Excessive heat may be generated, melting the fan-motor electrical connector, and possibly causing fan-motor components to ignite. **1995:** On some cars, passenger-airbag's inflator body is cracked and may not inflate properly; also, igniter end cap can separate, causing hot gases to be released. **1995:** Some outer tie-rod ends can fracture within 50,000 miles; may result in shake or shimmy and cause wheel to tuck inward or outward. **1996-01 w/manual transmission:** Vehicle could move unintentionally while in "Park." Dealers will modify parking-brake control. **1998 w/V8 engine:** Some cars have missing or inadequately brazed joints between fuel-rail body and mounting brackets; separation can result in leakage. **1998:** Some rack-and-pinion steering gears may have damaged shaft bearings. **1998-99:** Speed-control cable on certain vehicles can interfere with servo pulley, preventing throttle from returning to idle when disengaging the speed control. **1999-00 Cobra R:** Ball-joint assembly could cause knuckle casting to fail. If this occurs, the lower control arm could contact the inside of the rear wheel. In some cases, steering of the vehicle could be reduced. **1999-00:** Seatbelt retractor may have incorrectly formed pin shaft that could, in some circumstances, prevent seatbelt webbing from being extracted. **2000 GT (w/4.6-liter engine):** A coolant-flow blockage exists at the intake manifold heater-core nipple, resulting in no coolant flow to the heater and, therefore, no warm airflow from the heater or windshield defroster.

PRICES

	Good	Average	Poor
1994 Conv., GT Coupe	$4,200-5,300	$3,400-4,300	$1,400-1,700
GT Convertible	5,700-6,500	4,900-5,600	2,300-2,700
Mustang	3,200-3,800	2,500-3,000	800-900
1995 Conv., GT Coupe	4,800-5,600	4,000-4,700	1,800-2,100
GT Convertible	6,700-7,500	5,900-6,600	3,100-3,500
Mustang	3,600-4,300	2,900-3,400	1,000-1,200
1996 Cobra Convertible	10,700-12,000	9,600-10,800	5,700-6,400
Conv., GT Coupe	5,500-6,400	4,700-5,500	2,300-2,600
GT Convertible	7,500-8,500	6,800-7,700	3,800-4,300
Mustang	4,000-4,700	3,300-3,900	1,300-1,500
Mustang Cobra	9,200-10,200	8,300-9,200	4,800-5,300
1997 Cobra Convertible	12,200-13,500	11,000-12,200	6,800-7,600
Conv., GT Coupe	6,100-7,500	5,300-6,500	2,600-3,200
GT Convertible	8,600-9,600	7,700-8,600	4,500-5,000
Mustang	4,600-5,300	3,800-4,400	1,700-2,000
Mustang Cobra	10,500-11,700	9,500-10,500	5,600-6,200
1998 Cobra Convertible	14,500-15,800	13,200-14,400	9,000-9,800
Conv., GT Coupe	7,300-9,000	6,600-8,100	3,600-4,400
GT Convertible	10,000-11,000	9,000-9,900	5,200-5,700
Mustang	5,500-6,300	4,700-5,400	2,300-2,600
Mustang Cobra	12,500-13,500	11,300-12,200	7,100-7,700
1999 Cobra Convertible	16,500-18,000	15,000-16,400	10,600-11,500
Conv., GT Coupe	9,000-10,500	8,100-9,500	4,700-5,500
GT Convertible	12,000-13,000	10,800-11,700	6,700-7,300
Mustang	7,000-7,800	6,200-6,900	3,400-3,700
Mustang Cobra	14,500-15,500	13,200-14,100	9,000-9,600

2000 Conv., GT Coupe	$10,500-12,000	$9,500-10,800	$5,600-6,400
GT Convertible	14,000-15,200	12,700-13,800	8,500-9,300
Mustang	8,500-9,400	7,700-8,500	4,400-4,900
2001 Bullitt Coupe	16,500-18,000	15,000-16,400	10,600-11,500
Cobra Convertible	23,000-24,500	21,200-22,500	15,000-15,900
Conv., GT Coupe	12,500-14,000	11,300-12,600	7,100-8,000
GT Convertible	16,000-17,500	14,600-15,900	10,200-11,200
Mustang	10,000-11,000	9,000-9,900	5,200-5,700
Mustang Cobra	21,000-22,500	19,300-20,700	13,700-14,600
2002 Cobra Convertible	26,000-28,000	24,200-26,000	17,200-18,500
Conv., GT Coupe	14,500-16,200	13,200-14,700	9,000-10,000
GT Convertible	18,000-19,500	16,600-17,900	11,500-12,500
Mustang	11,700-12,700	10,500-11,400	6,400-7,000
Mustang Cobra	23,200-25,000	21,300-23,000	15,100-16,300
2003 Cobra Convertible	31,000-33,000	28,800-30,700	21,700-23,100
Conv., GT Coupe	16,500-18,500	15,000-16,800	10,600-11,800
GT Convertible	21,000-23,000	19,300-21,200	13,700-15,000
Mustang	13,500-14,700	12,300-13,400	8,000-8,700
Mustang Cobra	27,500-29,500	25,600-27,400	18,400-19,800
Mustang Mach 1	22,000-23,500	20,200-21,600	14,300-15,300

For detailed information on this vehicle visit
http://used.consumerguide.com and enter code 2037

1993-97 FORD PROBE

CLASS: Sporty coupe
BUILT IN: USA
PROS: Acceleration (V6)
• Antilock brakes (optional)
• Cargo room
• Steering/handling (GT)
• Visibility
CONS: Automatic-transmission performance • Rear-seat room • Ride (GT)

EVALUATION: Acceleration is excellent with the GT's V6 and standard 5-speed gearbox. Action from the 4-cylinder engine is adequate, at least with manual shift. Performance lags with optional 4-speed automatic, which is also slow to downshift. The engine's low-end torque simply isn't sufficient to move the car off with any degree of real vigor. Even the V6 engine feels somewhat sluggish with automatic.

Base-model handling is secure and sporty. Firm suspension tuning and low-profile tires give the GT sharp, agile handling and a secure grip. In exchange, you can expect to endure a harsher, more jittery ride. A Probe GT jiggles on roads that feel smooth in the MX-6 LS. That level of roughness can lead to fatigue on a long trip. Base Probes are softer suspended for a better ride, without losing much handling competence. Ford softened the GT's suspension for 1996, but tires are still stiff so the ride isn't a whole lot better.

FORD

Visibility is better than in most sport coupes, due to the low cowl and relatively slim roof pillars. Space is adequate up front. Space is scant in back for grownups. Cargo room ranks as generous, especially with the split rear seatback folded down, though the rear sill is quite tall. The modern dashboard is neatly laid out, though climate and radio controls don't fall too easily to hand.

VALUE FOR THE MONEY: Significantly improved over the first (1989-92) generation, the latest Probe delivers plenty of punch and prowess for its price.

TROUBLE SPOTS

Engine stalling: If the engine stalls when the transmission is shifted into drive, the problem may be a cracked mass airflow snorkel tube. (1993-94)

Fuel gauge: The fuel gauge may only read $3/4$ full when the tank is full because the fuel return line is bent and interferes with the sender in the tank. (1995-96)

Transmission leak: Automatic transmission fluid leaks from the vent and gives the appearance of a leak at the cooler lines or main control cover. (1994-96)

AVERAGE REPLACEMENT COSTS

A/C Compressor	$875	CV Joints	$780
Alternator	380	Exhaust System	485
Automatic Trans.	1,075	Radiator	430
Brakes	275	Shocks and/or Struts	770
Clutch	590	Timing Chain/Belt	180

NHTSA RECALL HISTORY

1993: Lower pivot pin that joins liftgate gas strut to body can separate from mounting bracket due to undersized rivet head; liftgate could descend suddenly, resulting in potential injury. **1994:** Passenger-side airbag on small number of cars can detach from, and deform, the mounting bracket if it deploys during an accident and no one is occupying that seating position. **1995:** On some cars, passenger airbag may not inflate properly; also, igniter end cap can separate, causing hot gases to be released. **1996:** Supplementary inflatable restraint caution label on driver's sunvisor does not contain proper warning that rearward-facing child safety seats should not be installed in front passenger seat position. **1997:** External spring in timing belt tensioner can break, get caught in belt, and result in engine stalling.

PRICES	Good	Average	Poor
1993 Probe	$2,000-2,600	$1,400-1,800	$300-400
Probe GT	2,400-3,000	1,800-2,200	500-600
1994 Probe	2,300-2,900	1,700-2,100	400-600
Probe GT	2,800-3,400	2,100-2,600	600-700
1995 Probe	2,600-3,200	1,900-2,400	500-700
Probe GT	3,200-3,800	2,500-3,000	800-900
1996 Probe GT	3,500-4,200	2,800-3,400	900-1,100
Probe SE	2,900-3,400	2,200-2,700	700-800
1997 Probe GT	4,000-4,700	3,300-3,900	1,300-1,500
Probe SE	3,300-4,000	2,600-3,200	800-1,000

For detailed information on this vehicle visit
http://used.consumerguide.com and enter code **2040**

1993-97 FORD RANGER

CLASS: Compact pickup truck

BUILT IN: USA

PROS: Acceleration (V6)
• Reliability • Ride

CONS: Control layout
• Fuel economy (V6)

EVALUATION: Acceleration is about the same as in the prior generation. Though adequate with a 5-speed, the 4-cylinder engine labors under a heavy load and generally feels lethargic with automatic. Ranger's 4.0-liter V6 uses only slightly more fuel than the 3.0-liter, and delivers good low-speed punch; but the 4.0 is somewhat coarse and noisy. A 4.0 should perform most tasks with relative ease, and it works well with the automatic to furnish prompt passing power. We averaged 16.5 mpg in a 4WD Splash SuperCab with the 4.0-liter V6.

Rangers ride nicely and handle well (for a truck, that is). The suspension absorbs most big bumps without jarring, and the truck is stable in turns. Steering feedback and response are top-notch, and the Ranger has a notably solid feel overall.

Gauges are unobstructed, and the climate controls and radio are grouped efficiently. However, some buttons on optional stereos are too small, and climate controls demand quite a reach around the steering wheel. A regular-cab interior lacks space behind the seat. Also, the steering wheel protrudes too far, leaving no surplus of space for larger drivers.

VALUE FOR THE MONEY: Ford sought a more carlike look and feel for its Ranger—and succeeded. Some rugged truck characteristics may have been gone, but we view the changes as improvements. Ranger remained one of the best in its class, but we recommend that you shop all three domestic brands—including the Dodge Dakota and Chevrolet S-Series—before deciding.

TROUBLE SPOTS

Air conditioner: Water may drip onto the floor when the air conditioner is operated because the evaporator strip seals were not properly positioned at the factory. (1995-96)

Hard starting: If the engine does not want to start or cranks for a long time then stalls, the idle air control valve may be sticking. (1995-96)

Radiator: The radiator may leak in cold weather because of a bad seal between the tank and core. (1995-96)

Vehicle noise: Loose frame rivets should be replaced with bolts (welding is not approved). (1993-96)

Vehicle noise: A chattering noise that can be felt coming from the rear during tight turns after highway driving is caused by a lack of friction modifier or over-shimming of the clutch packs in the Traction-Lok differential. (1993-96)

FORD

AVERAGE REPLACEMENT COSTS

A/C Compressor	$425	Exhaust System	$215
Alternator	280	Radiator	340
Automatic Trans.	745	Shocks and/or Struts	285
Brakes	300	Timing Chain/Belt	395
Clutch	390	Universal Joints	90

NHTSA RECALL HISTORY

1993-94 sold or registered in specified southern California counties: Studs that attach master cylinder to power-brake-booster assembly can develop stress corrosion cracking after extended period; if one or both studs fractures, master cylinder could separate from booster when brakes are applied, preventing brakes from activating. **1993-94 w/2.3-liter engine, registered in AK, ME, MI (upper peninsula), MN, MT, ND, NH, NY, VT, or WI:** During extreme cold in northern winters, ice can form in throttle body, causing throttle plate to remain in highway cruising position after accelerator is released or speed control is deactivated. **1993-94 w/V6 engine:** Flexible hose in front fuel line is susceptible to cracking. **1993-94 w/manual shift :** Parking brake might not hold. **1996:** Certification label shows incorrect rear-tire-inflation pressure.

PRICES

	Good	Average	Poor
1993 Ranger	$2,300-3,800	$1,700-2,700	$400-700
Ranger SuperCab	3,000-4,300	2,300-3,300	700-1,000
1994 Ranger	2,600-4,500	1,900-3,300	500-900
Ranger SuperCab	3,400-5,200	2,700-4,100	900-1,400
1995 Ranger	2,900-5,400	2,200-4,100	700-1,200
Ranger SuperCab	3,900-6,400	3,200-5,200	1,200-2,000
1996 Ranger	3,200-6,200	2,500-4,800	800-1,500
Ranger SuperCab	4,400-7,400	3,700-6,100	1,500-2,600
1997 Ranger	3,500-7,000	2,800-5,600	900-1,900
Ranger SuperCab	5,000-8,500	4,300-7,200	2,000-3,400

For detailed information on this vehicle visit http://used.consumerguide.com and enter code **2039**

1998-03 FORD RANGER

BEST BUY CG

CLASS: Compact pickup truck

BUILT IN: USA

PROS: Acceleration (4.0-liter V6) • Optional ABS (XLT, Splash) • Handling • Ride

CONS: Acceleration (4-cylinder) • Interior room (regular cab) • Rear-seat comfort

CONSUMER GUIDE®

EVALUATION: Four-cylinder Rangers struggle to gain speed, especially with an automatic transmission. We recommend the 4.0-liter V6, which uses only slightly more fuel than the 3.0 V6 and costs only slightly more. Although the 4.0 liter is a bit coarse and noisy, it offers plenty of low-speed torque and should perform most tasks with ease. That engine also works well with Ford's 5-speed automatic transmission and furnishes prompt passing power. None of these engines is quiet, though the sixes are slightly smoother than the four. Gas mileage is passable, too. We averaged 15.6 mpg in a long-term test of a 4WD SuperCab with the 4.0 and automatic.

Like its Mazda B-Series cousin, Ranger rides and handles admirably for a truck. Yes, it jiggles more on rough roads than most cars. Still, the suspension absorbs most bumps without jarring the occupants, and provides stable cornering with moderate body lean.

Slightly roomier than before, with more behind-the-seat storage space, Ranger's regular-cab interior is still not spacious. The longer regular cab allows the seatback to be tilted farther back than before, but taller drivers may find the SuperCab a necessity for comfort. Some shorter drivers may declare the bottoms of the bucket seats to be too long, catching them behind the knees.

The 4-door SuperCab option is a big plus, but those rear-hinged back doors are narrow and cannot be opened unless the front door has been opened first. Even with a bench seat, three adults would be a tight squeeze up front. Entry/exit borders on awkward in the higher-riding 4x4s and 2WD Edge models. SuperCabs have a pair of child-sized rear seats that flip down from the sidewalls, but that area is more useful for cargo than people. Controls are positioned within easy reach, in a carlike interior, though the climate panel is recessed too much for quick adjustment. Radio controls are easier to use than in the past. Solid in build, Rangers use better quality interior materials than might be expected in a compact pickup.

VALUE FOR THE MONEY: Yes, Ranger lacks the V8 of a Dodge Dakota and the smooth V6 offered by Chevy. Nevertheless, the Ranger is refined, well-built, and priced sensibly. No wonder Ranger has been the top-selling compact truck. Because Mazda's B-Series does not sell as well, however, prices might be a bit lower without the Ford badge.

TROUBLE SPOTS

Air conditioner: The air-conditioner hose may rub against the radiator hose and one, or both, develop leaks. (1998)
Audio system: The in-tank fuel pump causes a whining or buzzing noise to come through the radio speakers. (1998-99)
Battery: The battery tray may have burrs that cut into the battery causing it to leak and eventually fail. (1998)
Engine misfire: Hesitation or surging when accelerating is caused by a faulty mass airflow sensor. (1998-99)
Engine misfire: The truck may feel like it is thumping or jerking under acceleration due to a problem with the driveshaft requiring replacement. (1998-99)
Vehicle noise: A hammering noise occurs due to steam forming in the cooling system requiring a coolant-bypass retrofit kit. (1998-00)

FORD

AVERAGE REPLACEMENT COSTS

A/C Compressor	$450	Exhaust System	$245
Alternator	250	Radiator	430
Automatic Trans.	580	Shocks and/or Struts	445
Brakes	420	Timing Chain/Belt	95
Clutch	415	Universal Joints	145

NHTSA RECALL HISTORY

1998 4-wheel drive w/off-road option: Tire and rim identification information is incorrect. **1998 w/4.0-liter engine:** Flexible section of chassis-mounted fuel line on some trucks could contact exhaust manifold; might potentially result in damage to fuel line or, in some cases, cause a fuel leak. **1998-99:** Cruise-control cable can interfere with servo pulley and not allow throttle to return to idle. **1999 w/3.0-liter engine:** O-ring seal in fuel-injection pulse damper to fuel-rail joint could be damaged, allowing fuel leakage. **2000 w/2.5-liter engine:** Engine-coolant circulation through heater circuit is prevented by plugged return tube at water pump. **2000-01:** Hood striker could fracture causing the hood to fly open while the vehicle is being driven. **2001:** Driver's and/or front-passenger's outboard seatbelt buckle may not fully latch. In the event of a crash, the restraint system may not provide adequate occupant protection. **2002 w/manual transmission and FX4 Package:** The rear-axle differential case could fracture, possibly resulting in wheel lock-up.

PRICES

	Good	Average	Poor
1998 Ranger 2WD	$4,000-5,500	$3,300-4,500	$1,300-1,800
Ranger 4WD	5,800-7,500	5,000-6,500	2,400-3,200
SuperCab 2WD	5,700-7,300	4,900-6,300	2,300-3,000
SuperCab 4WD	7,500-9,000	6,800-8,100	3,800-4,500
1999 Ranger 2WD	4,600-6,000	3,800-5,000	1,700-2,200
Ranger 4WD	6,500-8,000	5,700-7,000	2,900-3,600
SuperCab 2WD	6,400-8,000	5,600-7,000	2,800-3,500
SuperCab 4WD	8,500-10,200	7,700-9,200	4,400-5,300
2000 Ranger 2WD	5,300-7,000	4,600-6,000	2,200-2,900
Ranger 4WD	7,700-9,200	6,900-8,300	3,900-4,600
SuperCab 2WD	7,600-9,200	6,800-8,300	3,800-4,600
SuperCab 4WD	10,200-12,000	9,200-10,800	5,300-6,200
2001 Ranger 2WD	6,200-8,000	5,400-7,000	2,700-3,400
Ranger 4WD	9,000-10,500	8,100-9,500	4,700-5,500
SuperCab 2WD	9,000-10,800	8,100-9,700	4,700-5,600
SuperCab 4WD	11,700-13,600	10,500-12,200	6,400-7,500
2002 Ranger 2WD	7,500-9,500	6,800-8,600	3,800-4,800
Ranger 4WD	10,200-12,100	9,200-10,900	5,300-6,300
SuperCab 2WD	10,000-12,300	9,000-11,100	5,200-6,400
SuperCab 4WD	13,000-15,200	11,800-13,800	7,500-8,800
2003 Ranger 2WD	9,500-12,000	8,600-10,800	4,900-6,200
Ranger 4WD	12,500-14,500	11,300-13,100	7,100-8,300
SuperCab 2WD	11,500-15,000	10,400-13,500	6,300-8,300
SuperCab 4WD	14,500-17,500	13,200-15,900	9,000-10,900

For detailed information on this vehicle visit
http://used.consumerguide.com and enter code **2306**

1990-95 FORD TAURUS

CLASS: Midsize car

BUILT IN: USA

PROS: Acceleration (V6)
• Antilock brakes (optional)
• Handling/roadholding
• Passenger and cargo room
• Ride

CONS: Acceleration (4-cylinder) • Fuel economy (V6) • Radio controls

EVALUATION: Taurus feels composed over bumps and in corners. Steering is precise, and suspension movements are well-controlled. Taurus is sure-footed and agile, with balanced handling in turns and minimal body lean. The firm, Euro-style ride is just right, even if you can expect a few bumps on rougher surfaces.

The weak, noisy 4-cylinder engine just isn't strong enough to power a Taurus. A 3.0-liter V6 promises much brisker passing, and the optional 3.8-liter V6 noticeably stronger acceleration from a standstill, plus better midrange response. Harsh shifts from the automatic transmission do occur occasionally in low-speed driving. Neither V6 is frugal: One Taurus averaged just 17.9 mpg in commuting and expressway driving. For excitement behind the wheel of a seemingly sedate midsize sedan, SHO is the way to go. Acceleration rivals that of the world's leading sports sedans.

Variable-assist power steering was modified in 1992, resulting in a less-precise feel at highway speed. Also on the downside, Taurus tires thump loudly over bumps.

Head room is ample all around, and sedans have a deep, wide trunk. Analog gauges are clearly marked, but the stereo sits low and has small, poorly marked controls.

VALUE FOR THE MONEY: We rank the early '90s Taurus/Sable among the most impressive domestic cars: solid, roomy, great to look at, and a joy to drive.

TROUBLE SPOTS

Blower motor: Squeaking or chirping blower motors are the result of defective brush holders. (1990-94)

Engine noise: The motor mounts are prone to wear out prematurely so Ford has issued a voluntary recall (number 92M77) to replace the right front and right rear mounts. The coverage is 6 years or 60,000 miles. (1992-93)

Hard starting: If the engine does not start or cranks for a long time then stalls, the idle air control valve may be sticking. (1995)

Oil leak: Ford extended the warranty on the 3.8-liter Taurus to 7/100,000 and may compensate owners for repairs related to head gasket failures. (1994-95)

Suspension problems: The stabilizer bar links wear rapidly due to lack of grease fittings, especially if a technician is careless when servicing the MacPherson struts. (1990-95)

FORD

Tire wear: Premature tire wear and cupping is caused by rear wheel misalignment. (1990-95)

Tire wear: Inner edge of rear tires wear excessively from camber problems corrected with a revised rear suspension adjuster kit. (1990-95)

Vehicle noise: A popping noise comes from the front due to the strut rod bushing mountings moving in the frame. (1990-95)

AVERAGE REPLACEMENT COSTS

A/C Compressor	$455	Exhaust System	$365
Alternator	440	Radiator	525
Automatic Trans.	930	Shocks and/or Struts	495
Brakes	230	Timing Chain/Belt	210
CV Joints	505		

NHTSA RECALL HISTORY

1990-91: Front brake rotors on cars sold in 14 northeastern and Great Lakes states may suffer severe corrosion, resulting in reduced braking effectiveness. **1990-95 sold or registered in 24 states or D.C.:** Rear lower subframe mount plate nut can experience corrosion cracking if subjected to long-term exposure to road salt; can result in fracture. **1991-95 w/3.8-liter engine in 23 states:** Water can accumulate within speed-control conduit; if cable has frozen, throttle can stick and not return to idle. **1992 wagon:** Children can accidentally lock themselves in footwell area of rear-facing third seat or in storage compartment in wagons that lack optional third seat; self-latching assembly should be replaced with a unit that can be closed only with a key. **1992 wagon:** Secondary liftgate latch mechanism on some cars may not function, possibly allowing liftgate to open while car is in motion. **1992-93:** On cars sold in 14 Midwestern and Northeastern states, body mounts at rear subframe corners (which support engine/transmission) may detach due to corrosion, allowing subframe to drop; could result in clunking noise or altered steering-wheel alignment or, if both corners drop, could make steering very difficult. **1992-95 w/3.0- or 3.8-liter engine, in AK, IA, MN, NE, ND, or SD:** During high winds, heavy snow, and low temperatures, engine fan may become blocked or frozen; can cause smoke/flame. **1993 in 21 states:** Front coil springs can fracture as a result of corrosion in combination with small cracks. **1993:** Controllers intended for rear-drive vehicles (instead of front-drive) may have been installed in a few cars with optional antilock braking. **1993-94:** Headlights can flash intermittently as a result of a circuit-breaker opening. **1995 w/3.0-liter and 3.8-liter engines:** The engine cooling fan bearing can seize. Excessive heat may be generated, melting the fan motor electrical connector, and possibly causing fan motor components to ignite. **1995:** On some cars, retainer that holds master cylinder pushrod to brake pedal arm is missing or not fully installed; can result in loss of braking.

PRICES

	Good	Average	Poor
1990 Taurus	$1,000-1,600	$600-1,000	$100-200
Taurus SHO	1,700-2,300	1,100-1,500	300
1991 Taurus	1,200-1,800	700-1,100	100-200
Taurus SHO	2,000-2,600	1,400-1,800	300-400

1992 Taurus	$1,400-2,100	$900-1,300	$200-300
Taurus SHO	2,400-3,000	1,800-2,200	500-600
1993 Taurus	1,600-2,300	1,100-1,500	400-600
Taurus SHO	2,800-3,500	2,100-2,600	600-800
1994 Taurus	1,900-2,600	1,300-1,800	300-400
Taurus SHO	3,000-3,700	2,300-2,800	700-900
1995 Taurus	2,200-2,900	1,600-2,100	400-600
Taurus SHO	3,500-4,200	2,800-3,400	900-1,100

For detailed information on this vehicle visit
http://used.consumerguide.com and enter code **2043**

1996-99 FORD TAURUS

CLASS: Midsize car

BUILT IN: USA

PROS: Acceleration (LX, SHO) • Optional antilock brakes • Passenger and cargo room • Steering/handling

CONS: Automatic-transmission performance (G, GL) • Rear visibility • Ride (SHO)

EVALUATION: An LX accelerates with greater authority than its less-potent G/GL siblings. That 200-horsepower engine is smooth, refined, and potent at higher engine speeds. Low-speed torque is lacking, however, so you must floor the throttle to achieve brisk passing. The LX transmission shifts smoothly.

Not only is the G/GL V6 engine less powerful, but it's noisier, rougher, and slower. Its transmission often stumbles, shifts roughly, and is slow to downshift for passing. Low-speed power is also lacking in the SHO's V8, though it's plenty potent at higher speeds. You simply have to wait until engine speed reaches 3000 rpm or so before much happens.

Steering is light and precise. Both models corner with good grip and commendable composure. Ride quality has improved somewhat, but the suspension does not absorb bumps well and feels too stiff on rough roads. Beware: The SHO's ride is stiff at all times. Wind and road noise have been reduced compared to previous Tauruses.

The modern-looking control panel for the climate and audio systems is easy to see and reach, but buttons are overly abundant and many look alike. With optional automatic air conditioning, that control pad gets packed full.

Interior space is better all around than before, especially in the rear, where leg room has grown substantially. Sitting three across, however, will crowd everyone—in both front and rear. The sedan trunk is roomy—wide, deep, and reaching well forward. The driver enjoys a clear view to the front and sides, but it's difficult to see the trunk of the sedan.

VALUE FOR THE MONEY: Though not perfect, Taurus is roomy, well-built, and enjoyable to drive. Prices went up for this generation, but Tauruses remained a good value and an excellent choice, new or used.

FORD

TROUBLE SPOTS

Air conditioner: The air conditioning may not cool properly because the lines leak at the spring-lock couplings. Larger O-rings are available. (1996-97)

Automatic transmission: Vehicles with the AX4S automatic transmission may shift harshly from first to second gear. (1996-97)

Dashboard lights: The check-engine lightcomes on for a variety of reasons including bad gasoline, a wobbling accessory drive pulley, or bad spark plugs. (1996-97)

Steering problems: The power steering gets harder to turn when decelerating from about 50 miles per hour or when shifting form reverse to drive requiring replacement of the control module and/or transmission range sensors. (1996)

Suspension noise: The sway bar links wear prematurely causing a clunking noise. Revised parts are available. (1996-97)

Tire wear: Rear tires wear prematurely due to incorrect rear alignment (toe and camber). (1996-97)

Tire wear: Inner edge of rear tires wear excessively from camber problems corrected with a revised rear suspension adjuster kit. (1996-97)

Vehicle noise: Rattling and buzzing from under the car is common due to loose heat shields on the catalytic converter and/or muffler. (1996-97)

Vehicle noise: Noises from the front end (popping, clunking, knocking) result from worn sway bar links. Countermeasure links have been issued by the carmaker. (1996-97)

Water leak: Water leaks onto the front floor because of poor sealing of the cabin air filter cowl inlet. (1996-98)

AVERAGE REPLACEMENT COSTS

A/C Compressor	$440	Exhaust System	$415
Alternator	350	Radiator	585
Automatic Trans.	1,115	Shocks and/or Struts	600
Brakes	280	Timing Chain/Belt	350
CV Joints	605		

NHTSA RECALL HISTORY

1996: Brake-fluid indicator can malfunction. **1996:** Vacuum diaphragm in fuel-pressure regulator was damaged during manufacture; if it tears or ruptures, liquid fuel could be released from air-cleaner assembly or exhaust system. **1996-97:** "Park"-pawl abutment bracket has sharp edge, which can cause pawl to hang up and not engage gear; vehicle can then move, even though indicator shows "Park." **1997 w/AX4S automatic transaxle:** Low/intermediate servo cover can separate while vehicle is moving, allowing transmission fluid to contact the hot catalytic converter. **1997-98:** Headlamp-aiming instruction in owner's manual is not sufficiently clear. **1998-99 w/manual seat tracks:** Front-seatbelt-buckle attaching stud may have been improperly heat-treated, resulting in cracks. **1999 w/"California" Emissions:** Incorrect transmission-oil-cooler line was installed, which contacts ABS module bracket and, over time, can wear and develop a leak. **1999:** Retainer clip can disengage from accelerator cable and fall into pedal-arm pivot area; engine may not fully return to idle, and insulator could interfere with cable. **1999**: Seatbelt retractor may have incorrectly formed pin shaft that could, in some circumstances, prevent seatbelt webbing from being extracted.

PRICES

	Good	Average	Poor
1996 Taurus SHO	$4,500-5,400	$3,700-4,500	$1,600-1,900
Taurus sedan	2,600-3,300	1,900-2,400	500-700
Taurus wagon	3,100-3,700	2,400-2,900	700-900
1997 Taurus SHO	5,500-6,500	4,700-5,600	2,300-2,700
Taurus sedan	3,000-3,800	2,300-2,900	700-900
Taurus wagon	3,600-4,200	2,900-3,400	1,000-1,200
1998 Taurus SHO	7,000-8,000	6,200-7,100	3,400-3,800
Taurus sedan	3,600-4,400	2,900-3,500	1,000-1,200
Taurus wagon	4,400-5,000	3,700-4,200	1,500-1,800
1999 Taurus SHO	8,500-9,500	7,700-8,600	4,400-4,900
Taurus sedan	4,500-5,300	3,700-4,400	1,600-1,900
Taurus wagon	5,400-6,200	4,600-5,300	2,200-2,500

For detailed information on this vehicle visit http://used.consumerguide.com and enter code **2191**

2000-03 FORD TAURUS

CLASS: Midsize car
BUILT IN: USA
PROS: Cargo room
• Handling/roadholding
• Rear-seat comfort
CONS: Low-speed acceleration

EVALUATION: Taurus delivers plenty of performance for a mainstream midsize car, though it lacks class-leading acceleration. Both engines run smoothly, but neither moves all that swiftly beyond midrange speeds. Each V6 can accelerate suitably from a standstill, but a Chevrolet Impala with the base engine responds better to the throttle than a Taurus, at 25-50 mph. Fuel economy with the twincam engine averaged 18.4 mpg. Road manners are another story. Taurus feels balanced, secure, and predictable even in rapid directional changes. Steering has fine on-center sense, but turning effort is not as linear as some drivers might like. Resistance to wallow and float is impressive, but rough-road ride is not. Stopping power feels strong and easily modulated. Family focused space is a strong point, including excellent back-seat room and comfort. Rear head clearance is generous, helped by the revised roof shape. Leg/foot space also is plentiful. The back seat is substantial and comfortably contoured, but the wagon's fold-away rear-racing third seat is for children under 80 pounds. Front outboard seating positions are uncrowded, but the bench's center spot is mighty snug. The new adjustable pedals work easily via a control on the seat

FORD

bottom. Shorter drivers can sit farther from the steering-wheel airbag. Gauges are unobstructed, but their analog markings are small. On bucket-seat models, the only gear indicator is near the console floor shift. Audio and climate controls are easy to see and use, but lack selectable air conditioning or recirculation modes. Luggage space is generous in either body style.

VALUE FOR THE MONEY: Taurus returned to its roots as family transportation with the 2000 redesign. Fully contemporary in styling, a Taurus delivers fine road manners, great utility, and an appealing array of safety features, at competitive prices. Despite acceleration limitations and imperfect ride comfort, Taurus deserves a place on any midsize-car shopping list.

TROUBLE SPOTS

Audio system: Noise (whine or buzz) in the radio speakers is probably due to interference from the in-tank fuel pump requiring a RFI filter on the pump assembly. (2000-01)

Engine misfire: Cam failures can lead to failure on V8 engines installed on SHO models. It is possible to weld the cams prior to the failure. (1996-99)

Fuel odors: Gasoline odor is probably due to a bad gasket on the lower intake manifold on the 3.0-L Duratec engine. (2000-01)

Vehicle shake: Harsh downshifts or shudder, especially on curves, can be caused by the transmission-fluid level being below the fullest level as shown on the dipstick. (2000)

AVERAGE REPLACEMENT COSTS

A/C Compressor	$405	Exhaust System	$300
Alternator	535	Radiator	405
Automatic Trans.	1,120	Shocks and/or Struts	1,100
Brakes	240	Timing Chain/Belt	180
CV Joints	990		

NHTSA RECALL HISTORY

2000: Headlamp-switch knob can fracture and separate from the headlamp switch. **2000:** On certain vehicles, "vehicle capacity weight" and "designated seating capacity" information was not printed on safety-certification labels. **2000-01 w/adjustable pedals:** Grease from the adjustable-pedal assembly enters the stoplamp switch and can contaminate the contacts, leading to carbon buildup and a potential short circuit. **2000-01:** A switch located in the plastic cover of the wiper-motor gear case could malfunction and overheat, potentially resulting in loss of wiper function or fire. **2000-01:** Stoplamp can illuminate (at reduced intensity) even though the service brakes have not been applied. **2001:** Child-safety-seat anchor-latch fasteners on certain vehicles do not have adequate residual torque; road vibrations could cause a nut to loosen and separate. **2001:** Owner's guides may not identify center rear seating position as having LATCH-compatible lower anchorages. **2002 w/adjustable pedals:** Pedals are not far enough apart and must be separated to at least 50 mm to avoid depressing one or the other, or both, unintentionally. **2003:** Some windshields may have been mounted improperly, leading to increased wind noise and leakage. Dealer will inspect and replace these windshields.

PRICES	Good	Average	Poor
2000 Taurus sedan	$6,000-7,600	$5,200-6,600	$2,500-3,200
Taurus wagon	7,200-8,200	6,400-7,300	3,500-4,000
2001 Taurus sedan	7,200-9,200	6,400-8,200	3,500-4,500
Taurus wagon	8,700-10,000	7,800-9,000	4,500-5,200
2002 Taurus sedan	8,700-11,200	7,800-10,100	4,500-5,800
Taurus wagon	10,500-12,000	9,500-10,800	5,600-6,400
2003 Taurus sedan	11,000-13,700	9,900-12,300	5,900-7,400
Taurus wagon	13,000-15,000	11,800-13,700	7,500-8,700

For detailed information on this vehicle visit
http://used.consumerguide.com and enter code **2374**

1995-98 FORD WINDSTAR

CLASS: Minivan

BUILT IN: Canada

PROS: Antilock brakes
• Passenger and cargo room
• Ride/handling

CONS: Fuel economy
• Instruments/controls
• Rear-seat entry/exit
• Steering feel

EVALUATION: Start-up acceleration with the 3.8-liter engine is okay, but the relatively heavy Windstar fails to feel truly lively. The automatic transmission typically pauses before downshifting to pass, and often shifts roughly. The stronger 1996 version of the 3.8-liter doesn't improve performance dramatically, but its extra passing power is appreciated. The 3.0-liter V6 has to struggle, and feels sluggish when passing. Gas mileage is not the greatest either way. We averaged 15.9 mpg with one Windstar and just 13.8 with another. A 3.0-liter Windstar averaged 16 mpg in urban driving and 20-21 mpg on the highway.

The absorbent suspension delivers a comfortable, stable ride at highway speeds and also on bumpy urban streets. Body lean is moderate, and tires grip well in spirited cornering. On the downside, steering feels loose and imprecise.

Getting in and out of the front seats is just about as easy as in most passenger cars. Climbing into the rear requires ducking around a shoulder belt for the middle seat. The rear seat must be pushed all the way back on its 7-inch track to produce adequate leg space.

Major controls are backlit at night, and the dashboard is conveniently laid out. The stereo is easy to reach, but controls are small and hard to decipher. Round dials for the climate system are easy to use. With all seats in place, Windstar offers 16 cubic feet of cargo room—more than a Grand Caravan/Voyager.

VALUE FOR THE MONEY: Windstars haven't proven to be quite as successful as Ford had hoped, but Ford's front-drive model equals or beats Chrysler's minivans in key areas of performance and accommodations. Therefore, Windstar is well worth a try.

TROUBLE SPOTS

Air conditioner: Moaning air conditioners are repaired by replacing the A/C compressor clutch and pulley. (1995-97)

Airbags: Diagnostic trouble codes for the airbag system flash intermittently requiring reprogramming. (1995)

Audio system: Whining noises in the radio speakers are caused by the fuel pump in the gas tank. An electronic noise filter must be installed on the fuel pump. (1995-96)

Brakes: The parking brake may fail to release because the release rod breaks. (1995-98)

Engine noise: A clunk heard and/or felt from the floor on acceleration, deceleration, or turns is caused by movement between the body and subframe, which is corrected by installing revised insulators. (1995-96)

Oil leak: Ford extended the warranty on 3.8-liter Windstars to 7/100,000 and may compensate owners for repairs related to head gasket failures. (1995)

Poor transmission shift: Vehicles with the AX4S automatic transmission may shift harshly from first to second gear. (1996-97)

AVERAGE REPLACEMENT COSTS

A/C Compressor	$380	Exhaust System	$425
Alternator	430	Radiator	425
Brakes	320	Shocks and/or Struts	515
CV Joints	476	Timing Chain/Belt	520

NHTSA RECALL HISTORY

1995 in certain hot-weather states: Cracks can develop in standard 20-gallon fuel tank. **1995:** Improperly tightened alternator-output wire may result in overheating and possible fire. **1995:** Some passenger airbags may not inflate properly; also, igniter end cap can separate, releasing hot gases. **1995:** Wiring-harness insulation can abrade on a brace between instrument panel and cowl, resulting in short-circuit and possible fire. **1995-96:** Tearing of bond between inner and outer hood panels during minor front-end collisions can result in gap at leading edge of hood; could lead to total separation of outer hood panel. **1996:** Due to improperly torqued fasteners, driver's seat on a few minivans may not hold properly in an accident. **1996:** Park-pawl abutment bracket has sharp edge, which can cause pawl to hang up and not engage gear; vehicle can move even though indicator shows Park. **1996-98:** Brake master cylinder on certain vehicles is oriented so warning statements are not entirely visible by direct view. **1996-98:** Certain off-lease vehicles, Canadian in origin but sold in the U.S., have daytime running lights that do not meet U.S. Specifications. **1997:** Servo cover can separate, causing transmission fluid to leak and contact catalytic converter; could result in fire. **1997-98:** Front coil springs could fracture as a result of corrosion. Some tires have deflated due to contact with a broken spring. **1998:** Damaged bearings on a few minivans can increase steering effort.

PRICES

	Good	Average	Poor
1995 Windstar GL	$2,700-3,400	$2,000-2,600	$600-700
Windstar LX	3,400-4,200	2,700-3,300	900-1,100

1996 Windstar GL	$3,200-4,000	$2,500-3,100	$800-1,000
Windstar LX	4,200-5,000	3,400-4,100	1,400-1,700
1997 Windstar LX	5,000-5,800	4,300-4,900	2,000-2,300
Windstar, GL	3,700-4,800	3,000-3,900	1,100-1,400
1998 Windstar 3.0L, GL	4,200-5,500	3,400-4,500	1,400-1,800
Windstar LX	5,800-6,600	5,000-5,700	2,400-2,800
Windstar Limited	6,600-7,400	5,800-6,500	3,000-3,300

For detailed information on this vehicle visit
http://used.consumerguide.com and enter code 2162

1999-03 FORD WINDSTAR

CLASS: Minivan
BUILT IN: Canada
PROS: Passenger and cargo room
CONS: Fuel economy

EVALUATION: Windstar has been, and continues to be, one of the better all-around minivan performers. The 3.0-liter engine struggles to provide adequate acceleration, making the quieter, smoother 3.8-liter V6 a stronger and better choice. That engine furnishes sufficient power even with a full load of passengers, and should not consume much more fuel than the overworked 3.0 liter. Both engines are gruff under hard throttle. With the longest wheelbase of any mini-van, Windstar provides a stable, carlike ride, though it does not absorb bumps quite as well as a Toyota Sienna. Handling is confident and better than Sienna's. Even so, steering feels artificial and does not respond as quickly as General Motors minivans or the Honda Odyssey. Brake-pedal feel is good, but overall stopping power is about average. One test SEL exhibited annoying torque steer in brisk take-offs. A friendly dashboard and comfortable, roomy seating carry over from the previous (1995-98) Windstar, with improvements evident in several areas. Power sliding doors are a true convenience. Even the manual sliders are unusual-ly easy to open and close, thanks to easy-to-grip interior handles. Rear hatches raise and lower easily, though separate-opening rear glass was not available. Substantial, supportive seats are heavy, so removal and installation demand muscle and technique, despite new rear rollers. Seatbacks do fold forward and recline, allowing great cargo and passenger versatility. Audio controls are too "busy," but the climate system's ability to run air conditioning in all vent modes is a benefit. If installed, the Reverse Sensing System is a valuable safeguard against unseen objects directly behind. That's helpful, because the base of the Windstar's rear window is not visible to the driver, complicating backing up.

VALUE FOR THE MONEY: Chrysler, Honda, and Toyota minivans have been ranked Best Buys, but the solid, easy-driving Windstar also is a fine choice, boasting some significant new safety and convenience features.

TROUBLE SPOTS

FORD

Air conditioner: Insufficient air conditioning may be due to a loose fitting at the condenser allowing the refrigerant to escape. (1999)

Climate control: Lack of climate-control temperature adjustment may be due a defective heater-control head or binding blend door. (1999)

Doors: Corroded relay contacts in the controller prevent the power sliding door from closing. (1999-00)

Engine knock: Engine knock may be due to oil getting into the intake manifold leading to a buildup of carbon in the cylinders. A redesigned valve cover alleviates the problem. (1999-00)

Seat: Drivers weighing more than 275 lbs. can pinch the electrical harness between the seat and frame shorting out the power seat circuit and blowing the fuse. (1999)

AVERAGE REPLACEMENT COSTS

A/C Compressor	$415	Exhaust System	$320
Alternator	535	Radiator	395
Automatic Trans.	1,120	Shocks and/or Struts	1,200
Brakes	240	Timing Chain/Belt	180
CV Joints	990		

NHTSA RECALL HISTORY

1999: Brake master cylinder on certain vehicles is oriented so warning statements are not entirely visible by direct view. **1999:** On certain vehicles, brake-fluid warning statement embossed on top of filler cap, and also on side of master-cylinder reservoir body, is not entirely visible by direct view. **1999-00:** Certain instrument clusters without a "message center" fail to comply with Federal safety requirements. **1999-01:** Auxiliary air-conditioning blower motor stops turning while in the medium-low blower speed setting, there is the potential that the resistor may become hot and smoke. **1999-01:** Wiper-motor gear case could malfunction and overheat, causing loss of wiper function or fire. **2000:** Certain minivans may have incorrect fuel-line end forms that result in insufficient pull-apart force for the fuel-line connection. **2000:** Some minivans may have incorrect urethane, resulting in an adhesive bond rather than the intended molecular bond for the front windshield and rear liftgate glass. If the bond deteriorates, it could provide less than the intended level of glass retention in a crash. **2000-01 w/adjustable pedals:** Driver's floormat could interfere with accelerator pedal, potentially resulting in stuck throttle. **2001:** Certain vehicles were built with a newly designed restraint-control module that, in some cases, does not recognize certain system faults that could result in airbag or seatbelt pretensioner unexpectedly activating during the self-test sequence at start-up time. **2001:** Driver- and/or font passenger-outboard seatbelt buckle may not fully latch. **2001:** Restraint-control module or crash sensor may have one or more screws missing, which could affect performance of occupant restraint. **2001-03:** Lower seat-to-floor latches on second- and third-row seats may fail in a crash resulting in occupant injury.

PRICES	Good	Average	Poor
1999 Windstar	$5,500-8,500	$4,700-7,300	$2,300-3,500
Windstar SEL	10,200-11,500	9,200-10,400	5,300-6,000
2000 SEL, Limited	$12,500-14,000	$11,300-12,600	$7,100-8,000

Windstar	7,500-10,500	6,800-9,500	3,800-5,300
2001 SEL, Limited	15,300-17,000	13,900-15,500	9,800-10,900
Windstar	10,000-13,200	9,000-11,900	5,200-6,900
2002 SEL, Limited	18,200-20,000	16,700-18,400	11,600-12,800
Windstar	12,500-15,500	11,300-14,000	7,100-8,800
2003 SEL, Limited	21,000-23,500	19,300-21,600	13,700-15,300
Windstar	15,000-18,000	13,700-16,400	9,500-11,300

For detailed information on this vehicle visit
http://used.consumerguide.com and enter code **2375**

1990-98 GEO/CHEVROLET TRACKER

CLASS: Compact sport-utility vehicle
BUILT IN: Canada, Japan
PROS: Fuel economy • 4WD traction (4WD)
CONS: Noise • Rear-seat room • Ride

EVALUATION: The initial 80-horsepower engine has sufficient power for decent acceleration and passing on the 2-door model. With automatic, you have to push the pedal to the floor often to keep up with traffic. That's true even with the 95-horsepower engine. In addition, four-doors are so sluggish with automatic that passing maneuvers have to be planned with care. Gas mileage is fine. We've averaged 24 mpg in a 4-wheel-drive convertible and 28.6 mpg with 2-wheel drive.

Tall and narrow, a Tracker must be driven with care through turns due to a high center of gravity. Even if it's not quite as precarious as it may seem while cornering, the abundant body lean quickly grows frightening. The ride is undeniably choppy, and noise levels are high. Two-wheel-drive Trackers are softer suspended for easier going on rough pavement, but even they get choppy.

A Tracker's interior is roomy for two in front, but the back seat is best for children. The driver's seat lacks much rearward travel, and suffers minimal space past one's left shoulder. Cargo space behind the rear seat is minuscule, but at least you can fold the seat forward if a load of parcels has to be transported. Controls operate smoothly; gauges are simple. Four-door wagons offer lots of head room, adequate rear leg space, and ample cargo area.

VALUE FOR THE MONEY: More modern and refined than the paramilitary Jeep Wrangler, Trackers are appealing in many ways. Still, Trackers and Suzuki Sidekicks are just too rough and noisy for service as daily drivers.

TROUBLE SPOTS

See the 1990-98 Suzuki Sidekick.

AVERAGE REPLACEMENT COSTS

See the 1990-98 Suzuki Sidekick.

NHTSA RECALL HISTORY

1990-91: Front-seatbelt release button can break and pieces can fall inside, causing improper operation. **1995:** Steering-wheel hub to spoke weld on some vehicles can fracture, allowing steering wheel to separate. **1996 4-door:** Fuel tank can puncture during rear-end collision.

PRICES	Good	Average	Poor
1990 Tracker 4WD	$1,500-2,000	$1,000-1,300	$200-300
1991 Tracker 2WD	1,100-1,700	700-1,000	100-200
Tracker 4WD	1,700-2,300	1,100-1,500	300
1992 Tracker 2WD	1,200-1,800	700-1,100	100-200
Tracker 4WD	1,900-2,500	1,300-1,700	300-400
1993 Tracker 2WD	1,400-2,000	900-1,300	200
Tracker 4WD	2,100-2,700	1,500-1,900	400-500
1994 Tracker 2WD	1,600-2,200	1,100-1,500	200-300
Tracker 4WD	2,300-3,000	1,700-2,200	400-600
1995 Tracker 2WD	1,800-2,400	1,200-1,600	300-400
Tracker 4WD	2,600-3,300	1,900-2,400	500-700
1996 Tracker 2WD	2,100-3,000	1,500-2,100	400-500
Tracker 4WD	3,100-3,800	2,400-3,000	700-900
1997 Tracker 2WD	2,600-3,700	1,900-2,700	500-800
Tracker 4WD	3,600-4,600	2,900-3,700	1,000-1,300
1998 Tracker 2WD	3,200-4,100	2,500-3,200	800-1,000
Tracker 4WD	4,200-5,400	3,400-4,400	1,400-1,800

For detailed information on this vehicle visit
http://used.consumerguide.com and enter code **2046**

1990-94 GMC JIMMY

CLASS: Midsize sport-utility vehicle

BUILT IN: USA

PROS: Acceleration • Antilock rear brakes • 4WD traction • Passenger room

CONS: Fuel economy • Noise • Rear-seat entry/exit (2-doors) • Ride

EVALUATION: The V6 develops considerable torque at low engine speeds for strong around-town acceleration and ample towing ability. Gas mileage is nothing to rave about with either transmission. Dramatic differences in ride/handling are noticeable between a model with the base suspension and tires, and one with off-road equipment. Expect a punishing ride with the latter. A 2-door tends to bounce and bang over bumpy roads. The 4-door's longer wheelbase improves ride quality, but this vehicle's suspension is among the least competent in its class. Interior noise also gets bothersome on the highway.

Interior room is good, though not as spacious as an Explorer or Grand Cherokee. Getting in or out is easy because there's hardly any step up. Because its back seat is ahead of the rear wheelwells, the 4-door offers 15 more inches of hip room than the 2-door.

Cargo space isn't as vast as might be expected with the rear seatback up and inside spare tire in place. Although the dashboard layout is good, some controls are a long reach, and radio buttons are small. The driving position is okay, but the optional gauge cluster is hard to read at a glance, day or night.

VALUE FOR THE MONEY: Offering satisfactory refinement and safety, and more carlike manners than the imports, GM's near-twins are reasonably good choices in a smaller sport-utility.

TROUBLE SPOTS

See the 1990-94 Chevrolet S10 Blazer.

AVERAGE REPLACEMENT COSTS

See the 1990-94 Chevrolet S10 Blazer.

NHTSA RECALL HISTORY

1990-91: Fuel tank sender seal may be out of position; could result in fuel leakage. **1991:** Rear-seatbelt-buckle release button can stick in unlatched position. **1991-94 4WD w/ABS:** Increased stopping distances can occur during ABS stops while in 2WD mode. **1993:** Rear seatbelts may not meet government requirements. **1994 w/VR4 weight-distribution trailer hitch option:** Trailer-hitch attaching bolts were not tightened adequately.

PRICES

	Good	Average	Poor
1990 Jimmy 2WD	$1,200-1,900	$700-1,200	$100-200
Jimmy 4WD	1,900-2,500	1,300-1,700	300-400
1991 Jimmy 2WD	1,500-2,300	1,000-1,500	200-300
Jimmy 4WD	2,300-3,000	1,700-2,200	400-600
1992 Jimmy 2WD	1,800-3,000	1,200-2,000	300-500
Jimmy 4WD	2,700-3,700	2,000-2,800	600-800
Typhoon	6,500-7,500	5,700-6,600	2,900-3,400
1993 Jimmy 2WD	2,100-3,400	1,500-2,400	400-600
Jimmy 4WD	3,000-4,200	2,300-3,200	700-1,000
Typhoon	7,800-9,300	7,000-8,400	4,000-4,700
1994 Jimmy 2WD	2,400-3,800	1,800-2,800	500-800
Jimmy 4WD	3,400-5,000	2,700-4,000	900-1,300

For detailed information on this vehicle visit
http://used.consumerguide.com and enter code **2248**

1995-01 GMC JIMMY/ENVOY

CLASS: Midsize sport-utility vehicle

BUILT IN: USA

PROS: Acceleration • Antilock brakes • 4WD traction • Passenger and cargo room • Ride

CONS: Fuel economy • Rear-seat comfort

EVALUATION: A more rigid body structure permits the use of softer suspension settings, which improves ride quality. The standard suspension easily cushions most bumps, but allows too much bouncing at highway speeds. The "luxury-ride" suspension available on 4-door models gives the best blend of comfort and control. An optional "Euro ride" suspension sharpens cornering ability, but not by enough to recommend that choice.

Passenger space is about the same as before, which means good room for four adults in both body styles. Five can fit in the 4-door. Step-in height is low, but getting into the rear seat of the 4-door demands some twisting to negotiate the narrow doorway. Getting into and out of the 2-door's back seat is a chore. The rear seat has a short, hard backrest. Cargo room in the 4-door is improved by mounting the spare tire beneath the rear end and by the 2001 Cargo Management System that fits into the floor of the cargo area, providing storage compartments and partitions.

Acceleration is more than adequate—brisk, really. Promising ample passing power, the latest Jimmy ranks above average for a sport-ute. Gas mileage is likely to be less than 15 mpg in town, and close to 20 mpg on the highway. We averaged 16.4 mpg with a 4WD 4-door. Some engine roar remains in hard acceleration, but road and wind noise now are well-muffled.

VALUE FOR THE MONEY: Although the GMC Jimmy and similar Chevrolet Blazer are not at the front of the compact sport-utility field, they're close enough to the leaders to deserve a close look.

TROUBLE SPOTS

See the 1995-03 Chevrolet Blazer.

AVERAGE REPLACEMENT COSTS

See the 1995-03 Chevrolet Blazer.

NHTSA RECALL HISTORY

1995 4WD: A few upper-ball-joint nuts were undertorqued; stud can loosen and fracture. **1995 w/air conditioning:** Fan-blade rivets can break and allow blade to separate from hub. **1995:** Brake-pedal bolt on some vehicles might disengage, causing loss of braking. **1995-96 4WD w/ABS:** Increased stopping distances can occur during ABS stops while in 2WD mode. **1995-96 AWD/4WD:** During testing, prop shaft contacted fuel tank, rupturing the tank; fuel leakage was beyond permissible level. **1995-96:** Windshield wipers may work intermittently. **1996-97 2-door w/manual locking recliner bucket seats:** Outboard-seatbelt webbing can separate during frontal impact. **1996-97:** Failure of an upper- and lower-control-arm ball-joint assembly could occur due to corrosion, resulting in impaired steering or steering loss, or a partial or complete collapse of the front suspension. **1997:** During a severe crash, seat belt buckles with an energy absorbing loop may malfunction, leading t full or partial ejection from the vehicle. Dealer will inspect and replace affected buckles. **1997:** On certain vehicles, the outside rearview mirror switch may short circuit. Dealer will inspect and replace affected parts. **1998 w/4WD or AWD:** On a few vehicles, one or both attaching bolts for lower control arm could separate from frame, resulting in loss of control. **1998:** Daytime running lights are not deactivated when turn-signal or hazard lamps are activated. **1998:** Fatigue fracture of rear-axle brake pipe can occur, causing slow fluid leak and resulting in soft brake pedal; if pipe breaks, driver would face sudden loss of rear-brake performance. **2000 w/2WD:** Right ABS module feed pipe and/or brake crossover pipe tube nuts on certain vehicles could have been improperly tightened; seals could have been broken, resulting in leakage. **2000-01:** Brake lights and rear hazard flashers may fail if the multi-function switch develops an open circuit condition. **2000-01:** Some seatbelt assemblies were not properly heat treated and do not pass the load-bearing requirement. **2001:** Console cover could come unlatched at less than the required load of the standard.

PRICES

	Good	Average	Poor
1995 Jimmy 2WD	$2,800-4,100	$2,100-3,100	$600-900
Jimmy 4WD	4,000-5,100	3,300-4,200	1,300-1,600
1996 Jimmy 2WD	3,200-4,100	2,500-3,200	800-1,000
Jimmy 4WD	4,400-5,800	3,700-4,800	1,500-2,000
1997 Jimmy 2WD	3,700-6,000	3,000-4,900	1,100-1,700
Jimmy 4WD	5,000-7,200	4,300-6,100	2,000-2,900
1998 Envoy	9,000-11,000	8,100-9,900	4,700-5,700
Jimmy 2WD	4,400-6,700	3,700-5,600	1,500-2,300
Jimmy 4WD	5,700-7,900	4,900-6,800	2,300-3,200
1999 Envoy	10,500-11,500	9,500-10,400	5,600-6,100
Jimmy 2WD	5,800-8,100	5,000-7,000	2,400-3,400
Jimmy 4WD	7,400-9,300	6,700-8,400	3,600-4,600
2000 Envoy	12,200-13,500	11,000-12,200	6,800-7,600
Jimmy 2WD	7,500-9,700	6,800-8,700	3,800-4,900
Jimmy 4WD	9,000-12,000	8,100-10,800	4,700-6,200
2001 Jimmy 2WD	9,700-12,000	8,700-10,800	5,000-6,200
Jimmy 4WD	11,200-14,000	10,100-12,600	6,000-7,600

For detailed information on this vehicle visit
http://used.consumerguide.com and enter code **2163**

1990-03 GMC SAFARI

CLASS: Minivan

BUILT IN: USA

PROS: Antilock brakes • Cargo room (extended-length) • Optional all-wheel-drive traction • Passenger room • Trailer-towing capability

CONS: Entry/exit • Fuel economy • Ride

EVALUATION: Spacious inside with either the regular- or extended-length body, Safari vans can be fitted to tow up to 6000 pounds and seat up to eight. With those eight seats, regular-length models have little rear cargo room. Optional rear "Dutch doors" make loading more convenient and improve visibility. Standard full swing-out doors have a large center blind spot due to their thick vertical bar.

Rear-drive is great for hauling, but Safari/Astro rides and handles more like a truck than a car. The rear axle hops around on bumpy roads, making it difficult to remain on course. The suspension pounds over broken pavement and allows too much floating on wavy roads.

Although the standard V6 has plenty of torque for hauling heavy loads, that muscle does not translate into brisk pickup. Best to pick a Safari with the optional engine, or a later model if performance matters. An extended AWD Safari averaged 18.3 mpg.

VALUE FOR THE MONEY: Safari is fine if you need a beast of burden, but don't want a full-size van. As a daily people-mover, however, a front-drive minivan would be wiser.

TROUBLE SPOTS

See the 1990-03 Chevrolet Astro.

AVERAGE REPLACEMENT COSTS

See the 1990-03 Chevrolet Astro.

NHTSA RECALL HISTORY

1990-91: Bucket seat's knob-recliner mechanism may loosen and cause bolt failure, allowing seatback to recline suddenly. **1995:** Fuel lines at tank were improperly tightened and could loosen. **1995:** On a few vans, left lower control-arm bolt could loosen, fatigue, and break. **1995-97:** The windshield-wiper motor may fail on certain vehicles. Dealer will inspect and replace affected parts. **1996-97:** Outboard-seatbelt webbing on right rear bucket seat can separate during crash. **1996-98 w/integrated child seats:** Seatbelt-retractor clutch spring and/or pawl spring in child seat may be missing. **1998:** On certain vehicles, the outside-rearview-mirror switch may short circuit. Dealer will inspect and replace affected parts. **1998-99:** Audible "fasten seatbelt" warning may not sound or may terminate too soon. **2003:** Poorly manufactured steering knuckles on some vehicles may allow for road contamination to enter and wear down the ball joint, resulting in difficulty controlling the vehicle

PRICES

	Good	Average	Poor
1990 Safari	$1,500-2,300	$1,000-1,500	$200-300
Safari AWD	2,000-2,700	1,400-1,900	300-500
1991 Safari	1,800-2,800	1,200-1,900	300-400
Safari AWD	2,300-3,200	1,700-2,300	400-600
1992 Safari	2,300-3,300	1,700-2,400	400-600
Safari AWD	2,600-3,800	1,900-2,800	500-800
1993 Safari	2,300-3,800	1,700-2,700	400-700
Safari AWD	3,000-4,600	2,300-3,500	700-1,100
1994 Safari	2,900-4,500	2,200-3,400	700-1,000
Safari AWD	3,600-5,000	2,900-4,000	1,000-1,400
1995 Safari	3,600-5,000	2,900-4,000	1,000-1,400
Safari AWD	4,400-5,700	3,700-4,700	1,500-2,000
1996 Safari	4,400-5,500	3,700-4,600	1,500-1,900
Safari AWD	5,400-6,500	4,600-5,600	2,200-2,700
1997 Safari	5,100-6,400	4,300-5,400	2,000-2,600
Safari AWD	6,200-7,400	5,400-6,400	2,700-3,200
1998 Safari	6,100-7,500	5,300-6,500	2,600-3,200
Safari AWD	7,200-8,500	6,400-7,600	3,500-4,200
1999 Safari	7,600-9,400	6,800-8,500	3,800-4,700
Safari AWD	9,200-10,600	8,300-9,500	4,800-5,500
2000 Safari	9,300-11,000	8,400-9,900	4,800-5,700
Safari AWD	11,000-12,500	9,900-11,300	5,900-6,800
2001 Safari	11,200-12,900	10,100-11,600	6,000-7,000
Safari AWD	12,700-14,300	11,400-12,900	7,400-8,300
2002 Safari	13,200-14,800	12,000-13,500	7,700-8,600
Safari AWD	14,700-16,200	13,400-14,700	9,100-10,000
2003 Safari	15,200-17,000	13,800-15,500	9,600-10,700
Safari AWD	17,200-19,000	15,800-17,500	11,000-12,200

For detailed information on this vehicle visit
http://used.consumerguide.com and enter code 2167

1990-98 GMC SIERRA

CG BEST BUY

CLASS: Full-size pickup truck
BUILT IN: Canada, USA
PROS: Acceleration (V8) • Antilock brakes (later models) • Passenger and cargo room • Trailer-towing capability • Visibility
CONS: Climate controls (early) • Fuel economy • Noise • Ride

GMC

EVALUATION: We're wary of trying much work with the base V6. A 5.0- or 5.7-liter V8 is more appropriate for rugged duty, and better suited for automatic. The 5.7-liter V8 feels livelier, furnishing a stronger kick in low-speed acceleration and highway passing. In fact, it's our favorite Sierra engine. All V8s guzzle; expect under 15 mpg in urban driving.

Ride quality suffers when the cargo box is empty, and is less pleasing in models with higher payload ratings. The latest Ford F-150, redesigned for '97, rides better. Sadly, unladen stopping distance from 60 mph averaged over 200 feet. And, despite standard antilock braking, rear-wheel lockup was difficult to avoid.

Forward visibility is good from a wide, spacious-feeling cab with ample room for even the largest occupants. Early heat/vent controls are complicated, but otherwise, the dashboard is neat and functional. The glovebox is tiny, but optional bucket seats came with a console that included a storage bin. The optional rear door on late models requires a V8, automatic, and SLE or SLT package. Regular-cab models don't offer much room for reclining the seatback or storing items behind the seat, so they trail the latest Dodge Ram and Ford F-150 in that area. The rear seat in extended-cab models is wide, but the seatback is uncomfortably vertical, and knee room is tight.

VALUE FOR THE MONEY: GM, Ford, and Dodge are closely matched in powertrain, body style, trim, and payload choices. Therefore, many buying decisions boil down to personal preference. Before deciding, be sure to try all three.

TROUBLE SPOTS

See the 1990-98 Chevrolet C/K Pickup.

AVERAGE REPLACEMENT COSTS

See the 1990-98 Chevrolet C/K Pickup.

NHTSA RECALL HISTORY

1990 diesel: Fuel lines can contact automatic-transmission linkage shaft or propshaft. **1994:** Brake-pedal retainer may be missing or mispositioned. **1994:** Brake-switch contacts can wear prematurely; may result in loss of brake lights without warning. **1994:** Some driver's seats could loosen. **1994-95:** Extended C10/15 with high-back buckets or 60/40 bench: Seatback might recline suddenly. **1994-96 C15:** Solder joints can crack, causing windshield wipers to work intermittently. **1995:** Steering-column nut could detach. **1995-96 w/gas engine:** Throttle cable may contact dash mat and bind. **1995-98 C15 crew-cab:** Front inner corner of fuel tank can contact body sill, wearing a hole in or cracking the tank; can result in fuel leakage. **1996 C-10/15 w/7.4-liter engine:** Fuel may leak. **1996:** Rear-axle U-bolts could loosen and eventually fall off. **1996:** The windshield wiper motor may fail on certain vehicles. Dealer will inspect and replace affected parts. **1997 C-15/25:** One or two of the front seat mounting bolts were not installed; seat will not protect occupant properly in the event of a crash. **1998 C10753 extended-cab:** Rear brake line can contact left front fender wheelhouse inner panel; a hole could be worn in brake line, allowing loss of fluid and reducing rear brake effectiveness. **1998 extended-cab and 4-door utility:** Steering-gear bolt can loosen and fall out, resulting in separation of shaft from gear. **1998:** On some trucks, one or both front brake rotor/hubs may have out-of-spec gray iron that can fail during life of vehicle.

PRICES

	Good	Average	Poor
1990 Sierra 1500 2WD	$2,100-3,700	$1,500-2,600	$400-700
Sierra 1500 4WD	2,800-4,100	2,100-3,100	600-900
Sierra 2500 2WD	2,800-3,900	2,100-2,900	600-900
Sierra 2500 4WD	3,500-4,400	2,800-3,500	900-1,200
1991 Sierra 1500 2WD	2,400-4,000	1,800-2,900	500-800
Sierra 1500 4WD	3,100-4,700	2,400-3,700	700-1,100
Sierra 2500 2WD	3,500-4,500	2,800-3,600	900-1,200
Sierra 2500 4WD	4,100-5,000	3,400-4,100	1,400-1,700
1992 Sierra 1500 2WD	2,800-4,700	2,100-3,500	600-1,000
Sierra 1500 4WD	3,500-5,400	2,800-4,300	900-1,500
Sierra 2500 2WD	3,900-4,800	3,200-3,900	1,200-1,500
Sierra 2500 4WD	4,700-5,700	3,900-4,800	1,700-2,100
1993 Sierra 1500 2WD	3,200-5,400	2,500-4,200	800-1,300
Sierra 1500 4WD	4,400-6,600	3,700-5,500	1,500-2,300
Sierra 2500 2WD	4,500-6,000	3,700-5,000	1,600-2,200
Sierra 2500 4WD	5,900-7,100	5,100-6,200	2,500-3,000
1994 Sierra 1500 2WD	3,600-6,300	2,900-5,000	1,000-1,800
Sierra 1500 4WD	4,800-7,900	4,000-6,600	1,800-3,000
Sierra 2500 2WD	5,300-6,800	4,600-5,800	2,200-2,800
Sierra 2500 4WD	6,700-8,000	5,900-7,000	3,100-3,700
1995 Sierra 1500 2WD	4,100-7,100	3,400-5,800	1,400-2,300
Sierra 1500 4WD	5,400-8,600	4,600-7,400	2,200-3,500
Sierra 2500 2WD	5,700-7,700	4,900-6,600	2,300-3,200
Sierra 2500 4WD	7,200-9,600	6,400-8,500	3,500-4,700
1996 Sierra 1500 2WD	4,500-8,300	3,700-6,900	1,600-3,000
Sierra 1500 4WD	6,100-10,300	5,300-9,000	2,600-4,400
Sierra 2500 2WD	6,400-8,700	5,600-7,700	2,800-3,800
Sierra 2500 4WD	8,100-10,700	7,300-9,600	4,100-5,500
1997 Sierra 1500 2WD	5,200-9,200	4,400-7,800	2,100-3,700
Sierra 1500 4WD	6,900-11,200	6,100-10,000	3,200-5,300
Sierra 2500 2WD	7,400-10,300	6,700-9,300	3,600-5,000
Sierra 2500 4WD	9,300-11,500	8,400-10,400	4,800-6,000
1998 Sierra 1500 2WD	6,000-10,400	5,200-9,000	2,500-4,400
Sierra 1500 4WD	7,700-12,200	6,900-11,000	3,900-6,100
Sierra 2500 2WD	8,300-11,000	7,500-9,900	4,300-5,700
Sierra 2500 4WD	10,100-12,800	9,100-11,500	5,300-6,700

For detailed information on this vehicle visit
http://used.consumerguide.com and enter code **2168**

1999-03 GMC SIERRA

CG BEST BUY

CLASS: Full-size pickup truck

BUILT IN: Canada

PROS: Acceleration (V8)
• Instruments/controls

CONS: Fuel economy
• Ride

EVALUATION: GMC Sierra and Chevrolet Silverado pickups outperform their predecessors, if not dramatically so. All-around performance easily matches Ford's F-150. New V8s are smooth and capable, but yield slightly less torque than previous engines, so acceleration and throttle response are similar. The Tow/Haul mode and optional adjustable suspension are welcome features, since most big pickups haul or tow at times. Although it's a smooth runner, the V6 struggles under heavy loads or up long grades. The 5.3-liter V8 offers good power under all conditions, though it trails Ford's 5.4 liter in torque. An alert, fuss-free automatic transmission helps. A 2WD Sierra with the 5.3 V8 averaged 12.6 mpg.

Brakes deliver good stopping power with firm, progressive pedal action, unlike the previous model's mushy feel. Steering is more precise, if overboosted. The Quadrasteer 4-wheel steering system, made available in 2002, is a revelation, giving this big pickup the close-quarters maneuverability of a small car as well as enhancing high-speed tracking and towing stability. A stiffer structure helps improve ride quality, which is more compliant than Ford's, though the tail still stutters over bumps when the bed is empty. Road, wind, and engine noise levels are mild.

In design, feel, and location, gauges and controls are best-in-class. GM also supplements the odometer with an engine-hour meter. Front seats are roomy and supportive. Integrated seatbelts move comfortably with the seats themselves. Some drivers might have trouble squeezing between the door panel and seat, to reach some controls. A Sierra or Silverado soundly trounces Ford and Dodge pickups in rear-seat accommodations, with more leg clearance. A contoured cushion and reclined backrest approach sedanlike comfort, and doors open wider.

VALUE FOR THE MONEY: General Motors refined its big pickups capably, while introducing plenty of worthy improvements. No extended-cabs are more comfortable. Both makes deliver high value for performance, comfort, and design, and beat Ford in 4WD convenience. GMC models tend to cost just a tad more then Silverados. Few C3 models are likely to be found, and they'll be expensive.

TROUBLE SPOTS

See the 1999-03 Chevrolet Silverado.

AVERAGE REPLACEMENT COSTS

See the 1999-03 Chevrolet Silverado.

NHTSA RECALL HISTORY

1999-00: Clearance between front right-hand brake pipe and body cross sill could decrease and allow contact, which could result in damage and loss of brake fluid and pressure. **2000 w/4-wheel disc brakes:** Out-of-spec spring clip in antilock brake system could allow motor bearing to become misaligned; eventually, ABS would be nonfunctional and dynamic-rear-proportioning system would become inoperative.

PRICES

	Good	Average	Poor
1999 Sierra 1500 2WD	$8,700-13,000	$7,800-11,700	$4,500-6,800
Sierra 1500 4WD	10,500-14,500	9,500-13,100	5,600-7,700
2000 Sierra 1500 2WD	9,500-13,800	8,600-12,400	4,900-7,200
Sierra 1500 4WD	12,000-16,200	10,800-14,600	6,700-9,100
2001 Sierra 1500 2WD	11,000-16,000	9,900-14,400	5,900-8,600
Sierra 1500 4WD	13,500-19,000	12,300-17,300	8,000-11,200
Sierra 1500 C3 AWD	22,000-23,500	20,200-21,600	14,300-15,300
2002 Sierra 1500 2WD	12,500-19,000	11,300-17,100	7,100-10,800
Sierra 1500 4WD	15,400-21,500	14,000-19,600	9,900-13,800
Sierra 1500 Denali AWD	26,500-28,500	24,600-26,500	17,500-18,800
2003 Sierra 1500 2WD	14,500-25,500	13,200-23,200	9,000-15,800
Sierra 1500 4WD	17,000-27,000	15,600-24,800	10,900-17,300
Sierra 1500 Denali AWD	30,000-32,500	27,900-30,200	21,000-22,800

For detailed information on this vehicle visit
http://used.consumerguide.com and enter code **2376**

1994-03 GMC SONOMA

CLASS: Compact pickup truck

BUILT IN: USA

PROS: Acceleration (V6) • Optional third door (later models) • Instruments/controls • Passenger room

CONS: Rear-seat room • Ride (some models) • Seat comfort (front passenger)

EVALUATION: A V6 is virtually essential if you want an automatic transmission or expect to do even occasional hauling. The 4-cylinder engine works best with manual shift, providing adequate acceleration for light-duty chores.

With an empty cargo bed, the Sonoma's back wheels tend to hop over sharp bumps and ridges in the road. Otherwise the basic "smooth-ride" suspension handles most pavement imperfections with little harshness and minimal bounding. Body lean is evident in turns, but the truck feels balanced and poised, providing fine resistance to gusty crosswinds. Power steering has a natural feel. Four-wheel antilock braking, standard on all late models, is a definite bonus. However, the brake pedal is spongy and has plenty of play before you feel any stopping power.

The optional rear door is easy to use and a genuine convenience, allowing unprecedented access to the rear of extended-cab models. A Sonoma equipped with that door, however, lacks the second jump seat. The 2001 Crew Cab's independent front hinged rear doors are more convenient than any extended-cab's rear-hinged doors, but its seat is low to the floor and there isn't a lot of legroom.

VALUE FOR THE MONEY: We rate Ford's Ranger a notch above the GMC and Chevrolet compact pickups, due to its slightly more polished feel. Dodge's latest Dakota, as redesigned for 1997, is bigger yet and even more polished, with stronger hauling ability and an available V8 engine. Even so, most buyers will find plenty to like in the GMC/Chevrolet compacts.

TROUBLE SPOTS

See the 1994-03 Chevrolet S-Series.

AVERAGE REPLACEMENT COSTS

See the 1994-03 Chevrolet S-Series.

NHTSA RECALL HISTORY

1994 w/2.2-liter engine: Vacuum hose can detach from power-brake-booster check valve as a result of backfire. **1994-96 w/ABS:** Increased stopping distances can occur during ABS stops while in 2WD mode. **1994-97:** Seatbelt webbing on certain models can separate during frontal impact. **1995 w/air conditioning and 4.3-liter engine:** Rivets can break and allow fan blade to separate from hub; if hood were open, a person could be struck by blade and be injured. **1995-00:** When the hazard flasher switch is used to turn the hazard-flashers on or off, the retained accessory power feature can be activated without a key in the ignition. **1995-96:** Windshield wipers may work intermittently. **1996 2WD manual shift w/2.2-liter engine:** Drive wheels could seize and lock while truck is moving. **1996:** Top coat of paint on a few trucks peels severely. **1996-97 w/4.3-liter engine:** Front brake line can contact oil pan, causing wear that may result in fluid loss. **1998:** Daytime running lights do not comply with FMVSS No. 108 requirements. **1998:** Fatigue fracture of rear-axle brake pipe can occur, causing slow fluid leak and resulting in soft brake pedal; if pipe breaks, driver would face sudden loss of rear-brake performance. **1998:** Wiring-harness clip can melt and drip onto exhaust manifold, possibly resulting in fire. **1998-00:** Left-hand safety-belt retractor may not meet the retractor locking requirements of the standard. **2000 w/2WD:** Right ABS module-feed pipe and/or brake-crossover-pipe tube nuts on certain vehicles could have been improperly tightened; seal could have been broken, resulting in leakage. **2000 w/all-disc brakes:** Out-of-spec spring clip in ABS motor could allow bearing to become misaligned; ABS and dynamic-rear-proportioning system would become inoperative. **2001:** Seatbelt buckles were not properly heat treated and do not pass the load-bearing requirement of the standard.

PRICES	Good	Average	Poor
1994 Sonoma 2WD	$2,100-3,900	$1,500-2,800	$400-700
Sonoma 4WD	3,300-4,600	2,600-3,600	800-1,200
1995 Sonoma 2WD	2,500-4,400	1,800-3,200	500-900
Sonoma 4WD	3,900-5,700	3,200-4,600	1,200-1,800

1996 Sonoma 2WD	$3,100-5,000	$2,400-3,900	$700-1,200
Sonoma 4WD	4,700-6,900	3,900-5,800	1,700-2,600
1997 Sonoma 2WD	3,700-6,000	3,000-4,900	1,100-1,700
Sonoma 4WD	5,600-8,000	4,800-6,900	2,300-3,300
1998 Sonoma 2WD	4,400-7,000	3,700-5,800	1,500-2,500
Sonoma 4WD	6,300-9,000	5,500-7,900	2,800-4,000
1999 Sonoma 2WD	5,000-8,000	4,300-6,800	2,000-3,200
Sonoma 4WD	7,000-10,200	6,200-9,100	3,400-4,900
2000 Sonoma 2WD	5,900-9,000	5,100-7,800	2,500-3,800
Sonoma 4WD	8,200-11,500	7,400-10,400	4,200-5,900
2001 Sonoma 2WD	6,800-10,500	6,100-9,300	3,200-4,900
Sonoma 4WD	9,700-13,500	8,700-12,200	5,000-7,000
2002 Sonoma 2WD	8,000-12,000	7,200-10,800	4,100-6,100
Sonoma 4WD	11,100-15,500	10,000-14,000	6,000-8,400
2003 Sonoma 2WD	9,800-14,000	8,800-12,600	5,100-7,300
Sonoma 4WD	13,000-17,500	11,800-15,900	7,500-10,200

For detailed information on this vehicle visit
http://used.consumerguide.com and enter code **2247**

1992-99 GMC SUBURBAN

CLASS: Full-size sport-utility vehicle
BUILT IN: Mexico, USA
PROS: Acceleration (7.4-liter) • Passenger and cargo room • Highway ride • Trailer-towing capability
CONS: Acceleration (early models) • Fuel economy • Rear-seat entry/exit

EVALUATION: Though front- and middle-row passengers have ample room in the Suburban, there's not enough room for adults to stretch out in the back. Still, each seat is wide enough for three to fit easily. The rear bench does not fold flat, but it's removable. Step-in height is a lot lower than in prior Suburbans. Cargo space is cavernous. Access to the optional third seat demands serious stooping. Visibility is fine, from a car-like seating position.

Acceleration with the 5.7-liter V8 is sufficient for most requirements, but only adequate in town, and the transmission is reluctant to downshift. The extra 50 horsepower delivered by the Vortec engine, introduced for 1996, gives the Suburban a welcome boost. Still, a 7.4-liter gasoline V8, or the 6.5-liter turbodiesel, is better for heavy-duty tasks. Gasoline V8s guzzle heavily. Expect no more than 10-12 mpg in city driving, or 16-18 on the highway.

Suburbans are smooth, capable, and comfortable on the highway, absorbing bumps well with only moderate floating. On the negative side, substantial body lean in turns at any speed encourages drivers to slow down. Simulated panic stops can produce pronounced nosedive, and occasional rear-wheel lockup.

VALUE FOR THE MONEY: If you must have space for nine occupants and a heavy load of luggage, or need to tow a trailer or boat, only Ford's Expedition comes close. But we prefer the more-nimble GMC Yukon.

TROUBLE SPOTS

See the 1992-99 Chevrolet Suburban.

AVERAGE REPLACEMENT COSTS

See the 1992-99 Chevrolet Suburban.

NHTSA RECALL HISTORY

1992: Brake-pedal pivot bolt can disengage. **1994:** Brake-switch contacts can wear prematurely; may result in loss of brake lights without warning. **1994-96:** Solder joints can crack, causing windshield wipers to work intermittently. **1995 w/automatic transmission:** External transmission leak can occur. **1995 w/automatic transmission:** When shift lever is placed in Park position, its indicator light may not illuminate. **1995-96 w/gasoline engine:** Throttle cable may contact dash mat and bind. **1997-98:** On certain vehicles, the outside rearview mirror switch may short circuit. Dealer will inspect and replace affected parts. **1998:** On some vehicles, one or both front brake rotor/hubs may have out-of-spec gray iron that can fail during life of vehicle. **1999:** In a crash, right-front-passenger-restraint systems may not meet neck-extension requirements.

PRICES	Good	Average	Poor
1992 Suburban 2WD	$5,100-6,100	$4,300-5,200	$2,000-2,400
Suburban 4WD	$5,900-6,900	$5,100-6,000	$2,500-2,900
1993 Suburban 2WD	5,500-6,700	4,700-5,800	2,300-2,700
Suburban 4WD	6,500-7,800	5,700-6,900	2,900-3,500
1994 Suburban 2WD	6,000-7,100	5,200-6,200	2,500-3,000
Suburban 4WD	7,100-8,400	6,300-7,500	3,500-4,100
1995 Suburban 2WD	6,700-8,700	5,900-7,700	3,100-4,000
Suburban 4WD	7,900-10,000	7,100-9,000	4,000-5,100
1996 Suburban 2WD	7,400-9,400	6,700-8,500	3,600-4,600
Suburban 4WD	8,600-11,000	7,700-9,900	4,500-5,700
1997 Suburban 2WD	8,200-10,500	7,400-9,500	4,200-5,400
Suburban 4WD	9,800-12,000	8,800-10,800	5,100-6,200
1998 Suburban 2WD	9,600-11,500	8,600-10,400	5,000-6,000
Suburban 4WD	11,000-13,500	9,900-12,200	5,900-7,300
1999 Suburban 2WD	11,100-14,100	10,000-12,700	6,000-7,600
Suburban 4WD	12,300-15,600	11,100-14,000	7,000-8,900

For detailed information on this vehicle visit
http://used.consumerguide.com and enter code **2170**

1992-00 GMC YUKON/DENALI

CLASS: Full-size sport-utility vehicle

BUILT IN: Mexico, USA

PROS: Antilock brakes
• Passenger and cargo room
• Quietness • Ride (4-door)
• Trailer-towing capability

CONS: Entry/exit (2-door & 4WD) • Fuel economy • Maneuverability • Ride (2-door)

EVALUATION: Until it added 50 horsepower for 1996, the 5.7-liter V8 was on the sluggish side, especially when passing or climbing hills. Improved transmission shift quality helped, though the automatic still is slow to downshift. Gas mileage is no bonus. In tests, we've barely topped 14 miles per gallon, even when driving mainly on the highway.

Quieter-running than before, Yukon offers improved behavior on the road. Suspensions of 4-door models are tuned for on-the-road comfort, resulting in an absorbent ride. The 2-door's ride is more choppy, tending toward rocking-horse motions. Though overassisted, steering is precise. Body lean in curves is still noticeable, but less troubling. Grip in corners is reassuring. Antilock brakes are a bonus, but you can expect severe nosedive in hard stops.

Occupants enjoy plenty of space to sit three abreast, with lots of head and leg room. A 4-door, in particular, offers interior space and towing power that's simply not available from compact sport-utility vehicles. Climbing aboard is easier than it used to be, too. The dashboard and control layout is modern and convenient. All controls are well-positioned, with large buttons that are easy to use while driving.

VALUE FOR THE MONEY: Yukons offer the strength and toughness of a full-size truck, but carlike comfort and a full load of convenience features. Before turning to Yukon or Tahoe, however, take a look at Ford's Expedition.

TROUBLE SPOTS

See the 1992-00 Chevrolet Blazer/Tahoe.

AVERAGE REPLACEMENT COSTS

See the 1992-00 Chevrolet Blazer/Tahoe.

NHTSA RECALL HISTORY

1992: Brake-pedal pivot bolt can disengage, resulting in loss of brake control. **1994-96:** Solder joints can crack, causing windshield wipers to work intermittently. **1995 w/automatic transmission:** When shift lever is placed in Park position, indicator may not illuminate. **1995-96 w/gas engine:** Throttle cable may contact dash mat and bind; engine speed might then not return to idle. **1998:** Lower steering pinch bolt may be "finger loose" or missing, allowing bolt to loosen and fall out; can result in off-center steering wheel and separation of shaft from steering gear. **1998:** On some vehicles, one or both front brake rotor/hubs may have out-of-spec gray iron that can fail during life of vehicle. **1998-00 C10:** Rear brake line can contact left front fender wheelhouse inner panel; a hole could be worn in brake line, allowing loss of fluid and reducing rear brake effectiveness. **1999:** In a crash, right front passenger restraint systems may not meet neck extension requirements. **2000 Yukon:** Airbag sensing diagnostic module may contain an anomaly that could prohibit the airbags from deploying in some frontal crashes. **2000 Yukon:** Rear Wheelhouse plugs may be loose or missing and could allow exhaust gases to flow into the passenger compartment. **2000:** When second-row head restraints are folded rearward as the seat is folded down, fingers could be trapped and pinched between the headrest and the seatback. Dealers will install protective covers.

PRICES

	Good	Average	Poor
1992 Yukon 4WD	$4,500-5,800	$3,700-4,800	$1,600-2,100
1993 Yukon 4WD	5,300-6,800	4,600-5,800	2,200-2,800
1994 Yukon 4WD	6,100-7,600	5,300-6,600	2,600-3,300
1995 Yukon 2WD 4-door	6,000-7,900	5,200-6,900	2,500-3,300
Yukon 4WD	7,300-8,900	6,600-8,000	3,600-4,400
1996 SLE, SLT 2WD	7,600-8,800	6,800-7,900	3,800-4,400
SLE, SLT 4WD	8,800-9,800	7,900-8,800	4,600-5,100
Yukon SL 2WD	7,000-7,800	6,200-6,900	3,400-3,700
Yukon SL 4WD	8,300-9,300	7,500-8,400	4,300-4,800
1997 SLE, SLT 2WD	8,500-9,500	7,700-8,600	4,400-4,900
SLE, SLT 4WD	9,800-10,800	8,800-9,700	5,100-5,600
Yukon SL 2WD	7,800-8,700	7,000-7,800	4,000-4,400
Yukon SL 4WD	9,700-10,700	8,700-9,600	5,000-5,600
1998 Yukon 2WD	10,000-11,200	9,000-10,100	5,200-5,800
Yukon 4WD	11,500-12,800	10,400-11,500	6,300-7,000
Yukon Denali 4WD	13,000-15,000	11,800-13,700	7,500-8,700
1999 Yukon 2WD	11,800-13,400	10,600-12,100	6,600-7,500
Yukon 4WD	13,500-15,000	12,300-13,700	8,000-8,900
Yukon Denali 4WD	16,000-18,000	14,600-16,400	10,200-11,500
2000 Yukon Denali 4WD	19,500-21,500	17,900-19,800	12,700-14,000

For detailed information on this vehicle visit
http://used.consumerguide.com and enter code **2171**

2000-03 GMC YUKON/DENALI

CLASS: Full-size sport-utility vehicle

BUILT IN: USA

PROS: Acceleration (Denali) • Passenger and cargo room • Trailer towing capacity

CONS: Entry/exit (Denali) • Fuel economy • Steering feel

EVALUATION: Though mainly evolutionary, Yukon advances brought some noticeable improvements. New V8s feel slightly smoother than the engines they replaced, but not much stronger. Acceleration is adequate, aided by the smooth automatic's astute shifting, but the 4.8 liter feels strained in towing or heavy hauling. Gas mileage is dismal. A Denali XL averaged only 9.8 mpg, though models with smaller engines will do a little better.

Big SUVs don't corner like cars, but handling is better than their size might suggest. They feel balanced in directional changes, and are fairly easy to maneuver. Steering is reasonably precise, but road feel is only adequate. Ride quality and brake feel are the most noted improvements. The suspension absorbs bumps well and is sure-footed on rough pavement. Stopping power is strong, with firm, progressive pedal action. Wind rush is not intrusive. Tire noise is low for a full-size SUV, but audible at highway speeds.

The dashboard layout is logical and handy, with clear gauges and easily accessed controls. Drivers get a commanding view, while moving the spare tire beneath the rear undercarriage improved visibility and cargo space. Front- and second-row space is generous. Differences between regular and XL Yukons are most evident in the third row. XLs have ample head, shoulder, and leg room for two grownups, but leg and head clearance in the shorter Yukon's third-row seat suggests children and occasional use. Entry/exit is somewhat hampered by modest back-door openings. A Yukon has only enough room for a single row of grocery bags behind the third row, but Yukon XLs are more sizable. Third-row seats fold easily, and have wheels for removal. The XL's heavy bench takes two people to remove, while the Yukon's third row is in two sections.

VALUE FOR THE MONEY: GM's impressive new full-size SUVs are capable, comfortable, and easy to live with. Though too big for a lot of buyers, their size fits nicely into the gap between Ford's Expedition and Excursion. Don't buy a big SUV without trying a GMC or Chevrolet.

TROUBLE SPOTS

See the 2000-03 Chevrolet Tahoe and Suburban.

AVERAGE REPLACEMENT COSTS

See the 2000-03 Chevrolet Tahoe and Suburban.

NHTSA RECALL HISTORY

2001: Misrouted positive-battery-cable assembly could come in contact with the steering-shaft universal joint. Over time, this contact could cause a wear-through of the cable-assembly conduit and cable insulation, exposing the wire core and resulting in intermittent electrical shorting or battery discharge. **2001:** Outboard-seatbelt retractors for the 2nd and 3rd row of seats could be cracked. With repeated actuation of the locking mechanism, the crack could spread to the point such that the seatbelt would no longer lock. **2001:** Rear wheelhouse plugs may be loose or missing, allowing exhaust gases to flow forward under certain conditions and accumulate in rear wheelhouse. **2002:** Fingers can get pinched and trapped between the rear head restraints and the seatback when folding the seat down. Dealers will install protective covers. **2003 Yukon XL:** In certain extreme impacts, frame cross member could tear fuel tank resulting in fuel leakage. Dealers will install a fuel-tank shield on affected vehicles.

PRICES

	Good	Average	Poor
2000 Yukon 2WD	$17,500-19,000	$16,100-17,500	$11,200-12,200
Yukon 4WD	19,000-21,000	17,500-19,300	12,400-13,700
Yukon XL 1500 2WD	18,000-19,000	16,600-17,500	11,500-12,200
Yukon XL 1500 4WD	20,000-21,500	18,400-19,800	13,000-14,000
Yukon XL 2500 2WD	19,000-21,000	17,500-19,300	12,400-13,700
Yukon XL 2500 4WD	20,500-23,000	18,900-21,200	13,300-15,000
2001 Yukon 2WD	20,000-22,700	18,400-20,900	13,000-14,800
Yukon 4WD	22,500-24,800	20,700-22,800	14,600-16,100
Yukon Denali	29,000-31,000	27,000-28,800	20,000-21,400
Yukon XL 1500 2WD	21,500-23,500	19,800-21,600	14,000-15,300
Yukon XL 1500 4WD	23,500-25,500	21,600-23,500	15,300-16,600
Yukon XL 2500 2WD	22,500-24,500	20,700-22,500	14,600-15,900
Yukon XL 2500 4WD	24,000-26,200	22,300-24,400	15,600-17,000
Yukon XL Denali	30,000-32,000	27,900-29,800	21,000-22,400
2002 Yukon 2WD	23,000-26,200	21,200-24,100	15,000-17,000
Yukon 4WD	25,000-28,200	23,300-26,200	16,500-18,600
Yukon Denali	32,000-34,000	29,800-31,600	22,400-23,800
Yukon XL 1500 2WD	23,000-26,200	21,200-24,600	15,000-17,400
Yukon XL 1500 4WD	25,000-28,500	23,300-26,500	16,500-18,800
Yukon XL 2500 2WD	24,200-27,200	22,500-25,300	15,700-17,700
Yukon XL 2500 4WD	26,200-29,200	24,400-27,200	17,300-19,300
Yukon XL Denali	33,000-35,000	30,700-32,600	23,400-24,900
2003 Yukon 2WD	26,500-30,000	24,600-27,900	17,500-19,800
Yukon 4WD	28,500-32,400	26,500-30,100	19,400-22,000
Yukon Denali	36,000-38,000	33,500-35,300	25,600-27,000
Yukon XL 1500 2WD	26,500-30,500	24,600-28,400	17,500-20,100
Yukon XL 1500 4WD	28,500-32,000	26,500-29,800	19,400-21,800
Yukon XL 2500 2WD	27,500-31,500	25,600-29,300	18,400-21,100
Yukon XL 2500 4WD	29,500-33,000	27,400-30,700	20,400-22,800
Yukon XL Denali	37,000-39,500	34,400-36,700	26,300-28,000

For detailed information on this vehicle visit
http://used.consumerguide.com and enter code 2377

1994-97 HONDA ACCORD

CLASS: Midsize car

BUILT IN: Japan, USA

PROS: Acceleration (V6) • Passenger and cargo room • Ride • Steering/handling

CONS: Acceleration (4-cylinder) • Antilock brakes (limited availability) • Road noise

EVALUATION: The 1994 to '96 models feel much more substantial than their predecessor. Four-cylinder performance is adequate for most driving needs, but the V6's added punch comes in quite handy in passing situations. The automatic transmission still lags behind the competition in shift quality, but it's now at least acceptable. Steering is firm and the car tracks effortlessly. There's also less wind noise than before, though tires whine at expressway speeds.

The body, now three inches wider than before, significantly increases the interior's feeling of spaciousness. Leg room is good both front and rear, but head room is only average at best. The driver's seat provides a commanding view of the road, thanks to thin pillars and a low cowl. A wider trunk opening is also greatly appreciated. And while the rear seatback drops forward to allow the transport of large and bulky objects, it does not fold fully flat.

VALUE FOR THE MONEY: Overall, the Accord continues to be a fine, solid-feeling family car with a refined, sporty manner. In fact, this was the best Accord to date. The new V6 was most welcome, but long overdue. There was much stronger competition among midsize family sedans today than ever before, with Honda's rivals making noticeable strides in the areas of styling, powertrain sophistication, chassis dynamics, ergonomics, and creature comforts. Yet, Accord came through in fine fashion.

TROUBLE SPOTS

Audio system: If the CD changer in the trunk will not eject, the company will exchange the CD magazines with a redesigned one. (All)

Automatic transmission: Cars with high mileage may begin to shift more harshly, which may be corrected by adding a bottle of Lubeguard conditioner to the automatic transmission fluid. (1994-96)

Brakes: The parking brake may not fully release because a rivet on the brake rod is too tight. (1994)

Dashboard lights: The heater control panel lights do not glow when the switch is pressed because of breaks in the circuit board solder joints. (1994-95)

Engine noise: The gasket for the mid-exhaust pipe sticks, causing a buzzing noise. (1994-95)

Fuel gauge: The fuel gauge may not read full even though the tank is filled due to excessive resistance in the sending unit in the tank. (1994-95)

Manual transmission: If the transmission grinds when shifting into fifth gear, the fork, sleeve set, and mainshaft gear must be replaced. (1994-95)

Vehicle noise: A noise coming from the passenger footwell is most likely due to the air conditioning high pressure line vibrating against the power steering fluid line. (1995)

AVERAGE REPLACEMENT COSTS

A/C Compressor	$530	CV Joints	$670
Alternator	380	Exhaust System	540
Automatic Trans.	1,055	Radiator	485
Brakes	250	Shocks and/or Struts	545
Clutch	550	Timing Chain/Belt	350

NHTSA RECALL HISTORY

1994: Some tire valve stems were damaged during assembly, resulting in sudden loss of air pressure and/or loss of control. **1995:** Some supplemental restraint system electronic control units can cause unexpected airbag deployment. **1995-97 except DC and V6 models:** Improperly routed wire harness

HONDA

for factory-installed air conditioner can allow wires to rub against each other, which can eventually cause short circuit that may lead to overheating, smoke, and possible fire. **1997:** Certain ball joints can wear out prematurely and, in worst case, would separate, causing front suspension to collapse.

PRICES

	Good	Average	Poor
1994 Accord	$3,400-4,500	$2,700-3,600	$900-1,200
Accord EX	4,700-5,400	3,900-4,500	1,700-2,000
1995 Accord	3,800-5,400	3,100-4,400	1,100-1,600
Accord EX	5,200-6,000	4,400-5,100	2,100-2,400
1996 Accord	4,200-5,800	3,400-4,800	1,400-1,900
Accord EX	6,200-7,500	5,400-6,500	2,700-3,200
1997 Accord	4,800-6,900	4,000-5,800	1,800-2,600
Accord EX	7,400-9,000	6,700-8,100	3,600-4,400

For detailed information on this vehicle visit
http://used.consumerguide.com and enter code **2048**

1998-02 HONDA ACCORD

CG BEST BUY

CLASS: Midsize car

BUILT IN: USA

PROS: Acceleration (V6)
• Instruments/controls
• Steering/handling

CONS: Automatic-transmission performance

EVALUATION: Engines are silky, revvy, quiet, and packed with punch. The V6 provides quick getaways and ample passing power. Much of the time, you also get smooth and responsive downshifts for passing or merging. At times, though, the automatic shifts with a jerk and can be painfully slow to drop down a gear for passing. Gas mileage is a bonus, especially with the 4-cylinder engine. Our test 5-speed coupe averaged 23.8 mpg in hard urban driving. An automatic 4-cylinder got 24.7 mpg. Test sedans with the V6 engine averaged 24.0 and 20.7 mpg.

The ride is comfortable and controlled. Handling, on the other hand, is noticeably more precise than before, with less body lean and better grip in tight corners. You can expect little wind noise in any model, though some tire hum is audible on coarse pavement. Overall, noise levels rank about average.

An Accord sedan is just as roomy inside as a Toyota Camry or Ford Taurus. Like those competitors, too, Accords are more comfortable for four adults than for five. In any of those models, the center rear position lacks sufficient width for an average-sized grown-up. Seat comfort ranks as first-rate, especially up front. Wider doors ease entry/exit on sedans, but rear access in coupes demands a certain amount of crouching and crawling.

Dashboards are models of functional simplicity. Power window and lock switches are not illuminated, however. Sedans have a deep, wide trunk with a flat floor and a large lid, which opens to bumper level. Liftover is a bit higher in coupes, which also have slightly less trunk volume. All models have a handy split-folding rear seat.

VALUE FOR THE MONEY: If you're in the market for a top-notch midsize family sedan (or coupe), don't buy until you've test-driven an Accord. Resale values tend to be on the high side, however, so don't expect fantastic bargains.

TROUBLE SPOTS

Brakes: The brake light may not go off. The cause is a saturated float in the master cylinder that should be replaced under warranty or beyond. (1998)

Paint/body: If the car is driven on rough roads, the spoiler on the trunk can rub through the paint unless spacer pads are installed between the spoiler and trunklid. (1998)

Suspension noise: Loose nuts on the rear stabilizer bar cause it to rattle. (1998)

Vehicle noise: Noises come from the top of the windshield and rear window because the teeth for the glass fasteners aren't engaged. The teeth must be trimmed and a wool felt installed. (1998)

AVERAGE REPLACEMENT COSTS

A/C Compressor	$775	CV Joints	$1,405
Alternator	460	Exhaust System	610
Automatic Trans.	1,110	Radiator	585
Brakes	520	Shocks and/or Struts	920
Clutch	845	Timing Chain/Belt	475

NHTSA RECALL HISTORY

1998: Irregularity in transmission cover can allow car to roll down an incline while transmission is in "Park." **1998-99:** Worn ignition switch may cause interlock to fail, allowing key to be removed without shifting into "Park." **2000:** Airbags may not deploy correctly, due to improper welding. **2000:** Rear suspension lower arms and/or control arms could break, due to improper welding. **2000-01:** Certain rear seatbelt buckles were improperly manufactured and may be difficult to unfasten after a crash. **2001:** Broken plastic piece of air cleaner box cover could travel into the intake chamber. If the piece lodges in the throttle body, the throttle could stick in a partially open position. **2002 w/V6 engine:** Engine will stall if timing belt breaks due to a misaligned tensioner pulley on the water pump.

PRICES

	Good	Average	Poor
1998 Accord DX	$6,000-6,700	$5,200-5,800	$2,500-2,800
Accord EX	9,500-11,000	8,600-9,900	4,900-5,700
Accord LX	7,500-8,800	6,800-7,900	3,800-4,400
1999 Accord DX	7,200-8,000	6,400-7,100	3,500-3,900
Accord EX	11,000-12,500	9,900-11,300	5,900-6,800
Accord LX	9,000-10,500	8,100-9,500	4,700-5,500
2000 Accord DX	8,500-9,300	7,700-8,400	4,400-4,800
Accord EX	12,700-14,700	11,400-13,200	7,200-8,400
Accord LX, SE	10,500-12,000	9,500-10,800	5,600-6,400

HONDA

2001 Accord DX, Value	$10,200-11,000	$9,200-9,900	$5,300-5,700
Accord EX	14,500-16,500	13,200-15,000	9,000-10,200
Accord LX	12,000-14,000	10,800-12,600	6,700-7,800
2002 Accord DX, Value	12,200-13,000	11,000-11,700	6,800-7,300
Accord EX	16,200-18,700	14,700-17,000	10,400-12,000
Accord LX, SE	14,000-16,000	12,700-14,600	8,500-9,800

For detailed information on this vehicle visit
http://used.consumerguide.com and enter code **2289**

1992-95 HONDA CIVIC

CLASS: Subcompact car

BUILT IN: Canada, Japan, USA

PROS: Acceleration (EX and Si) • Fuel economy • Handling/roadholding • Ride (4-door)

CONS: Acceleration (CX and VX) • Cargo room (hatchback) • Noise (hatchback) • Rear-seat room (hatchback)

EVALUATION: All four engines are weak on low-end torque, lacking in zest. Although they pull smoothly enough in the middle gears, they fail to exhibit much overall gusto—especially with automatic transmissions. To climb hills and keep up with highway traffic you'll have to shift gears often and push hard on the gas pedal. Automatic transmissions shift neatly, lacking the harsh jolt of earlier models. Fuel economy is great. Over a long-term trial, a 5-speed EX sedan averaged 29.6 mpg. Wind and exhaust sounds are reduced, especially in sedans, though tire noise is a problem.

Civics ride smoothly for a subcompact, although sedans have a much better ride than coupe and hatchback models. Handling can best be described as modest, if agile, with the narrow tires and softer suspension leaning over in tight turns. The steering and brakes work well.

Interior room is surprisingly good for a subcompact. Four adults can stretch out in modest comfort. Interior controls are thoughtfully designed and easy to use. Cargo space is good as well, but the hatchbacks' split opening makes loading and unloading difficult.

VALUE FOR THE MONEY: You pay a hefty price for a nice Civic, but in this case the expenditure might well be worth it. Flaws are few in these refined, quietly impressive subcompacts, overwhelmed by some highly tempting virtues. Civics stand apart from the crowd because of their nimble handling, smooth running, enjoyable operation, and miserly gas mileage.

TROUBLE SPOTS

Air conditioner: If the air-conditioner belt repeatedly comes off, the splash shield under the engine is probably knocking it off when the car goes over a parking curb, etc. (1992-95)

Audio system: If the CD changer in the trunk will not eject, the company will exchange the CD magazines with a redesigned one. (All)

Automatic transmission: Cars with high mileage may begin to shift more harshly, which may be corrected by adding a bottle of Lubeguard conditioner to the automatic-transmission fluid. (1992-95)

Trunk latch: There may not be sufficient clearance on the trunk latch making it hard to open with the key. (1992-95)

Water leak: There may be water leaking into the passenger footwell because of insufficient sealer on the seam at the firewall. Look for rust on the floor pan and run water over the right lower corner of the windshield to watch for water leaks before buying the car. (1992-95)

AVERAGE REPLACEMENT COSTS

A/C Compressor	$470	CV Joints	$550
Alternator	310	Exhaust System	428
Automatic Trans.	750	Radiator	360
Brakes	180	Shocks and/or Struts	580
Clutch	455	Timing Chain/Belt	190

NHTSA RECALL HISTORY

1992-94: Retaining clip at automatic transmission can come off, so position of lever does not match actual transmission gear range. **1994:** Passenger-side airbag module on small number of cars may contain incorrect inflator, therefore unable to provide adequate protection.

PRICES

	Good	Average	Poor
1992 Civic	$1,600-2,500	$1,100-1,700	$200-400
Civic EX	2,700-3,300	2,000-2,500	600-700
Civic Si	2,400-3,000	1,800-2,200	500-600
1993 Civic	2,000-2,900	1,400-2,000	300-500
Civic EX	3,100-3,700	2,400-2,900	700-900
Civic Si	3,200-3,700	2,500-2,900	800-900
1994 Civic	2,500-3,400	1,800-2,500	500-700
Civic EX	3,600-4,300	2,900-3,400	1,000-1,200
Civic Si	3,700-4,200	3,000-3,400	1,100-1,200
1995 Civic	3,000-4,000	2,300-3,100	700-900
Civic EX	4,200-4,800	3,400-3,900	1,400-1,600
Civic Si	4,300-4,800	3,500-3,900	1,500-1,600

For detailed information on this vehicle visit
http://used.consumerguide.com and enter code **2049**

1996-00 HONDA CIVIC

CG BEST BUY

CLASS: Subcompact car

BUILT IN: Canada, USA

PROS: Antilock brakes • Fuel economy • Ride • Visibility

CONS: Rear-seat entry/exit • Road noise

HONDA

EVALUATION: Based on interior volume, the sedan now qualifies as a compact car, whereas the coupe and hatchback rank as subcompacts. Rear space in any body style is adequate for most people (up to about 6 feet tall) to fit without squeezing. Hatchbacks gained the most interior space. Thinner roof pillars and a bigger rear window improved visibility on all body styles. The driver faces a low steering wheel and easy-to-read gauges. Split folding rear seatbacks on all Civics expanded cargo capacity. The '01 redesign brought obvious gains in space, refinement, and comfort.

Acceleration is liveliest with the EX, but all Civics perform at least adequately. Gas mileage also is a bonus: An EX with automatic reached 36 mpg on the highway, averaging 29 mpg in suburban commuting. Engine noise has been quieted, but road noise is still prominent at highway speeds.

Except for some overreaction to wavy surfaces, ride comfort is pleasing—well above average for a small car, with few jolts and minimal bounciness. Easy to maneuver, stable, and well-controlled on the highway, the Civic delivers superior steering feedback and excellent response.

VALUE FOR THE MONEY: This generation continues Civic's long-standing tradition of reliability and durability. Largely for that reason—coupled with the high new-car prices of LX and EX models, in particular—their resale prices as used vehicles tend to stay high.

TROUBLE SPOTS

Audio system: Installing an aftermarket radio can result in loss of dome lights and keyless entry. Those two systems are tied into the Honda radio. (1997)

Cupholders: The cupholder lid sticks closed or will not close due to missing latch. (1996-97)

Seatbelts/safety: Seatbelts may not retract or may retract slowly. Also, the button that keeps the seatbelt tongue from sliding down breaks. The belts should be serviced under the Honda Lifetime Seat Belt Limited Warranty. (1996-97)

Water leak: Water leaks onto the front floor (either or both sides) due to insufficient sealer on body seams. (1996-97)

AVERAGE REPLACEMENT COSTS

A/C Compressor	$465	CV Joints	$590
Alternator	310	Exhaust System	405
Automatic Trans.	800	Radiator	515
Brakes	185	Shocks and/or Struts	690
Clutch	470	Timing Chain/Belt	185

NHTSA RECALL HISTORY

1996: Soapy lubricant used to insert brake-booster check valve into vacuum hose causes sticky valve and loss of power assist. **1996-98 w/accessory floormats:** Mispositioned floormat could interfere with accelerator pedal. **1997-98:** Some passenger airbag modules were improperly assembled; could prevent proper deployment. **1999-00:** Electrical contacts in the ignition switch can degrade, making the engine stall, due to high electrical current passing through the switch at startup. **2000:** Certain rear-seatbelt buckles were improperly manufactured and may be difficult to unlatch after a crash.

PRICES

	Good	Average	Poor
1996 Civic	$3,500-4,800	$2,800-3,800	$900-1,300
Civic EX	5,500-6,200	4,700-5,300	2,300-2,500
1997 Civic	4,000-5,800	3,300-4,800	1,300-1,900
Civic EX	6,200-6,900	5,400-6,000	2,700-3,000
1998 Civic	4,600-6,800	3,800-5,600	1,700-2,500
Civic EX	7,500-8,200	6,800-7,400	3,800-4,100
1999 Civic	5,400-7,800	4,600-6,700	2,200-3,200
Civic EX	8,700-9,500	7,800-8,600	4,500-4,900
Civic Si	10,500-11,500	9,500-10,400	5,600-6,100
2000 Civic	6,500-9,000	5,700-7,900	2,900-4,100
Civic EX	10,000-10,900	9,000-9,800	5,200-5,700
Civic Si	12,000-13,200	10,800-11,900	6,700-7,400

For detailed information on this vehicle visit
http://used.consumerguide.com and enter code **2172**

2001-03
HONDA CIVIC

CG BEST BUY

CLASS: Compact car

BUILT IN: Canada, England, Japan, USA

PROS: Acceleration (Si) • Build quality • Fuel economy • Handling (Si) • Visibility

CONS: Rear-seat entry/exit (coupes, Si) • Steering feel (except Si)

EVALUATION: Civic has long been tops for small-car refinement and driving fun, and the current generation shapes up as the best one yet. Honda claims greater structural rigidity in this generation.

Though not as quiet as the league-leading VW Jetta, Civics beat most subcompacts in noise control. Road noise and engine boom occur at high rpm, but engines are smooth and Civics deliver a generally solid feel.

Manual gearboxes remain a model of slick, light precision. Civics are fairly quick with a manual transmission and adequate with automatic. Some sedans have felt sluggish off the line, were slow to rev, and suffered resonance above 4000 rpm. Automatic transmissions respond well enough, but sometimes shift with a jolt. The CVT is always smooth and keeps the engine working with impressive efficiency—with less engine revving and consequent noise than early CVTs.

Extended-use EX sedans with automatic have averaged 30.5 mpg. In an even mix of city/highway driving, an LX/automatic sedan averaged 26.8 mpg, an EX/manual sedan got 26.5, and an HX CVT managed 28.9 mpg. A 2003 Civic Hybrid sedan squeezed out 47.6 mpg.

Handling remains nimble and assured. Firmer-damped EX models have the best body control, but cornering lean is evident in all models. Tires furnish only modest grip, and allow mild wander in crosswinds and along road grooves. Steering is a bit numb and overassisted.

Coupes and sedans ride better than the subcompact norm. Suspension tuning is on the soft side, so there's mild float over large humps and dips. Most bumps register, but few are jarring. Braking with ABS is generally good, but a non-ABS LX exhibited mediocre performance.

The sporty Si feels spirited, and avoids the float of other models. Though its suspension is tauter than other Civics, the Si never feels harsh, though it tends to fidget on fast freeways. Despite noticeable body lean, the Si has sharp reflexes and good grip in fast turns.

With its added interior volume, Civic moved from the EPA's subcompact to its compact-size category, augmented by a flat rear-seat floor area. Shoulder room is still lacking for three grown-ups in back, but sedans have comfortable head room. Coupes offer less rear head room and much less rear leg room than sedans. Sedans have good space up front, but coupes have a bit less head clearance and the Si even less. Entry/exit is simple in sedans, aided by their elevated roofline, but a squeeze to the rear in coupes.

Civic drivers sit on slightly higher and wider seats than before, which should aid long-distance comfort. Visibility is clear to all quarters, though the driver cannot see the car's rear corners when parking. Most gauges and controls are high and handy. Honda's exemplary ergonomics keep everything simple.

Trunks are spacious for the car's exterior size, but old-fashioned sickle-shaped hinges steal space and could crunch cargo, while the aperture won't swallow big boxes.

VALUE FOR THE MONEY: Improved in most respects, this Civic delivers more car for the money. With its fine reliability records, Honda's solidly built subcompact is a hands-down Best Buy, despite a few workmanship glitches on test models. Competitors cannot match Civic's blend of comfort, refinement, excellent ergonomics, and fuel thrift. Strong resale values keep secondhand prices high.

TROUBLE SPOTS

Climate control: The adjuster tabs for the center vents in the dash break off. (2001)

Seat: The rear seatback lock may not turn or is hard to turn, requiring lock rod replacement. (2001-02)

Steering problems: The steering wheel may be hard to turn or make noise due to a faulty power-steering pump. (2001)

Suspension noise: Front coil springs clash, causing a popping, or knocking noise. (2001)

Transmission slippage: The shift cable corrodes at the end near the transmission, making it difficult to shift and/or causing it to pop out of second or fifth gear. (2001)

Water leak: Water may leak into the trunk because there was insufficient seam sealer applied to the fenders at the factory. (2001)

AVERAGE REPLACEMENT COSTS

A/C Compressor	$670	CV Joints	$990

Alternator	$340	Exhaust System	$800
Automatic Trans.	1,895	Radiator	200
Brakes	400	Shocks and/or Struts	815
Clutch	465	Timing Chain/Belt	180

NHTSA RECALL HISTORY

2001 sedan: A small amount of water in electrical connection of fuel pump could lead to corrosion and engine stalling. Dealers will inspect and replace affected parts. **2001:** Fuel-filler neck may have insufficient clamping and could become dislodged in an accident resulting in fuel leakage and fire. Dealers will inspect and adjust hose clamps. **2001:** Two recalls for defective rear seatbelt buckles. Dealers will inspect and, if necessary, replace defective buckles. **2001-02:** Air-cleaner box cover may be damaged resulting in a broken piece possibly lodging in throttle linkage. This could lead to erratic throttle behavior. Dealers will inspect air-cleaner box for damage, locate and remove broken piece, and replace cleaner-box lid.

PRICES	Good	Average	Poor
2001 Civic	$9,000-10,500	$8,100-9,500	$4,700-5,500
Civic EX	11,000-12,000	9,900-10,800	5,900-6,500
2002 Civic	10,200-12,500	9,200-11,300	5,300-6,500
Civic EX	12,300-13,300	11,100-12,000	7,000-7,600
Civic Si	13,500-14,500	12,300-13,200	8,000-8,600
2003 Civic	11,500-13,000	10,400-11,700	6,300-7,200
Civic EX	14,000-15,200	12,700-13,800	8,500-9,300
Civic Hybrid	16,500-18,000	15,000-16,400	10,600-11,500
Civic Si	16,000-17,200	14,600-15,700	10,200-11,000

For detailed information on this vehicle visit
http://used.consumerguide.com and enter code **4484**

1997-01 HONDA CR-V

CG BEST BUY

CLASS: Compact sport-utility vehicle
BUILT IN: Japan
PROS: Entry/exit
• Passenger and cargo room
CONS: Acceleration
• Rear-seat comfort

EVALUATION: Performance is not a "plus" with the CR-V, at least with an automatic transmission. Acceleration to 60 mph in an early model with automatic took a leisurely 11.3 seconds, with only the driver aboard. Manual shift cuts about a second from that figure. Go-power sags even further when climbing steep upgrades, or with a full load. Overall gas mileage of 19.7 mpg fell short of expectations, too.

CR-V is pleasantly (and predictably) carlike to drive. Wind noise is unusual-

HONDA

ly well-suppressed at cruising speeds, and tire sounds are minor. Even though the engine begins to boom above 4000 rpm or so, it's never throbby or irritating. Body lean ranks as modest through tight turns, so the CR-V can be tossed around much like any small wagon. Ride comfort is generally good, but some road undulations result in an annoying tendency to wheel-hop.

Head and leg room are ample, but three adults don't fit comfortably in back. Step-in is low despite an 8-inch ground clearance, so entry/exit is easy, although rear doors are narrow for larger people. Though rather bus-like, the driving stance is accommodating, thanks to a standard tilt steering wheel and manual seat-height adjuster. The column-mounted shifter sits awkwardly behind the wiper stalk, but otherwise the driving environment is simple and convenient—quite similar to riding in a Civic.

The CR-V's 50/50 split rear seat can fold down to form a flat load floor. With the seat in use, you have space for about 10 grocery bags. Cargo bay access isn't the best, however, as you have to get past an external spare-tire carrier, glass liftgate, and swing-out tailgate.

Solid, rattle-free construction has been evident during test drives, even when rolling through rough surfaces. Panel fit and paint finish have been excellent, inside and out.

VALUE FOR THE MONEY: Except for a lack of power, the CR-V almost approaches perfection. As it stands, this is a handy and well-built compact wagon with carlike manners and a 4WD system that never needs to be thought about. Even though it can't match the space or brawn of bigger SUVs, Honda's CR-V is clearly the nicest of the "baby-size" 4x4s.

TROUBLE SPOTS

Brakes: The ABS light comes on because one (or both) of the rear-wheel speed sensors fails. Revised sensors are available to replace them. (1997)

Headlights: The fog light housing is prone to cracking and, when this happens, the lens falls out. (1997)

Mirrors: The power mirrors were not properly sealed to the body on some vehicles causing wind noise. (1997)

AVERAGE REPLACEMENT COSTS

A/C Compressor	$705	CV Joints	$930
Alternator	600	Exhaust System	415
Automatic Trans.	1,265	Radiator	495
Brakes	280	Shocks and/or Struts	940
Clutch	840	Timing Chain/Belt	545

NHTSA RECALL HISTORY

1998-99: Improperly routed under-dash wire harness on some vehicles could be damaged by contact with brake-light switch, possibly resulting in blown fuse.

PRICES	Good	Average	Poor
1997 CR-V 4WD	$7,600-8,300	$6,800-7,500	$3,800-4,200
1998 CR-V 2WD	8,400-9,300	7,600-8,400	4,400-4,800
CR-V 4WD	9,300-10,200	8,400-9,200	4,800-5,300
1999 CR-V 2WD	9,500-10,500	8,600-9,500	4,900-5,500
CR-V 4WD	10,500-11,700	9,500-10,500	5,600-6,200

2000 CR-V 2WD	$10,700-11,700	$9,600-10,500	$5,700-6,200
CR-V 4WD	12,000-13,500	10,800-12,200	6,700-7,600
2001 CR-V 2WD	12,000-13,000	10,800-11,700	6,700-7,300
CR-V 4WD	13,500-15,500	12,300-14,100	8,000-9,100

For detailed information on this vehicle visit
http://used.consumerguide.com and enter code 2173

1999-03 HONDA ODYSSEY

CG BEST BUY

CLASS: Minivan
BUILT IN: Canada
PROS: Acceleration • Entry/exit • Passenger and cargo room
CONS: Navigation-system controls • Rear visibility

EVALUATION: Honda's competent minivan has a lot to offer. Standing-start acceleration is spirited. Passing maneuvers are aided by a transmission that generally shifts promptly and smoothly—if a bit slow to downshift at full throttle from low and midrange speeds. A test EX reached 60 mph in a bit over 9 seconds. Only Toyota's Sienna offers a more refined powertrain. The new engine is smooth and quiet. Premium fuel is recommended, but Honda has said it will run on regular with only a slight power loss. An absorbent but taut ride is coupled with alert, confident handling that's at or near the top of the minivan class, resulting in excellent road manners. Steering has good feel but is slightly heavy at low speeds, lightening up quickly and feeling very communicative. Even at highway speeds, little engine, road, or wind noise intrudes. Braking is strong and stable. Drivers enjoy a comfortable, commanding position. Other seating positions enjoy plenty of head room. Middle seats offer enough leg space for average adults, but rear seats are most appropriate for children, who will have an easier time climbing into the back. A versatile seating arrangement allows for numerous combinations of people and cargo. The fold-away rear seat is especially handy. Easy front and second-row access is provided, via low step-in and large doorways. Gauges and controls are well-placed. A head-rest for every seating position leaves few clear sight lines to sides and rear, but most minivans have a similar setup. The "space-saver" spare tire is housed in a covered well, ahead of the middle-row seats. If one of the full-size tires goes flat, it will have to be transported in the rear cargo area.

VALUE FOR THE MONEY: When Honda finally broke into the mini-van mainstream, sales took off in a hurry. A solid value, it's roomy, refined, and performs well. Odysseys ranked as virtual bargains when new, but resale values are on the high side.

HONDA

TROUBLE SPOTS

Doors: If the junction switch in the B-pillar is not properly grounded, the sliding door alarm may sound when driving on rough roads. (1999-00)

Doors: A replacement fuel-door clip may be required if the left sliding door will not stay locked. (1999)

Engine misfire: The EGR port in the intake manifold clogs requiring installation of a revised PCV hose and manifold end cap. (1999)

AVERAGE REPLACEMENT COSTS

A/C Compressor	$775	Exhaust System	$775
Alternator	410	Radiator	700
Automatic Trans.	1,305	Shocks and/or Struts	1,555
Brakes	745	Timing Chain/Belt	710
CV Joints	1,290		

NHTSA RECALL HISTORY

1999 EX: Excessive grease in remote power-lock actuator could cause slow return of lever to proper latching position, preventing sliding door from latching. **1999:** On certain LX and EX models, in cold, wet weather, ice can form in throttle body, preventing return to idle position even though driver's foot is no longer on accelerator pedal. **1999:** On certain LX and EX models, sliding doors could open unexpectedly while vehicle is in motion. **1999:** Worn ignition switch may cause interlock to fail, allowing key to be removed without shifting into "Park." **1999-00:** Dimmer control for instrument panel lights on certain minivans can fail. **1999-00:** Sliding doors on some minivans may not latch properly because latches were not correctly riveted. **1999-00:** Wire harness in engine compartment could be damaged by contact with metal pipe, possibly resulting in blown fuse; if fuse blows, engine power, or operation of any or all electrical components (including lights, wipers, horn, and antilock function of brakes) can be lost. **2002 w/V6 engine:** Engine will stall if timing belt breaks due to a misaligned tensioner pulley on the water pump. **2003:** Some fuel tanks have imperfections that could allow leaking. Dealer will inspect and replace affected fuel tanks.

PRICES

	Good	Average	Poor
1999 Odyssey EX	$15,500-17,000	$14,100-15,500	$9,900-10,900
Odyssey LX	14,000-15,000	12,700-13,700	8,500-9,200
2000 Odyssey EX	17,700-19,200	16,300-17,700	11,300-12,300
Odyssey LX	16,000-17,000	14,600-15,500	10,200-10,900
2001 Odyssey EX	20,000-21,500	18,400-19,800	13,000-14,000
Odyssey LX	18,000-19,500	16,600-17,900	11,500-12,500
2002 Odyssey EX	22,000-24,000	20,200-22,100	14,300-15,600
Odyssey LX	20,000-21,500	18,400-19,800	13,000-14,000
2003 Odyssey EX	24,700-27,000	23,000-25,100	16,300-17,800
Odyssey LX	22,500-24,000	20,700-22,100	14,600-15,600

For detailed information on this vehicle visit
http://used.consumerguide.com and enter code **2378**

1994-97 HONDA PASSPORT

CLASS: Midsize sport-utility vehicle

BUILT IN: USA

PROS: Optional antilock brakes • 4WD traction (optional) • Passenger and cargo room

CONS: Fuel economy • No shift-on-the-fly • Noise

EVALUATION: The V6 engine is smoother and quieter, and delivers stronger acceleration than the four. Though lacking the low-speed muscle of 6-cylinder engines in rivals from Jeep, Ford, and General Motors, the V6 furnishes sufficient go-power, even with an automatic transmission. Gas mileage is less pleasing. We averaged just 14.6 mpg with a V6 and automatic, with about one-third of the driving on expressways. Engine noise is moderate, but road and wind noise can interfere with conversations.

A Passport is tough enough for off-roading, but the ride gets stiff and bouncy over ruts and potholes, failing to absorb bumps well. Steering is tight, with good feel—easy to correct to stay on course in gusty winds, and delivering more positive control during off-road treks.

Head/leg room are plentiful, but rear entry is tight through narrow doors. Climbing aboard also demands a rather high step-up. The rear seat folds flat to create a wide cargo floor, but a full-size spare tire eats into space. Initial models had overly complex multibutton controls for lighting and wipers. Also, the radio sat too low for easy adjustments while driving. The new dashboard added in mid-1995 has a more convenient control layout. All models have plenty of handy bins and storage pockets.

VALUE FOR THE MONEY: Though not lacking in features or capabilities, neither the Passport nor its Rodeo near-duplicate is quite in the league of a Chevrolet S10 Blazer or Ford Explorer.

TROUBLE SPOTS

See the 1991-97 Isuzu Rodeo.

AVERAGE REPLACEMENT COSTS

See the 1991-97 Isuzu Rodeo.

NHTSA RECALL HISTORY

1994: Camshaft-seal end plug can become dislodged from cylinder head, allowing oil to leak; can cause engine damage and fire. **1994:** Latch in seatbelt buckle could engage only partially, causing tongue to come out during collision or hard braking.

PRICES

	Good	Average	Poor
1994 Passport 2WD	$3,000-3,800	$2,300-2,900	$700-900
Passport 4WD	4,200-5,200	3,400-4,300	1,400-1,700

HONDA

1995 Passport 2WD	$3,700-5,500	$3,000-4,500	$1,100-1,600
Passport 4WD	5,200-6,500	4,400-5,500	2,100-2,600
1996 Passport 2WD	4,400-6,200	3,700-5,100	1,500-2,200
Passport 4WD	6,000-7,200	5,200-6,300	2,500-3,000
1997 Passport 2WD	5,500-7,000	4,700-6,000	2,300-2,900
Passport 4WD	7,000-8,000	6,200-7,100	3,400-3,800

For detailed information on this vehicle visit
http://used.consumerguide.com and enter code 2175

1998-02 HONDA PASSPORT

CLASS: Midsize sport-utility vehicle
BUILT IN: USA
PROS: Acceleration
• Antilock brakes • Cargo room • Passenger room
CONS: Fuel economy
• Road noise

EVALUATION: A shorter wheelbase, lighter weight, and more power helped make the latest Passport more nimble, but it set no new SUV standard. The suspension produces a generally stable ride, without pitching or bouncing. Small bumps and imperfections register in occupant consciousness, but don't intrude, though the ride can get choppy at times—not exactly a surprise in this class. Larger bumps and potholes are not absorbed nearly as well as they should be, resulting in a rather harsh experience. Among the more agile midsize SUVs, Passports suffer plenty of body lean and tire squeal in tight turns.

The V6 engine delivers brisk acceleration and good passing power. Passport's automatic transmission shifts smoothly and downshifts quickly. A 4-wheel-drive LS averaged 15.8 mpg in mixed driving, which is about on track for this league. Isuzu-engineered part-time push-button 4-wheel-drive is convenient to use, but most current rivals offer 4WD systems that don't need to be disengaged on dry pavement.

Passenger space is good, except for a shortage of rear toe room. The driver enjoys a commanding position, even though the seat is not height-adjustable and its positioning does not suit everyone. The firmly-padded driver's seat earns high marks, however. A simple dashboard layout is marred only by undersized audio controls—recessed and positioned a bit too far away for no-distraction use by the driver.

Step-in height is a little lower than the midsize-SUV norm, making it reasonably easy to get in and out. Back doors allow passengers to slip through easily, but narrow openings hinder exiting. Forward visibility is excellent, thanks to a low cowl and hood, but the optional outside spare tire interferes with the rearward view. The side-opening tailgate demands cumbersome 2-handed operation. To open it, you must first raise the window; to close, you must reach into the hinge area and release a bare-metal lever to free the door.

VALUE FOR THE MONEY: Like the Rodeo, Honda's SUV emphasizes the "sport" in sport-utility. But Isuzu's version has outsold the Passport by almost 3-to-1. Lack of outstanding features sets neither one above the competition, and high prices are an obstacle.

TROUBLE SPOTS

See the 1998-03 Isuzu Rodeo.

AVERAGE REPLACEMENT COSTS

See the 1998-03 Isuzu Rodeo.

NHTSA RECALL HISTORY

1998: Improperly crimped ground connection terminal in engine-wiring harness can eventually cause stress fracture, causing powertrain control module to receive an erroneous signal that may result in "no-start" condition or possible engine stalling. **1998-99:** Insufficient paint hardness on rear axles, due to uneven application, could result in loosening of nut for lower link bracket bolt, possibly leading to separation of link from axle. **2001:** Passenger-side airbag modules were shipped without enough generant and missing a necessary component—a check-valve pin. The airbag will not inflate properly.

PRICES	Good	Average	Poor
1998 Passport EX	$8,200-9,500	$7,400-8,600	$4,200-4,800
Passport LX	7,000-8,000	6,200-7,100	3,400-3,800
1999 Passport EX	10,200-11,700	9,200-10,500	5,300-6,100
Passport LX	9,000-10,500	8,100-9,500	4,700-5,500
2000 Passport EX	12,500-14,200	11,300-12,800	7,100-8,100
Passport LX	11,000-12,500	9,900-11,300	5,900-6,800
2001 Passport EX	14,500-16,500	13,200-15,000	9,000-10,200
Passport LX	13,000-14,500	11,800-13,200	7,500-8,400
2002 Passport EX	16,500-18,500	15,000-16,800	10,600-11,800
Passport LX	15,000-16,500	13,700-15,000	9,500-10,400

For detailed information on this vehicle visit
http://used.consumerguide.com and enter code **2339**

1997-01 HONDA PRELUDE

CLASS: Sporty coupe
BUILT IN: Japan
PROS: Acceleration • Build quality • Steering/handling
CONS: Cargo room • Rear-seat room

EVALUATION: This Prelude rides more softly and muffles the VTEC engine better than the old one did, so it doesn't feel—or sound—as sporty this time around. On the other hand, the new Prelude drives more securely through turns and over lumpy surfaces. There's also a satisfying exhaust note when the engine revs high—which it definitely likes to do. The ride is reasonably supple for a sports coupe, though uneven surfaces induce notable jiggle. Engine, wind, and road noise are low while cruising, but "tire slap" might be heard even in around-town driving.

Acceleration is lively with either transmission. Our test Preludes accelerated from 0-60 mph in 8.5 seconds with SportShift, and a swifter-yet 7.6 seconds with the 5-speed manual gearbox in an SH. While the you-do-it SportShift gear changes are crisp and immediate, high-rpm downshifts usually occur with a jerky lunge. On the plus side, SportShift's manual-shift capability gives the driver helpful control over engine speeds. Prelude's 5-speed is a slick-shifting, sheer delight, mating masterfully to smooth and easy clutch action. An SH averaged only 19.4 mpg, though a base car with automatic got a more appealing 23.2 mpg. Premium fuel is mandatory either way.

The current Prelude is not usefully bigger in size. A longer wheelbase adds some rear foot room, but no more functional backseat space than in prior Preludes. Therefore, the rear seat is again best used to carry children or parcels—though it's no worse than most rivals. Visibility is uncluttered all around. The new dashboard features simple, logically grouped analog gauges.

VALUE FOR THE MONEY: New styling gave this Prelude an airier cabin than before, and the base model has been better equipped than its predecessor. Workmanship is pleasing, but the interior decor is closer to economy-car basic than to suave sports machine. Still, energetic performance on the road can help make a Prelude appealing.

TROUBLE SPOTS

Dashboard lights: The active torque transfer system (ATTS) light may come on and the system will shut down. A revised control unit is available to replace the original one. (1997)

Dashboard lights: The malfunction indicator light comes on because the transmission-control module is damaged by electrical spikes from the ignition switch. (1997)

Manual transmission: Because of a manufacturing defect in the shift fork, the transmission may grind going into fifth gear. (1997)

Seatbelts/safety: The button on the seatbelt that prevents the male half of the buckle breaks, and the buckle slides down to the floor. (1997-98)

Vehicle noise: The rear corners of the headliner rub against the rear window causing a rattle, especially on rough roads. (1997)

Vehicle noise: Rattles or buzzing from under the car may result from the heat shield being too close to the active torque transfer system (ATTS). (1997)

AVERAGE REPLACEMENT COSTS

A/C Compressor	$390	CV Joints	$680
Alternator	425	Exhaust System	685

Automatic Trans.	$1,035	Radiator	$505
Brakes	270	Shocks and/or Struts	855
Clutch	540	Timing Chain/Belt	250

NHTSA RECALL HISTORY

1997-98: Certain ball joints can wear out prematurely and, in worst case, would separate, causing front suspension to collapse.

PRICES

	Good	Average	Poor
1997 Prelude	$8,800-9,800	$7,900-8,800	$4,600-5,100
Prelude SH	9,500-10,200	8,600-9,200	4,900-5,300
1998 Prelude	10,200-11,200	9,200-10,100	5,300-5,800
Prelude SH	11,000-12,000	9,900-10,800	5,900-6,500
1999 Prelude	12,000-13,000	10,800-11,700	6,700-7,300
Prelude SH	13,000-14,000	11,800-12,700	7,500-8,100
2000 Prelude	14,000-15,000	12,700-13,700	8,500-9,200
Prelude SH	15,000-16,000	13,700-14,600	9,500-10,100
2001 Prelude	16,000-17,000	14,600-15,500	10,200-10,900
Prelude SH	17,000-18,200	15,600-16,700	10,900-11,600

For detailed information on this vehicle visit
http://used.consumerguide.com and enter code **2265**

1995-99 HYUNDAI ACCENT

CLASS: Subcompact car

BUILT IN: South Korea

PROS: Optional antilock brakes • Fuel economy • Instruments/controls • Visibility

CONS: Passing power • Noise • Driving position

EVALUATION: Acceleration from the base engine is adequate around town with either manual or automatic shift. Highway passing, on the other hand, requires a long stretch of open road. The engine also strains hard when going up even small hills. Automatic-transmission downshifts are not harsh, and only seldom abrupt at all. Although the GT's engine, with 13 extra horsepower, performs with greater spirit, it does not transform the Accent into anything approaching a mini hot rod. Gas mileage is great. We've averaged more than 30 miles per gallon.

Hyundai made great strides in improving the suspension. The ride is now above average for a small automobile. The suspension absorbs most bumps well and has good stability at highway speeds. Large bumps produce a loud thump; but most smaller obstacles are taken in stride. Handling ability is adequate, but the Accent's skinny tires easily lose their grip.

Interior space is good in front for adults, but the back seat is too small for anyone taller than 5-foot-10. The dashboard is neat and legible, with easy-to-read gauges and logical controls, but some drivers find the fixed-position steering wheel to be too high for comfort. Outward visibility is good on both body styles. A large glovebox and long door pockets help with interior storage.

VALUE FOR THE MONEY: Because an Accent is also more satisfying to drive than some rivals, it can be a reasonable buy, provided that you can get beyond the interior noise problem. Reliability is also a question. All told, we recommend something larger for everyday transportation.

TROUBLE SPOTS

Automatic transmission: Automatic transmission may flare between second and third or downshift poorly. There is a modified transmission-control module available. (1996-97)

Automatic transmission: If the transmission slips or will not go into fourth gear, the end clutch needs to be replaced. (1995-96)

Hard starting: Hard starting may be due to a cracked in-tank fuel line. (1995-97)

Poor transmission shift: Harsh 4-3 downshifts when coming to a stop below 10 mph due to build problems with the original transmission. (1995-96)

Steering problems: The power-steering bracket may interfere with the coolant reservoir causing a buzzing noise or possible reservoir damage. A new bracket is available. (1995-97)

AVERAGE REPLACEMENT COSTS

A/C Compressor	$595	CV Joints	$330
Alternator	315	Exhaust System	250
Automatic Trans.	810	Radiator	390
Brakes	190	Shocks and/or Struts	550
Clutch	300	Timing Chain/Belt	175

NHTSA RECALL HISTORY

1995 w/manual shift: Engine-control module wiring harness can be contacted by clutch-pedal assembly; insulation damage can cause fuse to blow and engine to stall. **1995-96 cars sold/used in Puerto Rico:** Through contact with road hazards and curbs, lower control arm can shift from original position. **1995-97 in 20 "salt belt" states:** Road salt can result in corrosion that causes pits to form on lower coil of front springs, allowing cracks to develop and possible breakage. **1996-97:** Wipers may not operate, due to contamination in contacts. **1999 w/automatic transmission:** Pressure-control solenoid valve seals can allow transmission fluid to leak, resulting in slippage.

PRICES

PRICES	Good	Average	Poor
1995 Accent	$1,100-1,700	$700-1,000	$100-200
1996 Accent	1,300-2,200	800-1,400	200-300
1997 Accent	1,500-2,400	1,000-1,600	200-300
1998 Accent	1,800-2,900	1,200-2,000	300-400
1999 Accent	2,200-3,400	1,600-2,400	400-600

For detailed information on this vehicle visit
http://used.consumerguide.com and enter code 2177

2000-03 HYUNDAI ACCENT

CLASS: Subcompact car
BUILT IN: South Korea
PROS: Fuel economy
• Visibility
CONS: Acceleration
• Noise • Rear-seat
entry/exit (2-dr) • Ride

EVALUATION: Acceleration is barely acceptable with the 1.5-liter engine, even with manual shift. A test model took 11.2 seconds to reach 60 mph.

The optional automatic transmission performs well and does a nice job of resisting erratic shifting on hills. Passing with either transmission will require noisy, full-throttle operation. An automatic Accent struggles quite hard on significant upgrades, succeeding only after considerable huffing and puffing.

Economy is a plus. A 2000 GS hatchback averaged 29.6 mpg, while a similar sedan reached 30.4 mpg.

Small bumps are absorbed acceptably well, but like most subcompacts, the Accent can be a rough rider at times. Large potholes transmit jolts, and the going gets jiggly on washboard surfaces.

Cornering grip is modest, thanks to underachiever tires, but the Accent handles with predictable assurance. Body lean is moderate. Simulated panic stops without ABS are passable, despite some rear-wheel lockup. Hyundai keeps noise and vibration to competitive levels, but engine and road sounds do intrude.

Front seats are comfortable and supportive for everyday commuting, though longer trips may prove tiring. Taller drivers might feel crowded, as the seat does not offer much rearward travel. The back seat is too narrow for three adults, too flat to provide good support, and too cramped to give anyone six feet tall much leg or head room. Rear-seat entry/exit is tight, even in the four-door model.

Clearly marked controls are within easy reach. A rather high rear deck pinches the view through the back window, but visibility is good otherwise. Trunk space also is good, beneath a short, narrow lid. On the whole, the Accent is solid, well-detailed, and decently built.

VALUE FOR THE MONEY: Affordable without seeming cheap, an Accent is worth considering as a bargain-basement commuter car. Because it trails most non-Korean brands in resale value, used-car prices can be appealing. Most rivals offer better performance and refinement for a little more money.

TROUBLE SPOTS

Dashboard lights: The check-engine light may come on and the diagnostic code may indicate a lean fuel condition requiring mass-airflow sensor replacement. (2000-01)

Hard starting: The engine may not start (but starter cranks) due to a shorted overdrive-switch wire. (2000)

Poor transmission shift: Transmission may not shift out of park due to blown fuse, bad brake-light switch or transmission shift-lock solenoid. (1999)

Transmission slippage: Poor shifting, slippage or a transmission that will not shift out of third gear can often be traced to corroded connectors or other problems in the wiring, which may require replacement of the wiring harness. Other shifting problems may be caused by a problem with the transmission-fluid temperature sensor or pulse generator. (2000-01)

AVERAGE REPLACEMENT COSTS

A/C Compressor	$435	CV Joints	$670
Alternator	205	Exhaust System	270
Automatic Trans.	1,030	Radiator	155
Brakes	260	Shocks and/or Struts	440
Clutch	470	Timing Chain/Belt	280

NHTSA RECALL HISTORY

2000: Ball-joint connection can disengage rendering the windshield wipers inoperative. **2000-01:** Throttle valve may not close fully due to steady driving in cold temperatures, causing the vehicle to idle at higher than normal speed. **2000-02:** Head injury may result from contact with the A-pillar in a collision.

PRICES	Good	Average	Poor
2000 Accent GS, GL	$3,300-4,200	$2,600-3,300	$800-1,100
Accent L	2,700-3,300	2,000-2,500	600-700
2001 Accent GS, GL	4,200-5,000	3,400-4,100	1,400-1,700
Accent L	3,500-4,200	2,800-3,400	900-1,100
2002 Accent GS, GL	5,600-6,500	4,800-5,600	2,300-2,700
Accent L	4,800-5,500	4,000-4,600	1,800-2,100
2003 Accent	6,300-7,200	5,500-6,300	2,800-3,200
Accent GL	7,300-8,700	6,600-7,800	3,600-4,300

For detailed information on this vehicle visit
http://used.consumerguide.com and enter code **2454**

1992-95 HYUNDAI ELANTRA

CLASS: Subcompact car
BUILT IN: South Korea
PROS: Control layout
• Passenger and cargo room
• Visibility
CONS: Noise • Radio controls • Ride

EVALUATION: Early Elantras with the smaller engine exhibit fairly spirited performance with manual shift. But with the automatic transmission, you must use a heavy foot to keep up with traffic. Performance is better with the 1.8-liter engine that debuted for 1993. Though relatively smooth, the 1.6-liter engine isn't truly quiet. The 1.8-liter engine is smoother but not much quieter. Gas mileage isn't as great as might be expected. An automatic GLS averaged only 22.5 mpg. Road and wind noise is excessive for a modern small car.

Elantras have a floaty ride. The suspension does not absorb bumps well, and the ride can get rough over broken pavement. Wavy surfaces yield a bouncy and disjointed sensation. Body lean is excessive in sharp directional changes, and the front tires tend to resist turning. Brakes are adequate, if a bit overassisted. The addition of optional antilock braking for 1994 was a sensible move, though ABS was available only on the GLS.

Passenger space is generous for a car in this class. Six-footers can sit comfortably in back, though the seat is too narrow for three adults. Head room is adequate all around. Except for low-mounted radio gauges, controls are well laid out. Visibility is good to all directions. Out back, the large trunk has a low, bumper-height liftover.

VALUE FOR THE MONEY: Overall, Elantra rates no higher than average, but came better equipped than most competitors. Workmanship cannot match that of most rivals, so be sure any Elantra is inspected carefully before you make a purchase.

TROUBLE SPOTS

Automatic transmission: The transmission may shift poorly between first and second or develop harsh shifting. It can be corrected by adjusting the kickdown servo. (1992-95)

Automatic transmission: If the transmission slips or will not go into fourth gear, the end clutch needs to be replaced. (1992-95)

Brakes: Brake-pedal pulsation is often due to brake-disc-thickness variations. (1992-95)

Engine misfire: In cool weather, the engine may stall or run rough. A replacement computer might fix the problem. (1992)

Hard starting: A cold-start repair kit can aid 1.6-liter engines that do not start in temperatures below 10 degrees (F). (1992-94)

Hard starting: Hard starting may be due to a cracked in-tank fuel line. (1992-95)

Manual transmission: Manual transaxles may grind when attempting to shift into reverse due to a problem with either the reverse idle-gear bushing and reverse shift lever, reverse synchronizer, or a weak wave spring. (1992-94)

AVERAGE REPLACEMENT COSTS

A/C Compressor	$565	CV Joints	$355
Alternator	315	Exhaust System	295
Automatic Trans.	810	Radiator	390
Brakes	190	Shocks and/or Struts	595
Clutch	310	Timing Chain/Belt	195

NHTSA RECALL HISTORY

1994-95: Driver-side airbag warning light could illuminate because of increased electrical resistance; might prevent airbag from activating during a crash.

PRICES	Good	Average	Poor
1992 Elantra	$800-1500	$500-800	$100-200
1993 Elantra	1,000-1,600	600-1,000	100-200
1994 Elantra	1,100-1,700	700-1,000	100-200
1995 Elantra	1,300-1,900	800-1,200	200

> For detailed information on this vehicle visit
> http://used.consumerguide.com and enter code **2178**

1996-00 HYUNDAI ELANTRA

CLASS: Subcompact car
BUILT IN: South Korea
PROS: Dual airbags
• Optional antilock brakes
• Fuel economy • Passenger room
CONS: Passing power (automatic) • Small trunk opening • Noise

EVALUATION: Hyundai's second-generation Elantra took a giant leap forward in roominess, quiet running, and all-around competence on the road. Not only is this version quieter than the prior Elantra at highway speeds, but the engine becomes raucous only when pushed hard. Acceleration is good with either transmission, and passing power is brisk in around-town driving. On the downside, the automatic transmission shifts abruptly at times, and passing power above 60 mph is meager. Fuel economy is good. We averaged more than 25 mpg.

The suspension absorbs most bumps neatly, providing a stable highway ride. Unfortunately, you must cope with an abundance of suspension and tire thumping. Steering feels a trifle loose, but an Elantra handles competently, maneuvering nimbly with good grip. Brakes have a solid pedal feel, but a panic stop in an Elantra without ABS produced plenty of tire squeal and even a threat to swerve.

Visibility is clear in all directions. Head and leg room are generous in front for medium-sized adults. Backseat space is adequate, with acceptable head and leg room, but not enough width to hold three occupants comfortably. Sedans have passable trunk space, but a small opening, so loading of bulky items could be easier. The split-rear seatback on the GLS model folds for additional cargo space. The station wagon's rear seatback folds to create a flat cargo floor.

VALUE FOR THE MONEY: Value-conscious shoppers might want to take a close look at this latest, greatly improved Elantra, which flaunts a friendly demeanor. Though not flawless, moderate secondhand prices can make it tempting.

TROUBLE SPOTS

Automatic transmission: Automatic transmissions may flare between second and third or downshift poorly. There is a modified transmission-control module available. (1996-97)

Automatic transmission: If the transmission slips or will not go into fourth gear, the end clutch probably needs to be replaced. (1996)

Hard starting: Hard starting may be due to a cracked in-tank fuel line. (1996-97)

AVERAGE REPLACEMENT COSTS

A/C Compressor	$565	CV Joints	$355
Alternator	315	Exhaust System	355
Automatic Trans.	810	Radiator	390
Brakes	170	Shocks and/or Struts	595
Clutch	295	Timing Chain/Belt	195

NHTSA RECALL HISTORY

1996-97: Evaporative emissions control system can apply excessive vacuum to fuel tank, resulting in minor tank distortion; small crack could develop, allowing fuel to escape. **1996-97:** Wipers may not operate, due to contamination. **1999 w/automatic transmission:** Pressure control solenoid-valve seals can allow transmission fluid to leak, resulting in slippage. **2000:** Intermittent low-speed engine stalling occurs if the mass airflow sensor electrical signal is interrupted due to engine vibration transmitted to the MAF sensor-connector wiring harness.

PRICES	Good	Average	Poor
1996 Elantra	$1,600-2,400	$1,100-1,600	$200-300
1997 Elantra	2,100-3,000	1,500-2,100	400-500
1998 Elantra	2,700-3,800	2,000-2,900	600-800
1999 Elantra	3,500-4,800	2,800-3,800	900-1,300
2000 Elantra	4,600-5,700	3,800-4,700	1,700-2,100

For detailed information on this vehicle visit
http://used.consumerguide.com and enter code **2179**

2001-03 HYUNDAI ELANTRA

CLASS: Subcompact car
BUILT IN: South Korea
PROS: Fuel economy
• Maneuverability
CONS: Acceleration
(w/automatic transmission)
• Cargo room (sedan)

HYUNDAI

EVALUATION: In performance, maneuverability, and ride comfort, the Elantra scores reasonably well for a car of its caliber. Manual-shift models have accelerated to 60 mph in 8.4 seconds, which is brisk for a subcompact. Automatic-transmission versions have only adequate pickup, though the transmission is reasonably smooth and responsive. Fuel economy with manual shift averaged 25.2 to 25.9 mpg.

Ride quality in any model is surprisingly composed for a low-end subcompact, and suspensions absorb most rough stuff with ease. Some jiggle occurs on freeways, but not severely. The GT's sport suspension makes little difference in ride comfort.

Steering/handling in the GLS is dull but competent. An Elantra corners with noticeable body lean but good stability.

Without ABS, one sedan showed moderate dive and good modulation in hard stops, but also suffered early left-front-wheel lockup. The GT's sport suspension again makes little difference. The Elantra's engine makes unpleasant high-rpm snarl, and tire noise is noticeable on coarse pavement. Instruments and controls are ordinary but well laid out. The steering wheel may not tilt high enough for some drivers. A few cheap-looking plastic bits spoil the basically nice cabin decor.

Although an Elantra is not midsize-car spacious, six-footers will have no complaints, though tall drivers might like more rearward seat travel. A height-adjustable seat is standard.

Visibility is fine in the sedan, and a bit better in the sloped-tail hatchback. Another pleasant surprise is rear room/comfort. Though too narrow for three adults, head and leg room are good for two, along with adequate foot space. Narrowish rear-door thresholds don't severely impede entry/exit.

The sedan trunk isn't of class-leading size, but is adequately roomy. The GT combines hatchback versatility with four-door convenience.

VALUE FOR THE MONEY: In features, comfort, and even road manners, an Elantra is a budget alternative to the class-leading (but costlier) Honda Civic and Ford Focus. Cars from this South Korean automaker haven't earned a reputation for long-term reliability, but their resale values have been low. That can actually be good news for used-car shoppers.

TROUBLE SPOTS

Clutch: A squeak or squawk when the clutch pedal is pressed or released requires revised bushings for the release shaft. (2001-02)

Electrical problem: The electrical connector in the door(s) may corrode, especially where salt is used on the roads, causing failure of the speakers, power windows, power locks, etc. (2001)

Engine noise: Although not a failure, the valves can get noisy on the 2.0-liter engine and should be checked and adjusted as necessary every 60,000 miles.

Poor transmission shift: The shift from park to reverse or drive is harsh in many models, but if it is extremely harsh, a revised transmission control module may be required. Likewise, harsh shifts in other gears may also require a new module. (2001-02)

Poor transmission shift: A shift flare (engine racing between shifts) may be corrected by reprogramming the transmission-control module. (2001-02)

AVERAGE REPLACEMENT COSTS

A/C Compressor	$880	CV Joints	$1,240
Alternator	390	Exhaust System	775
Automatic Trans.	1,110	Radiator	365
Brakes	260	Shocks and/or Struts	850
Clutch	400	Timing Chain/Belt	190

NHTSA RECALL HISTORY

2001: Side-airbag satellite sensors might be improperly manufactured, resulting in airbag-warning-light illumination and nondeployment of side airbags in an impact. Dealers will replace the affected parts. **2001-03:** Rear brake tubes could contact steering box. Contact could cause wear and corrosion that could result in brake failure. Dealers will reposition brake tubes and apply anticorrosion material to tubes in areas where contact might have occurred.

PRICES	Good	Average	Poor
2001 Elantra GLS	$6,200-6,900	$5,400-6,000	$2,700-3,000
Elantra GT	7,500-8,300	6,800-7,500	3,800-4,200
2002 Elantra GLS	8,000-8,700	7,200-7,800	4,100-4,400
Elantra GT	9,500-10,500	8,600-9,500	4,900-5,500
2003 Elantra GLS	10,000-11,000	9,000-9,900	5,200-5,700
Elantra GT	11,500-13,000	10,400-11,700	6,300-7,200

For detailed information on this vehicle visit
http://used.consumerguide.com and enter code **4483**

2001-03 HYUNDAI SANTA FE

CLASS: Compact sport-utility vehicle

BUILT IN: South Korea

PROS: Cargo room
- Entry/exit
- Instruments/controls
- Ride/handling

CONS: Acceleration
- Interior materials

EVALUATION: Santa Fes function well in several areas, but performance is not among them. A test AWD LX accelerated to 60 mph in a middling 10.3 seconds, and was low on passing muscle, suggesting that this V6 won't have much in reserve with a sizable load. Slightly lighter weight makes the 2WD GLS feel marginally quicker.

On the plus side, an AWD LX averaged a commendable 22.3 mpg, despite gas-eating performance runs. A 2WD GLS averaged 14.5 to 19.3 mpg, with more city driving.

Although the ride is comfortably absorbent on undemanding surfaces, sharp ridges and expansion joints can jolt. Body lean is apparent in tight, fast corners, but far from alarming. Front-drive versions have surprisingly poor traction on wet surfaces, but all-wheel drive provides good all-weather grip.

With ABS, a test LX made short work of simulated emergency stops, but sluggish, mushy pedal action does not inspire confidence. The V6 engine groans at full throttle, but is decently quiet otherwise. Wind rush and tire roar are well-controlled.

Instruments are clear and controls accessible, but shorter drivers might find some gauges obscured. Also, some switches have unusual shapes. Similarly, the dashboard and door panels are molded with needless contours. The grade of interior materials is nothing special.

Front room/comfort is at least class-competitive, especially in head room. Step-in is decently low, despite a tall stance, which contributes to fine visibility. Limited rearward seat travel, on the other hand, spoils a basically good driving position, and some seat adjustments are tedious.

In the rear, the Santa Fe rivals many midsize SUVs for leg space, even with the front seats pushed back. Still, space is too narrow for three adults. Slim door bottoms impede entry/exit.

Cargo room challenges some midsize SUVs, but there's not much floor length behind the rear seat. A standard separate-opening tailgate window is convenient. That's not true of the wind-down spare tire, which is mounted beneath the body.

VALUE FOR THE MONEY: Hyundai's SUV needs more V6 muscle and better interior detailing, but Santa Fe is a high features-per-dollar vehicle with a generous 5-year/60,000-mile basic warranty and 10/100,000-mile powertrain coverage.

TROUBLE SPOTS

Crankshaft: On early production models with V6 engines, the crankshaft-position sensor was failing and was being replaced under recall. (2001)

Engine noise: The 2.4-liter engine's hydraulic lash adjusters, although functional, may be too noisy for some people and quieter replacements are available with larger oil holes. (2001-02)

Engine stalling: The 2.7-liter V6 engine may stall and not restart when idling for extended times with the air conditioner running requiring reprogramming of the engine control module and/or replacement of the oxygen sensors. (2001-02)

Poor transmission shift: The transmission may not shift when the "D" mode is selected or may not upshift or downshift when the "sport" mode is selected due to a faulty switch in the console shifter housing. (2001-02)

Poor transmission shift: The shift from park to reverse or drive is harsh in many models, but if it is extremely harsh, a revised transmission control module may be required. Likewise, harsh shifts in other gears may also require a new module. (2001-02)

Radiator: On vehicles with an automatic transmission, a clamp for the battery cable may wear through the lower radiator hose and the clamp should be replaced with a plastic cable tie. (2001)

Transmission leak: Fluid may leak from the four-wheel-drive transfer case breather plug requiring a length of hose be installed. (2001-02)

AVERAGE REPLACEMENT COSTS

A/C Compressor	$540	CV Joints	$730
Alternator	250	Exhaust System	300
Automatic Trans.	1,890	Radiator	470
Brakes	330	Shocks and/or Struts	875
Clutch	450	Timing Chain/Belt	300

NHTSA RECALL HISTORY

2001-02 V6: Two separate recalls for improperly manufactured crankshaft-position sensors could result in engine stalling while driving. Dealers will replace affected parts.

PRICES

	Good	Average	Poor
2001 Santa Fe 2WD	$12,000-13,500	$10,800-12,200	$6,700-7,600
Santa Fe AWD	13,500-14,800	12,300-13,500	8,000-8,700
2002 Santa Fe 2WD	14,000-15,500	12,700-14,100	8,500-9,500
Santa Fe AWD	16,000-17,500	14,600-15,900	10,200-11,200
2003 Santa Fe 2WD	16,000-18,200	14,600-16,600	10,200-11,600
Santa Fe AWD	18,500-20,500	17,000-18,900	11,800-13,100

For detailed information on this vehicle visit
http://used.consumerguide.com and enter code **4491**

1995-98 HYUNDAI SONATA

CLASS: Midsize car

BUILT IN: South Korea

PROS: Acceleration (V6)
• Optional antilock brakes
• Passenger and cargo room
• Ride

CONS: Automatic-transmission performance
• Wind noise

EVALUATION: The V6 engine furnishes more-than-adequate acceleration from a standing start, capable of reaching 60 mph in just over 9 seconds and delivering welcome passing response. A 4-cylinder Sonata with automatic is sluggish, but gets excellent fuel economy—a credible 23.8 mpg, versus 20.5 mpg for a V6 sedan. Wind noise is prominent around the side windows at highway speeds, making long drives more fatiguing.

Ride quality is impressive. The suspension is firm enough to provide a stable, comfortable highway ride and absorbent enough to soak up most bumps. On the other hand, the ride can get jumpy when rolling over bad roads. A Sonata is easy to drive, but handling ranks just about average—acceptable, that is, but nothing to boast about.

While the previous Sonata was spacious, this one is noticeably roomier.

HYUNDAI

Partly due to its longer wheelbase, the Sonata's rear seat looks huge compared to space inside some competitors. Expect plenty of head, leg, and elbow room up front, and also in the rear. Cargo space is generous. The new dashboard has a more convenient design than its predecessor, with easy-to-read gauges and an ample-size glovebox. Panel fit isn't always top-notch, but Sonatas appear to be tight and well-built.

VALUE FOR THE MONEY: Anyone seeking a low-priced family car with plenty of interior space should look over a Sonata before deciding on a purchase. Just don't expect it to shine above the competition.

TROUBLE SPOTS

Automatic transmission: If the transmission slips or will not go into fourth gear, the end clutch needs to be replaced. (1995-96)

Automatic transmission: Automatic transmissions may suffer shift shock or harsh shifting when accelerating from a stop due to a problem with the transmission-control module. (1995-97)

Brakes: The brakes may pulsate under light application. A revised set of brake pads plus a hardware kit are available. (1995-97)

Engine misfire: Rough idle, speed vacillations, shock shifting from park, and hard upshifts and downshifts may result from misadjusted throttle-position sensor and idle switch. (1995-97)

Manual transmission: Manual transaxles may grind when attempting to shift into reverse. The problem is corrected with a new reverse idle-gear bushing and reverse shift lever (1995) or reverse synchronizer. (1995-96)

AVERAGE REPLACEMENT COSTS

A/C Compressor	$950	CV Joints	$650
Alternator	365	Exhaust System	345
Automatic Trans.	1,010	Radiator	420
Brakes	170	Shocks and/or Struts	760
Clutch	325	Timing Chain/Belt	285

NHTSA RECALL HISTORY

1995: On 356 cars with gas-filled shock absorbers, one or both lower rear spring seats are not securely attached. **1996-97:** Wipers may not operate, due to contamination in contacts. **1998:** A crack could develop in the upper fuel-tank surface, allowing fuel to leak.

PRICES

	Good	Average	Poor
1995 Sonata	$1,700-2,400	$1,100-1,600	$300-400
1996 Sonata	2,000-2,800	1,400-2,000	300-500
1997 Sonata	2,500-3,400	1,800-2,500	500-700
1998 Sonata	3,300-4,500	2,600-3,600	800-1,100

> For detailed information on this vehicle visit
> http://used.consumerguide.com and enter code **2181**

1999-01 HYUNDAI SONATA

CLASS: Midsize car
BUILT IN: South Korea
PROS: Cargo room • Ride
CONS: Automatic transmission performance • Rear-seat comfort

EVALUATION: Sonata's suspension easily irons out most bumps, and the sedan rivals larger, more costly cars for overall comfort. Poor control of body motions is the penalty to be paid, a result of soft damping. Dips and creases can induce moderate bounding, and lane changes at highway speeds are sloppy. Nosedive also is significant, in emergency stops.

Off-the-line punch with the V6 is decent. With automatic, a test V6 Sonata accelerated to 60 mph in 9 seconds, but passing power is modest. In addition, the automatic transmission is reluctant to kick down for passing, and "hunts" too much between gears in hilly terrain. As for economy, a V6 GLS averaged 22.4 mpg. All-disc brakes in a GLS provide stabile, reasonably short stops even without ABS. Tire thrum is noticeable on coarse pavement and some wind noise is evident, but otherwise the Sonata is fairly quiet. Front seats are sufficiently roomy and supportive for this sedan's class. Rear leg room is good but head room only adequate for 6-footers, who occupy a short, low cushion that compels a knees-up stance. The driving position is comfortably high and sufficiently adaptable, with good visibility except for rear corners. Entry/exit is easy up front but tight in the back. Switches are easy to see and use, but audio controls are on the small side. Interior storage includes front-door map pockets, a decently sized glovebox, and a useful center console. Trunk space is ample, with a low sill. Standard folding rear seatbacks are handy, though the trunk pass-through isn't very large.

VALUE FOR THE MONEY: Though uninspiring, the Sonata is a well-equipped sedan, straddling the line between compact and midsize, which offers fair value. Despite several drawbacks, including tepid acceleration and unsporty handling, it's worth a try. Mediocre resale value translates into appealing prices on the secondhand market.

TROUBLE SPOTS

Audio system: If the CD player locks up, it can be reset by removing the "short connector" in the fuse panel for ten seconds or longer. (1999)

Automatic transmission: Automatic transmissions may not go into drive or reverse after the car has been parked several hours because the torque converter drains down through the front pump. Hyundai was replacing the transmission under warranty. (1999)

Fuel pump: A restriction in the on-board vapor-recovery line may cause gas-station fuel pumps to click off when refueling. (1999-2000)

HYUNDAI

Manual transmission: A countermeasure synchronizer, first and second gear and shift-fork kit is required to correct hard-shifting manual transmissions. (1999-2000)

AVERAGE REPLACEMENT COSTS

A/C Compressor	$880	CV Joints	$1,040
Alternator	370	Exhaust System	775
Automatic Trans.	710	Radiator	465
Brakes	260	Shocks and/or Struts	850
Clutch	435	Timing Chain/Belt	190

NHTSA RECALL HISTORY

1999-2000: Certain sedans with 2.5-liter V6 engines may experience intermittent low-speed engine stalling. **1999-2001:** Unusual motion of the side-impact airbag wiring harness and side-impact airbag wiring harness connector can cause the airbag warning light to illuminate.

PRICES

	Good	Average	Poor
1999 Sonata	$4,500-5,600	$3,700-4,600	$1,600-2,000
2000 Sonata	5,800-7,000	5,000-6,100	2,400-2,900
2001 Sonata	7,500-9,000	6,800-8,100	3,800-4,500

For detailed information on this vehicle visit
http://used.consumerguide.com and enter code **2379**

1997-01 HYUNDAI TIBURON

CLASS: Sporty coupe

BUILT IN: South Korea

PROS: Fuel economy • Ride • Steering/handling

CONS: Acceleration • Engine noise • Entry/exit • Rear-seat room • Road noise

EVALUATION: Though the 2.0-liter engine is a little smoother and quieter than the first-year 1.8-liter four, it also disappoints, generating a loud, crude growl during even moderate acceleration. The growling does not smooth out fully when cruising, either. Furthermore, road noise and suspension thumping grow annoying, making Tiburon quite unpleasant on a long trip. Acceleration from a standstill and from midrange speeds qualifies only as adequate—not lively enough to satisfy the enthusiastic driver. An automatic transmission slows progress substantially. An automatic Tiburon averaged an appealing 25 mpg in a mix of urban commuting and rush-hour expressway driving.

Handling is one of the car's greatest strengths—sporty and secure, with well-managed body lean through turns. A Tiburon pulls through sweeping curves with good grip and stability. Firm steering has plenty of road feel, centering quickly after turns. Large bumps and dips can yield mild float, however. A comfortable ride is another of this coupe's prime attributes. The ride is taut, but without lapsing into harshness.

The driver gets a low, snug driving position, facing a well-arranged dashboard. Back-seat space is no more than a joke, for anyone above toddler size. Entry/exit isn't so easy, even into front seats. Visibility is above average for a sports coupe, despite the car's curvy shape.

VALUE FOR THE MONEY: Attractively and distinctively styled, the Tiburon can be a good bargain-priced alternative to Ford's Probe as well as the Nissan 200SX. Although Tiburon ranks far ahead of the old Scoupe, however, it does no more than score dead even with other small sporty coupes, and behind some of them.

TROUBLE SPOTS

Automatic transmission: Harsh automatic transmission 4-3 downshifts when decelerating may require the transmission-control module or entire transaxle to be replaced. (1997-98)

Clutch: The clutch may drag (manual transmission), especially after long-term storage due to grease in the hydraulic line. Flushing and refilling the system cures the problem. (1997)

Sunroof/moonroof: The edge of the sunroof lip rusts because the weatherstrip does not seal properly. (1997-98)

Timing belt: The timing chain may be noisy and wear out prematurely. (1997-98)

AVERAGE REPLACEMENT COSTS

A/C Compressor	$555	CV Joints	$455
Alternator	380	Exhaust System	360
Automatic Trans.	970	Radiator	370
Brakes	210	Shocks and/or Struts	810
Clutch	375	Timing Chain/Belt	290

NHTSA RECALL HISTORY

1997: Evaporative-emissions control system can apply excessive vacuum to fuel tank, which could result in minor tank distortion; small crack could develop, allowing fuel to escape. **1997:** Wipers may not operate, due to contamination in contacts. **1997-2001:** The driver and front passenger seatbelts may not extend and retract smoothly through the d-ring guides mounted on the body pillars aft of the doors. **1999 w/automatic transmission:** Pressure-control solenoid-valve seals can allow transmission fluid to leak, resulting in slippage. **1999:** Tire-pressure placard contains incorrect tire sizes, seating capacity, and luggage capacity. **2000-01:** Seatbelts may not extend and retract smoothly, making them inconvenient to use.

PRICES

	Good	Average	Poor
1997 Tiburon	$2,800-3,600	$2,100-2,700	$600-800
1998 Tiburon	3,700-4,600	3,000-3,700	1,100-1,300
1999 Tiburon	4,800-5,800	4,000-4,900	1,800-2,200

2000 Tiburon	$6,500-7,500	$5,700-6,600	$2,900-3,400
2001 Tiburon	8,300-9,300	7,500-8,400	4,300-4,800

> For detailed information on this vehicle visit
> http://used.consumerguide.com and enter code **2266**

1991-96 INFINITI G20

CLASS: Near-luxury car

BUILT IN: Japan

PROS: Acceleration (manual) • Antilock brakes • Steering/handling

CONS: Acceleration (early automatic transmission)
• Climate controls • Engine noise • Ride (early models) • Road noise

EVALUATION: The 5-speed gearbox blends neatly with the fast-revving engine for a lively feel, whether off the line or meandering through tight, twisty roads. However, the automatic transmission cuts rather sharply into performance, shifting too often even on moderate uphill grades and impairing standing-start action. As for economy, we averaged 21.7 mpg with an automatic G20.

Though wind noise is low, road and engine noise can be a problem. However, the G20 suffers a stiff, jolting ride as soon as any big bumps appear. On the plus side, softer suspension bushings, introduced in mid 1993, deliver a ride that's still firm, but no longer too stiff on bumpy roads. In any year, body lean is minimal, power steering is quick and responsive, and brakes respond eagerly.

Space is more than adequate for four adults, and the handsome dashboard is well-organized. Gauges are clearly marked; controls handy, except for a low heat/vent panel. A low beltline and thin roof pillars contribute to a commanding driving position and good visibility. Firm front bucket seats offer good support. Six-footers can ride in back without feeling cramped. The ample trunk has a long, flat floor, and its lid opens from bumper height to more than 90 degrees.

VALUE FOR THE MONEY: Though capable and well-designed, the small Infiniti's lack lies in its engine department—neither as quiet nor as quick as expected, especially with automatic—and in the overly taut suspension. Even so, it's a spirited machine with a sensible design, thus worth a test-drive.

TROUBLE SPOTS

Automatic transmission: If the transmission won't upshift to third or fourth or slips on acceleration, the high clutch assembly may be burnt and debris gets lodged in the valve body. (1991-93)

Automatic transmission: The dropping resistor on the inner left fender can be damaged by rain or windshield-washer fluid causing harsh, noisy, or jerky transmission shifts. A new resistor, with a protective cover, is required to fix the problem. (1994)

Automatic transmission: A campaign was conducted to improve automatic-transmission life by installing an inline filter and auxiliary oil cooler. (1991)

Dashboard lights: If the check-engine light comes on, but the technician can find no faulty components, there may be inductive interference on the wiring harness leading to the onboard computer. Separating and isolating the wires from one another cures the problem. (1994-95)

Engine stalling: If a cold engine stalls when coming to a stop and is hard to restart, replacing the hydraulic-valve lash adjusters may restore performance. (1991-92)

Fuel odors: Fuel odors on cold start can be solved by a free repair that may include new fuel injectors, hoses, fuel rails, regulator, and wiring. (1991-92)

Transmission noise: If the automatic transmission chirps when shifting from second to third, a redesigned input shaft and high clutch assembly with an improved friction material should eliminate the problem. (1991)

Trunk latch: The electric trunk-release solenoid may stick in the open position, preventing the trunk from closing properly. (1992-94)

AVERAGE REPLACEMENT COSTS

A/C Compressor	$710	CV Joints	$430
Alternator	790	Exhaust System	520
Automatic Trans.	940	Radiator	480
Brakes	200	Shocks and/or Struts	820
Clutch	485	Timing Chain/Belt	615

NHTSA RECALL HISTORY

1991-92: Rear seatbelt buckle may engage only partially. **1991-96 19 states and D.C.:** Fuel-filler tube assembly can corrode, resulting in leakage. **1993-95:** Harness-connector protector near seatbelt pretensioner can ignite, due to proximity to combustion gas generated by pretensioner when device is triggered; fire can then occur in passenger compartment.

PRICES	Good	Average	Poor
1991 G20	$1,800-2,400	$1,200-1,600	$300-400
1992 G20	2,300-3,000	1,700-2,200	400-600
1993 G20	2,800-3,500	2,100-2,600	600-800
1994 G20	3,500-4,200	2,800-3,400	900-1,100
1995 G20	4,100-4,800	3,400-3,900	1,400-1,600
1996 G20	4,800-5,600	4,000-4,700	1,800-2,100

For detailed information on this vehicle visit
http://used.consumerguide.com and enter code **2060**

1996-99 INFINITI I30

CG BEST BUY

CLASS: Near-luxury car

BUILT IN: Japan

PROS: Acceleration
• Antilock brakes
• Steering/handling

CONS: Fuel economy • Rear-seat comfort • Rear visibility

INFINITI

EVALUATION: The V6 engine produces plenty of torque at low speeds, yielding quick takeoffs and brisk passing sprints. Accelerating to 60 mph takes about 8 seconds. Fuel economy is disappointing. Our test I30 averaged under 19 mpg, and premium gasoline is recommended.

The basic I30's suspension is firm, yet soaks up most bumps easily. Rear-seat passengers actually feel bumps and tar strips more than those seated in front. Steering is firm and precise, offering good feedback. Stable front-drive competence lets an I30 take high-speed corners with little body lean and taut road grip. Because the I30t has a firmer suspension than other models, coupled with high-performance tires, its handling is more responsive—quite agile for a big car. The I30t also suffers a stiffer ride, however, as well as greater tire noise at highway speeds.

Gauges and controls are well-marked and easy to reach while driving. Visibility is good to the front and sides, but large rear headrests block the view directly backward. Interior space is ample for four adults. Rear-seat backrests are too inclined to suit some passengers. The trunk is spacious, and is augmented by a folding pass-through section.

VALUE FOR THE MONEY: With more standard features than a Maxima, the I30 is well-equipped and a good alternative to the more expensive Lexus ES 300—a superior road car for long trips.

TROUBLE SPOTS

See the 1995-99 Nissan Maxima.

AVERAGE REPLACEMENT COSTS

See the 1995-99 Nissan Maxima.

NHTSA RECALL HISTORY

1998: Alternator diode may have been damaged when built, eventually resulting in failure and electric short that could melt plastic housing.

PRICES

	Good	Average	Poor
1996 I30	$5,700-6,500	$4,900-5,600	$2,300-2,700
1997 I30	7,500-8,500	6,800-7,700	3,800-4,300
1998 I30	9,500-10,500	8,600-9,500	4,900-5,500
1999 I30	11,500-12,500	10,400-11,300	6,300-6,900

For detailed information on this vehicle visit
http://used.consumerguide.com and enter code **2182**

1990-96 INFINITI Q45

CLASS: Luxury car
BUILT IN: Japan
PROS: Acceleration
• Antilock brakes
• Passenger room • Ride
• Steering/handling
CONS: Cargo room • Fuel economy

EVALUATION: Among the first items to be noticed behind a Q45's wheel is its quiet, silky, responsive powertrain. Not only is refinement high, but you experience lively off-the-line pickup and the crisp-shifting transmission helps it thread easily through traffic. A sporty growl emanates from beneath the hood, but the V8 runs smoothly. Fuel economy is not a "plus." We averaged only 16.6 mpg, even with a lot of highway miles, and costly premium fuel is required. Traction control is essential for preventing wheel slip on slick surfaces.

Though not quite as smooth-riding as an LS 400 or Jaguar XJ6, the Q45 easily equals the big BMW and Mercedes in that department, yielding a stable, comfortable highway experience. Handling and braking are good, though mild understeer (resistance to turning) is evident and body lean is noticeable. The big (11-inch) brakes work well in routine use.

Though spacious for four, a Q45 isn't vast when you consider its outside dimensions. Entry/exit is a snap. Rear leg room is ample, but there's no space for feet under the front seats. Though it's wide and has a flat floor, the trunk isn't very long or deep.

VALUE FOR THE MONEY: A worthy alternative to the big BMW or Mercedes, the Q45 lacks the charm of those European sedans but is beautifully built and lavishly appointed. It might not quite match Lexus for refinement, but you'd be wise to try both.

TROUBLE SPOTS

Automatic transmission: A campaign was conducted to improve automatic-transmission life by installing an inline filter and auxiliary oil cooler. (1991)

Brakes: To fix brake judder and/or a groaning noise when coming to a stop, new front brake pads were developed. (1990-94)

Engine knock: A knocking noise when the engine is cold, is probably coming from the ASCD cable rattling in the bracket near the firewall and is corrected by tie-wrapping the cable to the bracket. (1990-93)

Engine misfire: If the idle quality gradually deteriorates, feeling like the idle is set too low, a revised ECM (computer) should solve the problem. (1994-95)

Engine stalling: Stalling during coast-down idling is due to a loose connection at the air-flow meter. (1990-96)

Radiator: The radiator filler neck was prone to breakage and the radiator was redesigned so that the neck is a one-piece, die-cast design. A new cap is also required. (1990-92)

Vehicle shake: Engine vibration felt through the steering wheel, seat, and floor with the brakes on and the transmission in drive, may be corrected by replacing two motor mounts and engine-control computer. If the vibration is worse when the A/C is on, the compressor may also have to be replaced. (1990-91)

AVERAGE REPLACEMENT COSTS

A/C Compressor	$875	Radiator	$545
Alternator	395	Shocks and/or Struts	910
Automatic Trans.	975	Timing Chain/Belt	1,160
Brakes	235	Universal Joints	750
Exhaust System	1,680		

NHTSA RECALL HISTORY

1991-92 w/Bose speakers and integral amplifier: Conductive bridge can form on circuit board due to electrolyte leakage in high humidity; can result in overheating and possible smoke, flame, or fire.

PRICES

	Good	Average	Poor
1990 Q45	$3,000-3,700	$2,300-2,800	$700-900
1991 Q45	3,500-4,200	2,800-3,400	900-1,100
1992 Q45	4,200-5,000	3,400-4,100	1,400-1,700
1993 Q45	5,000-6,000	4,300-5,100	2,000-2,400
1994 Q45	6,000-7,000	5,200-6,100	2,500-2,900
1995 Q45	7,000-8,000	6,200-7,100	3,400-3,800
1996 Q45	8,000-9,200	7,200-8,300	4,100-4,700

> For detailed information on this vehicle visit
> http://used.consumerguide.com and enter code **2061**

1997-01 INFINITI Q45

CLASS: Luxury car
BUILT IN: Japan
PROS: Acceleration • Build quality • Quietness
CONS: Cargo room • Fuel economy • Price

EVALUATION: A test Q45 accelerated to 60 mph in a brisk 7.2 seconds. Midrange power is similarly ample, aided by a velvety-smooth, responsive and refined automatic transmission. Fuel economy is less inspiring. We averaged only 15.4 mpg in a driving mix that included a lot of rush-hour commuting, and 17.6 mpg in a session that covered more highway miles.

Compared to the prior Q45, the new standard model is less agile. Road manners are competent enough, but hardly sporty. This version also feels more roly-poly on tight, twisty roads—closer to the Lexus LS than to BMW's 5-Series, for instance. Slightly numb on-center steering feel doesn't help on this score, either. Suspension damping is soft enough to allow a fair amount of nosedive during hard braking. Otherwise, the brakes perform admirably. At the same time, you can expect something close to a "magic carpet" ride, with outstanding impact absorption. Body control is better in the Touring edition, however.

This "Q" is quiet, without question. Cruising is hushed, with little noise intruding from the road, wind, or engine. Passing over railroad tracks and other hazards generally produces a feeling of solidity. Though smaller outside than the prior "Q," this one is a little roomier inside. Despite the dimensions, though, lanky back-seat occupants must ride with knees-up if a tall passenger happens to occupy the front seat. Head room in back is only adequate, too. Front seats are roomy and comfortable, with enough

---

adjustments to accommodate occupants of nearly any stature. Visibility is good except over-the-shoulder, where wide rear roof pillars serve as obstacles. Although the dashboard looks somewhat uninspired, it's orderly and convenient, though a few controls are cryptic or hidden. The sedan's trunk is wide but not very long, offering space for about four medium suitcases plus a few odds and ends.

VALUE FOR THE MONEY: Though impressive overall and appealing in a number of ways, bland styling and inadequate cargo room help make the latest Q45 a less-than-scintillating competitor.

TROUBLE SPOTS

Brakes: Brakes make a clunking sound and may also pulsate after the engine is first started, but this is a function of the ABS brakes, not a malfunction. (1997-98)

Fuel economy: Fuel economy may be lower after an oil change if the proper SAE grade (5W-30) is used. (1997-98)

Hard starting: May be hard to start in cold weather unless the preferred procedure of depressing the accelerator 1/3 to the floor during cranking. (1997-98)

AVERAGE REPLACEMENT COSTS

A/C Compressor	$860	Exhaust System	$1,740
Alternator	390	Radiator	545
Automatic Trans.	975	Shocks and/or Struts	910
Brakes	245	Timing Chain/Belt	1,160
CV Joints	760		

NHTSA RECALL HISTORY

1997-98: Alternator diode may have been damaged when built, eventually resulting in failure and electric short that could melt plastic housing. **1997-98:** Ignition key can be removed when engine is turned off, without placing transmission shift lever in "Park" position. **2000-01 vehicles with 17-inch alloy wheels:** Certain 17-inch alloy wheels were made with defects could result in the wheel falling off. Dealer will inspect and replace affected wheels.

PRICES

	Good	Average	Poor
1997 Q45	$11,000-12,000	$9,900-10,800	$5,900-6,500
1998 Q45	14,500-16,000	13,200-14,600	9,000-9,900
1999 Q45	18,000-19,500	16,600-17,900	11,500-12,500
2000 Q45	21,500-23,500	19,800-21,600	14,000-15,300
2001 Q45	25,500-27,500	23,700-25,600	16,800-18,200

For detailed information on this vehicle visit
http://used.consumerguide.com and enter code **2267**

1997-00 INFINITI QX4

CLASS: Luxury sport-utility vehicle

BUILT IN: Japan

PROS: Build quality • Passenger and cargo room

CONS: Engine noise • Fuel economy • Rear-seat entry/exit • Rear-seat room

EVALUATION: Claims that a QX4 drives like a car rather than a truck are essentially accurate. The luxury wagon's firm suspension absorbs bumps better than many competitive SUVs. You also enjoy relatively low noise levels, plus confident cornering ability with good grip and little body lean. Don't be misled: The QX4 does not ride like a luxury sedan.

Also, the V6 engine sounds and feels rough when worked hard. Unfortunately, that's exactly what is needed to provide decent passing power. Acceleration is adequate in any case, aided by an automatic transmission that shifts smoothly, but sometimes hesitates to kick down into a lower gear for passing or merging. Gas mileage is not a bonus. We averaged only 12.5 miles per gallon in a mix of city and freeway driving, reaching a high of 15.2 mpg on the highway.

Step-in is high even with the standard running boards. Rear access is complicated even further by back doors that are narrow at the bottom and don't open to an angle close to 90 degrees. Once inside, all-around head and leg room are adequate for four adults (but not five), though rear passengers have virtually no under-seat foot space.

Cargo room, on the other hand, is plentiful even with the 60/40 rear seat in place. Conversion requires swinging the cushion forward and removing the headrests, but the seatbacks then lie flat to create a long, wide deck.

The driver can expect good visibility and a convenient, easy-to-understand dashboard layout. Standard dual power front seats combine with a tilt steering wheel for easy tailoring of the driver's position to suit just about anyone.

VALUE FOR THE MONEY: Considered in terms of value, the QX4 does not look particularly competitive against such rivals as the Mercedes-Benz ML320, which is roomier and rides more smoothly; or the very car-like Lexus RX 300. In fact, a well-equipped Nissan Pathfinder delivers just about as much as the QX4 for markedly fewer dollars, either new or used.

TROUBLE SPOTS

See the 1996-00 Nissan Pathfinder.

AVERAGE REPLACEMENT COSTS

See the 1996-00 Nissan Pathfinder.

NHTSA RECALL HISTORY

2000: Improperly seated key-cylinder cap can disengage causing the steering wheel to lock.

PRICES	Good	Average	Poor
1997 QX4	$10,000-11,000	$9,000-9,900	$5,200-5,700
1998 QX4	12,000-13,200	10,800-11,900	6,700-7,400
1999 QX4	13,700-15,000	12,500-13,700	8,200-9,000
2000 QX4	16,500-18,000	15,000-16,400	10,600-11,500

For detailed information on this vehicle visit
http://used.consumerguide.com and enter code 2268

2001-03 INFINITI QX4

CLASS: Luxury sport-utility vehicle
BUILT IN: Japan
PROS: • Passenger and cargo room • Build quality
CONS: Fuel economy• Rear seat entry/exit

EVALUATION: In performance and accommodations, the QX4 is similar to Nissan's Pathfinder, which costs less. Test models did 0-60 mph in 9 seconds, which is good for a midsize six-cylinder SUV. Calling on full power requires a determined throttle foot, though, and the automatic transmission can be slow to downshift for passing.

As for economy, test QX4s and Pathfinders have averaged 14.2-16.5 mpg, depending on conditions. That's about par for this class, but premium-grade fuel is required.

Both the QX4 and the Pathfinder ride firmly, though the QX4 is acceptably comfortable over bumps and ridges that feel jarring in a Pathfinder. A taut suspension aids control, keeping body lean in turns moderate. Steering feels properly weighted in turns, but suffers vague on-center feel at highway speeds. The turning radius is larger than on most rivals. The QX4's all-surface four-wheel-drive system performs well.

Wind and road noise are well-muffled. The V6 emits a throaty roar in hard acceleration, but cruises quietly enough.

A functionally sound dashboard goes on both the QX4 and Pathfinder. The nicely integrated navigation system works well, once you master its programming. Cabin decor is classy in the QX4.

Room and comfort are ample for adults up front. The driving position is good, and sufficiently adjustable, but thick roof pillars impede visibility.

Rear leg space is barely adequate for adults, if front seats are more than halfway back. The rear bench is low to the floor and deficient in back support. Step-in height is relatively high. Narrow door openings further impede entry/exit. Cargo room is good and flip-up back glass is useful, but the folding rear seat is somewhat complicated.

VALUE FOR THE MONEY: Infiniti has offered its new-vehicle owners "red carpet" customer service, and the QX4's all-wheel-drive system is a bonus. All told, though, neither the QX4 nor the Pathfinder has what it takes to be a compelling value against the competition.

TROUBLE SPOTS

See the 2001-03 Nissan Pathfinder.

AVERAGE REPLACEMENT COSTS

See the 2001-03 Nissan Pathfinder.

NHTSA RECALL HISTORY

2001: Defective ignition-lock assembly could cause key-cylinder cap to disengage, possibly locking the steering wheel while vehicle is in motion. Dealers will inspect lock assemblies and repair or replace them. **2001:** Some brackets used to attach the two gas struts to the rear hatch may have been improperly made, resulting in the struts detaching from the bracket(s) when opening or closing the rear door. Dealers will replace the strut brackets.

PRICES	Good	Average	Poor
2001 QX4 2WD	$21,000-22,500	$19,300-20,700	$13,700-14,600
QX4 4WD	22,500-24,000	20,700-22,100	14,600-15,600
2002 QX4 2WD	23,000-24,500	21,200-22,500	15,000-15,900
QX4 4WD	24,500-26,000	22,800-24,200	15,900-16,900
2003 QX4 2WD	25,500-27,000	23,700-25,100	16,800-17,800
QX4 4WD	27,500-30,000	25,600-27,900	18,400-20,100

For detailed information on this vehicle visit
http://used.consumerguide.com and enter code **2472**

1991-97 ISUZU RODEO

CLASS: Midsize sport-utility vehicle

BUILT IN: USA

PROS: Antilock brakes (4-wheel opt. after '96) • 4WD traction • Passenger and cargo room • Ride

CONS: Entry/exit • Fuel economy • No shift-on-the-fly (pre '96) • Road noise • Wind noise

EVALUATION: Acceleration is adequate but less than brisk with the early V6 and automatic. The 3.2-liter V6, made available in 1993, is an improvement in terms of smoothness and quietness. That V6 works well with automatic, which changes gears smoothly and downshifts promptly for passing. Gas mileage is nothing to boast about. One test Rodeo averaged just 13.9 mpg.

Ride is firm yet surprisingly comfortable, as the absorbent suspension handily soaks up just about every flaw on paved roads. Braking distances are acceptable, though a 2WD Rodeo turned out to be prone to abrupt front-wheel lockup. Road noise is prominent at highway speeds.

Occupants are treated well in a Rodeo. Rear leg room is ample, even with the front seats all the way back. Head clearance is good all around, and the driving position is comfortable for most people. Back doors are quite narrow at sill level, and open only about 70 degrees, so larger folks might feel squeezed when getting in and out. The full-size spare tire mounted inside many models cuts considerably into cargo space, but the back seat folds flat to create a wide cargo floor. Except for too many confusing buttons controlling lights and wipers, and a low-mounted radio, the dashboard is fine.

VALUE FOR THE MONEY: The need to stop the vehicle to engage 4WD, then stop and back up to disengage it, is an inconvenience. Otherwise, the competent and tightly constructed Rodeo deserves a serious look, as it just might be the best Isuzu model on the market.

TROUBLE SPOTS

Air conditioner: The air conditioner gradually becomes warmer due to ice forming on the evaporator. The root problem is a mispositioned thermostat. (1993)
Cruise control: The cruise control may not let the transmission shift down out of overdrive on hills. (1991)
Keys: The ignition key can be hard to remove because the lens over the shift lever interferes with the shift cable. (1992)
Steering noise: A knocking noise when the steering wheel is turned requires a steering-column repair kit. (1991-94)
Steering noise: Lack of grease causes squeaks in column. (1994)
Transmission noise: Lack of lube on the clutch shift fork pivot ball causes noises and squeaks. (1991-94)

AVERAGE REPLACEMENT COSTS

A/C Compressor	$685	Exhaust System	$320
Alternator	295	Radiator	660
Automatic Trans.	1,375	Shocks and/or Struts	200
Brakes	280	Timing Chain/Belt	100
Clutch	595	Universal Joints	120

NHTSA RECALL HISTORY

1991 w/V6: Incorrect transmission-fluid dipstick may have been installed. **1993-94:** Camshaft plug can become dislodged, allowing oil to leak; can cause engine damage and fire. **1994:** Latch in seatbelt buckle could engage only partially, causing tongue to come out during collision or hard braking. **1995:** Excess electrical charge in the alternator can result in engine-control malfunction due to an improperly manufactured integrated circuit in the voltage regulator.

PRICES	Good	Average	Poor
1991 Rodeo S	$1,700-2,600	$1,100-1,700	$300-400
Rodeo XS, LS	2,000-2,900	1,400-2,000	300-500
1992 Rodeo S	2,000-2,900	1,400-2,000	300-500
Rodeo XS, LS	2,300-3,200	1,700-2,300	400-600
1993 Rodeo LS	2,800-3,700	2,100-2,800	600-800
Rodeo S	2,400-3,400	1,800-2,500	500-700

ISUZU

1994 Rodeo LS	$3,200-4,200	$2,500-3,300	$800-1,000
Rodeo S	2,800-3,800	2,100-2,900	600-800
1995 Rodeo LS	3,900-5,400	3,200-4,400	1,200-1,700
Rodeo S	3,200-4,500	2,500-3,500	800-1,100
1996 Rodeo LS	4,700-6,000	3,900-5,000	1,700-2,200
Rodeo S	3,700-5,200	3,000-4,200	1,100-1,500
1997 Rodeo LS	5,500-7,000	4,700-6,000	2,300-2,900
Rodeo S	4,200-6,200	3,400-5,100	1,400-2,000

For detailed information on this vehicle visit
http://used.consumerguide.com and enter code **2185**

1998-03 ISUZU RODEO

CLASS: Midsize sport-utility vehicle

BUILT IN: USA

PROS: Acceleration (V6)
• Standard antilock braking
• Passenger and cargo room

CONS: Engine noise • Fuel economy • Road noise

EVALUATION: Rodeo's suspension produces a stable ride without pitching or bouncing, though small bumps and imperfections produce unpleasant choppiness. Larger bumps and potholes are not absorbed nearly as well as they should be, as the ride becomes downright harsh.

Lack of power with the 4-cylinder engine and manual shift isn't a big drawback. Rodeos with the V6 feel considerably livelier than before, promising brisk acceleration and good passing power. The automatic transmission shifts smoothly and downshifts promptly. An LS 4WD averaged 15.8 mpg in mixed driving—about on target for its class.

Interior space is greater than before, with good passenger room all around, except for a shortage of rear toe space. Even though the seat is not height adjustable and may not suit everyone, the driver enjoys a commanding position. The firmly padded seat earns high marks on its own. Controls for the climate and audio systems are recessed and demand a little too much of a stretch for no-distraction use by the driver. Stereo controls are too small, though the simple dashboard is otherwise pleasing.

Step-in height is a little lower than the midsize-SUV norm, so getting in and out is no great chore. Rear doors permit passengers to slip through fairly easily, though we'd be more pleased if they opened a bit wider. Forward visibility is fine thanks to the low cowl and hood line. Looking rearward, however, the optional outside spare tire interferes with the driver's view. Operation of the new side-opening tailgate is a cumbersome, two-handed process.

VALUE FOR THE MONEY: With the V6, a Rodeo accelerates better than most Japanese rivals, leaning toward the "sport" side of sport utility. Prices are not cheap, however, and Rodeo has no standout features that put it above the competition. That makes it an acceptable choice, but not a compelling one.

TROUBLE SPOTS

Doors: Unless the front-fender liners have been replaced, ice and snow can build up between the door and fender which caused door damage when it is opened. (1998)

Fuel gauge: The gas gauge may indicate full after a fill-up, then not move until the tank is half empty. (1998)

Steering problems: The steering wheel may shimmy or vibrate unless a steering-yoke spring kit is installed. (1998)

Transmission slippage: Delayed transmission engagement, after sitting overnight, may occur due to torque-converter draindown. (1998-99)

AVERAGE REPLACEMENT COSTS

A/C Compressor	$685	Exhaust System	$320
Alternator	295	Radiator	660
Automatic Trans.	620	Shocks and/or Struts	200
Brakes	280	Timing Chain/Belt	100
Clutch	1,110	Universal Joints	120

NHTSA RECALL HISTORY

1998 w/optional floormat: Repeated movement of feet can result in shifting of mat, which could interfere with gas pedal. **1998:** Ground terminal was not properly crimped in engine-wiring harness, which will eventually cause stress fracture; could result in "no-start" or engine stalling. **1998-99:** Paint was applied unevenly on rear axles of certain vehicles; could cause loosening of nut at lower-link bracket bolt. **1998-99:** The rear-axle lower link may become separated from the rear axle. **1999:** Vehicles fail to comply with federal requirement for "Occupant Protection in Interior Impact." **2000-01:** Airbag inflators may contain too much generant. Exploding airbag module could cause severe injury. **2000-01:** Airbag will not inflate properly due to the absence of a necessary component known as a check-valve pin. **2001:** The fuel-return hose does not meet ozone-resistant specifications and could crack, causing fuel leakage.

PRICES	Good	Average	Poor
1998 Rodeo 2WD	$5,500-7,000	$4,700-6,000	$2,300-2,900
Rodeo 4WD	7,000-8,500	6,200-7,600	3,400-4,100
1999 Rodeo 2WD	6,500-8,500	5,700-7,500	2,900-3,800
Rodeo 4WD	8,000-9,500	7,200-8,600	4,100-4,800
Rodeo LSE 2WD	9,000-10,000	8,100-9,000	4,700-5,200
Rodeo LSE 4WD	10,500-11,500	9,500-10,400	5,600-6,100
2000 Rodeo 2WD	7,800-10,000	7,000-9,000	4,000-5,100
Rodeo 4WD	9,500-11,200	8,600-10,100	4,900-5,800
Rodeo LSE 2WD	11,000-12,000	9,900-10,800	5,900-6,500
Rodeo LSE 4WD	12,500-14,000	11,300-12,600	7,100-8,000
2001 Rodeo 2WD	9,500-11,500	8,600-10,400	4,900-6,000
Rodeo 4WD	11,500-13,200	10,400-11,900	6,300-7,300
Rodeo LSE 2WD	13,000-14,500	11,800-13,200	7,500-8,400
Rodeo LSE 4WD	14,500-16,000	13,200-14,600	9,000-9,900

2002 Rodeo 2WD	$11,500-14,000	$10,400-12,600	$6,300-7,700
Rodeo 4WD	13,500-16,000	12,300-14,600	8,000-9,400
Rodeo LSE 2WD	15,500-17,000	14,100-15,500	9,900-10,900
Rodeo LSE 4WD	16,500-18,300	15,000-16,700	10,600-11,700
2003 Rodeo 2WD	13,500-17,500	12,300-15,900	8,000-10,300
Rodeo 4WD	16,000-19,000	14,600-17,300	10,200-12,200

For detailed information on this vehicle visit
http://used.consumerguide.com and enter code **2308**

1992-02 ISUZU TROOPER

CLASS: Full-size sport-utility vehicle

BUILT IN: Japan

PROS: Antilock brakes • 4WD traction • Passenger and cargo room

CONS: Entry/exit • Fuel economy • Lack of shift-on-the-fly (pre '96)

EVALUATION: All three V6 engines are silky and quiet, if not quite frisky. An early automatic LS wagon accelerated to 60 mph in a wholly adequate 11.7 seconds, but speed trails off fast on steep grades. Although the automatic transmission hunts busily between gears in urban driving, it's smooth and responsive. Gas mileage isn't great—we averaged just 15.8 mpg.

The 4-door has a stable, pleasantly supple ride, dealing with most bumps in a manner comparable to a large station wagon. It fails to soak up big bumps well, though, and feels somewhat harsh on rough pavement. A Trooper easily tackles tough off-road terrain. Quick highway cornering induces mild body lean, but little of the typical tall-4WD queasiness. Tire roar is low, but wind noise high. Braking is above average for the sport-utility class.

Troopers rank among the roomiest sport-utility vehicles, though getting inside can be a chore due to the tall step-up. Head room is bountiful, and the back seats three adults comfortably. Visibility is great. The driver's area is attractive and convenient. Isuzu's 70/30 rear cargo door opens onto a tall, long cargo area.

VALUE FOR THE MONEY: Rating high on our list of upscale 4x4s, early Troopers trail such rivals as the Ford Explorer and Jeep Grand Cherokee mainly in their omission of shift-on-the-fly 4WD (on 1992-95 models) and an airbag (1992-94 models).

TROUBLE SPOTS

Keys: The ignition key can be hard to remove because the lens over the shift lever interferes with the shift cable. (1992)

Suspension noise: The differential may chatter in turns requiring the oil to be drained and refilled including a bottle of limited-slip additive. (1992-93)

Windows: The fuse for the power windows, cruise control, and instrument panel may blow due to an intermittent short in the three-four gear switch for the transmission. (1994)

AVERAGE REPLACEMENT COSTS

A/C Compressor	$1,260	Exhaust System	$370
Alternator	295	Radiator	740
Automatic Trans.	1,465	Shocks and/or Struts	320
Brakes	340	Timing Chain/Belt	100
Clutch	660	Universal Joints	190

NHTSA RECALL HISTORY

1992-94: Camshaft plug can become dislodged from cylinder head, allowing oil to leak; can cause engine damage and fire. **1996:** Certain vehicles have incorrect rear center-seatbelt buckle; tongue cannot be inserted. **1996-97:** Left front brake line can be damaged, resulting in fluid leakage, reduced brake effectiveness, and longer stopping distance. **1998:** Improperly installed transfer-gearbox nuts may loosen; propeller shaft can then separate, resulting in sudden loss of drive to wheels and possible damage to critical components. **2000-01 w/TOD:** In certain high-speed frontal crashes, movement of engine-compartment components can cause the potential for fuel leakage.

PRICES	Good	Average	Poor
1992 Trooper	$3,200-3,900	$2,500-3,000	$800-900
1993 Trooper	3,600-4,400	2,900-3,500	1,000-1,200
1994 Trooper	4,000-4,900	3,300-4,000	1,300-1,600
1995 Trooper	4,700-6,000	3,900-5,000	1,700-2,200
1996 Trooper	5,500-7,000	4,700-6,000	2,300-2,900
1997 Trooper	6,300-8,200	5,500-7,200	2,800-3,600
1998 Trooper	7,600-9,500	6,800-8,600	3,800-4,800
1999 Trooper	8,800-10,800	7,900-9,700	4,600-5,600
2000 Trooper	10,000-13,500	9,000-12,200	5,200-7,000
2001 Trooper	11,500-15,200	10,400-13,700	6,300-8,400
2002 Trooper	13,500-18,000	12,300-16,400	8,000-10,600

For detailed information on this vehicle visit
http://used.consumerguide.com and enter code **2186**

2000-02 JAGUAR S-TYPE

CLASS: Luxury car

BUILT IN: England

PROS: Acceleration (V8)
• Handling/roadholding
• Quietness • Ride

CONS: Automatic-transmission performance (V6)
• Cargo room • Navigation-system controls

JAGUAR

EVALUATION: As expected of a Jaguar, the base suspension delivers a plush, supple ride with excellent bump absorption and little tire rumble, even on rough pavement. Large humps induce a trace of "float," yet body lean is modest in fast corners, where the sedan grips well and inspires confidence.

Quick, informative steering is helpful, though a trifle more effort might achieve better high-speed control. The Sport Package doesn't increase effort, but sharpens most other reflexes and its wider tires yield still more grip, suffering only a slight penalty in ride quality and road noise.

Both engines are smooth and hushed, rising to a muted, appealing growl when pushed hard. Performance is satisfying, too. Jaguar claimed a 3.0 sedan could accelerate to 60 mph in 8 seconds, whereas the V8 needed only 6.6 seconds. Both engines demand premium fuel, and an S-Type with the V6 averaged 19.5 mpg.

When it's cooperating, the automatic transmission shifts promptly and smoothly enough. But in hard driving, it seems to change gears illogically, and can take a while to do so at all—even when using the manual mode of the 2-slot "J-gate" shifter.

Passenger and cargo space could be better, but at least 6-footers have decent head clearance all around. Tall occupants will sit knees-up in back, though foot room is adequate and the seat is properly firm and contoured. The cabin is too narrow to fit three adults in back. Up-front ambience also is cozy, but comfort is excellent.

Rear visibility isn't the best, but big mirrors help. All-button audio and climate controls are handy but "busy." The glovebox is tough to access. Interior storage is so-so. The trunk is rather small, though usefully shaped and easy to load. Despite leather and wood, the interior's plastic trim imparts a generic feel that's not found in other Jaguars.

VALUE FOR THE MONEY: Blending traditional Jaguar charm with modern engineering, the S-Type ranks as good value in an upper-crust sedan, though it's not as sporty as BMW's 5-Series. Reliability under Ford's jurisdiction should be better than Jaguars of the past.

TROUBLE SPOTS

See the 2000-02 Lincoln LS.

AVERAGE REPLACEMENT COSTS

See the 2000-02 Lincoln LS.

NHTSA RECALL HISTORY

2000-01: Front-suspension lower ball joints were not tightened to specification. Vehicle control could be affected, increases the risk of crash. **2000-01:** Seatbelt buckles were not properly heat treated and do not pass the load-bearing requirement of the standard.

PRICES

	Good	Average	Poor
2000 S-Type 3.0	$21,500-24,000	$19,800-22,100	$14,000-15,600
S-Type 4.0	24,000-25,500	22,300-23,700	15,600-16,600
2001 S-Type 3.0	24,500-26,000	22,800-24,200	15,900-16,900
S-Type 4.0	27,000-28,500	25,100-26,500	18,100-19,100

| 2002 S-Type 3.0 | $28,500-31,000 | $26,500-28,800 | $19,400-21,100 |
| S-Type 4.0 | 31,500-33,500 | 29,300-31,200 | 22,100-23,500 |

For detailed information on this vehicle visit
http://used.consumerguide.com and enter code **2457**

1990-96 JEEP CHEROKEE

CLASS: Midsize sport-utility vehicle
BUILT IN: USA
PROS: Acceleration (6-cylinder) • Wet-weather traction (4WD) • Passenger and cargo room
CONS: Acceleration (4-cylinder) • Fuel economy • Noise

EVALUATION: The base 4-cylinder Cherokee's engine is adequate with manual shift, weak under a heavy load, and downright feeble and unresponsive if hooked to an automatic transmission. With either transmission, the robust 6-cylinder engine lets you sprint away from stoplights and quickly pass other vehicles. Expect about 17 mpg with a manual-shift six, or 15 mpg with automatic. All models have higher-than-average wind, road, and engine noise.

These vehicles are spacious inside for their modest exterior dimensions—though not quite comparable to the Grand Cherokee or a Ford Explorer. Four sit in comfort. Head room is generous all around, and with a little squeezing, back seats accommodate three adults. Folding that rear seatback produces great luggage space, with a long and flat floor, and volume is acceptable with the seatback up. The long steering column puts the wheel too close to the driver's chest.

VALUE FOR THE MONEY: Cherokees offer a lot of temptations, serving as an excellent alternative for those who cannot afford a Grand Cherokee or Explorer. Next to something like the latest Chevrolet Blazer, though, they do seem a step behind in civility.

TROUBLE SPOTS

Air conditioner: If the air conditioner gradually stops cooling, the computer (PCM) may not be sending a signal to the compressor-clutch relay to cycle off, which causes the A/C evaporator to freeze up. (1991-95)

Automatic transmission: If the transmission will not engage when first started, chances are the torque converter is draining down. A check valve in the fluid line leading to the transmission cooler should fix the problem. (1993) If the transmission won't upshift for about the first quarter mile in cool weather, it is probably due to defective cast-iron seal rings in the governor drive. (1993-94)

Oil leak: The rear main seals on 2.5- and 4.0-liter engines are prone to leakage if the vehicle is operated in dirty conditions. (1991-96)

Transmission leak: Automatic-transmission fluid leaks from the speed sensor in the transmission. (1993-94)

AVERAGE REPLACEMENT COSTS

A/C Compressor	$390	Exhaust System	$270
Alternator	355	Radiator	380
Automatic Trans.	680	Shocks and/or Struts	190
Brakes	265	Timing Chain/Belt	185
Clutch	495	Universal Joints	145

NHTSA RECALL HISTORY

1990 w/4.0-liter engine and automatic: Could have intermittent high idle speed. **1990 w/ABS:** Hydraulic fluid may be contaminated. **1990-91 w/ABS:** Hydraulic control unit for antilock braking system can experience excessive brake-actuator piston-seal wear, which could lead to loss of antilock function and reduced power assist. **1990-91 w/ABS:** Improper insertion/crimping of hose fittings can result in loss of ABS function. **1990-96 in 15 states and Washington, D.C.:** Front-disc brake rotors can experience severe corrosion if operated for extensive period in "salt belt"; can eventually compromise structural integrity, allowing wear surface to separate from hub. **1991 w/ABS:** Brake-fluid tube may contact steering shaft and result in leakage. **1991:** Jounce bumper could contact and collapse left rear brake tube. **1993:** Retainer clip that secures master-cylinder rod to brake pedal was not installed properly. **1993-96:** High steering loads can cause steering-gear bolts to break or frame to crack. **1994:** Rear-seatbelt bolts may not support passengers in sudden stop. **1995:** Certain airbags might not deploy in an accident. **1995:** Parking-brake handle-release button can separate, so parking brake may not hold and vehicle could roll inadvertently. **1996:** Fasteners that secure alternator fuse could have improper clamp load; arcing could cause fire in engine compartment.

PRICES

	Good	Average	Poor
1990 Cherokee 2WD	$1,100-2,000	$700-1,200	$100-200
Cherokee 4WD	1,700-2,800	1,100-1,900	300-400
1991 Cherokee 2WD	1,300-2,400	800-1,500	200-300
Cherokee 4WD	2,100-3,500	1,500-2,500	400-600
1992 Cherokee 2WD	1,500-2,700	1,000-1,800	200-400
Cherokee 4WD	2,400-4,000	1,800-2,900	500-800
1993 Cherokee 2WD	1,700-3,300	1,100-2,200	300-500
Cherokee 4WD	2,500-4,300	1,800-3,100	500-900
1994 Cherokee 2WD	2,000-3,800	1,400-2,700	300-600
Cherokee 4WD	2,900-4,800	2,200-3,600	700-1,100
1995 Cherokee 2WD	2,300-4,500	1,700-3,200	400-900
Cherokee 4WD	3,400-5,500	2,700-4,300	900-1,400
1996 Cherokee 2WD	2,600-5,000	1,900-3,700	500-1,100
Cherokee 4WD	3,800-6,300	3,100-5,100	1,100-1,900

For detailed information on this vehicle visit
http://used.consumerguide.com and enter code **2052**

1997-01 JEEP CHEROKEE

CLASS: Midsize sport-utility vehicle

BUILT IN: USA

PROS: Acceleration (6-cylinder) • Optional antilock brakes • Cargo room • Passenger room

CONS: Acceleration (4-cylinder) • Fuel economy

EVALUATION: Chrysler Corporation (now DaimlerChrysler) has done an admirable job of keeping a basically solid design fresh enough for today's tougher market. Most models that date back to 1984, as the Cherokee does, would have faded away long before.

Cherokee's 4-cylinder engine provides only adequate acceleration with the 5-speed manual transmission, and is overmatched with automatic in anything other than gentle cruising. Of course, most Cherokees on the market are 6-cylinder. That engine is strong throughout the speed range, and delivers fuel economy typical of a midsize SUV: about 15 mpg with automatic and 17 mpg with manual shift.

Cherokee suffers powertrain and road resonances that are absent in most competitive sport-utility vehicles. Wind noise at speed is prominent, too.

Good balance and tidy dimensions make the Cherokee quite maneuverable in most situations. The firm base suspension provides a solid ride that absorbs all but the worst bumps, without jarring. An "Up Country" option, if installed, makes for a rough ride. Optional antilock braking feels strong and natural.

A Cherokee really shows its age in interior accommodations. Less roomy than a Grand Cherokee or a Ford Explorer, it does carry four adults in comfort. However, the low-roof passenger compartment has no surplus of front shoulder room, a shortage of rear knee clearance, and fairly lofty step-in. Rear entry/exit is tight, too, thanks to narrow lower doorways.

On the plus side, the dashboard is modern and convenient. Outward vision is good, though larger door mirrors would help when lane changing.

Mounting the spare tire inside eats up cargo room, but there's still decent space with the rear seat in use, and a long load floor with that seat folded. An outside spare was available at Jeep dealerships, so look for one of that kind if cargo space is a major concern.

Some Cherokees we tested when new had occasional interior rattles, as well as wider-than-usual panel gaps around the hood and tailgate.

VALUE FOR THE MONEY: Convenient 4-wheel-drive systems, commendable off-road capability, and civilized on road manners—for less than a Grand Cherokee or an Explorer—make the Cherokee an above average value. Despite an aging design and strong competition, Cherokees sold well in the late '90s and are not too expensive today unless you go for a fully equipped model. Still, Cherokee is behind the times in room, ride, and refinement.

TROUBLE SPOTS

Air conditioner: The air conditioner gradually stops blowing cool air because the evaporator ices up. Replacing the low-pressure cycling switch usually fixes it. (1997-99)

Brake noise: Grinding and scraping noises under hard braking are caused by the driveshaft hitting the floor pan and is fixed by replacing the front lower control arm. (1997)

Brakes: The brake friction material transfers to the rotors (especially in warm, moist climates) causing brake-pedal pulsation when stopping. New pads should correct it. (1997-99)

Fuel gauge: The fuel gauge may show ⅛ to ¼ full but the vehicle will run out of gas because of a defective sending unit that must be replaced. (1997)

Vehicle shake: Vibration at speeds over 60 mph may be due to a misaligned or defective driveshaft. (1997-98)

Windshield washer: Because of a bad check valve, windshield washer fluid drips from the nozzle for the rear window and can cause paint staining. (1997)

AVERAGE REPLACEMENT COSTS

A/C Compressor	$470	Exhaust System	$395
Alternator	350	Radiator	350
Automatic Trans.	1,215	Shocks and/or Struts	410
Brakes	375	Timing Chain/Belt	240
Clutch	380	Universal Joints	270

NHTSA RECALL HISTORY

1997: Accuracy of fuel-tank-mounted fuel-level sending unit can degrade over time, indicating significantly more fuel in reserve than is actually present. **1997-99 sold or registered in 15 states or Washington, D.C.:** Front-disc brake rotors can experience severe corrosion if operated for extensive period in the "salt belt." **1997-99:** Water and/or road salt in proximity of airbag-control module could lead to corrosion and possible inadvertent deployment. **1998:** Due to improperly hardened front-seatbelt shoulder turning-loop anchors, front-seat occupant might not be properly restrained in a crash. **1998:** Power-brake booster-vacuum reservoir diaphragm can split or tear, causing increase in engine-idle speed and loss of power assist during brake application. **2000 w/4.0-liter engine:** Debris can accumulate in the intake and exhaust manifolds, increasing the risk of fire. **2001:** Some of the owner's manuals for these vehicles are missing instructions for properly attaching a child restraint system's tether strap to the tether anchorage.

PRICES

	Good	Average	Poor
1997 Cherokee 2WD	$3,200-5,200	$2,500-4,100	$800-1,200
Cherokee 4WD	4,000-6,200	3,300-5,100	1,300-2,000
1998 Cherokee 2WD	3,700-6,200	3,000-5,000	1,100-1,800
Cherokee 4WD	4,800-7,500	4,000-6,300	1,800-2,900
1999 Cherokee 2WD	4,500-7,500	3,700-6,200	1,600-2,700
Cherokee 4WD	5,600-8,700	4,800-7,500	2,300-3,600
2000 Cherokee 2WD	5,700-9,000	4,900-7,700	2,300-3,700
Cherokee 4WD	6,800-10,000	6,100-8,900	3,200-4,700

| 2001 Cherokee 2WD | $7,000-10,500 | $6,200-9,300 | $3,400-5,000 |
| Cherokee 4WD | 8,200-12,000 | 7,400-10,800 | 4,200-6,100 |

For detailed information on this vehicle visit
http://used.consumerguide.com and enter code **2359**

1993-98 JEEP GRAND CHEROKEE

CLASS: Midsize sport-utility vehicle

BUILT IN: USA

PROS: Antilock brakes • Wet-weather traction (4WD) • Passenger and cargo room

CONS: Engine noise • Fuel economy • Reliability (early models)

EVALUATION: Base-engine power is adequate for most drivers, but the 5.2-liter V8 is much better, especially in low-speed acceleration. It delivers strong off-the-line pickup as well as brisk passing response. The 5.9-liter in the Limited model has even more power at low speeds. We averaged 16.5 mpg in a 6-cylinder Grand Cherokee, and a meager 13.3 mpg with a V8. All three engines can get noisy, though they're much quieter when cruising.

Interior room is good, though the spare tire takes up space. Head and leg room are generous all around, and three adults fit in the rear seat. Entry/exit to the front requires only a slight step up. Rear doors are narrow at the bottom and don't open wide enough to allow large people to get in or out without bending a little. With the rear seatback up, luggage space isn't much greater than in a midsize car. Even with the child seat that became available during 1994, rear seatbacks can be folded down to create a long cargo floor.

VALUE FOR THE MONEY: We rate the Grand a step behind the Ford Explorer, but both lead the field in refinement, ability, and overall quality. An Explorer is more trucklike, a trait that some buyers like and others do not, but the Grand Cherokee offers impressive on- and off-road performance, plus a broad range of engine and 4WD choices. Early Grand Cherokees suffered some reliability problems, so a later model might be a better bet.

TROUBLE SPOTS

Air conditioner: If the air conditioner gradually stops cooling, the computer (PCM) may not be sending a signal to the compressor-clutch relay to cycle off, which causes the A/C evaporator to freeze up. (1993-95)

Automatic transmission: If the transmission will not engage when first started, chances are the torque converter is draining down. A check valve in the fluid line leading to the transmission cooler should remedy the problem. (1993)

Automatic transmission: The transmission won't upshift for about the first quarter mile in cool weather due to defective cast-iron seal rings in the governor drive. (1993-94)

Engine misfire: Rough idle and stalling can be traced to a defective idle-air-control motor. (1993-94)

Oil consumption and engine knock: Oil-pump-gear wear results in bucking and surging when the engine is warm and lack of lubrication when the engine is cold. (1993)

Oil leak: The rear main seals on 4.0-liter engines are prone to leakage if the vehicle is operated in dirty conditions. (1993-96)

Oil leak: A chronic oil leak at the filter on 5.2-liter engine is likely due to a warped adapter plate. (1995)

Transmission leak: Automatic-transmission fluid leaks from the speed sensor in the transmission. (1993-94)

AVERAGE REPLACEMENT COSTS

A/C Compressor	$390	Exhaust System	$270
Alternator	360	Radiator	380
Automatic Trans.	700	Shocks and/or Struts	155
Brakes	300	Timing Chain/Belt	195
Clutch	375	Universal Joints	135

NHTSA RECALL HISTORY

1993: Eccentric cam-adjuster bolts in both front lower-suspension arm-to-front axle-bracket attachments may fail, causing vehicle to pull to one side. **1993:** Molded plastic pin that connects upper and lower steering-column shafts may be sheared; shafts could separate, causing total loss of steering control. **1993:** Retainer clip that secures master-cylinder input rod to brake pedal could work loose, allowing separation, which may cause loss of braking. **1993-98 in 15 states and Washington, D.C.:** Front-disc brake rotors can experience severe corrosion if operated for extensive period in "salt belt"; can eventually compromise structural integrity, allowing wear surface to separate from hub. **1995:** Parking-brake release button can separate, so brake may not hold and vehicle could roll inadvertently. **1996 w/Quadra-Trac, temporary spare tire, and 225/70R16 or 245/70R15 tires:** When temporary spare tire is in use, front axle can overheat; can force fluid out of seals, increasing risk of fire. **1996:** Fasteners that secure alternator fuse could have improper clamp load; arcing could cause fire in engine compartment. **1997:** Airbag could deploy inadvertently when ignition is shut off. **1997:** Fuel-level sending unit degrades over time, causing gauge to show significantly more fuel in tank than is actually present. **1998:** Power-brake booster-vacuum reservoir diaphragm can split or tear; may cause increase in engine idle speed and loss of power brake assist.

PRICES

	Good	Average	Poor
1993 Grand Cherokee 2WD	$2,500-3,200	$1,800-2,300	$500-700
Grand Cherokee 4WD	3,500-4,500	2,800-3,600	900-1,200
1994 Grand Cherokee 2WD	3,000-3,700	2,300-2,800	700-900
Grand Cherokee 4WD	4,000-5,200	3,300-4,300	1,300-1,700
1995 Grand Cherokee 2WD	3,700-4,800	3,000-3,900	1,100-1,400
Grand Cherokee 4WD	4,800-6,200	4,000-5,200	1,800-2,400
1996 Grand Cherokee 2WD	4,500-5,600	3,700-4,600	1,600-2,000
Grand Cherokee 4WD	5,700-7,200	4,900-6,200	2,300-3,000

1997 Grand Cherokee 2WD	$5,500-7,000	$4,700-6,000	$2,300-2,900
Grand Cherokee 4WD	6,600-8,200	5,800-7,200	3,000-3,800
1998 Grand Cherokee 2WD	6,800-8,500	6,100-7,600	3,200-4,000
Grand Cherokee 4WD	7,900-10,500	7,100-9,500	4,000-5,400

For detailed information on this vehicle visit
http://used.consumerguide.com and enter code 2053

1999-03 JEEP GRAND CHEROKEE

CLASS: Midsize sport-utility vehicle

BUILT IN: USA

PROS: Acceleration
• Cargo room

CONS: Fuel economy
• Reliability (early models)

EVALUATION: Handling and off-road ability are top Grand Cherokee strengths. Control in directional changes is good, despite a fair amount of body lean. Steering feels natural, though small corrections are needed at highway speeds. No midsize SUV rides more comfortably. The revised suspension handles all but the worst potholes with ease, but permits queasy fore-and-aft and side-to-side pitching motions through uneven pavement. And even the worst terrain elicits no squeaks or rattles from the stiffened body structure.

Acceleration is adequate with the 6 cylinder engine, robust with the V8, and the new 4.7 liter is far smoother than the old 5.2-liter V8. The reworked 6-cylinder also is much quieter. A 6-cylinder 4WD Laredo averaged 16.1 mpg. Wind rush and tire roar may intrude at highway speeds, but the quieter engines help lower overall interior noise levels. Transmissions shift with prompt smoothness. Braking is strong and smooth. Selec-Trac or Quadra-Trac furnish more than enough traction on even the most slippery streets, but Quadra-Drive offers the ultimate in 4WD grip. A Quadra-Drive Grand Cherokee can climb in and out of places that leave rivals spinning their tires, though gear whine is intrusive.

Four adults get plenty of space. Grand Cherokees still aren't wide enough to seat three adults comfortably in back, and the rear seatback is too upright for best comfort, with little toe space ahead. All seats are too soft for best support. Large outside mirrors are helpful, but roof pillars are too thick for full outward vision. Generously sized bins and pockets provide plenty of storage space for small items. Relocating the spare tire opened up more luggage room, but it's still only adequate and rear seats are somewhat difficult to fold. Back-seat entry/exit is hampered by narrow door bottoms.

VALUE FOR THE MONEY: An even better dollar value than the old Grand Cherokee, this version offers good performance and overall design. Long-term mechanical reliability is still a question mark.

TROUBLE SPOTS

Engine misfire: The powertrain-control module (engine computer) may have to be reprogrammed or replaced if the engine sags with the A/C on. (1999)

Fuel odors: The gas tank may fill slowly because of a problem with the filler pipe, which has been revised, and there is also a revised gas cap to replace binding ones. (1999)

Hard starting: Engine may be hard to start due to an internal leak or bits of plastic wedged inside the fuel-pump assembly. A new sealing ring or complete pump assembly could be required. (1999-2000)

Vehicle noise: Replacing the rear driveshaft eliminates a whining sound above 40 mph. (1999-2000)

Vehicle noise: Popping/snapping noises are usually corrected by replacing the front driveshaft. In many cases, that unit probably has a dry universal joint. (1999)

AVERAGE REPLACEMENT COSTS

A/C Compressor	$555	Exhaust System	$405
Alternator	340	Radiator	620
Automatic Trans.	1,125	Shocks and/or Struts	1,240
Brakes	490	Timing Chain/Belt	400
CV Joints	1,405		

NHTSA RECALL HISTORY

1999: Front-seatbelt retractor on certain vehicles does not work properly. **1999:** Rear-outboard seatbelt retractor spring can disengage from rewind mechanism, disabling retractor function and preventing belt from fitting snugly around occupant. **1999-00:** Inadequately manufactured shoulder seatbelt height-adjustable turning-loop top mounting bolt may not withstand sufficient force to function properly in certain impact situations. **2000:** Improperly heat-treated end-of-travel stops in some steering-gear units could result in sticking, binding, or seizing of the steering gear. **2000:** Passenger-airbag inflator assembly in small number of cars contains incorrect inflator charge amount, which could increase risk of passenger injury under certain crash conditions. **2000-02:** Fuel tank on some vehicles may have suspect vent-tube welds; separation of tube weld could result in fuel leakage. **2001:** Some owner's manuals are missing full instructions for properly attaching a child-restraint system's tether strap. **2002:** Debris can accumulate in the intake and exhaust manifolds, increasing the risk of fire. **2002:** Fuel may spill out of the filler tube upon refueling the tank due either to a misrouted fuel-recovery vent or a stuck inlet check valve. **2002:** Instrument cluster could become inoperative due to a software error. **2002:** Passenger-airbag wiring harness was improperly manufactured and may not deploy properly.

PRICES	Good	Average	Poor
1999 Grand Cherokee Laredo	$10,000-12,000	$9,000-10,800	$5,200-6,200
Grand Cherokee Ltd.	11,500-13,500	10,400-12,200	6,300-7,400
2000 Grand Cherokee Laredo	12,000-14,000	10,800-12,600	6,700-7,800
Grand Cherokee Ltd.	14,000-16,000	12,700-14,600	8,500-9,800
2001 Grand Cherokee Laredo	14,000-16,000	12,700-14,600	8,500-9,800
Grand Cherokee Ltd.	17,000-19,000	15,600-17,500	10,900-12,200

2002 Grand Cherokee Laredo	$16,000-18,200	$14,600-16,600	$10,200-11,600
Grand Cherokee Ltd.	19,500-21,500	17,900-19,800	12,700-14,000
Grand Cherokee Overland	24,000-26,000	22,300-24,200	15,600-16,900
Grand Cherokee Sport	16,500-18,500	15,000-16,800	10,600-11,800
2003 Grand Cherokee Laredo	18,000-21,000	16,600-19,300	11,500-13,400
Grand Cherokee Ltd.	22,000-25,000	20,200-23,000	14,300-16,300
Grand Cherokee Overland	26,500-29,000	24,600-27,000	17,500-19,100

For detailed information on this vehicle visit
http://used.consumerguide.com and enter code **2381**

1990-95 JEEP WRANGLER

CLASS: Compact sport-utility vehicle

BUILT IN: Canada

PROS: Acceleration (6-cylinder) • Antilock brakes (optional with 6-cylinder) • Wet-weather traction • Maneuverability

CONS: Cargo room • Engine noise • Entry/exit • Fuel economy • Instruments/controls • Ride/handling • Road noise • Wind noise

EVALUATION: Acceleration and drivability are only adequate from the initial 6-cylinder engine; gas mileage mediocre. Meager is the word for acceleration from the 4-cylinder engine. Performance got a welcome boost from the fuel-injected six of 1991. Jeep claimed a 0-60-mph acceleration time of 9.7 seconds, versus 14.3 seconds for the old carbureted 6-cylinder engine.

A stiff suspension makes for jarring travel over most surfaces. The Wrangler's narrow stance and short wheelbase promise good manueverability, but demand conservative cornering speeds.

Climbing aboard isn't so easy, as it's a tall step over the doorsills. Once inside, you get a cramped rear seat and tiny cargo area (unless the rear seat is tilted out of the way). Tall people have ample head room all around to sit comfortably upright. Once aboard, you can expect to be assaulted by road noise and wind buffeting—whether the top is up or down. Gauges and controls are strung across the dashboard in a haphazard manner.

VALUE FOR THE MONEY: Seriously consider how you would use the vehicle, and if the compromises in on-road ride, handling, and fuel economy are worth it in the end. Also look at an Isuzu Amigo, which lacks the Jeep's classic image but feels just about as tough, as well as the Geo Tracker/Suzuki Sidekick, with their friendlier ergonomics. But none of those rivals have a muscular 6-cylinder engine like Wrangler's. We don't recommend any mini 4x4 as a daily driver, but plenty of people love them.

TROUBLE SPOTS

Automatic transmission: If the transmission will not engage when first started, chances are the torque converter is draining down. A check valve in the fluid line leading to the transmission cooler should remedy the problem. (1993) If the transmission won't upshift for about the first quarter mile in cool weather, it is probably due to defective cast-iron seal rings in the governor drive. (1992-94)

Oil leak: The rear main seals on 2.5- and 4.0-liter engines are prone to leakage if the vehicle is operated in dirty conditions. (1991-95)

Transmission leak: Automatic-transmission fluid leaks from the speed sensor in the transmission. (1992-94)

AVERAGE REPLACEMENT COSTS

A/C Compressor	$375	Exhaust System	$255
Alternator	315	Radiator	355
Automatic Trans.	690	Shocks and/or Struts	180
Brakes	275	Timing Chain/Belt	185
Clutch	690	Universal Joints	130

NHTSA RECALL HISTORY

1990-91 in 15 states and Washington, D.C.: Front-disc brake rotors can experience severe corrosion if operated for extensive period in "salt belt"; can eventually compromise structural integrity, allowing wear surface to separate from hub. **1990-92:** Front brake hoses can wear due to contact with splash shields. **1990-94:** Plastic fuel tank's sending-unit gasket can crack, resulting in fuel and vapor leaks. **1991-93 w/manual shift:** Salt corrosion between starter solenoid wire and battery feed may short these connections. **1994-95 w/manual transmission:** Parking brake can release without warning.

PRICES

	Good	Average	Poor
1990 Wrangler 6-cyl.	$3,300-4,000	$2,600-3,200	$800-1,000
Wrangler S 4-cyl.	2,700-3,300	2,000-2,500	600-700
1991 Wrangler 6-cyl.	3,800-4,700	3,100-3,800	1,100-1,400
Wrangler S 4-cyl.	3,100-3,700	2,400-2,900	700-900
1992 Wrangler 6-cyl.	4,300-5,500	3,500-4,500	1,500-1,900
Wrangler S 4-cyl.	3,500-4,100	2,800-3,300	900-1,100
1993 Wrangler 6-cyl.	4,900-6,000	4,200-5,100	1,900-2,300
Wrangler S 4-cyl.	3,900-4,600	3,200-3,700	1,200-1,400
1994 Wrangler 6-cyl.	5,500-6,700	4,700-5,800	2,300-2,700
Wrangler S 4-cyl.	4,300-5,000	3,500-4,100	1,500-1,700
1995 Wrangler 6-cyl.	6,000-7,500	5,200-6,500	2,500-3,200
Wrangler S 4-cyl.	5,000-5,800	4,300-4,900	2,000-2,300

For detailed information on this vehicle visit
http://used.consumerguide.com and enter code **2054**

1997-03 JEEP WRANGLER

CLASS: Compact sport-utility vehicle

BUILT IN: USA

PROS: Optional antilock brakes • 4WD versatility • Maneuverability

CONS: Acceleration (4-cylinder) • Fuel economy • Noise

EVALUATION: Wranglers really are more carlike than before—far better in ride quality and ergonomics. Occupant comfort is vastly improved, though few would call the Wrangler experience comfortable. The new suspension is a lot more absorbent, true, but it still reacts abruptly to dips and bumps. Unless the pavement really gets nasty, though, the ride isn't jarring.

Original 4-cylinder Wrangler with manual shift has trouble merging or overtaking fast-moving freeway traffic. Performance in a 5-speed Wrangler with the 6-cylinder engine gets reasonably vigorous—though accompanied by considerable engine and gear noise. New 4 cyl is more refined than the 6 cyl, and though it's somewhat sluggish away from a stop, it has adequate merging and passing response. Fuel economy is tolerable, but no bonus. A 5-speed Sahara with the 6-cylinder engine averaged 19.3 mpg.

Wind noise is abundant where the roof meets the windshield frame. Doors seal poorly too, with the canvas top in place. That canvas top also flutters, while the optional hardtop "drums" at highway speeds. Taking the top up and down is easier than before, but still a frustrating chore. Full instruments now are clustered in front of the driver, not spread out as in prior Wranglers. Two adults now fit in back without squeezing, but the cushion and backrest are hard and short. Interior storage is better than in earlier Wranglers. Space behind the back seat is modest.

VALUE FOR THE MONEY: True Wrangler fans don't fret about its flaws. For other potential owners, the great strides made in safety, ride quality, and refinement in this generation bring Wrangler closer than before to serving as an everyday vehicle.

TROUBLE SPOTS

Doors: The doors may not unlock with the key, requiring replacement of the door latches. (1997)

Fuel gauge: The gas-gauge needle may not point to full, may show 1/8 to ¼ full when the tank is empty. (1997)

Fuel odors: The gas tank may fill slowly or the pump nozzle will keep shutting off due to a problem with the fuel-tank venting system. (1997)

Steering problems: Fluid leaks from the power-steering reservoir. (1997)

JEEP

Water leak: Water may leak onto the passenger-side front floor due to leaks in the heater and air-conditioner housing or from a problem with the evaporator drain tube. (1997)

AVERAGE REPLACEMENT COSTS

A/C Compressor	$375	Exhaust System	$220
Alternator	315	Radiator	300
Automatic Trans.	930	Shocks and/or Struts	190
Brakes	270	Timing Chain/Belt	200
Clutch	2,165	Universal Joints	220

NHTSA RECALL HISTORY

1997 w/manual steering: Driver's airbag-wiring harness can break when steering wheel is turned to "full lock" position; in crash, airbag would not deploy. **1997:** Airbag could deploy inadvertently when ignition is shut off. **1997:** Airbag-control module on some vehicles contains an error that can delay deployment in certain crash situations. **1998:** Front-seatbelt shoulder anchors were not properly heat treated and hardened; in a crash, occupant may not be properly restrained. **1998:** Power-brake booster-vacuum reservoir diaphragm can split or tear; may cause increase in engine-idle speed and loss of power brake assist. **1999:** Instrument-panel ground-attachment screws could loosen over time, possibly affecting gauges and/or defroster. **2001:** Some of the owner's manuals for these vehicles are missing instructions for properly attaching a child-restraint system's tether strap to the tether anchorage. **2001-02:** Water may leak into the ignition switch, causing a short circuit and possibly a fire. **2002 w/4.0-liter engine:** Debris can accumulate in the intake and exhaust manifolds, increasing the risk of fire.

PRICES

	Good	Average	Poor
1997 Wrangler 6-cyl.	$8,000-9,200	$7,200-8,300	$4,100-4,700
Wrangler SE 4-cyl.	6,000-6,700	5,200-5,800	2,500-2,800
1998 Wrangler 6-cyl.	9,400-11,000	8,500-9,900	4,900-5,700
Wrangler SE 4-cyl.	7,200-8,000	6,400-7,100	3,500-3,900
1999 Wrangler 6-cyl.	10,500-12,200	9,500-11,000	5,600-6,500
Wrangler SE 4-cyl.	8,500-9,300	7,700-8,400	4,400-4,800
2000 Wrangler 6-cyl.	12,500-14,500	11,300-13,100	7,100-8,300
Wrangler SE 4-cyl.	9,800-10,700	8,800-9,600	5,100-5,600
2001 Wrangler 6-cyl.	14,000-16,000	12,700-14,600	8,500-9,800
Wrangler SE 4-cyl.	11,000-12,000	9,900-10,800	5,900-6,500
2002 Wrangler 6-cyl.	15,500-17,500	14,100-15,900	9,900-11,200
Wrangler SE 4-cyl.	12,500-13,500	11,300-12,200	7,100-7,700
Wrangler X	14,000-15,000	12,700-13,700	8,500-9,200
2003 Wrangler 6-cyl.	17,200-20,000	15,800-18,400	11,000-12,800
Wrangler SE 4-cyl.	14,000-15,000	12,700-13,700	8,500-9,200
Wrangler X	15,500-17,000	14,100-15,500	9,900-10,900

For detailed information on this vehicle visit
http://used.consumerguide.com and enter code **2189**

2001-03 KIA OPTIMA

CLASS: Compact car

BUILT IN: South Korea

PROS: Instruments/controls • Ride

CONS: Automatic-transmission performance • Rear-seat room/comfort

EVALUATION: In performance and accommodations, Optimas mirror comparably equipped Sonatas. Optimas and Sonatas with the four-cylinder engine have modest acceleration: about 10 seconds to reach 60 mph. Acceleration with a V6 is noticeably quicker. A 2001 model with the 2.5-liter V6 did 0-60 mph in a reasonably brisk 8.5 seconds with the automatic transmission. The 2.7-liter models feel slightly stronger.

Automatic transmissions are fairly smooth, and the manual-shift feature helps make up for its tardy kick-down action that lengthens midrange passing response. The automatic is also too eager to upshift, which makes use of the manual shift gate more appealing.

As for economy, 2001 sedans with V6/automatic averaged 18.7 to 20.2 mpg. A four cylinder will be slightly thriftier. Both engines use regular fuel.

Compliant suspensions soak up most bumps with ease, though these sedans float a bit over large dip and humps. Comfort-biased tires keep impact harshness pleasantly low.

Steering/handling is modest but predictable, despite noticeable body lean in fast corners. Later Optimas have 15-inch wheels.

Simulated panic stops were only class-average short, even with ABS. Brake-pedal feel is a bit numb, and brakes are a bit touchy in routine use. Non-ABS systems resist lockup, however, and nosedive is well-checked.

Road noise is louder than wind noise at highway speeds, but not objectionable. Bumps come through with a loud thump. The V6 is quiet at idle, and produces a muted whine under full throttle. Still, both engines are on the coarse side, compared to Japanese rivals.

Dashboard design places everything within easy reach. Most buttons and dials are large and easy to use. All power-window switches are lit at night. Materials are hard to fault for the price. Higher-line models feature glossy woodgrain plastic trim.

Front head and leg room are ample. Seats are comfortable and offer either manual or power height adjustment, for a commanding view. Top-line models were available with leather upholstery that lacks richness.

Back seats are wide enough for only two adults, who have marginal foot room and just-acceptable head room, and must sit knees-up if the front seats are pushed far back. Seat cushions are somewhat low and a bit too soft for best support, but the rear has a fold-down center armrest.

The flat-floor trunk has a smallish opening but good volume, and hinges don't dip into the load area. The seatback folds easily but not quite flat, and the pass-through is not full-width. Interior storage is generous, with a two-tier console box, two covered cupholders, console and dash bins, map pockets, and a decent-size glovebox.

KIA

VALUE FOR THE MONEY: In terms of equipment and comfort, Optima and Sonata offer impressive value for the money. Both serve as bargain-priced Camry alternatives that have little need for apologies. Both have suffered from low resale values associated with South Korean cars, which can be good news for used-car shoppers. Generous warranties, however, do not offset the quality concerns.

TROUBLE SPOTS

Engine stalling: Problems in the wiring to the throttle-position sensor may cause drivability concerns such as momentary stalling. (2001)

AVERAGE REPLACEMENT COSTS

A/C Compressor	$710	CV Joints	$1,215
Alternator	345	Exhaust System	355
Automatic Trans.	925	Radiator	435
Brakes	220	Shocks and/or Struts	1,300
Clutch	475	Timing Chain/Belt	265

NHTSA RECALL HISTORY

2001: Side-airbag wiring harness could be misrouted, possibly rendering the airbag inactive in the event of an impact. Dealers will inspect and replace any affected parts. **2001-02 w/V6:** Two separate recalls for improperly manufactured crankshaft-position sensors could result in engine stalling while driving. Dealers will replace affected parts.

PRICES

	Good	Average	Poor
2001 Optima LX	$6,500-7,400	$5,700-6,500	$2,900-3,300
Optima SE	8,200-9,200	7,400-8,300	4,200-4,700
2002 Optima LX	8,000-9,000	7,200-8,100	4,100-4,600
Optima SE	9,700-10,700	8,700-9,600	5,000-5,600
2003 Optima LX	10,500-12,000	9,500-10,800	5,600-6,400
Optima SE	12,300-13,800	11,100-12,400	7,000-7,900

For detailed information on this vehicle visit
http://used.consumerguide.com and enter code **4482**

2001-03 KIA RIO

CLASS: Subcompact car
BUILT IN: South Korea
PROS: Fuel economy
CONS: Acceleration
• Rear-seat entry/exit
• Rear-seat room (sedan)

EVALUATION: Rios cope adequately with city/suburban traffic, but struggle to reach highway speed, even at full throttle. The automatic transmission hunts annoyingly between gears, to maintain a pace on even moderate grades. One test car took a slow 11.5 seconds to accelerate to

60 mph, with an automatic transmission. The Rio feels little faster with manual shift, but the automatic wagon is more sluggish than the sedan.

Fuel economy is unimpressive, given the car's light weight and mediocre power. Test Rios have averaged 25.2 mpg with an automatic transmission, 22.9 mpg with manual.

Ride quality benefited from the switch to 14-inch tires for 2002. Around town, the Rio's suspension is absorbent enough to avoid jarring on broken and patchy surfaces. It's choppy on scalloped freeways, though mild bounce occurs over only the largest bumps and dips.

Steering has a troublingly rubbery feel, and there's plenty of body lean and front-end plowing in turns. Poor directional stability at highway speeds occurs with any crosswind. Simulated emergency stops were no problem, with or without optional ABS.

The engine moans and drones in hard acceleration, or when cruising above 55 mph or so. Wind rush is tolerably low, but tires are noisy even on fairly smooth pavement.

Instruments and controls are part of an uninspired design, but logical and convenient, except for smallish audio controls. Sedans lack a tachometer and a trunklid release, but intermittent wipers have been standard. Cabin materials are slightly better than entry-level pricing would suggest. One test sedan's rear parcel shelf vibrated loudly when a rear door or the trunklid was slammed.

Front head room is good, because seats are low to the floor. A height-adjustable driver's seat has been standard, though the optional tilt wheel does not lift that high and larger drivers may feel confined. A standard fold-down driver's armrest is a nice touch. Rearward visibility is poor on both body styles.

Back seats are very tight for adult legs, unless front passengers move well ahead; even then, toe space is minimal. Wagons seem to have slightly more head room than the sedan's bare minimum. No rear cupholders are supplied. Entry/exit is tight because doors have narrow bottoms and do not open wide.

Sedan trunk space is good for such a small car, but the opening won't swallow large boxes, and no fold-down rear seatback has been offered. Wagons have a split-folding rear seat, roomy cargo hold, and convenient pull-down tailgate handle, but a high floor lip hinders easy loading.

VALUE FOR THE MONEY: Rios offer "cheap wheels" economy and a generous warranty, but Kia's resale values are low, partly due to its unproven record of reliability and low ratings on independent surveys of customer satisfaction. Toyota's Echo might be more desirable, but low resale values on a Kia translate to more appealing used-car prices.

TROUBLE SPOTS

Dashboard lights: The transmission-control module program had problems with the lockup-converter strategy on some early build vehicles that illuminate the check-engine light. A revised module corrects the problem. (2001)

Dashboard lights: The check-engine light may come on (and phantom trouble codes stored) due to a software glitch in the transmission-control module. A new module is available. (2001)

Hood/trunk: The fuse-panel cover tends to fall off whenever the hood latch is pulled. A revised cover is available. (2000)

KIA

AVERAGE REPLACEMENT COSTS

A/C Compressor	$590	CV Joints	$1,330
Alternator	310	Exhaust System	445
Automatic Trans.	1,540	Radiator	315
Brakes	200	Shocks and/or Struts	520
Clutch	430	Timing Chain/Belt	570

NHTSA RECALL HISTORY

2001: Fuel leaks could develop at fuel-distributor assembly. Dealers will inspect and replace affected assemblies.

PRICES

	Good	Average	Poor
2001 Rio sedan	$3,500-4,200	$2,800-3,400	$900-1,100
2002 Rio Cinco	5,500-6,400	4,700-5,500	2,300-2,600
Rio sedan	5,000-5,900	4,300-5,000	2,000-2,400
2003 Rio Cinco	7,600-8,500	6,800-7,700	3,800-4,300
Rio sedan	7,000-8,000	6,200-7,100	3,400-3,800

For detailed information on this vehicle visit
http://used.consumerguide.com and enter code **4480**

1994-03 KIA SEPHIA/SPECTRA

CLASS: Subcompact car
BUILT IN: South Korea
PROS: Optional antilock braking (certain later models) • Fuel economy • Price
CONS: Build quality • Noise • Stereo location

EVALUATION: Sephias broke no new technical ground, but offered competent—if unremarkable—performance. Even in its latest form, though, Sephia is a mediocre performer compared to most budget-range rivals. Acceleration is so-so, as are ride and handling. Even fuel economy has been unremarkable, as a recent test LS sedan with 5-speed averaged a nothing-special 22.7 mpg. An earlier GS model, in contrast, averaged almost 31 mpg, driving 40 percent of the time on the highway. Noise also has been a problem, and refinement lags way behind that of the class-leading Hondas and Toyotas.

Engine noise is moderate, but road and wind noise are prominent. Ride quality isn't bad for a subcompact, though the suspension tends to "hammer" over bumps instead of absorbing them.

Sephias boast more interior space than many subcompacts, especially in back. Trunk space is also good. Except for the stereo, which was mounted low and had small, hard-to-use buttons, the early dashboard was well laid out.

VALUE FOR THE MONEY: Prices have been attractive on the new-car market, and similarly tempting on used-car lots. Kia spokespersons claim their cars' resale value has been strong, but it's definitely not in the same league as a Toyota or Honda. That could be good news for used-car shoppers, but there's more to value than price—especially when reliability is a question mark. Refinement, too, lags well behind the class-leading Toyota Corolla and Honda Civic.

On the whole, we've been underwhelmed by Sephia and Spectra. But as of 2001, Kias were covered by the industry's most comprehensive warranties, which adds to owner peace of mind. When that tempting price is factored into the equation, this South Korean subcompact might be a credible choice for the budget conscious.

TROUBLE SPOTS

Fuel odors: Gasoline burps back out of the filler pipe during refueling. (1998-99)

AVERAGE REPLACEMENT COSTS

A/C Compressor	$330	CV Joints	$750
Alternator	290	Exhaust System	265
Automatic Trans.	660	Radiator	190
Brakes	270	Shocks and/or Struts	200
Clutch	440	Timing Chain/Belt	400

NHTSA RECALL HISTORY

1994: Electronic-speedometer sensor can seize, causing speedometer and cruise control (if equipped) to stop functioning. **1998-99:** A valve on the fuel-filler assembly could cause fuel shut-off before the tank reaches 95 percent of capacity. **1998-99:** Ball socket on windshield-wiper link may be out of tolerance, resulting in link disengaging under load. Also, wiper-arm retaining nut could be inadequately tightened. **1998-99:** If exposed to moisture, two connectors could corrode; over time, fuel pump will not receive enough current to operate, causing engine to stall. **1998-99:** If pin tension in fuel pump's ground connector is poor, or bolt securing connector to floor is not tightened sufficiently, poor connection as pump operates can create heat, which in turn increases resistance. Eventually, the pump may fail to operate, causing engine to stall.

PRICES

	Good	Average	Poor
1994 Sephia	$1,000-1,600	$600-1,000	$100-200
1995 Sephia	1,200-1,800	700-1,100	100-200
1996 Sephia	1,400-2,000	900-1,300	200
1997 Sephia	1,700-2,500	1,100-1,700	300-400
1998 Sephia	2,100-2,800	1,500-2,000	400-500
1999 Sephia	2,500-3,300	1,800-2,400	500-700
2000 Sephia	3,000-3,800	2,300-2,900	700-900
2001 Sephia	4,200-5,000	3,400-4,100	1,400-1,700
2002 Spectra sedan	5,500-6,300	4,700-5,400	2,300-2,600
2003 Spectra sdn/hatchback	7,000-8,200	6,200-7,300	3,400-3,900

For detailed information on this vehicle visit
http://used.consumerguide.com and enter code **2312**

1994-98 LAND ROVER DISCOVERY

CLASS: Luxury sport-utility vehicle
BUILT IN: England
PROS: Antilock brakes • Ride
CONS: Entry/exit • Fuel economy • Noise • Price

EVALUATION: Acceleration is fairly lively in a Discovery, but no quicker than the 6-cylinder Jeep Grand Cherokee or Ford Explorer. Gas mileage is nothing to brag about. We averaged just 13 mpg in a blend of expressway and suburban driving.

Expect plenty of road noise and mechanical sounds, with constant gear whining.

The Discovery's firm suspension manages to absorb most bumps smartly and does a good job of reducing body lean. Even so, it leans more in turns than a Grand Cherokee or Explorer, and the steering demands too much muscle at low speeds. Tall ground clearance is an advantage when off-road, but a hindrance to climbing aboard or exiting, and you tend to drive with your shoulder shoved against the door. Adults will feel comfortable in Discovery's first two rows of seats, but the jump seats are best left to children.

Gauges are easy to see and well-lit at night. Cargo space is abundant. As for assembly quality, our test vehicles have felt rock-solid.

VALUE FOR THE MONEY: Range Rover/Land Rover is perceived to be a luxury vehicle by some people, but that's definitely not the case with a Discovery. Interiors are surprisingly basic, unless the vehicle is fitted with leather upholstery. Before spending a wad of money on this vehicle, look at upscale versions of the Ford Explorer and Jeep Grand Cherokee.

TROUBLE SPOTS

Climate control: The electrical connector for the rear defroster can short to the center high-mount stoplamp (CHMSL) and blow a fuse. When this happens, the transmission cannot be shifted out of park. (All)

Doors: The sound-insulation pads in the doors can shift and plug the water drain holes which could lead to rust through. (All)

Hard starting: Starting difficulty in cold weather has been traced to oil that is too thick and a computer PROM with the wrong calibration. (1994-95)

Sunroof/moonroof: The sunroof may leak and water may drip from the latch or motor or front edge. (1994-96)

Transaxle leak: The front-axle stub seals and the rear-axle hub seals tend to leak. (1994-96)

Vehicle shake: The vehicle may vibrate when accelerating, especially between 30-40 mph due to a bad harmonic balancer or engine mount. (1994-95)

AVERAGE REPLACEMENT COSTS

A/C Compressor	$1,390	CV Joints	$235
Alternator	635	Exhaust System	440
Automatic Trans.	3,000	Radiator	820
Brakes	390	Shocks and/or Struts	680
Clutch	1,210	Timing Chain/Belt	840

NHTSA RECALL HISTORY

1994-98: Chafing of cruise-control wire against steering-wheel coupler can cause insulation to fail; electrical grounding could then cause driver's airbag to deploy. **1995:** Wrong-sized driveshaft nuts on some vehicles can loosen, ultimately causing one or both driveshafts to disconnect. **1995-96:** Right front door may not latch fully, causing door to "bounce" back off seals; could open while vehicle is moving.

PRICES

	Good	Average	Poor
1994 Discovery	$6,000-7,000	$5,200-6,100	$2,500-2,900
1995 Discovery	6,700-7,700	5,900-6,800	3,100-3,500
1996 Discovery	7,500-8,700	6,800-7,800	3,800-4,400
1997 Discovery	8,500-10,000	7,700-9,000	4,400-5,200
1998 Discovery	11,000-12,500	9,900-11,300	5,900-6,800

> For detailed information on this vehicle visit
> http://used.consumerguide.com and enter code **2190**

1999-03 LAND ROVER DISCOVERY II

CLASS: Luxury sport-utility vehicle

BUILT IN: England

PROS: Build quality • Cargo room • Exterior finish • Passenger room • Ride

CONS: Entry/exit • Fuel economy • Noise • Instruments/controls

EVALUATION: Without Active Cornering Enhancement (ACE), this tall, relatively narrow sport-utility vehicle suffers copious body lean in tight turns. With ACE, it corners with fine control and balance. Too bad the ACE technology has only been available on top-line models. Although the Discovery's ride gets choppy on closely spaced bumps, most imperfections are soaked up without jarring. Braking is sure and acceleration is acceptable for this premium-SUV class, though fuel economy is likely to be painful. A test model with the 4.0-liter engine accelerated to 60 mph in 10.2 seconds, but averaged only 12.5 mpg using the required premium fuel. Test SE did 0-60 mph in 9.1 sec, a useful improvement over the 4.0-liter version's 10.2. The added

LAND ROVER

torque provides a needed boost in midrange passing response, too.

Wind, engine, and axle noise are intrusive. The optional 3rd-row seat feels cramped, but overall, both people and package space are good. A tall step-in and narrow doorways make entry/exit tough, even for an SUV—especially into the rear compartment. Workmanship is on the patchy side, compared to the Discovery's main competitors. Quality, in fact, has been a longtime concern with respect to products from the British Land Rover company. One test Discovery model, for instance, suffered numerous squeaks and rattles.

VALUE FOR THE MONEY: The Discovery's optional 7-passenger capacity is a bonus. Regardless, the BMW X5, Mercedes-Benz M-Class, and Lexus RX 300 offer better performance, handling, road manners, refinement, and quality—without the Discovery's foolish eccentricities. Basically, it's an old soldier that sells mainly due to its off-road prowess and the toney Land Rover name. In the less-trucky SUV group, the nicely polished (if only 5-passenger) Lexus RX 300 ranks as a top alternative.

TROUBLE SPOTS

Coolant leak: Heater hoses may leak due to insufficiently tightened clamps causing coolant to puddle on intake manifold of 4.0-L engine. (1999)

Sunroof/moonroof: Sunroof may jam and dealers were replacing both the front and rear assemblies at no charge. (1999)

Water leak: Plugged drain holes (excess sealant) in the fresh-air intake plenum causes water to enter passenger compartment during torrential rains and/or carwashes. (1999)

Windows: The rear-window glass may break from stress caused by the CHMSL (center high-mounted stoplamp) housing. (1999)

AVERAGE REPLACEMENT COSTS

A/C Compressor	$915	CV Joints	$1,150
Alternator	1,025	Exhaust System	745
Automatic Trans.	910	Radiator	810
Brakes	505	Shocks and/or Struts	1,340
Clutch	400	Timing Chain/Belt	500

NHTSA RECALL HISTORY

1999-00 w/active cornering enhancement: The high-pressure hydraulic pipe could fracture, resulting in loss of hydraulic fluid which could lead to loss of engine auxiliary functions. **1999-00:** Engine-idler pulley can fracture and fail, causing the pulley to throw off the serpentine belt. Loss of engine auxiliary functions could result. **1999-01:** The antilock braking system's electronic-control unit can misinterpret the sensor signal, resulting in inappropriate ABS activation. **1999-02:** Chafing of the accelerator cable could lead to breakage of the interior cable strands, making the throttle stick in the open position. **2000-01:** The power-interrupt solenoid in the winch assembly could experience excessive heat, which could lead to fire.

PRICES

PRICES	Good	Average	Poor
1999 Discovery II	$13,000-16,000	$11,800-14,600	$7,500-9,300
2000 Discovery II	16,000-18,500	14,600-16,800	10,200-11,800

2001 Discovery II	$19,000-22,000	$17,500-20,200	$12,400-14,300
2002 Discovery II	22,000-25,000	20,200-23,000	14,300-16,300
2003 Discovery II	24,500-29,000	22,800-27,000	15,900-18,900

For detailed information on this vehicle visit
http://used.consumerguide.com and enter code **2458**

1990-96 LEXUS ES 250/300

CG BEST BUY

CLASS: Near-luxury car

BUILT IN: Japan

PROS: Acceleration
• Antilock brakes
• Passenger and cargo room
• Ride/handling

CONS: Automatic-transmission performance (ES 250)
• Fuel economy • Rear visibility • Road noise (ES 250)

EVALUATION: The ES 250 has a comfortable ride, soaking up bumps with little notice. It also tends to display good control and stability at high speed, while the standard antilock brakes provide strong, safe stops with good control. Tire whine and road noise are intrusive, however. The ES 250 also provides a bright, airy interior with tall windows, which give the driver excellent visibility, though it's hard to see the trunk while backing up. Leg room is generous both front and back, but head room is about average.

More-distinctive styling and a 3.0-liter V6 gave the rebadged ES 300 both the extra size and power it needed. The 300 provides outstanding responsiveness and handling. The same smooth and quiet ride that has become a Lexus hallmark is quite evident in the ES 300. However, body roll is noticeable and the steering is on the light side. While not quite up to full European standards in the suspension or steering departments, the ride and handling should not be an issue with most buyers. Except in straight highway driving, we got under 20 mpg in an ES 300, which demands premium fuel.

On the plus side, the ES 300 offers more passenger space than its compact external dimensions suggest. Leg room and head room are generous, even with the optional sunroof. Drivers enjoy a comfortably upright stance ahead of a tilt steering wheel and an attractive, well-arranged dashboard that mimics the panel design of the big LS 400. Some rear-seat space is sacrificed, however, for the sake of trunk room, which is more than adequate.

VALUE FOR THE MONEY: Much more than a glorified Camry, the ES 250/300 helped Lexus maintain a solid image in the luxury car market. Particularly in ES 300 form, this Lexus feels and behaves like the costlier, more luxurious automobile that it is.

LEXUS

TROUBLE SPOTS

See the 1992-96 Toyota Camry.

AVERAGE REPLACEMENT COSTS

See the 1992-96 Toyota Camry.

NHTSA RECALL HISTORY

1992: Secondary hood-latch mechanism could accumulate dust or debris that would keep the latch from engaging properly. **1994-96 ES 300:** Steering-wheel set nut may not have been sufficiently tightened; could result in vibration and looseness in steering wheel, and ultimately separation.

PRICES	Good	Average	Poor
1990 ES 250	$2,200-2,800	$1,600-2,000	$400-500
1991 ES 250	2,800-3,500	2,100-2,600	600-800
1992 ES 300	4,800-5,600	4,000-4,700	1,800-2,100
1993 ES 300	5,900-6,700	5,100-5,800	2,500-2,800
1994 ES 300	6,900-7,800	6,100-6,900	3,200-3,700
1995 ES 300	7,800-8,800	7,000-7,900	4,000-4,500
1996 ES 300	8,500-9,500	7,700-8,600	4,400-4,900

For detailed information on this vehicle visit
http://used.consumerguide.com and enter code **2055**

1997-01
LEXUS ES 300

CG BEST BUY

CLASS: Near-luxury car
BUILT IN: Japan
PROS: Acceleration • Build quality • Passenger and cargo room • Quietness • Ride
CONS: Price • Rear visibility

EVALUATION: Acceleration is more than adequate. We timed an ES 300 at 7.6 seconds, accelerating from a standstill to 60 mph. Better yet, the engine is silent at idle speed, and almost silkily silent when rolling along under power. Quietness, in fact, might be this Lexus's single greatest asset. Wind rush is no more than a whisper at highway speeds, and road noise rarely amounts to more than a muted hum. This is one truly quiet sedan.

Gas mileage isn't bad. Even hard city driving failed to push our overall figure below 20 mpg, though premium fuel is required.

Steering is firmer than before, and quick, but lacks some road feel. In the same way, the Lexus suspension furnishes capable handling and offers more isolation from bumps and holes than a BMW 3-Series or Mercedes-Benz C-Class, yet the ES 300 is not as nimble as those competitors. Braking is swift and sure, except for marked nosedive in "panic" stops.

The additional 1.3 inches of rear leg room is barely noticeable, but the Lexus interior is as inviting for four adults as any luxury automobile's. Six-footers can sit comfortably in tandem, although the back-seat occupants must ride with knees raised and have little toe room beneath the front seats. Visibility is fine all around, except that the high parcel shelf and narrow rear window eliminate any view of the trunk and rear corners while backing up. The driving position is excellent, with clear gauges and handy switchgear. Cargo room shrunk by 1.3 cubic feet with the redesign, but the trunk still qualifies as roomy and usefully shaped. Workmanship is first-rate.

VALUE FOR THE MONEY: The ES 300 does just about everything a sedan of its class should, and does it very well. For shoppers who value comfort and elegance over sporty road manners, there's no better near-luxury sedan on the market.

TROUBLE SPOTS

See the 1997-01 Toyota Camry/Solara.

AVERAGE REPLACEMENT COSTS

See the 1997-01 Toyota Camry/Solara.

NHTSA RECALL HISTORY

1997: In extreme cold, accumulated moisture can temporarily freeze in brake-vacuum hose. **1997-98:** Steering-wheel set nut may not have been sufficiently tightened; could result in vibration and looseness in steering wheel, and ultimate-separation.

PRICES

	Good	Average	Poor
1997 ES 300	$10,500-11,500	$9,500-10,400	$5,600-6,100
1998 ES 300	12,700-14,000	11,400-12,600	7,200-8,000
1999 ES 300	15,000-16,500	13,700-15,000	9,500-10,400
2000 ES 300	18,000-19,500	16,600-17,900	11,500-12,500
2001 ES 300	21,000-23,000	19,300-21,200	13,700-15,000

For detailed information on this vehicle visit
http://used.consumerguide.com and enter code **2271**

1993-97 LEXUS GS 300

CLASS: Luxury car
BUILT IN: Japan
PROS: Acceleration
• Antilock brakes
• Steering/handling
CONS: Cargo room • Fuel economy • Price • Rear visibility

EVALUATION: Even with the latest 5-speed automatic transmission, the 6-cylinder engine is sluggish off the line, but then pulls strongly and smoothly to deliver brisk acceleration at higher speeds. Passing power is good, and the automatic transmission downshifts quickly out of overdrive. Gas mileage isn't so great. We averaged 17.3 mpg, and the engine demands premium fuel.

A GS 300 sedan handles adeptly, with a moderately firm ride that's never harsh. However, it lacks the library-quiet highway ride that's characteristic of the LS 400 and ES 300. Road noise isn't a problem, but the suspension and tires "thump" prominently over bumps and ruts.

Leg room is indeed ample all around, but rear head room is limited when the car is equipped with the optional power moonroof. A large driveline hump limits the back seat to two passengers. Large rear pillars and a narrow rear window restrict the driver's view, hiding the trunk. Although the trunk is wide and flat, it's too short to hold much, and liftover height is above bumper level. The dashboard layout is similar to that of the LS 400.

VALUE FOR THE MONEY: This deft-handling, if expensive, premium sedan is definitely worth a look. But before buying, also consider the BMW 3-Series or 5-Series, Infiniti J30, Cadillac Seville, and Mercedes-Benz C-Class or E-Class. Except for the Seville, all of those are rear-wheel drive, like the GS 300.

TROUBLE SPOTS

Audio system: Static or electrical noises from the turn signals, brake lights, etc. may be heard through the speakers when listening to an AM radio station due to a poor ground for the radio antenna. (1993-96)

Climate control: Because of an intermittent open condition in the temperature-sensor circuit, the ambient temperature display shows -22 degrees (F) and the climate control misbehaves. The display will not change until the fuse for the air conditioning control unit is removed briefly. (1993-95)

Suspension noise: Clunking noises from the front end on rough roads is caused by the design of the upper shock mount. A redesigned mount and shock are available. (1993-94)

AVERAGE REPLACEMENT COSTS

A/C Compressor	$1,490	Exhaust System	$680
Alternator	455	Radiator	480
Automatic Trans.	1,200	Shocks and/or Struts	640
Brakes	370	Timing Chain/Belt	200
CV Joints	1,000		

NHTSA RECALL HISTORY

1993-94: Spherical portions of certain lower ball joints are not smooth, causing friction that can lead to ball joint separation. **1995-97:** Due to inadequate lubrication, excessive wear can cause damage to lower ball joints; separation from steering-knuckle arms could occur.

PRICES	Good	Average	Poor
1993 GS 300	$8,000-9,000	$7,200-8,100	$4,100-4,600
1994 GS 300	9,500-10,500	8,600-9,500	4,900-5,500
1995 GS 300	10,800-12,000	9,700-10,800	5,800-6,500
1996 GS 300	11,800-13,000	10,600-11,700	6,600-7,300
1997 GS 300	14,000-15,500	12,700-14,100	8,500-9,500

For detailed information on this vehicle visit
http://used.consumerguide.com and enter code **2251**

1998-03 LEXUS GS 300/400/430

CLASS: Luxury car

BUILT IN: Japan

PROS: Acceleration • Build quality • Side airbags • Exterior finish • Interior materials • Quietness • Steering/handling

CONS: Fuel economy • Navigation-system controls

EVALUATION: With any engine, these sedans have silky powertrains, ultralow noise levels, ample midrange punch, and powerful, undramatic braking. The automatic transmission is smooth and responsive and the "E-shift" buttons on the GS 400 do their job well enough. Wind and mechanical noise are minimal enough so tire roar becomes noticeable, especially with the optional low-profile 17-inch tires. Both engines demand premium fuel. Test GS 400 sedans have averaged 17.9 to 19.0 mpg, while a GS 300 returned 17.2 mpg (with more city driving).

These sedans offer a higher level of control than prior Lexus models. Both GS models blaze ahead with ironlike stability at high speed. Unlike other Lexus sedans, they also corner with grippy precision, aided by firm and responsive steering. You can expect a trifle more body lean than in a 5-Series BMW, and the GS isn't quite as "tossable" on curvy roads. At the same time, you get a ride that's comfortably supple over most any surface, though the GS 400 can turn fidgety and thumpy over tar strips and expansion joints.

Passenger and cargo room are better than before, though not by much, in a rather cozy interior. Rear entry/exit isn't the best either, though all doors open exceptionally wide, and back-seat head room remains tight for 6-footers. Otherwise, space is ample for four adults, or five in a pinch (perhaps literally). Though not exceptionally roomy, the trunk is satisfactory. GS drivers face a well-arranged Lexus dashboard that presents large gauges and large, simple minor controls.

Like all Lexus models, this one is solidly built and carefully finished, crafted of top-quality materials, though we noted a couple of uncharacteristic interior rattles in a GS 400. Cabins are trimmed in supple leather and gorgeous wood.

VALUE FOR THE MONEY: All told, GS is the only true Japanese alternative to taut-handling German sport sedans, without losing the posh, smooth ride of a Lexus. Prices are a drawback, but the GS is still worth a look if you're shopping in the Lexus level. We prefer the BMW 540i and Mercedes-Benz E430 over the GS 400, which makes the GS 300 our pick as the better value of the duo.

TROUBLE SPOTS

Air conditioner: The A/C fails to operate accompanied by failure of the temperature gauge, transmission-selector light, and the outside-temperature indicator just displays two dashes, but the system returns to normal if

LEXUS

the key is switched off and on, requiring replacement of the A/C electronic-control unit. (1998)

Audio system: If the CD player stops working, but returns to normal when the key is cycled, or the there is cross-talk on the AM band, the company will replace the radio-tuner assembly. (1998)

Electrical problem: Using the wrong cigar-lighter element (wrong size for the socket) can cause a short circuit. (1998-2000)

AVERAGE REPLACEMENT COSTS

A/C Compressor	$810	Exhaust System	$810
Alternator	540	Radiator	630
Automatic Trans.	1,195	Shocks and/or Struts	1,605
Brakes	535	Timing Chain/Belt	420
CV Joints	1,410		

NHTSA RECALL HISTORY

1998: Due to manufacturing defect of yaw-rate sensor, Vehicle Stability Control system can operate improperly if sensor is affected by certain electromagnetic waves, as from a cellular phone; should this occur, brake may operate unexpectedly, affecting steering and speed control.

PRICES	Good	Average	Poor
1998 GS 300	$17,000-18,500	$15,600-17,000	$10,900-11,800
GS 400	19,000-20,500	17,500-18,900	12,400-13,300
1999 GS 300	20,000-21,500	18,400-19,800	13,000-14,000
GS 400	23,000-24,500	21,200-22,500	15,000-15,900
2000 GS 300	23,000-25,000	21,200-23,000	15,000-16,300
GS 400	26,500-28,500	24,600-26,500	17,500-18,800
2001 GS 300	26,500-28,500	24,600-26,500	17,500-18,800
GS 430	32,000-34,000	29,800-31,600	22,400-23,800
2002 GS 300	30,500-32,500	28,400-30,200	21,400-22,800
GS 430	36,500-38,500	33,900-35,800	25,900-27,300
2003 GS 300	34,200-36,200	31,800-33,700	24,300-25,700
GS 430	40,500-43,000	37,700-40,000	29,200-31,000

For detailed information on this vehicle visit
http://used.consumerguide.com and enter code **2311**

1999-03 LEXUS RX 300

CLASS: Luxury sport-utility vehicle

BUILT IN: Japan

PROS: Build quality • Exterior finish • Interior materials • Passenger and cargo room • Ride

CONS: Audio and climate controls • Wind noise

EVALUATION: Whether it has front-drive or all-wheel drive, an RX 300 delivers snappy off-the-line acceleration and has plenty of power throughout the speed range. The V6 is a model of refinement, augmented by flawless transmission behavior—though some early units exhibited uneven shifting until warmed up. An early 2WD model did 0-60 mph in 8.2 seconds and averaged 16.3 mpg—short of EPA estimates but better than most midsize SUVs. All-wheel drive doesn't slow it down much. An RX 300 feels like no other SUV—more like a luxury car or a minivan, unlike the posh but truck-flavored Mercedes M-Class. The ride is impressive, smothering large and small bumps with ease—better than many cars and less bouncy than most SUVs on scalloped freeways. An RX 300 corners with fine stability and little body lean for an SUV, helped by responsive steering. Still, it's too big and heavy to be a truly sporty handler. Routine braking is good, though the pedal might be a trifle spongy. Some tire noise occurs on coarse pavement, but the RX 300 is pleasingly quiet overall—except with the sunroof open, when wind rushes past with a mighty roar. Entry/exit is a simple matter of stepping in and out. Five adults can ride without complaint, and the center-rear position matches the comfort of the supportive outboard seats. The driver sits commandingly high, but roof pillars may be too thick for best outward vision. The tilt steering wheel does not adjust to suit everyone. Though it works well enough, the video-screen display for climate and audio settings is unorthodox and a little gimmicky. Other instruments and controls are attractively arranged, large, and functional.

Conversion of the back seat is convenient, but the load floor isn't so long with seats up, and liftover is relatively high.

VALUE FOR THE MONEY: Essentially a "suburban utility vehicle" rather than a traditional SUV, the RX 300 is posh, refined, roomy, and pleasant to drive. Strong demand keeps prices high, but we recommend it highly.

TROUBLE SPOTS

Audio system: Noises from the speakers (Nakamichi unit) can be corrected by exchanging the amplifiers under warranty. (1999)

Exhaust system: A booming noise from the exhaust system is corrected by installing a damper weight. (1999)

Wind noise: A throbbing wind noise from the moonroof is due to the location of the luggage-rack cross bars. Repositioning them may reduce the sound. (1999)

AVERAGE REPLACEMENT COSTS

A/C Compressor	$555	Exhaust System	$550
Alternator	310	Radiator	600
Automatic Trans.	955	Shocks and/or Struts	350
Brakes	380	Timing Chain/Belt	425
CV Joints	915		

NHTSA RECALL HISTORY

1999 w/optional traction control: If one of the dual brake lines fails and driver applies brake, vehicle will feel unstable compared to vehicles with proper brake distribution. **1999:** Headlights and taillights may not automatically illuminate in low ambient light, when headlight switch is placed in "Auto" position.

PRICES	Good	Average	Poor
1999 RX 300	$17,500-19,000	$16,100-17,500	$11,200-12,200
2000 RX 300	20,500-22,000	18,900-20,200	13,300-14,300
2001 RX 300	23,500-25,500	21,600-23,500	15,300-16,600
2002 RX 300	27,000-29,000	25,100-27,000	18,100-19,400
2003 RX 300	31,000-33,000	28,800-30,700	21,700-23,100

For detailed information on this vehicle visit
http://used.consumerguide.com and enter code **2382**

1990-94 LINCOLN CONTINENTAL

CLASS: Near-luxury car
BUILT IN: USA
PROS: Antilock brakes
• Passenger and cargo room
• Quietness • Ride
CONS: Fuel economy
• Instruments/controls

EVALUATION: The six-passenger interior is quite accommodating and the 19.1 cubic feet of trunk space is generous, but the missing ingredient was the kind of powertrain that could inspire confidence. With nearly all luxury rivals boasting V6 and V8 engines with at least 200 horsepower on tap, the Continental failed to generate much enthusiasm. Despite this drawback, the car's standard computer-controlled suspension soaks up most bumps and ruts easily, providing a stable highway ride. The body tends to float over wavy surfaces, even though the suspension is calibrated to stiffen automatically to control bounce. The steering feels light and numb, but it centers easily after turns. Though the all-season tires are not designed for slalom racing, they grip well on wet surfaces and the front-drive Continental feels sure-footed in tight turns. Many accessory switches are difficult to see at night, because they're unlit.

VALUE FOR THE MONEY: Even with its big-car looks, posh interior, limousine-style rear seat, and aerodynamic styling, the Continental lacks the performance needed to compete against other premium front-drive sedans.

TROUBLE SPOTS

Automatic transmission: If the transmission shudders or vibrates when accelerating above 35 mph, the torque-converter clutch is most likely the problem. The fix is to replace the EEC-IV processor (computer) and the fluid. (1991)

Blower motor: Squeaking or chirping blower motors are the result of defective brush holders. (1990-94)

Engine noise: Motor mounts are prone to premature wear causing a clunking noise. (1992-93)

Oil leak: Ford extended the warranty on 3.8-liter Taurus's to 7/100,000 and may compensate owners for repairs related to head-gasket failures. (1994)

Tire wear: Rapid rear tire wear is caused by poor rear wheel alignment. Kits are available to provide camber adjustment to correct the problem. (1990-94)

AVERAGE REPLACEMENT COSTS

A/C Compressor	$450	Exhaust System	$840
Alternator	420	Radiator	610
Automatic Trans.	950	Shocks and/or Struts	1,595
Brakes	195	Timing Chain/Belt	290
CV Joints	585		

NHTSA RECALL HISTORY

1990: Front-outboard seating position seatbelt buckles can fail to latch or unlatch. **1990-94 sold or registered in 24 states or D.C.:** Rear-lower subframe-mount plate nut can experience corrosion cracking if subjected to long-term exposure to road salt; can result in fracture. **1991-94 in 23 specified states:** Water can accumulate within the speed-control cable conduit; if unit is activated and cable has frozen, throttle may not return to idle. **1992-94 registered in AK, IA, MN, NE, ND, or SD:** During high winds, heavy drifting snow, and low temperatures, engine fan may become blocked or frozen and fail to rotate; and can cause smoke/flame. **1993-94:** Headlights can flash intermittently as a result of circuit-breaker opening. **1994:** Brake pedal push rod retainer may be missing or improperly installed, which can cause loss of braking ability.

PRICES

	Good	Average	Poor
1990 Continental	$1,600-2,100	$1,100-1,400	$200-300
1991 Continental	1,900-2,600	1,300-1,800	300-400
1992 Continental	2,200-2,900	1,600-2,100	400-600
1993 Continental	2,500-3,300	1,800-2,400	500-700
1994 Continental	3,000-3,800	2,300-2,900	700-900

For detailed information on this vehicle visit
http://used.consumerguide.com and enter code **2057**

1995-02 LINCOLN CONTINENTAL

CLASS: Near-luxury car
BUILT IN: USA
PROS: Acceleration
• Antilock brakes
• Instruments/controls
• Passenger and cargo room
CONS: Climate controls
• Fuel economy • Noise
• Electronic steering and suspension

EVALUATION: Helped by its new V8 engine, this Continental is a lot quicker, a bit more agile—and loaded with electronic gadgetry. In acceleration, the

LINCOLN

newly energetic Continental can match a Cadillac Seville SLS. At 16.3 mpg, gas mileage has not improved and premium fuel is recommended.

Despite its multiple adjustments, Lincoln's high-tech electronic suspension/steering fails to succeed fully. High mode makes the steering stiffer, without increasing feel; Low mode leaves the steering rather light and vague. The suspension also works best in Normal, as the other two modes have little effect on absorption of bumps.

Interior space is great. Occupants have plenty of leg space front and rear, while head room is adequate for 6-footers, even with the optional moonroof. Storage space is fine. The Continental's trunk is wide, deep, and long.

Reflecting off a mirror above the instrument cluster, the dramatic virtual image gauges are strikingly bright at night, but hard to read in bright sunlight. Controls are plentiful, and most are handy, but climate controls and seat heaters are recessed into the dashboard and hard to reach.

VALUE FOR THE MONEY: Lincoln evidently attempted to make the Continental both a sports sedan and a traditional luxury car. It's not quite either, but worth a look anyway. Because sales have been tepid, used-car prices may be appealing.

TROUBLE SPOTS

Air conditioner: Air conditioner output may be low or nonexistent because of a problem with the compressor clutch. (1995)

Hard starting: The engine may be hard to start or may stall after hot soak due to the idle-air control valve sticking (1995-96), or a poor connection at the crank position sensor. (1995-97)

Steering noise: The steering grunts or groans after making right hand turns, requiring replacement of the steering gear. (1995-97)

Suspension noise: Clunking from the front end may be due to premature wear of the sway-bar links. (1995-97)

AVERAGE REPLACEMENT COSTS

A/C Compressor	$435	Exhaust System	$540
Alternator	510	Radiator	290
Automatic Trans.	870	Shocks and/or Struts	1,165
Brakes	320	Timing Chain/Belt	795
CV Joints	470		

NHTSA RECALL HISTORY

1995-96: "Autolamp" control module may fail. **1996:** Vehicle can move even though indicator shows Park. **1998:** Text and/or graphics for headlamp aiming instructions, provided in owner guides, are not sufficiently clear. **1999:** Fuel-rail crossover hose was damaged during assembly, allowing fuel leakage. **1999-00:** Due to defective airbag sensors, the driver and/or passenger airbag might deploy as a result of minor bumps in the road and such. Dealer will inspect and recalibrate all defective sensors. **2000:** Due to incorrectly formed pin shaft in seatbelt retractor, switching mechanism could become nonfunctional in some circumstances, preventing seatbelt webbing from being extracted. **2000-01:** A switch located in the plastic cover of the wiper-motor gear case could malfunction and overheat, potentially resulting in loss of wiper function or fire.

PRICES

PRICES	Good	Average	Poor
1995 Continental	$4,000-4,800	$3,300-3,900	$1,300-1,500
1996 Continental	4,800-5,600	4,000-4,700	1,800-2,100
1997 Continental	6,000-6,900	5,200-6,000	2,500-2,900
1998 Continental	8,500-9,500	7,700-8,600	4,400-4,900
1999 Continental	11,000-12,000	9,900-10,800	5,900-6,500
2000 Continental	14,000-15,500	12,700-14,100	8,500-9,500
2001 Continental	17,000-18,500	15,600-17,000	10,900-11,800
2002 Continental	21,000-22,500	19,300-20,700	13,700-14,600

For detailed information on this vehicle visit
http://used.consumerguide.com and enter code **2194**

2000-02 LINCOLN LS

CLASS: Near-luxury car
BUILT IN: USA
PROS: Acceleration (V8)
• Ride/handling • Seat
comfort
CONS: Automatic-trans-
mission performance
• Climate controls

EVALUATION: European in flavor, the LS is the dynamic equal of some cost-ly import sedans. Low-speed steering feel could be firmer, but an LS turns crisply, cornering with grippy precision and modest body lean. Highway stability is impressive even in gusty crosswinds. The optional Sport Package controls body motions better than the base suspension, yet the ride remains pleasantly supple.

Acceleration with the V8 feels strong. A test LS reached 60 mph in 7.3 seconds. An automatic-transmission V6 takes 9.3 seconds, according to Lincoln—not outstanding, yet the car feels adequately powered except on steep inclines or when real passing punch is required. Lincoln's automatic transmission can delay in responding to throttle inputs, though not as much as the S-Type's, and is slow to kick down for passing. Overall shift smoothness isn't the best, especially compared with BMW and Audi automatics. Lincoln's manual gearbox also lags, with notchy shift action and indistinct clutch movement. A V8 LS averaged 16.3 mpg using premium fuel, while a manual-shift V6 got 19.6 mpg. Engine sounds are muted, but tire noise intrudes on some coarse surfaces, which also yields some minor body drumming. Braking is swift and sure, despite indecisive pedal action. Although the interior feels less cramped than the S-Type's, the practical limit is four adults. Head clearance is so-so, but rear leg space is good even behind tall front occupants. An all-button climate system is not so easy to use. Large mirrors offset visibility lost to thickish rear roof pillars. Inside storage is limited, and only small suitcases stand upright in the trunk, which lacks fore/aft depth and has bulky hinges.

VALUE FOR THE MONEY: Highly capable and mannerly on the road, an LS delivers a lot of features for the money. In addition, few near-luxury rivals are

LINCOLN

available with a V8 engine. Though not perfect, marred by rather ordinary interior furnishings, the LS can easily be compared with cars that cost a lot more.

TROUBLE SPOTS

Engine misfire: Poor engine performance or a no-start condition may be the result of a loose fuel-hose clamp causing an internal leak. (2000)

Steering problems: Replacement steering wheels (on cars shipped with the wrong wheel) may have been installed without sufficiently tightening the locking nut. (2000)

Vehicle noise: A droning noise at highway speeds while in 5th gear was being corrected by replacing the halfshafts. (2000)

Windows: The rear-window regulator cable may break, making it impossible to open or close the window. (2000-01)

AVERAGE REPLACEMENT COSTS

A/C Compressor	$410	CV Joints	$900
Alternator	385	Exhaust System	465
Automatic Trans.	1,095	Radiator	450
Brakes	345	Shocks and/or Struts	1,975
Clutch	615	Timing Chain/Belt	610

NHTSA RECALL HISTORY

2000-01: Front-suspension lower ball joints on some vehicles were not tightened to specifications and could loosen and, ultimately, result in fracture of ball-joint stud.

PRICES

	Good	Average	Poor
2000 LS V6	$13,000-15,000	$11,800-13,700	$7,500-8,700
LS V8	14,800-16,500	13,500-15,000	9,300-10,400
2001 LS V6	16,000-18,000	14,600-16,400	10,200-11,500
LS V8	18,500-20,500	17,000-18,900	11,800-13,100
2002 LS V6	19,500-22,000	17,900-20,200	12,700-14,300
LS V8	22,000-24,000	20,200-22,100	14,300-15,600

For detailed information on this vehicle visit
http://used.consumerguide.com and enter code **2383**

1998-02 LINCOLN NAVIGATOR

CLASS: Luxury sport-utility vehicle

BUILT IN: USA

PROS: Standard antilock braking • Cargo room • Instruments/controls • Passenger room

CONS: Entry/exit • Fuel economy • Maneuverability

CONSUMER GUIDE®

LINCOLN

EVALUATION: Though too big and heavy to drive like a car, Navigator does have good scoot for a large sport utility. The latest 300-horsepower engine is stronger than Expedition's, promising robust acceleration and plenty of low-speed muscle for swift passing. Even better, though not really agile, it handles with surprising poise on twisty roads. Body lean is modest, at least at reasonable cornering velocities. On the down side, steering feels too light and divorced from the road, especially on 4x4 models. Those 4x4s also yield a stiff and jiggly ride that's absent on 2WD models, which ride nearly as smooth as some regular passenger cars. Both versions are quiet in highway driving.

Navigator offers the same towing brawn and convenient Control Trac 4WD operation as the Expedition, with a simple dashboard switch to select 2WD, automatic 4WD (which shifts automatically between 2WD/4WD, locked-in 4WD High, and 4WD Low). Demerits include dismal fuel economy—just over 12 mpg in our tests, with 2WD or 4WD. Some drivers have found seats to be too hard and low, lacking in lumbar support. Accessing the third-row seat is difficult, however, so it's best left to preteens. Front-seat space is bountiful, and the Navigator is wide enough for comfortable 3-across adult seating in the second row. A nearly flat floor means no one has to straddle a hump.

Sheer size makes the Navigator difficult to park. Overall height, especially in 4WD form, may prevent the big SUV from fitting in some garages. Getting inside is a task, due to the tall step-up into the interior, even on 2WD models. It's worse yet on 4x4s, despite the air suspension that lowers the vehicle an inch when the ignition is turned off. That inch just isn't enough to make a difference.

Instruments and controls are well laid-out, and the steering wheel holds a nice array of duplicate radio and climate controls. Cargo space is skimpy with the third seat in place, but immense if it's removed. Because it's heavy, though, removal is a 2-person task. Interior storage possibilities are unmatched: two gym-bag-sized center consoles, plus bins and pockets galore—though nothing is lockable. Visibility is good to the front and sides, but hindered to the rear by a forest of large headrests. Touches of wood trim highlight rich-looking interior materials.

Two options are worth looking for: The new Reverse Sensing System is helpful, sounding a warning of unseen objects while backing up. Shorter drivers are likely to favor the adjustable-pedal cluster, which moves the unit forward by as much as 3 inches.

VALUE FOR THE MONEY: A hot seller from the start, Navigator drew buyers in their 40s—markedly younger than usual for Lincoln. Some observers derided the Navigator's blatantly excessive body trim, but plenty of shoppers loved it. All told, Navigator might be a good buy—not much more costly than the highly rated Expedition, and loaded with amenities. A Navigator contains every luxury a semireasonable hedonist could covet—as well as real stretch-out space, in both front and rear.

TROUBLE SPOTS

See the 1997-02 Ford Expedition.

AVERAGE REPLACEMENT COSTS

See the 1997-02 Ford Expedition.

LINCOLN

NHTSA RECALL HISTORY

1998: Certain off-lease vehicles, Canadian in origin but sold in the U.S., have daytime running lights that do not meet U.S. Specifications. **1998:** Main battery cable can contact body panel in trunk, resulting in damage to cable insulation that could lead to short circuit, loss of electrical supply, or fire. **1998:** Text and/or graphics for headlamp-aiming instructions, provided in owner guides, are not sufficiently clear. **1998-00:** Bolts that attach trailer-hitch assembly to frame could lose their clamp load; hitch could then separate from vehicle. **1999 w/4WD and 17-inch chrome steel wheels:** Clamp load can be lost on wheel lugs, due to insufficient wheel contact area with hub; in some cases, contact area can deform, resulting in loss of lug-nut torque that can cause vibration or separation of wheel/tire from vehicle. **1999:** Fuel-line assemblies on some vehicles may have been damaged by supplier during manufacture, allowing leakage. **1999:** Retainer clip that holds master-cylinder pushrod to brake-pedal arm may be missing or partially installed, causing increased stopping distances. **2000-01:** A switch located in the plastic cover of the wiper-motor gear case could malfunction and overheat, potentially resulting in loss of wiper function or fire. **2000-01:** Some of the owner's manuals for these vehicles are missing instructions for properly attaching a child restraint system. **2001:** Driver- and/or front passenger-outboard seatbelt buckle may not fully latch. In the event of a crash, the restraint system may not provide adequate occupant protection. **2002 4.2-liter:** Rear-tire pressure is listed incorrectly on label.

PRICES	Good	Average	Poor
1998 Navigator 2WD	$14,000-15,500	$12,700-14,100	$8,500-9,500
Navigator 4WD	15,500-17,000	14,100-15,500	9,900-10,900
1999 Navigator 2WD	16,500-18,000	15,000-16,400	10,600-11,500
Navigator 4WD	18,000-19,500	16,600-17,900	11,500-12,500
2000 Navigator 2WD	20,000-21,500	18,400-19,800	13,000-14,000
Navigator 4WD	21,500-23,000	19,800-21,200	14,000-15,000
2001 Navigator 2WD	23,500-25,000	21,600-23,000	15,300-16,300
Navigator 4WD	25,000-27,000	23,300-25,100	16,500-17,800
2002 Navigator 2WD	27,000-28,700	25,100-26,700	18,100-19,200
Navigator 4WD	29,000-31,000	27,000-28,800	20,000-21,400

For detailed information on this vehicle visit
http://used.consumerguide.com and enter code **2323**

1990-97 LINCOLN TOWN CAR

CLASS: Luxury car
BUILT IN: USA
PROS: Antilock brakes (optional) • Passenger and cargo room
CONS: Fuel economy • Maneuverability • Rear visibility

LINCOLN

EVALUATION: Despite its new V8 engine, the Town Car can hardly be classified as a sprinter, given the fact it tips scales at over two tons, but once underway, there's strong acceleration and passing power. One drawback to brisk acceleration seems to be the 4-speed automatic, which is slow to downshift at times. As for economy, we've averaged an unimpressive 17 mpg in city/expressway driving.

New suspension and further upgrades designed to improve the car's handling arrive in the form of a Ride Control Package. The car retains much of its penchant for excessive body roll and the kind of pillowy ride characteristics preferred by domestic luxury-car buyers. If you're not particular about handling, and need a spacious car, you've come to the right place. The Town Car is wide enough to accommodate six adults comfortably, while the large doors make entry and exit maneuvers effortless. For long trips, you can count on the spacious 22.3-cubic foot trunk to hold nearly all your worldly goods.

Most controls are mounted high on the dashboard where they're easy to see and reach while driving. Though the power window, door lock, and mirror controls are grouped on the driver's door, they aren't backlit at night. Huge rear roof pillars hinder the view while backing up.

VALUE FOR THE MONEY: Big sedans like the Town Car and its main rival, the Cadillac Fleetwood, are plush, quiet, and comfortable. However, newer luxury models are now available that offer comparable luxury, more agility, and better overall economy.

TROUBLE SPOTS

Air springs: Air springs are prone to leaks caused by the bag rubbing against the axle or control arm. (Any so-equipped)

Alternator belt: The drive-belt tensioner pulley or idler-pulley bearings are apt to make a squealing noise when the engine is started in cold weather. (1993-96)

Automatic transmission: The transmission may slip and the engine may flare when the transmission shifts into fourth gear, which can often be traced to a bad TR/MLP sensor. (1992-95)

Automatic transmission: Transmission shudder or vibration can be caused by improper transmission fluid. It requires that the transmission fluid (including fluid in the torque converter) be changed and that only Mercon fluid be used. (1992-94)

Hard starting: If the engine does not want to start or cranks for a long time then stalls, the idle-air control valve may be sticking. (1996)

Hard starting: The connector at the starter solenoid tends to corrode resulting in a "no-crank" condition. (1991-94)

Oil leak: The oil filter balloons and leaks because the oil-pump relief valve sticks. (1991-94)

Vehicle noise: A broken gusset or weld separation at the frame crossmember causes a rattle from the rear or the car. (1990-92)

Vehicle noise: A chattering noise that can be felt coming from the rear during tight turns after highway driving is caused by a lack of friction modifier or over-shimming of the clutch packs in the Traction-Lok differential. (1990-96)

LINCOLN

AVERAGE REPLACEMENT COSTS

A/C Compressor	$390	CV Joints	$140
Alternator	375	Exhaust System	690
Automatic Trans.	700	Shocks and/or Struts	365
Brakes	265	Timing Chain/Belt	330

NHTSA RECALL HISTORY

1990-91 cars in 25 states: Corrosion of hood-latch striker causes detachment, so hood can open unexpectedly. **1990-97 police/fleet/natural gas:** Bearing within lower ball joint can weaken slowly during use and eventually crack; could result in separation, allowing control arm to drop to the ground. **1991:** Distorted fuel lines may contact steering-column universal joint and be damaged. **1991-92:** Secondary hood latch may not engage; if primary latch releases when car is moving, hood could fly up. **1992-93:** Speed-control deactivation switch can develop short that could result in underhood fire, whether or not engine is running. **1994:** Brake-pedal pushrod retainer may be missing or improperly installed, which can cause disengagement and loss of braking. **1994:** Nuts and bolts that attach rear brake adapter to axle-housing flange can loosen and separate, allowing damage to ABS sensor, hydraulic line, and parking-brake cable. **1995:** Seal between fuel-filler pipe and tank may not be fully cured, which could allow fuel to leak. **1995:** Some passenger-side airbags may not inflate properly; also, igniter cap can separate, releasing hot gases. **1995-96 fleet cars only:** Corrosion of inadequately lubricated Pitman arms can cause abnormal wear of joint, resulting in separation. **1995-97:** Passenger vehicles that have had the driver's airbag module replaced after April 5, 2000 may have modules with inflators that lack insufficient welds and may prevent proper inflation of the airbag. **1996:** Driver's door, when closed only to secondary latched position, may not sustain the specified 1000-pound transverse load. **1996:** Wrong parts may have been used to service seatbelts with switchable retractor for child restraints. **1996-97:** Replacement seatbelts made by TRW and sold by Ford may not restrain occupant in a collision. **1997:** Driver's airbag module could stay in position during deployment, but leave the steering wheel cavity afterward.

PRICES

	Good	Average	Poor
1990 Town Car	$2,300-2,900	$1,700-2,100	$400-600
1991 Town Car	2,700-3,400	2,000-2,600	600-700
1992 Town Car	3,100-3,900	2,400-3,000	700-900
1993 Town Car	3,600-4,400	2,900-3,500	1,000-1,200
1994 Town Car	4,300-5,200	3,500-4,300	1,500-1,800
1995 Town Car	5,000-6,000	4,300-5,100	2,000-2,400
1996 Town Car	5,800-7,200	5,000-6,300	2,400-3,000
1997 Town Car	7,000-9,000	6,200-8,000	3,400-4,300

For detailed information on this vehicle visit
http://used.consumerguide.com and enter code **2059**

1998-02 LINCOLN TOWN CAR

CLASS: Luxury car
BUILT IN: USA
PROS: Cargo room
• Standard side airbags
(1999-2002) • Passenger
room • Quietness
CONS: Fuel economy
• Rear visibility

EVALUATION: With a tad more horsepower and a little less weight than before, the latest Town Car moves off the line in a fairly spirited manner. Even so, acceleration cannot match that of a Northstar-equipped Cadillac DeVille. A Cartier edition with the stronger engine took a somewhat leisurely 9.5 seconds to reach 60 mph. The reworked automatic transmission still upshifts seamlessly, but now it also downshifts more promptly for passing—though the latter task sometimes demands a hefty shove on the gas pedal.

Ride quality remains smooth—velvety and absorbent, in fact—but the Town Car is now less floaty over pavement irregularities and more controlled than in the past, thanks to a revised suspension. Minor wheel pattering at speed can be expected, however, on some freeway surfaces. Handling also has improved, so the big sedan is no longer as wallowy and boatlike as Town Cars of the past. Less body roll in turns and sharper steering response help it tolerate spirited driving—if not exactly encourage such exuberant behavior.

Accommodations always were spacious. Even though the latest Town Car is a bit trimmer, interior room has not suffered. Large doors make it easy to get in and out of both the front and rear seats. Head room is generous all around. Leg room is good but not great, and the car isn't really wide enough to fit six adults without real squeezing. Quietness is another long-standing Town Car tradition. If anything, the new model is even more serene inside than its predecessors, with almost no road or wind noise intruding, and no more than a muted roar from the engine.

Gauges now are analog (needle-type) rather than digital, and very legible. User-friendly climate and audio controls are easy to see, reach, and use. Outward visibility is compromised by thick side and rear roof pillars and a tall rear deck. Trunk room is down about 10 percent. That still leaves a lot of luggage space, though much of the volume is again within a deep center well—which can be a strain when you need to load and remove heavy objects. Workmanship on our test Cartier sedan was flawless, though materials felt less-expensive than in some rivals.

VALUE FOR THE MONEY: Lincoln's Town Car is the last remaining American-brand, rear-drive, full-size luxury sedan. So, potential buyers aren't overloaded with alternatives. Fortunately, the refined Town Car

LINCOLN

continues to offer the traditional luxury-car values of spaciousness and splendid riding isolation, as well as a load of comforts and conveniences. Although we give higher marks to the latest front-drive Cadillac DeVille as a domestically built luxury automobile, the Town Car is worth considering—and priced far below imported competitors.

TROUBLE SPOTS

Exhaust system: The engine idles rough due to the exhaust system vibrating. Installing a damper on the right side of the Y-pipe corrects it. (1998-99)

Steering problems: The steering wheel may vibrate and/or buzz. Power-steering hose must be replaced. (1998)

Vehicle noise: The heat shields come loose on the catalytic converter and muffler causing a rattling and buzzing noise. (1998-99)

Windshield: Water may leak from the windshield area because of a gap in the sealer. (1998-99)

AVERAGE REPLACEMENT COSTS

A/C Compressor	$435	Radiator	$460
Alternator	265	Shocks and/or Struts	1,315
Automatic Trans.	875	Timing Chain/Belt	415
Brakes	410	Universal Joints	195
Exhaust System	525		

NHTSA RECALL HISTORY

1998: Text and/or graphics for headlamp-aiming instructions, provided in owner guides, are not sufficiently clear. **1998-00:** Jacking instructions are incorrect and, if followed, could result in vehicle dropping suddenly. **1998-99 limousine w/ball joint containing one-piece bearing:** Bearing within lower control-arm ball joint can weaken slowly during use; eventually, crack could result in separation, allowing control arm to drop to ground. **2000-01:** A switch located in the plastic cover of the wiper-motor gear case could malfunction and overheat, potentially resulting in loss of wiper function or fire. **2001:** A restraint-control module (RCM) or a side- or front-crash sensor may have been assembled with one or more of the screws that mount the circuit board in the housing missing. **2001:** Driver- and/or front passenger-outboard seatbelt buckle may not fully latch. In the event of a crash, the restraint system may not provide adequate occupant protection.

PRICES

	Good	Average	Poor
1998 Town Car	$9,500-11,500	$8,600-10,400	$4,900-6,000
1999 Town Car	11,500-14,000	10,400-12,600	6,300-7,700
2000 Town Car	14,500-17,500	13,200-15,900	9,000-10,900
2001 Town Car	17,500-22,000	16,100-20,200	11,200-14,100
2002 Town Car	20,500-26,000	18,900-23,900	13,300-16,900

For detailed information on this vehicle visit
http://used.consumerguide.com and enter code **2324**

1993-97 MAZDA 626

CG BEST BUY

CLASS: Compact car
BUILT IN: USA
PROS: Acceleration (V6) • Fuel economy • Steering/handling
CONS: Automatic-transmission performance • Road noise

EVALUATION: A V6 and 5-speed deliver willing, capable performance and spirited acceleration. Both engines are smooth, free-revving, and fairly quiet, but neither has enough low-speed torque for pleasant, vigorous running with automatic. Automatics also are slow to downshift for passing. Worse yet, they suffer jerky full-throttle downshifts, especially with 4-cylinder power.

A 4-cylinder achieved nearly 24 mpg, and a manual-transmission V6 averaged 20.7 mpg.

Ride quality is good, with the suspension filtering out most pavement imperfections. The sedan also handles better than you might expect. Body lean is moderate in turns, but the car feels secure and composed in spirited driving. "Panic" braking is swift and stable.

Rear seating disappoints, and rear doors could be bigger. Head room is adequate for tall people, even with a power sunroof installed. Leg space is ample all around. Space also is adequate for rear passengers' feet under front seats. Split rear seatbacks fold down for additional cargo space. Wind noise is low on the highway, though the 4-cylinder gets a little loud at higher speeds. Outward visibility is good, and the driver faces clear, simple control panels.

VALUE FOR THE MONEY: All told, the solidly built 626 sedan is a strong contender against the Honda Accord and Toyota Camry, though the latter are quieter and more luxurious.

TROUBLE SPOTS

Air conditioner: Poor A/C performance caused by defective relay will not let compressor cycle off on V6 models. (1993-95)

Door handles: The outer door handles may come loose and rattle. Replace the original retaining nuts with ones that won't come loose. (1993-95)

Engine knock: Cars with a V6 engine built before March 1993 may have engine knock, especially when cold, due to carbon buildup in the combustion chamber. (1993-94)

Engine mounts: Original motor mounts are prone to breakage. Mazda offers redesigned mounts as a replacement. (1993-94)

Engine noise: A metallic tapping noise from the rear of the engine could be due to slippage between the exhaust-camshaft driven gear and friction gear. (1993-95)

Engine stalling: If the engine stalls when the transmission is shifted into drive, the problem may be a cracked mass-airflow snorkel tube. (1993-94)

MAZDA

Power seats: The insulation on the wires for the power seat can wear through causing a short circuit disabling the power seat. (1993-94)

Transaxle leak: A damaged torque-converter hub seal allows fluid to leak from the automatic transmission. (1994-96)

Vehicle shake: Vibration in the steering wheel, shift lever, and floor is probably caused by mispositioned radiator dampers. (1993-95)

Wipers: The welds holding the wiper-arm support bracket break causing a creak or rattle when the wipers are running. (1993-95)

AVERAGE REPLACEMENT COSTS

A/C Compressor	$360	Exhaust System	$495
Alternator	245	Radiator	410
Automatic Trans.	1,075	Shocks and/or Struts	670
Brakes	245	Timing Chain/Belt	160
Clutch	625		

NHTSA RECALL HISTORY

1994: Headlight wire that runs through turn-signal lever can fail where it is soldered to switch, causing loss of headlights. **1995:** Some passenger-side airbags may not inflate properly; also, igniter cap can separate, causing hot gases to be released. **1995-97:** Airbag could deploy as a result of minor undercarriage impact. **1997:** Spring in timing-belt tensioner can break and get caught, resulting in possible engine stalling.

PRICES	Good	Average	Poor
1993 626 DX, LX	$1,600-2,200	$1,100-1,500	$200-300
626 ES	2,400-3,000	1,800-2,300	500-600
1994 626 DX, LX	1,900-2,600	1,300-1,800	300-400
626 ES	2,800-3,500	2,100-2,600	600-800
1995 626 DX, LX	2,200-3,000	1,600-2,100	400-600
626 ES	3,300-4,000	2,600-3,200	800-1,000
1996 626 DX, LX	2,600-3,500	1,900-2,600	500-700
626 ES	3,800-4,500	3,100-3,600	1,100-1,400
1997 626 DX, LX	3,200-4,400	2,500-3,400	800-1,100
626 ES	4,700-5,400	3,900-4,500	1,700-2,000

For detailed information on this vehicle visit
http://used.consumerguide.com and enter code **2063**

1998-02 MAZDA 626

CG BEST BUY

CLASS: Compact car

BUILT IN: USA

PROS: Acceleration (V6)
• Build quality
• Steering/handling

CONS: Automatic-transmission performance • Road noise

EVALUATION: Mazda wanted a quiet, refined compact for the next generation—and mostly succeeded in that quest. Engine and wind noise are well-muffled, though tire roar is too audible over coarse pavement. Ride quality is firm, but absorbent. The longer wheelbase helps reduce pitch and hop on scalloped freeways, though high-speed dips induce some float. Cornering is still decisive and sporty, with only mild body lean and stable front-drive responses. Quick, precise steering is helpful, but directional changes aren't really sport-sedan crisp. Braking is good, with little nosedive and steady tracking in hard stops.

Four-cylinder performance is at least adequate with manual shift, but sluggish with automatic, whereas V6 models are lively either way. With either engine, though, the automatic can downshift with a jerk at times. A manual-shift model averaged a pleasing 22.5 mpg. Though a compact, the 626 rivals some midsize sedans, with space for 6-footers to sit in tandem without rear riders' knees digging into the front seats. Underseat foot room also is good. The cabin is still a bit narrow for uncrowded three-abreast grownup travel in back, but large doorways ease entry/exit. In terms of visibility, driving, seating, and dashboard layout; the 626 is competitive, but not terrific. Tall drivers might want a little more rearward seat travel to get further from the steering wheel. Interior decor has a tasteful, understated look. Small-items stowage is better than average, with roomy compartments in the dashboard and console, as well as map pockets. A 626 feels reassuringly stout on rough roads.

VALUE FOR THE MONEY: A competent family 4-door, more mainstream than its predecessor, the 626 lost some of its sporting flair but still tops most rivals—especially with the V6 engine. LX versions offer the best combination of features and value in this competitive segment. Because it's often overlooked, prices are appealing.

TROUBLE SPOTS

Coolant leak: Early production models with the 4-cylinder engine may leak coolant from the optional block heater. A redesigned heater, made of cast brass, can be retrofitted. (1998-99)

Sunroof/moonroof: A variety of sunroof problems may be due to broken or missing panel-bumper clips, loose guides, or motor and cable problems. (1999)

Vehicle noise: The vapor-emission control valve makes a clicking or tapping noise in the rear of the vehicle and can be quieted with a redesigned bracket. (1998-2000)

AVERAGE REPLACEMENT COSTS

A/C Compressor	$405	CV Joints	$670
Alternator	305	Exhaust System	270
Automatic Trans.	1,030	Radiator	505
Brakes	260	Shocks and/or Struts	440
Clutch	470	Timing Chain/Belt	280

NHTSA RECALL HISTORY

1999-00: Certain reservoir tank caps on brake master cylinder lack ventilation holes; as a result, pressure in tank can drop gradually as brake pad or shoe wears and ambient temperature drops. Also, pressure could reach

MAZDA

a point where brake caliper and drum cylinder are pulled back by vacuum when vehicle is parked for a long time.

PRICES

	Good	Average	Poor
1998 626 4-cylinder	$4,200-5,000	$3,400-4,100	$1,400-1,700
626 V6	5,400-6,100	4,600-5,200	2,200-2,500
1999 626 4-cylinder	5,500-6,300	4,700-5,400	2,300-2,600
626 V6	6,300-7,200	5,500-6,300	2,800-3,200
2000 626 4-cylinder	7,000-7,800	6,200-6,900	3,400-3,700
626 V6	8,000-9,000	7,200-8,100	4,100-4,600
2001 626 4-cylinder	8,500-9,400	7,700-8,500	4,400-4,900
626 V6	9,500-10,700	8,600-9,600	4,900-5,600
2002 626 4-cylinder	10,000-11,000	9,000-9,900	5,200-5,700
626 V6	11,200-12,200	10,100-11,000	6,000-6,600

For detailed information on this vehicle visit http://used.consumerguide.com and enter code **2384**

1992-95 MAZDA 929

CLASS: Near-luxury car
BUILT IN: Japan
PROS: Antilock brakes
• Braking ability • Quietness
• Steering/handling
CONS: Wet-weather traction • Passenger and cargo room • Driving position

EVALUATION: Not quite as lively or silky as the Lexus ES 300 or Nissan Maxima, a 929 isn't quite as nimble either. You can expect a bit more body lean in corners, though the car is generally well-controlled. Steering feels tight and responsive, but is a shade light for best high-speed control. Braking prowess ranks among the best in its class.

The 929's V6 engine delivers more than adequate acceleration, capable of reaching 60 mph in 9.4 seconds. Smooth and quiet on the road, the engine sounds harsh when it's cold and feels a little rough. We averaged 19 mpg, and the 4-speed automatic transmission shifts smoothly and promptly.

Interior noise levels are low, and slim roof pillars permit good visibility. A bumper-height opening allows easy access to the trunk, but space is somewhat limited. The interior is also less roomy than might be expected. Front seats aren't that spacious, and the driver's seat doesn't have enough rearward travel. In addition, tall people are likely to find their heads against the ceiling, and the steering wheel lacks a tilt feature. Rear leg room is good, but head room is limited and a center person must straddle the driveline hump. Conveniently positioned controls and large, clear analog gauges sit on an attractive dashboard.

VALUE FOR THE MONEY: Overall, the 929 pales when compared to the Acura Legend, Lexus ES 300, or Nissan Maxima. Its V6 lacks the refinement and verve and the 929 comes up short in too many areas to be a prime choice among used luxury cars.

TROUBLE SPOTS

Engine misfire: Using a replacement distributor cap can cause high idle with erroneous trouble codes blaming the crankshaft sensor and/or distributor. (1992-95)

Engine misfire: Fuel-injector seals may leak causing an electrical problem resulting in an engine miss. (1993)

Engine temperature: Overheating may be due to plastic water-pump impeller coming loose or breaking. (1992)

Oil leak: A crack in the oil gallery in the 3.0-liter cylinder head allows oil to seep into the coolant. (1992-95)

AVERAGE REPLACEMENT COSTS

A/C Compressor	$1,535	CV Joints	$705
Alternator	250	Exhaust System	680
Automatic Trans.	780	Radiator	540
Brakes	260	Shocks and/or Struts	1,040
Clutch	500	Timing Chain/Belt	315

NHTSA RECALL HISTORY

None to date.

PRICES	Good	Average	Poor
1992 929	$2,500-3,200	$1,800-2,300	$500-700
1993 929	3,000-3,800	2,300-2,900	700-900
1994 929	3,700-4,500	3,000-3,600	1,100-1,300
1995 929	4,500-5,500	3,700-4,600	1,600-2,000

For detailed information on this vehicle visit
http://used.consumerguide.com and enter code **2202**

1994-97 MAZDA B-SERIES

CG BEST BUY

CLASS: Compact pickup truck

BUILT IN: USA

PROS: Acceleration (4.0-liter V6) • Antilock brakes • Build quality • Payload capacity

CONS: Acceleration (4-cylinder) • Fuel economy • Passenger room (reg. cab)

EVALUATION: The 4.0-liter engine is indeed the best choice, though most buyers will be satisfied with 3.0-liter V6, especially when equipped with manual shift. Using only a little more fuel than the 3.0-liter engine, the 4.0-liter V6 delivers good low-speed punch, though it can get coarse and noisy. A 4-cylinder engine provides acceptable power with the 5-

MAZDA

speed manual gearbox, but is sluggish when driving an automatic transmission. It's an unwise choice for towing or hauling heavy payloads.

All models ride rather nicely, and road manners are good. You won't be assaulted by undue tire, engine, or wind noise, either. Off-road setups make for a stiff ride on 4x4s, but suspensions on other models absorb most big bumps without jarring the occupants.

Interiors are well-designed, though the rear jump seats are usable only by small children. Ranger and B-Series were the only compact pickups to offer a passenger-side airbag, added for 1996 as an option.

VALUE FOR THE MONEY: Choosing between a Ford Ranger and Mazda B-Series is mainly a matter of styling details and price. Both the B-Series and its Ranger counterpart rank among the best in their class, but look also at the Chevrolet S10 or GMC Sonoma.

TROUBLE SPOTS

See the 1993-97 Ford Ranger.

AVERAGE REPLACEMENT COSTS

See the 1993-97 Ford Ranger.

NHTSA RECALL HISTORY

1994 V6: Flexible hose in front fuel line is susceptible to cracking. **1994 in Southern California:** Studs that attach master cylinder to power brake booster can develop stress cracking after extended period. **1994 w/manual shift:** Parking brake might not hold.

PRICES

	Good	Average	Poor
1994 B2300	$2,000-2,600	$1,400-1,800	$300-400
B3000 2WD	2,500-3,500	1,800-2,600	500-700
B3000 4WD	3,000-3,800	2,300-2,900	700-900
B4000 2WD	3,200-4,000	2,500-3,100	800-1,000
B4000 4WD	4,200-5,500	3,400-4,500	1,400-1,800
1995 B2300 2WD	2,200-3,700	1,600-2,600	400-700
B2300 4WD	3,500-4,400	2,800-3,500	900-1,200
B3000 2WD	2,800-4,000	2,100-3,000	600-900
B3000 4WD	4,500-5,300	3,700-4,400	1,600-1,900
B4000 2WD	3,700-4,500	3,000-3,600	1,100-1,300
B4000 4WD	5,000-6,500	4,300-5,500	2,000-2,600
1996 B2300 2WD	2,600-4,500	1,900-3,300	500-900
B2300 4WD	4,200-5,000	3,400-4,100	1,400-1,700
B3000 2WD	4,500-5,300	3,700-4,400	1,600-1,900
B3000 4WD	6,000-6,800	5,200-5,900	2,500-2,900
B4000 2WD	4,800-5,500	4,000-4,600	1,800-2,100
B4000 4WD	5,800-7,000	5,000-6,100	2,400-2,900
1997 B2300 2WD	3,100-5,300	2,400-4,100	700-1,300
B2300 4WD	4,500-5,300	3,700-4,400	1,600-1,900
B4000 2WD	5,500-6,500	4,700-5,600	2,300-2,700
B4000 4WD	6,200-8,000	5,400-7,000	2,700-3,400

> For detailed information on this vehicle visit
> **http://used.consumerguide.com** and enter code **2195**

1998-03 MAZDA B-SERIES/TRUCK

CG BEST BUY

CLASS: Compact pickup truck

BUILT IN: USA

PROS: Acceleration (B4000)
• Build quality • Passenger room (regular cab)

CONS: Acceleration (B2500) • Engine noise • Rear-seat comfort (extended cab)

EVALUATION: Engines make the difference under B-Series hoods. Four-cylinder trucks struggle to gain speed when loaded with cargo or aimed uphill, especially with an automatic transmission. Even with manual shift, a 2WD 4-cylinder model took nearly 13 seconds to reach 60 mph. Fuel economy is more pleasing. We averaged 20.1 mpg in a 4-cylinder B2500.

We recommend the 4.0-liter V6, which uses only slightly more fuel than the 3.0 V6 and costs only slightly more. Although the 4.0 liter is a bit coarse and noisy, it offers plenty of low-speed torque and should perform most tasks with ease. That engine also works well with the 5-speed automatic transmission and furnishes prompt passing power. None of these engines is quiet, though the sixes are slightly smoother than the four. The OHC V6, added in 2001, is smooth, quieter than previous gruff 4.0.

Like its Ford Ranger cousin, the Mazda B-Series rides and handles admirably for a truck. Yes, it jiggles more on rough roads than most cars. Still, the suspension absorbs most bumps without jarring the occupants, and provides stable cornering with moderate body lean. The 4WD system cannot be used on dry pavement, but is otherwise as convenient as they come. A dashboard knob switches between 2- and 4-wheel drive while on the move.

Slightly roomier than before, with more behind-the-seat storage space, the regular-cab interior is still not spacious. The longer regular cab allows the seatback to be tilted farther back than before, and seat travel is greater than in some rivals. Still, taller drivers may find the Cab Plus layout a necessity for comfort. Some shorter drivers may declare the bottoms of the bucket seats to be too long, catching them behind the knees. The 4-door Cab Plus 4 option is a big plus, but those rear-hinged back doors are narrow and cannot be opened unless the front door has been opened first.

Even with a bench seat, three adults would be a tight squeeze up front. Entry/exit borders on awkward in the higher-riding 4x4s. Cab Plus models have a pair of child-sized rear seats that flip down from the sidewalls, but that area is more useful for cargo than people. Controls are positioned within easy reach, in a carlike interior, though the climate panel is recessed too much for quick adjustment. Radio controls are easier to use than in the

MAZDA

past. Solid in build, Mazda trucks use better quality interior materials than might be expected in a compact pickup.

VALUE FOR THE MONEY: Yes, Mazda pickups lack a few features available on rivals, including a third door (on extended-cab GM pickups) and the V8 option and full-time 4WD of a Dodge Dakota. Nevertheless, the B-Series is refined, well-built, and priced sensibly. No wonder Ranger has been the top-selling compact truck. Because Mazda's B-Series does not sell as well as the Ford Ranger, prices are likelier to be a bit lower than trucks wearing a Ford badge.

TROUBLE SPOTS
See the 1998-03 Ford Ranger.

AVERAGE REPLACEMENT COSTS
See the 1998-03 Ford Ranger.

NHTSA RECALL HISTORY
1998 B4000 w/2WD and 4.0-liter engine: Flexible section of fuel line is too close to exhaust manifold; could result in damage to fuel line, and possible leakage. **1998-99 w/cruise control:** Cable can interfere with speed-control-servo pulley and not allow throttle to return to idle when disengaging cruise control. **2000:** Seatbelt assemblies were not properly heat treated and therefore do not meet the load-bearing requirement of the standard. **2001:** Passenger's seatbelt buckle may not fully latch.

PRICES

	Good	Average	Poor
1998 B2500	$3,800-6,000	$3,100-4,900	$1,100-1,800
B3000 2WD	6,000-6,900	5,200-6,000	2,500-2,900
B3000 4WD	5,800-8,000	5,000-7,000	2,400-3,400
B4000 2WD	6,300-7,200	5,500-6,300	2,800-3,200
B4000 4WD	8,500-9,500	7,700-8,600	4,400-4,900
1999 B2500	4,300-7,000	3,500-5,700	1,500-2,400
B3000 2WD	7,000-8,000	6,200-7,100	3,400-3,800
B3000 4WD	7,300-9,500	6,600-8,600	3,600-4,700
B4000 2WD	6,000-8,000	5,200-7,000	2,500-3,400
B4000 4WD	9,200-10,500	8,300-9,500	4,800-5,500
2000 B2500	4,900-7,500	4,200-6,400	1,900-2,900
B3000 2WD	5,500-8,500	4,700-7,300	2,300-3,500
B3000 4WD	7,500-10,000	6,800-9,000	3,800-5,000
B4000 2WD	8,500-9,800	7,700-8,800	4,400-5,100
B4000 4WD	10,500-11,500	9,500-10,400	5,600-6,100
2001 B2500	5,600-8,000	4,800-6,900	2,300-3,300
B3000 2WD	6,500-9,500	5,700-8,400	2,900-4,300
B3000 4WD	8,500-11,000	7,700-9,900	4,400-5,700
B4000 2WD	10,000-11,000	9,000-9,900	5,200-5,700
B4000 4WD	12,000-13,000	10,800-11,700	6,700-7,300
2002 B2500	6,500-8,200	5,700-7,200	2,900-3,700
B3000 2WD	8,000-11,000	7,200-9,900	4,100-5,600
B3000 4WD	11,000-12,500	9,900-11,300	5,900-6,800
B4000 2WD	11,000-12,500	9,900-11,300	5,900-6,800
B4000 4WD	13,200-14,500	12,000-13,200	7,700-8,400

2003 B2500	$8,000-10,700	$7,200-9,600	$4,100-5,500
B3000 2WD	9,500-11,500	8,600-10,400	4,900-6,000
B3000 4WD	12,000-14,000	10,800-12,600	6,700-7,800
B4000 2WD	12,500-14,000	11,300-12,600	7,100-8,000
B4000 4WD	15,000-17,000	13,700-15,500	9,500-10,700

For detailed information on this vehicle visit
http://used.consumerguide.com and enter code **2325**

1990-97
MAZDA MIATA

CG BEST BUY

CLASS: Sports car
BUILT IN: Japan
PROS: Acceleration
(w/manual transmission)
• Antilock brakes (optional)
• Fuel economy
• Steering/handling
CONS: Cargo room
• Road noise

EVALUATION: The Miata is lively, agile, simple, and fun-to-drive. While off-the-line acceleration is not terrific (0-60 in about 8.3 seconds), it shows flashes of brilliance in 2nd and 3rd gear, and it gets great mileage, with 25-27 mpg possible on a regular basis. The Miata maneuvers beautifully, is easy to handle, and hugs the road snugly. The ride can be choppy at times, given the fact body flex is the bane of all convertibles. Extra bracing added for the 1994 model year seems to improve the situation, however.

Though the prominent exhaust note isn't inappropriate given the Miata's mission, there are also above-average quantities of wind and road noise. The cozy cockpit has well-placed gauges and controls, plus enough space to give tall people adequate room, permitting full enjoyment of the car's attributes. This is true despite the lack of any steering-wheel adjustment. Leg room is not a problem, but head room is tight.

One golf bag or a couple of gym bags and the tonneau cover are about all that will fit in the small trunk, which also holds the mini-spare. There's also usable storage behind the seats (perhaps as much as afforded by the trunk).

VALUE FOR THE MONEY: The first-generation Miata still looks and feels as good as it did when it arrived in 1989. If you're looking for an affordable, fun-to-drive sports car, there's little need to search further.

TROUBLE SPOTS

Audio system: If tapes get stuck in the Panasonic radio/tape player, the unit must be removed and sent to a factory service center. (1990)

Engine noise: A ticking noise from the top of the engine is likely due to inadequate hydraulic lash adjusters for the valves. (1990-93)

Oil leak: Early models often developed an oil leak at the plug in the drain pan unless the plug was tightened by hand with the gasket squarely in place before snugging with a wrench. (1990)

Timing belt: There is a revised, more-robust timing-belt tensioner pulley to replace the original. (1990-94)

Windows: The windows may not fully open because a cable comes loose blocking the window's travel. (1992-94)

AVERAGE REPLACEMENT COSTS

A/C Compressor	$435	Exhaust System	$290
Alternator	245	Radiator	500
Automatic Trans.	940	Shocks and/or Struts	645
Brakes	245	Timing Chain/Belt	205
Clutch	455	Universal Joints	380

NHTSA RECALL HISTORY

1990-91: Rear turn-signal lamps may have insufficient amount of reflecting paint on inner surface. **1990-93 w/optional hardtop:** Plastic buckles on optional hoist accessory kit can break, causing hardtop to fall. **1991 w/ABS:** Return-fluid line of front-brake system on some cars is misconnected to return; when antilock comes into use, all fluid from front brakes goes to rear system, which may lead to increased stopping distance. **1995:** Airbag could deploy as a result of minor undercarriage impact.

PRICES

	Good	Average	Poor
1990 Miata	$2,500-3,100	$1,800-2,300	$500-700
1991 Miata	3,000-3,700	2,300-2,800	700-900
1992 M-Edition	3,800-4,400	3,100-3,600	1,100-1,300
Miata	3,500-4,200	2,800-3,400	900-1,100
1993 M-Edition	4,400-5,000	3,700-4,200	1,500-1,800
Miata	4,000-4,800	3,300-3,900	1,300-1,500
1994 M-Edition	5,100-5,700	4,300-4,800	2,000-2,300
Miata	4,500-5,300	3,700-4,400	1,600-1,900
1995 M-Edition	5,700-6,400	4,900-5,500	2,300-2,600
Miata	5,000-5,800	4,300-4,900	2,000-2,300
1996 M-Edition	6,500-7,200	5,700-6,300	2,900-3,200
Miata	5,700-6,600	4,900-5,700	2,300-2,700
1997 M-Edition	7,800-8,500	7,000-7,700	4,000-4,300
Miata	6,800-7,700	6,100-6,900	3,200-3,600

For detailed information on this vehicle visit
http://used.consumerguide.com and enter code **2065**

1999-03
MAZDA MIATA

CG BEST BUY

CLASS: Sports car
BUILT IN: Japan
PROS: Acceleration
• Fuel economy
• Steering/handling
CONS: Cargo room
• Entry/exit • Noise

EVALUATION: In its modestly modified form, the Miata preserved its original fun-to-drive nature while adding a little muscle. Quite simply, Miatas represent front-engine sports-car tradition—in contrast to the Toyota MR2 Spyder, introduced for 2000, which is a midengine model. Both are terrific fun to drive. Mazda offers more cargo space, as well as brisk performance—especially at low speeds and when passing. An early example accelerated to 60 mph in about 8 seconds.

There seems to be no great difference in performance between the 5- and 6-speed manual transmission, but automatic-equipped Miatas are not nearly so responsive. As for economy, an early 5-speed model yielded 25.8 mpg.

Road, wind, and engine noise are prominent, but normal conversation is possible at 60 mph with the top down. Stopping power is strong and easily modulated. Over rippled pavement, some body flex and cowl shake is inevitable.

Handling is sheer delight—reflexes razor-sharp, with steering a model of accuracy. Stability on straightaways and in turns was improved. Factory-type tires, on the other hand, furnish poor traction on snow-covered pavement. Good winter tires are a far better choice.

Though not quite as spacious inside as the MR2, the Miata offers decent room for two medium-size adults, though six-footers have no excess of leg space. Entry/exit is a matter of bending and twisting, as in most true sports cars. The console lid release is hard to reach, and its cover must be open to use the poorly designed cupholders.

Small windows hamper visibility, but the defrosting glass back window is welcome. The trunk holds a couple of soft overnight bags. Workmanship is good, using quality materials and tight assembly.

VALUE FOR THE MONEY: Especially in base form, the Miata represents greater value than, say, a Toyota MR2 Spyder—partly due to its greater cargo capacity, which makes it a more practical driver. On the fun-per-dollar scale, a Miata is unmatched.

TROUBLE SPOTS

Cigarette lighter: The cigarette lighter can be easily damaged if an accessory with the wrong-size plug is installed in the outlet. (1999-01)

Cruise control: The cruise control may not hold steady (varying upward), or the decel feature may not work due to failed transistors in the control unit. (1999)

Engine noise: The bearing caps on some early production 1.8-L engines may not have been machined properly, causing a rattling noise from the engine requiring a new block. (1999)

Exhaust system: Muffler may rattle because the inner shell vibrates and a countermeasure muffler has been released with padding between the parts. (1999)

AVERAGE REPLACEMENT COSTS

A/C Compressor	$810	CV Joints	$890
Alternator	310	Exhaust System	350
Automatic Trans.	1,235	Radiator	300
Brakes	345	Shocks and/or Struts	955
Clutch	475	Timing Chain/Belt	265

NHTSA RECALL HISTORY

2001-03: Fog lights may have been installed improperly, and they may fall down into the bumper, causing it to burn. Dealer will inspect and replace all affected parts.

PRICES	Good	Average	Poor
1999 Miata	$10,000-11,500	$9,000-10,400	$5,200-6,000
2000 Miata	11,500-13,500	10,400-12,200	6,300-7,400
2001 Miata	13,200-15,200	12,000-13,800	7,700-8,800
2002 Miata	15,000-17,500	13,700-15,900	9,500-11,000
2003 Miata	17,000-20,000	15,600-18,400	10,900-12,800

For detailed information on this vehicle visit
http://used.consumerguide.com and enter code **2459**

2000-03 MAZDA MPV

CLASS: Minivan
BUILT IN: Japan
PROS: Cargo room
• Handling/roadholding
• Instruments/controls
• Passenger room
CONS: Acceleration
(2000-01) • Automatic-
transmission performance

EVALUATION: Because the MPV serves Mazda globally, exterior dimensions aim mainly at European and Asian use. Therefore, it's smaller than American minivan buyers might prefer.

Trimmer size brings performance benefits, however, led by good handling. With 16-inch wheels, an MPV carves corners with outstanding balance and grip. Close-quarters maneuverability also is impressive. Steering is faithful and communicative, antilock braking is linear and strong, the ride is flat, and bumps are absorbed capably.

On the down side, until the 3.0-liter V6 arrived for 2002, the vehicle was simply too heavy for its engine. Progress is okay from a standing start and in flatland cruising, but the early MPV feels underpowered in hilly terrain and when passing. In addition, its automatic transmission tends to settle into the least-optimal gear, then downshifts too late to be of much value. The 2.5-liter V6 also emits a coarse growl under even moderate throttle, though other sound levels are pleasantly low.

Despite its relative compactness, the MPV doesn't feel cramped. Front seating is spacious. Front- and second-row cushions are comfortably thick and supportive, though the third-row bench is flat and hard. The sliding second-row arrangement is useful, but exposed floor tracks may collect debris. Second- and third-row knee clearance is adequate for 6-footers.

Mazda's clever "tumble-under" rear bench, like that in Honda's Odyssey, flips to create rear-facing tailgate-party seating. It folds with little effort, and easily removable second-row seats weigh just 37 pounds each.

Attractive, readable gauges and simple controls are pleasing, though the gear selector blocks some radio buttons. Entry/exit isn't so convenient because side doors don't open far.

Performance definitely improved (though not dramatically so) with the bigger 2002 engine, though air-conditioner output is modest.

VALUE FOR THE MONEY: Although the small 2000-01 engine is easily overtaxed, the MPV does an admirable job of packaging people and cargo, while delivering sporty handling. Still, a Caravan or Odyssey is roomier and more powerful.

TROUBLE SPOTS

Dashboard lights: On early production vehicles, the check-engine light may come on reporting a problem with the oxygen sensors which are not the problem, but the powertrain-control module is misprogrammed. (2000)
Information stickers/paperwork: A recall was issued because the tire-specifications label on the door and in the owner's manual was incorrect. Owners were sent stickers to update the information which buyers should look for to avoid replacing the tires with the wrong size. (2000)
Paint/body: As a result of crash tests done by the Insurance Institute for Highway Safety, the carmaker will install front bumper supports at no cost. (2000)

AVERAGE REPLACEMENT COSTS

A/C Compressor	$650	CV Joints	$750
Alternator	410	Exhaust System	450
Automatic Trans.	1,200	Radiator	475
Brakes	465	Shocks and/or Struts	140
Clutch	410	Timing Chain/Belt	350

NHTSA RECALL HISTORY

2000: Fuel injectors were not properly matched to the lower intake manifold and may allow fuel leakage. **2000:** Rear doors may not lock completely when the childproof locking system is engaged due to accumulation of dust in the locking mechanism. **2000-01:** Due to inappropriate brake-pipe layout, some vehicles do not meet the brake stopping-distance requirements of the standard. **2001:** Some passenger-airbag modules were not properly welded and may not deploy in a collision. **2002:** The gross axle-weight rating (GAWR) is listed incorrectly on the certification label. **2002-03:** Improper wiring of front fog lights on certain vehicles may cause a fire. Dealer will inspect and replace affected parts.

PRICES	Good	Average	Poor
2000 MPV DX, LX	$10,000-11,200	$9,000-10,100	$5,200-5,800
MPV ES	12,000-13,200	10,800-11,900	6,700-7,400
2001 MPV DX, LX	12,000-13,500	10,800-12,200	6,700-7,600
MPV ES	14,500-15,700	13,200-14,300	9,000-9,700
2002 MPV ES	16,800-18,000	15,500-16,600	10,800-11,500
MPV LX	14,500-16,000	13,200-14,600	9,000-9,900

2003 MPV ES	$20,000-22,500	$18,400-20,700	$13,000-14,600
MPV LX	17,200-19,000	15,800-17,500	11,000-12,200

> For detailed information on this vehicle visit
> http://used.consumerguide.com and enter code **2460**

1990-92 MAZDA MX-6

CLASS: Sporty coupe
BUILT IN: Japan, USA
PROS: Acceleration (GT)
• Fuel economy
CONS: Automatic-transmission performance
• Torque steer (GT)

EVALUATION: Four-cylinder coupes produce reasonably brisk acceleration and enthusiastic passing power. Reluctant downshifting from the automatic transmission makes a manual-shift model the better choice, however. For a real kick in an MX-6, pick the GT with its turbocharged 4-cylinder engine, which delivers 145 horses. Gas mileage is a pleasant bonus with either transmission, though, as expected, an MX-6 is more frugal with stick shift.

These competent coupes feel roomier inside than before and deliver a soft, supple ride—if stiffer than a typical family car. Only the GT's ride might be considered harsh through rough surfaces. Handling and road-holding are capable enough, even in the DX version, suffering only moderate body lean in turns. Wind and tire noise can grow annoying. Engine noise also is stronger than in some Japanese-brand rivals.

Because the MX-6 coupe rides a shorter wheelbase than its 626 sedan sibling, rear leg room is a bit tighter. Cargo space also is above average for the car's class.

VALUE FOR THE MONEY: All in all, this is a nicely refined rival to the 2-door Honda Accord or Toyota Camry, and also a better daily driver than a rear-drive Ford Mustang or Chevrolet Camaro.

TROUBLE SPOTS

Suspension noise: A knocking noise from the front end when driving over speed bumps caused by defective spring seats. (1990-92)
Oil consumption: A plugged drainback hole in the cylinder head causes high oil consumption. (1991)

AVERAGE REPLACEMENT COSTS

A/C Compressor	$545	Exhaust System	$535
Alternator	235	Radiator	400
Automatic Trans.	1435	Shocks and/or Struts	700
Brakes	210	Timing Chain/Belt	180
Clutch	600		

NHTSA RECALL HISTORY

None to date.

PRICES

	Good	Average	Poor
1990 MX-6 DX, LX	$1,200-1,800	$700-1,100	$100-200
MX-6 GT, 4WS	1,500-2,100	1,000-1,400	200-300
1991 MX-6 DX, LX	$1,400-2,100	$900-1,300	$200-300
MX-6 GT	1,900-2,500	1,300-1,700	300-400
1992 MX-6 DX, LX	1,700-2,400	1,100-1,600	300-400
MX-6 GT	2,300-2,900	1,700-2,100	400-600

For detailed information on this vehicle visit
http://used.consumerguide.com and enter code 2198

1993-97 MAZDA MX-6

CLASS: Sporty coupe
BUILT IN: USA
PROS: Acceleration (V6)
• Antilock brakes (optional)
• Steering/handling
CONS: Automatic-transmission performance • Rear-seat room • Ride (LS)

EVALUATION: While we prefer the V6, be aware that the 4-cylinder engine does have adequate performance and better fuel economy. Equipped with a V6 and 5-speed, the coupe delivers willing performance and spirited acceleration. The engine has plenty of low-end torque and revs freely to redline. While the V6 runs smoothly and quietly at all speeds, the automatic tends to stifle the car's performance, even becoming balky when asked to perform a full-throttle downshift. The 4-cylinder likewise delivers decent power with the manual, but as expected, turns sluggish when paired with the automatic.

Handling is crisp and responsive, with little body roll in tight corners. Ride quality on the LS suffers some from the standard performance tires, which are rated for speeds up to 149 mph. However, the ride is still better than that provided by the Ford Probe GT. You can also expect the stiff tires to offer poor traction in snow. The MX-6 is a snug 2+2. Front head room and leg room are adequate for 6-footers, the rear seats are so tiny that even some small children may complain about the lack of space.

VALUE FOR THE MONEY: Ford's Probe has the same mechanical features but at a lower price. Both the MX-6 and Probe are the cream of the crop among sports coupes, in our view.

TROUBLE SPOTS

Engine knock: Cars with a V6 engine built before March 1993 may have engine knock, especially when cold, due to carbon buildup in the combustion chamber. (1993-94)

Engine mounts: Broken motor mounts allow the engine to rock back and forth when accelerating, decelerating, or starting from a stop. (1993-94)

Engine noise: A metallic tapping noise from the rear of the engine could be due to slippage between the exhaust-camshaft driven gear and friction gear. (1993-95)

MAZDA

Power seats: The insulation on the wires for the power seat can wear through causing a short circuit. (1993-94)

Transmission leak: A damaged torque-converter hub seal allows fluid to leak from the automatic transmission. (1994-96)

Vehicle shake: Vibrations in the steering wheel, shift lever, and floor are probably caused by mispositioned radiator dampers. (1993-95)

Wipers: The welds holding the wiper-arm support bracket break, causing a creak or rattle when the wipers are running. (1993-95)

AVERAGE REPLACEMENT COSTS

A/C Compressor	$360	CV Joints	$780
Alternator	245	Exhaust System	485
Automatic Trans.	1,075	Radiator	410
Brakes	275	Shocks and/or Struts	770
Clutch	590	Timing Chain/Belt	180

NHTSA RECALL HISTORY

1994: Headlight wire that runs through turn-signal lever can fail where it is soldered to switch, causing loss of headlights. **1995-96:** Airbag could deploy as a result of minor undercarriage impact. **1997:** Spring in timing-belt tensioner can break and get caught, resulting in possible engine stalling.

PRICES	Good	Average	Poor
1993 MX-6	$2,300-3,000	$1,700-2,200	$400-600
MX-6 LS	2,700-3,400	2,000-2,600	600-700
1994 MX-6	2,700-3,400	2,000-2,600	600-700
MX-6 LS	3,200-3,900	2,500-3,000	800-900
1995 MX-6	3,300-4,000	2,600-3,200	800-1,000
MX-6 LS	3,800-4,400	3,100-3,600	1,100-1,300
1996 MX-6	4,000-4,800	3,300-3,900	1,300-1,500
MX-6 LS	4,700-5,300	3,900-4,500	1,700-2,000
1997 MX-6	5,000-5,800	4,300-4,900	2,000-2,300
MX-6 LS	5,800-6,500	5,000-5,700	2,400-2,700

For detailed information on this vehicle visit
http://used.consumerguide.com and enter code **2067**

1995-98 MAZDA PROTEGE

CLASS: Subcompact car

BUILT IN: Japan

PROS: Optional antilock brakes (LX, ES) • Fuel economy • Passenger room • Ride

CONS: Acceleration (w/automatic transmission) • Entry/exit • Handling • Radio controls (1995-96)

344   CONSUMER GUIDE®

EVALUATION: Mazda obviously tuned the Protege's suspension more toward ride comfort than handling finesse, though steering response is good and the car reacts well in urban driving. Bumps are easily absorbed, though they often produce a loud "thump." Hard cornering brings lots of body lean, and the narrow 13-inch tires on DX and LX models start squealing early. The 14-inch ES tires have noticeably better cornering grip.

Space inside is ample for four adults, with abundant front head and rear leg room. However, rear doors are narrow at the bottom, making it awkward to climb in and out. You get a good-sized trunk and an average-sized glovebox.

The 1.5-liter engine in DX and LX models delivers adequate acceleration with a manual transmission, though it's sluggish with automatic. With a full load, the 1.5-liter 4-cylinder might be short on strength. Surprisingly, the 1.8-liter engine in the ES doesn't seem that much stronger, despite its 30-horsepower advantage. Highway passing and merging are notably easier, however. Both engines should return above-average fuel economy. A manual-shift LX averaged 30.2 mpg.

The dashboard is well laid out, with clear gauges and stalk-mounted light and wiper controls. Until the 1997 model year, however, the radio sat too low. Small buttons require a long look away from the road to make any adjustments. The radio moved to the top of the dashboard in 1997. Visibility is fine in all directions.

VALUE FOR THE MONEY: Exceptionally easy to drive, Protege provides a rewarding mixture of maneuverability, economy, and quietness, coupled with solid assembly quality.

TROUBLE SPOTS

Engine knock: If engine knock occurs in hot weather, there is a revised engine-control computer that will correct the problem. (1995-96)

Exhaust system: There is a new tailpipe tip available to eliminate a hooting noise from the exhaust. (1995-96)

Steering problems: The steering wheel may be off center requiring adjustment of the alignment (tie rods). (1995)

AVERAGE REPLACEMENT COSTS

A/C Compressor	$420	Exhaust System	$555
Alternator	350	Radiator	500
Automatic Trans.	1,460	Shocks and/or Struts	600
Brakes	230	Timing Chain/Belt	190
CV Joints	840		

NHTSA RECALL HISTORY

1995 w/1.5-liter engine: Valve springs can develop minute cracks and break; can cause engine chatter, piston damage, and stalling. **1995:** Headlight wire can fail, causing loss of headlights with or without prior warning.

PRICES	Good	Average	Poor
1995 Protege	$1,800-2,500	$1,200-1,700	$300-400
1996 Protege	2,200-3,200	1,600-2,300	400-600

MAZDA

1997 Protege	$2,800-4,000	$2,100-3,000	$600-900
1998 Protege	3,500-4,500	2,800-3,600	900-1,200

For detailed information on this vehicle visit
http://used.consumerguide.com and enter code **2200**

1999-03 MAZDA PROTEGE

CG BEST BUY

CLASS: Subcompact car

BUILT IN: Japan

PROS: Fuel economy
• Ride

CONS: Acceleration (w/automatic transmission)

EVALUATION: With the Protege, Mazda favors handling ability over ride comfort, unlike the tamer, softer Honda Civic or Toyota Corolla. Offering sportier road manners than many rivals, Proteges give a gener ally favorable impression, though the tradeoff is a slightly stiffer ride and markedly higher level of engine, road, and wind noise. Still, DX and LX editions take most bumps with firm control and yield a supple ride, with adequate steering and agile handling. Although the ES sedan shares their suspension, its high-profile tires—which sharpen handling—don't smother small road imperfections as well. Tepid acceleration is the foremost flaw of 1999-00 models. Both engines offered in that period are slow from a stop. Acceleration does improve at about 20 mph, but passing power is lacking. Performance is adequate with manual shift, and a 5-speed ES scoots through traffic well enough, but automatic is disappointing. The extra horsepower available in 2001 provides a modest but welcome improvement. Visibility is good all around. Bodies are solid, and paintwork and exterior trim equal Honda/Toyota quality.

Protege is one of the most spacious subcompact sedans, with relatively abundant front head room and rear leg room. Wide back doors make it easy to slide feet in and out. Rotary climate knobs are just out of the driver's reach, but the dashboard is well laid out. Open and covered bins, two cupholders, front-door map pockets, and a large glovebox provide good storage room. Trunk space is about average, though all models have a 60/40 split folding rear seatback.

VALUE FOR THE MONEY: Proteges often are overlooked by subcompact buyers. Too bad, because their roominess and driving pleasure equal—and even exceed—a Civic, Corolla, or Chevrolet Prizm. DX sedans, in particular, are a cut above most base-model subcompacts, with rich-looking plastic surfaces and appealing fabrics inside. Limited-edition MazdaSpeed models sell for considerably more than other models and really appeal only to enthusiasts.

TROUBLE SPOTS

Automatic transmission: The automatic transmission may not shift out of second or third gear due to a defective solenoid (the system stores the wrong trouble code often making diagnoses incorrect). The powertrain control module was being replaced under the standard warranty. (1999)

Battery: The battery may go dead due to excessive current drains from memories in components (like the radio memory or engine control computer). (1999)

Doors: The power door locks may malfunction if contacts get wet or corrode. Countermeasure switches with rubber seals are available and were being installed under the normal warranty. (1999)

Exhaust system: A booming noise from the exhaust system is corrected by installing a stiffener over the front muffler and a damper weight near the rear muffler. (1999-2000)

Keys: The key may be hard to insert or turn in the door lock because the flap breaks off and falls into the lock cylinder. (1999)

AVERAGE REPLACEMENT COSTS

A/C Compressor	$810	CV Joints	$1,200
Alternator	295	Exhaust System	355
Automatic Trans.	925	Radiator	435
Brakes	220	Shocks and/or Struts	1,300
Clutch	475	Timing Chain/Belt	265

NHTSA RECALL HISTORY

2000-01: Brake-fluid leakage could occur on certain vehicles, causing brake performance to be degraded.

PRICES

	Good	Average	Poor
1999 Protege DX, LX	$4,500-5,200	$3,700-4,300	$1,600-1,900
Protege ES	5,300-6,000	4,600-5,200	2,200-2,500
2000 Protege DX, LX	5,700-6,500	4,900-5,600	2,300-2,700
Protege ES	6,600-7,300	5,800-6,400	3,000-3,400
2001 Protege DX, LX	6,500-7,300	5,700-6,400	2,900-3,300
Protege ES	7,800-8,500	7,000-7,700	4,000-4,300
Protege MP3	10,500-11,500	9,500-10,400	5,600-6,100
2002 Protege DX, LX	8,000-8,900	7,200-8,000	4,100-4,500
Protege ES	9,300-10,000	8,400-9,000	4,800-5,200
Protege5	10,500-12,000	9,500-10,800	5,600-6,400
2003 Mazdaspeed Protege	15,500-17,000	14,100-15,500	9,800-10,700
Protege DX, LX	10,000-11,000	9,000-9,900	5,200-5,700
Protege ES	11,300-12,300	10,200-11,100	6,200-6,800
Protege5	12,500-14,000	11,300-12,600	7,100-8,000

For detailed information on this vehicle visit
http://used.consumerguide.com and enter code **2385**

2001-03
MAZDA TRIBUTE

CG BEST BUY

CLASS: Compact sport-utility vehicle
BUILT IN: USA
PROS: Cargo room
CONS: Control layout (2001) • Noise

EVALUATION: Tribute's performance and accommodations mirror those of similarly equipped Escapes. No four-door compact SUV has as much power as a V6 Tribute. Therefore, V6 models are among the quickest compact SUVs, taking just 8.9 seconds to accelerate to 60 mph. More important, you get ample power for stress-free passing and merging, though some drivers might like more muscle on long upgrades. Not only is acceleration satisfying, but the automatic transmission shifts smoothly.

An extended-use AWD V6 Tribute averaged 19.5 mpg, including some long highway trips. Regular fuel is used by both engines.

Tributes and Escapes have different suspension tuning, but both feel markedly taut, without wallow or float over dips and swells at highway speeds. Some sharp bumps can register abruptly, however.

Steering and handling beat most rivals. Directional stability is impressive, even in gusty crosswinds. In fast cornering, balance and grip are quite good. As in most SUVs, the body leans and the nose plows in quick, sharp turns. Otherwise, the Tribute is balanced and confident in directional changes. The Tribute has firmer steering than an Escape, but both are exceptionally direct.

Brakes have good stopping power, but some drivers might find nosedive excessive in hard stops. Noise levels are generally acceptable, but wind noise is prominent at speed and the tires whine on coarse pavement.

Instruments and controls are legible and generally well-placed. Climate and audio controls are high, within easy reach. Early automatic-transmission shift levers interfered with the driver's reach to the radio. The Ford-designed climate system does not allow independent control of air recirculation or air conditioning.

Tribute interiors feel slightly upscale, compared to the Escape's. Both are solid, with attractive materials.

Seats are firm and supportive. Taller riders might want more front head room in sunroof-equipped models, but clearance is otherwise generous. The airy, comfortable cabin belies the compact SUV's exterior dimensions. Driver views are unimpeded to sides and rear.

Not only is the Tribute more comfortable in back than any other compacts, it offers more rear knee and foot room than most midsize SUVs. The rear bench is tall and well-contoured, even at the inboard position. The floor is nearly flat, and the cabin is wide enough for three-adult comfort on short trips. Doorways are wide but step-in is higher than most compact SUVs.

Cargo room is generous. Rear seatbacks fold flat, once the headrests are removed and the seat bottoms tilted forward. The standard separate-opening rear glass is an added convenience.

VALUE FOR THE MONEY: Solid, substantial feeling, roomy, comfortable, and even fun to drive, the Tribute and its Escape cousin rank as compact SUV all-stars. They are also eminently sensible alternatives to any number of midsize SUVs, especially truck-based wagons, which are less efficient in their use of space and fuel.

TROUBLE SPOTS

Coolant leak: The low coolant light may come on in vehicles with the 3.0-liter engine because the float sinks in the coolant recovery tank and a revised assembly is available. (2001)

Engine stalling: During closed-throttle deceleration, the 3.0-liter engine may stall and may not illuminate the check-engine light. (2001-03)

Rough idle: When driving over 75 mph, some 2.0-liter engines may lose power then, once at idle, may run rough due to a problem with the speed-limiter algorithm in the computer which should be reprogrammed. (2001)

AVERAGE REPLACEMENT COSTS

A/C Compressor	$410	CV Joints	$1,950
Alternator	340	Exhaust System	385
Automatic Trans.	1,920	Radiator	455
Brakes	370	Shocks and/or Struts	1,132
Clutch	455	Timing Chain/Belt	450

NHTSA RECALL HISTORY

2001 2WD w/o antilock brakes: Improper rear hubs may cause rear wheels to separate from vehicle. Dealers will inspect and replace if necessary. **2001 w/cruise control:** The speed-control cable can have a cracked or missing servo cap. Over time, corrosion could interfere with the function of the speed control. Dealers will inspect and replace affected caps. **2001:** Incorrect steering-wheel nut can lead to steering-wheel separating from steering column. Dealers will inspect and replace affected steering-wheel assemblies. **2001:** O-ring seats in the fuel line might be damaged, causing an odor or fire. Dealers will inspect and replace affected fuel lines. **2001:** Owner's manuals do not indicate which seats are equipped child-restraint anchorages. Owners will be provided with revised owner manuals. **2001:** Windshield-wiper linkage can disengage, resulting in possible loss of wiper function. Dealers will inspect and replaced affected wiper linkages.

PRICES

	Good	Average	Poor
2001 Tribute 2WD	$10,700-13,500	$9,600-12,200	$5,700-7,200
Tribute 4WD	12,000-15,000	10,800-13,500	6,700-8,400
2002 Tribute	12,300-15,500	11,100-14,000	7,000-8,800
Tribute 4WD	13,800-17,500	12,600-15,900	8,400-10,700
2003 Tribute 2WD	14,000-18,200	12,700-16,600	8,500-11,100
Tribute 4WD	16,000-20,500	14,600-18,700	10,200-13,100

For detailed information on this vehicle visit
http://used.consumerguide.com and enter code **4489**

1990-95 MERCEDES-BENZ 300/E-CLASS

CLASS: Luxury car
BUILT IN: Germany
PROS: Antilock brakes
• Ride • Steering/handling
CONS: Automatic-transmission performance • Fuel economy • Price

EVALUATION: Acceleration with 6-cylinder engines ranges from tepid to adequate. Gathering passing power at 40-60 mph requires flooring the throttle at times, and then you endure a long pause before the transmission reacts. An early 300E 4Matic averaged 18.7 mpg. Adding a V8 engine was just what was needed to make the Mercedes-Benz sedans match the acceleration of the Japanese-built Lexus LS 400 and Infiniti Q45. Throttle response at midrange speeds is noticeably stronger than in 6-cylinder models, though the automatic transmission sometimes shifts with an unseemly jerk.

E-Class sedans are not very space-efficient, considering their 110.2-inch wheelbase. Front leg room is generous, but in the back it's only adequate. Because of rear-wheel-drive, with its intrusive drive-shaft tunnel and a rather narrow interior, three adults will find a tight fit in the back seat. Trunk space is adequate, however.

You can expect a stable, well-controlled highway ride, as well as precise steering and capable handling. With 4Matic 4-wheel-drive (available until 1994), it's virtually impossible to break the wheels loose. Even when you try to do so on wet pavement, this car sticks like glue. For drivers who don't need that much traction, ASD and ASR provide additional grip when it's needed, helping to maintain steering control.

VALUE FOR THE MONEY: Service and maintenance can be expensive, but the assurances of longevity compensate in the long run. Strong resale value keeps prices high on the secondhand market.

TROUBLE SPOTS

Automatic transmission: Harsh and erratic shifts are often due to a damaged dust cover on the vacuum modulator for the transmission. (1990-94)

Automatic transmission: The transmission may delay shifting into Drive or Reverse, and may be corrected by installing reformulated Mercedes-Benz transmission fluid. (1990)

Brakes: Brake squeal at low speeds (under 10 mph) may activate the antilock brake system. (1990-93)

Convertible top: The locking tabs for the convertible top tend to wear and should be checked every 15,000 miles. (1990)

Exhaust system: Possible exhaust leak at the oxygen sensor caused by damaged catalytic converter. (1990-91 diesel)

Oil leak: Oil enters the air filter. There are revised valve covers with improved oil separators available for the 3.0-liter engine. (1990)

AVERAGE REPLACEMENT COSTS

A/C Compressor	$925	Radiator	$400
Alternator	440	Shocks and/or Struts	1,440
Automatic Trans.	1,060	Timing Chain/Belt	645
Brakes	190	Universal Joints	685
Exhaust System	870		

NHTSA RECALL HISTORY

1990 300: Bolts used for brake-strut support do not meet specification and may break, resulting in deterioration of steering and braking. **1990 300:** Under certain operating conditions, plastic cover of preresistor for auxiliary fan may melt, which could result in underhood fire. **1991-92 400E:** If car is restarted soon after shutoff and charcoal canister is saturated with fuel, fuel vapor may be expelled onto electric-auxiliary radiator-fan preresistor; under certain conditions, that preresistor could become hot enough to ignite the fuel. **1992 w/"ASR" automatic slip control:** Plastic brake-hydraulic hose was misrouted too close to preresistor for auxiliary cooling fan, which becomes hot under certain conditions; could cause hose to melt and leak brake fluid onto hot preresistor, resulting in possible fire. **1992-95 E Class 124:** Front passenger metal footrest can, over time, abrade through wiring harness, causing short circuit; wires might then overheat, engine may stall, or airbag could inadvertently deploy.

PRICES

	Good	Average	Poor
1990 260E, 300D/E sedan	$4,500-6,000	$3,700-5,000	$1,600-2,200
300CE coupe	8,000-9,000	7,200-8,100	4,100-4,600
300TE wagon	7,500-8,400	6,800-7,600	3,800-4,200
1991 300CE coupe	9,000-10,000	8,100-9,000	4,700-5,200
300D/E sedan	5,200-7,000	4,400-6,000	2,100-2,800
300TE wagon	8,500-9,500	7,700-8,600	4,400-4,900
1992 300CE coupe	11,000-12,000	9,900-10,800	5,900-6,500
300D/E sedan	6,500-8,500	5,700-7,500	2,900-3,800
300TE wagon	9,500-10,500	8,600-9,500	4,900-5,500
400E sedan	9,800-11,000	8,800-9,900	5,100-5,700
500E sedan	14,000-15,500	12,700-14,100	8,500-9,500
1993 300CE convertible	20,500-22,500	18,900-20,700	13,300-14,600
300CE coupe	12,500-13,800	11,300-12,400	7,100-7,900
300D/E sedan	8,000-10,000	7,200-9,000	4,100-5,100
300TE wagon	11,000-12,500	9,900-11,300	5,900-6,800
400E sedan	11,000-12,500	9,900-11,300	5,900-6,800
500E sedan	17,000-18,500	15,600-17,000	10,900-11,800
1994 E320	10,000-13,500	9,000-12,200	5,200-7,000
E320 convertible	23,000-25,000	21,200-23,000	15,000-16,300
E420	12,500-14,000	11,300-12,600	7,100-8,000
E500	21,000-23,000	19,300-21,200	13,700-15,000

MERCEDES-BENZ

1995 E300D/320	12,000-17,000	10,800-15,300	6,700-9,500
E320 convertible	26,000-28,000	24,200-26,000	17,200-18,500
E420	14,500-16,000	13,200-14,600	9,000-9,900

For detailed information on this vehicle visit
http://used.consumerguide.com and enter code **2205**

1994-00 MERCEDES-BENZ C-CLASS

CLASS: Near-luxury car

BUILT IN: Germany

PROS: Acceleration (C280, C36) • Antilock brakes • Steering/handling

CONS: Wet-weather traction • Rear-seat room • Road noise

EVALUATION: Both the 4- and 6-cylinder engines are quiet and refined, even when pushed hard, but suffer rather leisurely acceleration from a standing start. Both of the 2001 V6 engines are quite smooth. The older engines do gather steam quickly and deliver strong passing power—especially the C280. A C280 sedan accelerated to 60 mph in a brief 8.3 seconds. The C320, introduced in 2001, did 0-60 in just 7.2 sec. The automatic transmission downshifts promptly to deliver passing power when it's needed, though upshifts can feel sloppy during hard acceleration.

Steering response is excellent, and handling is balanced with fine grip through turns. You'll feel most of the bumps in either of these cars, even though the firm suspension absorbs the worst of the impacts. Road noise intrudes on the pleasure, too—especially emanating from the rear tires.

Controls are laid out in a user-friendly manner, and you get a comfortable driving position. Though more spacious than its 190 predecessor, the C-Class isn't exactly roomy. Tall drivers might lack sufficient head or leg room, even with the seat position considerably rearward. Moving the driver's seat all the way back drastically cuts into rear leg space, which is only adequate even under the best conditions. Cargo space is good in a usefully square trunk, and an optional folding rear seatback provides extra space.

VALUE FOR THE MONEY: All told, we've been impressed with the C-Class. This sedan is well worth a look if you're shopping in the luxury end of the compact-car league.

TROUBLE SPOTS

Brake noise: Brake squeal at low speeds (under 10 mph) may activate the antilock brake system. (1994-97)

Clock: The clock on the C220 may reset itself when starting the engine due to a faulty instrument-cluster voltage regulator. (1994)

Dashboard lights: The EC warning light may come on indicating loss of A/C refrigerant caused by a faulty refrigerant pressure sensor. (1997)

Fuel gauge: Erroneous fuel-gauge readings are often due to a bad potentiometer on the fuel-level sensor. (1994-96)

Hard starting: The starter may corrode due to the windshield water draining onto it. (1994-96)

AVERAGE REPLACEMENT COSTS

A/C Compressor	$865	Radiator	$445
Alternator	330	Shocks and/or Struts	1,200
Automatic Trans.	1,035	Timing Chain/Belt	305
Brakes	200	Universal Joints	545
Exhaust System	650		

NHTSA RECALL HISTORY

1994 C220: Cruise-control linkage may be inadequately lubricated, subject to binding, so throttle will not return to closed position when pedal is released. **1994-95 C220/C280, C36:** In minor frontal impact, hood-latch hook may not function properly as secondary safety catch. **1996 C280:** Drive-belt pulley of a few 6-cylinder engines can develop fatigue cracks and break; car would then lack engine cooling, battery charging, and/or power steering. **1998-99 w/Hoppecke battery:** Battery-maintenance schedule could be less than needed to maintain proper electrolyte levels. Low electrolyte levels could result in battery explosion.

PRICES

	Good	Average	Poor
1994 C220	$7,200-8,100	$6,400-7,200	$3,500-4,000
C280	8,500-9,500	7,700-8,600	4,400-4,900
1995 C220	8,000-9,000	7,200-8,100	4,100-4,600
C280	9,500-10,500	8,600-9,500	4,900-5,500
C36	15,000-16,500	13,700-15,000	9,500-10,400
1996 C220	9,000-10,000	8,100-9,000	4,700-5,200
C280	10,700-12,000	9,600-10,800	5,700-6,400
C36	16,800-18,300	15,500-16,800	10,800-11,700
1997 C230	10,500-11,700	9,500-10,500	5,600-6,200
C280	12,500-13,800	11,300-12,400	7,100-7,900
C36	19,000-20,500	17,500-18,900	12,400-13,300
1998 C230	12,500-14,000	11,300-12,600	7,100-8,000
C280	14,500-16,000	13,200-14,600	9,000-9,900
C43	22,000-23,500	20,200-21,600	14,300-15,300
1999 C230	15,000-16,500	13,700-15,000	9,500-10,400
C280	17,000-18,500	15,600-17,000	10,900-11,800
C43	24,500-26,500	22,800-24,600	15,900-17,200
2000 C230	17,500-19,000	16,100-17,500	11,200-12,200
C280	20,000-21,500	18,400-19,800	13,000-14,000
C43	28,500-31,000	26,500-28,800	19,400-21,100

For detailed information on this vehicle visit
http://used.consumerguide.com and enter code **2204**

1996-02 MERCEDES-BENZ E-CLASS

CG BEST BUY

CLASS: Luxury car
BUILT IN: Germany
PROS: Acceleration (gas engines) • Build quality
• Quietness • Ride/handling
CONS: Fuel economy (except diesel)
• Instruments/controls • Price

EVALUATION: All E-Class sedans are more athletic than most luxury 4-door models, if not so nimble as, say, a 5-Series BMW or Lexus GS. Steering is firm and precise, body lean modest in hard cornering. The taut suspension provides a comfortable highway ride and smothers most bumps and ruts around town. Silence is another virtue, so these sedans cruise quietly at highway speeds.

Space is ample for four adults in any E-Class sedan, though a bulky transmission tunnel precludes true long-distance comfort for the person in the center rear position. All models offer good cargo capacity, flat load floors, large trunk openings, and low liftovers. The wagon's third seat easily folds flush with the cargo deck, but it's sized more for youngsters than grownups. The E-Class pilot gets good visibility from a comfortable, easily tailored driver's position. Gauges and controls are well-designed and well laid out, though markings on too many of the switches are not obvious.

Acceleration is satisfying even in the Turbodiesel model, and brisk in the E320, which uses a smooth and responsive 6-cylinder gas engine. Moving up a notch, a recent E430 delivers stirring highway passing power. The automatic transmission downshifts promptly to deliver strong passing response.

Fuel mileage is best with a diesel. An E320 sedan with the inline gas six got a so-so average of 21.1 mpg, with more than half the driving on highways. The V8 E420 amounts to a Teutonic muscle car, but it gets quite thirsty for fuel. Workmanship, as expected, is top-notch.

VALUE FOR THE MONEY: With its exceptional quality and strong performance, the E-Class deserves strong consideration among premium sedans. Best choice for value is the E320. With any model, high resale values translate to hefty prices on the used-car market.

TROUBLE SPOTS

Dashboard lights: A malfunction in the fuel-tank pressure sensor or the purge-control valve (or both) will cause the check-engine light to come on. (1997-98)

Headlights: Headlight and parking-light bulbs burn out prematurely on E300 models and a kit with new sockets and bulbs is available. (1996-97)

AVERAGE REPLACEMENT COSTS

A/C Compressor	$390	Exhaust System	$845
Alternator	480	Radiator	440

Automatic Trans.	$1,190	Shocks and/or Struts	$1,630
Brakes	330	Timing Chain/Belt	710
CV Joints	845		

NHTSA RECALL HISTORY

1996 E320: Drive-belt pulley on some cars can break. **1997:** Some passenger vehicles have experienced side airbag deployments in the absence of a crash. **1999:** Due to the installation of an incorrect clamp, the side airbag may not deploy fully in a collision.

PRICES	Good	Average	Poor
1996 E300D	$14,000-15,000	$12,700-13,700	$8,500-9,200
E320	15,000-16,000	13,700-14,600	9,500-10,100
1997 E300D	16,500-17,500	15,000-15,900	10,600-11,200
E320	17,500-19,000	16,100-17,500	11,200-12,200
E420	19,000-20,500	17,500-18,900	12,400-13,300
1998 E300TD	19,000-20,500	17,500-18,900	12,400-13,300
E320	20,000-21,500	18,400-19,800	13,000-14,000
E430	22,000-24,000	20,200-22,100	14,300-15,600
1999 E300TD	21,500-23,000	19,800-21,200	14,000-15,000
E320	22,500-24,000	20,700-22,100	14,600-15,600
E430	25,000-27,000	23,300-25,100	16,500-17,800
E55	35,000-37,500	32,600-34,900	24,900-26,600
2000 E320	27,500-30,500	25,600-28,400	18,400-20,400
E430	30,000-32,000	27,900-29,800	21,000-22,400
E55	40,000-42,500	37,200-39,500	28,800-30,600
2001 E320	31,500-35,500	29,300-33,000	22,100-24,900
E430	35,000-37,000	32,600-34,400	24,900-26,300
E55	45,500-48,500	42,800-45,600	33,700-35,900
2002 E320	35,500-39,500	33,000-36,700	25,200-28,000
E430	39,500-42,500	36,700-39,500	28,400-30,600
E55 AMG	51,000-54,000	47,900-50,800	38,300-40,500

For detailed information on this vehicle visit
http://used.consumerguide.com and enter code **2273**

1998-01 MERCEDES-BENZ M-CLASS

CLASS: Luxury sport-utility vehicle

BUILT IN: USA

PROS: Acceleration (ML430, ML55 AMG) • Build quality • Cargo room • Steering/handling

CONS: Fuel economy • Ride (ML430, ML55 AMG)

MERCEDES-BENZ

EVALUATION: Seeking to create an SUV that drives like a car, Mercedes-Benz took a clear lead. A Lexus RX 300 or BMW X5 feels more carlike, but few true SUVs are more pleasant to drive than an M-Class. Though an ML320 isn't that snappy moving from a stop, the smooth, responsive automatic transmission helps get the best out of its V6 engine. V8 models are noticeably quicker. Off-the-line-punch isn't great, but the ML430 gathers speed quickly and has good passing power. An ML320 accelerated to 60 mph in 9.1 seconds and averaged 13.9 to 15 mpg. An ML430 averaged 15.7 mpg, but the high-performance ML55 got only 12.9 mpg.

Wind and road noise are low for an SUV, if higher than those of the RX300. Both V8 engines emit a throaty roar under hard throttle, but the V6 sounds coarse when pushed.

Poised and stable in tight turns, the ML320 moves with far less body lean than most SUVs. Steering is precise and linear, though self-centering is weak. Braking is strong and stable. A smooth, supple, on-road ride is the rule in an ML320. Firmer suspensions and low-profile tires make other models stiff over bumps and broken pavement. Although the unique 4ETS system works transparently in light-duty, off-pavement driving, it's not as effective as traditional 4WD setups in heavy snow or on demanding off-road trails. Four adults have ample room, and three can almost fit comfortably in back. The rear seat slides forward about 3 inches for extra cargo space, but rear leg room then becomes tight. Step-in height is much lower than the SUV norm. Unusually wide doors provide easy entry/exit. Controls are easy to find and use, though some markings are not obvious. Outward vision is fine forward, but a bit cluttered by headrests directly astern. Load volume is ample and easy to use, with a low, flat floor. Sturdy construction is evident, despite occasional body shudder on rough surfaces.

VALUE FOR THE MONEY: Mercedes leads the true-SUV pack for its blend of refinement, handling, overall competence, and carlike convenience. Strong resale values keep prices high.

TROUBLE SPOTS

Engine knock: A knocking noise from the accessory drive belt or water pump is caused by the idler pulley not providing even tension. A countermeasure pulley with a smaller diameter will correct the problem. (1998)

Engine misfire: Engine roughness, miss, or stalling may be due to a damaged mass-airflow sensor (MAF). This dirt may be getting past the air cleaner due to a damaged gasket, loose cover or improperly installed air cleaner. (1998)

Fuel gauge: The fuel gauge may not read full although the tank is full. The fuel-sending unit was being replaced under warranty. (1998)

Oil leak: Engine oil may weep from the head gasket. Gaskets are being replaced under warranty. (1998)

AVERAGE REPLACEMENT COSTS

A/C Compressor	$915	Exhaust System	$775
Alternator	1,025	Radiator	810
Automatic Trans.	910	Shocks and/or Struts	990
Brakes	565	Timing Chain/Belt	515
CV Joints	1,750		

NHTSA RECALL HISTORY

1998-99: Latching mechanism on seatbelt assembly was not assembled correctly. If plastic cover is loose during engagement of buckle tongue, the buckle could unlatch. **2000:** Seatbelt anchor in rear-folding middle seating position may fail in a crash. **2001:** Faulty AAM II units could cause failure of high-beam lights, instrument cluster, door locks, and wiper systems.

PRICES

	Good	Average	Poor
1998 ML320	$15,500-17,000	$14,100-15,500	$9,900-10,900
1999 ML320	18,500-20,000	17,000-18,400	11,800-12,800
ML430	20,500-22,500	18,900-20,700	13,300-14,600
2000 ML320	22,000-23,500	20,200-21,600	14,300-15,300
ML430	24,500-26,500	22,800-24,600	15,900-17,200
ML55 AMG	35,000-37,000	32,600-34,400	24,900-26,300
2001 ML320	25,000-26,500	23,300-24,600	16,500-17,500
ML430	28,000-30,000	26,000-27,900	19,000-20,400
ML55 AMG	39,500-41,500	36,700-38,600	28,400-29,900

> For detailed information on this vehicle visit
> http://used.consumerguide.com and enter code **2386**

1998-03 MERCEDES-BENZ SLK

CLASS: Sports car
BUILT IN: Germany
PROS: Acceleration • Build quality • Side airbags • Steering/handling
CONS: Cargo room • Engine noise

EVALUATION: Acceleration off the line is a bit leisurely, but speed gathers quickly once the supercharger hits full puff, at about 3000 rpm. Test manual SLK320 ran 0-60 mph in brisk 7.4 sec. The SLK230 takes 8.4 and can feel sleepy, though it goes well once its supercharger starts delivering. Midrange power is strong and satisfying, but in some situations, you get a lag between flooring the throttle and feeling extra thrust—a delay that can be frustrating in city driving. The automatic transmission furnishes the right gear for most occasions, and smooth, generally prompt shift action. It also helps fuel economy. We averaged nearly 24 mpg in fast highway driving. Expect 17-18 mpg in city/suburban driving with a light right foot.

Despite having a long first-to-second shift "throw" and a rubbery feel, the manual gearbox made available in 1999 gives the SLK stronger sports-car credibility. Even if that 5-speed does not shift as crisply as some, it does make the car feel more sporty.

MERCEDES-BENZ

Though smooth for a four, the engine emits an unbecoming, coarse growl when worked hard. Exhaust sound is audible too, but things settle down to a low hum at cruising speeds. Wind noise is modest, with the top and windows raised. Road rumble is prominent, except on glassy asphalt—a penalty of the car's aggressive tires. Those tires also make for a thumpy roar over expansion joints and broken pavement, but big ruts and bumps are smothered quite well.

Entry/exit is tricky, with the low-slung build. The driving position is snug. Even so, 6-footers won't complain in either seat, both of which are firm and comfortable for long drives. Gauges are "retro" stylish, informative, and very readable. Controls are conveniently laid out, but we've been dismayed by door windows that don't quite lower all the way, leaving a half-inch ridge of glass. The hardtop lowers in a trice, but cuts trunk space by two-thirds, to little more than three cubic feet below a pull-out vinyl cover. That cover must be deployed to operate the top, because it's actually a safety switch to prevent the roof from accidentally crushing luggage. Top up, the trunk's 9.5 cubic feet will carry soft baggage for two on a long weekend, but the space is very oddly shaped.

Some minor body tremors may be noticed with the top down, but only on very rough roads. Too bad the dashboard's pop-out cupholder is so rickety, and the radio reception can be surprisingly mediocre.

VALUE FOR THE MONEY: Early buyers had to put their names on a waiting list, due to the SLK's popularity. Mercedes' coupe/roadster isn't cheap, but there's nothing else quite like the SLK on any road.

TROUBLE SPOTS

Fuel pump: When refueling at a rapid rate, fuel may spit back from the filler neck as the tank approaches full. (1999)

AVERAGE REPLACEMENT COSTS

A/C Compressor	$770	Exhaust System	$880
Alternator	490	Radiator	700
Automatic Trans.	1,245	Shocks and/or Struts	1,295
Brakes	610	Timing Chain/Belt	415
CV Joints	1,435		

NHTSA RECALL HISTORY

2000: A safety-improvement campaign to fix side airbags that may suddenly deploy in hot weather is offered by Mercedes-Benz. **2001-02:** Owner's manual does not contain the proper headlamp-aiming instructions.

PRICES

	Good	Average	Poor
1998 SLK230	$19,500-21,000	$17,900-19,300	$12,700-13,700
1999 SLK230	22,000-23,500	20,200-21,600	14,300-15,300
2000 SLK230	24,500-26,000	22,800-24,200	15,900-16,900
2001 SLK230	27,000-28,500	25,100-26,500	18,100-19,100
SLK320	30,000-32,000	27,900-29,800	21,000-22,400
2002 SLK230	30,000-32,000	27,900-29,800	21,000-22,400
SLK32 AMG	40,000-43,000	37,200-40,000	28,800-31,000
SLK320	34,000-36,500	31,600-33,900	24,100-25,900

2003 SLK230	$35,000-37,000	$32,600-34,400	$24,900-26,300
SLK32 AMG	46,000-49,000	43,200-46,100	34,000-36,300
SLK320	39,000-42,000	36,300-39,100	28,100-30,200

For detailed information on this vehicle visit
http://used.consumerguide.com and enter code **2328**

1999-02 MERCURY COUGAR

CLASS: Near-luxury car
BUILT IN: USA
PROS: Exterior finish
• Ride (base suspension)
CONS: Rear-seat room
• Rear visibility

EVALUATION: Reasonably peppy with the base engine, a Cougar gains some low-end muscle if equipped with the V6, but passing power is unimpressive. So is acceleration, with almost 10 seconds needed to reach 60 mph in an automatic-transmission Cougar. The automatic shifts fluidly, but hunts annoyingly between gears in hilly terrain and lacks a provision to lock out overdrive fourth gear. Neither engine matches Japanese-brand rivals for refinement or high-revving fun. As for economy, we averaged 19.9 mpg with a five-speed V6, and 20.7 with automatic. Cougars handle well, gripping nicely in sweeping turns, but lack the twisty-road agility and poise offered by most import brands. A long wheelbase (for a coupe) hampers nimbleness, but helps the base suspension yield a relatively comfortable ride. The V6 Sport Group improves roadability, but at the expense of a thumpy, nervous ride. Brake-pedal feel has been inconsistent, ranging from mushy to touchy on new test models, though stopping power is adequate. Road rumble and exhaust noise are intrusive. Front head and leg room are adequate in a rather claustrophobic interior. Bucket seats afford good lateral support, but aren't the most comfortable. The cramped rear seat is for preteens, with poorly shaped cushions. Split folding rear seatbacks provide generous cargo space, but liftover is high. Lack of a redline on the tachometer, and low radio controls, mar an otherwise appealing dashboard. In addition, the cabin abounds with hard, cheap-looking plastic.

VALUE FOR THE MONEY: With their "new-edge" look, Cougars earn points for style and originality in the trendy sports-coupe segment, but score weaker in practical virtues and driving satisfaction. Most competitive threat is the Mitsubishi Eclipse, which was much improved for 2000 and handles better. A Dodge Avenger/Stratus coupe is roomier, and an Acura CL or Honda Prelude costs considerably more.

TROUBLE SPOTS

Automatic transmission: Automatic-transmission fluid may leak from the vent hose. A redesigned hose is available. (1999-2000)

Climate control: The blower may not work if the blower resistor goes bad. It is being replaced under warranty up to 6 years or 72,000 miles. (1999-2000)

Engine misfire: The 2.5L and 3.0L engines were built with the timing marks for the camshafts in the wrong place and if replacement timing chains are installed using the marks, severe engine damage will result. (1999)

Hard starting: The engine may not start if the windshield-wiper switch is in the low or intermittent position because the wiper wiring was installed too close to the antitheft control module. (1999-2000)

Sunroof/moonroof: If the sunroof rattles, there are revised guide shoes available. (1999)

AVERAGE REPLACEMENT COSTS

A/C Compressor	$395	CV Joints	$850
Alternator	535	Exhaust System	650
Automatic Trans.	790	Radiator	405
Brakes	455	Shocks and/or Struts	1,300
Clutch	390	Timing Chain/Belt	560

NHTSA RECALL HISTORY

1999: An open circuit in the wiring harness could lead to electrical arcing that could melt the connector housing material, increasing the potential for a fire. **1999:** Brake-lamp-switch terminals could overheat, potentially causing either loss of brake-lamp function or continuously illuminated brake lamps. **1999:** In high humidity, door-latch pawl on certain cars may stick in open or unlatched position, and door will not latch when closed. **1999:** Rough surface of heater-blower resistor's stainless-steel blades can damage the copper surface of wiring-harness connector, eventually resulting in increased resistance and an open circuit, leading to electrical arcing. **1999-00 w/V6:** Battery cable may be misrouted and attachment to alternator cable under-torqued. If misrouted, cable could contact power-steering line and insulation could wear, resulting in electrical short. **2000-01 w/adjustable pedals:** If grease from pedal assembly enters stoplamp switch, it can contaminate contacts leading to carbon buildup and, potentially, a short circuit.

PRICES

	Good	Average	Poor
1999 Cougar	$6,000-7,200	$5,200-6,300	$2,500-3,000
2000 Cougar	7,200-8,700	6,400-7,700	3,500-4,300
2001 Cougar	8,700-10,500	7,800-9,500	4,500-5,500
2002 Cougar	10,500-12,500	9,500-11,300	5,600-6,600

For detailed information on this vehicle visit
http://used.consumerguide.com and enter code **2388**

1992-03 MERCURY GRAND MARQUIS

CLASS: Full-size car
BUILT IN: Canada
PROS: Acceleration
• Antilock brakes (optional)
• Passenger and cargo room
CONS: Climate controls
• Fuel economy • Radio controls (early models)
• Steering feel

EVALUATION: Mercury's flagship, the Grand Marquis, offers adult-size space front and rear with limousinelike entry and exit. Extra room is what you expect with the Grand Marquis, and you get it. There's over 20 cubic feet of cargo space in the deep trunk, but much of the volume is in a center well that doesn't easily accept bulky objects.

Under the hood sits Ford's overhead camshaft V8, which provides the car with more than adequate amounts of horsepower and torque. The engine is also quiet and enables the Grand Marquis to accelerate the way you expect a large car to do. Stoplight launches aren't exactly the best, but highway passing power is more than ample. We averaged a mediocre 17.3 mpg, with nearly half of the driving on highways and expressways. Marauder V8s move out with more authority—reminding us of the mid-90s Chevy Impala SS models. Surprisingly, we averaged 17.6 mpg with the high-output V8, but premium-grade fuel is required.

Steering on base model is feather-light, devoid of feel, and base suspension still tends to be on the soft side, so try to find a model equipped with the optional Handling Package, which includes a rear air suspension, larger stabilizer bar, tuned suspension parts, dual exhausts, a 3.27 rear axle ratio, and larger 225/60R16 tires mounted on alloy wheels. The beefed-up suspension helps reduce body roll and gives the car better cornering grip. Marauder models hold the road much better and have sharper steering, but their performance tires are not suited for winter driving.

VALUE FOR THE MONEY: The Grand Marquis stacks up just fine against its rivals from GM: the Buick Roadmaster and Chevrolet Caprice, both of which were eliminated in 1997. Overall, however, we recommend some of the more efficient front-drive full-size sedans, such as the Buick LeSabre, Pontiac Bonneville SSE, Chrysler LHS, and Dodge Intrepid.

TROUBLE SPOTS

See the 1992-03 Ford Crown Victoria.

AVERAGE REPLACEMENT COSTS

See the 1992-03 Ford Crown Victoria

NHTSA RECALL HISTORY

1992-93: Speed-control deactivation switch can develop short that could potentially result in underhood fire. **1994:** Nuts and bolts that attach rear brake adapter to axle-housing flange can loosen, allowing damage to ABS sensor, hydraulic line, or parking-brake cable. **1995:** Heads of rivets holding rear-outboard seatbelt D-rings may fracture under load, reducing belt's restraining capability in an accident. **1995:** Noncycling power-window circuit breaker and cycling-type headlamp breaker were interchanged; in the event of short or overload in circuit, both headlamps can go out without warning. **1995:** Seal between fuel-filler pipe and fuel tank may not be fully cured, which could allow fuel to leak. **1995:** Some passenger-side airbags may not inflate properly; also, igniter end cap can separate, causing hot gases to be released. **1996:** Driver's door, when closed only to secondary latched position, may not sustain the specified 1000-pound transverse load. **1996-00:** Replacement seatbelts made by TRW and sold by Ford may not restrain occupant in a collision. **1998-00:** Jacking instructions are incorrect and, if followed, could allow vehicle to drop suddenly. **2000:** During high-load conditions (ice, snow, or other debris), windshield wipers could become inoperative with no advance warning. **2000:** Left-rear seatbelt-retractor attaching bolts may have been incorrectly tightened. **2000:** Loose module could result in delayed airbag deployment. **2001:** A restraint-control module (RCM) or a side- or front-crash sensor may have been assembled with one or more of the screws that mount the circuit board in the housing missing. **2001:** Driver- and/or outboard front-passenger's seatbelt buckle may not fully latch. In the event of a crash, the restraint system may not provide adequate occupant protection.

PRICES

	Good	Average	Poor
1992 Grand Marquis	$2,400-3,000	$1,800-2,200	$500-600
1993 Grand Marquis	2,700-3,400	2,000-2,600	600-700
1994 Grand Marquis	3,100-3,800	2,400-3,000	700-900
1995 Grand Marquis	3,500-4,200	2,800-3,400	900-1,100
1996 Grand Marquis	4,000-4,900	3,300-4,000	1,300-1,600
1997 Grand Marquis	5,000-6,000	4,300-5,100	2,000-2,400
1998 Grand Marquis	6,300-7,400	5,500-6,500	2,800-3,300
1999 Grand Marquis	8,000-9,200	7,200-8,300	4,100-4,700
2000 Grand Marquis	9,500-10,700	8,600-9,600	4,900-5,600
2001 Grand Marquis	11,000-12,600	9,900-11,300	5,900-6,800
2002 Grand Marquis	13,500-15,500	12,300-14,100	8,000-9,100
2003 Grand Marquis	16,000-18,500	14,600-16,800	10,200-11,800

For detailed information on this vehicle visit
http://used.consumerguide.com and enter code **2069**

1997-01 MERCURY MOUNTAINEER

CLASS: Midsize sport-utility vehicle

BUILT IN: USA

PROS: Acceleration
• Antilock brakes • Passenger and cargo room • Visibility

CONS: Fuel economy • Ride

EVALUATION: Meager gas mileage is a major drawback. An early Mountaineer with the V8 averaged 16.1 mpg, and barely managed 18 mpg on the highway—roughly identical to the EPA estimates. Later models might not even do that well.

Virtues are the same as the Explorer's, including a roomy and comfortable interior, good visibility to all directions, and strong acceleration from the V8 engine. Permanent all-wheel drive is handy and works as promised, giving the Mountaineer good traction when needed, without any guesswork or action by the driver.

Although the V6 engine of 1998-99 cannot match the V8's muscle, its 5-speed automatic transmission does an admirable job of keeping the engine in its power band. Control Trac 4WD is more convenient than the systems offered by competitors.

A Mountaineer corners confidently, with less body lean than some rivals. At the same time, the ride can get more bouncy and trucklike than those competitors. Road and wind noise at highway speeds are not particularly intrusive. The interior is roomier than that of a Jeep Grand Cherokee or Chevrolet Blazer/GMC Jimmy. Space is ample for four adults, and three can sit in back for relatively short distances. Most switchgear is easy to reach, though climate controls are low on the dashboard. Deep side and rear windows and well-positioned outside mirrors give the driver a clear view of surrounding traffic.

VALUE FOR THE MONEY: We rate both the popular Explorer and its Mercury mate highly in the SUV league. Though engine choices aren't identical, the two models provide similar performance and accommodations, with sound ergonomics in a roomy cabin.

TROUBLE SPOTS

See the 1991-03 Ford Explorer/SportTrac/Sport.

AVERAGE REPLACEMENT COSTS

See the 1991-03 Ford Explorer/SportTrac/Sport.

NHTSA RECALL HISTORY

1997: After operation at highway speeds, at below -20 degrees (F), engine may not return to idle. **1997:** Gas-cylinder bracket may not properly support rear liftgate. **1997-98 w/4.0-liter engine:** A gap between the plate and bore of throttle body was too narrow, causing the throttle pedal to stick. **1997-98 w/SOHC 4.0-liter:** Fuel lines can be damaged and fire could result if vehicle is jump started and ground cable is attached to fuel-line bracket near battery. **1998-99:** Secondary hood latch on certain vehicles may corrode and stick in open position. **1998-99:** Speed-control cable on certain vehicles can interfere with pulley, preventing throttle from returning to idle when disengaging the speed control. **1999:** Right-front brake-line connection could separate, causing leakage when brake pedal is applied. **1999-00 w/4.0-liter engine and AWD:** Generic electronic module could "lock-up," so various functions (front wipers, interior lights, 4x4 system, etc.) could not be turned on or off. **2000 w/side airbags:** Side airbag could deploy if ignition key is in "run" position and seat-belt webbing is forcibly extracted from locked retractor with jerking motion.

PRICES

	Good	Average	Poor
1997 Mountaineer 2WD	$5,800-6,600	$5,000-5,700	$2,400-2,800
Mountaineer 4WD	6,800-7,500	6,100-6,700	3,200-3,500
1998 Mountaineer 2WD	7,000-8,000	6,200-7,100	3,400-3,800
Mountaineer 4WD	8,200-9,000	7,400-8,100	4,200-4,600
1999 Mountaineer 2WD	8,500-9,500	7,700-8,600	4,400-4,900
Mountaineer 4WD	9,800-10,800	8,800-9,700	5,100-5,600
2000 Mountaineer 2WD	10,800-12,000	9,700-10,800	5,800-6,500
Mountaineer 4WD/AWD	12,100-13,200	10,900-11,900	6,800-7,400
2001 Mountaineer 2WD	13,000-14,500	11,800-13,200	7,500-8,400
Mountaineer 4WD/AWD	14,200-15,700	12,900-14,300	8,700-9,600

For detailed information on this vehicle visit
http://used.consumerguide.com and enter code **2274**

1995-00 MERCURY MYSTIQUE

CLASS: Compact car
BUILT IN: Mexico, USA
PROS: Acceleration (V6)
• Optional antilock brakes
• Steering/handling
CONS: Stereo controls
• Engine noise (4-cylinder)
• Rear-seat room • Road noise

EVALUATION: Mystique and the similar Ford Contour are more like European sports sedans than American family cars. All models feel well-balanced and competent on twisting 2-lane roads.

Best powertrain combination is the V6 with automatic. The V6 has plenty of power and the new transmission shifts crisply and smoothly. Although automatic works just as well with the 4-cylinder, the base engine is noisier and has trouble mustering enough power to conquer hills. A

4-cylinder Mystique feels more than adequate with a 5-speed. As for economy, we averaged 23 mpg with the 4-cylinder. Road noise has been prominent on all models tested, but wind noise was low.

There's adequate room for adults in the front seat, but the rear seat lacks leg and head room for adults over five-foot-nine inches tall. The dashboard is functional and modern, but small poorly marked stereo controls are tough to use. The trunk opening is rather small, but the cargo area is wide at the rear and has a flat floor that reaches well forward. A standard 60/40 split rear seatback folds for additional luggage space.

VALUE FOR THE MONEY: Mystique is a highly competitive alternative to Japanese compact sedans and to the Chrysler Cirrus. Its biggest drawback is simply the lack of rear-seat room—especially in a family sedan.

TROUBLE SPOTS

See the 1995-00 Ford Contour.

AVERAGE REPLACEMENT COSTS

See the 1995-00 Ford Contour.

NHTSA RECALL HISTORY

1995: Front-seatbelt outboard-anchor tabs may be cracked. **1995:** Fuel-tank filler reinforcement can leak, resulting in fire. **1995:** Metal shield on plastic fuel-filler pipe can develop static charge during refueling; could serve as ignition source for fuel vapors. **1995:** Some passenger-side airbags may not inflate properly; also, igniter end cap can separate, releasing hot gases. **1995-96 w/V6:** Tightening of the engine-cooling fan-motor bearings can result in increased motor torque and higher-than-normal motor current and accompanying high motor temperatures. **1995-96 w/traction control:** Throttle cables were damaged during assembly, leading to fraying or separation; could prevent engine from returning to idle. **1995-98:** Automatic-transmission control can be damaged if subjected to certain interior cleaning products; gear indicator can deteriorate and incorrectly indicate actual gear position. **1996:** Fuel-filler pipe-vent hose may have less than intended level of ozone resistance, which could result in brittleness and cracking. **1996-98 w/o ABS:** Pressure-reducing valve in rear brakes may be subject to corrosion, which could result in malfunction when operated in areas that use salt compounds for deicing or dust control. **1996-98:** An open circuit in the wiring harness could lead to electrical arcing that could melt the connector housing material, increasing the potential for a fire. **1996-98:** Terminals at headlight switch and wiring harness can experience heat damage as a result of overheating. **1998:** Accelerator cable may have burr that could fray the core wire; cable could stick, bind, or cause high engine rpm. **1998:** Airbag-sensor wiring insulation can become brittle and crack over time; could cause airbag-warning light to illuminate and disable airbag system. **1998:** Front coil springs may fracture as a result of corrosion in high-corrosion environments. **1998:** Text and/or graphics for headlamp-aiming instructions, provided in owner guides, are not sufficiently clear. **1999 w/automatic transmission:** Ignition key can be rotated to "Lock" position and removed, without shift lever being in "Park" position. **2000:** Improper label was installed on some cars, with incorrect instructions for activation of childproof safety locks.

PRICES	Good	Average	Poor
1995 Mystique	$2,200-2,900	$1,600-2,100	$400-600
1996 Mystique	2,500-3,200	1,800-2,300	500-700
1997 Mystique	2,800-3,600	2,100-2,700	600-800
1998 Mystique	3,500-4,400	2,800-3,500	900-1,200
1999 Mystique	4,400-5,500	3,700-4,600	1,500-1,900
2000 Mystique	5,300-6,700	4,600-5,800	2,200-2,700

> For detailed information on this vehicle visit
> http://used.consumerguide.com and enter code **2207**

1990-95 MERCURY SABLE

CLASS: Midsize car

BUILT IN: USA

PROS: Acceleration (3.8-liter V6) • Antilock brakes (optional) • Passenger and cargo room • Ride

CONS: Fuel economy • Instruments/controls (electronic) • Radio controls

EVALUATION: Sable yields a firmer, more-controlled ride than most American family sedans. If possible, select a Sable with the optional 3.8-liter engine. The higher power at lower engine speeds translates into better around-town performance and extra passing power for highway driving. Fuel economy is less than great with the 3.8-liter engine, and the standard V6 isn't much thriftier.

Complaints are generally few and far between. The only area not above average is the placement of controls for the stereo. They're too low on the dashboard and are too small and poorly marked. Duplicate controls higher on the dash are designed to remedy the flaw. Optional digital instruments are hard to see in sunlight, and some auxiliary readouts are blocked by the steering wheel's rim.

VALUE FOR THE MONEY: The Mercury Sable and Ford Taurus, the best-selling sedan in the country for over four years, have remained popular with the buying public because they continue to represent a good value when compared to other midsize cars. They're roomy, well-built, have competent road manners, and sell at reasonable prices.

The quality of the Sable improved over the years, until the car was able to match or exceed the quality of its Japanese competitors.

TROUBLE SPOTS

See the 1990-95 Ford Taurus.

AVERAGE REPLACEMENT COSTS

See the 1990-95 Ford Taurus.

NHTSA RECALL HISTORY

1990-91: Front-brake rotors on "salt belt" cars may suffer corrosion, resulting in reduced braking effectiveness, abnormal pedal effort, loud noise, and possible increase in stopping distance. **1990-95 sold or registered in 24 states or D.C.:** Rear lower-subframe mount-plate nut can experience corrosion cracking if subjected to long-term exposure to road salt; can result in fracture. **1991-95 w/3.8-liter engine, in 23 states:** Speed-control cable could freeze, causing throttle to stick and not return to idle. **1992 wagon:** Secondary portion of liftgate latch on some cars may not function, possibly allowing liftgate to open while car is in motion if latch is not in primary position. **1992-95 in AK, IA, MN, NE, ND, or SD:** During high winds, heavy drifting snow, and low temperatures, engine fan may become blocked or frozen and fail to rotate; can cause smoke/flame. **1993 in 21 states:** Front coil springs can fracture as a result of corrosion combined with small cracks. **1993:** Controllers intended for use in rear-wheel-drive vehicles (instead of front drive) may have been installed on small number of cars with optional antilock braking, which could result in reduced braking ability. **1993-94:** Headlights can flash intermittently as a result of a circuit-breaker opening. **1995 w/3.0-liter and 3.8-liter engines:** The engine-cooling fan bearing can seize. Excessive heat may be generated, melting the fan-motor electrical connector, and possibly causing fan-motor components to ignite. **1995:** On some cars, retainer clip that holds master-cylinder pushrod to brake-pedal arm is missing or not fully installed; components can separate, resulting in loss of braking.

PRICES

	Good	Average	Poor
1990 Sable	$1,200-1,800	$700-1,100	$100-200
1991 Sable	1,400-2,000	900-1,300	200
1992 Sable	1,600-2,300	1,100-1,500	200-300
1993 Sable	1,800-2,500	1,200-1,700	300-400
1994 Sable	2,100-2,800	1,500-2,000	400-500
1995 Sable	2,500-3,300	1,800-2,400	500-700

For detailed information on this vehicle visit
http://used.consumerguide.com and enter code **2071**

1996-99 MERCURY SABLE

CLASS: Midsize car
BUILT IN: USA
PROS: Acceleration (LS)
• Optional antilock brakes
• Passenger and cargo room
• Steering/handling
CONS: Automatic-transmission performance (GS)
• Rear visibility

MERCURY

EVALUATION: Interiors are roomier than before, and construction feels more solid. Performance also has improved, due to the new engine that's installed in LS Sables. Quieter and smoother than the overhead-valve V6 in a Sable G or GS, that dual-cam V6 provides more-spirited acceleration and stronger passing power. Its electronically controlled transmission is smooth and responsive. Acceleration is adequate with the base engine, but its automatic vibrates when changing gears and is slower to downshift for passing.

Road and wind noise are better than in previous Sables. The firm suspension on all models feels stable at highway speeds, but a little too stiff on bumpy roads. Steering is lighter than before, but more precise, and a Sable can corner almost as well as some sports cars. All models use the same tires, and suspension differences are slight.

Front seats offer generous space. Rear leg room has grown considerably, and tall people can easily fit in the outboard positions. Although the flip-open armrest that comes with the front bench seat is useful, when it's open you cannot plug a cellular phone or other device into the cigarette lighter. Sedans have a roomy trunk with a wide, flat floor that reaches well-forward. Visibility is generally good, but it's difficult to see the sedan's trunk and the wagon's rear windows are narrow.

VALUE FOR THE MONEY: Showing significant gains in passenger accommodations and performance, the latest Sable is worth a test-drive.

TROUBLE SPOTS

See the 1996-99 Ford Taurus.

AVERAGE REPLACEMENT COSTS

See the 1996-99 Ford Taurus.

NHTSA RECALL HISTORY

1996: Brake-fluid indicator can malfunction. **1996:** Small number of cars were inadvertently equipped with 18-gallon fuel tank rather than 16-gallon as specified; displacement of tank's shipping plug could result in leakage. **1996-97 w/automatic transaxle:** "Park" pawl shaft was improperly positioned during assembly; could result in park pawl occasionally not engaging when selector lever is placed in "Park" position, allowing vehicle to roll if parking brake has not been applied. **1996-97:** "Park" pawl-abutment bracket has sharp edge which can cause pawl to hang up and not engage gear; vehicle can move even though indicator shows "Park." **1997:** Servo cover can separate, causing transmission fluid to leak and contact catalytic converter; could result in fire. **1997-98:** Headlamp-aiming instructions in owner's manuals are not sufficiently clear. **1998-99:** Front seatbelt-buckle attaching stud may have been improperly heat treated, resulting in cracks. **1999 w/California Emissions:** Incorrect transmission-oil cooler line was installed, which contacts ABS module bracket and, over time, can wear and develop a leak. **1999:** Retainer clip can disengage from accelerator cable and fall into pedal-arm pivot area; engine may not fully return to idle, and insulator could interfere with cable. **1999:** Seatbelt retractor may have incorrectly formed pin shaft that could, in some circumstances, prevent seatbelt webbing from being extracted.

PRICES

PRICES	Good	Average	Poor
1996 Sable sedan	$2,400-3,200	$1,800-2,300	$500-600
Sable wagon	2,900-3,500	2,200-2,700	700-800
1997 Sable sedan	3,000-3,800	2,300-2,900	700-900
Sable wagon	3,600-4,300	2,900-3,400	1,000-1,200
1998 Sable sedan	3,800-4,700	3,100-3,800	1,100-1,400
Sable wagon	4,600-5,400	3,800-4,500	1,700-2,000
1999 Sable sedan	4,900-5,900	4,200-5,000	1,900-2,300
Sable wagon	6,000-7,000	5,200-6,100	2,500-2,900

For detailed information on this vehicle visit
http://used.consumerguide.com and enter code **2208**

2000-03 MERCURY SABLE

CLASS: Midsize car
BUILT IN: USA
PROS: Cargo room
• Handling/roadholding
• Rear-seat comfort
CONS: Low-speed acceleration

EVALUATION: In most respects, the Sable is similar to Ford's Taurus. Both deliver plenty of performance, though they lack class-leading acceleration. Each engine runs smoothly, but neither can move the car all that swiftly beyond midrange speeds—the 25-50 mph range, when extra vigor is needed for passing. Either V6 can accelerate suitably from a standstill, however. A test Sable LS with the twincam engine did 0-60 mph in a brisk 8.2 seconds. Sables score higher in road manners, coming across as balanced, secure, and predictable even in rapid directional changes. Steering has fine on-center sense, though turning effort could be more linear. Resistance to wallow and float is impressive, but ride quality on rough pavement is unsatisfactory, with potholes and pavement patches registering sharply. Braking feels strong and easily modulated. Tire thrum is noticeable at highway speeds, but not especially annoying. Interior space is abundant, promising excellent rear-seat room and comfort, on a substantial and comfortably contoured bench. Rear head clearance is generous. Leg and foot space also are plentiful. Outboard front occupants are uncrowded if a bench seat is installed, but the center spot is snug.

Adjustable pedals work easily, teaming with the standard tilt steering wheel. If those pedals are installed, shorter drivers can sit farther away from the steering-wheel airbag. Gauges are unobstructed, but analog markings are small. Luggage space is generous in either body style. The sedan's trunk is among the largest in its class. Useful grocery-bag hooks are included, though hinges and brackets intrude into the cargo area and the opening isn't particularly large.

MERCURY

VALUE FOR THE MONEY: Sable and Taurus returned to their roots with the 2000 redesign. Now contemporary in styling, a Sable provides fine road manners, excellent utility, an array of safety features, with a modestly more luxurious feel than a Taurus. Despite acceleration limitations and marginal ride comfort, Sables are worth considering.

TROUBLE SPOTS

See the 2000-03 Ford Taurus.

AVERAGE REPLACEMENT COSTS

See the 2000-03 Ford Taurus.

NHTSA RECALL HISTORY

2000: Headlamp-switch knob on certain vehicles can fracture and separate, making it difficult to activate headlamps. **2000:** On certain vehicles, "vehicle capacity weight" and "designated seating capacity" information was not printed on the safety-certification labels. **2000-01 w/adjustable pedals:** Grease from the adjustable-pedal assembly enters the stoplamp switch and can contaminate the contacts leading to carbon buildup, and potentially, a short circuit. **2000-01:** A switch located in the plastic cover of the wiper-motor gear case could malfunction and overheat, potentially resulting in loss of wiper function or fire. **2000-02:** Adjustable pedals are not far enough apart and could be inadvertently depressed simultaneously. Dealers may adjust pedal spacing. **2001:** Child Safety Seat Anchor Latch fasteners on certain vehicles do not have adequate residual torque; road vibrations could cause nut to loosen and separate from its stud. **2001:** Owner guides may not identify center rear seating position as having LATCH-compatible lower anchorages. **2002-03:** Some windshields may have been mounted improperly, leading to increased wind noise and leakage. Dealer will inspect and replace these windshields.

PRICES

	Good	Average	Poor
2000 Sable GS	$6,400-7,500	$5,600-6,600	$2,800-3,300
Sable LS	7,000-8,700	6,200-7,700	3,400-4,200
2001 Sable GS	7,800-9,000	7,000-8,100	4,000-4,600
Sable LS	8,500-10,500	7,700-9,500	4,400-5,500
2002 Sable GS	9,500-11,000	8,600-9,900	4,900-5,700
Sable LS	11,000-11,500	9,900-10,400	5,900-6,200
2003 Sable GS	11,700-13,500	10,500-12,200	6,400-7,400
Sable LS	13,700-16,000	12,500-14,600	8,100-9,400

For detailed information on this vehicle visit
http://used.consumerguide.com and enter code **2387**

1991-96 MERCURY TRACER

CLASS: Subcompact car
BUILT IN: Mexico, USA
PROS: Fuel economy
• Price
CONS: Control layout
• Engine noise • Rear-seat
room • Road noise

EVALUATION: Based on Mazda Protege chassis and running gear, the car delivers a good ride and above-average build quality. While fit-and-finish are good, all models could use more insulation, as road and engine are noticeably present in the Tracer.

Visibility from the airy cabin is improved and there's more ample passenger space. The only exception is the tighter head room on models equipped with the optional sunroof. Our primary gripe focuses on an instrument panel with controls that seem too far away, too small, and a little confusing.

VALUE FOR THE MONEY: Our favorite Tracer is the LTS, which offers more-spirited acceleration with its dual-cam Mazda engine, plus improved handling and performance, thanks to the upgraded suspension package. Also included are 4-wheel disc brakes, styled wheels, and available antilock brakes.

TROUBLE SPOTS

See the 1991-96 Ford Escort.

AVERAGE REPLACEMENT COSTS

See the 1991-96 Ford Escort.

NHTSA RECALL HISTORY

1991: Interference may occur between bolt that secures fuel-line shield to lower dash and gas pedal, causing pedal to stick wide open. **1991:** On some cars, fatigue crack can develop in solder joint between fuel return tube and fuel-pump sending unit. **1992:** Pins securing ignition lock in steering-column housing can separate or move out of position, causing steering column to lock up. **1992:** Stoplamp switch could intermittently malfunction. **1993:** Driver's seat in some cars may not engage fully in its track; could move in event of crash. **1994-95:** A few driver-side airbags may have inadequately welded inflator canister, causing improper deployment and expelling hot gases. **1995 cars in certain states:** Cracks can develop in plastic fuel tank, resulting in leakage.

PRICES

	Good	Average	Poor
1991 Tracer	$1,100-1,600	$700-1,000	$100-200
1992 Tracer	1,200-1,700	700-1,100	100-200

1993 Tracer	$1,400-1,900	$900-1,200	$200
1994 Tracer	1,600-2,200	1,100-1,500	200-300
1995 Tracer	1,800-2,400	1,200-1,600	300-400
1996 Tracer	2,000-2,700	1,400-1,900	300-500

For detailed information on this vehicle visit
http://used.consumerguide.com and enter code 2072

1997-99 MERCURY TRACER

CLASS: Subcompact car
BUILT IN: Mexico, USA
PROS: Optional antilock brakes • Fuel economy • Price
CONS: Rear-seat room • Road noise

EVALUATION: Acceleration is adequate with either transmission, though a Tracer feels livelier with manual shift. Low-speed power is good, which is a bonus in Tracers that are equipped with automatic. The automatic transmission shifts more smoothly with the new engine, and also downshifts faster for passing and merging. The new engine is quieter than the previous 4-cylinder, but road noise is prominent on all models.

An LS sedan with manual shift averaged an impressive 31.2 mpg, with about two-thirds of the driving on highways. In a more even mix of urban and highway driving, mileage will naturally be lower.

A well-tuned suspension helps the Tracer absorb bumps better than most subcompact sedans and wagons. Handling is competent rather than sporting, though steering feels natural in turns and its on-center sense contributes to stable cruising.

Front seats have ample head room for adults and adequate leg room. The rear seat is short of space for anyone over 5-foot-8 or so. Rear knee room is tight, but toe space is good. Tracer's new dashboard places the audio and climate controls in an oval control panel, which is easy to reach and decipher while driving. Cargo space is adequate, and the rear seatback on all models folds down for additional room. Visibility is good on the whole, but the sedan's rear roof pillars are thick enough to block the driver's over-the-shoulder view.

VALUE FOR THE MONEY: Neither the Tracer nor its Escort sibling set any new standards for subcompacts. Even so, they're more refined than before, with more standard features, sensible design, competent road manners, and reasonable prices—whether new or secondhand.

TROUBLE SPOTS

See the 1997-03 Ford Escort/ZX2.

AVERAGE REPLACEMENT COSTS

See the 1997-03 Ford Escort/ZX2.

NHTSA RECALL HISTORY

None to date.

PRICES	Good	Average	Poor
1997 Tracer sedan	$2,500-3,100	$1,800-2,300	$500-700
Tracer wagon	2,700-3,300	2,000-2,500	600-700
1998 Tracer sedan	3,000-3,700	2,300-2,800	700-900
Tracer wagon	3,400-4,000	2,700-3,200	900-1,000
1999 Tracer sedan	3,800-4,500	3,100-3,600	1,100-1,400
Tracer wagon	4,300-5,000	3,500-4,100	1,500-1,700

For detailed information on this vehicle visit
http://used.consumerguide.com and enter code 2275

1993-98 MERCURY VILLAGER

CLASS: Minivan
BUILT IN: USA
PROS: Passenger room (front) • Steering/handling
CONS: Control layout • Wind noise

EVALUATION: Although the 3.0-liter Nissan engine is adequate, it can't quite match the muscle provided by the larger V6s in the front-drive minivans from Ford, GM, and Chrysler. While engine and road noise are within a reasonable range, when the Villager reaches highway speeds the wind noise can become quite pronounced. A wide turning circle makes the Villager harder to maneuver in tight spots than most cars, but in most other situations the Villager feels remarkably carlike. When compared with other minivans, body lean is quite modest. The suspension is firm enough to minimize bouncing on wavy roads, and it absorbs most bumps without breaking a sweat.

Front head room and leg room are both quite good, but only adequate for the middle- and rear-seat passengers. With all seats in their normal positions, the rear cargo area is quite small. Trying to improve the Villager's hauling capacity requires removing the truly cumbersome center seats. Stereo and climate controls are a stretch for the driver, and too small to operate easily.

VALUE FOR THE MONEY: Compared with other minivans, the Villager has less interior room. It also lacks many of the standard features found on its rivals. Nevertheless it's a good choice if you need more than a midsize station wagon but don't require the interior space provided in one of the larger minivans.

TROUBLE SPOTS

Blower motor: Squeaking or chirping blower motors are the result of defective brush holders. (1993-94)

Crankshaft: The crankshaft breaks behind the front pulley if the belts are overtightened. (1993-96)

AVERAGE REPLACEMENT COSTS

A/C Compressor	$345	Exhaust System	$265
Alternator	420	Radiator	505
Automatic Trans.	555	Shocks and/or Struts	544
Brakes	270	Timing Chain/Belt	185
CV Joints	615		

NHTSA RECALL HISTORY

1993: Brake master cylinder on some vans was improperly assembled or could have been damaged during assembly, which can result in loss of braking at two wheels, causing increased pedal travel, higher pedal effort, and increased stopping distance. **1993:** Fuel-filler hoses may have been cut prior to installation by knife used to open shipping box; fuel leakage could result, leading to fire if exposed to ignition source. **1993:** Leaves and other foreign matter can enter through cowl-panel air intake during operation of front heater and/or air conditioner, resulting in buildup in the plenum that can lead to noise, odors, or even a vehicle fire. **1993:** One or both bolts securing automatic seatbelt-restraint system tracks to B-pillars were not adequately tightened on some vans, increasing risk of injury in the event of a collision or sudden maneuver. **1995 w/sliding third-row bench seats:** Cable that connects seat-adjustment level to latch might be pinched in roller assembly, preventing latch on left side from fully engaging seat rail. **1995:** Rear lamp will not illuminate if the metal socket moves or separates from the plastic socket housing. This can result in failure of the stop or rear running lamps. **1996:** Power windows can be closed after ignition key is turned to "off" position and right front door is opened. **1997:** Fuel-line hoses could crack or split, resulting in leakage. **1997-98 w/battery supplied by GNB Technologies:** Defective negative battery post can cause acid leakage and related corrosion damage; could lead to engine fire or battery explosion. **1998:** Cracks have developed in the vent hose, allowing a fuel leak.

PRICES

	Good	Average	Poor
1993 Villager	$2,600-3,400	$1,900-2,500	$500-700
1994 Villager	3,000-4,200	2,300-3,200	700-1,000
1995 Villager	3,500-5,000	2,800-4,000	900-1,400
1996 Villager	4,100-5,800	3,400-4,800	1,400-1,900
1997 Villager	4,800-6,500	4,000-5,500	1,800-2,500
1998 Villager	5,600-7,500	4,800-6,500	2,300-3,100

For detailed information on this vehicle visit
http://used.consumerguide.com and enter code **2073**

1999-02 MERCURY VILLAGER

CLASS: Minivan
BUILT IN: USA
PROS: Control layout
• Passenger and cargo room
CONS: Fuel economy
• Interior materials

EVALUATION: Villagers earn about the same ratings in performance and accommodations as their Nissan Quest cousins. Acceleration is reasonably snappy from a standstill, but unimpressive in the 35-55 mph range. Highway passing response borders on inadequate with a full load and the air conditioner working. Engine roar under heavy throttle is significant, though wind and tire noise are on par for this class. So is fuel economy. Relatively compact in size, the Villager (and Quest) offer above-average minivan maneuverability, helped by firm steering with ample feel. Cornering response is crispest with the Estate and Sport, which roll on 16-inch tires. The suspension soaks up bumps decently, but overall ride quality does not match that of longer-wheelbase minivans like the Dodge Grand Caravan and Toyota Sienna. Relatively cozy inside, the Villager has scant clearance between any of the seats. Front seatbacks are narrow, though supportive cushions improve overall comfort. Step-in height is low, but third-row entry/exit is rather tight due to a relatively low roof and narrow passageways. Cargo room is slim with the third seat in its normal position, though the available parcel shelf is handy. The third-row bench does not remove, but can slide forward to free up a large cargo hold, though its release handle is difficult to reach. Second-row seats remove easily. Interior storage includes a removable net between the front seats, double front-door pockets, and numerous bins and beverage holders. Despite targeting upscale buyers, Villager and Quest have an abundance of hard-surfaced interior plastic items inside, along with industrial-look switchgear and unfinished edges.

VALUE FOR THE MONEY: Smaller outside and inside than most rivals, the Villager and equivalent Nissan Quest are more maneuverable. Both trail the competition in refinement and acceleration. Villagers have not held their value as well as Quests, and are therefore cheaper secondhand.

TROUBLE SPOTS

Doors: The power door locks may activate by themselves due to water getting into the wiring harness in the door, or because there is too much solder on the door switch. (1999-2000)

Vehicle noise: Gear whine between 40-70 mph is from the automatic-transmission shift cable. It must be rerouted and a damper must be installed. (1999-2001)

AVERAGE REPLACEMENT COSTS

A/C Compressor	$500	Exhaust System	$385
Alternator	350	Radiator	410
Automatic Trans.	1,320	Shocks and/or Struts	900
Brakes	370	Timing Chain/Belt	455
CV Joints	1,150		

NHTSA RECALL HISTORY

1999: Fuel-tank retention strap (two per minivan) on some vehicles can break at spot welds, causing underbody rattle; if welds fail, there may be fuel leakage and/or separation of fuel tank from vehicle. **1999:** Taillight socket's locking tab may have insufficient force to retain bulb. **1999-00:** One or more of the five bolts that mount the rack-and-pinion steering gear may have been incorrectly tightened; could result in steering looseness and noise or vibration. Eventually, bolts could fracture or fall out. **2001:** Plastic trim cover around base of front seatbelt buckle may become trapped, eventually allowing bolt to loosen.

PRICES	Good	Average	Poor
1999 Sport, Estate	$8,500-9,500	$7,700-8,600	$4,400-4,900
Villager	7,500-8,500	6,800-7,700	3,800-4,300
2000 Sport, Estate	10,300-11,500	9,300-10,400	5,500-6,100
Villager	9,000-10,000	8,100-9,000	4,700-5,200
2001 Sport, Estate	12,000-13,500	10,800-12,200	6,700-7,600
Villager	10,500-11,500	9,500-10,400	5,600-6,100
2002 Sport, Estate	14,000-15,700	12,700-14,300	8,500-9,600
Villager	12,000-13,200	10,800-11,900	6,700-7,400

For detailed information on this vehicle visit
http://used.consumerguide.com and enter code **2389**

1995-99 MITSUBISHI ECLIPSE

CLASS: Sporty coupe

BUILT IN: USA

PROS: Acceleration (GS-T, GSX) • All-wheel drive (GSX) • Optional antilock brakes • Steering/handling

CONS: Acceleration (RS, GS w/automatic) • Cargo room • Rear-seat room • Road noise

EVALUATION: The base engine revs smoothly and quickly without excess noise, but it's no powerhouse. Therefore, acceleration with the automatic transmission is marginal for freeway on-ramps and in passing sprints. Progress is livelier with the slick-shifting 5-speed manual gearbox. Turbos are decidedly faster. Unfortunately, Eclipse still suffers from some "turbo lag."

All Eclipse models offer nimble handling, good grip, and quick, accurate steering. On the downside, the ride turns choppy on freeways and rough roads, especially on turbocharged models. You also must endure plenty of road noise. All-wheel-drive models are capable of exhibiting race carlike moves, of the sort matched only by big-buck coupes.

Front occupants have adequate head room but may still feel crowded. The tiny back seat is strictly for preteens. The dashboard is well laid out, except for a center-mounted stereo unit that's too low. Cargo space is adequate, but with a tall liftover for loading and unloading.

Spyder convertibles look sharp, and deliver fun-in-the-sun driving at a comparatively reasonable price. Unfortunately, several convertibles we've driven have suffered from serious shakiness, even when rolling down smooth roads.

VALUE FOR THE MONEY: Though still one of the best sports coupes, the competition caught up with Eclipse during its second generation. Other than the all-wheel-drive model, this version of the Eclipse offers nothing you can't get for less money somewhere else.

TROUBLE SPOTS

Air springs: The front springs make creaking, popping, or squeaking noises when going over bumps requiring insulators to be installed on the upper coils. (1995-99)

Engine misfire: Misfiring is common due to carbon on the spark plugs and is corrected by replacing the plugs and plug wires. (1995)

Fuel pump: Noisy fuel pump may be result of a bad fuel-pressure regulator. (1995)

Fuel pump: The vehicle is sensitive to fuel starvation caused by a clogged in-tank filter. (1995-97)

Rear axle noise: Squeaking, rubbing, knocking, or tapping noises from the rear are eliminated by replacing the trailing-arm bushings (1995-97) or the shock-absorber insulator assembly. (1997-98)

AVERAGE REPLACEMENT COSTS

A/C Compressor	$600	CV Joints	$770
Alternator	360	Exhaust System	350
Automatic Trans.	975	Radiator	470
Brakes	310	Shocks and/or Struts	520
Clutch	415	Timing Chain/Belt	260

NHTSA RECALL HISTORY

1995-96: Incorrectly installed gaskets for fuel pump and/or gauge unit could allow fuel or fumes to escape. **1995-96:** Rubber boots on lower ball joint can become damaged, allowing dirt and water intrusion, which can cause excessive wear and possible separation. **1995-98 w/AWD:** Lockup of transfer case can occur, due to insufficient lubrication. **1997:** On a few cars, improperly welded passenger head-restraint support bracket on passenger side can break. **1998:** Dash-panel pad can shift, interfering with throttle-cable control. **1999:** The battery-cable wiring harness can become heat damaged, leading to malfunctions in the turn signals and oil-pressure lamp. **1999:** The steering-column multifunction switch levers can become loose or break.

PRICES

	Good	Average	Poor
1995 Eclipse GS-T, GSX	$4,200-5,200	$3,400-4,300	$1,400-1,700
Eclipse RS, GS	$3,000-4,000	$2,300-3,100	$700-900
1996 Eclipse GS-T, GSX	5,500-7,000	4,700-6,000	2,300-2,900
Eclipse RS, GS	3,700-5,000	3,000-4,100	1,100-1,500
Spyder convertible	5,700-6,800	4,900-5,800	2,300-2,800
1997 Eclipse GS-T, GSX	6,300-7,800	5,500-6,900	2,800-3,400
Eclipse base, RS, GS	4,500-5,700	3,700-4,700	1,600-2,100
Spyder convertible	6,700-8,200	5,900-7,200	3,100-3,800
1998 Eclipse GS-T, GSX	7,400-9,500	6,700-8,600	3,600-4,700
Eclipse RS, GS	5,500-6,700	4,700-5,800	2,300-2,700
Spyder convertible	8,000-9,500	7,200-8,600	4,100-4,800
1999 Eclipse GS-T, GSX	8,800-11,200	7,900-10,100	4,600-5,800
Eclipse RS, GS	6,500-8,000	5,700-7,000	2,900-3,600
Spyder convertible	9,500-11,200	8,600-10,100	4,900-5,800

For detailed information on this vehicle visit
http://used.consumerguide.com and enter code 2209

2000-03
MITSUBISHI ECLIPSE

BEST BUY CG

CLASS: Sporty coupe

BUILT IN: USA

PROS: Acceleration (V6) • Handling/roadholding • Front-seat comfort

CONS: Rear-seat entry/exit • Rear-seat room • Rear visibility • Road noise

EVALUATION: More mature and refined than their rough-and-tumble predecessors, Eclipses deliver a pliant, comfortable, sporty-coupe ride. Handling is alert and responsive with little cornering lean and grippy front-drive predictability, though maneuvers are hampered by a large turning circle. Wheel patter still turns up on washboard surfaces, but it's not bothersome. Engines are much improved. Whereas the old 2.0-liter fours were throbby and loud, the new 2.4 liter is generally smooth and quiet. It packs respectable punch, at least with manual shift—which is a pleasure to use. The V6-powered GT doesn't rocket away like the old turbocharged models, but it's plenty quick—and naturally, suffers no irritating turbo lag. A GT with automatic reached 60 mph in 8.3 seconds and averaged 21.8 mpg. Surprisingly, the V6 is hardly quieter than the 4 cylinder. Furthermore, the body transmits noticeable tire noise except on glassy pavement. Wind rush is nicely tamed, even with the frameless door glass.

Despite a more spacious cabin feel, Eclipses remain cozy 2+2 models with a teeny back seat and wiggle-in entry/exit. Front buckets hug one's torso, and should be comfortable on long rides. Driving positions are low-slung,

MITSUBISHI

and visibility remains difficult directly aft and over the shoulder. Taller drivers might wish the standard tilt steering wheel moved higher. Gauges and controls are clear and handy, but air-conditioner buttons are hard to see in daylight. Luggage space is generous in coupes with the back seat folded, limited in Spyders, but the load lip is lofty and the hatch lid heavy. Bulky doors may close with a tinny clang. Cowl shake occurs over bumps with a Spyder, but structural stiffness is acceptable and its soft top seals tightly.

VALUE FOR THE MONEY: Though not quite as inspiring as a Honda Prelude, Eclipses compare well against most anything in their class. A GT might be the best choice, but few will feel penalized in one of the less-expensive 4-cylinder models. Spyders have no direct rivals in their price league.

TROUBLE SPOTS

Audio system: A short causes popping noises from the speakers when the power seat is operated. A jumper harness with a filter has been released for installation under the seat. (1999-2001)

Automatic transmission: The automatic transmission may shudder, surge, or vibrate due to thermal breakdown of the original transmission fluid (SPII). The system must be flushed and refilled with revised fluid (SPIII). (1999-2001)

Hard starting: The starter may not run due to a faulty theft-alarm relay (automatic transmission) or a faulty starter relay (manual transmission). Revised relays are available to fix the problem. (2000)

Sunroof/moonroof: The sunroof may skip/stick during operation requiring a countermeasure drive-cable assembly. (2000-01)

Vehicle noise: Banging, creaking, and popping noises from the front end are usually due to dry stabilizer-bar bushings. Revised bushings are available as replacements. (1999-2000)

AVERAGE REPLACEMENT COSTS

A/C Compressor	$585	CV Joints	$1,220
Alternator	620	Exhaust System	370
Automatic Trans.	1,025	Radiator	495
Brakes	350	Shocks and/or Struts	1,010
Clutch	460	Timing Chain/Belt	340

NHTSA RECALL HISTORY

2000 V6: Power-steering pipe could wear through, allowing fluid leakage. Can result in a fire and continued loss of fluid will result in a loss of power assist, increasing the risk of a crash. **2001:** Bulge in fuel tank caused by manufacturing process on small number of vehicles resulted in thinning of material, increasing risk of fuel leakage.

PRICES

	Good	Average	Poor
2000 Eclipse GT coupe	$10,000-11,000	$9,000-9,900	$5,200-5,700
Eclipse RS, GS coupe	8,200-9,200	7,400-8,300	4,200-4,700
2001 Eclipse GT coupe	11,500-12,500	10,400-11,300	6,300-6,900
Eclipse RS, GS coupe	9,500-10,500	8,600-9,500	4,900-5,500
Spyder GT conv.	14,500-16,000	13,200-14,600	9,000-9,900
Spyder convertible	13,000-14,500	11,800-13,200	7,500-8,400

MITSUBISHI

2002 Eclipse GT coupe	$13,000-14,200	$11,800-12,900	$7,500-8,200
Eclipse RS, GS coupe	11,000-12,500	9,900-11,300	5,900-6,800
Spyder GT conv.	16,500-18,000	15,000-16,400	10,600-11,500
Spyder convertible	15,000-16,500	13,700-15,000	9,500-10,400
2003 Eclipse GT/GTS coupe	15,500-17,000	14,100-15,500	9,900-10,900
Eclipse RS, GS coupe	13,200-14,700	12,000-13,400	7,700-8,500
Spyder GT/GTS conv.	19,000-21,000	17,500-19,300	12,400-13,700
Spyder convertible	17,500-19,000	16,100-17,500	11,200-12,200

For detailed information on this vehicle visit
http://used.consumerguide.com and enter code **2391**

1992-94 MITSUBISHI EXPO/EXPO LRV

CLASS: Minivan
BUILT IN: Japan
PROS: All-wheel drive (Expo AWD) • Optional antilock brakes • Passenger and cargo room
CONS: Acceleration (LRV/automatic) • Handling • Noise

EVALUATION: Pleasant and easy to drive, both Expos perform in a similar manner. While acceleration is adequate, climbing hills or passing with a full load can be exciting. Also, the LRV's smaller engine lacks sufficient torque to keep the automatic transmission from frequent gear-hunting. We averaged 24.3 mpg with an LRV and 24.6 mpg with the Expo.

Wind noise is a problem above 40 mph, and road rumble is invariably noticed. Maneuverability is great for urban tasks, but cornering ability is modest. Tight corners produce marked body roll and tire squeal. On the plus side, you can expect a comfortably pliant ride. Both Expos tend to get blown around by strong crosswinds, though staying on course seldom becomes a problem.

Getting inside is no problem at all, and passenger space is plentiful. All around head room is nothing short of towering, and leg space in back is decent. The dashboard design is generally convenient, though the radio sits too low to see or reach easily.

VALUE FOR THE MONEY: Each breed of Expo is worth a look, and definitely versatile for passengers and cargo. But don't expect too much beyond their practical merits.

TROUBLE SPOTS

See the 1992-96 Eagle Summit Wagon.

AVERAGE REPLACEMENT COSTS

See the 1992-96 Eagle Summit Wagon.

NHTSA RECALL HISTORY

1992-93 sold in Caribbean: Shoulder-belt anchorage could remain at A-pillar when door was closed. **1992-93:** Automatic-seatbelt system may fail to operate correctly during crash.

PRICES

	Good	Average	Poor
1992 Expo	$1,800-2,400	$1,200-1,600	$300-400
Expo LRV	1,500-2,000	1,000-1,300	200-300
1993 Expo	2,200-2,800	1,600-2,000	400-500
Expo LRV	1,800-2,500	1,200-1,700	300-400
1994 Expo	2,600-3,300	1,900-2,400	500-700
Expo LRV	2,200-2,900	1,600-2,100	400-600

For detailed information on this vehicle visit
http://used.consumerguide.com and enter code **2210**

1994-98 MITSUBISHI GALANT

CLASS: Compact car
BUILT IN: USA
PROS: Antilock brakes
• Passenger and cargo room
• Ride
CONS: Engine noise • Fuel economy • Rear visibility

EVALUATION: The Galant's 141-horsepower 4-cylinder has more than adequate acceleration and passing power with the automatic transmission. It shifts smoothly and downshifts without argument when it comes time to pass. The 160-horsepower unit found on 1994 GS models feels stronger still. Engine noise is abundant during hard acceleration.

Galant's suspension absorbs bumps easily, while providing a stable, competent ride at highway speeds. The car handles corners with ease and the precise steering feel gives drivers a sense of confidence.

Firm, supportive seats and a generous front cabin area are Galant strong points. However, rear-seat passengers have only adequate head room, and an inch less leg room than the previous model. The dashboard has an attractive four-dial gauge cluster, and climate controls are stacked atop the center stereo controls in the center console. In a welcome departure for Mitsubishi, the stereo is mounted high enough for easy operation, even when driving. The trunk provides ample space plus a wide flat floor and low liftover. Visibility is good, but wide rear roof pillars force the driver into neck-stretching during lane changes.

VALUE FOR THE MONEY: This generation of the Galant has several good qualities, and we consider it a solid buy. Nevertheless, it lacks a single distinguishing feature to help it stand out in the crowded field of midsize domestic and imported sedans, particularly given the absence of a V6 option.

MITSUBISHI

TROUBLE SPOTS

Dashboard lights: The headlights and dash lights may dim during deceleration because the computer switches on the electric cooling fan. (1994-95)

Exhaust system: A revised Vehicle Emission Control Information (VECI) label was mailed to all owners who were to place it over the old one that contained incorrect information. (1994)

Steering problems: Cars that drift or pull to the right may be cured by replacing the lower control arm with one having rear bushing with a built-in offset. (1994-95)

Transaxle leak: Transaxle end-clutch oil seals could leak leading to a loss of overdrive (fourth gear). (1994)

Vehicle shake: Vibrations on automatic transmission models are probably due to the upper radiator-mounting posts not being centered in the mounting brackets. (1994)

AVERAGE REPLACEMENT COSTS

A/C Compressor	$610	CV Joints	$725
Alternator	335	Exhaust System	500
Automatic Trans.	865	Radiator	595
Brakes	220	Shocks and/or Struts	460
Clutch	560	Timing Chain/Belt	290

NHTSA RECALL HISTORY

1994-95: Grease was inadvertently applied to contact of stoplamp switch, causing it to heat up and allowing internal elements to melt; switch will stick on or off, causing ABS warning to disappear. **1995-98:** Rubber boots on lower ball joint can become damaged, allowing dirt and water intrusion, which can cause excessive wear and possible separation.

PRICES

	Good	Average	Poor
1994 Galant	$1,800-2,500	$1,200-1,700	$300-400
Galant LS, GS	2,300-2,900	1,700-2,100	400-600
1995 Galant	2,100-2,800	1,500-2,000	400-500
Galant LS	2,700-3,300	2,000-2,500	600-700
1996 Galant	2,500-3,200	1,800-2,300	500-700
Galant LS	3,200-3,800	2,500-3,000	800-900
1997 Galant	3,100-3,900	2,400-3,000	700-900
Galant LS	4,000-4,700	3,300-3,900	1,300-1,500
1998 Galant	3,900-4,600	3,200-3,700	1,200-1,400
Galant LS	4,900-5,600	4,200-4,800	1,900-2,200

For detailed information on this vehicle visit
http://used.consumerguide.com and enter code **2076**

1999-03 MITSUBISHI GALANT

CLASS: Compact car
BUILT IN: USA
PROS: Ride
• Steering/handling
CONS: Rear-seat
entry/exit

EVALUATION: Surprisingly entertaining on the road, especially with V6 power, the Galant delivers solid driving feel. Both engines are smooth performers. The 4 cylinder delivers brisk takeoffs and cruises without strain at highway speeds, becoming vocal only at higher rpm. As expected, the V6 is somewhat smoother, quieter, and punchier, but commands premium fuel. A 4-cylinder model accelerated to 60 mph in 10.3 seconds, while a GTZ V6 did it 2 seconds quicker. The V6 works well with the transmission to deliver throttle response as good as any in its class. Wind rush is muted, but tire roar is noticeable on coarse pavement. Handling is front-drive balanced and predictable, while the Galant's ride is calm, controlled, and absorbent—apart from minor tail hop over sharp lateral ridges. The GTZ model telegraphs small bumps more clearly than less-sporty Galants, but exhibits more precise steering and slightly less body lean in tight corners. Steering feel on lesser models is a bit numb. Simulated "panic" stops are short, true, and level, even without antilock braking. Interior space is sufficient, but with only average room for four adults on a longer ride. Adults in back lack leg space to avoid knees-up riding. Rear-seat entry/exit could be better, but front seats are long-haul supportive. Gauges and controls are well-positioned and obvious. Visibility is hindered only to the rear by the Galant's high-tail styling. With a flat floor and low liftover, the trunk is spacious enough but its lid feels flimsy. All models except the base DE have split folding rear seatbacks. On the whole, interior decor is pleasant but on the bland side.

VALUE FOR THE MONEY: Though not quite a standout, the Galant is a pleasant, agreeably competent family 4 door that should be on the tentative shopping list of anyone considering an Accord or Camry. Packed with features for the money, the Galant mimics much of the driving satisfaction, if not the top-notch engineering, of Honda and Toyota models.

TROUBLE SPOTS

Audio system: A short causes popping noises from the speakers when the power seat is operated. A jumper harness with a filter has been released for installation under the seat. (1999-2001)

Automatic transmission: The automatic transmission may shudder, surge, or vibrate due to thermal breakdown of the original transmission fluid (SPII). The system must be flushed and refilled with revised fluid (SPIII). (1999-2001)

Vehicle noise: Banging, creaking, and popping noises from the front end are usually due to dry stabilizer-bar bushings. Revised bushings are available as replacements. (1999-2000)

MITSUBISHI

AVERAGE REPLACEMENT COSTS

A/C Compressor	$695	Exhaust System	$280
Alternator	290	Radiator	380
Automatic Trans.	810	Shocks and/or Struts	860
Brakes	250	Timing Chain/Belt	465
CV Joints	1,430		

NHTSA RECALL HISTORY

1999-00 w/V6: On certain cars, battery-cable wiring harness can become heat-damaged by front exhaust manifold, which could cause grounded circuits. This failure could cause any of the following to occur: (1) engine will not start because main fuse will blow if power lead is grounded; (2) low oil-pressure warning lamp will illuminate if signal wire is grounded; (3) air conditioner will become inoperative if lead to magnetic clutch is grounded; and (4) turn signal/hazard lamps will become inoperative if voltage-monitor lead is grounded. **1999-00:** Steering-column multifunction switch levers can become loose or break over time; loosening or cracking can cause directional lamps that do not self-cancel or operate, headlamps that do not turn off, windshield washers that operate continuously, and/or windshield wipers that do not operate. **2000:** Power-steering pipe could wear through, allowing fluid leakage. Can result in a fire and continued loss of fluid will result in a loss of power assist, increasing the risk of a crash. **2001:** Bulge in fuel tank on small number of vehicles resulted in thinning of material, increasing risk of fuel leakage. **2002:** Front harness may be routed so that it comes into contact with a rough edge, possibly causing grounded circuits, loss of stop- or turn-signal lamp operation and/or engine hesitation. **2003:** Excessive fuel pressure could lead to fuel leak and fire.

PRICES

	Good	Average	Poor
1999 Galant	$5,000-6,300	$4,300-5,400	$2,000-2,500
Galant LS, GTZ	7,000-8,000	6,200-7,100	3,400-3,800
2000 Galant	6,000-7,500	5,200-6,500	2,500-3,200
Galant LS, GTZ	8,500-9,700	7,700-8,700	4,400-5,000
2001 Galant	7,200-8,800	6,400-7,800	3,500-4,300
Galant LS, GTZ	10,000-11,500	9,000-10,400	5,200-6,000
2002 Galant	9,000-11,000	8,100-9,900	4,700-5,700
Galant LS, GTZ	11,200-13,000	10,100-11,700	6,000-7,000
2003 Galant	11,000-13,500	9,900-12,200	5,900-7,300
Galant LS, GTZ	13,000-16,000	11,800-14,600	7,500-9,300

For detailed information on this vehicle visit
http://used.consumerguide.com and enter code **2390**

1997-02 MITSUBISHI MIRAGE

CLASS: Subcompact car
BUILT IN: Japan
PROS: Fuel economy
• Price • Visibility
CONS: Acceleration (DE)
• Rear-seat room (coupes)

EVALUATION: Unusually easy to drive, the latest Mirage scores well in a number of areas. Bonuses include a comfortable driving position, no-nonsense dashboard and sensibly placed controls, commanding visibility all around, and competitive passenger and cargo space. The only exception is the coupe's back seat, which is too small for adults to occupy comfortably.

Ride, handling, and braking all rank as acceptable, but not outstanding. A Mirage corners nimbly and predictably, with front-drive security. Ride comfort is good, and quite nice indeed on the highway. But the experience can begin to get choppy when rolling through broken surfaces and freeway expansion joints. On coarse pavement too, tire noise gets to be a problem. Wind rush is not excessive at highway speeds.

On the negative side, engine noise remains relatively strong. Acceleration isn't so lively, except with the bigger engine and manual transmission. The new automatic transmission is a lot smoother in operation and more responsive than the old one, but because models with the smaller engine lack sufficient power, we'd avoid automatic. In fact, we'd avoid the smaller engine entirely, due to its minimal gusto. An LS coupe with the bigger engine averaged 30.9 mpg in mostly highway driving. An LS sedan with automatic achieved 26 mpg in a mix of city and highway operation.

As expected, it's considerably easier to get into a 4-door than a 2-door, and the sedan offers more usable rear passenger space. Even so, leg and foot room out back are necessarily tight when sitting behind a tall front-seater. All models have a reasonably sized trunk with a flat floor. The LS coupe adds the extra versatility of a split folding backseat (which was available as an option package for sedans).

VALUE FOR THE MONEY: Mirage is definitely worth a test drive if you're shopping in the Civic/Corolla neighborhood and wouldn't mind saving a few dollars.

TROUBLE SPOTS

Spark plugs: Spark plugs tend to foul if the vehicle is driven only short distances in cold weather. (1997-98)

AVERAGE REPLACEMENT COSTS

A/C Compressor	$560	CV Joints	$1,230
Alternator	430	Exhaust System	230
Automatic Trans.	1,020	Radiator	360

MITSUBISHI

Brakes...............................	$330	Shocks and/or Struts.........	$715
Clutch...............................	440	Timing Chain/Belt.............	210

NHTSA RECALL HISTORY

1998: Poorly manufactured vacuum-check valve in hose between intake manifold and brake-vacuum booster. **1999-2001:** The bolt securing the crankshaft pulley can loosen. If the pulley falls off the vehicle, there will be a loss of power-steering assist.

PRICES

	Good	Average	Poor
1997 Mirage DE	$2,100-2,700	$1,500-1,900	$400-500
Mirage LS	2,500-3,100	1,800-2,300	500-700
1998 Mirage DE	2,400-3,200	1,800-2,300	500-600
Mirage LS	2,800-3,500	2,100-2,600	600-800
1999 Mirage DE	2,900-3,700	2,200-2,800	700-900
Mirage LS	3,300-4,000	2,600-3,200	800-1,000
2000 Mirage DE	3,600-4,500	2,900-3,600	1,000-1,300
Mirage LS	4,200-4,900	3,400-4,000	1,400-1,600
2001 Mirage DE, ES	4,500-5,500	3,700-4,600	1,600-2,000
Mirage LS	5,200-6,000	4,400-5,100	2,100-2,400
2002 Mirage coupe	6,000-7,000	5,200-6,100	2,500-2,900

For detailed information on this vehicle visit
http://used.consumerguide.com and enter code **2277**

1992-00 MITSUBISHI MONTERO

CLASS: Full-size sport-utility vehicle

BUILT IN: Japan

PROS: Acceleration (215-horsepower engine) • 4WD traction • Passenger and cargo room • Quietness • Ride

CONS: Acceleration (151-horsepower engine) • Entry/exit • Fuel economy

EVALUATION: The 3.0-liter V6 is smooth and quiet, but could use a bit more muscle. Acceleration with the base engine, even in 177-horsepower form, is adequate rather than spirited. Passing power also ranks as adequate. With automatic, steep grades cause noticeable slowing and a lot of busy shifting. Fuel economy is on the dismal side: we averaged 16.5 mpg in city/highway driving. An SR with the 215-horsepower engine accelerated to 60 mph in a brisk 10.0 seconds. Economy sagged to a gloomy 13.8 mpg. Mitsubishi's Active-Trac 4WD system is convenient and easy to use.

Montero is still one of the better-riding 4x4s, even more stable in corners than earlier versions, thanks to a slightly wider stance. A Montero doesn't feel as agile as a Jeep Grand Cherokee, however, showing more body lean in turns and even a slight tipsy sensation. Wavy surfaces produce little bouncing, but the firm suspension does not absorb bumps well.

The dashboard made everything easy to see, reach, and use, but the Multi Meter is little more than a gimmick. Passenger and cargo space are abundant, but the Montero sits high off the ground, so it's difficult to get in and out. Montero has more than enough cargo space for several grocery bags. Stowing the jump seats against the sidewalls creates a long, wide cargo area.

VALUE FOR THE MONEY: Despite some appealing features, Montero has not been at the top of our sport-utility list, when compared with such domestic rivals as the Ford Explorer, Jeep Grand Cherokee, and Chevrolet Blazer/GMC Jimmy, which tend to be more carlike.

TROUBLE SPOTS

Dashboard lights: The check-engine light may come on when the vehicle is driven at wide-open throttle. (1997)

Manual transmission: Hard shifting, gear clash, may come from the manual transmission due to a failure of the first-second gear synchronizers, while screeching noises are due to failed second-third synchros. (1992-95)

Paint/body: Paint on the roof rack fades and peels. (1992-93)

Steering problems: Shudder while cornering may be minimized by adding Mitsubishi Limited Slip Differential Additive to the rear differential. (1997)

AVERAGE REPLACEMENT COSTS

A/C Compressor	$825	Exhaust System	$370
Alternator	410	Radiator	665
Automatic Trans.	930	Shocks and/or Struts	300
Brakes	330	Timing Chain/Belt	405
Clutch	645	Universal Joints	1,180

NHTSA RECALL HISTORY

1992-93: During conditions of full-lock steering and full-suspension travel, front brake hose can crack, resulting in leakage. **1992-94 sold in Puerto Rico:** Front brake hose can crack during full-lock steering and full suspension travel, resulting in fluid leakage. **1994-98:** Accessory cargo mats interfere with latching integrity of the folding third seats. **1997-98:** Front brake lines can develop pinholes due to chafing; brake fluid can leak, resulting in deteriorated performance and illumination of indicator lamp. **1999 w/4WD and automatic:** Transmission fluid could be vented onto hot exhaust system as a result of unanticipated heat generation.

PRICES

	Good	Average	Poor
1992 Montero	$3,200-4,500	$2,500-3,500	$800-1,100
1993 Montero	3,800-5,300	3,100-4,300	1,100-1,600
1994 Montero	4,600-5,600	3,800-4,600	1,700-2,100
1995 Montero	5,500-6,500	4,700-5,600	2,300-2,700
1996 Montero	6,500-7,700	5,700-6,800	2,900-3,500
1997 Montero	7,500-8,800	6,800-7,900	3,800-4,400
1998 Montero	10,000-11,000	9,000-9,900	5,200-5,700

1999 Montero	$12,000-13,000	$10,800-11,700	$6,700-7,300
2000 Montero	14,000-15,500	12,700-14,100	8,500-9,500

For detailed information on this vehicle visit
http://used.consumerguide.com and enter code **2212**

2001-03 MITSUBISHI MONTERO

CLASS: Full-size sport-utility vehicle

BUILT IN: Japan

PROS: Cargo room
• Passenger room

CONS: Acceleration • Fuel economy • Ride
• Steering/handling

EVALUATION: Acceleration with a Montero borders on sluggish. The automatic transmission can be manually shifted to help keep pace with fast-moving traffic, but the Montero really needs a brawnier V8, as in most rivals.

Fuel economy is tolerable, however. A test Limited averaged 17.1 mpg using regular fuel.

Ride quality and handling earn no prizes. You get a curiously stiff ride, and the big tires clearly transmit even small bumps to the SUV's occupants. Still, the suspension does limit wallowing that allows only minor fore/aft pitching.

Steering is precise if slightly overassisted, but the Montero is not happy on curvy roads. A slightly tippy sensation will compel many drivers to slow down. Gusty crosswinds induce mild wandering a highway speeds.

Engines are decently quiet for cruising, but rather raucous when pushed. Tire roar is significant, except on smooth asphalt. Wind rush rises sharply with speed, too.

Although the dashboard looks busy, it works well enough, though small icons for "doors ajar" and 2WD/4WD operation are hard to see at times. Interior materials feel sturdy and controls have smooth action.

Front seats are comfortably spacious. Driver positioning is high and commanding, but some long-legged drivers might prefer more rearward seat travel. The second-row bench carries three adults with little crowding.

Narrow floor passages impede entry/exit, but the relatively low step-in is appreciated. So is the Montero's convenient fold-away third-row seat, though it's cramped except for preteens.

Cargo room is abundant. Some people won't like the right-hinged cargo door, but load height is reasonably low and seat-folding is easy. Inside are two roomy dashboard gloveboxes, map pockets, and a handy between-the-seats cubby.

VALUE FOR THE MONEY: Three rows of seats, solid construction, and reasonable fuel economy for a full-size SUV are among the Montero's attractions. Unfortunately, those benefits are overshadowed by mediocre acceleration; too much body lean in turns; and a harsh, trucky ride.

TROUBLE SPOTS

Audio system: Using novelty-type CDs, copied CDs, or those with poorly affixed labels may severely damage the player. (2001-03)

Dashboard lights: If the transmission overheats and turns on the "A/T TEMP" light, the oil pan should be replaced with a larger one. (2000-01)

Power seat: The wiring harness under the driver's seat may chafe and short out blowing a fusible link causing loss of power seat, power windows, and power sunroof. (2001-02)

Transmission leak: The transmission cooler (inside the radiator) may crack and leak, allowing transmission fluid into the coolant and coolant into the transmission. The company recalled early production models to replace the radiator. (2001)

Wheels: Shifting into or out of four-wheel drive while moving may cause it to get stuck in 4H (4-wheel high) range unless the shift forks are adjusted to prevent the problem. (2001)

AVERAGE REPLACEMENT COSTS

A/C Compressor	$410	CV Joints	$1,490
Alternator	375	Exhaust System	455
Automatic Trans.	1,915	Radiator	555
Brakes	375	Shocks and/or Struts	665
Clutch	455	Timing Chain/Belt	310

NHTSA RECALL HISTORY

2001: Some vehicle's passenger-side outside mirrors may not comply with the requirements of FMVSS 111. Dealers will replace the rearview mirror.
2001: The hydraulic brake-booster accumulator may have been improperly manufactured and could leak, resulting in an abnormal noise from the left side of the dash panel when the brakes are applied, and possibly a delayed first-time brake-boost assist after the vehicle has been parked for a period of time. Dealers will install an improved accumulator.

PRICES

	Good	Average	Poor
2001 Montero Limited	$19,500-21,000	$17,900-19,300	$12,700-13,700
Montero XLS	16,000-17,500	14,600-15,900	10,200-11,200
2002 Montero Limited	22,000-23,500	20,200-21,600	14,300-15,300
Montero XLS	18,500-20,000	17,000-18,400	11,800-12,800
2003 Montero Limited	25,000-27,000	23,300-25,100	16,500-17,800
Montero XLS	21,500-23,500	19,800-21,600	14,000-15,300

For detailed information on this vehicle visit
http://used.consumerguide.com and enter code **4499**

1997-03 MITSUBISHI MONTERO SPORT

CLASS: Midsize sport-utility vehicle
BUILT IN: Japan
PROS: Build quality
• Instruments/controls
CONS: Entry/exit • Fuel economy • Noise • Ride

EVALUATION: A 4-cylinder engine isn't sufficient for a vehicle of this size and weight. With the 3.0-liter V6, acceleration from a standstill is only a little less sluggish, even with a light load aboard. Modest upgrades slow progress considerably, which can present a problem even when merging onto certain expressways. The 3.5-liter V6 in the '99 Limited yields more satisfying performance. We managed about 17 mpg in city/highway driving with one Sport, but another example—driven somewhat harder—couldn't beat 15 mpg.

Use of the big Montero's chassis gives the Sport a stiff and lively ride on the highway. Overly light power steering is on the vague side. Although a Sport is far more stable than the bigger Montero in cornering, thanks to its lower stance, body lean is definitely noticeable in tight turns.

Noise levels reach beyond the SUV norm. Large door mirrors generate plenty of turbulence on the highway, and the engine fan whines loudly at higher speeds. Tire noise is prominent, too.

Ample ground clearance can be helpful for off-road operation, but the Sport's tall step-in makes getting in and out a chore, especially into the back seat. Four adults can ride without feeling claustrophobic, even when accompanied by a sizable load of luggage. Still, a low roofline limits head room for 6-footers, and rear leg space is no more than adequate. On some models, the spare tire mounts under the load deck so it doesn't cut into cargo space. Although the driver gets a commanding view, thick rear roof pillars hinder parking and lane changes. Instruments are large and legible. Most minor controls are within easy reach.

VALUE FOR THE MONEY: All told, the Montero Sport is too slow, noisy, and stiff-riding to truly satisfy the driver who spends more time on suburban roads than rural trails.

TROUBLE SPOTS

Engine knock: Models sold in California may have engine knock indicating possible welding flash entering the cylinders. (1997-98)

Engine noise: Valve tap for a couple minutes after startup is considered normal. (1997-98)

Vehicle shake: The vehicle may shudder when making low-speed turns and the condition may be corrected by adding a limited-slip differential additive. (1997)

AVERAGE REPLACEMENT COSTS

A/C Compressor	$825	Exhaust System	$350
Alternator	410	Radiator	650
Automatic Trans.	930	Shocks and/or Struts	800
Brakes	330	Timing Chain/Belt	405
Clutch	645	Universal Joints	560

NHTSA RECALL HISTORY

1999 w/4WD and automatic: Automatic-transmission fluid could be vented onto hot exhaust system. **1999-2001 w/3.5-liter engine:** Brake-vacuum hoses may fail causing a loss of power assist to the brakes and increase stopping distances.

PRICES

	Good	Average	Poor
1997 Montero Sport ES, LS	$4,200-6,200	$3,400-5,100	$1,400-2,000
Montero Sport XLS	7,000-8,000	6,200-7,100	3,400-3,800
1998 Montero Sport ES, LS	5,500-8,000	4,700-6,900	2,300-3,300
Montero Sport XLS	8,200-9,200	7,400-8,300	4,200-4,700
1999 Montero Sport ES, LS	7,000-10,000	6,200-8,900	3,400-4,800
Montero Sport Ltd.	11,000-12,500	9,900-11,300	5,900-6,800
Montero Sport XLS	9,500-11,000	8,600-9,900	4,900-5,700
2000 Montero Sport ES, LS	8,500-11,500	7,700-10,400	4,400-6,000
Montero Sport Ltd.	12,500-14,000	11,300-12,600	7,100-8,000
Montero Sport XLS	11,000-12,300	9,900-11,100	5,900-6,600
2001 Montero Sport ES, LS	10,000-13,200	9,000-11,900	5,200-6,900
Montero Sport Ltd.	14,000-15,500	12,700-14,100	8,500-9,500
Montero Sport XS, XLS	12,500-14,000	11,300-12,600	7,100-8,000
2002 Montero Sport ES, LS	11,500-15,000	10,400-13,500	6,300-8,300
Montero Sport Ltd.	16,200-18,000	14,700-16,400	10,400-11,500
Montero Sport XLS	14,500-16,500	13,200-15,000	9,000-10,200
2003 Montero Sport ES, LS	14,000-17,500	12,700-15,900	8,500-10,700
Montero Sport Ltd.	19,000-21,500	17,500-19,800	12,400-14,000
Montero Sport XLS	16,800-18,800	15,500-17,300	10,800-12,000

For detailed information on this vehicle visit
http://used.consumerguide.com and enter code **2278**

1995-98 NISSAN 240SX

CLASS: Sporty coupe

BUILT IN: Japan

PROS: Optional antilock brakes • Instruments/controls • Steering/handling

CONS: Cargo room • Noise • Rear-seat room • Ride (SE)

EVALUATION: Acceleration is nothing special for a sports coupe. A base-model 240SX with the automatic transmission took 10 seconds flat

NISSAN

to reach 60 mph. Takeoffs are strong enough at first, but acceleration tapers off at higher speeds. The engine produces a sporty but loud snarl under hard acceleration. Road noise also is prominent. As for gas mileage, we averaged 20.8 mpg with automatic and 25.2 mpg with a 5-speed.

Sharp steering and agile reactions are the bonuses of this coupe's rear-drive chassis, but poor traction on slippery roads remains a sore spot. Ride comfort depends on the model. The firmer SE suspension rides more harshly than the base version, which does a better job of absorbing bumps and tar strips.

Despite the lengthened wheelbase and wider body, the 240SX still suffers from a snug interior. Space is considerably less than the car's outside dimensions suggest, and the wraparound cockpit gives a somewhat closed-in feeling. Head room is limited for tall drivers. Even children will lack space in the rear seat, especially in terms of leg room. Seats are nicely supportive. Visibility is good all around, except past somewhat thick windshield pillars.

VALUE FOR THE MONEY: We've not been overwhelmed by either the styling or the performance of the 240SX, before or after the '97 facelift.

TROUBLE SPOTS

Air conditioner: Poor air-conditioner performance due to compressor-joint seals that tend to leak. (1995-96)

Brakes: Nissan issued a voluntary recall to replace a defective diode that will not turn on the low-brake-fluid-warning light. (1995)

Dashboard lights: The check-engine light may come on and set an erroneous trouble code for the crankshaft position sensor if certain wires in the computerized engine-control circuits are not kept separated from one another. (1995)

Engine temperature: The engine tends to overheat if any air trapped in the cooling system is not properly bled. (1995)

AVERAGE REPLACEMENT COSTS

A/C Compressor	$695	CV Joints	$430
Alternator	290	Exhaust System	180
Automatic Trans.	810	Radiator	380
Brakes	220	Shocks and/or Struts	460
Clutch	335	Timing Chain/Belt	660

NHTSA RECALL HISTORY

1995: Brake-warning light will not illuminate when fluid level drops.

PRICES	Good	Average	Poor
1995 240SX	$3,000-3,900	$2,300-3,000	$700-900
1996 240SX	3,900-4,800	3,200-3,900	1,200-1,500
1997 240SX	5,300-7,000	4,600-6,000	2,200-2,900
1998 240SX	6,900-8,800	6,100-7,800	3,200-4,100

For detailed information on this vehicle visit
http://used.consumerguide.com and enter code **2219**

1993-97 NISSAN ALTIMA

CLASS: Compact car

BUILT IN: USA

PROS: Antilock brakes (optional) • Fuel economy • Instruments/controls • Steering/handling

CONS: Automatic-transmission performance • Engine noise • Road noise • Wind noise

EVALUATION: Performance and fuel economy from the standard 150-horsepower 2.4-liter 4-cylinder engine are more than adequate. Even with the automatic transmission, passing response is fine. But when called upon to pass quickly or make a merging maneuver, aggressive use of the accelerator is required to coax the automatic to make its one- or two-gear downshift.

Benefiting from its wide standard tires (205/60R-15s), the Altima is more athletic and nimble than all but the Accord. Ride quality is comfortable, if firm, and braking is strong and progressive. Also contributing to the car's handling prowess is its crisp steering response. The only potential drawback is a cabin that could use a bit more sound insulation.

The interior provides adequate head room for all passengers and enough space for two adults in the rear seat. The trunk has a wide, flat floor, giving the Altima good cargo room for its size.

VALUE FOR THE MONEY: Overall, we rate Nissan's compact sedan highly and encourage buyers to give it a close look before buying anything in its league.

TROUBLE SPOTS

Air conditioner: Poor air-conditioner performance may be caused by a refrigerant leak at the compressor-joint connector and is fixed by replacing the O-ring. (1993-95)

Automatic transmission: If the transmission does not shift properly until warmed up, make sure it is filled only with Nissanmatic "C" transmission fluid. (All)

Automatic transmission: Burnt transmission fluid or no reverse gear signal a defective rear control valve and low/reverse brake. (1993-94)

Automatic transmission: If the gauges quit working, the check-engine light comes on, or the transmission shifts harshly, then a wiring harness may be chafing on the top of the transmission under the battery tray or the instrument-wiring harness is chafing on the airbag-harness support bracket. (1995)

Brakes: Inspect the right-rear brake hose for chafing on the rear suspension, which could lead to a leak and brake failure. (1995)

Oil leak: Oil leaking from the front of the engine could be caused by a bad O-ring between the timing cover and the engine block. (1993-95)

AVERAGE REPLACEMENT COSTS

A/C Compressor	$510	CV Joints	$385
Alternator	275	Exhaust System	475

NISSAN

Automatic Trans.	$900	Radiator............................	$280
Brakes................................	200	Shocks and/or Struts.........	540
Clutch................................	440	Timing Chain/Belt.............	755

NHTSA RECALL HISTORY

1993-94: Engine movement can cause throttle-cable housing to pull out of its guide; engine may then not return to idle when gas pedal is released. **1994-95:** Air bags in certain vehicles are causing eye injuries. Dealer will replace all affected air bags. **1995 w/automatic:** Shift-lever lock plate can be broken; movement of lever without driver's knowledge can result in unexpected vehicle movement. **1995:** On a few cars, right-rear brake hose may contact suspension component, causing abrasion and eventual leakage. **1997:** Seatbelts might not restrain occupant during a collision.

PRICES

	Good	Average	Poor
1993 Altima	$1,900-2,500	$1,300-1,700	$300-400
Altima SE, GLE	2,300-2,900	1,700-2,100	400-600
1994 Altima	2,300-3,000	1,700-2,200	400-600
Altima SE, GLE	2,800-3,400	2,100-2,600	600-700
1995 Altima	2,800-3,500	2,100-2,600	600-800
Altima SE, GLE	3,300-4,000	2,600-3,200	800-1,000
1996 Altima	3,300-4,000	2,600-3,200	800-1,000
Altima SE, GLE	3,800-4,400	3,100-3,600	1,100-1,300
1997 Altima	3,800-4,500	3,100-3,600	1,100-1,400
Altima SE, GLE	4,300-5,000	3,500-4,100	1,500-1,700

For detailed information on this vehicle visit
http://used.consumerguide.com and enter code **2077**

1998-01 NISSAN ALTIMA

BEST BUY CG

CLASS: Compact car

BUILT IN: USA

PROS: Passenger room • Quietness • Ride

CONS: Automatic-transmission performance

EVALUATION: Acceleration is little-changed from the prior generation—in short, nothing to shout about. Our test GLE ran 0-60 mph in a so-so 10 seconds with automatic transmission. The 2000 models should be a bit swifter. There's also little change in the transmission's reluctance to downshift promptly, or in its abruptness when it does. Our test GXE returned a somewhat disappointing 20.3 mpg, while our GLE averaged 23.4 mpg, despite hard city driving and performance testing.

Expect a smooth, absorbent ride except on washboard surfaces, where minor wheel pattering disturbs the calm. Alas, the ride exacts a tradeoff in mediocre body control over big humps and dips, plus more body lean in tight turns than we prefer. Even so, Altima handling is competently agile, aided by quick steering with good feedback. Braking with ABS proved to be safe and undramatic, if unexceptional by today's standards.

Unlike previous Altimas, the current generation allows 6-footers to sit comfortably in tandem. The cabin still is not wide enough for three adults in back, but leg, knee, and foot space are all good, as is overall head room even with a power moonroof installed. Front bucket seats in the 2000 models are more supportive and better bolstered.

The dashboard is nicely laid out, with clean gauges and convenient, guess-free controls that complement a comfortable driver's post. Commuters should welcome the new console-mounted dual cupholders—much more useful than the rickety pull-out contraption of old. Visibility is good except over-the-shoulder, due to high tail styling and wide rear roof posts. Trunk space is good, but not great. A wide rear-bumper shelf makes for some back-straining reaches, and the lid hinges intrude into the cargo area. The cabin has plenty of places for bric-a-brac, though not accessible to rear seaters.

VALUE FOR THE MONEY: Acceptably solid and well-finished, Altima remains a must-see for value-minded buyers, due largely to its low noise levels and soft ride. Trunklids have felt tinny, however. Though unexceptional, Altima ranks as a nice family compact—less bland after the 2000 revamp.

TROUBLE SPOTS

Keyless entry: The remote keyless-entry system is difficult to program. (1998)
Vehicle noise: A broken BTV valve bracket causes a rattle under the hood. (1999-2000)

AVERAGE REPLACEMENT COSTS

A/C Compressor	$610	CV Joints	$1,235
Alternator	320	Exhaust System	180
Automatic Trans.	745	Radiator	330
Brakes	205	Shocks and/or Struts	525
Clutch	430	Timing Chain/Belt	775

NHTSA RECALL HISTORY

None to date.

PRICES

	Good	Average	Poor
1998 Altima SE, GLE	$5,400-6,100	$4,600-5,200	$2,200-2,500
Altima XE, GXE	4,800-5,500	4,000-4,600	1,800-2,100
1999 Altima SE, GLE	6,900-7,600	6,100-6,800	3,200-3,600
Altima XE, GXE	6,000-7,000	5,200-6,100	2,500-2,900
2000 Altima SE, GLE	8,500-9,500	7,700-8,600	4,400-4,900
Altima XE, GXE	7,500-8,500	6,800-7,700	3,800-4,300
2001 Altima SE, GLE	10,200-11,500	9,200-10,400	5,300-6,000
Altima XE, GXE	9,000-10,000	8,100-9,000	4,700-5,200

For detailed information on this vehicle visit
http://used.consumerguide.com and enter code 2329

2002-03 NISSAN ALTIMA

CLASS: Midsize car

BUILT IN: USA

PROS: Acceleration (3.5 SE) • Handling/roadholding • Instruments/controls

CONS: Engine noise (4-cyl)

EVALUATION: There's a lot to like about the latest Altimas. Nissan forecasted that four-cylinder engines would account for 80 percent of Altima sales. Early tests put automatic transmission versions at 8.6 seconds for 0-60 mph acceleration. That's competitive with rival four cylinder Honda Accords and Volkswagen Passats, and slightly quicker than Toyota Camrys. But Altima's four-cylinder is unrefined compared to its rivals', being buzzy and coarse in all but gentle cruising.

The robust V6 is as smooth and responsive as any competitor's. Acceleration to 60 mph in 6.9 seconds, with automatic, places the 3.5 SE among the quickest midsize sedans.

EPA gas-mileage estimates are similar to those of Accord and Camry, which have less horsepower. A 2.5 S averaged 23.9 mpg in mostly highway driving. An SE with automatic got only 17.6 mpg including performance testing, but 24.9 mpg when traveling mainly on the highway. Altima's 20-gallon fuel tank is the largest in the midsize class. Nissan recommends premium fuel for the V6.

A rigid structure and smart suspension design pay off in a comfortable, controlled ride. Four-cylinder models feel particularly absorbent over ruts and crests. More-aggressive tires firm up the 3.5 SE's ride, but it's not jarring.

Handling is good overall, despite overly sensitive straightline steering feel. Confident roadholding and good balance in turns help make the 3.5 SE crisper in all respects, thanks to its wider, lower-profile tires. On the other hand, a wide turning circle frustrates around-town driving and parking. Also, torque steer can make the 3.5 SE feel a little too spirited during brisk acceleration. Braking is strong, and easily modulated in ABS-equipped models.

The growling, vibratory four-cylinder engine offsets fine suppression of road and wind noise. Some sedan bodies suffered a metallic drumming resonance on coarse pavement.

Gauges are deep-set in instrument-panel coves, but brightly backlit for great readability even in daylight. Dashboard design is clean, contemporary, and user-friendly. The wiggle worm automatic-transmission shift gate invites easy manual gear changes, but doesn't suit everyone. Manual gearboxes on early models worked crudely.

An arching roof creates generous head room. Leg room also is good, as is seat comfort and bolstering. The driver gets height adjustment in all but base models. All Altimas have handy height-adjustable center armrests. Separate levers for steering-wheel tilt and telescoping adjustments is unorthodox, but provides greater-than-usual range of motion. Outward visibility is hampered slightly by a tall rear deck and by occasional reflections off light-colored dashboard tops.

Large, wide rear door openings ease entry/exit. Comfortable well-contoured seating offers plenty of knee and toe space. But head room for those over 5-feet-8 is constrained, and three-across adult seating is a squeeze. Two cupholders sit in the folding center armrest. Low-grade plastics inside, and a tinny clang of the trunklid, proved disappointing.

Altimas have a wide trunk with low liftover, but lid hinges dip into the cargo area. All models have a 60/40 split fold-down rear seatback for added versatility.

VALUE FOR THE MONEY: Nissan finally got a genuine Camry/Accord alternative in the moderately priced midsize class. Strong on features for the money, the Altima gained a spunky personality, especially in sporty 3.5 SE guise. Not as refined or well-built as a Camry, Accord or Passat, the latest Altima is nevertheless strongly recommended. Four-cylinder models satisfy most needs.

TROUBLE SPOTS

Air conditioner: On some early production vehicles, the manual adjuster for the air conditioner fails because the gear that controls the air blend door falls off. (2002)

Clutch: On some early build cars, the original-equipment clutch disc causes a howling sound during release (pedal being depressed) and a countermeasure disc with different friction is available. (2002)

Electrical problem: The exhaust manifold heat shield on early production cars cuts the oxygen sensor wires, resulting in lack of engine power. (2002)

Engine stalling: A problem with the ignition coils causes stumbling during light throttle cruise or stalling at idle, requiring installation of a resistor between the coils and spark plugs. (2002)

Wheels: The wheel covers chirp or squeak because they rub on the wheel (balance) weights which must be covered with felt tape to prevent the noise. (2002)

AVERAGE REPLACEMENT COSTS

A/C Compressor	$705	CV Joints	$1,125
Alternator	310	Exhaust System	395
Automatic Trans.	1,895	Radiator	380
Brakes	325	Shocks and/or Struts	630
Clutch	635	Timing Chain/Belt	460

NHTSA RECALL HISTORY

2002: On certain vehicles, driver's-side-airbag electrical connector may come loose. If the connector comes loose, the supplemental airbag warning light flashes intermittently. In this situation, the driver's-side airbag will not deploy in the event of a crash. Dealers will install a retaining clip on the clock-spring electrical connector. **2002:** One of the sensors for the airbag system does not work as well as expected in high-speed offset crash situations. Dealers will replace the airbag sensor. **2002-03 in cold climates:** Moisture in fuel tank could freeze and form ice crystals that may obstruct the suction opening of the fuel pump causing the vehicle to stop running. Dealers will install a screen at the suction opening of the fuel pump. **2002-03 w/2.5-liter engine:** Exhaust-pipe hanger pin may catch debris from that could be ignited by contact with the main catalyst. Dealers will remove the protruding pin and install heat shield(s).

NISSAN

For detailed information on this vehicle visit
http://used.consumerguide.com and enter code **4488**

1998-2003 NISSAN FRONTIER

CLASS: Compact pickup truck

BUILT IN: USA

PROS: Standard 4-wheel antilock brakes (selected models) • Control layout • Ride/handling

CONS: Acceleration (4-cylinder) • Rear-only ABS on 2WD models • Rear-seat comfort

EVALUATION: Nissan's coarse 2.4-liter twin-cam four-cylinder engine does not have enough get-up-and-go for even base model 2WD regular cabs. However, manual-transmission clutch and shift actions are light and smooth and the automatic shifts crisply and kicks down quickly for more passing power. The new V6 engine made available for 1999 brought a welcome power boost for 4x4s, but was needed almost as much in 4x2 models. Though stronger than a 4 cylinder, however, the V6 engine still is less robust than most rivals. The Supercharged V6 introduced in 2001 gives Frontier a needed shot in the arm, even though it feels little faster than the top V6s in most rival compact pickups. A 4x4 King Cab V6 with manual shift took a leisurely 11.2 seconds to hit 60 mph, while the Supercharged V6 with automatic did 0-60 mph in an estimated 9.2 sec.

Ride and handling are strong points, both ranking with the best small pickups. Bumps are taken in stride, and there's only moderate body lean in corners. Stopping power is only adequate with rear-only antilock braking, but swift and stable with the all-wheel system. Beware of the optional Off-Road Package, which makes the going a lot bouncier.

Frontier has a fresh, carlike interior. That's pleasing, but the old-fashioned pull-out, umbrella-style hand brake is not. In addition, the automatic transmission's column-shift lever interferes with wiper stalk and climate controls. Climate and radio controls are mounted high, and within easy reach. All told, the interior design is far more modern than that of Nissan's previous pickup.

Front head and leg room are generous for even 6-footers. As in every other extended-cab compact pickup, the King Cab's jump seats are child size. Crew

Cabs, added for 2000, maneuver just as easily as King Cab models. The Crew Cab's aft entryways are quite narrow, and there's little leg room ahead of the hard back bench unless a front seat is shoved far forward. Entry/exit is good to the front, and 4WD Frontiers do not have as high a step-in as some competing 4x4 models. Interiors use plenty of hard plastic. All but the base 2WD model have front-door map pockets. Cloth trim on seats and door panels is more upscale than in the typical compact pickup.

VALUE FOR THE MONEY: Neither the brawniest nor the most refined compact truck of them all, Frontier is still worth a close look. If the truck you find fits your needs, Frontier rates among the better small pickups.

TROUBLE SPOTS

Engine noise: Engine rattle at startup is corrected by installing new camshaft bolts and a timing-chain tensioner. (1998-99)

AVERAGE REPLACEMENT COSTS

A/C Compressor	$725	Exhaust System	$260
Alternator	410	Radiator	285
Automatic Trans.	850	Shocks and/or Struts	470
Brakes	355	Timing Chain/Belt	180
Clutch	570	Universal Joints	330

NHTSA RECALL HISTORY

1998 w/automatic transmission: Securing pin inside transmission-control assembly of some trucks can loosen, allowing shift lever to be inadvertently moved out of the "Park" position with key in ignition. **1998 w/bucket seats:** In frontal crash, front seatbelt can slip between seat and seatback-recliner handle, where it can be cut by sharp edge of lever. **1999-00:** Taillight socket may have been improperly molded, resulting in locking tab having insufficient force to retain bulb. **2001:** Fuel-tank shutter valves may be faulty on certain vehicles, resulting in possible fuel leakage. Dealers will inspect and replace affected parts. **2002:** Under certain conditions, on vehicles equipped with a supercharger, faulty airflow meters may have been installed, resulting in the illumination of the malfunction indicator lamp and decreased engine speed. Dealer will inspect and reprogram affected meters. **2003 XE:** Some vehicles may have spare tires with incorrect size rims, resulting in deteriorating brake performance. Dealer will inspect and replace affected rims.

PRICES

	Good	Average	Poor
1998 Frontier 2WD	$4,000-7,000	$3,300-5,700	$1,300-2,200
Frontier 4WD	6,000-8,500	5,200-7,400	2,500-3,600
1999 Frontier 2WD	5,200-7,800	4,400-6,600	2,100-3,100
Frontier 4WD	7,200-10,500	6,400-9,300	3,500-5,100
2000 Frontier 2WD	6,200-11,000	5,400-9,600	2,700-4,700
Frontier 4WD	9,500-13,000	8,600-11,700	4,900-6,800
2001 Frontier 2WD	7,500-13,500	6,800-12,200	3,800-6,800
Frontier 4WD	11,500-15,500	10,400-14,000	6,300-8,500
2002 Frontier 2WD	9,500-16,000	8,600-14,400	4,900-8,300
Frontier 4WD	14,000-18,000	12,700-16,400	8,500-11,000

2003 Frontier 2WD	$11,200-18,500	$10,100-16,700	$6,000-10,000
Frontier 4WD	16,000-20,000	14,600-18,200	10,200-12,800

> For detailed information on this vehicle visit
> http://used.consumerguide.com and enter code **2330**

1990-94 NISSAN MAXIMA

CLASS: Midsize car
BUILT IN: Japan
PROS: Acceleration
• Antilock brakes (optional)
• Handling/roadholding
• Instruments/controls • Ride
CONS: Fuel economy
• Head room (w/optional sunroof)

EVALUATION: With 190 horsepower on tap, the SE is a potent and sporty performer that matches up well when compared with higher-priced European models. Those preferring a touch of luxury will discover the GXE is also well worth considering. Maxima comes with a well-organized instrument panel and comfortable driving position. It provides the kind of poised front-drive handling and competent road manners that others have tried to emulate, coupled with a comfortable ride. With its softer suspension the GXE leans a bit more in the turns than the firmer SE, but both models respond to steering inputs quickly and precisely.

Especially worthy of praise is the twin-cam V6 that powers the SE model. It's smoother, quieter, and feels stronger than engines offered by most of the Maxima's rivals. It propels the Maxima SE to 60 mph in under 9.0 seconds with the manual transmission, while the GXE equipped with the mannerly 4-speed automatic performs the task in about 10.5 seconds. The interior has ample head room in front and back, plus enough leg room for tall people to stretch out comfortably. Our only complaints focus on the slow addition of airbags—dual airbags didn't become standard until 1995.

VALUE FOR THE MONEY: This verdict is a simple one: the Maxima heads our must-drive list of near-luxury sedans from the early 1990s.

TROUBLE SPOTS

Airbags: A voluntary recall was issued to replace an airbag sensor to reduce the possibility of the bag deploying when it is not needed. (1992-93)

Automatic transmission: If the transmission does not shift properly until warmed up, make sure it is filled only with Nissanmatic "C" transmission fluid. (all)

Automatic transmission: Burnt transmission fluid and no reverse gear may signal a defective rear-control valve and low/reverse brake. (1993-94)

Clutch: The clutch plate, pressure plate, and release fork must be replaced if there is clutch judder. (1990-92)

Coolant leak: Coolant may leak from the front of the cylinder head, which may appear to be a head gasket, but comes from a threaded plug in the front of the head. (1990-94)

Engine noise: Noise from the top of the engine can be traced to a problem with the spring assembly in the variable-valve timing control (VTC). (1992-94)

Heater core: Poor heater performance is likely after the coolant is changed due to air trapped in the heater core. (1990)

Manual transmission: If the manual transmission slips, the clutch disc will be replaced with a revised one. (1994)

Rough idle: Idle fluctuation may result from the use of the wrong air-filter, or if the original air-filter housing was not replaced with a revised unit for a funnel-shaped filter. (1990)

AVERAGE REPLACEMENT COSTS

A/C Compressor	$655	CV Joints	$475
Alternator	240	Exhaust System	315
Automatic Trans.	935	Radiator	500
Brakes	190	Shocks and/or Struts	1,385
Clutch	545	Timing Chain/Belt	370

NHTSA RECALL HISTORY

1990-94 registered in CT, DE, DC, IA, IL, IN, MA, MD, ME, MI, MN, NH, NJ, NY, OH, PA, RI, VT, WI, and WV: Mixture of mud and salt could become trapped between fuel-filler tube and wheel housing; corrosion could result in fuel leakage. **1992-93 w/driver-side airbag:** In some underbody impacts, sensor activates and causes airbag to inflate when not needed. **1993-94 GXE w/aluminum wheels:** Excessive clear-coating may position wheel nuts too far away from hub when tightened.

PRICES	Good	Average	Poor
1990 Maxima	$1,900-2,500	$1,300-1,700	$300-400
1991 Maxima	2,300-3,000	1,700-2,200	400-600
1992 Maxima	2,700-3,400	2,000-2,600	600-700
1993 Maxima	3,100-3,800	2,400-3,000	700-900
1994 Maxima	3,600-4,400	2,900-3,500	1,000-1,200

For detailed information on this vehicle visit
http://used.consumerguide.com and enter code **2078**

1995-99 NISSAN MAXIMA

CLASS: Midsize car
BUILT IN: Japan
PROS: Acceleration
• Optional antilock brakes
• Ride • Steering/handling
CONS: Fuel economy
• Rear-seat comfort

EVALUATION: Performance leads off the car's strong points, ranking as little short of stunning. We timed a GXE with the automatic transmission at 7.9 seconds to 60 mph. Tromp the gas pedal to the floor, and a Maxima nearly leaps ahead. Only modest engine roar is heard on such occasions, as the Maxima is otherwise quiet-running. Passing power also is impressive, but the automatic unit is slow to downshift for passing at times, and occasionally shifts harshly. As for fuel economy, we averaged 24.1 mpg with one GXE and 21.4 mpg with another.

Maxima offers a comfortable and stable ride, precise steering, and crisp handling. Body lean is noticeable in high-speed lane changes and when cornering swiftly, but the Maxima maintains a tight grip on the road surface.

Maxima feels really big inside—more so than its outside appearance suggests. With a little more head room and rear leg room than its predecessor, the latest Maxima is more accommodating for tall passengers. The wide trunk has a flat floor that provides plenty of cargo space. Instruments and controls are well-positioned and easy to see and use while driving. The low dashboard permits a great view of the road ahead. Stereo and climate controls are in a slanted panel that's easy to reach. Round analog gauges are large.

VALUE FOR THE MONEY: If you're searching for a midsize sedan that reaches above the run-of-the-mill offerings, a Maxima of any 1995-99 vintage is definitely worth a trial run.

TROUBLE SPOTS

Automatic transmission: The original automatic-transmission (model F04) shift solenoids allowed slipping and premature wear. (1997)

Brake noise: Groaning from the rear brakes is caused by the parking brakes not fully releasing, requiring new brake cables and pads. (1995-99)

Brake noise: Rear brakes rattle on rough road. (1995)

Clutch: The clutch may slip when accelerating hard in 4th or 5th gear due to a problem with the friction material. (1995)

Engine knock: Spark knock or ping may result from a defective onboard computer. (1995-97)

Engine noise: Noise from the front of the engine may be caused by excessive play in the timing chain for which a new tensioner and chain guide are required. (1995-96)

Hard starting: If the engine does not start on the first attempt, the engine may crank very slowly on the second attempt because of a problem with the engine-control computer. (1995)

Hard starting: Hard starting, stalling, or stumbling under load could be caused by corrosion of the coolant sensor. (1995-96)

Rough idle: Several problems (no-start, no A/C, rough running, etc.) can be traced to broken wires in the engine compartment where the harness bends near the right strut tower. (1995-97)

AVERAGE REPLACEMENT COSTS

A/C Compressor	$625	CV Joints	$1,145
Alternator	450	Exhaust System	375
Automatic Trans.	1,080	Radiator	445
Brakes	210	Shocks and/or Struts	1,530
Clutch	515	Timing Chain/Belt	1,305

NHTSA RECALL HISTORY

1997-98: One of the diodes in the alternator may be damaged and could fail, leading to an electrical short which could melt the plastic housing.

PRICES	Good	Average	Poor
1995 Maxima	$4,200-5,300	$3,400-4,300	$1,400-1,700
1996 Maxima	4,800-6,000	4,000-5,000	1,800-2,300
1997 Maxima	6,200-7,700	5,400-6,700	2,700-3,300
1998 Maxima	8,000-9,500	7,200-8,600	4,100-4,800
1999 Maxima	9,800-11,500	8,800-10,400	5,100-6,000

For detailed information on this vehicle visit
http://used.consumerguide.com and enter code **2214**

2000-03 NISSAN MAXIMA

CG BEST BUY

CLASS: Midsize car
BUILT IN: Japan
PROS: Acceleration
• Ride • Steering/handling
CONS: Manual shift action

EVALUATION: Redesigning improved what was already a smooth, swift, and polished performer. A Maxima corners with grippy assurance and only mild body lean. The sporty SE is a tad crisper thanks to its sport suspension, but all Maximas are agile and the driver benefits from quick, informative steering. On the negative side, the SE's tauter suspension results in a somewhat choppy ride over bumps that other models comfortably absorb. Braking is quick and consistent, with excellent control.

A responsive powertrain yields 0-60 mph acceleration in 7.9 seconds. In fact, the V6 feels truly muscular, delivering fine punch off the line and strong passing power. Test Maximas have averaged 20-22.5 mpg, but premium fuel is recommended. Automatic transmissions are free of lurching in full-throttle downshifts—a malady suffered by earlier Maximas. Manual-transmission models suffer from imprecise clutch takeup and slightly stiff shift action. Unless the front wheels are perfectly straight too, there's some annoying steering-wheel tub during hard takeoffs.

Although the practical limit is four grownups inside, each has a bit more wiggle room than in the past. Taller adults get enough head clearance beneath the optional moonroof, and a more upright rear seatback improves comfort on long trips. Still, 6-footers need to ride knees-up in back if a taller person is occupying the front seat ahead. Visibility is good except directly to the rear. Gauges and controls are simple and inviting, though look-alike knobs for audio volume and temperature could confuse. Rearward seat travel is good; power seat controls easy to reach. The trunk has a wide, low opening.

NISSAN

VALUE FOR THE MONEY: Quiet and athletic, the Maxima offers an appealing blend of performance, handling, and ride comfort, with refinement and amenities approaching the near-luxury class. Nissan's top sedan fares well against such tough adversaries as the Honda Accord and Toyota Camry.

TROUBLE SPOTS

Audio system: Popping and crackling noises in the audio system are often due to cell phones plugged into the cigarette lighter. Using a different power source or moving the phone often helps. (2000)

Cold-starting problems: The engine may idle too slowly or stall when first started (below 40 degrees F). Reprogramming of the powertrain-control module is required. (2000)

Sunroof/moonroof: The headliner may sag near the sunroof because the Velcro does not hold sufficiently. Additional clips were being installed under warranty. (2000)

Vehicle noise: Noises from the right front strut require replacement of the rubber spring seat. (2000)

AVERAGE REPLACEMENT COSTS

A/C Compressor	$705	CV Joints	$740
Alternator	290	Exhaust System	480
Automatic Trans.	1,310	Radiator	380
Brakes	455	Shocks and/or Struts	470
Clutch	635	Timing Chain/Belt	460

NHTSA RECALL HISTORY

2001-02: The pin on the lower control arm could break, causing a knocking sound and abnormal steering. **2002 w/electronic throttle-control system:** Due to the incorrect design of the accelerator-pedal stopper, the pedal can "overtravel," causing the check-engine light to come on and/or reducing engine speed.

PRICES

	Good	Average	Poor
2000 Maxima GXE	$12,000-13,000	$10,800-11,700	$6,700-7,300
Maxima SE, GLE	13,500-14,700	12,300-13,400	8,000-8,700
2001 Maxima GXE	13,500-14,700	12,300-13,400	8,000-8,700
Maxima SE, GLE	15,000-16,200	13,700-14,700	9,500-10,200
2002 Maxima GXE	15,000-16,500	13,700-15,000	9,500-10,400
Maxima SE, GLE	16,500-17,700	15,000-16,100	10,600-11,300
2003 Maxima GXE	17,500-19,000	16,100-17,500	11,200-12,200
Maxima SE, GLE	19,000-21,500	17,500-19,800	12,400-14,000

For detailed information on this vehicle visit
http://used.consumerguide.com and enter code **2393**

1990-95 NISSAN PATHFINDER

CLASS: Midsize sport-utility vehicle
BUILT IN: Japan
PROS: Acceleration
• Antilock brakes (optional)
• Wet-weather traction (4WD) • Passenger and cargo room
CONS: Entry/exit • Fuel economy

EVALUATION: Early Nissan Pathfinder models seemed to ride smoothly, with less of the rough bounce customary on some of the new truck-based compact sport-utility vehicles. Adequate power finally arrived in 1990 when the 3.0-liter engine switched to multipoint fuel injection, giving the Pathfinder 180 horsepower, but low-end torque still is not sufficient to help the Pathfinder keep pace with the Explorer or Cherokee when called upon to climb hills or haul heavy loads.

Given that the Pathfinder was not significantly changed after 1990, the newer Ford Explorer and Jeep Cherokee have provided more popular carlike features and handling, making Nissan's older design feel dated, too stiff, and unsophisticated. Gas mileage is dismal as well. In our test we only achieved 14.7 mpg with the automatic. The Pathfinder's 4WD system is another drawback. Since it lacks full shift-on-the-fly capability, it's far less convenient than most competitive part-time systems used by an ever-growing number of rivals.

The handling is safe and predictable, but ranks far below the head of the class. Also, narrow rear doors that combine with a high step-up made entering and exiting a bit of a chore.

VALUE FOR THE MONEY: To its credit, the Pathfinder provides precise steering and ample cargo room. It's also rugged and as durable as a Swiss Army knife. Unfortunately, the compact sport-utility market has stampeded forward toward more carlike vehicles, effectively leaving the Pathfinder in the dust.

TROUBLE SPOTS

Air conditioner: Rattling or rumbling from the blower may be caused by leaves and other debris that are not stopped by the fresh-air grille. (1993-95)

Automatic transmission: If the transmission does not shift properly until warmed up, make sure it is filled only with Nissanmatic "C" transmission fluid. (1990-95)

Coolant leak: Coolant may leak from the front of the cylinder head, which may appear to be a head gasket, but comes from a threaded plug in the front of the head. (1990-95)

Hard starting: If the engine is hard to start at high altitudes, it is flooding from too much fuel and a revised water-temperature sensor will cure the problem. (1990-95)

NISSAN

Oil leak: Oil leaks from the manual transmission are likely coming from the breather vent. (1990-93)

Oil leak: There is a revised pinion seal to correct oil leaks at both front and rear differentials on 2WD and 4WD models. (1992)

Poor drivability: A check-engine light accompanied by poor drivability could be caused by water in the wiring connector for the oxygen sensor. (1995)

AVERAGE REPLACEMENT COSTS

A/C Compressor	$540	Exhaust System	$275
Alternator	250	Radiator	460
Automatic Trans.	830	Shocks and/or Struts	295
Brakes	225	Timing Chain/Belt	375
Clutch	470	Universal Joints	170

NHTSA RECALL HISTORY

1990-91: Front-seatbelt release button can break and pieces can fall inside. **1994:** Latch plate in seatbelt buckle could engage only partially, causing tongue to come out of buckle during collision or hard braking.

PRICES	Good	Average	Poor
1990 Pathfinder 2WD	$2,000-2,600	$1,400-1,800	$300-400
Pathfinder 4WD	2,500-3,300	1,800-2,400	500-700
1991 Pathfinder 2WD	2,400-3,100	1,800-2,300	500-600
Pathfinder 4WD	2,900-3,700	2,200-2,800	700-900
1992 Pathfinder 2WD	2,800-3,500	2,100-2,600	600-800
Pathfinder 4WD	3,400-4,200	2,700-3,300	900-1,100
1993 Pathfinder 2WD	3,200-3,900	2,500-3,000	800-900
Pathfinder 4WD	3,800-4,600	3,100-3,700	1,100-1,400
1994 Pathfinder 2WD	3,600-4,400	2,900-3,500	1,000-1,200
Pathfinder 4WD	4,300-5,500	3,500-4,500	1,500-1,900
1995 Pathfinder 2WD	4,200-5,200	3,400-4,300	1,400-1,700
Pathfinder 4WD	4,800-6,000	4,000-5,000	1,800-2,300

For detailed information on this vehicle visit
http://used.consumerguide.com and enter code **2079**

1996-00 NISSAN PATHFINDER

CLASS: Midsize sport-utility vehicle

BUILT IN: Japan

PROS: Instruments/controls • Passenger and cargo room • Ride • Steering/handling

CONS: Engine noise • Fuel economy • Rear-seat entry/exit • Rear leg room

EVALUATION: Softer-riding than before, with additional rear seat and cargo room, the new Pathfinder also delivers better acceleration and has a more modern dashboard. Because of its relatively low ride height, getting in and out of the front seats is easy. Despite large rear doors, however, the back seat presents more of a challenge, partly because those doors do not open 90 degrees. There's little room to swing your feet and legs through the narrow opening.

The V6 engine is smoother than in the previous model, though a heavy throttle foot yields a loud engine roar—too gruff and growly when worked hard. The 2001 V6 brought Pathfinder/QX4 up to par with the competition. '01 Nissans claimed 0-60 mph in 8.8 sec—2.1 sec faster than earlier models. Low-speed response is good, though a Pathfinder cannot beat its domestic rivals—with V8 engines—in all-out acceleration. Fuel economy is on the dismal side, like most SUVs. An SE 4x4 with automatic averaged a meager 14.1 mpg in a combination of city, suburban, and highway driving.

Ride and handling rank among the most carlike in the sport-utility field. A tight suspension and linear steering contribute to a sense of control. Even so, you get a surprising amount of body lean and tire squeal during fast turns. The ride is firm, but devoid of harshness over bumps. Road and wind noise are low.

The Pathfinder's dashboard is one of the most user-friendly you can find, with all controls easy to see and reach. Head room is good all around, if not exceptional, but the rear seat offers barely enough leg room for anyone taller than about 5-foot-10. Worse yet, toe room is scant under the front seats. Cargo space is good, but folding the rear seats requires tilting the cushion, then removing the head restraints so the backrests can lie flat. Thick side roof pillars might impair the driver's over-the-shoulder views.

VALUE FOR THE MONEY: Pathfinders are not cheap, but largely because of excellent road manners and truck-tough construction, they're worth a look before buying an SUV in this class.

TROUBLE SPOTS

Airbags: Airbag-indicator light may flash, indicating a failure. Dealer will replace the SRS (supplemental restraint system) sensor under warranty. (1996)

Audio system: The radio may loose its presets and the clock its time due to voltage spikes. A replacement radio, less susceptible to this problem, is available. (1996)

Brake noise: A high-pitched squeal or whistle from the area of the front brakes is eliminated by replacing the baffle plate on both sides. (1996-98)

Suspension noise: The front suspension squeaks on rough roads due to a problem between the strut rod and rubber bumper. (1996)

Vehicle shake: Vibrations at 30-40 mph are often the result of the front driveshaft being installed out of phase. (1996-97)

Wheels: The black anodized lug nuts' surfaces corrode (looking light white dust spots). Nissan will replace them with chrome lug nuts. (1996)

AVERAGE REPLACEMENT COSTS

A/C Compressor	$660	Exhaust System	$460
Alternator	460	Radiator	610
Automatic Trans.	1,115	Shocks and/or Struts	490

NISSAN

Brakes	$670	Timing Chain/Belt	$490
Clutch	610	Universal Joints	310

NHTSA RECALL HISTORY

1996: Carpet padding on some vehicles could be too thick, catching driver's right foot. **1996:** Due to type of lubricant used, steering-wheel effort at low ambient temperatures could increase.

PRICES	Good	Average	Poor
1996 Pathfinder 2WD	$5,000-6,500	$4,300-5,500	$2,000-2,600
Pathfinder 4WD	5,800-7,500	5,000-6,500	2,400-3,200
1997 Pathfinder 2WD	6,000-7,500	5,200-6,500	2,500-3,200
Pathfinder 4WD	6,900-8,500	6,100-7,600	3,200-4,000
1998 Pathfinder 2WD	7,800-9,500	7,000-8,600	4,000-4,800
Pathfinder 4WD	8,700-10,500	7,800-9,500	4,500-5,500
1999 Pathfinder 2WD	10,000-12,000	9,000-10,800	5,200-6,200
Pathfinder 4WD	10,800-13,000	9,700-11,700	5,800-7,000
2000 Pathfinder 2WD	12,500-14,500	11,300-13,100	7,100-8,300
Pathfinder 4WD	13,600-15,500	12,400-14,100	8,000-9,100

For detailed information on this vehicle visit
http://used.consumerguide.com and enter code **2290**

2001-03 NISSAN PATHFINDER

CLASS: Midsize sport-utility vehicle
BUILT IN: Japan
PROS: Acceleration • Build quality • Cargo room
CONS: Rear-seat entry/exit • Rear-seat room

EVALUATION: Previously a performance also-ran, the Pathfinder is now more than competitive in its class. Test Pathfinders and QX4s have accelerated to 60 mph in 9.0 seconds, which is good for midsize six-cylinder SUVs. Still, tapping full power requires a determined throttle foot, and the automatic transmission can be slow to downshift for passing.

Pathfinders and QX4s have averaged 14.2 to 16.5 mpg, depending on conditions. That's about par for this class, but premium-grade gasoline is required. Both the Nissan and Infiniti ride firmly, though the QX4 is acceptably comfortable over bumps and ridges that feel jarring in a Pathfinder.

A taut suspension aids control, and keeps body lean in corners moderate. Steering feels properly weighted in turns, but suffers vague on-center feel at highway speeds, and the turning radius is larger than most rivals'. The QX4's all-surface 4WD is welcome on the Pathfinder LE. An SE's old-fashioned 4WD setup is far less convenient.

Wind and road noise are well-muffled. The V6 emits a throaty roar in hard acceleration, but cruises quietly.

The Pathfinder and QX4 share a functionally sound dashboard. The nicely integrated navigation system works well, once you master its programming. Cabin decor is classy in the QX4 and in leather-equipped Pathfinders, but quite ordinary otherwise.

Front space is ample and comfortable for adults. The driving position is good, and adequately adjustable, but thick roof pillars impede visibility.

Rear leg space is barely adequate for adults, if front seats are more than halfway back. The seat is low to the floor and deficient in back support. Step-in height is relatively high. Narrow door openings further complicate entry/exit.

Cargo volume is good, and the flip-up back glass is useful. The folding rear seat is overly complicated.

VALUE FOR THE MONEY: An antiquated 4WD system weighs against the Pathfinder, unless it's the top-of-the-line LE with the QX4's system. Neither of these SUVs has what it takes to be a compelling value. Available side-impact protection and antiskid security could be a plus in 2003 models.

TROUBLE SPOTS

Automatic transmission: Automatic transmission may flare (seem to drop out of gear) between shifts requiring replacement of the transmission control module. (2001)

Engine noise: A rumbling, bearinglike noise from the transfer case is corrected by replacing the companion flange with a redesigned component. (2001)

Suspension problems: Stones tend to lodge in between the right rear shock absorber and its top mounting bracket requiring insertion of a piece of foam to keep stones out. (2001)

AVERAGE REPLACEMENT COSTS

A/C Compressor	$555	CV Joints	$510
Alternator	610	Exhaust System	370
Automatic Trans.	1,995	Radiator	420
Brakes	445	Shocks and/or Struts	1,035
Clutch	410	Timing Chain/Belt	335

NHTSA RECALL HISTORY

2001: Some brackets used to attach the two gas struts to the rear hatch may have been improperly made, resulting in the struts detaching from the bracket(s) when opening or closing the rear door. Dealers will replace the strut brackets.

PRICES	Good	Average	Poor
2001 Pathfinder 2WD	$15,000-17,500	$13,700-15,900	$9,500-11,000
Pathfinder 4WD	16,500-19,000	15,000-17,300	10,600-12,200
2002 Pathfinder 2WD	18,000-20,000	16,600-18,400	11,500-12,800
Pathfinder 4WD	19,700-21,500	18,100-19,800	12,800-14,000
2003 Pathfinder 2WD	21,000-24,000	19,300-22,100	13,700-15,600
Pathfinder 4WD	23,000-26,000	21,200-23,900	15,000-16,900

For detailed information on this vehicle visit
http://used.consumerguide.com and enter code 2473

NISSAN
1993-98 NISSAN QUEST

CLASS: Minivan
BUILT IN: USA
PROS: Antilock brakes
(optional) • Passenger room
• Steering/handling
CONS: Acceleration (with
load) • Control layout
• Wind noise

EVALUATION: Quest is a carlike, luxury-oriented people mover that stresses comfort over hauling. As a result, the Quest has a low step-in height that allows easy entry and exit. It also provides a very comfortable driving position, good visibility, and an ample supply of cupholders and cubbies.

Although the 3.0-liter engine is adequate, it can't quite match the muscle provided by the larger V6s in front-drive minivans from Ford, GM, and Chrysler. When loaded, maneuvers such as merging onto freeways or passing slower traffic cannot be accomplished with quite the same ease. But, compared with other minivans, body lean is quite modest. Actually, Quest handles with more poise than some regular passenger cars. Ride quality is commendable, too—absorbent, yet stable and comfortable at highway speeds. The suspension is firm enough to minimize bouncing on wavy roads, and it soaks up most bumps without breaking a sweat. On the negative side, wind and road noise are excessive at highway speeds.

Front head room and leg room are both quite good, but only adequate for the middle- and rear-seat passengers. Stereo and climate controls are low on the dashboard and a long reach, hampered by small buttons. With all seats in their normal positions, the rear cargo area is tight. Trying to improve the Quest's hauling capacity requires removing the truly cumbersome center seats.

VALUE FOR THE MONEY: Compared with other minivans, the Quest has less interior room. It also lacks many of the standard features found on its rivals. Nevertheless, it's a good choice if you need more than a midsize station wagon but don't need the interior space provided in one of the bigger minivans.

TROUBLE SPOTS
See the 1993-98 Mercury Villager.

AVERAGE REPLACEMENT COSTS
See the 1993-98 Mercury Villager.

NHTSA RECALL HISTORY
1993: Fuel-filler hoses may have been cut prior to installation by knife used to open shipping box; fuel leakage could result, leading to fire if exposed to ignition source. **1993:** Leaves and other foreign matter can enter through cowl panel air intake during operation of front heater

and/or air conditioner, resulting in build-up in the plenum that can lead to noise, odors, or even a vehicle fire. **1993:** Master cylinder on some vans was improperly assembled or damaged during assembly, which can result in loss of braking at two wheels, causing increased pedal travel and effort and increased stopping distance. **1993:** One or both bolts securing automatic seatbelt tracks to B-pillars were not adequately tightened on some vans, increasing risk of injury in collision or sudden maneuver. **1993-98:** Cracks have developed in the vent hose, allowing a fuel leak. **1995 with sliding third-row bench seats:** Cable that connects seat-adjustment level to latch might be pinched in roller assembly, preventing latch on left side from fully engaging seat rail. **1995:** Rear lamp socket may not illuminate, resulting in malfunction or stoplamp or rear running lamps. **1996:** Power windows can be closed after ignition key is turned to "off" position and right front door is opened. **1997:** Some batteries have a defective negative post that can cause acid leakage and corrosion. **1997-98:** Fuel in the tank can expand into the vent hose and leak due to cracks in the hose.

PRICES

	Good	Average	Poor
1993 Quest	$3,100-4,000	$2,400-3,100	$700-1,000
1994 Quest	3,700-4,500	3,000-3,600	1,100-1,300
1995 Quest	4,300-5,200	3,500-4,300	1,500-1,800
1996 Quest	4,900-6,000	4,200-5,100	1,900-2,300
1997 Quest	5,600-6,800	4,800-5,800	2,300-2,800
1998 Quest	6,400-8,200	5,600-7,200	2,800-3,600

For detailed information on this vehicle visit
http://used.consumerguide.com and enter code 2080

1999-02 NISSAN QUEST

CLASS: Minivan
BUILT IN: USA
PROS: Control layout
• Passenger and cargo room
CONS: Interior materials

EVALUATION: In performance and accommodations, Quests differ little from their Mercury Villager counterparts. Acceleration is reasonably peppy from a standstill, but unimpressive in the 35-55 mph range. In fact, highway passing response borders on inadequate with a full load and the air conditioner working. Engine roar under heavy throttle is notable, though wind and tire noise are on par for this class. So is fuel economy. A test Quest, when new, averaged a less-than-frugal 16.9 mpg. Relatively compact in size, the

NISSAN

Quest (and Villager) offer above-average minivan maneuverability, helped by firm steering with ample feel. Cornering response is crispest with the SE edition, which rides 16-inch tires instead of the usual 15-inch. The Quest's suspension soaks up bumps decently, but overall ride quality does not match that of longer-wheelbase minivans like the Dodge Grand Caravan and Toyota Sienna. Relatively cozy, the Quest's interior has scant clearance between any of the seats. Front seatbacks are narrow, though supportive cushions improve overall comfort. Low step-in height is pleasing, but third-row entry/exit is rather tight due to a low roof and narrow passageways. Cargo room is slim with the third seat in its normal position, though the available adjustable-height parcel shelf is handy. The third-row bench can slide forward to free up a large cargo hold, but its release handle is difficult to reach. Second-row seats remove easily. Interior storage includes a removable net between front seats, double door pockets, and numerous bins. Despite targeting upscale buyers, the Quest and Villager contain a lot of hard-surfaced interior plastic items inside, along with industrial-look switchgear and unfinished edges.

VALUE FOR THE MONEY: Smaller outside and inside than most rivals, Nissan's Quest and the equivalent Mercury Villager are more maneuverable. Both trail the competition in refinement and acceleration. Quests have held their value more strongly, thus cost more secondhand.

TROUBLE SPOTS

See the 1999-02 Mercury Villager.

AVERAGE REPLACEMENT COSTS

See the 1999-02 Mercury Villager.

NHTSA RECALL HISTORY

1999: Fuel-tank retention strap (two per minivan) can break at spot welds, causing underbody rattle; if welds fail, there may be fuel leakage and/or separation of fuel tank from vehicle. **1999:** Second-row captain's chair on right side of some minivans may have inadequate lubrication of easy-entry/exit latch system, and actuator spring could deform, causing latch to remain in unlatched position; seat would then slide freely on track, and springs would move seat to easy-entry position. **1999:** Taillight socket's locking tab may have insufficient force to retain the bulb. **1999-00:** One or more of the five bolts that mount rack-and-pinion steering gear may have been incorrectly tightened; could result in steering looseness and noise or vibration. Eventually, bolts could fracture or fall out. **2001:** The seatbelt-buckle bolt could loosen, leaving the occupant improperly restrained in a collision.

PRICES

	Good	Average	Poor
1999 Quest	$9,800-11,500	$8,800-10,400	$5,100-6,000
2000 Quest	11,500-13,200	10,400-11,900	6,300-7,300
2001 Quest	13,500-15,200	12,300-13,800	8,000-9,000
2002 Quest	15,500-17,500	14,100-15,900	9,900-11,200

For detailed information on this vehicle visit
http://used.consumerguide.com and enter code **2395**

1995-99 NISSAN SENTRA

CLASS: Subcompact car

BUILT IN: USA

PROS: Optional antilock brakes (GXE, GLE) • Fuel economy • Ride

CONS: Acceleration (w/automatic transmission) • Rear-seat entry/exit • Rear-seat room • Seat comfort

EVALUATION: In terms of quietness and solidity, the 1995 redesign moved Sentra from the middle to near the front of the subcompact class. Even when driven over the roughest roads, Sentras act and feel far more substantial than most small cars, with a supple yet well-controlled ride and a notable absence of body drumming and road rumble. Although wind noise rises appreciably above 60 mph, the little engine doesn't thrash or boom at most speeds.

You'll need to work the 1.6-liter engine hard when mated to the automatic transmission. But, when mated to the slick-shifting 5-speed manual, the Sentra feels frisky. The 140-horsepower engine in the SE has good acceleration with automatic and feels even more lively with the 5-speed.

Despite a bigger interior than prior models, Sentra remains practical for only four adults. Three grownups simply cannot fit comfortably in the back seat for longer trips. A functional, attractive dashboard gives the Sentra driver a user-friendly environment, but seats are flat and hard. Cargo space isn't the greatest, but the trunk has a flat floor and low opening at bumper level.

VALUE FOR THE MONEY: Solid and refined, Sentra looks like a good value in the small-car hunt. We'd even place it on a par with the Toyota Corolla—today's standard of comparison in the subcompact league.

TROUBLE SPOTS

Air conditioner: Poor air conditioning may be due to refrigerant leaking from the service fitting valves. (1996)

Audio system: Cellular phones can interfere and cause noise from the radio speakers if the phone is plugged into the cigarette-lighter socket near the radio rather than another 12-volt accessory socket. (1995-99)

Brake noise: The rear drum brakes may squeal, grind, or groan due to being overadjusted. (1995)

Dashboard lights: The check-engine light comes on due to a problem with the rear heated oxygen sensor. (1995-96)

Fuel gauge: The gauge may not register full due to the pump wires interfering with the float arm. (1995)

Hard starting: Starting difficulty and/or flooding while starting in cold weather at higher altitudes may require a revised powertrain-control module (PCM). (1997-99)

Horn: The horn may sound when the wheel is turned due a spring slipping out of place in the steering column. (1995-99)

NISSAN

Sunroof/moonroof: The sunroof may tilt up, but not slide back due to a problem with the lifter mechanism. (1995-96)

AVERAGE REPLACEMENT COSTS

A/C Compressor	$610	Exhaust System	$320
Alternator	310	Radiator	300
Brakes	290	Shocks and/or Struts	460
Clutch	390	Timing Chain/Belt	620
CV Joints	1,120		

NHTSA RECALL HISTORY

1995 w/antilock brakes: Hydraulic actuator was not properly purged of all air; bubbles can cause increased pedal travel and stopping distances. **1995-96:** Front coil springs may not have sufficient corrosion resistance in areas where significant amounts of deicing salts are applied to roads. **1995-98:** Water can enter and displace grease in wiper arm linkage joint, resulting in gradual wear over a period of time that could lead to separation of wiper linkage assembly. **1996:** Does not meet illumination requirements for brake light. **1996-97:** Stop/taillamps do not meet illumination requirements of Federal Motor Vehicle Safety Standard (FMVSS) No. 108.

PRICES

	Good	Average	Poor
1995 Sentra	$2,200-3,000	$1,600-2,100	$400-600
1996 Sentra	2,500-3,500	1,800-2,600	500-700
1997 Sentra	2,900-4,200	2,200-3,200	700-1,000
1998 Sentra	3,500-5,000	2,800-4,000	900-1,400
1999 Sentra	4,400-5,800	3,700-4,800	1,500-2,000

For detailed information on this vehicle visit http://used.consumerguide.com and enter code **2215**

2000-03 NISSAN SENTRA

CLASS: Subcompact car
BUILT IN: Mexico
PROS: Fuel economy
CONS: Rear-seat entry/exit

EVALUATION: Sentras don't exactly feel underpowered. SE-Rs are among the quickest subcompact cars: 7.8 sec 0-60 for SE-R, 7.0 sec for Spec V, Nissan says. Still, a test GXE with a manual transmission needed a relatively leisurely 9.9 seconds to reach 60 mph. Automatic adds at least a second to that pace. With its bigger engine, the SE is quicker—but not by all that much unless it has the 5 speed, which helps this small sedan feel quite spirited. Automatic transmissions are smooth and responsive enough, but some 5 speeds have suffered imprecise shift action and overly sharp clutch engagement, which makes smooth driving tricky. As for economy, a GXE averaged 24.9 mpg, while an SE managed 28.5 mpg. Both had manual shift.

Sentra's base suspension delivers safe, predictable front-drive handling, but only modest cornering grip on its standard all-season tires. Some bounding at higher speeds is noticeable, as is marked wheel patter on washboard-surfaced freeway segments. Although the ride isn't really bad, the suspension is less absorbent than that of a Honda Civic, Volkswagen Jetta, or Toyota Echo. A firmer suspension gives the SE sportier handling, with a slight loss of ride comfort. No model is really quiet, with tire roar higher than the class norm. Even without ABS, a GXE stopped in reasonably short distances with little nosedive and easy pedal modulation, but some sudden wheel lockup.

Interior space could be more generous. The lack is most noticeable in back, where 6-footers can sit upright but have little leg or foot space if the front seat is pushed all the way back. Front seats don't move far, either, so tall drivers might also feel cramped. Entry/exit is hindered by small rear door openings. Gauges and controls are simple and handy. The radio is high, but smallish buttons and markings make it a little hard to use. Interior storage is above average, but trunk space is not, aggravated by a moderate-size opening and scant height beneath the parcel shelf.

VALUE FOR THE MONEY: Not as refined as a Civic or as roomy as a Ford Focus, Nissan's "entry-level" sedan is solid enough—and priced right on the secondhand market.

TROUBLE SPOTS

Air conditioner: If the air conditioner does not cool, the thermocouple in the evaporator may be at fault. A new probe must be installed in a different location. (2000-01)

Audio system: Popping and crackling noises in the audio system are often due to cell phones plugged into the cigarette lighter. Using a different power source or moving the phone often helps. (2000)

Steering noise: Squeaks or rattles from the front end when turning are often due to misaligned, and damaged, strut bearing not fully seated in its recess. It was being replaced under warranty. (2000)

Water leak: The driver's-side floor gets wet because the air-conditioner evaporator drain hose has a tendency to fall off the pipe at the evaporator case. A hose clamp may help. (2000)

AVERAGE REPLACEMENT COSTS

A/C Compressor	$610	CV Joints	$1,230
Alternator	320	Exhaust System	345
Automatic Trans.	740	Radiator	325
Brakes	200	Shocks and/or Struts	520
Clutch	430	Timing Chain/Belt	770

NHTSA RECALL HISTORY

2000-01: Steel wheels could fail and separate from the mounting hub without prior warning. **2000-02:** May be missing tamperproof caps meant to prevent horizontal headlamp adjustment. **2003:** Corrosion on resistor in ECM could cause check-engine light to come on or cause the engine to stop. **2001:** Bolts used to attach each front-suspension lower control arm to the body on the left and right sides may not have been properly manufactured and could fracture, increasing the risk of a crash. **2002 2.5 liter:** Exhaust-pipe hanger pin may catch debris from that could be ignited by contact with the main catalyst. Dealers will remove the protruding pin and install heat shield(s).

PRICES

	Good	Average	Poor
2000 Sentra SE	$6,900-7,600	$6,100-6,800	$3,200-3,600
Sentra XE, GXE	6,000-6,800	5,200-5,900	2,500-2,900
2001 Sentra SE	8,300-9,000	7,500-8,100	4,300-4,700
Sentra XE, GXE	7,200-8,000	6,400-7,100	3,500-3,900
2002 Sentra SE-R	11,000-12,200	9,900-11,000	5,900-6,600
Sentra XE, GXE	8,500-9,500	7,700-8,600	4,400-4,900
2003 Sentra Limited Edition	11,500-13,000	10,400-11,700	6,300-7,200
Sentra SE-R	12,500-14,000	11,300-12,600	7,100-8,000
Sentra XE, GXE	10,000-11,000	9,000-9,900	5,200-5,700

For detailed information on this vehicle visit
http://used.consumerguide.com and enter code **2392**

2000-03 NISSAN XTERRA

CLASS: Midsize sport-utility vehicle
BUILT IN: USA
PROS: Cargo room
CONS: Acceleration (4-cylinder) • Rear-seat entry/exit • Ride/handling • Wind noise

EVALUATION: Nissan intended the Xterra to be backpack-functional and contemporary cool, yet in some ways it's rather stodgy. Acceleration is plodding with the 4 cylinder, but adequate with the V6. The automatic transmission works well, as do the brakes. An automatic 2WD SE reached 60 mph in 9.6 seconds. Even in 2WD form, the suspension is stiff enough to cause notable jiggle on bumpy pavements, though it won't pummel a person's kidneys. Cornering grip is decent for a high, narrow SUV, but steering is vague on-center. Compared to the nimble Honda CR-V, an Xterra feels rather ponderous. Fuel economy is midsize-level, not compact-frugal. One new 2WD V6 averaged 17.2 mpg; another just 14.6 mpg in harder driving, while a 4WD SE S/C averaged just 13.4 mpg with the supercharged V6.

While it doesn't match a CR-V or Toyota RAV4 in convenient all-surface 4WD, an Xterra—which has a Low range—is designed to lead those rivals in off-road capability. An Xterra eagerly tackles difficult mountain trails, but its V6 drones under hard throttle, and a nagging wind whistle from the roof rack adds to intrusive noise levels. Nissan's no-frills approach is evident in utilitarian cabin furnishings.

Most interior trim panels are noticeably thin, as is the door glass, though seat fabrics look durable. The simple dashboard works well, though lanky drivers might crave more rearward seat travel and using the "umbrella handle" parking brake is an old-fashioned chore. Lowish front bucket seats promise good head room for tall occupants, but impel a slightly legs-out posture. Rear head room is terrific, because the kicked-up roofline allows the bench seat to stand higher. Sadly, three grownups won't fit easily in back. Rear leg room is minimal unless front seats are pushed forward, and the back bench is hard. Step-in is high, and rear door bottoms are so narrow that entry/exit is a real squeeze. Cargo space beats a CR-V or RAV4 with the rear seat up.

VALUE FOR THE MONEY: Though less pleasant for everyday driving than the CR-V and RAV4, an Xterra offers truck toughness and off-road ability, along with V6 power. A V6 Xterra costs less than one of those less roomy 4-cylinder competitors.

TROUBLE SPOTS

Audio system: Popping and crackling noises in the audio system are often due to cell phones plugged into the cigarette lighter. Using a different power source or moving the phone often helps. (2000)

Dashboard lights: The check-engine light comes on due to a poor electrical ground between the intake manifold and cylinder head on V6 engines. (2000)

Engine misfire: Poor idle quality when coasting with the clutch depressed was being corrected by reprogramming the powertrain-control module. (2000)

Vehicle noise: Clunking or hammering noise under the floor can be traced to a loose torsion bar anchor at the crossmember. Spacer washers were being installed under warranty. (2000)

AVERAGE REPLACEMENT COSTS

A/C Compressor	$590	CV Joints	$730
Alternator	290	Exhaust System	300
Automatic Trans.	1,490	Radiator	670
Brakes	330	Shocks and/or Struts	875
Clutch	450	Timing Chain/Belt	400

NHTSA RECALL HISTORY

2000 w/automatic: Shift-cable lock plate may be too brittle and could break, so transmission would not shift out of "Park" position and gear indicated may differ from gear that is actually engaged. **2001:** Fuel-tank shutter valves may be faulty on certain vehicles, resulting in possible fuel leakage. Dealers will inspect and replace affected parts. **2002 Supercharger:** Under certain conditions, on vehicles equipped with a supercharger, faulty airflow meters may have been installed, resulting in the illumination of the malfunction indicator lamp and decreased engine speed. Dealer will inspect and reprogram affected meters. **2002:** Certain cars may have faulty clock-spring connectors, resulting in airbag nondeployment. Dealer will inspect and replace affected parts.

PRICES

	Good	Average	Poor
2000 Xterra 2WD	$10,000-12,500	$9,000-11,300	$5,200-6,500
Xterra 4WD	13,500-15,000	12,300-13,700	8,000-8,900

2001 Xterra 2WD	$11,500-14,200	$10,400-12,800	$6,300-7,800
Xterra 4WD	15,000-16,500	13,700-15,000	9,500-10,400
2002 Xterra 2WD	13,300-16,500	12,100-15,000	7,800-9,700
Xterra 4WD	16,800-18,700	15,500-17,200	10,800-12,000
2003 Xterra 2WD	15,500-19,500	14,100-17,700	9,900-12,500
Xterra 4WD	19,200-22,000	17,700-20,200	12,500-14,300

For detailed information on this vehicle visit
http://used.consumerguide.com and enter code **2394**

1992-97 OLDSMOBILE ACHIEVA

CLASS: Compact car
BUILT IN: USA
PROS: Acceleration
• Antilock brakes (optional)
• Steering/handling
CONS: Entry/exit • Ride

EVALUATION: Ever since its introduction in 1992, Oldsmobile has been striving to provide a 4-cylinder engine that matches the refinement of its Japanese rivals. The early versions delivered brisk acceleration and strong off-the-line performance, but were noisy and generated annoying vibrations that could be felt through the steering column. So up until 1995 and 1996, the V6 engines are a better choice, providing lots of torque at low speeds and delivering the best all-around performance.

Achieva's suspension feels crude compared to Japanese rivals, banging and clanking over bumps that others absorb easily. The Computer Command Ride exhibits little noticeable difference between the soft and sport modes. In either setting, handling and stability were commendable, without any severe impact harshness.

Inside, gauges are grouped into four round pods in a concave "wrap-around" instrument panel. A center panel holds the radio and climate-control switches, which are clearly marked and easy to reach. Overall, interior appointments are a cut above previous Oldsmobile compacts. Thick rear C-pillars and a smaller rear window tend to restrict visibility rearward on the 4-doors, but interior comfort is generally good, with adequate head room and leg room to go around. Rear doors on 4-door models are narrow at the bottom, so you might have to bend and twist to slip inside.

VALUE FOR THE MONEY: While the Achieva is much more competitive than the previous Calais, it has no "stand out" features that make it exceptional. On the plus side, fully equipped Achievas cost hundreds, even thousands, less than comparable versions of Japanese rivals.

TROUBLE SPOTS

See the 1992-96 Buick Skylark.

AVERAGE REPLACEMENT COSTS

See the 1992-96 Buick Skylark.

NHTSA RECALL HISTORY

1994: Welds in rear assembly of fuel tank may be insufficient to prevent leakage in certain rear-impact collisions, increasing risk of fire. **1996:** During deployment of the passenger airbag, the airbag can snag on a reinforcement inside the instrument panel. This might cause the airbag to not deploy properly. **1996:** Front and/or rear hazard warning lamps might not work. **1996:** If the key is held in the "start" position for an extended period, high current flowing through the ignition switch can melt internal switch parts. **1996:** Interior lamps might come on unexpectedly while vehicle is being driven. **1997:** Omitted fuse cover could result in short circuit and possible fire.

PRICES	Good	Average	Poor
1992 Achieva	$1,300-1,900	$800-1,200	$200
1993 Achieva	1,500-2,100	1,000-1,400	200-300
1994 Achieva	1,700-2,400	1,100-1,600	300-400
1995 Achieva	1,900-2,600	1,300-1,800	300-400
1996 Achieva	2,100-2,800	1,500-2,000	400-500
1997 Achieva	2,500-3,300	1,800-2,400	500-700

> For detailed information on this vehicle visit
> http://used.consumerguide.com and enter code **2082**

1999-03 OLDSMOBILE ALERO

CLASS: Compact car
BUILT IN: USA
PROS: Acceleration (V6)
• Control layout
• Quietness
CONS: Engine noise (4-cylinder) • Rear-seat entry/exit (coupe) • Rear visibility (coupe)

EVALUATION: Although the 2.4-liter 4-cylinder engine delivers plenty of power, it lacks refinement, vibrating at idle and getting loud in hard acceleration. A brief test drive indicated that the 2.2-liter 4 cyl trades a little power for slightly smoother, quieter operation, but it should be strong enough for most driving situations. The V6 adds some welcome low-speed muscle and runs a lot smoother and quieter than the 2.4 liter. It's strong from a standing start and responds quickly for passing. Torque steer (pulling to the side under hard acceleration) came as a penalty for the

CONSUMER GUIDE®   419 zesty V6 engine, however. Aleros with the V6 averaged 21.6 to 23.7 mpg. Alero's automatic transmission is about as slick-operating as any, offering smooth, prompt downshifts with little tendency to "hunt" between gears. Manual shift adds a dash of sportiness, but does not shift as smoothly as the gearboxes in a Honda or Toyota.

Capable road manners combine with comfort, as a result of the Alero's rigid structure and supple suspension. Still, despite good grip in steady cornering, an Alero cannot match import-brand sport sedans. Though it feels athletic in curves, Oldsmobile's compact is less nimble than, say, a Ford Contour SE. Steering feels artificially heavy and the car can feel unsure in quick transitions, though directional stability is great otherwise. Neither suspension rides harshly over bumps, but compliance and control don't really stand out. Wind noise is low, but tires thrum on all but the smoothest surfaces.

Large, legible gauges and well-placed controls ease the driving experience. Front bucket seats are a bit narrow, with insubstantial padding and without much lateral support, but are comfortable anyway. Front head and leg room are good. Rear-seat space in sedans rivals some midsized cars, but entry/exit isn't so easy with the coupe. Visibility is good in sedans, but thick roof pillars impede over-the-shoulder views in coupes. A small opening and high liftover impairs trunk loading.

VALUE FOR THE MONEY: Satisfying in ordinary use, the Alero behaves admirably on twisting roads and feels more mature than its Pontiac Grand Am cousin. Acceleration with the V6 is another "plus," but Aleros cannot match import-brand rivals in refinement. Value is enhanced by its long list of standard features.

TROUBLE SPOTS

See the 1999-03 Pontiac Grand Prix.

AVERAGE REPLACEMENT COSTS

See the 1999-03 Pontiac Grand Prix.

NHTSA RECALL HISTORY

1999-00: Console cover may not stay closed in a crash. **2001:** Owner's manual doesn't adequately explain child-restraint anchorage system. Dealers will send vehicle owners a supplement to their manual. **2001:** When the vehicle is shifted from 5th gear into reverse, a shift inhibitor causes the transmission to be in 4th gear even though the lever indicates reverse gear.

PRICES	Good	Average	Poor
1999 Alero	$5,000-6,000	$4,300-5,100	$2,000-2,400
Alero GLS	6,500-7,300	5,700-6,400	2,900-3,300
2000 Alero	6,200-7,200	5,400-6,300	2,700-3,100
Alero GLS	8,000-9,000	7,200-8,100	4,100-4,600
2001 Alero	7,500-8,700	6,800-7,800	3,800-4,400
Alero GLS	9,600-10,600	8,600-9,500	5,000-5,500

2002 Alero	$8,700-10,200	$7,800-9,200	$4,500-5,300
Alero GLS	11,200-12,200	10,100-11,000	6,000-6,600
2003 Alero	10,000-12,000	9,000-10,800	5,200-6,200
Alero GLS	13,000-15,000	11,800-13,700	7,500-8,700

For detailed information on this vehicle visit
http://used.consumerguide.com and enter code **2396**

1995-99 OLDSMOBILE AURORA

CLASS: Near-luxury car

BUILT IN: USA

PROS: Acceleration
• Antilock brakes
• Passenger room
• Steering/handling

CONS: Fuel economy
• Rear visibility (1995)
• Wind noise

EVALUATION: Although the engine will not snap anyone's head back at takeoff, it delivers brisk acceleration and ample passing power. A test Aurora accelerated to 60 mph in a swift 8.2 seconds. The transmission shifts so smoothly, you'll seldom notice anything happening. Gas mileage is slightly better than expected: We averaged 20.3 mpg, but premium gasoline is required.

Road noise is noticeable, but not excessive. However, wind noise has been prominent around the side windows on Auroras that have been tested. Ride control is commendable at high speeds. Optional V-rated tires make the ride noticeably stiffer, however. With either tires, an Aurora offers sporty handling, displaying only minimal body roll in turns and excellent grip.

The Aurora's roomy interior has ample space for four adults. Controls are easy to reach and clearly labeled; analog gauges large and easy to read in a well-designed dashboard. Luggage space is ample, with a long, flat trunk floor, though the opening is too small to load bulky objects.

VALUE FOR THE MONEY: Carrying Oldsmobile a big step forward, Aurora is competitive with Japanese and European sedans that cost thousands more when new. We recommend that you give it a trial run if you're shopping in the luxury-sedan league.

TROUBLE SPOTS

Battery: The floor pan rusts due to the battery venting or an overflow of acid. (1995-99)

Brake noise: The brakes make noise due to a problem with the rotors for which there are replacements. (1997)

OLDSMOBILE

Electrical problem: The door locks may quit working and the instrument-panel fuse may blow due to a short circuit caused by a bolt inside either front door chafing the wiring harness. (1995)

Electrical problem: The plugs on some aftermarket devices will short out the accessory outlet or cigarette lighter blowing the fuse. (1995-99)

Keyless entry: The keyless remote has a rather short range and can be corrected with a new module. (1996-97)

Mirrors: The automatic parking-assist outside mirrors may point too high. (1997)

Poor transmission shift: The transmission-cooler hose gets twisted near the radiator, preventing the transmission from shifting into forward or reverse. (1997-99)

Seat: The front seat does not heat, requiring replacement of the heating element in the seat or back cushions. (1995-99)

Vehicle noise: A problem with the power brake-booster check valve causes a noise from the dashboard. (1995-97)

AVERAGE REPLACEMENT COSTS

A/C Compressor	$500	Exhaust System	$295
Alternator	380	Radiator	385
Automatic Trans.	1,070	Shocks and/or Struts	500
Brakes	430	Timing Chain/Belt	505
CV Joints	905		

NHTSA RECALL HISTORY

1995: Rear shoulder belt(s) do not retract. **1996:** Damaged capacitor may cause failure of "Key in the Ignition" and driver seatbelt-unbuckled warnings, and other functions. **1999:** Brake-booster to pedal-assembly nuts may be loose. **1999:** Incorrect brake-caliper assembly, brake pads, and caliper-mounting bracket might be installed.

PRICES	Good	Average	Poor
1995 Aurora	$4,700-5,400	$3,900-4,500	$1,700-2,000
1996 Aurora	5,400-6,200	4,600-5,300	2,200-2,500
1997 Aurora	6,500-7,200	5,700-6,300	2,900-3,200
1998 Aurora	8,300-9,200	7,500-8,300	4,300-4,800
1999 Aurora	10,000-11,200	9,000-10,100	5,200-5,800

> For detailed information on this vehicle visit
> http://used.consumerguide.com and enter code **2220**

1996-01 OLDSMOBILE BRAVADA

CLASS: Midsize sport-utility vehicle

BUILT IN: USA

PROS: Acceleration
• Antilock brakes
• Passenger and cargo room
• Ride

CONS: Fuel economy
• Rear-seat comfort

EVALUATION: The 4.3-liter V6 has more than enough power and the automatic transmission shifts smoothly. Though we saw 18-plus mpg, expect only about 15 mpg around town. GM boasts inline-6 has V8 power and 6-cyl fuel economy. That engine is strong, with good passing performance, but doesn't feel as potent as power ratings might imply. Permanent 4-wheel drive is another bonus. It lets you concentrate solely on driving, while a computer determines how to apportion power among the four wheels. You never have to give the system a thought.

Ride quality also is impressive for a sport-utility vehicle, as the Bravada's suspension absorbs bumps more effectively than that of an Explorer or Grand Cherokee.

The Bravada's interior layout is virtually identical to Blazer/Jimmy, which means ample space for four adults. Cargo space also is abundant. Front bucket seats are comfortable for long drives, but the rear bench has a low cushion. Therefore, back-seat occupants are forced to sit with knees pointed toward the ceiling. The dashboard has clear gauges and convenient, easy-to-use controls, highlighted by easy dials for the climate system. Interiors also feature numerous cupholders, while the split rear seat folds easily, providing more cargo storage space, without removing headrests.

VALUE FOR THE MONEY: Except for its posh extras, Bravada isn't really better than a Blazer or Jimmy. None of the three sport utilities ranks at the front of the compact sport-utility field, but they're close enough to deserve a look and a trial run.

TROUBLE SPOTS

See the 1995-03 Chevrolet Blazer.

AVERAGE REPLACEMENT COSTS

See the 1995-03 Chevrolet Blazer.

NHTSA RECALL HISTORY

1996 w/AWD or 4WD: During testing, prop shaft contacted fuel tank, rupturing the tank; fuel leakage was beyond permissible level. **1996:** Solder joints can crack, causing windshield wipers to work intermittently. **1996:** The windshield wiper motor may fail on certain vehicles. Dealer will inspect and replace affected parts. **1996-97:** Failure of an upper and lower control arm ball joint assembly could occur due to corrosion, resulting in impaired steering or steering loss, or a partial or complete collapse of the front suspension. **1997:** During a severe crash, seat belt buckles with an energy absorbing loop may malfunction, leading t full or partial ejection from the vehicle. Dealer will inspect and replace affected buckles. **1998 w/AWD or 4WD:** On a few vehicles, one or both attaching nuts for lower control arm were not properly torqued; can result in separation from frame and loss of control. **1998:** Fatigue fracture of rear-axle brake pipe can occur, causing slow fluid leak and resulting in soft brake pedal; if pipe breaks, driver would face sudden loss of rear-brake performance. **2000-01:** Brake lights and rear hazard flashers may fail if the multifunction switch develops an open circuit condition.

PRICES

	Good	Average	Poor
1996 Bravada	$6,000-6,800	$5,200-5,900	$2,500-2,900
1997 Bravada	7,200-8,000	6,400-7,100	3,500-3,900
1998 Bravada	8,500-9,500	7,700-8,600	4,400-4,900
1999 Bravada	10,000-11,000	9,000-9,900	5,200-5,700
2000 Bravada	11,700-13,000	10,500-11,700	6,400-7,200
2001 Bravada	14,000-15,300	12,700-13,900	8,500-9,300

For detailed information on this vehicle visit
http://used.consumerguide.com and enter code **2221**

1997-99 OLDSMOBILE CUTLASS

CLASS: Midsize car
BUILT IN: USA
PROS: Acceleration
• Standard antilock brakes
• Passenger and cargo room
CONS: Engine noise
• Steering feel

EVALUATION: Acceleration is strong off the line and around town, and the V6 engine is smooth, but Cutlass does not feel markedly more energetic at highway speeds. The automatic transmission shifts without jarring. Our main complaint has been the coarse-sounding 3.1-liter V6 engine, failing to exhibit the refinement of a Camry or Accord.

Charging down a freeway off-ramp may produce substantial body lean, as well as tire scrubbing. Steering is a little slow and vague, too, during spirited cornering. Most owners aren't likely to push it that hard. In daily driving situations, Cutlass feels agile, maneuverable, and secure. Most of the time, steering response is quick and handling competent. Cutlasses ride comfortably and stably on the highway. Although the well-controlled suspension prevents Cutlass from floating as much as some other GM cars and absorbs rough pavement quite well, there's a lot of suspension and tire thumping over ruts and potholes. Wind noise is tolerable, but the level of engine and tire noise yields less-than-serene cruising. Braking power is adequate, with good pedal modulation and moderate nosedive in hard braking.

For four adults, Cutlass is spacious for its size. Front head room is adequate and leg room more than adequate all around. Rear head room is sufficient for folks under 6 feet tall. Front bucket seats are firm and nicely contoured, but the rear bench is harder and flatter than it should be. The interior has an airy feeling, thanks to large windows. Gauges are large and clear. Radio and climate controls are easy to reach and use, as are convenient stalks for wipers and headlamps. Interior storage space ranks above average, including a large glovebox, generously sized center console/armrest, and front-door map pockets.

Trunk space is generous, helped by a flat floor, huge opening, and a near-bumper-level sill to ease loading. Thin roof pillars and large outside mirrors offer good visibility. However, the rear parcel shelf is high enough to block the driver's view of the trunk while backing up.

VALUE FOR THE MONEY: Unlike the midsize Intrigue that debuted for 1998, Oldsmobile's Cutlass catered to conservative American tastes. Performance and accommodations are similar to the Chevrolet V6 Malibu. Offering an admirable blend of utility, driving fun, and features, Cutlass and its Chevrolet Malibu counterpart are intermediate-sized sedans that warrant serious consideration. They score well in both quality and value.

TROUBLE SPOTS

See the 1997-03 Chevrolet Malibu.

AVERAGE REPLACEMENT COSTS

See the 1997-03 Chevrolet Malibu.

NHTSA RECALL HISTORY

1997-98: A buildup of snow or ice restricts the movement of the passenger-side windshield-wiper arm, the pivot housing can crack and the wipers will not operate.

PRICES	Good	Average	Poor
1997 Cutlass	$3,500-4,200	$2,800-3,400	$900-1,100
1998 Cutlass	4,300-5,100	3,500-4,200	1,500-1,700
1999 Cutlass	5,500-6,600	4,700-5,700	2,300-2,700

For detailed information on this vehicle visit
http://used.consumerguide.com and enter code **2331**

1990-96 OLDSMOBILE CUTLASS CIERA

CLASS: Midsize car

BUILT IN: USA

PROS: Acceleration (V6 engine) • Passenger and cargo room • Quietness

CONS: Acceleration (4-cylinder) • Ride

EVALUATION: It's best to avoid the 4-cylinder models if possible. While they provide good economy, they simply can't provide adequate power for a car of this size and weight. You may save some, but are always penalized with puny performance. The V6 versions are much smoother and more satisfying, providing ample torque for both off-the-line acceleration and highway passing.

When compared to the Supreme, or competitors like the Ford Taurus and Buick Regal, the Ciera's suspension is much softer. While some prefer this softer ride, it bounces over wavy roads and doesn't absorb rough pavement well. It also doesn't corner as well as the Toyota Camry or Honda Accord, which provide better grip and handle turns with much greater ease. On the positive side, the Ciera is a pleasant and quiet family car with plenty of interior and cargo room.

VALUE FOR THE MONEY: Much to the confusion of many, including product planners at Oldsmobile, the conservatively styled Cutlass Ciera constantly outsold the sleek and aerodynamic Cutlass Supreme. The Ciera prevailed, primarily because it still offers good utility as both a sedan and wagon, and could be reasonably equipped for as much as $4000 less than comparable midsize domestic and import models.

TROUBLE SPOTS

See the 1990-96 Buick Century.

AVERAGE REPLACEMENT COSTS

See the 1990-96 Buick Century.

NHTSA RECALL HISTORY

1990 w/Kelsey-Hayes steel wheels: Cracks may develop in wheel mounting surface; if severe, wheel could separate from car. **1990-91 w/six-way power seats or power recliner:** Short circuit could set seats on fire. **1990-96:** Rear-outboard seatbelt anchorages may not withstand required load; in collision, metal may tear and allow anchor to separate from body. **1992 wagon:** Remote-entry module may have a fault that causes actuation of interior lamps, door locks, and/or release of tailgate. **1993:** Right-front brake hose on some cars is improperly manufactured. **1994 w/3.1-liter V6:** If primary accelerator control spring fails, backup spring will not return throttle to closed position. **1994:** Improperly tightened spindle nut can cause premature wheel-bearing failure. **1994:** Water can cause short circuit in power-lock assembly.

PRICES	Good	Average	Poor
1990 Cutlass Ciera	$1,300-2,000	$800-1,300	$200
1991 Cutlass Ciera	1,600-2,300	1,100-1,500	200-300
1992 Cutlass Ciera	1,900-2,600	1,300-1,800	300-400
1993 Cutlass Ciera	2,200-2,900	1,600-2,100	400-600
1994 Cutlass Ciera	2,500-3,200	1,800-2,300	500-700
1995 Cutlass Ciera	2,800-3,500	2,100-2,600	600-800
1996 Cutlass Ciera	3,000-3,800	2,300-2,900	700-900

For detailed information on this vehicle visit
http://used.consumerguide.com and enter code **2084**

1990-97 OLDSMOBILE CUTLASS SUPREME

CLASS: Midsize car
BUILT IN: USA
PROS: Passenger and cargo room
CONS: Engine noise (4-cylinder) • Rear-seat comfort

EVALUATION: Many of the early Quad 4 engines—while eager—produced little power at low speeds. But when revved for optimum power, they became much noisier than either the 3.1-liter or 3.4-liter V6. The 24-valve V6 runs smoothly and quietly, revving quickly to higher speeds—even with the automatic. And the 3.1-liter V6 was gradually improved, with power rising from 135 horsepower in 1990 to 160 in 1994.

Cutlass Supreme has a firm sports-oriented base suspension. While it provides good handling and stability, its firmness generates noticeable harshness over rough roads. The FE3 suspension in the International Series models (1990-1994) is even stiffer. Braking with standard 4-wheel disc and antilock brakes is good. Improvement in build quality means that road noise and harshness are under control, and the car offers fairly good ride comfort.

Interior leg and head room are adequate, but the rear-seat cushions are too low and soft on long-distance comfort. There's also a roomy trunk and a handy cargo net on later models. The dual airbag instrument panel on 1995 models is a big improvement, putting the Supreme on par with its competition.

VALUE FOR THE MONEY: Despite all the changes that occurred, the final generation of the Cutlass Supreme was never quite able to catch up with the competition, even within GM. Only if the price really is right does this one deserve preference over, say, a Ford Taurus or Honda Accord.

TROUBLE SPOTS

Automatic transmission: Model TH-125 or 440-T4 automatic transmissions may shift late or not upshift at all. The problem is a stuck throttle valve inside the transmission. (1990-94)

OLDSMOBILE

Automatic transmission: 4T60E transmissions may drop out of drive while cruising, shift erratically, have no third or fourth gear, or no second and third gear because of a bad ground connection for the shift solenoids. (1991-94)

Cold-starting problems: A tick or rattle when the engine is started may be due to too much wrist-pin-to-piston clearance. (1993-95)

Engine noise: A rattling noise from the engine that lasts less than a minute when the car is started after sitting is often caused by automatic-transmission pump starvation or a sticking pressure-regulator valve. According to GM, no damage occurs and it does not have a fix for the problem. (1991-95)

Steering noise: The upper-bearing mount in the steering column can get loose and cause a clicking, requiring a new bearing spring and turn-signal cancel cam. (1994-96)

Transaxle leak: The right front-axle seal at the automatic transaxle is prone to leak and GM issued a revised seal to correct the problem. (1992-94)

Valve cover leaks: The plastic valve covers on the 3.1-liter engine were prone to leaks and should be replaced with redesigned aluminum valve covers. (1993-95)

AVERAGE REPLACEMENT COSTS

A/C Compressor	$555	Exhaust System	$470
Alternator	215	Radiator	340
Automatic Trans.	1,070	Shocks and/or Struts	1,855
Brakes	200	Timing Chain/Belt	170
CV Joints	470		

NHTSA RECALL HISTORY

1990: Brake lights may not illuminate. **1990:** Front shoulder-belt guide-loop fastener may pull through door-mounted anchor plate. **1990-91 in 15 states:** Due to corrosion of retainers for front engine-cradle bolts, where road salt usage is heavy, steering shaft could separate. **1991-92:** Front safetybelts may not meet standard. **1992:** Reverse servo pin of automatic transmission may bind. **1993:** Manual recliner mechanisms on some front seats will not latch under certain conditions, causing seatback to recline without prior warning. **1993-94:** Brake lines can contact transmission bracket and wear through. **1994-95:** Wiper/washer may not operate. **1995:** Center-rear seatbelt anchor plate could fracture in a crash. **1995:** Seatbelt anchor can fracture during crash. **1995-96:** Due to corrosion over time, airbag deployment could occur during vehicle startup, while parked or idling, or while in operation.

PRICES

	Good	Average	Poor
1990 Convertible	$2,700-3,300	$2,000-2,500	$600-700
Cutlass Supreme	1,400-2,100	900-1,300	200-300
1991 Convertible	3,200-3,800	2,500-3,000	800-900
Cutlass Supreme	1,700-2,500	1,100-1,700	300-400
1992 Convertible	3,700-4,400	3,000-3,600	1,100-1,300
Cutlass Supreme	2,000-3,000	1,400-2,100	300-500
1993 Convertible	4,200-5,000	3,400-4,100	1,400-1,700
Cutlass Supreme	2,300-3,500	1,700-2,500	400-700
1994 Convertible	4,800-5,600	4,000-4,700	1,800-2,100
Cutlass Supreme	2,600-3,500	1,900-2,600	500-700

1995 Convertible	$5,500-6,400	$4,700-5,500	$2,300-2,600
Cutlass Supreme	2,900-3,800	2,200-2,900	700-900
1996 Cutlass Supreme	3,400-4,200	2,700-3,300	900-1,100
1997 Cutlass Supreme	4,000-4,800	3,300-3,900	1,300-1,500

For detailed information on this vehicle visit
http://used.consumerguide.com and enter code **2085**

1992-99
OLDSMOBILE EIGHTY EIGHT/REGENCY

CG BEST BUY

CLASS: Full-size car
BUILT IN: USA
PROS: Acceleration
• Antilock brakes (optional)
• Automatic-transmission performance • Passenger and cargo room
CONS: Fuel economy
• Steering feel

EVALUATION: The Eighty Eight's base engine has ample energy for strong takeoffs and sufficient power for safe passing. Expect to realize 0-60 times around 9.0 seconds, which is very quick for a full-size family car. Fuel economy in our tests has been about 17 to 21 mpg. The optional supercharged engine available on the LSS has even stronger acceleration, but is just as refined. Fuel economy is slightly lower, and premium unleaded is required. Automatic-transmission performance is wonderfully smooth, especially on full-throttle shifts. It's eager to kick down for passing.

We feel the power steering on the base and LS models is too light and fails to provide adequate feedback. Also, the standard softly sprung suspension allows too much body roll, causing the Eighty Eight to lean excessively in turns. The LSS provides improved steering and a firmer, more-controlled ride.

The 6-passenger Eighty Eight provides easy entry/exit to all seats and ample cargo space. The dashboard is modern, with simple and logical controls for the stereo and climate control, making for more convenient operation of vehicle systems and amenities.

VALUE FOR THE MONEY: If you are searching for a big sedan, capable of holding lots of people and cargo, put the Eighty Eight at the top of your shopping list.

TROUBLE SPOTS
See the 1992-99 Pontiac Bonneville.

AVERAGE REPLACEMENT COSTS
See the 1992-99 Pontiac Bonneville.

NHTSA RECALL HISTORY

1992-93: Transmission-cooler line in cars with certain powertrains, sold in specified states, can separate at low temperature. **1994-95:** On some cars, spring in headlight switch can fail and lights would not remain illuminated. **1996 w/3.8-liter V6:** Backfire during engine starting can cause breakage of upper intake manifold, resulting in nonstart condition and possible fire. **1996:** Damaged capacitor may cause failure of "Key in the Ignition" warning chime and driver seatbelt-unbuckled warning chime and indicator lamp; other functions also may be impaired. **1999:** Clip that secures linkage of transmission-detent lever can loosen and disconnect; indicated gear would then differ from actual state of the transmission.

PRICES	Good	Average	Poor
1992 Eighty Eight	$2,200-2,900	$1,600-2,100	$400-600
1993 Eighty Eight	2,600-3,300	1,900-2,400	500-700
1994 Eighty Eight	3,000-3,700	2,300-2,800	700-900
1995 Eighty Eight	3,400-4,200	2,700-3,300	900-1,100
1996 Eighty Eight	3,900-4,800	3,200-3,900	1,200-1,500
LSS	4,900-5,600	4,200-4,800	1,900-2,200
1997 Eighty Eight	4,600-5,500	3,800-4,600	1,700-2,000
LSS	5,900-6,700	5,100-5,800	2,500-2,800
Regency	6,300-7,100	5,500-6,200	2,800-3,100
1998 Eighty Eight	5,500-6,500	4,700-5,600	2,300-2,700
LSS	7,000-7,900	6,200-7,000	3,400-3,800
Regency	7,500-8,500	6,800-7,700	3,800-4,300
1999 Eighty Eight	6,800-7,900	6,100-7,000	3,200-3,700
LSS	8,500-9,500	7,700-8,600	4,300-4,800

For detailed information on this vehicle visit
http://used.consumerguide.com and enter code **2086**

1998-02 OLDSMOBILE INTRIGUE

CLASS: Midsize car
BUILT IN: USA
PROS: Acceleration
• Standard antilock brakes
• Passenger and cargo room
• Ride • Steering/handling
CONS: Climate controls
• Engine noise (early models)

EVALUATION: Intrigue comes as close as any domestic sedan to equaling the feeling and philosophy of formidable import designs, such as the Nissan Maxima and Toyota Camry. It's inviting to drive, with little body lean and stable handling along twisty stretches. You also get plenty of "pull" from the 3.8-liter V6. An early GL accelerated to 60 mph in 7.6 seconds, averaging 21.7 mpg on regular fuel. Later models with the 3.5-liter engine turned out to be less frugal: in the 17.7 to 19.5 mpg neighborhood. The responsive automatic transmission is smooth-shifting and well-behaved.

A solid structure and taut suspension provide a stable ride and comfortable handling, with very good grip and balance in turns. Little floating or wallowing can be discerned over uneven pavement. Intrigue has better steering feel than the Camry, and a more controlled ride than either the Maxima or the Camry. Still, you can get tire and suspension thump over sharp bumps and ridges. The ride remains comfortably absorbent, even with the Autobahn Package—an option on the GL that included firmer tires and larger brakes. Tires in the Autobahn Package provide better grip and crisper cornering behavior. Stopping power is strong, though some drivers might consider brake-pedal feel to be numb.

Front bucket seats, which are firm and supportive, have ample fore/aft travel, giving tall folks room to stretch. Some shorter drivers might find the lower cushion a bit long. Others could consider the lumbar support to be too prominent. The rear seat is less spacious, though there's more than adequate head and leg room for most adults and the doors are wide enough for easy entry/exit. Intrigue's driving position is comfortable, commanding, and should suit most people. A tilt steering wheel has been standard, and a power driver's seat might be installed. Lexus could have designed the dashboard, which puts everything within easy sight and reach in a modern, attractive design. One exception: The automatic-temperature control panel on GL/GLS models is too low to reach easily while driving. Even more serious, it has difficulty defogging windows in some chilly, damp conditions. Cargo space is more than competitive for its class. The trunk floor is flat and wide, and there are no bulky hinges to intrude into the cargo area.

VALUE FOR THE MONEY: Intrigue is more sophisticated than the brash Grand Prix, and more nimble and poised than a Ford Taurus or Toyota Camry V6. If you're looking for an impressive midsize car with a thoughtful blend of features and performance, don't decide until you've driven this pleasant and surprising Olds.

TROUBLE SPOTS

Alarm system: If the key reminder continues to sound after the key is removed from the ignition and the power door locks do not work; the lock cylinder must be replaced. (1998-99)

Brake noise: During moderate application, the rear brakes make a moaning sound. New pads are available to correct the problem. (1998-99)

Engine misfire: The engine develops an ignition miss because the grease in the spark-plug boots causes them to crack. (1998)

Wipers: The windshield wipers may not park at the bottom of the windshield because water gets into the motor assembly and freezes. (1998)

AVERAGE REPLACEMENT COSTS

A/C Compressor	$460	Exhaust System	$425
Alternator	220	Radiator	215
Automatic Trans.	855	Shocks and/or Struts	910
Brakes	390	Timing Chain/Belt	220
CV Joints	795		

NHTSA RECALL HISTORY

1998-99: Some cars were built with rear-seat shoulder belts that could twist, allowing webbing to jam in retractor. **2000:** Internal fluid leaks in brake-control unit of some cars may prevent rear-brake proportioning, ABS, traction control, or stability control from performing as designed. **2000-01:** Some seatbelt assemblies were not properly heat treated and do not pass the load-bearing requirement.

PRICES	Good	Average	Poor
1998 Intrigue	$5,000-6,000	$4,300-5,100	$2,000-2,400
Intrigue GLS	6,200-7,000	5,400-6,100	2,700-3,000
1999 Intrigue	6,200-7,200	5,400-6,300	2,700-3,100
Intrigue GLS	8,000-9,000	7,200-8,100	4,100-4,600
2000 Intrigue	7,500-8,700	6,800-7,800	3,800-4,400
Intrigue GLS	9,700-10,700	8,700-9,600	5,000-5,600
2001 Intrigue	9,000-10,300	8,100-9,300	4,700-5,400
Intrigue GLS	11,500-12,500	10,400-11,300	6,300-6,900
2002 Intrigue	11,000-12,500	9,900-11,300	5,900-6,800
Intrigue GLS	13,500-15,000	12,300-13,700	8,000-8,900

For detailed information on this vehicle visit
http://used.consumerguide.com and enter code **2332**

1991-96 OLDSMOBILE NINETY EIGHT

CLASS: Near-luxury car

BUILT IN: USA

PROS: Acceleration
• Antilock brakes (optional)
• Automatic transmission performance • Passenger and cargo room

CONS: Fuel economy
• Visibility

EVALUATION: For those who still appreciate Oldsmobile's former conservative approach, the Ninety Eight provides everything you can ask for. That includes dual airbags (after 1994), standard antilock brakes, acres of passenger room, and excellent acceleration from GM's 3.8-liter V6, whether you choose the normally aspirated or supercharged versions. The engines deliver brisk acceleration off the line, and the automatic transmission downshifts quickly to make ample passing power available. Expect 16-18 mpg in urban driving, about 25 on the highway.

Head room and leg room are generous for all seating positions in the Ninety Eight, which has room for six adults, if everyone is willing to squeeze a little. Trunk space (over 20 cubic feet) is generous as well, with the flat, wide floor capable of holding several suitcases. The instrument panel has large, well-marked controls and gauges that are easy to read and convenient to use. While it's easy to see all four corners of the car for parking, thick rear pillars block the driver's over-the-shoulder view.

VALUE FOR THE MONEY: The Ninety Eight's conservative styling has clearly begun to limit its appeal, but it's a less-expensive alternative to V8 luxury sedans such as the Cadillac Fleetwood and Lincoln Town Car.

TROUBLE SPOTS

See the 1991-96 Buick Park Avenue.

AVERAGE REPLACEMENT COSTS

See the 1991-96 Buick Park Avenue.

NHTSA RECALL HISTORY

1991: Console-mounted shift lever may disengage, causing loss of gearshift operation. **1991:** Parking-brake lever assembly may release when applied; parking brake may then not hold the vehicle. **1992-93:** Transmission-cooler line in cars with certain powertrains, sold in specified states, can separate at low temperature. **1994-95:** Headlight-switch spring can fail and prevent latching of headlamp in "On" position. **1995 w/Twilight Sentinel:** Current leakage can cause loss of headlights and parking lights; or lights may turn on while car is parked. **1996 w/3.8-liter V6:** Backfire during engine starting can cause breakage of upper intake manifold, and result in nonstart condition and possible fire. **1996:** Damaged capacitor may cause failure of "Key in the Ignition" warning chime and driver seatbelt-unbuckled warning chime and indicator lamp; other functions also may be impaired.

PRICES

	Good	Average	Poor
1991 Ninety Eight	$2,700-3,400	$2,000-2,600	$600-700
1992 Ninety Eight	3,000-3,800	2,300-2,900	700-900
1993 Ninety Eight	3,400-4,200	2,700-3,300	900-1,100
1994 Ninety Eight	3,800-4,600	3,100-3,700	1,100-1,400
1995 Ninety Eight	4,400-5,200	3,700-4,300	1,500-1,800
1996 Ninety Eight	5,000-6,000	4,300-5,100	2,000-2,400

For detailed information on this vehicle visit
http://used.consumerguide.com and enter code **2087**

1990-96 OLDSMOBILE SILHOUETTE

CLASS: Minivan

BUILT IN: USA

PROS: Acceleration (3.8-liter V6) • Antilock brakes (optional) • Passenger and cargo room

CONS: Climate controls • Visibility

OLDSMOBILE

EVALUATION: Early models with the standard 120-horsepower 3.1-liter V6 were obviously underpowered, especially when loaded with passengers and vacation luggage. The 1992 addition of standard antilock brakes and optional 170-horsepower V6 with 4-speed automatic were both welcome additions. The new powertrain gives the Silhouette needed vitality and is the obvious choice. While the 3.4-liter, with 10 more horsepower added for '96 seems like an improvement, it doesn't have as much low-speed power.

No minivan has seats that are easier to remove or rearrange than the lightweight (just 34 pounds) buckets in the Silhouette. Ride and handling qualities are a match for any large sedan, but the Silhouette offers far more passenger and cargo space. Poor visibility, however, remains the Silhouette's primary sore spot. The long dashboard stretches nearly four feet from the driver to the windshield, and obscures the front corners of the sloping nose. Adding to the distraction is the extra set of roof pillars needed to support the large glass windshield. Also, the climate control buttons on the dash are difficult to see and reach while driving.

VALUE FOR THE MONEY: Despite their hard-to-see front ends and view-obstructing front pillars, first-generation Silhouettes have many virtues. Some shoppers, however, might be more satisfied with the 1997-up model, which does away with the radical nose and incorporates more traditional styling, which should solve the visibility problem.

TROUBLE SPOTS

See the 1990-96 Chevrolet Lumina APV/Minivan.

AVERAGE REPLACEMENT COSTS

See the 1990-96 Chevrolet Lumina APV/Minivan.

NHTSA RECALL HISTORY

1990: Rear modular seat-frame hold-down hooks on some vans may not meet required pull force. **1990:** Right seat/shoulder-belt retractor may have been installed in second-row left-seat position. **1990-91 in 14 states:** Rear cradle bolts could pull through retainers, due to corrosion; if both bolts pull through, steering shaft could separate from steering gear. **1990-91:** Due to corrosion, shaft could separate from steering gear, resulting in crash. **1992-95:** Transmission-cooler line in cars with certain powertrains, sold in specified states, can separate at low temperature. **1993-94 w/optional power sliding door:** Second-row, right-hand shoulder belt can become pinched between seat and door frame pillar trim. **1994:** Pawl spring may be missing from retractors for rear-center lap belt. **1994:** Third-row seatbelt retractors may lock up when van is on a slope. **1995:** Brake-pedal arm can fracture during braking, resulting in loss of brake operation. **1996-98:** Faulty power steering bearings may have been installed on certain vehicles, resulting in difficulty turning the steering wheel. Dealers will inspect and replace all affected parts.

PRICES

PRICES	Good	Average	Poor
1990 Silhouette	$1,500-2,100	$1,000-1,400	$200-300
1991 Silhouette	1,800-2,500	1,200-1,700	300-400
1992 Silhouette	2,200-3,000	1,600-2,100	400-600

1993 Silhouette	$2,600-3,400	$1,900-2,500	$500-700
1994 Silhouette	3,000-3,800	2,300-2,900	700-900
1995 Silhouette	3,500-4,300	2,800-3,400	900-1,200
1996 Silhouette	4,000-4,800	3,300-3,900	1,300-1,500

For detailed information on this vehicle visit
http://used.consumerguide.com and enter code 2088

1997-03 OLDSMOBILE SILHOUETTE

CLASS: Minivan
BUILT IN: USA
PROS: Antilock brakes
• Passenger and cargo room
• Ride
CONS: Fuel economy

EVALUATION: Silhouette's ride is comfortable and the minivan handles more than competently. If not actually sporty in nature, it's at least at the top of minivan class, helped by particularly communicative steering. Yes, a firm suspension means you'll feel more bumps in a Silhouette than in a Chrysler Town & Country, for one; but the Oldsmobile's ride is never harsh.

Acceleration ranks as adequate with the 3.4-liter V6 engine, but low-speed power was better with the 3.8-liter V6 that had been available in '95 models. On the plus side, GM's 4-speed automatic transmission is one of the smoothest around, with prompt downshifts that help get the most out of the engine whenever a welcome burst of power is needed.

In a lengthy test run that included several highway trips, a Silhouette managed 19.2 mpg. Standard antilock brakes stop the Silhouette with minimal fuss, but the pedal tends to feel slightly mushy.

In a Silhouette, you get a comfortable driving position and a commanding view of the road. Passenger space is good, though taller adults might complain about leg room—especially in the farthest-back seats. Center and rear seats are low to the floor and do not feel as substantial or supportive as those in rivals.

Entry and exit to the back seats is awkward, and the pass-through between the front buckets is narrow. Cargo room behind the rear seats is good in the extended-length model, but only average in the regular-length version.

Radio and climate controls in the new dashboard are easy to see and reach, with large buttons and knobs. Gauges are amply sized and unobstructed.

Storage space is abundant, including more cupholders than most people will ever need, and handy cargo nets attached to the sides of the front seats. Paint in our test minivans has been smooth and glossy, though many body-panel gaps were uneven. Interior materials are pleasant in quality.

OLDSMOBILE

VALUE FOR THE MONEY: All told, Silhouette brings a lot of equipment for the money, along with convenient sliding doors and friendly driving manner. We recommend a test drive before buying any family minivan.

TROUBLE SPOTS

See the 1997-03 Chevrolet Venture.

AVERAGE REPLACEMENT COSTS

See the 1997-03 Chevrolet Venture.

NHTSA RECALL HISTORY

1997-2001 w/passenger-side sliding door: Door closes but may not be latched. If this happens, the sliding door can open while the vehicle is in motion. **1997-98 w/bucket seats or split bench seat in second or third row:** Seat-latch mechanism does not have protective covers; when activating release mechanism to roll a bucket seat forward, finger(s) could be severely injured, or severed, if they are not kept clear. **1997-98:** Windshield-wiper linkage arm can contact brake line connected to traction-control modulator valve; brake line can chafe, resulting in brake-fluid leakage. **1998:** Broken shift-cable fitting or loose shift linkage can occur; moving shift lever to "Park" position may not shift the transmission to "Park," and vehicle could roll. **1999:** Steering shaft on a few minivans could separate, as a result of collapsed sleeve. **2000 w/extended wheelbase:** Fuel-tank rollover valve on small number of minivans is inoperative. **2000:** Some seatbelt assemblies were not properly heat treated and do not pass the load-bearing requirement. **2001:** Seat-latch anchor-wire diameter may be wider than 6.1 mm, potentially inhibiting the installation of child restraints. **2002:** Driver's-side airbag inflator could fracture during deployment increasing the risk of serious injury.

PRICES	Good	Average	Poor
1997 Silhouette extended	$5,800-7,800	$5,000-6,800	$2,400-3,300
Silhouette regular	5,000-5,700	4,300-4,800	2,000-2,300
1998 Silhouette extended	7,700-9,200	6,900-8,300	3,900-4,600
Silhouette regular	7,000-7,800	6,200-6,900	3,400-3,700
1999 Silhouette Premiere	11,500-12,700	10,400-11,400	6,300-7,000
Silhouette extended	9,300-10,800	8,400-9,700	4,800-5,600
Silhouette regular	8,600-9,500	7,700-8,600	4,500-4,900
2000 Silhouette Premiere	13,500-15,000	12,300-13,700	8,000-8,900
Silhouette extended	10,400-12,000	9,400-10,800	5,500-6,400
2001 Silhouette Premiere	16,000-17,500	14,600-15,900	10,200-11,200
Silhouette extended	12,200-14,500	11,000-13,100	6,800-8,100
2002 Silhouette Premiere	18,200-19,700	16,700-18,100	11,600-12,600
Silhouette extended	14,000-17,500	12,700-15,900	8,500-10,700
2003 Silhouette Premiere	21,500-24,000	19,800-22,100	14,000-15,600
Silhouette extended	17,000-21,000	15,600-19,300	10,900-13,400

For detailed information on this vehicle visit
http://used.consumerguide.com and enter code **2279**

1990-95 PLYMOUTH ACCLAIM

CLASS: Compact car
BUILT IN: USA
PROS: Acceleration (V6)
• Antilock brakes (optional)
• Passenger and cargo room
CONS: Automatic-transmission performance
• Noise • Ride

EVALUATION: The Acclaim is best with the V6, which delivers ample power, smoothly and quietly. However, the 4-speed automatic transmission had sluggish, sloppy shift action in our tests of 1990 models. The base 2.5-liter is adequate with automatic transmission; the easy-shifting 5-speed manual coaxes a little more performance out of this engine.

Road noise is prominent at highway speeds. The base engine is too loud, even while cruising. Because the suspension does not absorb bumps well, an Acclaim bangs and bounds over rough pavement.

Acclaim's airy, pleasant interior is large enough for four adults to spread out and not feel cramped. Split folding rear seatbacks that flop down for extra cargo room are optional on the base model and standard on the others. The large trunk has a flat floor and a low liftover for easy loading. Acclaim also scored points for its standard airbag.

VALUE FOR THE MONEY: If you're a budget-minded shopper in the market for a no-nonsense family compact, be sure to put the Acclaim on your list of must-see models.

TROUBLE SPOTS

See the 1990-95 Dodge Spirit.

AVERAGE REPLACEMENT COSTS

See the 1990-95 Dodge Spirit.

NHTSA RECALL HISTORY

1990: Oil may leak from engine valve-cover gasket. **1991:** Both airbag-system front-impact sensors may not be secured to mounting brackets, so airbag would not deploy. **1991:** Front disc brake caliper-guide pin bolts may not be adequately tightened and could loosen. **1991:** Front-outboard seatbelt may become difficult to latch; latch may open in sudden stop or accident. **1992:** Zinc plating of some upper steering-column shaft-coupling bolts caused hydrogen embrittlement and breakage of the bolt. **1994:** Seatbelt assembly on small number of cars may fail in accident, increasing risk of injury.

PRICES	Good	Average	Poor
1990 Acclaim	$1,100-1,600	$700-1,000	$100-200
1991 Acclaim	1,300-1,800	800-1,100	200

PLYMOUTH

1992 Acclaim	$1,500-2,100	$1,000-1,400	$200-300
1993 Acclaim	1,700-2,400	1,100-1,600	300-400
1994 Acclaim	2,000-2,700	1,400-1,900	300-500
1995 Acclaim	2,300-3,000	1,700-2,200	400-600

For detailed information on this vehicle visit
http://used.consumerguide.com and enter code 2089

1996-00
PLYMOUTH BREEZE

CG BEST BUY

CLASS: Midsize car
BUILT IN: USA
PROS: Fuel economy
• Passenger and cargo room
CONS: Acceleration (2.0-liter w/automatic transmission) • Noise • Rear visibility

EVALUATION: Except for the lack of an alternative to its initial 2.0-liter engine, the first Breeze offered essentially the same virtues and demerits as the Cirrus and Stratus. That engine has adequate pep with manual shift, but feels sluggish with the automatic transmission, especially when you need a quick burst of speed for passing or merging into traffic. Even with the manual gearbox, it's necessary to downshift fairly often to get acceptable response for passing and merging, or when encountering modest upgrades. The 2.0-liter four also is noisy during hard acceleration.

A manual-shift Breeze got 30.2 mpg overall, while one with automatic managed 27 mpg in mostly highway driving.

Acceleration and passing power aren't dramatically better with the 2.4-liter engine, still ranking as adequate for daily driving. The bigger engine is not a lot quieter, either.

On the plus side, it's a roomy and well-designed family sedan that offers competent handling ability. Like its Chrysler Corporation cousins, the agile Breeze feels at home on twisting roads. A firm suspension tames body lean quite well and reduces bouncing at highway speeds, but it's less effective at absorbing the impact of bumpy pavement surfaces.

Space is ample at all seating positions, courtesy of the "cab-forward" design. Three medium-size adults can sit abreast in the back seat without feeling like sardines in a can. A spacious trunk holds plenty of cargo, and has a flat floor and low liftover. The modern dashboard has simple and convenient controls, positioned for maximum visibility and accessibility, but interior materials are of lower grade than usual for this class of car.

The rear seatback folds down, to add storage space. Visibility is excellent to most directions but restricted through the narrow rear window.

VALUE FOR THE MONEY: Less costly than many Japanese rivals, the competent Breeze also is better equipped and roomier than some other family sedans.

TROUBLE SPOTS

See the 1995-00 Dodge Stratus.

AVERAGE REPLACEMENT COSTS

See the 1995-00 Dodge Stratus.

NHTSA RECALL HISTORY

1996: Corrosion of ABS hydraulic control unit can cause solenoid valves to stick open; vehicle then tends to pull from a straight stop when brakes are applied. **1996-97:** Lower ball joint can separate due to loss of lubrication; could cause loss of control. **1996-97:** Secondary hood-latch spring can disengage if hood is slammed. **1996-98 w/automatic:** If operator presses button to shift out of Park with key in locked position, pin can break; "ignition-park" interlock would then be nonfunctional. **1996-98 w/automatic:** Improperly adjusted cable could disable "ignition-park" interlock system. **1998-99:** Right rear-brake tube can contact exhaust-system clamp and wear a hole in it; tube could then leak, reducing braking effectiveness. **2000:** A few cars were produced with unpainted fuel-tank straps. **2000:** Inadequate weld on some vehicles could result in fatigue damage of right front brake tube. **2000:** Incorrect child-lock instruction label could cause confusion as to whether the childproof safety lock was activated. **2000:** Some of the owner's manuals for these vehicles are missing instructions for properly attaching a child restraint system's tether strap to the tether anchorage.

PRICES	Good	Average	Poor
1996 Breeze	$2,200-2,800	$1,600-2,000	$400-500
1997 Breeze	2,700-3,400	2,000-2,600	600-700
1998 Breeze	3,500-4,200	2,800-3,400	900-1,100
1999 Breeze	4,400-5,100	3,700-4,200	1,500-1,800
2000 Breeze	5,500-6,200	4,700-5,300	2,300-2,500

> For detailed information on this vehicle visit
> http://used.consumerguide.com and enter code **2280**

1992-94 PLYMOUTH COLT VISTA

CLASS: Minivan

BUILT IN: Japan

PROS: All-wheel drive (AWD wagon) • Optional antilock brakes • Fuel economy • Passenger and cargo room

CONS: Acceleration • Noise

EVALUATION: A manual transmission helps the base engine achieve adequate acceleration, but an automatic makes it feel underpowered. The 2.4-liter engine is a far better choice than the feeble 1.8-liter—especially with the 20 horsepower added for 1993.

PLYMOUTH

Compact size, great visibility, and fine low-speed maneuverability makes the Colt Vista an excellent urban vehicle. In fast corners, however, the tall height and narrow track result in plenty of body lean and tire squeal. Grip improves with the AWD model, with its bigger tires. Ride quality is surprisingly supple. Braking feels strong and balanced, even if antilocking is not installed. Base-model Colt Vistas are not well-insulated against engine and wind noise.

Low step-in height and the sliding side door make entry/exit easy and inviting. Controls and gauges are logically laid out. Chair-height seats not only are comfortable, but they take advantage of the panoramic greenhouse to give a great view of the surroundings. Cargo space behind the back seat is tight, but the rear bench folds flat and can tumble forward to create a flat load floor from the tailgate forward.

VALUE FOR THE MONEY: An "in between" vehicle, the Colt Vista is an ideal choice for a small family on a budget. Not as versatile as a full-size minivan, the Vista is also not as expensive.

TROUBLE SPOTS

See the 1992-96 Eagle Summit Wagon.

AVERAGE REPLACEMENT COSTS

See the 1992-96 Eagle Summit Wagon.

NHTSA RECALL HISTORY

1992-93: Automatic seatbelt system may fail to operate correctly during crash. **1993-94 w/AWD:** Lockup of transfer case can occur.

PRICES

	Good	Average	Poor
1992 Colt Vista	$1,400-2,100	$900-1,300	$200-300
1993 Colt Vista	1,700-2,400	1,100-1,600	300-400
1994 Colt Vista	2,200-2,900	1,600-2,100	400-600

> For detailed information on this vehicle visit
> http://used.consumerguide.com and enter code **2224**

1995-99 PLYMOUTH NEON

CLASS: Subcompact car
BUILT IN: Mexico, USA
PROS: Optional antilock brakes • Fuel economy • Passenger and cargo room • Ride
CONS: Automatic-transmission performance • Noise

EVALUATION: Base-engine acceleration has been surprisingly swift: about 8.9 seconds to reach 60 mph. We also averaged more than 31 mpg,

driving mainly on expressways. However, it idles noisily and growls loudly during acceleration. The optional dual-cam engine feels only a little livelier than the base engine—not enough to make it a priority. Automatic-
transmission shift action is too abrupt with either engine.

Ride quality rivals that of many larger cars—especially with 14-inch tires
installed. The Neon's suspension takes bumps and potholes in stride, soaking up most of them without disturbing the occupants unduly. At the
same time, a Neon handles more like a sports car than a small sedan. Body
lean in hard cornering is minimal, and the Neon's tires grip tautly. The car
feels solid and well-planted on the road. Firm, responsive steering feels
natural and centers quickly.

Four 6-footers fit without squeezing in the spacious interior, which belies
the car's outer dimensions. Visibility is excellent to the front and sides but
because the rear parcel shelf is high the view to the rear is somewhat
obstructed. The Neon's trunk opens at bumper level, and the split rear
seatback folds down to expand the cargo area.

VALUE FOR THE MONEY: All told, whether it's wearing a Plymouth
or Dodge badge, Neon ranks as good value—and a sensible choice—
among subcompact cars.

TROUBLE SPOTS

See the 1995-99 Dodge Neon.

AVERAGE REPLACEMENT COSTS

See the 1995-99 Dodge Neon.

NHTSA RECALL HISTORY

1995: Corrosion at fuel and rear-brake tubes may lead to brake fluid or
fuel leakage. **1995:** Steering-column coupler can become disconnected
when vehicle sustains underbody impact. **1995-96 including "ACR competition" package:** Brake master cylinder can leak. **1996:** Wiring harness
in Mexican-built cars could short-circuit; can cause various malfunctions,
including stalling. **1997:** Airbag could deploy inadvertently when ignition
is shut off. **1998:** Rear-suspension crossmember on some cars may be
missing spot welds; can result in structural cracks in body, and reduced
rear-impact crash protection. **1999:** Front-suspension lower control arms
may have been inadequately welded and could separate.

PRICES	Good	Average	Poor
1995 Neon	$1,700-2,500	$1,100-1,700	$300-400
1996 Neon	2,000-2,900	1,400-2,000	300-500
1997 Neon	2,400-3,000	1,800-2,200	500-600
1998 Neon	3,100-3,800	2,400-3,000	700-900
1999 Neon	3,800-4,500	3,100-3,600	1,100-1,400

For detailed information on this vehicle visit
http://used.consumerguide.com and enter code **2226**

1990-94 PLYMOUTH SUNDANCE

CLASS: Subcompact car
BUILT IN: Mexico, USA
PROS: Acceleration (turbo, V6) • Antilock brakes (optional)
CONS: Engine noise • Rear-seat room

EVALUATION: Base models with the 2.2-liter engine are faster than most economy cars—though the engine tends to be on the noisy and rough side. The 2.5-liter version is smoother and more responsive, though it isn't quite as fuel efficient and not all much quieter. Most raucous of the engine trio, as expected, is the turbo four.

Dusters with V6 power have lively acceleration and, with wider tires and firmer suspension, make for a competent sporty package. Even the moderately firm base suspension delivers good cornering and grip, though it feels a bit harsh on bumpy roads.

Tall people won't complain about room in the front seats, but 6-footers are advised to avoid the rear seats, where both leg and head room are skimpy. Luggage space is adequate with the rear seatback up and generous when folded forward.

VALUE FOR THE MONEY: While not overly refined, Sundance is a low-cost vehicle that doesn't shout "economy car" when you open the door. It simply doesn't feel as puny and lightweight as other entry-level offerings, and has the added safety of an airbag.

TROUBLE SPOTS

See the 1990-94 Dodge Shadow.

AVERAGE REPLACEMENT COSTS

See the 1990-94 Dodge Shadow.

NHTSA RECALL HISTORY

1990: Engine valve-cover gasket may dislocate and allow oil leak. **1991:** Front-disc brake-caliper guide-pin bolts may not be adequately tightened and could loosen. **1991-92:** Lower seatback bolt on driver's seat can fail and separate. **1991-92:** Steering-wheel mounting armature can develop cracks and separate from the center hub attachment to the steering column; can result in loss of vehicle control. **1992:** Zinc plating of some upper steering-column shaft-coupling bolts caused hydrogen embrittlement and breakage of the bolt. **1993-94 2-door:** Bolt that attaches recliner mechanism to driver's seatback on certain cars could break; may result in seatback suddenly reclining.

PRICES	Good	Average	Poor
1990 Sundance	$1,000-1,500	$600-900	$100-200
1991 Sundance	1,100-1,700	700-1,000	100-200

1992 Sundance	$1,400-2,100	$900-1,300	$200-300
1993 Sundance	1,600-2,200	1,100-1,500	200-300
1994 Sundance	1,900-2,600	1,300-1,800	300-400

For detailed information on this vehicle visit
http://used.consumerguide.com and enter code 2090

1991-95 PLYMOUTH VOYAGER

CLASS: Minivan

BUILT IN: Canada, USA

PROS: Antilock brakes (later models) • Wet-weather traction (AWD) • Passenger and cargo room • Ride

CONS: Acceleration (4-cylinder) • Fuel economy

EVALUATION: The primary focus of their redesign was the interior, which shows marked improvements in important areas. First of all, key controls were moved so they no longer are blocked by the steering wheel. Headlamps and wiper/washer switches are now on two pods flanking the steering wheel. Among a variety of thoughtful touches, climate and radio controls were moved closer to the driver, a new center console now features pull-out cupholders, and a locking glovebox has been added to the passenger side. Visibility is better all around, but especially at the rear where the window dips further into the liftgate.

A recalibrated suspension shows up in reduced body roll in turns, making Voyager's road manners even more carlike. The Voyager steers precisely and has exceptional stability. On the road, Voyager is remarkably well-mannered for a minivan. Any of the 6-cylinder engines are preferable to the anemic 100-horsepower 4-cylinder. Power from the trio of V6s range from adequate with the 3.0-liter to impressive with the 3.8-liter. The 3.3-liter seems particularly smooth and responsive.

VALUE FOR THE MONEY: With all the revisions, Chrysler reasserted its minivan leadership against a growing number of serious competitors. They remained the best-in-class minivans because they were carlike to drive and offered a range of models and features that no rival yet matched.

TROUBLE SPOTS

See the 1991-95 Dodge Caravan.

AVERAGE REPLACEMENT COSTS

See the 1991-95 Dodge Caravan.

NHTSA RECALL HISTORY

1991 w/ABS: High-pressure hose in antilock braking system may leak or detach, which increases likelihood of brake lockup. **1991 w/ABS:** High-pressure pump of antilock braking system may be porous, resulting in increased stopping distances. **1991:** Liftgate-support attaching bolts can break, resulting in liftgate falling unexpectedly. **1991-92:** Steering-wheel mounting armature can develop cracks and separate from the center hub attachment to the steering column; can result in loss of vehicle control. **1991-93 w/ABS:** Piston seal in control unit can wear excessively; ABS could fail, and power assist might be reduced. **1991-93:** Due to improperly staked left windshield-wiper pivot drive arm, wipers could cease to function. **1991-93:** Seatbelt-release button can stick inside cover, so buckle is only partially latched; also, center rear-belt anchor clip can disconnect. **1992:** Bolts that attach gas strut to rear liftgate can accumulate fatigue damage, if loose; liftgate could fall suddenly. **1992:** Brake pedal pad attachment arm on small number of vehicles could break. **1992:** Brake-pedal pad attachment to pedal arm may not have adequate strength. **1992:** Fuel tank may drop, or lines may rupture near fuel tank, leading to possible fire. **1992:** Zinc plating of some upper steering-column shaft-coupling bolts caused hydrogen embrittlement and breakage. **1993-94:** Liftgate support attaching bolts can break, resulting in liftgate falling unexpectedly. **1993-94:** Lug nuts on optional 15-inch stamped steel wheels may have been improperly installed, which could lead to wheel separation. **1993-95:** Wiring that initiates driver and/or passenger airbag could short immediately after turning ignition key to "on" position, causing airbag to deploy inadvertently.

PRICES

	Good	Average	Poor
1991 Grand Voyager	$1,600-2,300	$1,100-1,500	$200-300
Grand Voyager LE	2,000-2,700	1,400-1,900	300-500
Voyager	1,200-1,800	700-1,100	100-200
Voyager LE	1,500-2,100	1,000-1,400	200-300
1992 Grand Voyager	1,800-2,500	1,200-1,700	300-400
Grand Voyager LE	2,500-3,200	1,800-2,300	500-700
Voyager	1,400-2,100	900-1,300	200-300
Voyager LE	2,000-2,700	1,400-1,900	300-500
1993 Grand Voyager	2,200-3,000	1,600-2,100	400-600
Grand Voyager LE	2,900-3,700	2,200-2,800	700-900
Voyager	1,700-2,600	1,100-1,700	300-400
Voyager LE	2,600-3,300	1,900-2,400	500-700
1994 Grand Voyager	2,500-3,300	1,800-2,400	500-700
Grand Voyager LE	3,400-4,200	2,700-3,300	900-1,100
Voyager	2,000-2,800	1,400-2,000	300-500
Voyager LE	2,900-3,600	2,200-2,700	700-800
1995 Grand Voyager	3,000-3,800	2,300-2,900	700-900
Grand Voyager LE	4,200-5,000	3,400-4,100	1,400-1,700
Voyager	2,300-3,000	1,700-2,200	400-600
Voyager LE	3,600-4,200	2,900-3,400	1,000-1,200

For detailed information on this vehicle visit
http://used.consumerguide.com and enter code **2091**

2001-03
PLYMOUTH VOYAGER

CLASS: Minivan

BUILT IN: USA

PROS: Entry/exit
• Interior storage space
• Passenger room

CONS: Acceleration (4-cyl)
• Fuel economy

CG BEST BUY

EVALUATION: Considering a Voyager? Then go for the 3.3-liter V6, which furnishes the power required by a vehicle this size. Fuel economy is less than frugal with either engine.

Otherwise, the Voyager offers many of the benefits of Chrysler's larger Town & Country minivan, and its Dodge Grand Caravan counterpart, for significantly fewer dollars. Still, there are important differences between the two Chrysler models, apart from their size.

Both versions are carlike and friendly, roomy and comfortable, with good steering feel. Ride quality is better in a Town & Country, but the Voyager isn't harsh. Bigger wheels and tires give the Town & Country an edge over Voyager in handling and roadholding. Because of its shorter wheelbase, the Voyager tends to be jumpier, and less forgiving when rolling through bad pavement.

Stopping power with the Voyager is adequate, though short of the Town & Country's with its antilock four-wheel disc setup. Voyagers rank as average in noise suppression, whereas the Town & Country is among the quietest minivans.

Voyager owners can expect a fine driving position. The Voyager's shorter wheelbase results in just-adequate leg room in the second- and third-row positions, and in unexceptional cargo space with all seats in place.

Third-row seats remove easily, but are less convenient than back seats in minivans with stowable seating. The available power side door's manual-override function is a surprising convenience. It stops and reverses direction quickly when encountering an obstruction. Chrysler's revamped dashboard moved controls closer to the driver, but the front cupholders block access to the in-dash CD changer.

VALUE FOR THE MONEY: DaimlerChrysler's multimodel lineup has handily dominated the American minivan market. Soon after the fourth-generation models reached dealerships, they accounted for 62 percent of sales under $20,000 and 37 percent of those over $30,000. That's compelling testimony to the appeal of the entry-level Voyager and the luxury Town & Country. Both versions, bolstered by the 2001 redesign, now rank as stronger values than ever, even in the wake of increased minivan competition.

TROUBLE SPOTS

Air conditioner: The A/C compressor may fail, causing a squealing or missing drive belt. The compressor fails from not turning on the rear A/C

PLYMOUTH

controls, but running only the front. After the A/C parts are replaced, the body-control computer requires reprogramming. (2001)

Doors: Loose weather strip tricks the power sliding door into thinking there is an obstruction making it misbehave during opening or closing. The weather strip must be replaced. (2001-02)

Engine stalling: The engine may lose power or stall, especially when the temperature is below freezing, requiring replacement of if the throttle-position sensor. (2001-02)

Fuel gauge: The fuel gauge may drop below the actual level while driving, but may return to the correct reading after sitting for about 10 minutes due to a kinked hose at the leak-detection pump filter. (2001-02)

Suspension noise: Knocking or squawking sounds from the front suspension are corrected by replacing the sway-bar links. (2001)

Water leak: Some early production (prior to April 2001) vehicles may have a serpentine belt that squeals of jumps off (in cold weather) the pulley caused by water leaking from the wiper module drain tube. In cold weather ice forms on the pulley. (2001)

Water leak: A wet passenger-side carpet is often due to condensation from the A/C drain tube blowing back into the passenger compartment. Replacing the tube with a longer one corrects the problem. (2001-02)

AVERAGE REPLACEMENT COSTS

A/C Compressor	$415	Exhaust System	$415
Alternator	535	Radiator	395
Automatic Trans.	1,620	Shocks and/or Struts	1,500
Brakes	440	Timing Chain/Belt	180
CV Joints	990		

NHTSA RECALL HISTORY

2002: Some owner's manuals are missing instructions for installing child seats. Owners will be provided with an addendum to the owners manual.

PRICES

	Good	Average	Poor
2001 Voyager	$9,000-10,000	$8,100-9,000	$4,700-5,200
Voyager LX	10,800-12,000	9,700-10,800	Δ5,800-6,500
2002 Voyager	10,500-12,000	9,500-10,800	5,600-6,400
Voyager LX	12,700-14,000	11,400-12,600	7,200-8,000
2003 Voyager	12,500-15,000	11,300-13,500	7,100-8,600
Voyager LX	15,500-18,000	14,100-16,400	9,900-11,500

For detailed information on this vehicle visit
http://used.consumerguide.com and enter code **4477**

2001-03 PONTIAC AZTEK

CLASS: Midsize sport-utility vehicle

BUILT IN: Mexico

PROS: Cargo room
• Interior storage space
• Passenger room

CONS: Interior materials
• Brake-pedal feel (2WD)

EVALUATION: If you aren't put off by Aztek's appearance, you can get a minivanlike experience on a smaller scale. Like its minivan parent, the front-drive Aztek offers smooth acceleration and good midrange response—though no surplus of either. The AWD version weighs about 264 pounds more and feels somewhat slower than the 2WD model, in most conditions.

Fuel economy is so-so. A test 2WD model averaged 18.7 mpg, while a 4WD Aztek that covered more highway miles averaged 19.4 mpg. Azteks use regular fuel.

An Aztek's suspension is generally absorbent and well-controlled, with its minivan roots yielding better bump absorption than most midsize SUVs manage. Heavier AWD models do not ride quite as smoothly. Some side-to-side body motions on uneven pavement have been evident in both.

Steering/handling also is minivanlike. Unstressed in routine driving, the Aztek delivers good cornering grip. Fast turns generate pronounced body lean, though, and strong crosswinds compromise the front-drive version's stability. Stopping power with ABS seems more than adequate, despite a mushy-feeling brake pedal on 2WD test models.

Relatively low noise levels are evident from the engine, wind, and road. Few true SUVs are this quiet.

Gauges and controls are functional, despite the dashboard's eccentric appearance, with unnecessary bulges and coves. Thick side roof pillars interfere with visibility over the shoulder, and the driver cannot easily see front body corners. A rear wiper has not been available, and the sloped hatchback glass is quickly coated in a wintertime film of salt and slush. Cabin materials are mostly budget-grade plastics.

Front seating is comfortable, though taller drivers may wish for more rearward travel. Step-in height is minivan-low, easing entry/exit.

Knee, leg and foot space in the rear should suit six-footers. The rear bench seat is more springy foam than supportive padding. Passengers must twist their feet to get in or out, and large doors are cumbersome in tight spaces.

Cargo space is cavernous and versatile. The console doubles as a cooler, and doors have map pockets with twin bottle holders. The rear bench easily removes in two sections, and the available sliding rear storage tray is clever and useful. An Aztek can carry 4x8-foot plywood sheets with the tailgate lowered, but the large glass liftgate is heavy and that tailgate does not open flat.

PONTIAC

VALUE FOR THE MONEY: Aztek is as comfortable as any SUV, and packed with features designed for active folks, but cannot venture far off-road. Assembly quality and budget-grade cabin materials won't please the discerning, however. Unorthodox styling has tended to keep new-car prices discounted and resale prices down a bit.

TROUBLE SPOTS

Electrical problem: There was a recall (nonsafety related) to repair the global positioning system for the On-Star system. (2001)

Fuel gauge: Water leaking onto the electrical connector below the driver's seat causes corrosion resulting in starting failures, stalling and/or malfunctioning fuel gauge. (2001-02)

Poor transmission shift: If beverages spill into the console, the shift-indicator slide gets damaged making it difficult or impossible to shift out of park. There is an improved replacement part to fix this. (2001-02)

Water leak: The air-conditioner evaporator case may not drain properly causing water to leak into the passenger-side foot well. (2001)

Wipers: The wiper blades strike one another near the bottom of the windshield. The right (passenger) side blade should be replaced with a shorter one. (2001)

AVERAGE REPLACEMENT COSTS

A/C Compressor	$530	Exhaust System	$335
Alternator	585	Radiator	355
Automatic Trans.	1,705	Shocks and/or Struts	810
Brakes	415	Timing Chain/Belt	210
CV Joints	610		

NHTSA RECALL HISTORY

2001: Seat-latch anchor-wire diameter may be greater than 6.1 mm standard. Dealers will inspect and repair the latch anchor wires. **2001-02:** Owner's manual does not explain the meaning of the location symbols for the lower universal-anchorage system. Owners will be provided with a supplement for their owner's manual. **2003:** Steering-column intermediate shaft could be too small, allowing the intermediate shaft to spin inside the steering column coupling, resulting in loss of steering control of the vehicle. Dealers will inspect, and replace if necessary, the steering-column intermediate shaft.

PRICES

PRICES	Good	Average	Poor
2001 Aztek 2WD	$10,500-11,700	$9,500-10,500	$5,600-6,200
Aztek 4WD	12,000-13,200	10,800-11,900	6,700-7,400
2002 Aztek 2WD	12,000-13,300	10,800-12,000	6,700-7,400
Aztek 4WD	13,700-15,000	12,500-13,700	8,200-9,000
2003 Azek 2WD	13,500-15,000	12,300-13,700	8,000-8,900
Aztek 4WD	15,500-17,500	14,100-15,900	9,900-11,200

> For detailed information on this vehicle visit
> http://used.consumerguide.com and enter code **4495**

CONSUMER GUIDE®

1992-99 PONTIAC BONNEVILLE

BEST BUY CG

CLASS: Full-size car
BUILT IN: USA
PROS: Acceleration
• Automatic transmission performance • Cargo room
CONS: Fuel economy
• Ride (SSE, SSEi)

EVALUATION: Even with the base engine, which currently delivers 205 horsepower, acceleration and passing response are brisk and sure. The supercharged version has all the feel of a burly V8, but requires the use of costlier premium unleaded. Expect real-world fuel economy of 17-18 in the city for the base engine, 25 on the highway. That drops to 15-16 city mileage for the supercharged version and 23-24 on the highway. Both engines team with an automatic that shifts promptly and smoothly. The CCR feature in the SSEi felt too loose and bouncy in Touring mode, and in Performance mode it failed to absorb bumps very well.

Bonneville has the same spacious interior and trunk as its more sedate siblings at Buick and Oldsmobile. There's ample room for both passengers and cargo. The trunk is wide, has a flat floor that extends well-forward, providing 18 cubic feet of storage. Inside, the seating is comfortable and the instrument panel is well-executed.

VALUE FOR THE MONEY: The Chrysler LH/LHS sedans are roomier and have more daring styling, but the Bonneville and its GM cousins are high-quality cars that can be tailored to suit a variety of tastes, from cushy luxury to sporty performance.

TROUBLE SPOTS

Automatic transmission: 4T60E transmissions may drop out of drive while cruising; shift erratically; or have no second, third, or fourth gear because of a bad ground connection for the shift solenoids. (1992-94)

Automatic transmission: The 4T60E automatic transmission can suddenly go into neutral at highway speeds due to a problem with internal shift valves. (1995-97)

Cruise control: If the cruise control doesn't stay engaged, or drops out of cruise, the brake switch can usually be adjusted. (1992-95)

Engine noise: A rattling noise from the engine when the car is started after sitting is often caused by automatic-transmission pump starvation, or a sticking pressure-regulator valve. (1992-95)

Engine noise: Bearing knock was common on many 3.3- and 3.8-liter engines due to too much clearance on the No. 1 main bearing. (1992-94)

Oil consumption and engine knock: 3.8-liter engines are prone to excessive oil consumption often accompanied by spark knock due to failure of the valve-stem seals. (1993-95)

PONTIAC

Steering noise: The upper-bearing mount in the steering column can get loose and cause a clicking, requiring a new bearing spring and turn-signal cancel cam. (1994-96)

Transaxle leak: The right front-axle seal at the automatic transaxle is prone to leak. GM issued a revised seal to correct the problem. (1992-94)

AVERAGE REPLACEMENT COSTS

A/C Compressor	$460	Exhaust System	$500
Alternator	190	Radiator	360
Automatic Trans.	970	Shocks and/or Struts	750
Brakes	230	Timing Chain/Belt	260
CV Joints	730		

NHTSA RECALL HISTORY

1992 w/console shift : Control cable on some cars may disengage from bracket and falsely indicate gear position. **1992:** Parking-brake lever may release one or more teeth when applied. **1992-93:** Transmission-cooler line in cars with certain powertrains, sold in specified states, can separate at low temperature. **1995 w/Twilight Sentinel :** Excess current leakage can cause loss of headlights and parking lights. **1996 w/3.8-liter V6 :** Backfire during engine starting can cause breakage of upper intake manifold, resulting in nonstart condition and possible fire. **1996:** Damaged capacitor may cause failure of "Key in the Ignition" warning chime and driver-seatbelt-unbuckled warning chime and indicator lamp; other functions may also be impaired. **1997:** Seat cover trim on a few cars does not meet flammability requirements. **1999 w/chromed aluminum wheels:** Studs on some wheels could break, causing tire/wheel assembly to separate. **1999:** Clip that secures linkage of transmission-detent lever can loosen and disconnect; indicated gear would then differ from actual state of the transmission.

PRICES	Good	Average	Poor
1992 Bonneville SE	$2,500-3,200	$1,800-2,300	$500-700
SSE, SSEi	3,300-4,000	2,600-3,200	800-1,000
1993 Bonneville SE	2,900-3,600	2,200-2,700	700-800
SSE, SSEi	3,900-4,700	3,200-3,800	1,200-1,500
1994 Bonneville SE	3,300-4,000	2,600-3,200	800-1,000
SSE, SSEi	4,400-5,200	3,700-4,300	1,500-1,800
1995 Bonneville SE	3,700-4,400	3,000-3,600	1,100-1,300
SSE, SSEi	5,200-6,000	4,400-5,100	2,100-2,400
1996 Bonneville SE	4,200-4,900	3,400-4,000	1,400-1,600
SSE, SSEi	5,700-6,900	4,900-5,900	2,300-2,800
1997 Bonneville SE	4,800-5,500	4,000-4,600	1,800-2,100
SSE, SSEi	6,500-7,700	5,700-6,800	2,900-3,500
1998 Bonneville SE	5,800-6,700	5,000-5,800	2,400-2,800
SSE, SSEi	7,800-9,000	7,000-8,100	4,000-4,600
1999 Bonneville SE	7,000-8,000	6,200-7,100	3,400-3,800
SSE, SSEi	9,200-11,000	8,300-9,900	4,800-5,700

For detailed information on this vehicle visit
http://used.consumerguide.com and enter code **2092**

2000-03 PONTIAC BONNEVILLE

CLASS: Full-size car
BUILT IN: USA
PROS: Acceleration
• Automatic-transmission performance • Cargo room
• Ride/handling
CONS: Fuel economy (SSEi) • Rear-seat comfort

EVALUATION: Dynamically, at least, Bonneville matches the best front-drive full-size sedans. Despite a weight hike, acceleration is strong in SE and SLE sedans, with good throttle response. Performance is outstanding with the supercharged SSEi. With either engine, the transmission changes gears smoothly and downshifts come quickly for passing. An SE averaged 20.6 mpg, while the SSEi got just 15.7 mpg on premium gasoline. Engines are smooth, but wind rush and suspension/tire noises over coarse surfaces may appear. Softest-riding version is the SE, which floats more over high-speed dips, but all are comfortable over bumps and nearly devoid of the front-end bobbing that sometimes plagued previous Bonnevilles. A standard load-leveling rear suspension improves stability. Handling is impressive—balanced and composed—sharpest in the SLE and SSEi. Watch out for torque steer (pulling to one side in hard acceleration) in the SSEi. Though the SSEi's StabiliTrak can get confused during rapid sawing of the steering wheel, it should help the Bonneville stay on course in emergency maneuvers. Space is abundant for four adults, in an interior that has a more sporty flair than most full-size sedans. Still, the lost inch of rear head room won't help taller passengers. A protruding center section in the rear seatback discourages 3-across seating, on a cushion that's soft and poorly shaped. Leather-covered buckets in the SSEi have 12 settings but aren't all that supportive. Instruments sit close to the driver, though the dashboard looks cluttered. Some plastic panels feel low-budget. Audio and climates controls are easy to reach and decipher. Entry/exit is easy through large doors. The trunk is large, but hinges dip into the load area.

VALUE FOR THE MONEY: Volume leader is the SE, which is a fine value. Supercharged power in the SSEi is satisfying, but at a far higher price—though Bonnevilles have not held their value especially well. Besides, a lot of cars on its level are more refined and promise more verve.

TROUBLE SPOTS

Automatic transmission: The column-mounted shift lever is hard to move out of park due to the interlock cable being too long. (2000)
Brake wear: The original-equipment rear brake pads cause a humming or moaning noise, especially when the brakes are hot or warm. (2000)
Horn: If the horn becomes difficult to operate or sounds by itself in cold temperatures, the airbag module will have to be replaced. (2000)

PONTIAC

Steering noise: A countermeasure high-pressure power-steering hose will reduce vibrations, shudders or moans from the steering wheel during slow-speed turns. (2000-01)

AVERAGE REPLACEMENT COSTS

A/C Compressor	$525	Exhaust System	$565
Alternator	275	Radiator	450
Automatic Trans.	895	Shocks and/or Struts	975
Brakes	485	Timing Chain/Belt	325
CV Joints	750		

NHTSA RECALL HISTORY

2000: Some cars have internal fluid leaks in brake hydraulic-control unit; when rear-brake proportioning, antilock braking, traction control, or stability-control feature is activated in some driving situations, feature may not perform as designed. **2002:** When shifting from 5th gear into reverse, a shift inhibitor causes the transmission to be in 4th gear, even though the lever indicates reverse gear. **2002-03 SSEi- supercharged V6:** Faulty fuel-tank sensors may have been installed in certain vehicles, leading to fuel leakage. Dealer will inspect and replace all affected parts.

PRICES	Good	Average	Poor
2000 Bonneville SE, SLE	$10,000-12,300	$9,000-11,100	$5,200-6,400
Bonneville SSEi	14,500-15,800	13,200-14,400	9,000-9,800
2001 Bonneville SE, SLE	11,800-14,500	10,600-13,100	6,600-8,100
Bonneville SSEi	17,000-18,500	15,600-17,000	10,900-11,800
2002 Bonneville SE, SLE	13,600-16,800	12,400-15,300	8,000-9,900
Bonneville SSEi	19,800-21,300	18,200-19,600	12,900-13,800
2003 Bonneville SE, SLE	16,000-20,000	14,600-18,200	10,200-12,800
Bonneville SSEi	22,500-24,500	20,700-22,500	14,600-15,900

For detailed information on this vehicle visit
http://used.consumerguide.com and enter code **2398**

1993-02 PONTIAC FIREBIRD

BEST BUY CG

CLASS: Sporty coupe
BUILT IN: Canada
PROS: Acceleration (V8s) • Antilock brakes • Steering/handling
CONS: Entry/exit • Fuel economy (V8s) • Noise • Rear-seat room • Rear visibility • Ride

EVALUATION: Few cars can match the level of performance of a

Firebird. V8 versions promise acceleration of the sort that shoves your spine right into the seatback. V6 powered 'birds aren't exactly slugs, either. With manual shift, in particular, they feel lively enough in everyday driving. The stronger 3.8-liter V6 delivers particularly brisk acceleration and strong passing power. Also, the V6 is considerably more fuel efficient, netting 17-20 mpg versus 15 for the V8 models. Available traction control on recent models helps deal with horrendous grip on slippery pavement.

Even a base-model Firebird holds the road well, though naturally not with the tenacious grip delivered by the Formula and Trans Am cars. On the downside, those low-profile tires on V8 models roar over most pavement surfaces. They also combine with stiff suspension, to produce a jarring ride over bumpy roads.

Firebird's low-slung cockpit is best for two adults. Getting into the rear and finding a comfortable home back there is a challenge. Even children might have trouble. Up front, a hump in the floor cuts into passenger leg room. Cargo space is adequate, as long as you don't expect too much.

Structural rigidity and assembly quality are much better than in prior Firebird generations.

VALUE FOR THE MONEY: Firebirds are styled more aggressively than Ford's Mustang, and exhibit more muscle-car character, though a Mustang is easier to live with for everyday driving.

TROUBLE SPOTS

See the 1993-02 Chevrolet Camero.

AVERAGE REPLACEMENT COSTS

See the 1993-02 Chevrolet Camero.

NHTSA RECALL HISTORY

1994: Misrouted V8 fuel line may contact "air" check valve; heat could damage line. **1995:** Lower coupling of steering intermediate shaft could loosen and rotate, resulting in loss of control. **1997:** Seatbelt retractors on some cars can lock-up on slopes. **1999 w/manual transmission:** Clutch master cylinder on a few cars may have incorrect retaining ring, preventing disengagement when clutch pedal is depressed. **2002:** Welds near the lower driver's-side door hinge do not meet specifications.

PRICES	Good	Average	Poor
1993 Firebird	$3,400-4,000	$2,700-3,200	$900-1,000
Formula, Trans Am	4,300-5,000	3,500-4,100	1,500-1,700
1994 Convertible	4,800-5,500	4,000-4,600	1,800-2,100
Firebird coupe	3,700-4,400	3,000-3,600	1,100-1,300
Formula, Trans Am	4,900-5,800	4,200-4,900	1,900-2,300
Trans Am convertible	6,000-6,800	5,200-5,900	2,500-2,900
1995 Convertible	5,300-6,000	4,600-5,200	2,200-2,500
Firebird coupe	4,100-4,800	3,400-3,900	1,400-1,600
Formula, Trans Am	5,600-6,500	4,800-5,600	2,300-2,700
Trans Am convertible	6,700-7,400	5,900-6,500	3,100-3,400

PONTIAC

1996 Convertible	$5,800-6,500	$5,000-5,700	$2,400-2,700
Firebird coupe	4,600-5,300	3,800-4,400	1,700-2,000
Formula, Trans Am	6,300-7,300	5,500-6,400	2,800-3,200
Trans Am convertible	7,500-8,500	6,800-7,700	3,800-4,300
1997 Convertible	7,000-7,800	6,200-6,900	3,400-3,700
Firebird coupe	5,700-6,400	4,900-5,500	2,300-2,600
Formula, Trans Am	7,800-8,800	7,000-7,900	4,000-4,500
Trans Am convertible	10,000-11,000	9,000-9,900	5,200-5,700
1998 Convertible	8,500-9,500	7,700-8,600	4,400-4,900
Firebird coupe	7,000-7,800	6,200-6,900	3,400-3,700
Formula, Trans Am	9,500-11,500	8,600-10,400	4,900-6,000
Trans Am convertible	12,000-13,200	10,800-11,900	6,700-7,400
1999 Convertible	10,000-11,200	9,000-10,100	5,200-5,800
Firebird coupe	8,700-9,600	7,800-8,600	4,500-5,000
Formula, Trans Am	11,700-13,700	10,500-12,300	6,400-7,500
Trans Am convertible	14,500-16,000	13,200-14,600	9,000-9,900
2000 Convertible	12,000-13,200	10,800-11,900	6,700-7,400
Firebird coupe	10,500-11,500	9,500-10,400	5,600-6,100
Formula, Trans Am	14,000-16,000	12,700-14,600	8,500-9,800
Trans Am convertible	17,000-18,500	15,600-17,000	10,900-11,800
2001 Convertible	14,000-15,300	12,700-13,900	8,500-9,300
Firebird coupe	12,500-13,500	11,300-12,200	7,100-7,700
Formula, Trans Am	16,500-19,000	15,000-17,300	10,600-12,200
Trans Am convertible	20,000-21,500	18,400-19,800	13,000-14,000
2002 Convertible	16,000-17,300	14,600-15,700	10,200-11,100
Firebird coupe	14,500-15,700	13,200-14,300	9,000-9,700
Formula, Trans Am	19,000-22,000	17,500-20,200	12,400-14,300
Trans Am convertible	22,500-24,500	20,700-22,500	14,600-15,900

For detailed information on this vehicle visit
http://used.consumerguide.com and enter code 2228

1992-98 PONTIAC GRAND AM

CLASS: Compact car
BUILT IN: USA
PROS: Acceleration (V6)
• Antilock brakes (optional)
• Steering/handling
CONS: Engine noise
• Rear-seat entry/exit
• Ride (GT) • Road noise

EVALUATION: Acceleration with the base 115/120-horsepower Quad OHC is only adequate, and the engine becomes rough and raucous above 3000 rpm. Later 4-cylinders and V6s provide excellent acceleration and both V6s are smooth. All engines are fairly fuel efficient, but still have a ways to go before they catch the Honda Accord or Toyota Camry.

The base suspension furnishes a fairly well-controlled ride, but allows lots of body lean in turns, and the base tires have only modest grip in the corners. The SE's optional handling suspension package and wider tires improve the Grand Am's road manners without adding undue ride harshness. The GT handles crisply during sudden changes in direction, but tends to jolt and thump more over bumps. The standard antilock brakes stop the Grand Am quickly and precisely.

Though interior dimensions change only fractionally, the rear seat feels more spacious, partly due to new thin-line front seatbacks, more toe room under the front cushions, and a rear seatback that's not as vertical as before. Entry into the sedan is tight because doors are narrow at the bottom. With the new instrument panel, all gauges are larger and provide unobstructed views. Also, radio and climate-control systems are closer to the driver. Access to the trunk benefits from a new lid that opens at a 90-degree angle.

VALUE FOR THE MONEY: Grand Am has been far more successful than its cousins at Buick and Oldsmobile because Pontiac provides the right blend of image and price.

TROUBLE SPOTS

See the 1992-96 Buick Skylark.

AVERAGE REPLACEMENT COSTS

See the 1992-96 Buick Skylark.

NHTSA RECALL HISTORY

1992 coupe: Passenger-side easy-entry seat adjuster on some cars may fail to fully lock into position after seatback has been tilted and seat slid forward. **1992:** Bolts and nuts that attach bearing-hub assembly to rear axle are insufficiently tightened on some cars. **1992:** Small number of cars have incorrect upper spring seat at right rear. **1994:** Welds in rear assembly of fuel tank may be insufficient to prevent leakage in certain rear-impact collisions, increasing risk of fire. **1996:** Front and/or rear hazard warning lamps might not work. **1996:** If the key is held in the "start" position for an extended period, high current flowing through the ignition switch can melt internal switch parts. **1996:** Interior lamps might come on unexpectedly while vehicle is being driven. **1996:** Steering-column lower pinch bolt was not properly tightened. This could cause loss of steering control. **1997:** Omitted fuse cover could result in short circuit and possible fire.

PRICES

PRICES	Good	Average	Poor
1992 Grand Am	$1,500-2,100	$1,000-1,400	$200-300
Grand Am GT	2,000-2,600	1,400-1,800	300-400
1993 Grand Am	1,700-2,400	1,100-1,600	300-400
Grand Am GT	2,300-2,900	1,700-2,100	400-600
1994 Grand Am	2,000-2,700	1,400-1,900	300-500
Grand Am GT	2,600-3,300	1,900-2,400	500-700
1995 Grand Am	2,300-3,000	1,700-2,200	400-600
Grand Am GT	3,100-3,700	2,400-2,900	700-900

PONTIAC

1996 Grand Am	$2,600-3,300	$1,900-2,400	$500-700
Grand Am GT	3,400-4,100	2,700-3,200	900-1,100
1997 Grand Am	3,000-3,700	2,300-2,800	700-900
Grand Am GT	4,000-4,800	3,300-3,900	1,300-1,500
1998 Grand Am	4,000-4,800	3,300-3,900	1,300-1,500
Grand Am GT	5,000-5,800	4,300-4,900	2,000-2,300

For detailed information on this vehicle visit
http://used.consumerguide.com and enter code **2094**

1999-03 PONTIAC GRAND AM

CLASS: Compact car
BUILT IN: USA
PROS: Acceleration (V6)
• Steering/handling
CONS: Engine noise (4-cylinder) • Radio controls
• Rear-seat entry/exit
(coupe) • Ride

EVALUATION: A Grand Am looks faster than it is in reality, though it's not really underpowered. The 2.4-liter 4-cylinder engine provides enough zip for most driving, though it generates some idle shake and groans loudly under hard throttle. Acceleration with the 2.2-liter 4 cyl is not as strong, but it's adequate for most situations—with the bonus of marginally smoother, quieter operation.The V6 is quiet and smooth, swifter in around-town driving, and gets good mileage. Test V6 Grand Ams, when new, averaged 19.4 to 21.5 mpg. The well-behaved automatic transmission downshifts quickly and rarely "hunts" between gears. Manual shift adds a sporty tone, despite its somewhat notchy action. With either engine, the droning note of the sporty exhaust grows tiresome. Road and wind noise are reasonable, but tires roar intrusively and thump loudly over tar strips. Expect a choppy ride over sharp ridges and broken pavement, but the Grand Am is generally stable and resists wallowing. On smoother surfaces, the ride is firm but not harsh. Handling isn't Eurosedan-precise, of course, but turn-in is reasonably quick, with firm steering as well as good grip and balance in corners. Stopping power is adequate, with good pedal feel.

Excess is the word for interior styling, with deeply recessed gauges and an overall cluttered look. Most controls are close at hand, though audio switches are small and poorly marked. Front leg room is generous and head room good, even with an optional sunroof. The supportive, comfortable driver's seat adjusts to most body types. Back-seat space beats the compact average, but the coupe's rear seat is narrower, with less head room. Rear visibility is hampered by the rear spoiler (if installed). Although the trunk is spacious, its opening is small with an unusually high liftover that makes loading a chore.

VALUE FOR THE MONEY: "Expressive" styling and a sporty nature draw a lot of customers to Grand Ams, but the compact isn't as far ahead in basic engineering and construction. Though less refined than some rivals, it's competent in most respects and exhibits enjoyable road manners.

TROUBLE SPOTS

Brakes: Pulsation felt in the steering wheel and brake pedal is caused by faulty brake pads and discs. Revised parts are available. (1999-2000)

Paint/body: The rear spoiler gets distorted in the hot sun. Also, water gets inside requiring drain holes to be drilled. (1999)

Water leak: Water leaks under the door and onto the floor due to a bad door gasket. A countermeasure gasket is being installed under warranty. (1999-2000)

AVERAGE REPLACEMENT COSTS

A/C Compressor	$500	Exhaust System	$455
Alternator	380	Radiator	450
Automatic Trans.	1,090	Shocks and/or Struts	535
Brakes	470	Timing Chain/Belt	505
CV Joints	905		

NHTSA RECALL HISTORY

1999-00: Console cover may not stay closed in a crash. **2001:** Owner's manual doesn't adequately explain child-restraint anchorage system. Dealers will send vehicle owners a supplement to their manual. **2001:** When shifting from 5th gear into reverse, a shift inhibitor causes the transmission to be in 4th gear, even though the lever indicates reverse gear.

PRICES

	Good	Average	Poor
1999 Grand Am	$5,300-6,000	$4,600-5,200	$2,200-2,500
Grand Am GT	6,800-7,500	6,100-6,700	3,200-3,500
2000 Grand Am	6,500-7,200	5,700-6,300	2,900-3,200
Grand Am GT	8,300-9,000	7,500-8,100	4,300-4,700
2001 Grand Am	8,000-8,800	7,200-7,900	4,100-4,500
Grand Am GT	10,000-10,800	9,000-9,700	5,200-5,600
2002 Grand Am	9,500-10,300	8,600-9,300	4,900-5,400
Grand Am GT	11,600-12,600	10,400-11,300	6,400-6,900
2003 Grand Am	11,000-12,000	9,900-10,800	5,900-6,500
Grand Am GT	13,500-15,200	12,300-13,800	8,000-9,000

For detailed information on this vehicle visit
http://used.consumerguide.com and enter code **2397**

1990-96 PONTIAC GRAND PRIX

CLASS: Midsize car
BUILT IN: USA
PROS: Antilock brakes (optional) • Handling
CONS: Engine noise • Rear-seat comfort • Ride (optional suspensions, tires) • Road noise

EVALUATION: It's best to avoid models with the noisy 4-cylinder engine. However, the 3.1-liter V6 provides ample acceleration with much less noise and vibration. Turbo engines provide outstanding acceleration, but suffer from "turbo lag" and poor fuel economy. The best engine choice is the dohc 3.4-liter V6, which provides the acceleration of the turbo engine without the lag and ruckus.

Inside, the cabin of the 1990-1993 Grand Prix with its backlit red gauge cluster works hard to emulate the continental flair of the BMW. However, Pontiac is not quite able to capture the European maturity or purposefulness. Revisions to the cabin in 1994 bring long overdue improvements. The new controls are both simpler to use and easier to reach. Large, soft-touch rotary dials replace the climate system's fussy, undersized switches and sliders. Select either the coupe or sedan and you should find the cabin capable of transporting four adults in relative pleasure—but the back seat is too low and uncomfortable.

Pontiac's suspension tuning gives the Grand Prix somewhat more composed road manners than the Lumina, Regal, and Cutlass Supreme, especially over bumps and dips. Cornering ability is especially impressive on cars equipped with the Y99 rally suspension package, but drivers must endure a harsher ride.

VALUE FOR THE MONEY: We rate the Ford Taurus, Mercury Sable, and Honda Accord higher overall. But with the gradual improvements bestowed on the Grand Prix, it is a good choice as well.

TROUBLE SPOTS

See the 1990-97 Oldsmobile Cutlass Supreme

AVERAGE REPLACEMENT COSTS

See the 1990-97 Oldsmobile Cutlass Supreme

NHTSA RECALL HISTORY

1990 w/Kelsey-Hayes steel wheels : Cracks may develop in wheel mounting surface. **1990:** Stoplamps may not illuminate. **1990-91 in 15 states:** Due to corrosion of front engine cradle bolts, where road-salt usage is heavy, steering shaft could separate from steering gear. **1991 coupe:** Fog lamps and low- and high-beam headlamps can be operated simultaneously on some cars, causing circuit breaker to overload and trip. **1991:** Front-door shoulder-belt guide loops may be cracked. **1992:** Reverse servo pin of 4-speed automatic transmission may bind. **1993:** Manual recliner mechanisms on some front seats will not latch under certain conditions, causing seatback to recline without prior warning. **1994-95:** Wiper/washer may operate intermittently, or not at all. **1995:** Center rear-seatbelt anchor plate could fracture in a crash. **1995:** Seatbelt anchor can fracture in crash.

PRICES

	Good	Average	Poor
1990 Grand Prix	$1,300-1,800	$800-1,100	$200
Grand Prix STE	2,000-2,500	1,400-1,800	300-400
1991 Grand Prix	1,500-2,100	1,000-1,400	200-300
Grand Prix GT, STE	2,200-2,800	1,600-2,000	400-500
1992 Grand Prix	1,800-2,500	1,200-1,700	300-400
Grand Prix GT, STE	2,500-3,100	1,800-2,300	500-700
1993 Grand Prix	2,100-2,800	1,500-2,000	400-500
Grand Prix GT, STE	2,800-3,500	2,100-2,600	600-800
1994 Grand Prix	2,400-3,100	1,800-2,300	500-600
1995 Grand Prix	2,700-3,400	2,000-2,600	600-700
1996 Grand Prix	3,000-3,800	2,300-2,900	700-900

For detailed information on this vehicle visit
http://used.consumerguide.com and enter code **2095**

1997-03 PONTIAC GRAND PRIX

CLASS: Midsize car
BUILT IN: USA
PROS: Acceleration • Cargo room • Passenger room • Steering/handling
CONS: Fuel economy (supercharged engine)

EVALUATION: Acceleration from a standing start is adequate with the 3.1-liter V6, strong with the 3.8-liter, and almost ferocious with the supercharged engine—with no loss of refinement. The transmission changes gears with world-class smoothness, and downshifts quickly for passing. Our test 3.8-liter SE averaged 22.7 mpg in mostly highway driving—including a high of 27 on the highway and a low of 15 mpg in urban commuting. The GTP returned only 17-18 mpg—on the required premium gasoline—so its supercharged performance does not come cheap.

Road noise is prominent on all models at highway speeds. Wind and engine noise are low, but tire thrum frequently intrudes. Braking is strong, but pedal modulation mediocre. Grand Prix feels agile and sure-footed on winding roads. Steering is more precise than before. The SE and GT have a stable, comfortable ride with little bouncing over wavy surfaces. Their firm suspension absorbs most bumps well and provides capable handling with little body lean. The GTP's tauter suspension gives slightly sharper handling and it reacts more abruptly to potholes, yielding more tire thump, but the ride still does not rate as harsh.

Head room is plentiful all around. There's ample room for four adults, and a fifth can squeeze into the rear seat. With front seats pushed all the way back, leg room is still adequate out back. The rear bench is low to the floor and provides little support. Doors open wide to allow easy entry/exit, though the rakish roofline provides a slight impediment. Overall, the dashboard looks busy and cluttered. Gauges and controls are well-illuminated by Pontiac's traditional red lighting, and most switchgear is clearly labeled, easy to find and use. Uplevel stereos have small buttons that are haphazardly arranged, making it hard to pick out any particular one in a hurry. Visibility is good to the front and sides, but the high parcel shelf blocks the driver's view of the trunk when backing up. You get ample luggage space in a fairly deep trunk.

VALUE FOR THE MONEY: Pontiac's reworked midsize was a big hit from the start. Sales of the '97 model ran more than 50 percent of 1996 levels, though naturally its popularity tapered off later. Brashly styled with a confident stance, Grand Prix is a highly capable, sporty midsize car that challenges the class leaders in overall value.

TROUBLE SPOTS

Brake noise: During moderate application, the rear brakes make a moaning sound. New pads are available to correct the problem. (1998-99)

Cruise control: If the cruise control cancels when the wipers are running, the cruise control module and ground wires must be replaced. (1997-98)

Door handles: On white cars, the door handles turn yellow from the lock-cylinder grease. The company will replace the cylinders under warranty and there is a colorless grease available. (1997-99)

Doors: The power door locks fail due to a rubber part breaking on the actuator arm inside the door. (1997)

Engine misfire: The 3800 engine develops an ignition miss because the grease in the spark-plug boots causes them to crack. (1997-98)

Poor transmission shift: The transmission may not shift out of third gear because the wires from the torque-converter switch rub and short out on the air-cleaner housing. (1998)

Tail/brake lights: If water leaks into the left taillight housing, it must be replaced with a countermeasure housing. (1997)

Wipers: The windshield wipers may not park at the bottom of the windshield because water gets into the motor assembly and freezes. (1997-98)

AVERAGE REPLACEMENT COSTS

A/C Compressor	$460	Exhaust System	$425
Alternator	220	Radiator	215
Automatic Trans.	855	Shocks and/or Struts	910
Brakes	390	Timing Chain/Belt	220
CV Joints	795		

NHTSA RECALL HISTORY

1997: Windshield wipers may stop working, due to separation between drive pin and crescent in crank-arm assembly. **1997-98:** Faulty power-steering bearings may have been installed on certain vehicles, resulting in difficulty turning the steering wheel. Dealers will inspect and replace all affected parts. **1997-99:** When the hazard-flasher switch is used to turn the hazard flashers on or off, the retained accessory power feature can be activated without a key in the ignition. **1999:** Driver's airbag-inflator modules could produce excessive internal pressure. In the event of a crash, the increased internal pressure can cause the inflator module to explode. **2000:** Front passenger-airbag modules in a few cars have undersized inflator orifice; in a crash, this can cause inflator module to explode. **2000:** Some seatbelt assemblies were not properly heat treated and do not pass the load-bearing requirement. **2001:** Passenger airbag-inflator modules may have been built without the correct amount of explosive. Airbag explosion or failure could occur. **2003:** Right rear brake hose may be too loose, resulting in loss of brake fluid. Dealer will inspect vehicle and tighten affected brake hoses.

PRICES	Good	Average	Poor
1997 Grand Prix	$4,200-5,700	$3,400-4,700	$1,400-1,900
1998 Grand Prix	5,000-6,800	4,300-5,800	2,000-2,700
1999 Grand Prix GT, GTP	7,500-8,800	6,800-7,900	3,800-4,400
Grand Prix SE	6,200-7,200	5,400-6,300	2,700-3,100
2000 Grand Prix GT, GTP	9,000-10,800	8,100-9,700	4,700-5,600
Grand Prix SE	7,500-8,500	6,800-7,700	3,800-4,300
2001 Grand Prix GT, GTP	10,500-13,000	9,500-11,700	5,600-6,900
Grand Prix SE	9,000-10,000	8,100-9,000	4,700-5,200
2002 Grand Prix GT, GTP	12,500-15,000	11,300-13,500	7,100-8,600
Grand Prix SE	10,500-11,500	9,500-10,400	5,600-6,100
2003 Grand Prix GT, GTP	14,500-18,000	13,200-16,400	9,000-11,200
Grand Prix SE	12,500-13,700	11,300-12,300	7,100-7,800

For detailed information on this vehicle visit
http://used.consumerguide.com and enter code **2315**

1995-03 PONTIAC SUNFIRE

CLASS: Subcompact car
BUILT IN: USA
PROS: Antilock brakes
• Fuel economy
• Instruments/controls
CONS: Noise • Rear-seat comfort • Rear visibility

PONTIAC

EVALUATION: The original engine is somewhat coarse under hard throttle, but acceleration is adequate with either manual or automatic shift. The Quad 4 and later Twin Cam engines are better—smoother, quieter, and more powerful. Acceleration off the line is lively, and they work well with the 4-speed automatic. You can expect about 25 mpg in the city and 30 mpg on the highway with either engine.

Through twisting roads, a GT corners with minimal body lean and tight grip. Under comparable conditions, an SE exhibited greater body lean, less grip, and slower reaction in its steering. Both Sunfires absorb bumpy surfaces handily, but can toss occupants around a bit on rough surfaces.

Interior space is adequate for four adults. A low rear-seat cushion forces an uncomfortable knees-up position, and head room is only marginal. Front head and leg room are a lot better. Gauges are unobstructed and controls operate smoothly. Forward visibility is fine, past a low dashboard. Backing up is difficult because of the Sunfire's high rear parcel shelf. The glovebox in Sunfire can hold a 12-pack of soda cans and front doors have map pockets. Trunk space is ample, too, but the 2-door's trunk opening is too small to easily load bulky cargo.

VALUE FOR THE MONEY: Well-equipped when new, Sunfires make good choices in the subcompact league. Except for sportier styling touches from Pontiac, however, differences between Sunfires and Cavaliers are modest.

TROUBLE SPOTS

See the 1995-03 Chevrolet Cavalier.

AVERAGE REPLACEMENT COSTS

See the 1995-03 Chevrolet Cavalier.

NHTSA RECALL HISTORY

1995: Automatic-transmission indicator may not reflect correct gear position. **1995:** Welds were omitted from lower control arms; excessive loads can result in separation. **1995-96:** Front or rear hazard warning lamps (four-way flashers), or both, do not flash when switch is activated. **1996:** If the key is held in the "start" position for an extended period, high current flowing through the ignition switch can melt internal switch parts. **1996:** Interior lamps might come on unexpectedly while vehicle is being driven. **1996:** Kinked accelerator cable in a few cars can result in unwanted acceleration. **1996-97:** Airbag could deploy inadvertently in a low-speed crash, or when an object strikes the floor pan. **1996-97:** Rear-suspension trailing-arm bolts can fatigue and break. **1996-98:** Faulty power-steering bearings may have been installed on certain vehicles, resulting in difficulty turning the steering wheel. Dealers will inspect and replace all affected parts. **1997:** Spare tire on a few cars may have incorrect rim. **1998:** Wheel lug nuts on a few cars were not tightened securely, resulting in fracture of studs. **1999:** Instrument-panel backlighting may not function after driver adjusts interior-light intensity.

PRICES	Good	Average	Poor
1995 Convertible	$3,200-4,000	$2,500-3,100	$800-1,000
Sunfire	2,100-2,700	1,500-1,900	400-500
Sunfire GT	2,700-3,300	2,000-2,500	600-700

1996 Convertible	$3,500-4,300	$2,800-3,400	$900-1,200
Sunfire	2,300-3,000	1,700-2,200	400-600
Sunfire GT	2,900-3,500	2,200-2,700	700-800
1997 Convertible	4,000-4,800	3,300-3,900	1,300-1,500
Sunfire	2,700-3,400	2,000-2,600	600-700
Sunfire GT	3,500-4,200	2,800-3,400	900-1,100
1998 Convertible	4,800-5,600	4,000-4,700	1,800-2,100
Sunfire	3,500-4,200	2,800-3,400	900-1,100
Sunfire GT	4,300-5,000	3,500-4,100	1,500-1,700
1999 Convertible	6,500-7,300	5,700-6,400	2,900-3,300
Sunfire	4,300-5,000	3,500-4,100	1,500-1,700
Sunfire GT	5,200-6,000	4,400-5,100	2,100-2,400
2000 Convertible	8,000-9,000	7,200-8,100	4,100-4,600
Sunfire	5,200-6,000	4,400-5,100	2,100-2,400
Sunfire GT	6,400-7,200	5,600-6,300	2,800-3,200
2001 Sunfire GT	7,500-8,500	6,800-7,700	3,800-4,300
Sunfire SE	6,200-7,000	5,400-6,100	2,700-3,000
2002 Sunfire GT	8,800-9,800	7,900-8,800	4,600-5,100
Sunfire SE	7,500-8,300	6,800-7,500	3,800-4,200
2003 Sunfire coupe	9,000-10,000	8,100-9,000	4,700-5,200

For detailed information on this vehicle visit
http://used.consumerguide.com and enter code 2229

1990-96 PONTIAC TRANS SPORT

CLASS: Minivan

BUILT IN: USA

PROS: Acceleration (3.8-liter V6) • Passenger and cargo room

CONS: Acceleration (3.1-liter V6) • Visibility

EVALUATION: Featuring a fiberglasslike composite shell bonded to a steel framework, rust isn't a problem, and the plasticlike bodies are good at absorbing parking-lot dings. However, the long sloping nose of the Trans Sport has proven less than popular with the public. The view from the driver's seat is also disconcerting. A restyling job in 1994 added a driver-side airbag and shortened the front somewhat.

The Trans Sport's handling is much more carlike than trucklike. Acceleration is a bit below average with the 3.1-liter V6 and three-speed automatic. However, performance improves with the arrival of GM's "3800" 3.8-liter V6 paired with a 4-speed automatic. Power is enhanced further in 1996 with the switch to the more fuel efficient 3.4-liter V6 engine.

The interior is roomy, and the removable bucket seats weigh only 36 pounds. Pontiac also gained a convenient power function for its sliding door, which can be activated either by a button inside the vehicle or with the remote-entry keyfob.

VALUE FOR THE MONEY: Overall, the Trans Sport is a capable and stylish minivan. It provides good interior room, the safety of an airbag and a power sliding door on newer models, plus less boxy styling. While the Trans Sport is no match overall for Chrysler's new minivans, it's reasonably priced and a good value in rust-belt areas that experience severe winters.

TROUBLE SPOTS

See the 1990-96 Chevrolet Lumina APV/Minivan.

AVERAGE REPLACEMENT COSTS

See the 1990-96 Chevrolet Lumina APV/Minivan.

NHTSA RECALL HISTORY

1990: Rear modular seat frame hold-down hooks may not meet the required pull force. **1990:** Right-seat/shoulder-belt retractor may have been installed in second-row left seat position. **1990-91 in 14 states:** Rear cradle bolts could pull through retainers, due to corrosion; if both bolts pull through, steering shaft could separate from steering gear. **1992-95:** Transmission-cooler line in cars with certain powertrains, sold in specified states, can separate at low temperature. **1993-94 w/optional power sliding door :** Shoulder belt can become pinched between seat and door-frame pillar trim. **1994:** Pawl spring may be missing from retractors for rear center lap belts. **1994:** Third-row seatbelt retractors may lock up when van is on a slope. **1995 w/3.1-liter engine:** Throttle-cable support brackets could contact throttle-lever system and inhibit throttle return; engine speed would then decrease more slowly than anticipated. **1995:** On some cars, brake-pedal arm can fracture during braking. **1996-98:** Faulty power steering bearings may have been installed on certain vehicles, resulting in difficulty turning the steering wheel. Dealers will inspect and replace all affected parts.

PRICES	Good	Average	Poor
1990 Trans Sport	$1,500-2,100	$1,000-1,400	$200-300
1991 Trans Sport	1,800-2,400	1,200-1,600	300-400
1992 Trans Sport	2,100-2,700	1,500-1,900	400-500
1993 Trans Sport	2,400-3,100	1,800-2,300	500-600
1994 Trans Sport	2,800-3,500	2,100-2,600	600-800
1995 Trans Sport	3,200-4,000	2,500-3,100	800-1,000
1996 Trans Sport	3,800-4,600	3,100-3,700	1,100-1,400

For detailed information on this vehicle visit
http://used.consumerguide.com and enter code **2097**

1997-03 PONTIAC TRANS SPORT/MONTANA

CLASS: Minivan
BUILT IN: USA
PROS: Antilock brakes
• Passenger and cargo room
• Ride
CONS: Fuel economy
• Rear-seat comfort

EVALUATION: You can expect a stable, comfortable ride as the standard suspension absorbs most road imperfections with ease. With the firmer suspension that's part of the Montana Package, you'll feel more bumps and the ride gets a little jittery on rough surfaces. Steering is firm and precise, and a Trans Sport corners with good grip and moderate body lean.

Smooth-running and fairly quiet, the 3.4-liter V6 produces sufficient acceleration for most conditions. When three or more people are aboard and you need a quick burst of power for passing, however, the minivan feels sluggish. The smooth-shifting automatic transmission downshifts quickly for passing. As for economy, we averaged 18.7 mpg, with a little more highway driving than urban miles. Wind noise around the mirrors is noticeable on the highway, but road and engine noise are minimal.

Low step-in height makes entry/exit easy—easier yet with the optional driver-side sliding door. Gauges are unobstructed, and the driver can reach the large radio and climate controls without much of a stretch.

Leg room is at least adequate all around. Most adults should fit in the middle and rear seats without scrunching, but some might complain because the seats are low to the floor, forcing some awkward bending of the knees.

Individual bucket seats are light enough to be removed by one person. So is the rear bench. Short-wheelbase models have only a narrow cargo area at the rear, when all seats are in place. Extended-wheelbase minivans have a much larger cargo area out back.

VALUE FOR THE MONEY: Even though we still consider Chrysler's minivans the best around, we've been impressed by the Trans Sport as well as its Chevrolet and Oldsmobile cousins.

TROUBLE SPOTS

See the 1997-03 Chevrolet Venture.

AVERAGE REPLACEMENT COSTS

See the 1997-03 Chevrolet Venture.

NHTSA RECALL HISTORY

1997-2001 w/passenger-side sliding door: Door closes but may not be latched. If this happens, the sliding door can open while the vehicle is in motion. **1997-98:** Windshield-wiper linkage arm can contact brake line connected to traction-control modulator valve; brake line can chafe, resulting in brake-fluid leakage. **1998:** Broken shift-cable fitting or loose shift linkage can occur; moving shift lever to "Park" position may not shift the transmission to "Park," and vehicle could roll. **1999 Montana:** Driver's-side-airbag inflator module could explode on deployment because of excessive internal pressure. **2000:** Some seatbelt assemblies were not properly heat treated and do not pass the load-bearing requirement. **2001 Montana:** Passenger-airbag inflator modules may have been built without the correct amount of explosive. Airbag explosion or failure could occur. **2001:** Seat-latch anchor-wire diameter may be wider than 6.1 mm, potentially inhibiting the installation of child restraints. **2002:** Driver's-side-airbag inflator could fracture during deployment, increasing the risk of serious injury. **2002-03:** Owner's manual doesn't adequately explain child-restraint anchorage system. Dealers will send vehicle owners a supplement to their manual.

PRICES

	Good	Average	Poor
1997 Trans Sport extended	$6,000-6,800	$5,200-5,900	$2,500-2,900
Trans Sport regular	5,000-5,800	4,300-4,900	2,000-2,300
1998 Trans Sport extended	7,500-8,400	6,800-7,600	3,800-4,200
Trans Sport regular	6,200-7,300	5,400-6,400	2,700-3,100
1999 Montana extended	9,200-10,200	8,300-9,200	4,800-5,300
Montana regular	7,700-8,900	6,900-8,000	3,900-4,500
2000 Montana extended	10,900-12,500	9,800-11,300	5,900-6,800
Montana regular	9,400-10,400	8,500-9,400	4,900-5,400
2001 Montana extended	12,500-14,500	11,300-13,100	7,100-8,300
Montana regular	11,000-12,200	9,900-11,000	5,900-6,600
2002 Montana extended	14,500-18,000	13,200-16,400	9,000-11,200
Montana regular	13,000-14,500	11,800-13,200	7,500-8,400
2003 Montana extended	16,800-22,000	15,500-20,200	10,800-14,100
Montana regular	15,000-16,500	13,700-15,000	9,500-10,400

For detailed information on this vehicle visit
http://used.consumerguide.com and enter code **2281**

1997-03 PORSCHE BOXSTER

CLASS: Sports car
BUILT IN: Germany
PROS: Acceleration • Side airbags (1998-up) • Steering/handling • Braking
CONS: Noise • Passenger room • Ride

EVALUATION: Looks are just the starting point of the Boxster's appeal. It may be the latest "budget" Porsche, but the Boxster is no less a thoroughbred sports car than its big-brother 911. This roadster entertains most on twisty roads, tracking with grippy sure-footed stability, little body lean, and sure control, aided by rifle-quick steering with ample feedback.

Unfortunately, the penalty for this handling prowess is an annoyingly stiff ride, with constant minor pitching on some freeways, and lots of thumpy jiggle over tar strips and patches. Add in marked noise from engine, wind, and tires, and the Boxster would be wearing on a long Interstate trip.

Although the engine is strongest at higher rpm, there's enough low-end torque for punchy standing starts and quick passing sprints. Still, our manual-shift test car disappointed slightly in the 0-60 mph test at 7.5 seconds (Porsche claims 6.7).

Fuel economy is excellent for the performance, however. We averaged a laudable 21.7 mpg in spirited city/highway driving. "Panic" braking is arresting-cable swift. Mash the pedal and the Boxster just hunkers down and stops.

Some drivers feel cramped in a Boxster, even with the top down, while others have no complaints. Audio and climate controls are handy but confusing. Many drivers would prefer a tilt steering wheel instead of the standard telescopic adjustment. As it is, the wheel rim tends to mask part of the tachometer face.

Additional gripes: an old-fashioned floor-hinged gas pedal; analog and digital speedometers; no in-dash glovebox; and no top-side engine access other than three "service" ports in the rear trunk.

On the plus side, the Boxster's two cargo holds (front and rear) take a fair bit of stuff for a 2-seater, the seats are supportively comfortable, and visibility is okay despite a "bathtub" driving position and the soft top's fairly blind rear quarters. That top works quickly and seals well, but isn't completely covered when folded under its lid. Also, the plastic rear window seems cheap at this price.

The optional behind-the-seats wind blocker is effective, but cumbersome to remove or install.

Boxster is solid and rattle-free for a modern ragtop. One test car had some body shake over railroad tracks, though paint was gorgeous and panel fits precise—a sharp contrast to the thin, cheap-looking black plastic used on the dashboard and console.

VALUE FOR THE MONEY: As a more affordable Porsche, the Boxster is mainly for those who appreciate a Porsche's special virtues. BMW's 6-cylinder Z3 2.8 is a more "traditional" sports car that's close in performance, while some observers favor the Mercedes-Benz as the best all-around machine. All are good in their way, and cost about the same, so take your pick. No, it's not perfect; but Boxster is a genuine sports car, and genuinely entertaining on the road.

TROUBLE SPOTS

Dashboard lights: The check-engine light may come on due to a loose gas cap or damaged gas-cap seal. (1998-99)

Engine misfire: An engine miss might be caused by water in the air-cleaner housing. A water-separator bowl must be installed in the housing intake. (1997)

Oil leak: A steel plug in the cylinder head may cause an oil leak. An aluminum plug is available to correct the problem. (1997)

Vehicle noise: On cars with a manual transmission, the power-steering-pump belt may squeal during parking maneuvers. Replacing the original aluminum pulley with a steel pulley eliminates the noise. (1997-98)

Vehicle shake: If the hardtop rattles, replacing the centering-pin caps with redesigned caps might correct the problem. (1997)

AVERAGE REPLACEMENT COSTS

A/C Compressor	$760	CV Joints	$2,150
Alternator	430	Exhaust System	870
Automatic Trans.	1,460	Radiator	890
Brakes	745	Shocks and/or Struts	1,600
Clutch	765	Timing Chain/Belt	850

NHTSA RECALL HISTORY

1997-98: Contact buckle supplied with child-seating system airbag-deactivation kit does not deactivate the airbag.

PRICES

	Good	Average	Poor
1997 Boxster	$20,000-21,500	$18,400-19,800	$13,000-14,000
1998 Boxster	22,000-24,000	20,200-22,100	14,300-15,600
1999 Boxster	24,000-26,000	22,300-24,200	15,600-16,900
2000 Boxster	27,000-29,000	25,100-27,000	18,100-19,400
Boxster S	31,500-33,500	29,300-31,200	22,100-23,500
2001 Boxster	30,000-32,000	27,900-29,800	21,000-22,400
Boxster S	35,000-37,000	32,600-34,400	24,900-26,300
2002 Boxster	34,000-36,000	31,600-33,500	24,100-25,600
Boxster S	39,000-41,000	36,300-38,100	28,100-29,500
2003 Boxster	38,500-41,000	35,800-38,100	27,300-29,100
Boxster S	45,000-48,000	42,300-45,100	32,900-35,000

For detailed information on this vehicle visit
http://used.consumerguide.com and enter code 2333

1994-98 SAAB 900

CLASS: Near-luxury car
BUILT IN: Sweden
PROS: Acceleration (V6, turbo) • Passenger and cargo room • Steering/handling
CONS: Ride • Road noise • Wind noise

EVALUATION: This new Saab retained its upright stance and stuck to its hatchback design. As a result, it preserved such virtues as generous head and leg room, plus enormous cargo space from what is basically a very compact car. However, mainstream buyers may find the key position is too disorienting and the cabin too narrow.

The dashboard is little changed, so most controls are close at hand. But the power-window buttons are mounted between the seats rather than on the door panels where they'd be more convenient to operate.

The V6 feels strong and smooth, and works particularly well with the new 4-speed automatic. It shifts quickly and consistently with no hesitation. It downshifts smoothly, eagerly providing all the passing power you need. The 900's 2.3-liter 4-cylinder has adequate power with the manual, but feels underpowered when paired with the automatic.

Body lean is evident when taking turns at speed, but these cars have a generally sporty feel, with precise steering and excellent grip. The taut suspension provides excellent control, but combines with the modest wheelbase for a ride that's choppy enough over rough pavement to deter some buyers. Wind and road noise are disconcerting at highway speeds.

VALUE FOR THE MONEY: Mainstream shoppers interested in a near-luxury car still aren't likely to put the Saab 900 on their must-see list, but we credit Saab with making a better 900 for those who love and appreciate its quirky nature.

TROUBLE SPOTS

Audio system: Scratches or microscopic cracks in the rear-window heater grid cause interference in the radio when the rear defroster is turned on. (All)

Engine fan: The battery may go dead because the cooling-fan relay, which allows the fan to run 10 minutes after the engine is turned off, keeps the fan on. (1994-96)

Hard starting: The turbo bypass valve is secured with plastic clamps that break, causing hard starting and poor drivability. (All)

Poor drivability: Stumble, stalling, or hesitation during the first minute after startup is corrected by replacing the engine-control computer. (1994-95)

Transmission leak: The gear-selector shaft seal is prone to leak on manual transmissions. (1994-96)

AVERAGE REPLACEMENT COSTS

A/C Compressor	$665	CV Joints	$485
Alternator	455	Exhaust System	640
Automatic Trans.	1,250	Radiator	395
Brakes	265	Shocks and/or Struts	990
Clutch	655	Timing Chain/Belt	630

NHTSA RECALL HISTORY

1994 hatchback: Weld omitted from manual driver's-seat rails. **1994:** On some manual front seats, trigger springs at fore/aft lever do not properly lock the seat rails. **1994:** Weld points for side-protection beam in rear door may be out of position. **1994-95 w/manual shift:** It is possible to move shift lever into reverse, remove key, and still be in neutral. **1994-95:** Welds on recliner may be missing, allowing seatback to fall backward when

SAAB

under load. **1994-97:** Corrosion can cause throttle lever to bind. **1994-98:** Instructions for properly aiming headlights were omitted. **1995 convertible:** Steering-column shaft may be misaligned. **1995 w/Bosch "Motronic 2.10.3":** Upon startup, engine speed may fluctuate for up to 30 seconds. **1995:** Some vehicles may have defective airbag electronic control units, causing an electrical short and possible deployment. Dealer will inspect and replace all affected parts. **1996:** Seatbelt anchorage on some cars may not properly secure the occupant in an accident. **1997-98:** Airbag alert label on driver's sunvisor was omitted. **1998:** Static electricity can build up within the passenger-side airbag module and create enough of a charge to cause an inadvertent airbag deployment.

PRICES

	Good	Average	Poor
1994 900	$3,700-4,800	$3,000-3,900	$1,100-1,400
900 Convertible	5,200-6,500	4,400-5,500	2,100-2,600
900 Turbo	4,800-5,500	4,000-4,600	1,800-2,100
1995 900	4,200-5,400	3,400-4,400	1,400-1,800
900 Convertible	6,200-7,700	5,400-6,700	2,700-3,300
900 Turbo	5,500-6,500	4,700-5,600	2,300-2,700
1996 900	4,700-6,000	3,900-5,000	1,700-2,200
900 Convertible	7,200-8,500	6,400-7,600	3,500-4,200
900 Turbo	6,000-7,000	5,200-6,100	2,500-2,900
1997 900	5,300-6,900	4,600-5,900	2,200-2,800
900 Convertible	8,500-10,000	7,700-9,000	4,400-5,200
900 Turbo	6,800-7,800	6,100-6,900	3,200-3,700
1998 900	6,200-7,500	5,400-6,500	2,700-3,200
900 Convertible	10,000-12,000	9,000-10,800	5,200-6,200
900 Turbo	7,500-8,500	6,800-7,700	3,800-4,300

For detailed information on this vehicle visit
http://used.consumerguide.com and enter code **2099**

1999-02 SAAB 9-3

CLASS: Near-luxury car
BUILT IN: Sweden
PROS: Acceleration
• Cargo room (except convertible) • Rear-seat room/comfort (convertible) • Brake performance
CONS: Turbo-engine performance • Build quality (convertible) • Rear-seat entry/exit (except 4-dr) • Rear visibility

EVALUATION: Compact Saabs deliver sporty driving in a space-efficient, if somewhat quirky, package. Overall acceleration is good. Base models are responsive but calm. A manual-transmission base car accelerated to 60 mph in 7.5 seconds, and averaged 19.4 mpg even in hard driving. High Output models are slightly faster. A 4-door averaged 21.3 mpg. Viggens react with serious spirit. On the downside, the turbocharger does not yield extra power until the engine reaches 3000 rpm or so, and "turbo lag" (delay after flooring the throttle) makes smooth driving difficult. Unruly steering-wheel tug occurs when pushed hard, too, unless front wheels are pointed dead-ahead. Handling is sporty, responsive, and predictable, with good cornering grip. SE models (and Viggens) ride quite stiffly. High-performance tires transmit a lot of irritating thump and jiggle on small, sharp bumps. Base models have softer tires and should be noticeably more compliant and comfortable on any road. Braking is swift and powerful. Relatively narrow and tall, hatchbacks have fairly ample space for five, plus cargo room that rivals a wagon. Convertibles seat only four, with very limited rear leg room. Rear visibility is so-so in hatchbacks and awful in top-up convertibles. Gauges and controls are well-located. The floor-mounted ignition switch is a longtime Saab hallmark. Sadly, so is the SE's obstinate automatic climate-control system. Detail finish is good and materials are classy. A test convertible suffered excessive body flex over bumps, but other Saabs have felt rigid and mostly rattle-free.

VALUE FOR THE MONEY: All models have their charms, but are compromised by turbo-engine performance. Saab loyalists are likely to love the quirky 9-3, but a Volvo S70 sedan or V70 wagon might be a more prudent choice for near-luxury motoring in the Swedish mode.

TROUBLE SPOTS

Automatic transmission: A recall was issued to replace the shift-lock solenoid that prevented the transmission from shifting out of park. (1999)

Brakes: If the brake-fluid reservoir cap is not installed properly, fluid can be sucked out of the reservoir through the cap's check valve. (1999-01)

Climate control: There were several problems with the HVAC controls ranging from stiff controls to ticking motors to loose knobs and broken spindles. New parts were being installed under warranty. (1999)

Oil consumption: A banjo bolt in the crankcase ventilation system should be replaced to prevent oil from possibly entering the combustion chamber (causing emissions) or starving the turbo bearing. (1999)

Wipers: The rear wiper may get loose or fall off unless thread-locking compound is applied to the hold-down nut. (1999)

AVERAGE REPLACEMENT COSTS

A/C Compressor	$775	CV Joints	$1,290
Alternator	410	Exhaust System	775
Automatic Trans.	1,100	Radiator	700
Brakes	745	Shocks and/or Struts	1,455
Clutch	830	Timing Chain/Belt	655

NHTSA RECALL HISTORY

1999 w/manual front seats, made March 4 - October 17, 1998: Failure of "Easy Entry" cable in front manual seats can cause seat fore/aft adjustable mechanism to be unlocked, reducing the restraint capability of the safetybelts in a crash. **2001:** Airbag alert labels may not be permanently affixed. **2002:** A loose tie rod could result in a sudden reduction or total loss of steering control.

PRICES

	Good	Average	Poor
1999 9-3 Convertible	$12,000-13,500	$10,800-12,200	$6,700-7,600
9-3 SE	9,000-10,000	8,100-9,000	4,700-5,200
9-3 Viggen	15,000-16,500	13,700-15,000	9,500-10,400
9-3 hatchback	7,500-8,500	6,800-7,700	3,800-4,300
2000 9-3 Convertible	16,000-18,000	14,600-16,400	10,200-11,500
9-3 SE	12,000-13,000	10,800-11,700	6,700-7,300
9-3 Viggen	18,000-19,500	16,600-17,900	11,500-12,500
9-3 hatchback	10,500-11,500	9,500-10,400	5,600-6,100
Viggen Convertible	20,000-22,000	18,400-20,200	13,000-14,300
2001 9-3 Convertible	20,000-22,000	18,400-20,200	13,000-14,300
9-3 SE	15,500-16,700	14,100-15,200	9,900-10,700
9-3 Viggen	21,500-23,000	19,800-21,200	14,000-15,000
9-3 hatchback	13,500-15,000	12,300-13,700	8,000-8,900
Viggen Convertible	25,000-27,500	23,300-25,600	16,500-18,200
2002 9-3 Convertible	24,000-26,000	22,300-24,200	15,600-16,900
9-3 SE	17,000-18,500	15,600-17,000	10,900-11,800
9-3 Viggen	25,000-27,000	23,300-25,100	16,500-17,800
Viggen Convertible	30,000-32,500	27,900-30,200	21,000-22,800

> For detailed information on this vehicle visit
> http://used.consumerguide.com and enter code **2399**

1991-96 SATURN COUPE

CLASS: Sporty coupe

BUILT IN: USA

PROS: Acceleration (SC2) • Antilock brakes (optional) • Fuel economy • Instruments/controls

CONS: Acceleration (SC1) • Engine noise • Entry/exit • Rear-seat room • Road noise

EVALUATION: If possible, select a base model (1995-96) with the 100-horsepower base engine paired with the manual 5-speed. Acceleration is sluggish with the automatic. Also, the revised base engine performs better than the previous 85-horsepower unit. The more powerful twin-cam engine in the SC2 performs well with either transmission. We timed one with the automatic at 9.1 seconds to 60 mph. The same car averaged 25 mpg from mainly urban driving. The SC1 should prove even more economical. However, both engines are still too noisy at higher speeds.

Like most other sports coupes, these two suffer from limited rear-seat room, though there's plenty of space in front for tall people. The gauges are clearly marked and well-lit at night, and the steering-column stalks for both lights and wipers are at the driver's fingertips. The early climate controls are too low in the center of the dashboard and require a long look away from the road to find the right switch.

VALUE FOR THE MONEY: Saturn coupes began to get lots of competition from rivals, but the used-car certification program from Saturn dealerships could help ensure that buyers will get a good deal on a used Saturn. You also have the promise of higher-than-average customer service on repairs and warranty work after the purchase.

TROUBLE SPOTS

Antenna: A whistling wind noise may be coming from the radio antenna. (1991-95)

Automatic transmission: If the automatic transmission shifts harshly, erratically, or sticks in gear or neutral, iron sediment in the valve body may be the problem. (1993-94)

Brake noise: Brakes that growl or grind during low speed stops are repaired by replacing the front pads and machining the rotors. (1991-95)

Cruise control: If the cruise control fluctuates at speeds over 64 mph, a new control-module assembly may be needed. (1991-95)

Doors: If the doors will not open, the door-latch assembly(s) will be replaced. (1991-93)

Engine noise: Squealing from the front of the engine when the temperature is below 40 degrees (F) will be fixed by replacing the drive-belt idler pulley with one having a revised bearing. (1991-95)

Tail/brake lights: A drop in fuel economy, brake noise, vehicle vibration, and/or increased brake-pedal travel could be caused by a misadjusted brake-light switch that does not allow the pedal to return to full release. (1991-93)

Trunk latch: If the trunk can be opened without the key, Saturn will fix the release mechanism. (1991-93)

AVERAGE REPLACEMENT COSTS

A/C Compressor	$390	CV Joints	$380
Alternator	350	Exhaust System	298
Automatic Trans.	905	Radiator	350
Brakes	190	Shocks and/or Struts	485
Clutch	530	Timing Chain/Belt	295

NHTSA RECALL HISTORY

1991-93: Generator-wiring harness could suffer excessive current flow. **1992:** Automatic transaxle-valve assemblies on some cars were improperly machined. **1993 SC2:** Battery-cable terminal at solenoid may be formed incorrectly. **1993:** Brake-booster housing on some cars could separate. **1994-95:** Some front seat-back-recliner gear teeth may wear excessively through repeated use; could cause seatback to slip partially rearward when force is applied. **1995 w/automatic:** Improperly adjusted cable makes it possible to shift from "Park" with key removed, or to remove key while lever is in position other than "Park." **1996:** Horn could become inoperable or activate without pressing button; under certain conditions, heat could build up, leading to underhood fire.

PRICES	Good	Average	Poor
1991 SC2	$1,600-2,100	$1,100-1,400	$200-300
1992 SC2	1,800-2,400	1,200-1,600	300-400
1993 SC1, SC2	2,100-2,700	1,500-1,900	400-500
1994 SC1, SC2	2,400-3,100	1,800-2,300	500-600
1995 SC1, SC2	2,700-3,400	2,000-2,600	600-700
1996 SC1, SC2	3,000-3,700	2,300-2,800	700-900

For detailed information on this vehicle visit
http://used.consumerguide.com and enter code **2100**

1997-02 SATURN COUPE

CG BEST BUY

CLASS: Sporty coupe
BUILT IN: USA
PROS: Acceleration (SC2) • Fuel economy
CONS: Acceleration (SC1 w/auto) • Entry/exit • Noise • Rear-seat room

EVALUATION: Acceleration with an SC1 is adequate with manual shift, but a little less satisfying with the 4-speed automatic transmission. When you need a quick burst of power, it might not be there. With either transmission, an SC2 coupe accelerates in a more lively manner. An SC2 with automatic takes off with some zest, though turning on the air conditioning takes a toll on performance. Highway passing power also is good with the SC2.

Fuel economy is appealing with any coupe, but the frugality champ is an SC1 with the 5-speed gearbox. We've averaged a miserly 31.9 mpg in mixed city/highway driving, versus 26 mpg with an SC2 that was equipped with the 5-speed.

Although noise levels are lower than before, both engines remain loud and rather coarse during hard acceleration. All Saturns corner with pleasing swiftness and control. Handling is sure-footed and competent in both models, but the SC1's steering is lighter and less precise. Ride quality is good with either coupe, but the SC1's softer suspension makes it more livable on urban roads. You pay a penalty for the SC2's sportier handling, which promises less body lean in turns.

Visibility is good to all directions, unlike most sports coupes, helped by thin roof pillars and large windows. Large, clear gauges inform the driver. Radio and climate controls are in a pod that protrudes from the dashboard, mounted too low for best access while driving. Power window and mirror controls are on the center console, unlit and difficult to find at night. Front seats offer plenty of room, but are rather low, surrounded by a high beltline and a vast dashboard top. Firm seats offer good lateral support. Leg room might have grown markedly in back, as measured with a ruler, but the rear-seat cushion is so low that most adults have to sit with their knees nearly pointing at the ceiling. Cargo space is adequate in a deep trunk.

VALUE FOR THE MONEY: All told, Saturns lack the refinement of most Japanese sports coupes. They're also noisier, but boast an impressive reliability record. The side-curtain airbags added for 2001 are unique in this class.

TROUBLE SPOTS

Air conditioner: The air conditioning may stop working when the car is driven for extended times on the highway because the evaporator freezes up. (1997-98)

Automatic transmission: Cars with automatic transmissions may leak fluid from the upper, left-hand corner where the case was not manufactured properly. (1997-98)

Electrical problem: Electrical accessories may quit working. The lock will have to be repaired. On some models, the key won't turn back to the lock position. (1997)

Engine misfire: The engine may stall or quit running as if it has run out of gas even though the gauge shows ⅛-¼ tank; caused by a plugged evaporative-emissions canister vent. (1997)

Hard starting: If a car with a manual transmission won't start, the wiring harness is probably damaged from rubbing on the clutch-pedal pivot causing a short circuit. (1997-98)

Windows: The side windows may not go up or down, or they may rattle because the glass comes loose from the regulator. (1997-98)

AVERAGE REPLACEMENT COSTS

A/C Compressor	$400	CV Joints	$390
Alternator	350	Exhaust System	310
Automatic Trans.	915	Radiator	350
Brakes	190	Shocks and/or Struts	490
Clutch	530	Timing Chain/Belt	300

NHTSA RECALL HISTORY

1997: Belted occupant in front passenger seat could experience seat movement during a moderate frontal impact. **1997:** Horn could become inoperable or activate without pressing button; leading to an underhood fire. **1997:** Ignition key can be removed while in "run" position. **1997:** Lock-up feature of seatbelt may not work properly. **1999-00:** Some seatbelt shoulder-guide anchor bolts were inadequately tightened at center pillar and could fall out. **2000:** Armrest latch may open during a crash. **2000:** Some brake-pipe-attachment nuts may not have been tightened properly, and leakage could occur. **2000:** Some rear-bumper fasteners could be loose or missing; rear bumper may not absorb energy properly in a rear-end collision.

SATURN

2000: Some welds in instrument-panel carrier assembly were not strong enough; occupant, especially if unbelted, may have increased risk of injury in frontal crash. **2000:** The fuel-tank Over Pressure Relief valve can become stuck open in a frontal collision, creating a fire hazard. **2001:** An improperly adjusted automatic-transaxle park-lock assembly could allow the vehicle to be shifted out of "Park" with the ignition key removed. **2001:** An inadequate weld at the top of the fuel tank could allow fuel leakage in a rollover.

PRICES	Good	Average	Poor
1997 SC1	$3,600-4,300	$2,900-3,400	$1,000-1,200
SC2	4,100-4,800	3,400-3,900	1,400-1,600
1998 SC1	4,200-5,000	3,400-4,100	1,400-1,700
SC2	4,800-5,500	4,000-4,600	1,800-2,100
1999 SC1	5,000-5,800	4,300-4,900	2,000-2,300
SC2	5,600-6,300	4,800-5,400	2,300-2,600
2000 SC1 3-door	5,900-6,700	5,100-5,800	2,500-2,800
SC2 3-door	6,500-7,200	5,700-6,300	2,900-3,200
2001 SC1 3-door	6,800-7,600	6,100-6,800	3,200-3,600
SC2 3-door	7,800-8,500	7,000-7,700	4,000-4,300
2002 SC1 3-door	7,800-8,600	7,000-7,700	4,000-4,400
SC2 3-door	9,000-10,000	8,100-9,000	4,700-5,200

For detailed information on this vehicle visit
http://used.consumerguide.com and enter code **2283**

2000-03 SATURN L-SERIES

CLASS: Midsize car
BUILT IN: USA
PROS: Acceleration (V6)
• Cargo room (wagon)
• Steering/handling
CONS: Noise • Rear-seat comfort

EVALUATION: A reasonably accomplished performer, the L-Series is distinguished by fine handling. Opel-derived suspension tuning pays off in impressive high-speed stability. These midsize Saturns corner with confidence and modest body lean. Steering is linear and communicative, though it may feel heavy at low speeds. Some 4-cylinder stick-shift models have felt too light at high speeds. Sedans and wagons handle nearly identically, though wagons ride marginally stiffer. Neither absorbs bumps as well as a Camry. Buyers get a firm, Eurostyle ride in exchange for sporty road manners. Stopping power and pedal feel are impressive. Saturn has claimed that the volume-leading LS1/L200 with automatic takes 9.8 seconds to reach 60 mph, while a V6/automatic LS2/L300 did it in 8.2. Some early V6 models showed poor throttle response at takeoff and slow downshifts when passing, but others felt spry even in hilly terrain. A test V6/automatic sedan averaged 19 mpg, while a 4-cylinder/automatic wagon got an impressive 26.6 mpg. L-Series models are as quiet as most competitors. Road, wind, and engine noise are well-muffled. The 4-cylinder engine sounds richer under hard throttle than the V6.

Four adults have as much room as in an Accord or Camry, even if the L-Series does not match their interior refinement. Cloth seats are more supportive than the optional leather. Rear leg space is ample, with head clearance for 6-footers, but the cushion is soft and low. Vision directly rearward is constricted by the high deck. Instruments are large and clear. Sedans have a large, accessible trunk. Interiors have a low-budget look. Door handles are uninviting plated plastic, and audio controls are small and plasticky.

VALUE FOR THE MONEY: Though not class leaders, L-Series models satisfy in most performance areas. Although cabins are roomy, they're furnished modestly. New-car prices undercut those of comparable Accord and Camry models, and Saturns are likely to remain lower than those competitors on the used-car market.

TROUBLE SPOTS

Climate control: The HVAC blower may only operate on high, requiring replacement of the resistor card. (2000)

Electrical problem: Chafed wires for the cooling fan cause the No. 1 fuse to blow. The wires were being lengthened with splices. (2000)

Hood/trunk: A shorter release cable is available for the hood release. (2000)

Oil consumption: The oil-filter cap can be damaged if an open-end wrench or adjustable wrench is used to remove the cap. Only a socket wrench or cap-style oil-filter tool are acceptable. (2000-01)

Seat: The power seat may stop working because the wiring harness chafes the seat assembly. (2000-01)

AVERAGE REPLACEMENT COSTS

A/C Compressor	$475	CV Joints	$770
Alternator	260	Exhaust System	370
Automatic Trans.	1,110	Radiator	350
Brakes	360	Shocks and/or Struts	490
Clutch	570	Timing Chain/Belt	280

NHTSA RECALL HISTORY

2000 LS: Certain vehicles have inoperative valve within fuel-tank assembly, which can result in fuel spillage in a rollover incident. **2000 LS:** Turn-signal lamps may not work, or work intermittently, when driver uses turn-signal lever or hazard-warning switch. **2000 w/TRW seatbelt-buckle assemblies:** Seatbelt-buckle assemblies fail to conform to Federal requirements, because buckle base was not properly heat treated. **2000 w/automatic transmission:** Transaxle shift-cable clip may be missing or improperly seated, allowing cable to slip out of bracket; driver may put lever into "Park," but transaxle may be in Reverse or Neutral. **2000:** Over Pressure Relief valve in fuel tank can become stuck open in a frontal collision; if vehicle rolls over, fuel spillage could occur. **2000-03 2.4L engines:** Ignition-control module may fail. The "Service Engine Soon" light will go on, and the vehicle will be hard to start. Dealers will inspect and replace all affected parts. **2001:** Small number of vehicles may have passenger-airbag-inflator module with incorrect amount of generant. **2003:** Windshield-wiper motor could fail, resulting in loss of visibility. Dealer will inspect and replace affected parts.

PRICES

	Good	Average	Poor
2000 LS, LS1, LW1	$6,100-7,800	$5,300-6,800	$2,600-3,400
LS2, LW2	8,000-9,000	7,200-8,100	4,100-4,600
2001 L100, L200, LW200	7,200-9,200	6,400-8,200	3,500-4,500
L300, LW300	9,500-10,500	8,600-9,500	4,900-5,500
2002 L100, L200, LW200	8,700-10,700	7,800-9,600	4,500-5,600
L300, LW300	11,000-15,500	9,900-14,100	5,900-9,000
2003 L200, LW200	10,700-13,000	9,600-11,700	5,700-6,900

For detailed information on this vehicle visit http://used.consumerguide.com and enter code **2400**

1991-95 SATURN SEDAN/WAGON

CG BEST BUY

CLASS: Subcompact car

BUILT IN: USA

PROS: Acceleration (SL2, SW2) • Antilock brakes (optional) • Fuel economy

CONS: Acceleration (base) • Engine noise • Rear-seat room • Road noise

EVALUATION: The single-cam engine in the SL1 and SW1 gives these cars adequate acceleration with the manual transmission, but with the automatic you often have to floor the throttle to keep up with traffic. The dual-cam engine provides lively acceleration and decent passing power with either transmission. Though some changes have been made over the years to decrease interior noise levels, engines still become loud and harsh at higher speeds.

Both the sedans and wagons have ample head room in front for 6-footers to sit comfortably, though the front buckets don't go back far enough for tall people to stretch out. Passengers in the back have just as much head room but less leg room. The wagon's firm rear seat has an upright backrest that some may find uncomfortable. Entry/exit is easy to the front, but tight through the narrow rear doors. The import-inspired dash is easy to use, and outward visibility is unobstructed. Trunk space is good for the class and the split-rear seatbacks fold for more cargo room.

Responsive handling and adept roadhandling are high points, particularly on the SL2 and SW2 models. And the addition of a softer suspension and tires for '93 on these level "2" models provide a noticeable improvement in ride quality.

VALUE FOR THE MONEY: Saturn sedans aren't the best choice in a subcompact, but overall they rank only slightly below the class-leading Honda Civic and Toyota Corolla.

TROUBLE SPOTS

Antenna: A whistling wind noise may be coming from the radio antenna. (1991-95)

Automatic transmission: If the automatic transmission shifts harshly, erratically, or sticks in gear or neutral, iron sediment in the valve body may be the problem. (1993-94)

Brake noise: Brakes that growl or grind during low speed stops are repaired by replacing the front pads and machining, or replacing the rotors. (1991-95)

Cruise control: If the cruise control fluctuates at speeds over 64 mph, a new control-module assembly must be installed. (1991-95)

Doors: If the doors will not open, the door-latch assembly(s) must be replaced. (1991-93)

Engine noise: Squealing from the front of the engine when the temperature is below 40 degrees (F) may be fixed by replacing the drive-belt idler pulley with one having a revised bearing. (1991-95)

Engine stalling: If the DOHC engine stalls and does not restart when coming to a stop, the oil may be the wrong viscosity. (1991-95)

Tail/brake lights: A drop in fuel economy, brake noise, vehicle vibration, and/or increased brake-pedal travel could be caused by a misadjusted brake-light switch that does not allow the pedal to return to full release. (1991-95)

AVERAGE REPLACEMENT COSTS

A/C Compressor	$390	CV Joints	$355
Alternator	350	Exhaust System	300
Automatic Trans.	905	Radiator	295
Brakes	190	Shocks and/or Struts	485
Clutch	530	Timing Chain/Belt	295

NHTSA RECALL HISTORY

1991-93: Generator-wiring harness could suffer excessive current flow. **1992:** Automatic transaxle-valve assemblies on some cars were improperly machined. **1993 SL2/SW2 :** Battery-cable terminal at starter solenoid may be formed incorrectly. **1993:** Brake-booster housing on some cars could separate. **1994-95:** Some front seatback-recliner gear teeth may wear excessively through repeated use; could cause seatback to slip partially rearward when force is applied. **1995 SL w/manual steering :** Some pinion shafts could fracture, causing total loss of steering control. **1995 w/automatic** : Improperly adjusted cable makes it possible to shift from "Park" with key removed, or to remove key while lever is in position other than "Park."

PRICES

	Good	Average	Poor
1991 SL1, SL2	$1,100-1,600	$700-1,000	$100-200
1992 SL, SL1, SL2	1,300-1,900	800-1,200	200
1993 SL, SL1, SL2	1,500-2,200	1,000-1,400	200-300
SW1, SW2 wagon	1,800-2,500	1,200-1,700	300-400
1994 SL, SL1, SL2	1,800-2,500	1,200-1,700	300-400
SW1, SW2 wagon	2,200-2,900	1,600-2,100	400-600
1995 SL, SL1, SL2	2,100-2,900	1,500-2,100	400-500
SW1, SW2 wagon	2,600-3,400	1,900-2,500	500-700

For detailed information on this vehicle visit
http://used.consumerguide.com and enter code **2101**

1996-02 SATURN SEDAN/WAGON

CG BEST BUY

CLASS: Subcompact car

BUILT IN: USA

PROS: Acceleration (SL2/SW2) • Optional antilock brakes and traction control • Fuel economy

CONS: Acceleration (SL/SL1/SW1 w/auto)

• Noise • Rear-seat comfort

EVALUATION: Engine and road noise were reduced with the 1996 redesign, but these cars still failed to head the subcompact class in terms of refinement. Both engines sound coarse and unrefined in hard acceleration. Engines did quiet down somewhat in 1998, but road noise remains considerable at highway speeds. The '99 models appear quieter yet—markedly closer to the competition, finally. Automatic-transmission operation also had been imperfect. Shift quality improved in this generation, and the 4-speed automatic is less harsh than before. This automatic transmission generally changes gears smoothly and downshifts promptly for passing. Acceleration is lively with an SL2 sedan or SW2 wagon with either transmission. Other models rank as adequate with manual shift, and markedly more sluggish with automatic. We've averaged more than 30 mpg in an SL2 with the 5-speed. A 1998 SL1 with manual shift averaged 28.9 mpg. An SL2 with automatic averaged a bit above 25 mpg.

Different tires gave the SL2/SW2 models a more comfortable ride, with less impact harshness and thumping on rough pavement. These sedans and wagons corner with pleasing swiftness and control. Body lean in turns is less in the SL2 and SW2, and their tires hold out longer before squealing in protest when you try an overly quick corner. On all models, the suspension absorbs minor bumps well, but rough roads can cause abrupt, even harsh reaction, which are felt by occupants.

Front head and leg room is sufficient for taller folks, and firm seats provide good lateral support. Back seat room is adequate for people under 5-foot-10 or so, provided the front seats aren't pushed back too far. The back seat is not particularly comfortable, and getting in and out is awkward because the door opening is narrow at the bottom. Dashboards flaunt large, clear gauges. Stereo and climate controls are mounted in a pod that protrudes from the dashboard, mounted too low for easiest access by the driver. Visibility is helped by the low dashboard and deep side windows, but the tail is too high to easily see straight rearward. Trunk space is adequate, and a low liftover eases the strain of loading/unloading luggage.

VALUE FOR THE MONEY: Despite some real improvements, these sedans and wagons still lag behind such rivals as the Civic and Corolla.

TROUBLE SPOTS

Air conditioner: The air conditioning may stop working when the car is driven for extended times on the highway because the evaporator freezes up. (1997-98)

Automatic transmission: Cars with automatic transmissions may leak fluid from the upper, left-hand corner where the case was not manufactured properly. (1997-98)

Electrical problem: Electrical accessories may quit working. The lock will have to be repaired. On some models, the key won't turn back to the lock position. (1997)

Engine misfire: The engine may stall or quit running as if it has run out of gas even though the gauge shows $\frac{1}{8}$-$\frac{1}{4}$ tank; caused by a plugged evaporative emissions canister vent. (1997)

Hard starting: If a car with a manual transmission won't start, the wiring harness was probably damaged by rubbing on the clutch-pedal pivot causing a short circuit. (1997-98)

Windows: The side windows may not go up or down, or they may rattle because the glass comes loose from the regulator. (1997-98)

AVERAGE REPLACEMENT COSTS

A/C Compressor	$400	CV Joints	$390
Alternator	350	Exhaust System	310
Automatic Trans.	915	Radiator	350
Brakes	190	Shocks and/or Struts	490
Clutch	530	Timing Chain/Belt	300

NHTSA RECALL HISTORY

1996 SL w/manual steering: Pinion gear could disengage from steering rack under high steering-system load conditions, such as parking or low-speed maneuvers. **1996 SW1/SW2:** Welds between roof and reinforcement pan-

SATURN

els do not meet specifications; flange sides could partially separate in a crash. **1996-97 SL w/manual steering:** Pinion-bearing cage in steering gear can separate, disengaging and causing loss of control. **1996-97:** Horn could become inoperable or activate without pressing button; heat could build up, leading to an underhood fire. **1997:** Ignition key can be removed while cylinder is in "run" position. **1999-00:** Some seatbelt shoulder-guide anchor bolts were inadequately tightened at center pillar and could fall out. **2000:** Armrest latch may open during a crash. **2000:** Some brake-pipe attachment nuts may have been improperly tightened; fluid leakage could occur. **2000:** Some rear-bumper fasteners could be loose or missing; rear bumper may not absorb energy as designed, in a rear-end collision. **2000:** Some welds in instrument-panel carrier assembly were not strong enough; occupant, especially if unbelted, may have increased risk of injury in frontal crash. **2000:** The fuel-tank Over Pressure Relief valve can become stuck open in a frontal collision, creating a fire hazard. **2001:** An improperly adjusted automatic transaxle park-lock assembly could allow the vehicle to be shifted out of "Park" with the ignition key removed. **2001:** An inadequate weld at the top of the fuel tank could allow fuel leakage in a rollover. **2002 sedan:** Welds between the door-striker and beltline do meet specifications. The seatbelt anchorage on the pillar could fail, increasing the risk of injury.

PRICES	Good	Average	Poor
1996 Saturn SL, SL1	$2,300-3,000	$1,700-2,200	$400-600
Saturn SL2	2,900-3,500	2,200-2,700	700-800
Saturn SW1 wagon	3,000-3,600	2,300-2,800	700-800
Saturn SW2 wagon	3,400-4,000	2,700-3,200	900-1,000
1997 Saturn SL, SL1	2,700-3,400	2,000-2,600	600-700
Saturn SL2	3,300-4,000	2,600-3,200	800-1,000
Saturn SW1 wagon	3,500-4,200	2,800-3,400	900-1,100
Saturn SW2 wagon	4,000-4,700	3,300-3,900	1,300-1,500
1998 Saturn SL, SL1	3,100-3,800	2,400-3,000	700-900
Saturn SL2	3,900-4,600	3,200-3,700	1,200-1,400
Saturn SW1 wagon	4,100-4,800	3,400-3,900	1,400-1,600
Saturn SW2 wagon	4,600-5,300	3,800-4,400	1,700-2,000
1999 Saturn SL, SL1	3,700-4,500	3,000-3,600	1,100-1,300
Saturn SL2	4,700-5,400	3,900-4,500	1,700-2,000
Saturn SW1 wagon	4,900-5,600	4,200-4,800	1,900-2,200
Saturn SW2 wagon	5,500-6,200	4,700-5,300	2,300-2,500
2000 Saturn SL, SL1	4,300-5,100	3,500-4,200	1,500-1,700
Saturn SL2	5,400-6,100	4,600-5,200	2,200-2,500
Saturn SW2 wagon	6,200-6,900	5,400-6,000	2,700-3,000
2001 Saturn SL, SL1	5,000-5,800	4,300-4,900	2,000-2,300
Saturn SL2	6,200-6,800	5,400-5,900	2,700-2,900
Saturn SW2 wagon	7,200-8,000	6,400-7,100	3,500-3,900
2002 Saturn SL, SL1	5,800-6,600	5,000-5,700	2,400-2,800
Saturn SL2	7,100-8,000	6,300-7,100	3,400-3,800

For detailed information on this vehicle visit
http://used.consumerguide.com and enter code **2284**

1998-02 SUBARU FORESTER

CLASS: Compact sport-utility vehicle

BUILT IN: Japan

PROS: Cargo room • Maneuverability • Ride • Visibility • Standard ABS (L, S)

CONS: Acceleration (automatic transmission) • Engine vibrations • Instruments/controls • Rear-seat room

EVALUATION: With all-wheel drive instead of 4-wheel drive, and built off a car rather than truck platform, Forester is not a true SUV. But any SUV owner who drives one will be immediately impressed by its blend of carlike manners and all-wheel-drive utility.

Subaru's flat-4 has good low-rpm power and feels more lively with manual shift, but performs acceptably with the automatic transmission. That transmission shifts smoothly and kicks down promptly, but passing power that feels adequate with just a driver aboard feels subpar with a load of passengers and luggage. A Forester accelerated to 60 mph in 9.3 seconds—almost 2 seconds quicker than Honda's CR-V. Gas mileage is a bonus, compared to truck-type SUVs. We averaged 17 mpg in one automatic-transmission Forester, and 20.9 mpg in a long-term trial.

Road and wind noise are constant highway companions, but to a lesser degree than in most other SUVs of any stripe. The engine is gruff when pushed hard, and the idle is lumpy with the air conditioning on. Handling isn't as nimble as a car's, but Forester is less ponderous than truck-based midsize SUVs and far more agile. Body lean is moderate in fast turns, and AWD provides reassuring grip. With a suspension tuned for the street and not the trail, Forester does not pitch or rock on uneven pavement, as do many true SUVs. Braking feels adequate, but pedal action is spongy. You can also expect a fair degree of nosedive in hard stops.

Forester looks like a small sport utility, but has the cabin space of a compact wagon. The driving position, while higher than in a traditional sedan, does not impart the "command-of-the-road" feeling of a true SUV. However, tall, thin roof pillars and a low cowl make for outstanding outward visibility to all directions. There's no step-up to speak of, and the doors open wide. So, entry and exit are inviting—though rear openings are quite narrow at the bottom. Head room is generous all around. Front leg room is good, but rear-seaters are squeezed for knee clearance and foot space. Forester's dashboard is well-designed, but some buttons hide behind the steering wheel and the radio controls are too small and low to operate easily while driving.

VALUE FOR THE MONEY: Forester is a worthy competitor for the better-publicized CR-V and RAV4. Hybrids are supposed to drive like cars, perform on-road like SUVs, and look like trucks. This one does.

SUBARU

TROUBLE SPOTS

Information stickers/paperwork: Subaru warns that its vehicles should not be emissions tested on some dynamometers because of the potential for serious damage. (1998-00)

Windshield: Windshield is easily chipped or scratched. (1998)

AVERAGE REPLACEMENT COSTS

A/C Compressor	$725	CV Joints	$730
Alternator	410	Exhaust System	260
Automatic Trans.	850	Radiator	285
Brakes	350	Shocks and/or Struts	470
Clutch	565	Timing Chain/Belt	180

NHTSA RECALL HISTORY

1998-99 w/antilock braking: In extremely cold weather, master-cylinder seals could fail; brake pedal might then go to the floor, increasing stopping distance. **2002-03:** Defective transmission parking rod assemblies were installed on certain vehicles with automatic transmissions. The vehicle may not remain in "Park." Dealer will inspect and replace all affected parts.

PRICES	Good	Average	Poor
1998 Forester	$7,000-8,500	$6,200-7,600	$3,400-4,100
1999 Forester	8,700-10,700	7,800-9,600	4,500-5,600
2000 Forester	11,000-12,500	9,900-11,300	5,900-6,800
2001 Forester	13,000-14,500	11,800-13,200	7,500-8,400
2002 Forester	15,000-16,700	13,700-15,200	9,500-10,500

For detailed information on this vehicle visit
http://used.consumerguide.com and enter code **2316**

1993-01 SUBARU IMPREZA

CLASS: Subcompact car

BUILT IN: Japan

PROS: Airbags, dual (later models) • All-wheel drive (AWD models) • Optional antilock brakes • Instruments/controls

CONS: Acceleration (early AWD models) • Cargo room • Rear-seat entry/exit • Rear-seat room

EVALUATION: With the 2.2-liter engine, acceleration of an AWD model is more than adequate with a manual transmission and adequate with automatic. Simply put, a 1.8-liter model lacks sufficient snap when you need to merge into expressway traffic or pass other cars on the highway. The 2.5-liter on the RS is probably the best all-around engine, providing ample acceleration and good passing power. All engines sound gruff and feel rough with manual shift. Our 1993 test wagon with AWD and a 5-speed felt sluggish from startup, while an AWD sedan with automatic was downright slow. We averaged 24.8 mpg overall with the early AWD wagon—very nice for an AWD car.

Interior space is comparable to that of a Honda Civic, Geo Prizm, or Toyota Corolla. That means sufficient space for four adults. But rear leg space is barely adequate if the front seats are pushed back. Tall drivers might want more seat travel to get farther from the steering wheel and pedals. Visibility is good to all directions. Cargo space isn't so great, even in the wagon. Rear entry/exit wins no prizes, either, as doors are quite narrow at the bottom and don't open very wide.

Dashboards are logically laid out, with controls grouped around the gauge cluster—easy to find and operate. On the downside, using the pull-out cupholder blocks access to the stereo controls.

VALUE FOR THE MONEY: With the exception of available AWD, the Impreza fails to stand apart. Later models might be more tempting—especially the Outback Sport wagon or the 2.5 RS coupe.

TROUBLE SPOTS

Dashboard lights: The hydraulic motor for the ABS system runs with the key turned off, which illuminates the ABS warning light on the dash. (1993-96)

Engine misfire: Bucking and jerking at slow speeds on all-wheel-drive cars is due to a defective transfer clutch. (1993-97)

Engine noise: The knock sensors in the cylinder heads may fail, which can cause pinging under load. (1993-95)

Hard starting: The engine may be hard to start after sitting in cold weather because ice forms on the fuel injectors. (1993-96)

AVERAGE REPLACEMENT COSTS

A/C Compressor	$725	CV Joints	$730
Alternator	410	Exhaust System	260
Automatic Trans.	850	Radiator	285
Brakes	350	Shocks and/or Struts	470
Clutch	565	Timing Chain/Belt	180

NHTSA RECALL HISTORY

1993 AWD: Fuel-filler system does not comply with federal leakage requirements. **1994-95:** Inadvertent airbag deployment could occur after undercarriage contact of tow hooks with curbs, dips, speed bumps, etc.

PRICES	Good	Average	Poor
1993 Impreza	$1,500-2,500	$1,000-1,600	$200-300
Impreza AWD	2,000-2,900	1,400-2,000	300-500
1994 Impreza	1,800-2,900	1,200-2,000	300-400
Impreza AWD	2,300-3,900	1,700-2,800	400-700
1995 Impreza	2,100-3,300	1,500-2,300	400-600
Impreza AWD	2,600-4,300	1,900-3,200	500-900

SUBARU

1996 Impreza	$2,400-4,000	$1,800-2,900	$500-800
Impreza LX, Outback	3,500-5,000	2,800-4,000	900-1,400
1997 Impreza	3,200-4,800	2,500-3,700	800-1,200
Impreza Outback	5,200-6,200	4,400-5,300	2,100-2,500
1998 Impreza	5,000-6,200	4,300-5,300	2,000-2,500
Impreza RS, Outback	7,200-8,200	6,400-7,300	3,500-4,000
1999 Impreza	6,500-7,700	5,700-6,800	2,900-3,500
Impreza RS, Outback	8,800-9,800	7,900-8,800	4,600-5,100
2000 Impreza	8,000-9,200	7,200-8,300	4,100-4,700
Impreza RS, Outback	10,200-11,200	9,200-10,100	5,400-5,900
2001 Impreza	9,500-10,800	8,600-9,700	4,900-5,600
Impreza RS, Outback	12,000-13,200	10,800-11,900	6,700-7,400

> For detailed information on this vehicle visit
> http://used.consumerguide.com and enter code **2231**

1995-99 SUBARU LEGACY

CLASS: Compact car
BUILT IN: Japan, USA
PROS: Antilock brakes (optional) • Wet-weather traction (traction control, AWD) • Passenger and cargo room • Visibility
CONS: Engine noise • Fuel economy (AWD)

EVALUATION: Legacy's 2.2-liter engine is adequate for most circumstances, but it throbs and feels strained in hard acceleration and in hilly country. It's also more gruff-sounding than most 4-cylinders. The dual-overhead-cam 2.5-liter engine is quieter and smoother, with both excellent acceleration and passing power. But note that fuel economy is unimpressive on the AWD models.

Legacy's suspension strikes an admirable balance between ride and handling, with ride comfort taking precedence. Bumps are absorbed easily and all models feel stable. Body lean is noticeable in spirited cornering maneuvers, and the front end tends to plow when pushed hard—more so on front-drive versions than AWD models. A low dashboard and narrow roof pillars provide clear visibility in all directions. Front head and leg room are ample. In back, people under six feet tall should have adequate room, and both body styles provide outstanding cargo space.

VALUE FOR THE MONEY: With the addition of dual airbags, the new Legacy was a more competitive entry in the compact class. But its trump card remained the competent line of all-wheel-drive sedans and wagons, which Subaru finally stressed in its advertising.

TROUBLE SPOTS

Alternator belt: The company issued a (nonsafety) recall to replace the alternators. (1996 and some later)

Automatic transmission: Severely cracked secondary pulleys and pump drives cause the ECVT to slip. (1995)

Automatic transmission: The automatic transmission dipstick may break requiring the broken bits to be removed. (1995-97)

Brake noise: There may be a buzzing sound coming from the ABS (antilock brake system) hydraulic unit motor and/or an ABS warning light glowing, caused by a faulty ABS relay for which there is a revised part. (1995-97)

Brakes: Some of the ABS (antilock brake system) hydraulic motors were faulty, causing them to run intermittently even after the key is turned off. (1995-98)

Dashboard lights: If the check-engine light comes on in cold weather it is likely due to ice forming in the vacuum line between the engine and transmission. (1995)

Oil leak: An oil leak between the oil pump and block is repaired by drilling out the oil return hole to 6mm diameter. (1995)

Poor transmission shift: Hesitation or poor acceleration may be due to the powertrain-control module (PCM) misinterpreting normal engine vibrations as knock, and retarding the ignition timing requiring a replacement PCM. (1999)

Rear axle noise: Vibration and noise from the rear when traveling over 65 mph on vehicles with AWD requires countermeasure dampers on the rear crossmember. (1997-99)

AVERAGE REPLACEMENT COSTS

A/C Compressor	$560	CV Joints	$460
Alternator	345	Exhaust System	565
Automatic Trans.	940	Radiator	360
Brakes	225	Shocks and/or Struts	615
Clutch	515	Timing Chain/Belt	195

NHTSA RECALL HISTORY

1995: Front coil springs were produced with poor paint quality which, after continued exposure to corrosive salt, can result in breakage of the spring. **1995-96:** Inadvertent airbag deployment could occur after undercarriage contact of tow hooks with curbs, dips, speed bumps, etc. **1996-97:** Due to improper welding, fractures can occur on support bracket of front transverse link, resulting in separation and failure of front suspension. **1997:** Hazard-warning switch can stick in intermediate position, so turn signals become inoperable. **1997:** Omitted bearing in throttle-body assembly could eventually lead to incomplete return of throttle, resulting in fast idle. **1997-98 w/automatic transmission:** Due to poor welds, ignition key can stick, shift lever/linkages can break, and improper movement of shift lever can occur. **1998-99 w/ABS:** In extremely cold weather, master-cylinder seals could fail; brake pedal might then go to floor, increasing stopping distance. **1998-99:** Purolator oil filter can fracture, causing vaporized oil spray and subsequent oil leak at hot exhaust system; could result in underhood fire.

PRICES

	Good	Average	Poor
1995 Legacy sedan	$2,700-5,200	$2,000-3,900	$600-1,100
Legacy wagon	3,400-6,000	2,700-4,700	900-1,600
1996 LSi, 2.5GT, Outback	5,000-7,000	4,300-6,000	2,000-2,800
Legacy	3,300-6,000	2,600-4,700	800-1,500
1997 Legacy	4,400-6,200	3,700-5,100	1,500-2,200
Legacy GT, LSi	6,500-8,500	5,700-7,500	2,900-3,800
Legacy Outback	7,500-8,500	6,800-7,700	3,800-4,300
1998 Legacy	5,500-7,300	4,700-6,300	2,300-3,000
Legacy GT	8,000-9,500	7,200-8,600	4,100-4,800
Legacy Outback	9,500-10,500	8,600-9,500	4,900-5,500
1999 Legacy	7,000-9,000	6,200-8,000	3,400-4,300
Legacy GT, SUS	9,500-11,000	8,600-9,900	4,900-5,700
Legacy Outback	10,000-11,500	9,000-10,400	5,200-6,000

For detailed information on this vehicle visit http://used.consumerguide.com and enter code **2104**

2000-03 SUBARU LEGACY/OUTBACK

CLASS: Compact car

BUILT IN: USA

PROS: All-wheel drive
• Cargo room (wagon)

CONS: Automatic-transmission performance • Seat comfort (Legacy)

EVALUATION: Acceleration is adequate with manual shift, but a Legacy/Outback/Baja feels sluggish with automatic. Though it shifts smoothly, the automatic usually maintains too high a gear—and then is reluctant to downshift. As for economy, a five-speed GT Limited sedan averaged a satisfying 22.5 mpg.

Base Legacy and Outback models soak up pavement irregularities better than some larger, more expensive cars. Sport versions and Baja have a ride that is slightly more stiff and jarring. Steering feel and highway tracking are excellent, but plenty of body lean is evident in turns, and tires on early Brighton and L models have modest grip. With their stiffer suspension settings and bigger tires, GTs furnish genuinely sporty handling, but at the expense of some sharp reactions over bigger bumps and tar strips. Brakes are easily modulated and provide terrific stopping power. Wind and road noise are easily managed, while the engine delivers a prominent snarl.

Front seats are comfortable for most drivers, though some may find them lacking in long-distance support. All controls are within easy reach. Outward visibility is very good. Rear head, leg, and foot room are plentiful for two adults, on a nicely supportive seat. Tall doors make getting in/out easy. The sedan's trunk is efficiently shaped and liftover is low, but volume is unimpressive. Outbacks blend a little SUV feeling with compact-car convenience, adding a ride that's more civilized and controlled than on any truck-based SUV. Despite copious body lean in turns, an Outback handles far more competently than any SUV. Four-cylinder acceleration is sluggish, and the automatic transmission is reluctant to downshift. Six-cylinder engines are smoother and deliver greater performance, but aren't quite as peppy as some might expect. Baja model makes little sense for practical use, and slow sales back that claim.

VALUE FOR THE MONEY: Considerably better than its predecessor, the Legacy isn't an attractive value apart from its AWD system. A six-cylinder Outback wagon stands out for SUV looks and all-wheel-drive traction, without the thirst and clumsiness of a truck-based vehicle.

TROUBLE SPOTS

Pedals: Some owners have complained about the brake pedal being too low or requiring too long a stroke. Dealers were adjusting the pedal height by changing the length of the pushrod. (2000)

Vehicle noise: Some early build models made a clicking noise under the dash when the HVAC was switched to "recirc" mode. (2000)

Water leak: Water may leak from the courtesy-light housing, especially on cars with the dual sunroof, due to a leaking seam. (2000)

AVERAGE REPLACEMENT COSTS

A/C Compressor	$410	CV Joints	$830
Alternator	490	Exhaust System	210
Automatic Trans.	1,015	Radiator	210
Brakes	220	Shocks and/or Struts	525
Clutch	530	Timing Chain/Belt	275

NHTSA RECALL HISTORY

2000 Legacy: Antirust coating could shrink, causing a torque decrease in the bolt that secures the transverse-link bracket to the vehicle body. If the bracket becomes too loose, the transverse link could separate from the vehicle. **2000 Legacy:** The left-side steering-knuckle arm was incorrectly assembled. Steering control could be lost, if left uninspected. **2000-03 Legacy/Outback:** Road salt may cause some vehicles' rear suspension subframe to rust, affecting control of the vehicle. Dealer will inspect and replace affected parts. **2001 Legacy:** A casting flaw in the right-front bearing housing could result in loss of steering control. **2001 Legacy:** Incorrect seatbelt was installed in the rear-center position. The belt is too short. **2001 Legacy:** Manual seats have been improperly welded. Latch mechanism can break, making seat adjustment impossible. **2001 Legacy:** Underhood fuel hoses can age and become less flexible, allowing fuel leakage at low temperatures. **2001-03 Legacy/Outback/Baja:** Defective transmission parking-rod assemblies were installed on certain vehicles with automatic transmissions. The vehicle may not remain in "Park." Dealer will inspect and replace all affected parts. **2002:** The brake master cylinders may not function properly at low temperatures. The brakes may not release after being applied.

PRICES

	Good	Average	Poor
2000 Legacy GT, Limited	$11,500-13,000	$10,400-11,700	$6,300-7,200
Legacy L, Brighton	8,500-10,000	7,700-9,000	4,400-5,200
Outback	12,500-14,000	11,300-12,600	7,100-8,000
2001 Legacy GT, Limited	13,000-14,500	11,800-13,200	7,500-8,400
Legacy L	10,500-12,000	9,500-10,800	5,600-6,400
Outback	14,000-15,500	12,700-14,100	8,500-9,500
Outback H6	17,000-19,500	15,600-17,900	10,900-12,500
2002 Legacy GT, Limited	15,000-16,500	13,700-15,000	9,500-10,400
Legacy L	12,500-14,000	11,300-12,600	7,100-8,000
Outback	16,000-17,500	14,600-15,900	10,200-11,200
Outback H6	19,000-21,000	17,500-19,300	12,400-13,700
2003 Legacy 2.5 GT	17,500-19,000	16,100-17,500	11,200-12,200
Legacy L	15,000-16,500	13,700-15,000	9,500-10,400
Outback	18,000-21,000	16,600-19,300	11,500-13,400
Outback H6	22,000-26,000	20,200-23,900	14,300-16,900

For detailed information on this vehicle visit
http://used.consumerguide.com and enter code **2465**

1995-02 SUZUKI ESTEEM

CLASS: Subcompact car
BUILT IN: Japan
PROS: Cargo room (wagon) • Fuel economy • Maneuverability
CONS: Noise • Rear visibility • Ride

EVALUATION: Best considered as an around-town runabout, Esteem lacks the power to keep up with fast-moving traffic. Ride quality also leaves a lot to be desired. Its short wheelbase makes the car pitch fore and aft on concrete expressways. The suspension does not absorb bumps well, so rough pavement translates to a harsh experience. There's also noticeable bouncing on wavy surfaces.

On the plus side, the sedan feels nimble and maneuverable. Brakes perform adequately, but rear-wheel lockup is evident on non-ABS models.

Although the Esteem is more substantial than the smaller Swift hatchback, its body panels feel tinny. Noise levels are lower, but you can still expect plenty of road noise and tire thumping. Also annoying is a loud, coarse growl from the engine.

A GLX with automatic accelerates adequately, but the transmission on a new test model vibrated when it changed gears, and downshifted harshly. We averaged 24.2 mpg with that model, in mostly urban rush-hour commuting.

Head room is ample up front and adequate for two comparatively short people in back, though the rear-seat padding is hard and the narrow back doors are difficult to enter. A small opening limits trunk utility, but cargo space is surprisingly large, with a flat floor that reaches well forward.

Controls are easy to see and reach. Visibility to the rear is impaired by wide roof pillars. A narrow rear window cuts off the driver's view of the trunk.

VALUE FOR THE MONEY: Unimpressive in most areas, except for fuel economy, the Esteem does not deliver acceptable value. For not too many extra dollars, several good alternatives can be found, including a Honda Civic, Geo Prizm, Chevrolet Cavalier, or Dodge/Plymouth Neon.

TROUBLE SPOTS

Brake wear: The bushings in the front brake calipers may be too small, allowing the brake pads to wear unevenly. Countermeasure bushings are available to fix this. (1995-96)

Fuel gauge: The fuel gauge is inaccurate, requiring replacement of the sending unit and fuel breather pipe. (1995)

Rough idle: The spark-plug wires on 16-valve, 1.6L engines deteriorate causing poor idle, stumbling, reduced fuel economy, etc. and should be replaced with improved wires. (1995)

AVERAGE REPLACEMENT COSTS

A/C Compressor	$385	CV Joints	$580
Alternator	420	Exhaust System	275
Automatic Trans.	710	Radiator	295
Brakes	350	Shocks and/or Struts	650
Clutch	350	Timing Chain/Belt	330

NHTSA RECALL HISTORY

2002: Windshield may not be properly secured to the vehicle. Dealer will inspect and replace affected windshields.

PRICES

	Good	Average	Poor
1995 Esteem	$1,300-2,000	$800-1,300	$200
1996 Esteem	1,700-2,400	1,100-1,600	300-400
1997 Esteem	2,100-2,800	1,500-2,000	400-500
1998 Esteem	2,600-3,400	1,900-2,500	500-700
1999 Esteem	3,100-4,000	2,400-3,100	700-1,000
2000 Esteem	3,800-4,700	3,100-3,800	1,100-1,400
2001 Esteem	4,700-5,700	3,900-4,800	1,700-2,100
2002 Esteem	5,800-6,800	5,000-5,900	2,400-2,900

For detailed information on this vehicle visit
http://used.consumerguide.com and enter code **2354**

1990-98 SUZUKI SIDEKICK

CLASS: Compact sport-utility vehicle

BUILT IN: Canada, Japan

PROS: 4WD traction
• Fuel economy
• Maneuverability

CONS: Acceleration (w/automatic transmission)
• Noise • Rear-seat room
• Ride

EVALUATION: Acceleration with 80-horsepower engine is on the leisurely side, and the power boost in 1992 does not help much. The Sport model's larger engine finally offers acceptable performance. That 1.8-liter 4-cylinder works well with the 4-speed automatic transmission. A late-model wagon with manual shift averaged 25.3 mpg, though automatic dropped the figure to a so-so 21.4 mpg. However, even the latest Sidekick engines growl loudly under throttle. Wind and road noise are abundant at highway speeds, too.

Reasonably stable in corners and on the highway, Sidekick suffers a somewhat stiff and jiggly ride on rough surfaces. Four-door models endure less choppiness, credited to their longer wheelbase, but they're not that much more comfortable overall. Tall and narrow, Sidekicks must be driven with care through turns. Sidekick's 4-wheel-drive system is not for use on dry pavement.

Head room is plentiful up front, but the rear bench seat holds only two adults, for 4-passenger capacity. Worse yet, it's hard, with little leg space when the front seats are all the way aft—though space is adequate otherwise. In the Sidekick's narrow cabin, doors sit close to the seats, leaving little outside shoulder room. Cargo space is best in the 4-door, with its swing-open rear door and fold-down back seat.

VALUE FOR THE MONEY: Though better than the tiny old Samurai, this is still not a good choice for everyday driving, even in 4-door form.

TROUBLE SPOTS

Automatic transmission: The automatic transmission may hunt between 40-45 mph. A time-delay module kit for the torque-converter clutch should correct the condition. (1990-95)

Automatic transmission: The transfer case binds and can be damaged if driven on dry roads in 4WD mode. (1990-97)

Engine misfire: Using premium fuel can trigger trouble codes and cause poor starting. (1996-97)

Hard starting: Hard starting below freezing, especially at high altitudes, requires a Cold Start Harness Set. (1990)

AVERAGE REPLACEMENT COSTS

A/C Compressor	$385	CV Joints	$280
Alternator	420	Exhaust System	175

Automatic Trans.	$515	Radiator............................	$295
Brakes................................	250	Shocks and/or Struts.........	650
Clutch................................	450	Timing Chain/Belt.............	230

NHTSA RECALL HISTORY

1990-91: Front-seatbelt button can break and pieces can fall inside. **1993:** The right rear and left axle-shaft housing tubes were improperly welded and can fracture, resulting in separation of the wheel assembly which could impede vehicle control and/or increase stopping distance. **1996 4-doors:** Fuel tank can puncture during rear-end collision. **1996-97:** Mounting bolts that attach upper end of front struts to vehicle body could break, causing loss of control.

PRICES

	Good	Average	Poor
1990 Sidekick 2WD conv.	$1,000-1,500	$600-900	$100-200
Sidekick 4WD conv.	1,400-2,000	900-1,300	200
1991 Sidekick 2WD conv.	1,100-1,700	700-1,000	100-200
Sidekick 4-door	1,800-2,300	1,200-1,600	300
Sidekick 4WD conv.	1,500-2,100	1,000-1,400	200-300
1992 Sidekick 2WD 4-door	1,500-2,100	1,000-1,400	200-300
Sidekick 2WD conv.	1,200-1,800	700-1,100	100-200
Sidekick 4WD 4-door	2,100-2,600	1,500-1,800	400-500
Sidekick 4WD conv.	1,900-2,400	1,300-1,700	300-400
1993 Sidekick 2WD 4-door	1,700-2,300	1,100-1,500	300
Sidekick 2WD conv.	1,400-2,000	900-1,300	200
Sidekick 4WD 4-door	2,300-2,900	1,700-2,100	400-600
Sidekick 4WD conv.	2,100-2,600	1,500-1,800	400-500
1994 Sidekick 2WD 4-door	1,900-2,500	1,300-1,700	300-400
Sidekick 2WD conv.	1,600-2,200	1,100-1,500	200-300
Sidekick 4WD 4-door	2,500-3,100	1,800-2,300	500-700
Sidekick 4WD conv.	2,300-2,900	1,700-2,100	400-600
1995 Sidekick 2WD 4-door	2,100-2,700	1,500-1,900	400-500
Sidekick 2WD conv.	1,800-2,400	1,200-1,600	300-400
Sidekick 4WD 4-door	2,900-3,500	2,200-2,700	700-800
Sidekick 4WD conv.	2,600-3,200	1,900-2,400	500-700
1996 Sidekick 2WD 4-door	2,500-3,100	1,800-2,300	500-700
Sidekick 2WD conv.	2,100-2,800	1,500-2,000	400-500
Sidekick 4WD 4-door	3,500-4,200	2,800-3,400	900-1,100
Sidekick 4WD conv.	3,100-3,700	2,400-2,900	700-900
1997 Sidekick 2WD 4-door	3,000-3,800	2,300-2,900	700-900
Sidekick 2WD conv.	2,600-3,300	1,900-2,400	500-700
Sidekick 4WD 4-door	4,000-5,000	3,300-4,100	1,300-1,600
Sidekick 4WD conv.	3,600-4,300	2,900-3,400	1,000-1,200
1998 Sidekick 2WD 4-door	3,700-4,500	3,000-3,600	1,100-1,300
Sidekick 2WD conv.	3,200-3,800	2,500-3,000	800-900
Sidekick 4WD 4-door	4,500-5,700	3,700-4,700	1,600-2,100
Sidekick 4WD conv.	4,200-4,900	3,400-4,000	1,400-1,600

For detailed information on this vehicle visit
http://used.consumerguide.com and enter code **2233**

1999-03 SUZUKI VITARA

CLASS: Compact sport-utility vehicle

BUILT IN: Japan

PROS: Off-road capability • Maneuverability

CONS: Acceleration • Rear-seat entry/exit • Rear-seat room • Visibility

---

EVALUATION: Four-cylinder Vitaras are slow, with coarse engines. A V6 Grand Vitara is a little quieter and quicker, but acceleration is only adequate, taking a leisurely 11.5 seconds to reach 60 mph. Automatic-equipped 4x4 models have averaged 17.9 to 20.7 mpg and furnish timely downshifts when coupled with the V6 engine. The manual gearshift is vague, with long throws.

Suzuki's 4WD system is less convenient than a permanently engaged unit used in the Honda CR-V, Ford Escape/Mazda Tribute, or Subaru Forester. Those rivals lack the Vitara's 4-Low range for off-road work.

All models deliver an uncomfortably choppy ride on all but smooth surfaces. Directional stability is compromised by crosswinds, and steering feel is indistinct. Hard cornering brings marked body lean and only moderate grip.

Braking fails to inspire confidence, yielding substantial nosedive, inconsistent pedal action and, even with ABS, rear-wheel lockup in simulated panic stops.

Interiors are not especially hospitable, even on Grand Vitaras. Chair-height front seats are short on thigh support and rearward travel for long-legged occupants. The rear bench in both body styles is hard, has an even shorter cushion, and offers scant leg space. Step-in height is reasonable, but rear entry/exit is hampered by very narrow door bottoms in wagons.

Although the dashboard layout is good, audio controls (until 2001) were small and poorly marked. Interior storage is adequate, but cargo floors are short and space is modest for a wagon, even with rear seats folded. Worse, the one-piece cargo door on both body styles opens to the right, blocking loading from the curb.

Visibility is poor to the rear, but otherwise good. The air conditioner struggles to cool the cabin on sunny days, and most interior materials have a low-buck feel.

VALUE FOR THE MONEY: Off-road ability is the Vitara's strongest quality. Both body styles have been priced to attract young buyers who crave a 4x4 image, but they're also-rans in room and comfort.

TROUBLE SPOTS

Fuel pump: Suzuki is recalling 59,888 Grand Vitara SUVs from the 1999-2001 model years. When temperatures drop below minus 13 degrees (F), moisture can freeze in the fuel-pressure regulator. That could lead to fuel leakage, which could cause a fire in the presence of an ignition source.

Keyless entry: Keyless-entry keyfob battery dies prematurely due to bad diode inside. Only applies to units with Suzuki name in white on fob. (1998-02)

Suspension problems: Vibrations from the front suspension and steering, especially at speeds in excess of 55 mph, make vehicle difficult to control. (1999-02)

AVERAGE REPLACEMENT COSTS

A/C Compressor	$530	CV Joints	$540
Alternator	430	Exhaust System	240
Automatic Trans.	765	Radiator	305
Brakes	220	Shocks and/or Struts	525
Clutch	430	Timing Chain/Belt	275

NHTSA RECALL HISTORY

1999: An electrical short circuit could occur due to pinched wires between the rear stereo speaker and the speaker retaining plate. **1999:** Brakes may be inoperative due to a malfunctioning lamp-actuating switch. **1999:** Seatbelts may not properly restrain occupants because of undertorqued lower-anchor bolts. **1999:** The steering shafts could separate due to a cracked coupling. Steering control could be lost without warning. **2000-01 Grand Vitara/Grand Vitara XL-7:** In cold weather, moisture can freeze and expand in the fuel-pressure regulator, causing fuel loss at the fuel-pipe/fuel-hose connection upon startup **2001 Grand Vitara:** Tire-information label is not permanently affixed as it should be. **2002-03 Grand Vitara:** Windshield may not be properly secured to the vehicle. Dealer will inspect and replace affected windshields.

PRICES

	Good	Average	Poor
1999 Grand Vitara	$5,000-7,000	$4,300-6,000	$2,000-2,800
Vitara Convertible	3,700-5,200	3,000-4,200	1,100-1,500
Vitara wagon	4,500-6,500	3,700-5,400	1,600-2,300
2000 Grand Vitara	6,300-8,500	5,500-7,500	3,000-4,000
Vitara convertible	4,800-7,000	4,000-5,900	1,800-2,700
Vitara wagon	5,700-7,600	4,900-6,500	2,300-3,100
2001 Grand Vitara	7,800-10,500	7,000-9,500	4,000-5,400
Vitara convertible	6,000-8,200	5,200-7,100	2,500-3,400
Vitara wagon	6,900-9,000	6,100-8,000	3,200-4,200
2002 Grand Vitara	10,000-13,000	9,000-11,700	5,200-6,800
Vitara convertible	8,000-10,000	7,200-9,000	4,100-5,100
Vitara wagon	8,900-10,500	8,000-9,500	4,600-5,500
2003 Grand Vitara	13,000-15,500	11,800-14,100	7,500-9,000
Vitara wagon	11,000-13,500	9,900-12,200	5,900-7,300

For detailed information on this vehicle visit
http://used.consumerguide.com and enter code **2466**

1990-95 TOYOTA 4RUNNER

CLASS: Midsize sport-utility vehicle

BUILT IN: Japan

PROS: Antilock brakes (optional) • Wet-weather traction (4WD) • Passenger and cargo room • Reliability • Ride (later models)

CONS: Acceleration • Entry/exit • Fuel economy • Handling • Noise

EVALUATION: The 4Runner's chief attractions are tight, thorough assembly quality and a commendable reputation for quality. However, the 4Runner is much smaller inside than the top-selling Ford Explorer and Jeep Grand Cherokee, with barely adequate space for four adults. Exit/entry are hurt by a higher-than-usual stance—nearly two feet off the ground. Also, fuel economy is very mediocre. We averaged just 13.8 mpg with a V6 model in our last test. Acceleration is nothing special either, even with the V6, which is hard-pressed to reach 60 mph in under 13 seconds. And you can forget the 4-cylinder, which is even slower.

Plus points include the convenient 4WDemand system and 4-wheel antilock brakes. Some Japanese rivals still have not adopted either shift-on-the-fly 4WD or 4-wheel ABS. Unfortunately, ABS was optional instead of standard.

VALUE FOR THE MONEY: High prices remain one of the 4Runner's biggest problems. We prefer domestic rivals such as the Ford Explorer, Jeep Grand Cherokee, Chevrolet Blazer, and GMC Jimmy, which have more room, a broader selection of features and models, plus better all-around performance for the money.

TROUBLE SPOTS

Clutch: A leaking or damaged direct clutch in the transfer case causes a slip or chatter on acceleration. (1990-92)

Clutch: Because of clutch judder, the pressure plate and disc were enlarged (from 9.00 in. to 9.5 in. diameter) for 4x4 models. (1990-94)

Exhaust system: In compliance with emission control regulations, the oxygen sensor should be replaced at 80,000 miles. (1993-94)

AVERAGE REPLACEMENT COSTS

A/C Compressor	$1,155	CV Joints	$155
Alternator	515	Exhaust System	261
Automatic Trans.	1,280	Radiator	515
Brakes	225	Shocks and/or Struts	190
Clutch	500	Timing Chain/Belt	615

NHTSA RECALL HISTORY

None to date.

PRICES	Good	Average	Poor
1990 4Runner	$3,200-4,000	$2,500-3,100	$800-1,000
1991 4Runner	3,600-4,500	2,900-3,600	1,000-1,300
1992 4Runner	4,200-5,200	3,400-4,300	1,400-1,700
1993 4Runner	4,800-6,000	4,000-5,000	1,800-2,300
1994 4Runner	5,400-6,600	4,600-5,700	2,200-2,700
1995 4Runner	6,000-8,000	5,200-7,000	2,500-3,400

For detailed information on this vehicle visit
http://used.consumerguide.com and enter code **2110**

1996-02 TOYOTA 4RUNNER

CG BEST BUY

CLASS: Midsize sport-utility vehicle

BUILT IN: Japan

PROS: Optional antilock brakes • Passenger and cargo room • Quietness • Ride

CONS: Entry/exit • Fuel economy • Price

EVALUATION: Because this version weighs less and also comes with stronger engines, it can charge up hills that would have overtaxed the old 4Runner. On-road performance is therefore more relaxed, especially when towing a trailer or hauling a full load of people and cargo. Acceleration with the smooth V6 is indeed snappy in town, though highway passing is more ordinary. We recommend a V6, because the 4-cylinder engine, despite being enlarged, still lacks the torque to propel such a heavy vehicle. Later models with the dealer-installed supercharger accelerate with authority—moving to the head of the midsize sport-utility class—aren't overly noisy, and don't consume much more fuel.

Solid-feeling on rough pavement, a 4Runner copes admirably when it encounters off-road terrain. Engine and tire noise are less noticeable than they used to be. The current suspension promises a comfortable ride on almost any surface. Steering is carlike and precise, delivering stable cornering.

Running boards on the Limited are a virtual necessity when climbing aboard, due to the uncomfortably high step-in level. Once inside, space is ample for four adults, and not bad at all for a fifth. Cargo room is generous, even with the rear seat in use, helped by a spare tire that's mounted beneath the cargo floor. The 4Runner's power liftgate window is a convenience that's not offered by any other compact sport utility.

TOYOTA

VALUE FOR THE MONEY: Domestic rivals such as the Ford Explorer, Chevrolet Blazer, and Jeep Grand Cherokee might be better bargains, but a 4Runner includes Toyota's reputation for reliability.

TROUBLE SPOTS

Oil leak: Head-gasket failures, particularly on higher mileage engines. In some cases, the company has issued a service campaign or extended warranty. (1996)

AVERAGE REPLACEMENT COSTS

A/C Compressor	$1,140	Exhaust System	$305
Alternator	485	Radiator	475
Automatic Trans.	940	Shocks and/or Struts	600
Brakes	220	Timing Chain/Belt	610
Clutch	400	Universal Joints	590

NHTSA RECALL HISTORY

1996: Some 2WD models could lose directional stability when hauling heavy loads and under severe driving maneuvers. Although 4WD models did not exhibit this condition, they were also recalled, to avoid confusion.
1996: Sticker alerting driver to "particular handling and maneuvering characteristics of utility vehicles" was not affixed to driver's sunvisor.
1997: Some 2WD models could lose directional stability when hauling heavy loads and under severe driving maneuvers. Although 4WD models did not exhibit this condition, they were also recalled, to avoid confusion.
1998: Some 2WD models could lose directional stability when hauling heavy loads and under severe driving maneuvers. Although 4WD models did not exhibit this condition, they were also recalled, to avoid confusion.
1998-99: Some wheel lug nuts are defective, causing loss of torque, fatigue fracture of wheel, and possible loss of wheel.

PRICES

	Good	Average	Poor
1996 4Runner 4-cyl.	$5,500-6,500	$4,700-5,600	$2,300-2,700
4Runner Limited	9,500-10,800	8,600-9,700	4,900-5,600
4Runner V6	7,500-8,500	6,800-7,700	3,800-4,300
1997 4Runner 4-cyl.	7,000-8,200	6,200-7,300	3,400-3,900
4Runner Limited	11,000-12,500	9,900-11,300	5,900-6,800
4Runner V6	9,500-11,000	8,600-9,900	4,900-5,700
1998 4Runner 4-cyl.	8,500-10,000	7,700-9,000	4,400-5,200
4Runner Limited	13,500-15,000	12,300-13,700	8,000-8,900
4Runner V6	11,500-13,000	10,400-11,700	6,300-7,200
1999 4Runner 4-cyl.	10,500-12,000	9,500-10,800	5,600-6,400
4Runner Limited	16,000-17,500	14,600-15,900	10,200-11,200
4Runner V6	14,000-15,500	12,700-14,100	8,500-9,500
2000 4Runner 4-cyl.	12,500-14,000	11,300-12,600	7,100-8,000
4Runner Limited	18,500-20,500	17,000-18,900	11,800-13,100
4Runner V6	16,000-18,000	14,600-16,400	10,200-11,500
2001 4Runner	17,500-19,500	16,100-17,900	11,200-12,500
4Runner Limited	20,500-22,500	18,900-20,700	13,300-14,600

2002 4Runner	$20,000-22,000	$18,400-20,200	$13,000-14,300
4Runner Limited	23,500-25,500	21,600-23,500	15,300-16,600

For detailed information on this vehicle visit
http://used.consumerguide.com and enter code **2243**

1995-99 TOYOTA AVALON

CLASS: Full-size car
BUILT IN: USA
PROS: Acceleration
• Optional antilock brakes
• Instruments/controls
• Passenger and cargo room
• Quietness
CONS: Fuel economy • Price

CG BEST BUY

EVALUATION: Except for more body lean and understeer on twisting roads, an Avalon drives much like the Toyota Camry. Although the Avalon's suspension is firmer, it still absorbs most bumps. Even on wavy roads, the sedan does not bounce or feel mushy. It also corners with good grip and moderate body lean.

Because there's a negligible weight difference between Avalon and the V6 Camry, don't expect a discernible difference in acceleration or passing sprints. A test Avalon accelerated to 60 mph in 8.5 seconds—just about exactly as swift as a Camry. Toyota's V6 engine is just as silky smooth in the Avalon as in the Camry, and nearly silent. Better yet, it's complemented by a smooth, responsive automatic transmission. As for gas mileage, an early model averaged 19.4 mpg, driving mostly in rush-hour commutes. The V6 engine requires premium fuel.

Space is ample for four adults, and six can tolerate shorter trips in models with the front bench seat. Leg space is generous in the backseat, and rear doors open wide for easy entry/exit. The trunk is wide and deep, with a long, flat floor. Low liftover height makes it easier to load and unload, too.

Avalon's dashboard layout and materials are first rate. Large round gauges are legible. Both the stereo and climate controls are high enough to easily see and reach while driving.

VALUE FOR THE MONEY: Roomy and competent, but markedly more costly than a Camry when new, Avalon might offer little excitement, but the sedan also suffers few faults. We've been impressed with the solid feel, good workmanship, and low noise levels.

TROUBLE SPOTS

Antenna: The radio may have poor reception or noise because of a poor antenna ground. (1997)

Brake noise: The front brakes make a groaning and grinding noise that is eliminated by replacing the brake rotors and installing special shims. (1997-99)

TOYOTA

Brake noise: The front or rear disc brakes may make a moaning noise that can be corrected with revised brake pads. (1995-97)

Climate control: The ambient temperature occasionally gets stuck on 22 degrees (F), and the climate-control system may not work properly. (1995-96)

Suspension noise: The front suspension is noisy when driving over speed bumps or washboard roads due to a bad rubber bushing in the upper strut mount. Countermeasure bushings have been released. (1997-99)

Vehicle noise: There is a kit to eliminate wind noise from the A-pillars. (1995-96)

AVERAGE REPLACEMENT COSTS

A/C Compressor	$880	Exhaust System	$365
Alternator	370	Radiator	465
Automatic Trans.	710	Shocks and/or Struts	850
Brakes	260	Timing Chain/Belt	190
CV Joints	1,100		

NHTSA RECALL HISTORY

1997 in specified states: In extreme cold, accumulated moisture can temporarily freeze in brake-vacuum hose.

PRICES

	Good	Average	Poor
1995 Avalon	$4,800-5,600	$4,000-4,700	$1,800-2,100
Avalon XLS	5,700-6,500	4,900-5,600	2,300-2,700
1996 Avalon	5,400-6,200	4,600-5,300	2,200-2,500
Avalon XLS	6,600-7,500	5,800-6,600	3,000-3,500
1997 Avalon	6,400-7,300	5,600-6,400	2,800-3,200
Avalon XLS	7,800-8,600	7,000-7,700	4,000-4,400
1998 Avalon	8,000-9,000	7,200-8,100	4,100-4,600
Avalon XLS	9,500-10,500	8,600-9,500	4,900-5,500
1999 Avalon	10,000-11,000	9,000-9,900	5,200-5,700
Avalon XLS	11,500-13,000	10,400-11,700	6,300-7,200

For detailed information on this vehicle visit
http://used.consumerguide.com and enter code **2236**

2000-03 TOYOTA AVALON

CG BEST BUY

CLASS: Full-size car

BUILT IN: USA

PROS: Acceleration • Automatic-transmission performance • Build quality • Passenger room • Quietness • Ride

CONS: Handling • Brake-pedal feel

EVALUATION: Toyota sought quieter running in the reworked Avalon, and handily achieved that goal. Except for mild tire rumble over very coarse pavement, this Avalon is a pleasantly hushed automobile. Even hard acceleration produces only a distant, rich engine sound. Acceleration is a tad better than before, thanks to little-changed weight and 10 extra horsepower—sufficient for nearly any situation. A test Avalon reached 60 mph in 8.3 seconds, and also averaged 21 mpg. The responsive automatic transmission is glassy smooth. Premium fuel is advised. Not only is the ride comfortable—close to plush, in fact—but drivers enjoy improved body control and firmer, more-communicative steering. The new Avalon dashes through twisty roads with almost sports-sedan poise—well-ahead of domestic rivals. Only a couple of quibbles have come up, including a bit of body drumming over rough patches, and slightly unprogressive pedal action in routine braking. In the seriously spacious interior, 6-footers can ride in tandem, with plenty of leg-stretching room for both. Higher-set seats are matched by a raised roofline that provides fine all-around head room. Three adults fit adequately on front and back seats, though middle riders must straddle a hump and may lack foot room. Rear entry/exit is easy enough, and all seats are comfortably supportive. Though not as long as the old Avalon's trunk, the new one is taller with plenty of space. Climate and audio controls couldn't be better, but the steering-wheel rim can obscure the tops of gauges without some juggling of seat and wheel. Abundant space is provided for small-item stowage, including a massive glovebox. Visibility is good despite hard-to-see rear body corners, and mirrors are usefully large.

VALUE FOR THE MONEY: Spacious and posh, quiet and smooth-riding, the Avalon delivers Lexus-like attributes at a family oriented price. Approaching the near-luxury league in features, comfort, and functional roadability, it could be the best full-size sedan on the market.

TROUBLE SPOTS

Sunroof/moonroof: The moon roof may make noise because the silencer pads come loose and get wedged in the slider assembly. A revised pad was being installed under warranty. (2000)

Water leak: Water leaks at the A-pillar (between windshield and front door) require sealing in the upper-corner joint area. (2000)

AVERAGE REPLACEMENT COSTS

A/C Compressor	$510	Exhaust System	$475
A/C Compressor	655	Radiator	410
Automatic Trans.	1,330	Shocks and/or Struts	900
Brakes	450	Timing Chain/Belt	340
CV Joints	950		

NHTSA RECALL HISTORY

2000: On certain cars, due to improper heat treatment, rear axle may not have adequate strength in some areas; shafts could fail or break after extended use. **2001:** Front-subframe assembly on small number of vehicles was not adequately welded and could fail.

PRICES	Good	Average	Poor
2000 Avalon XL	$14,500-15,500	$13,200-14,100	$9,000-9,600
Avalon XLS	16,500-17,500	15,000-15,900	10,600-11,200
2001 Avalon XL	16,700-18,000	15,200-16,400	10,700-11,500
Avalon XLS	18,700-20,000	17,200-18,400	12,000-12,800
2002 Avalon XL	19,000-20,500	17,500-18,900	12,400-13,300
Avalon XLS	21,000-22,500	19,300-20,700	13,700-14,600
2003 Avalon XL	22,000-24,000	20,200-22,100	14,300-15,600
Avalon XLS	25,000-27,500	23,300-25,600	16,500-18,200

> For detailed information on this vehicle visit
> http://used.consumerguide.com and enter code **2401**

1992-96
TOYOTA CAMRY

CG BEST BUY

CLASS: Midsize car
BUILT IN: Japan, USA
PROS: Acceleration (V6)
• Antilock brakes (optional)
• Passenger and cargo room
• Quietness • Ride
CONS: Fuel economy (V6)
• Rear-seat comfort

EVALUATION: The 4-cylinder engine is smooth and responsive, giving the Camry sedan adequate acceleration and passing power, even with the automatic transmission. We averaged 10.9 seconds to 60 mph in our test and nearly 23 mpg. The V6 is much quicker, but uses more fuel (we averaged about 18 mpg in our test). However, the V6 is perhaps the most polished engine in this class and works in concert with a highly refined automatic to deliver virtually vibration-free performance.

Camrys feature a soft, absorbent ride that soaks up most bumps and ruts quite easily. It also corners with good stability and has good traction on wet roads. While the Camry's 103.1-inch wheelbase put it in the compact class, it has more interior room than many midsize models. Note, however, that the rear seatbacks tend to be stiff and too reclined, making them uncomfortable for some people. The trunklid opens at bumper level to a wide, flat floor that reaches well-forward. Split rear seatbacks fold down to add cargo space.

VALUE FOR THE MONEY: There's a lot of the Lexus ES 300 in the Camry, which we believe set the standard for refinement among midsize and compact family cars. It's smoother, quieter, and built with higher levels of quality than some luxury sedans costing thousands more. New Camrys generally sold for more than its compact rivals, so expect pre-owned models to also be priced a bit more, given Toyota's generally high resale value and strong reputation for reliability.

TROUBLE SPOTS

Air conditioner: A problem with the expansion valve causes the air conditioner to gradually lose efficiency. (1992-93)

Automatic transmission: A-40 series automatic transmissions may shift harshly because rubber check balls become smaller, blow through the plate, and get dislodged. (1992-96)

Coolant leak: Head-gasket failures on 3.0-liter engines allows coolant to get into the cylinders. (All)

Hard starting: Hard starting after cold soak is due to ignition-coil voltage leaking to an inappropriate ground. (All)

Suspension noise: Front and rear sway-bar bushings were redesigned using a self-lubricating material. (1992-95)

Trunk latch: If the trunk won't stay open on sedans with a spoiler, the support torsion rod must be adjusted. (1992-96)

Water leak: Water leaks on the passenger side come from two sources: the SRS wiring-harness grommet and the fresh-air intake plenum. (1992-93)

AVERAGE REPLACEMENT COSTS

A/C Compressor	$865	CV Joints	$500
Alternator	375	Exhaust System	550
Automatic Trans.	1,067	Radiator	580
Brakes	145	Shocks and/or Struts	800
Clutch	600	Timing Chain/Belt	220

NHTSA RECALL HISTORY

1994-96: Insufficiently tightened steering-wheel nut may cause steering vibration and looseness; nut could eventually come off, leading to separation from shaft. **1996:** On some cars, when taillight bulb is lit, its holder can deform.

PRICES

	Good	Average	Poor
1992 Camry sedan	$2,100-3,200	$1,500-2,300	$400-600
Camry wagon	2,500-3,100	1,800-2,300	500-700
1993 Camry sedan	2,500-3,700	1,800-2,700	500-800
Camry wagon	3,000-3,700	2,300-2,800	700-900
1994 Camry coupe, sedan	2,900-4,300	2,200-3,300	700-1,000
Camry wagon	3,600-4,300	2,900-3,400	1,000-1,200
1995 Camry coupe, sedan	3,300-5,400	2,600-4,300	800-1,400
Camry wagon	4,300-5,400	3,500-4,400	1,500-1,800
1996 Camry coupe, sedan	3,800-6,200	3,100-5,000	1,100-1,900
Camry wagon	5,500-6,500	4,700-5,600	2,300-2,700

For detailed information on this vehicle visit
http://used.consumerguide.com and enter code **2105**

TOYOTA

2002-03 TOYOTA CAMRY

CG BEST BUY

CLASS: Midsize car

BUILT IN: USA

PROS: Acceleration (V6)
• Build quality • Interior
storage space • Quietness
• Ride

CONS: Navigation-system
controls

EVALUATION: All Camrys are pleasing, but about 75 percent of Camry sales have been four-cylinder models. A four-cylinder LE with automatic transmission accelerated to 60 mph in 9.2 seconds. That's competitive with class rivals and adequate for most any chore, aided by a smooth, alert automatic transmission. The V6 is strong and responsive, reaching 60 mph in 8.3 seconds.

Fuel economy also is a benefit. A four-cylinder LE with automatic averaged 23.3 mpg. Models with V6/automatic averaged 20.4 to 21.1 mpg. All figures included a mix of city/freeway driving. Toyota recommends regular-grade gasoline for the four-cylinder and premium for the V6.

Ride quality is comfortably supple and absorbent in all models, with very low impact harshness. The standard suspension suffers minor unwanted "float" over dips and swells. The more firmly damped SE suspension provides better body control, with no comfort penalty.

Handling is safe, predictable, and pleasant. Body lean is apparent in tight, fast turns, but not excessive. An SE is more confident, with slightly less lean and better stability, but far from sport-sedan nimble. Quick, precise steering needs better road feel in all models. Brakes are strong and easily modulated, but a Camry with ABS is your best bet.

As for quietness, the Camry tops its class in refinement. Minor tire thrum is evident on coarse pavement, but the impressive four-cylinder engine is almost as smooth and quiet as the V6.

Instruments and controls are simple and intuitive, placed in a stylish dashboard that puts most everything up high and close. The optional navigation system is easier to use than some, but requires effort to learn. Its screen tilts for viewing, but must be powered fully open to access CD and tape slots. Workmanship and materials are fine.

Front occupants get adult-size space, with comfortable bucket seats and a good range of adjustments, especially in the XLE edition. The driver sits higher than in past Camrys, but current styling somewhat impedes rearward visibility.

These Camrys feel slightly roomier in back than their predecessors, with ample head and knee space outboard, and enough for a middle rider on short trips. Entry/exit is easy.

The 2002 redesign enlarged the Camry's trunk by 2.7 cubic feet, for better volume than in many rival sedans, but the narrow aperture cannot swallow really bulky items. Interior storage is ample and handy, particularly in front.

VALUE FOR THE MONEY: Camry's redesign brought laudable new safety features and lifted comfort, convenience, and refinement to nearly Lexus levels. Although all these must-try midsizes still engage the head more than the heart, Toyota's proven reliability is tough to beat. Slightly lower new-car sticker prices made Camrys an even stronger value than before, but high resale figures tend to keep used-car prices on the high side. Don't buy a midsize car without considering Toyota's all-around excellent family sedan.

TROUBLE SPOTS

Engine stalling: The check-engine light may come on when the temperature is below freezing (32 degrees F) accompanied by poor engine performance. This requires replacement of the throttle body, gasket, and intake surge tank. (2002)

Fuel pump: If the gas cap gets stuck, it can be replaced with an improved cap. (2002)

Poor transmission shift: Early production vehicles with automatic transmissions may shift poorly. The revised engine-control module designed for 2003 models can be installed in older vehicles. (2002)

Valve cover leaks: If service personnel using bulk oil-fill equipment are not careful, the oil-fill nozzle may bend or break the oil baffle inside the valve cover. (2002-03)

AVERAGE REPLACEMENT COSTS

A/C Compressor	$655	Exhaust System	$475
Alternator	490	Radiator	510
Automatic Trans.	1,430	Shocks and/or Struts	900
Brakes	450	Timing Chain/Belt	375
CV Joints	950		

NHTSA RECALL HISTORY

2002 w/3-spoke steering wheel: During airbag deployment, it is possible that the bottom portion of the airbag cover may strike the driver causing personal injury. Dealers will replace the driver's-side airbag module.

PRICES

	Good	Average	Poor
2002 Camry 4 cyl	$13,800-16,000	$12,600-14,600	$8,400-9,800
Camry V6	15,000-17,000	13,700-15,500	9,500-10,700
2003 Camry 4 cyl	16,000-19,500	14,600-17,700	10,200-12,500
Camry V6	18,000-21,500	16,600-19,800	11,500-13,800

For detailed information on this vehicle visit
http://used.consumerguide.com and enter code **4485**

TOYOTA

1997-01 TOYOTA
CAMRY/SOLARA

CLASS: Midsize car
BUILT IN: Japan, USA
PROS: Acceleration (V6)
• Build quality • Quietness
• Ride
CONS: Rear visibility
• Steering feel

EVALUATION: All models have less wind and road noise than average. Suspensions readily iron out the rough stuff, while providing a stable and comfortable highway ride. Cornering is marked by moderate body lean, with good grip and safe front-drive responses. Steering is quick and centers well after turns, but effort is too low and road feel is too numb for the best control. In addition, even the more firmly suspended Solara coupe tends to "float" over uneven surfaces.

Smooth and quiet for a 4-cylinder, Camry's base engine provides adequate acceleration even with an automatic transmission. The V6 is far more impressive—smoother and quieter yet, yielding good pickup from low speeds as well as swift passing/merging action. An LE sedan with the V6 averaged a passable 20.4 mpg in hard city/freeway driving. A 4-cylinder model returned 22.5 mpg, despite more urban driving. Brakes work beautifully, capable of short, arrow-straight panic stops with little nosedive.

Back-seat space is greater than in the prior generation, but four adults will be more comfortable than five. Like most midsize cars, Camry does not have quite enough rear-cabin width to permit uncrowded three-abreast travel. Head and leg room are ample, however, in both front and rear. Entry/exit isn't a problem, either, except into the backseat of the Solara coupe, due to low, narrow rear passageways and lack of a slide-forward driver's seat. Camry cargo space is competitive, and all models have a handy split folding rear seatback. Solara's trunk opening is high, and space is not all that large.

Dashboards are typical Toyota, conveniently organized and attractively styled. Most instruments and controls are easy to see and reach. One exception involves the climate panel, which is too low in the center for the easiest operation while driving. Visibility is good, except for a minor over-the-right-shoulder blind spot, due to the wide rear roof posts and tall trunk. Solara coupes have more visibility troubles than the sedan.

VALUE FOR THE MONEY: Tight, careful assembly quality helps make the Camry a top-notch value, and a top choice in a midsize family sedan.

TROUBLE SPOTS

Audio system: The CD player may not accept or eject CDs. (1997)
Brake noise: Original-equipment brake pads are noisy causing groaning, grinding, squeaking, and vibration. A revised lining is available. (1997-98)
Doors: The fuel door does not open when the release is pulled due to weak spring. (1997-98)

Power seats: The front power seats may chatter requiring replacement of the seat-adjuster assembly (1997-98) or manually operated seat cushion on driver's side moves. (1997)

Sunroof/moonroof: The moonroof may rattle when it is opened about four inches or the glass panel may get skewed and will not retract. (1997)

Suspension noise: Noises from the front end when driving over dips in the road are a result of defective upper strut-tower cushions. (1997-98)

AVERAGE REPLACEMENT COSTS

A/C Compressor	$890	CV Joints	$510
Alternator	380	Exhaust System	570
Automatic Trans.	1,105	Radiator	585
Brakes	160	Shocks and/or Struts	840
Clutch	600	Timing Chain/Belt	260

NHTSA RECALL HISTORY

1997 in 19 states: In extreme cold for an extended period, accumulated moisture can temporarily freeze in brake-vacuum hose, resulting in elimination of power-brake assist. **1997:** Accumulated moisture can temporarily freeze in brake-vacuum hose. **1997:** Ignition key can be removed even when gearshift lever is not in "Park" position. **1997-98:** Insufficiently tightened steering-wheel nut may cause steering vibration and looseness; nut could eventually come off, leading to separation from shaft. **1998:** Audiovox Securikey+ Security System can malfunction causing electrical failure; can cause engine to run poorly and stall, and electrical components can intermittently fail. **1998:** Some wheel lug nuts are defective, causing loss of torque, fatigue fracture of wheel, and possible loss of wheel. **1998-2000 Camry made in KY:** Accelerator-cable housing could be deformed at the cruise-control actuator-to-throttle body connection. The accelerator inner-cable could wear away and eventually break, increasing the risk of a crash. **2000:** Due to improper heat treatment, certain rear-axle shafts could fail or break after extended use. **2001 Camry:** Front-subframe assembly was not adequately welded. This condition could cause failure of the assembly, increasing the risk of a crash.

PRICES

PRICES	Good	Average	Poor
1997 Camry CE, LE	$5,000-6,200	$4,300-5,300	$2,000-2,500
Camry XLE	6,800-7,500	6,100-6,700	3,200-3,500
1998 Camry CE, LE	6,200-7,500	5,400-6,500	2,700-3,200
Camry XLE	8,200-9,000	7,400-8,100	4,200-4,600
1999 Camry CE, LE	7,500-9,000	6,800-8,100	3,800-4,500
Camry Solara coupe	9,000-10,000	8,100-9,000	4,700-5,200
Camry XLE	9,500-10,700	8,600-9,600	4,900-5,600
Solara SLE coupe	11,200-12,500	10,100-11,300	6,000-6,800
2000 Camry CE, LE	9,000-11,000	8,100-9,900	4,700-5,700
Camry Solara conv.	15,500-17,000	14,100-15,500	9,900-10,900
Camry Solara coupe	10,500-11,700	9,500-10,500	5,600-6,200
Camry XLE	11,500-13,700	10,400-12,300	6,300-7,500
Solara SLE conv.	18,000-19,500	16,600-17,900	11,500-12,500
Solara SLE coupe	13,200-14,500	12,000-13,200	7,700-8,400

TOYOTA

2001 Camry CE, LE	$10,500-12,500	$9,500-11,300	$5,600-6,600
Camry Solara conv.	17,500-19,000	16,100-17,500	11,200-12,200
Camry Solara coupe	12,000-13,500	10,800-12,200	6,700-7,600
Camry XLE	13,000-14,500	11,800-13,200	7,500-8,400
Solara SLE conv.	20,000-21,500	18,400-19,800	13,000-14,000
Solara SLE coupe	15,000-16,500	13,700-15,000	9,500-10,400

> For detailed information on this vehicle visit
> http://used.consumerguide.com and enter code 2285

1994-99 TOYOTA CELICA

CG BEST BUY

CLASS: Sporty coupe
BUILT IN: Japan
PROS: Acceleration (GT)
• Optional antilock brakes
• Fuel economy
• Instruments/controls
• Steering/handling
CONS: Cargo room (exc. hatchback) • Engine noise • Rear-seat room

EVALUATION: Handling is where Toyota's Celica excels: crisp, responsive, with fine grip in corners and minimal body lean. You get a surprisingly supple ride too, even in a GT with the stiffly sprung Sports Package option. Sure, it's stiffer and choppier than other Celicas, but you get a little extra cornering precision with that Sport option. Braking is good too, though it would be better if more models had antilocking.

The 1.8-liter dual-cam 4-cylinder engine in an ST is smooth and lively with 5-speed manual shift, and economical, too. Optional 4-speed automatic saps its strength, because the engine lacks low-speed torque. The GT's 2.2-liter engine feels a lot stronger at all speeds, but makes plenty of noise doing it, roaring and throbbing in hard driving. As for economy, a GT hatchback with manual shift averaged 25.7 mpg. Tires aren't quiet, either—in any Celica.

This is a typical 2+2 layout, with little rear space for adults, and six-footers face marginal head clearance if a Celica coupe is sunroof-equipped. Controls and gauges are well laid out on a modern-styled, convenient dashboard. Trunk space is passable in notchback models, but the hatchback offers more cargo volume. The convertible's top is power-operated, but blocks the rear view substantially and robs rear-seat room and cargo space.

VALUE FOR THE MONEY: Even though the price may be high, if you want two-passenger fun and reliability, a Celica is worth the extra bucks—partly due to Toyota's reputation for quality.

TROUBLE SPOTS

Audio system: The Fujitsu 10-CD changer has a tendency to not accept or eject CDs. (1994-97)

Automatic transmission: Automatic transmissions may shift harshly due to rubber check balls in the valve body wearing out. (1994-99)

Brake noise: The original-equipment brake pads make squeaking noise. (1994-96)

Climate control: The rear-defroster terminals tend to break on convertibles. (1995-97)

Convertible top: Due to the balance rods rubbing, the convertible top wears at the sail panel near the rear window. (1995-97)

Vehicle noise: The fuel-door release cable rattles. Installing foam pads inside the fender usually quiets it. (1994)

Wheels: Proper wheel alignment may not be possible unless a special steering knuckle bolt is used. (1994-96)

AVERAGE REPLACEMENT COSTS

A/C Compressor	$880	CV Joints	$1,080
Alternator	340	Exhaust System	250
Automatic Trans.	710	Radiator	520
Brakes	210	Shocks and/or Struts	970
Clutch	425	Timing Chain/Belt	140

NHTSA RECALL HISTORY

None to date.

PRICES

	Good	Average	Poor
1994 Celica	$3,500-4,500	$2,800-3,600	$900-1,200
1995 Celica	4,100-5,200	3,400-4,300	1,400-1,700
Convertible	6,000-7,200	5,200-6,300	2,500-3,000
1996 Celica	4,800-6,000	4,000-5,000	1,800-2,300
Convertible	7,300-8,500	6,600-7,700	3,600-4,200
1997 Celica	5,700-7,200	4,900-6,200	2,300-3,000
Convertible	8,500-10,000	7,700-9,000	4,400-5,200
1998 Celica	7,800-8,800	7,000-7,900	4,000-4,500
Convertible	10,000-11,500	9,000-10,400	5,200-6,000
1999 Celica	10,000-11,000	9,000-9,900	5,200-5,700
Convertible	12,500-14,000	11,300-12,600	7,100-8,000

For detailed information on this vehicle visit
http://used.consumerguide.com and enter code **2154**

2000-03 TOYOTA CELICA

CG BEST BUY

CLASS: Sporty coupe

BUILT IN: Japan

PROS: Acceleration (GT-S 6-speed) • Handling/road-holding

CONS: Acceleration (GT w/automatic) • Entry/exit • Noise • Passenger room

TOYOTA

EVALUATION: Agile handling and grippy cornering are the big Celica bonuses, augmented by sharp, responsive steering. The penalty is engines that must rev madly to achieve top performance. That requires a heavy throttle foot with automatic, or a lot of manual shifting—a pleasant task with the short-throw gearbox. Even so, only the 6-speed GT-S comes close to being lively when pushing on the gas pedal. A GT coupe with automatic is sluggish on long upgrades, if adequate otherwise. A manual-shift GT-S averaged 24.2 mpg, but demands premium fuel. High rpm translates to plenty of noise except in gentle cruising, and the sounds aren't that pleasing. Wind rush is noticeable, and tire roar occurs on many pavements. As in most sporty cars, the ride is firm and rather "busy" on most surfaces. Braking is excellent if the Celica is equipped with ABS. Race car-type styling and shrinking of some exterior dimensions means the Celica's cabin is short on space. Even moderately tall occupants have limited head and leg room—enough to cramp some drivers. As expected, the back seat isn't really fit for people, and entry/exit is the crouch-and-crawl process typical in sporty coupes.

Drivers sit low, race car-style, and enjoy a good forward view as well as simple, handy controls and fine shifter/wheel/pedal spacing. Over-the-shoulder visibility is cluttered, due to the roofline, and the spoiler partly blocks traffic views at the rear. Gauges are legible, but the tachometer is not in the driver's direct line of sight, and warning lights are scattered. Interior stowage and cargo space are marginal.

VALUE FOR THE MONEY: Though capable and fun to drive, the Celica is noisy and lacks the low-end torque for decent acceleration with an automatic transmission. An Acura Integra offers similar high-rpm responses from a smoother 4-cylinder engine. Mitsubishi's Eclipse has a V6 option. Adventurous styling and Toyota's reputation for reliability help Celica appeal to the younger crowd, but prices are high.

TROUBLE SPOTS

Climate control: The knob for the heater-flow control may be hard to turn. A revised mechanism improves the feel. (2000)

Seatbelts/safety: The button that prevents the retractable portion of the seatbelt from going too far comes off. New buttons are available to fix this. (2000-01)

Wheels: The wheel covers on early production models clicked or squeaked and were being replaced under warranty. (2000)

AVERAGE REPLACEMENT COSTS

A/C Compressor	$405	CV Joints	$910
Alternator	535	Exhaust System	200
Automatic Trans.	690	Radiator	405
Brakes	220	Shocks and/or Struts	1,010
Clutch	395	Timing Chain/Belt	260

NHTSA RECALL HISTORY

2002-03: Faulty fuel-tank check valves were installed on certain vehicles, resulting in possible fire. Dealer will inspect and replace all affected parts.

PRICES

	Good	Average	Poor
2000 Celica GT	$11,200-12,200	$10,100-11,000	$6,000-6,600
Celica GT-S	12,800-14,000	11,600-12,700	7,400-8,100
2001 Celica GT	12,500-13,500	11,300-12,200	7,100-7,700
Celica GT-S	14,500-15,800	13,200-14,400	9,000-9,800
2002 Celica GT	14,000-15,500	12,700-14,100	8,500-9,500
Celica GT-S	16,000-17,500	14,600-15,900	10,200-11,200
2003 Celica GT	15,500-17,000	14,100-15,500	9,900-10,900
Celica GT-S	18,000-20,500	16,600-18,900	11,500-13,100

For detailed information on this vehicle visit
http://used.consumerguide.com and enter code **2402**

1993-97 TOYOTA COROLLA

CG BEST BUY

CLASS: Subcompact car

BUILT IN: Canada, Japan, USA

PROS: Antilock brakes (optional) • Fuel economy • Ride

CONS: Acceleration (w/automatic transmission) • Rear-seat room

EVALUATION: The 1.8-liter gives the Corolla DX and LE (pre-1996) models quicker acceleration and stronger passing power than the base sedan's 1.6-liter unit. We timed a Corolla with the 1.8-liter at 10.9 seconds to 60 mph, which is slower than a Honda Civic, but quicker than most other rivals. Though the automatic transmission generally works well with the 1.8-liter engine, it's slow to downshift for passing, unless you floor the throttle. The optional 3-speed automatic provided with the 1.6-liter engine is not only slow to downshift, it can be harsh at times. However, fuel economy is good with either engine—generally averaging about 30 mpg.

Corolla's suspension provides a stable highway ride and absorbs bumps better than some larger cars. Corolla is quieter than the similar Geo Prizm because Toyota includes more sound insulation in its cars. The car is roomier than most rivals, yet the rear seat is a tight fit for two adults, and more appropriate for children. Cargo space is adequate and can be expanded on DX models, thanks to the split folding rear seatback.

VALUE FOR THE MONEY: Corollas generally sold for more than comparable subcompact rivals, so expect preowned models to also be priced a bit more, given Toyota's generally high resale value and strong reputation for reliability.

TROUBLE SPOTS

Automatic transmission: A-40 series automatic transmissions may eventually shift harshly because rubber check balls become smaller, blow through the plate, and get dislodged. (1993-96)

Water pump: Water pumps leak due to a defective seal. (1993-94)

Windshield washer: Windshield-washer bottles frequently break. (1993-95)

AVERAGE REPLACEMENT COSTS

A/C Compressor	$925	CV Joints	$805
Alternator	415	Exhaust System	550
Automatic Trans.	1,025	Radiator	440
Brakes	200	Shocks and/or Struts	550
Clutch	515	Timing Chain/Belt	155

NHTSA RECALL HISTORY

1993-94: Snow or water can penetrate carpet and result in short and possible fire. **1993-95:** If liquid is spilled in console-box area, airbag warning light can illuminate during normal driving conditions and cause airbag to malfunction, deploying inadvertently. **1994:** Anchor straps in certain seatbelt assemblies were improperly heat treated and can break. **1995:** Battery may have defective weld inside positive or negative terminal, which can result in a no-start condition or explosion. **1997:** If airbag computer experiences mechanical shock within very short time after engine is started, airbag can deploy inadvertently.

PRICES	Good	Average	Poor
1993 Corolla	$2,200-3,000	$1,600-2,100	$400-600
1994 Corolla	2,500-3,400	1,800-2,500	500-700
1995 Corolla	3,000-4,400	2,300-3,100	700-900
1996 Corolla	3,500-4,400	2,800-3,500	900-1,200
1997 Corolla	4,000-4,800	3,300-3,900	1,300-1,500

For detailed information on this vehicle visit
http://used.consumerguide.com and enter code **2106**

1998-02 TOYOTA COROLLA

CG BEST BUY

CLASS: Subcompact car

BUILT IN: Canada, USA

PROS: Fuel economy • Maneuverability

CONS: Rear-seat room

EVALUATION: Although the new car feels stronger at higher engine speeds, automatic-transmission models feel somewhat sluggish at first, failing to deliver a sharp jump off the line from a standstill. Acceleration, in fact, ranks about average for a subcompact. In addition, turning on the air conditioner deadens performance noticeably. The 4-speed automatic transmission provides smooth, timely upshifts and prompt downshifts for passing, but seems to cut engine power slightly during gear changes.

Corolla suspensions are tuned to provide a comfortable ride, rather than sporty handling. Bumps are absorbed nicely, with good straightline stability, but high-speed turns produce excessive body roll. This drawback is especially noticeable in the 1998 VE and CE, which lacked the LE model's front stabilizer bar. The front stabilizer went into all 1999 models, but body roll remains apparent—though the car is agile and predictable.

All told, the ride is even quieter than before, with only moderate wind and road noise at highway speeds. Yes, the engine thrashes when worked hard, but it settles down nicely at cruising speeds. Braking with the optional ABS is swift and undramatic—just as it should be.

Like previous Corollas, this latest version is short on back-seat space, and not exactly bountiful up front, either. With average-sized folks seated up front, medium-sized adults can squeeze into the rear seats. Knee room will be snug, however. If front seats are moved more than halfway back, rear leg room becomes extremely tight. On the plus side, back doors are wide enough at the bottom so average-sized people slip easily through the openings.

A low cowl and beltline help to give the driver a commanding position. Reaching the radio and climate controls is a bit of a stretch, but all are simple to use and clearly marked. Though useful in size, the trunk has hinges that dip down into the load space when the lid is closed.

VALUE FOR THE MONEY: Ranked as a Best Buy for new-car shoppers, Corolla is also appealing secondhand—but prices aren't the lowest by any means in the subcompact league.

TROUBLE SPOTS

Airbags: On cars with side impact protection, the company advises that replacement seat covers (leather or cloth) not be installed or the side airbags may not work properly. (1998)

Cruise control: Some models may not shift into overdrive when the cruise control is on. A new cruise-control computer is available. (1998)

Doors: The dome light may not work when switched to "On," requiring replacement of the dome-light assembly. (1998)

Water leak: The rear quarter windows leak and a new molding strip will be installed under the normal warranty. (1998)

AVERAGE REPLACEMENT COSTS

A/C Compressor	$620	CV Joints	$1,400
Alternator	490	Exhaust System	610
Automatic Trans.	785	Radiator	670
Brakes	440	Shocks and/or Struts	1,080
Clutch	560	Timing Chain/Belt	455

NHTSA RECALL HISTORY

1998-99: Some lug nuts on cars distributed by Gulf States Toyota, Inc. Are defective, causing loss of torque, fatigue fracture of wheel, and possible loss of wheel.

PRICES

PRICES	Good	Average	Poor
1998 Corolla CE, LE	$5,000-5,600	$4,300-4,800	$2,000-2,200
Corolla VE	4,700-5,400	3,900-4,500	1,700-2,000

TOYOTA

1999 Corolla CE, LE	$6,200-6,800	$5,400-5,900	$2,700-2,900
Corolla VE	5,800-6,500	5,000-5,700	2,400-2,700
2000 Corolla CE, LE	7,300-8,000	6,600-7,200	3,600-3,900
Corolla VE	6,900-7,600	6,100-6,800	3,200-3,600
2001 Corolla CE, S	8,000-8,800	7,200-7,900	4,100-4,500
Corolla LE	8,400-9,100	7,600-8,200	4,400-4,700
2002 Corolla CE, S	9,200-10,000	8,300-9,000	4,800-5,200
Corolla LE	9,600-10,400	8,600-9,400	5,000-5,400

For detailed information on this vehicle visit
http://used.consumerguide.com and enter code **2291**

2000-03 TOYOTA ECHO

CLASS: Subcompact car

BUILT IN: Japan

PROS: Fuel economy
• Interior storage space
• Maneuverability

CONS: Acceleration
(w/automatic transmission)
• Rear-seat entry/exit (2-dr)

EVALUATION: Mechanically, Toyota's Echo is modern but ordinary, promising thrifty driving. Although its engine is no powerhouse, acceleration is almost brisk with manual shift. Automatic is generally smooth and responsive, though it may hesitate when asked to downshift at midrange speeds.

Noise suppression is nothing special, and exhaust boom occurs near peak engine rpm. Still, the Echo feels substantial for such a lightweight.

A tall, upright profile makes it feel different to drive. An Echo corners with good stability, but feels a tad tippy if pushed—aggravated by skinny tires. Front-end "plowing" sets in early. Close-quarters maneuverability is great, despite slightly dull steering action.

Ride comfort beats the small-car norm, with a little jiggle on washboard-surfaced freeways. Even at moderate speed, the bluff-sided Echo reacts to stiff crosswinds. Minor tire-induced wander can occur on grooved surfaces.

Even though it's one of the roomiest subcompacts, the cabin is too narrow for an adult in the center rear position, but leg room is no problem, rear foot space is good, and all-around head room ranks as generous. Seats are comfortable, if rather flat, and occupants sit higher than usual.

Rear-seat entry/exit isn't so easy in the 2 door. The high steering wheel is angled for a slightly minivanlike position. Visibility is commanding.

Less likable is the gimmicky central gauge pod, which is angled toward the driver but may be too distant for some eyes. Cargo room is ample, but the short tail leaves little fore-aft length without the optional split folding rear seat. Interior materials are attractive, but have an "entry-level" look and feel.

VALUE FOR THE MONEY: Pleasant and efficient, the Echo blends tempting prices with Toyota's strong reputation for quality and reliability. Sales have been tepid for such an affordable car, suggesting that the targeted young buyers have not taken to its styling. Performance is nothing special, but Echo is roomier than many rivals and the quirky look gives it a certain "character."

TROUBLE SPOTS

Climate control: The knob for the heater-flow control may be hard to turn. A revised mechanism improves the feel. (2000)

Seatbelts/safety: The button that prevents the retractable portion of the seatbelt from going too far comes off. New buttons are available to fix this. (2000-01)

Wheels: The wheel covers on early production models clicked or squeaked and were being replaced under warranty. (2000)

AVERAGE REPLACEMENT COSTS

A/C Compressor	$405	CV Joints	$910
Alternator	535	Exhaust System	200
Automatic Trans.	690	Radiator	405
Brakes	220	Shocks and/or Struts	1,010
Clutch	395	Timing Chain/Belt	260

NHTSA RECALL HISTORY

2000 w/automatic transmission: In cold ambient temperatures there is a possibility that the vacuum in the intake manifold could be insufficient for the brake booster, leading to increased stopping distance. **2000 w/speed control device:** E-clip that holds speed-control assembly to accelerator linkage could break; could result in accelerator sticking. **2001 registered in 19 specified states:** Condensed moisture from PCV port could seep toward brake-vacuum port inside intake manifold at freezing ambient temperatures, and start to freeze; vacuum assist to brakes would decrease and increased pedal pressure would be required. **2002:** Snow could accumulate inside the rear wheel and freeze, possible damaging the rear brake line and decreasing brake effectiveness by allowing brake fluid to leak.

PRICES

	Good	Average	Poor
2000 Echo	$5,800-6,700	$5,000-5,800	$2,400-2,800
2001 Echo	6,800-7,700	6,100-6,900	3,200-3,600
2002 Echo	8,000-9,000	7,200-8,100	4,100-4,600
2003 Echo	9,200-10,500	8,300-9,500	4,800-5,500

For detailed information on this vehicle visit
http://used.consumerguide.com and enter code **2403**

2001-03 TOYOTA HIGHLANDER

CG BEST BUY

CLASS: Midsize sport-utility vehicle

BUILT IN: Japan

PROS: Instruments/controls • Passenger and cargo room

CONS: Fuel economy

TOYOTA

EVALUATION: Capable all-around, the Highlander benefits from Toyota-style reliability. A Highlander V6 with AWD accelerated to 60 mph in a pleasing 8.5 seconds. Still, a fully loaded Highlander feels a bit lazy off the line and also in midrange passing, despite smooth, responsive automatic transmission.

With the V6 and AWD, Highlanders averaged 16.4 mpg in mostly city driving, and 17.6 mpg including performance testing. In a mix of urban/suburban commuting, fuel economy rose to 19 mpg. All are good figures for a midsize SUV. Toyota recommends premium fuel for the V6 and regular grade for the four cylinder.

A firmer suspension than in the RX 300 lets most every bump register, but the Highlander's ride is not jarring, always composed, and shuns the side-to-side wiggling motion that afflicts some SUVs.

Pleasant-handling Highlanders are maneuverable and stable. The body leans in turns, but overall control is among the best of any midsize SUV. Helping is steering with fine road feel, despite being slightly overassisted. Standard ABS with Brake Assist furnishes acceptable performance, but pedal action is mushy, and nosedive is evident in hard stops. The optional antiskid system provides appropriate corrections in slippery corners. AWD is not as capable off-road or in deep snow as traditional 4WD might be.

Engine noise is seldom intrusive. Wind noise rises sharply with speed, and coarse pavement tire drone causes rear-seat riders to raise their voices.

Main gauges are set deeper in "coves" than ideal for readability. They're still legible, though painted surrounds reflect sunlight. The gearshift sprouts from the dashboard, as in the RX 300; it's inviting to use, but can get knocked into Neutral by a driver's hand returning from cupholder to steering wheel. Cupholders are too large to secure a soda can.

Controls are positioned conveniently and move smoothly, though audio and climate system graphics aren't always obvious. The cabin is solidly assembled from durable materials, but ambience is middle-market austere even with leather.

Front space is generous in all dimensions, though the moonroof housing eats into head room. Seats are nicely supportive, but unexpectedly firm. The driver gets an elevated view of the road, over a long dashtop that's more minivanlike than SUV-style.

Entry/exit requires slight extra effort, due to SUV-like ground clearance. Rear head, shoulder, and knee clearance are spacious, but tight toe space tarnishes the advantages of a virtually flat floor. The rear seat is too firm if you equate deep cushioning with comfort. As in front, getting in/out demands a conscious step-up/down.

Absence of a third-row seat creates a tall, wide cargo hold. Split 60/40, the rear seat moves down and forward to form a nearly flat load floor. With headrests removed, front seatbacks fold rearward for sleeper-ready versatility. Storage bins are plentiful.

VALUE FOR THE MONEY: Aside from slightly elevated ground clearance, Highlander doesn't really do anything better than an AWD minivan would, sacrificing in the bargain such agreeable features as space- efficient sliding side doors and seven-passenger seating. That said, for most shoppers the Highlander is a far smarter choice than a truck-based SUV. Its all-around competence, pricing, and Toyota design make it more than a match for midsize SUVs of any stripe. New or used, it's an easy Best Buy.

TROUBLE SPOTS

Dashboard lights: Both the check-engine light and antilock-brake warning light may come on due to a problem with the skid-control computer for which there is an updated replacement. (2001-02)

AVERAGE REPLACEMENT COSTS

A/C Compressor	$550	Exhaust System	$470
Alternator	595	Radiator	355
Automatic Trans.	2,195	Shocks and/or Struts	1,435
Brakes	220	Timing Chain/Belt	410
CV Joints	930		

NHTSA RECALL HISTORY

2001: Brake master-cylinder cap may induce a vacuum, introducing air into the master-cylinder reservoir. This could cause abnormal brake noise and increased pedal stroke, resulting in longer stopping distances. Dealers will bleed the air from the brake lines and replace the reservoir-filler cap. **2001:** In a crash, fuel-breather hose at top of the fuel tank might contact the underside of the body, causing the nozzle to break. Possibly resulting in fuel leakage if the vehicle rolls over after a high-speed frontal crash. Dealers will rotate the specified clamp. **2003 in Southern states w/alloy wheels:** Spare tire may require the use of a different style of wheel nut to attach it to the vehicle, and using the wrong lug nuts could lead to a loose wheel. Owners will be provided with different style lug nuts, a warning label for the spare re/alloy wheel, and an owner's-manual addendum.

PRICES

	Good	Average	Poor
2001 Highlander	$17,000-20,000	$15,600-18,400	$10,900-12,800
Highlander Limited	20,500-23,000	18,900-21,200	13,300-15,000
2002 Highlander	19,000-22,500	17,500-20,700	12,400-14,600
Highlander Limited	22,700-25,000	20,900-23,000	14,800-16,300
2003 Highlander	21,500-25,500	19,800-23,500	14,000-16,600
Highlander Limited	25,500-28,000	23,700-26,000	16,800-18,500

For detailed information on this vehicle visit
http://used.consumerguide.com and enter code **4496**

1990-97 TOYOTA LAND CRUISER

CLASS: Luxury sport-utility vehicle

BUILT IN: Japan

PROS: 4WD traction • Antilock brakes (later models) • Passenger and cargo room

CONS: Acceleration (4.0-liter) • Entry/exit • Fuel economy • Price • Ride

EVALUATION: Steering was vague and overassisted in the early version, and the ride gets choppy, even on roads that look smooth. The 1991-97 version has a slightly wider stance, so it's a little less tipsy in corners. Still, don't expect to rush through fast curves or tight low-speed turns without plenty of body lean.

Acceleration from early models is nothing to shout about, either: on the order of 15.4 seconds to reach 60 mph. The 4.5-liter engine gets its job done, bringing enough power and torque to move this big rig rather smartly. Heavy weight helps make fuel consumption horrid. An early Land Cruiser got only 10.5 mpg; another with the 4.0-liter engine managed just 13 mpg. The permanently engaged 4-wheel-drive system installed in 1991 is a bonus, giving the driver the advantage of 4WD but no duties to perform.

Passenger space is ample all around. Seats are comfortable for long trips, and the cargo area is bountiful. A Land Cruiser stands tall, so step-up into the interior is high. Reaching the optional third seat is awkward because you have to clamber around the middle bench. It's kid-size, too, and leaves little cargo space at the rear. However, both the second and third seats pack up easily to expand cargo volume. Some controls in the pre-1991 model have a haphazard look, but full instrumentation was standard. The interior got a lot more modern in 1991, with instruments and controls handier and better organized. Overall, the interior has a sturdy, high-grade look, and body construction is tight and solid.

VALUE FOR THE MONEY: Expensive and sold in modest numbers, Land Cruisers continue to attract a modest but eager following. Still, most buyers find a Ford Explorer or Jeep Cherokee to be a better value.

TROUBLE SPOTS

Audio system: Static in the radio is caused by poor antenna ground. (1990-96)

Automatic transmission: Automatic transmissions have delayed engagement in reverse. (1990-96)

Radiator: The thermostat gasket had a tendency to leak in cold weather. (1990-95)

Vehicle noise: The transfer-case lever rattles and vibrates, and is corrected by installing a new boot and hardware. (1990-94)

AVERAGE REPLACEMENT COSTS

A/C Compressor	$1,055	Exhaust System	$330
Alternator	375	Radiator	435
Automatic Trans.	1,010	Shocks and/or Struts	510
Brakes	230	Timing Chain/Belt	885
Clutch	520	Universal Joints	520

NHTSA RECALL HISTORY

1990: Heavy loads and high temperatures can create high pressure in fuel tank, resulting in cracks and leakage.

PRICES	Good	Average	Poor
1990 Land Cruiser	$6,000-7,000	$5,200-6,100	$2,500-2,900
1991 Land Cruiser	7,200-8,200	6,400-7,300	3,500-4,000
1992 Land Cruiser	8,500-9,500	7,700-8,600	4,400-4,900

1993 Land Cruiser	$9,800-10,800	$8,800-9,700	$5,100-5,600
1994 Land Cruiser	11,000-12,200	9,900-11,000	5,900-6,600
1995 Land Cruiser	12,500-14,000	11,300-12,600	7,100-8,000
1996 Land Cruiser	14,000-15,500	12,700-14,100	8,500-9,500
1997 Land Cruiser	16,000-18,000	14,600-16,400	10,200-11,500

For detailed information on this vehicle visit
http://used.consumerguide.com and enter code **2239**

1991-97 TOYOTA PREVIA

CLASS: Minivan
BUILT IN: Japan
PROS: Antilock brakes (optional) • Passenger and cargo room
CONS: Climate controls • Engine noise • Fuel economy

EVALUATION: Acceleration is decent, but when worked hard the engine gets noisy and sends an annoying vibration through the floor. It's responsive in everyday driving, however, thanks to an automatic transmission that shifts smoothly and promptly, and seldom hunts between third and fourth gears. We averaged 15 mpg in one test and 19 mpg in another. Though the 161-horsepower supercharged version doesn't move the Previa into the fast lane, it does make this minivan more responsive, particularly in passing situations.

While the Previa holds the road well and seems composed going around corners, neither its ride nor overall handling match that of the class champion Chrysler minivans.

The wild-looking W-shaped dashboard actually works rather well, putting most controls within easy reach, though the climate controls are poorly marked. Only the rear-seat headrests keep outward vision from being absolutely panoramic. Passenger space is ample, though the split third seat is too tight to accommodate three adults, and head room beneath the sliding sunroof is only adequate for 6-footers. The center seat is removable and rear seat is split so that both halves can fold outward against the sides of the vehicle.

VALUE FOR THE MONEY: With its roomy, versatile nature and Toyota's reputation for reliability and durability, the Previa qualifies as a good family vehicle.

TROUBLE SPOTS

Air conditioner: A faulty expansion valve may cause the air conditioner to gradually lose efficiency. (1992-93)

Automatic transmission: A-40 series automatic transmissions may shift harshly because rubber check balls become smaller, blow through the plate, and get dislodged. (1992-94)

TOYOTA

Coolant leak: Core plugs in the cylinder head may leak coolant. (1991)
Exhaust system: In compliance with emission-control regulations, the oxygen sensor will be replaced free at the 80,000-mile maintenance. (1993-95)

AVERAGE REPLACEMENT COSTS

A/C Compressor	$860	Exhaust System	$337
Alternator	390	Radiator	555
Automatic Trans.	830	Shocks and/or Struts	500
Brakes	210	Timing Chain/Belt	890
Clutch	475	Universal Joints	135

NHTSA RECALL HISTORY

1991: Certain windshield-wiper components are subject to premature failure.
1991: Failure of component in Fujitsu-Ten radio causes short circuit that could result in fire. **1997:** Oil leakage can occur at continuous speeds above 75 mph.

PRICES

	Good	Average	Poor
1991 Previa	$2,800-3,600	$2,100-2,700	$600-800
Previa All-Trac	3,200-4,000	2,500-3,100	800-1,000
1992 Previa	3,400-4,300	2,700-3,400	900-1,100
Previa All-Trac	3,900-4,800	3,200-3,900	1,200-1,500
1993 Previa	4,000-4,900	3,300-4,000	1,300-1,600
Previa All-Trac	4,600-5,500	3,800-4,600	1,700-2,000
1994 Previa	4,700-5,800	3,900-4,900	1,700-2,100
Previa All-Trac	5,300-6,500	4,600-5,600	2,200-2,700
1995 Previa	5,500-6,700	4,700-5,800	2,300-2,700
Previa All-Trac	6,300-7,500	5,500-6,600	2,800-3,300
1996 Previa	6,200-7,400	5,400-6,400	2,700-3,200
Previa All-Trac	7,100-8,300	6,300-7,400	3,400-4,000
1997 Previa	7,500-9,000	6,800-8,100	3,800-4,500
Previa All-Trac	8,500-10,000	7,700-9,000	4,400-5,200

> For detailed information on this vehicle visit
> http://used.consumerguide.com and enter code **2107**

1996-00 TOYOTA RAV4

CLASS: Compact sport-utility vehicle
BUILT IN: Japan
PROS: Maneuverability • Visibility
CONS: Noise • Rear-seat room

EVALUATION: The RAV4 delivers a softer, more-compliant ride as well as more-responsive steering than truck-based SUVs. Unlike the Sidekick/Tracker, which often feels ready to lean over, the RAV4 feels stable and carlike while cornering swiftly, and robust when traversing rough roads. Its permanent 4-wheel-drive system is more convenient than the on-demand systems used by the early competition. Still, you can expect some choppiness on scalloped freeways and over patchy pavement, especially with the shorter-length 2-door model.

Tire roar is always noticeable, and wind rush rises sharply as speed increases. The engine becomes quite boomy when worked hard, too.

RAV4 also lags behind most small cars in terms of performance. A manual-shift 4WD 2-door accelerated to 60 mph in 10.5 seconds, but an automatic 4-door needed about 13 seconds—and that was without a load. We've averaged a disappointing 20.8 mpg from an automatic 4WD 4-door in city/highway driving. The lighter-weight front-drive models should be a little thriftier, and also quicker.

Four adults fit comfortably inside a 4-door RAV, but back-seaters don't get much leg or knee room. Rear entry/exit is a squeeze for larger folks, too. The 2-door is best enjoyed with two adults up front and two children in back, because its rear seat is even tighter than the 4-door's. Rear access also is more difficult, despite a slide-forward feature on the right-front seat.

Cargo space is good in both body styles, considering their exterior dimensions.

Though not as commanding as in some SUVs, the driving stance allows clear views all around, in either hardtop body style. In the recent convertible, however, the over-the-shoulder view is impaired when the rear roof is in place. On the plus side, the convertible's top fits well, though it takes a while to raise or lower.

Most people are likely to be satisfied inside, though more rearward seat travel would be nice—especially for taller folks. The carlike dashboard is simple and convenient.

VALUE FOR THE MONEY: Despite the RAV4's pluses, Honda's CR-V is roomier, quieter, and more practical—a better compact wagon and miniSUV than Toyota's offering.

TROUBLE SPOTS

Audio system: Static can be heard on the AM band when other electrical items such as wipers or turn signals are used due to a bad ground for the antenna. (1996)

Audio system: The CDs get stuck and may not eject from the Fujitsu-Ten CD player. (1997)

Brake noise: The rear brakes make a whining noise because the backing plate is too thin. A thicker one is available. (1996)

AVERAGE REPLACEMENT COSTS

A/C Compressor	$810	CV Joints	$500
Alternator	475	Exhaust System	560
Automatic Trans.	1,080	Radiator	580
Brakes	160	Shocks and/or Struts	800
Clutch	610	Timing Chain/Belt	220

NHTSA RECALL HISTORY

1998: Audiovox Securikey+ Security Systems can malfunction causing electrical failure; can cause engine to run poorly and stall, and electrical components can intermittently fail. **2000:** If the vehicle is repeatedly parked by shifting into "P" without applying the parking brake, the lock rod could break rendering the parking-lock system inoperative. **2000:** The front disc-brake rotor can develop stress fractures if the lug nuts are too tight. If the disc rotor breaks, braking action on that wheel will be lost, increasing the risk of a crash.

PRICES

	Good	Average	Poor
1996 RAV4 2WD	$4,000-5,000	$3,300-4,100	$1,300-1,600
RAV4 4WD	4,800-6,000	4,000-5,000	1,800-2,300
1997 RAV4 2WD	4,800-5,800	4,000-4,900	1,800-2,200
RAV4 4WD	5,700-7,000	4,900-6,000	2,300-2,900
1998 RAV4 2WD	6,000-7,200	5,200-6,300	2,500-3,000
RAV4 4WD	7,100-8,500	6,300-7,600	3,400-4,100
1999 RAV4 2WD	7,300-8,800	6,600-7,900	3,600-4,300
RAV4 4WD	8,500-10,000	7,700-9,000	4,400-5,200
2000 RAV4 2WD	9,500-11,000	8,600-9,900	4,900-5,700
RAV4 4WD	10,800-12,500	9,700-11,300	5,800-6,800

For detailed information on this vehicle visit
http://used.consumerguide.com and enter code **2286**

2001-03 TOYOTA RAV4

CLASS: Compact sport-utility vehicle

BUILT IN: Japan

PROS: Instruments/controls • Maneuverability • Visibility

CONS: Acceleration • Engine noise • Rear-seat room

EVALUATION: Acceleration is adequate unless this compact SUV is carrying a heavy load or needs to pass. Either way, you can expect laborious highway passing. An all-wheel-drive RAV4 with manual shift accelerated to 60 mph in 9.6 seconds, which is comparable to the 2002-up Honda CR-V but slower than a V6-powered Ford Escape. Automatic models add about a second to the figure. With all-wheel drive and a manual gearbox, a RAV4 averaged 21.7 mpg, including some gas-guzzling performance tests. Another RAV4 with automatic, driven mainly on the highway, averaged 23 mpg.

Although the RAV4 never rides uncomfortably, it does bound a bit over big bumps and feels unsettled on washboard surfaces. Honda's CR-V rides better overall. Quick steering is accompanied by good feedback, but the RAV4 can be buffered by gusty crosswinds. Low-speed handling is competent. Hard cornering induces a fair amount of body lean and tire scrub, but not the tipsy sensation that plagues many SUVs. Simulated emergency stops are marked by nosedive and mild wander. Wind and road noise intrude, but they're no louder than in most subcompact cars. The engine suffers from high-rpm boominess, though it's relaxed enough in top-gear cruising. Again, CR-V is quieter overall.

Instruments and controls are simple and convenient, including the old-fashioned radio tuning knob and dial-type climate controls. More than most

Toyotas, the cabin exhibits some design flair, with a pleasing mix of textures and shades, classy low-grain molded plastic, legible semiretro gauges, and a sporty, thick-rimmed steering wheel. Entry/exit into the front is easy, with good room for adults. Seats are very firm but comfortable enough, though taller drivers may wish for more rearward travel and a greater range for the tilt steering wheel. Visibility is fine, partly because the external spare tire mounts low enough to avoid interference. Rear head room is good but leg, toe, and shoulder space are limited. The rear bench seat reclines but isn't all that comfortable. Narrow rear-door passages impede entry/exit, too. The back seat folds or removes easily, leaving enough room behind it for at least a dozen plastic grocery bags. The swing-out tail door can be clumsy, however, and unlike some competitors, the RAV4 has no separate-opening window.

VALUE FOR THE MONEY: On the whole, a RAV4 is more suited to suburban errand-running than to long-distance people-hauling or even moderate off-roading. Still, it's an attractive compact SUV. Many rivals offer more space and stronger performance, but only Honda matches Toyota's reputation for quality and durability. High resale value, on the other hand, means used-RAV4 prices will be high. Don't buy without also giving the CR-V a trial run.

TROUBLE SPOTS

Brake noise: The front brakes may groan and revised brake pads were made available. The rear brakes may squeal which is corrected by installing revised brake drums. (2001-02)

Vehicle noise: Squeaks and rattles from the A-pillars, rear windows and glovebox require felt inserts that are being covered under the 36/36,000 warranty. (2001)

Wind noise: If the roof rack rattles or buzzes, there is an improved crossbar that has an additional thumbscrew for better attachment. (2001)

AVERAGE REPLACEMENT COSTS

A/C Compressor	$825	CV Joints	$670
Alternator	710	Exhaust System	755
Automatic Trans.	1,995	Radiator	720
Brakes	755	Shocks and/or Struts	860
Clutch	560	Timing Chain/Belt	420

NHTSA RECALL HISTORY

None to date.

PRICES

PRICES	Good	Average	Poor
2001 RAV4 2WD	$12,000-13,500	$10,800-12,200	$6700-7600
RAV4 4WD	13,500-15,000	12,300-13,700	8000-8900
2002 RAV4 2WD	14,000-15,200	12,700-13,800	8500-9300
RAV4 4WD	15,700-17,000	14,300-15,500	10,000-10,900
2003 RAV4 2WD	16,000-17,500	14,600-15,900	10,200-11,200
RAV4 4WD	17,700-19,200	16,300-17,700	11,300-12,300

For detailed information on this vehicle visit http://used.consumerguide.com and enter code **4493**

TOYOTA

1998-03 TOYOTA SIENNA

CLASS: Minivan
BUILT IN: USA
PROS: Standard antilock brakes • Build quality • Side airbags (LE, XLE)
CONS: Fuel economy • Radio placement

EVALUATION: With several hundred pounds more weight to carry, the V6 that feels strong in a Camry feels merely adequate in a Sienna—and loses some of its snap with the air conditioning on. The transmission shifts smoothly and downshifts quickly for passing, so Sienna seldom feels underpowered. Acceleration time to 60 mph of 8.9 seconds affirms that opinion. Hard takeoffs induce mild steering-wheel tug that highlights the Sienna's lack of traction control. We averaged 15.9 mpg. A long-term Sienna returned 19.4 mpg, including a substantial amount of highway driving. Toyota recommends premium fuel.

Suspension settings favor a smooth ride over sporty handling, but that's appropriate for this type of vehicle. Bumps are absorbed with little impact, and body lean in turns is moderate for a minivan. Overall road manners are composed and predictable, though Sienna can feel a little nose-heavy when entering freeway on-ramps. Braking is swift and stable. Road and wind noise are subdued, leaving the cabin serene at highway speeds.

Sienna boasts a well-thought-out and pleasant cabin. The low floor makes it easy to climb in and out, yet the standard height-adjustable driver's seat affords a commanding view of the road. Front seats are spacious. Second-row passengers do not have an abundance of leg room if the front seats are pushed very far back, but knee clearance is generally good even in the rear row. Actually, adults can be comfortable anywhere if no seats are moved fully aft. Climate controls are easily accessed, but the radio is mounted low and recessed into the dashboard, requiring a long look away from the road to reach while driving. Numerous storage bins and drink holders of various sizes handle interior storage nicely. There's room for a double row of grocery bags in the back with all seats in place. The individual seats can be removed fairly easily though they're heavy, so it's a 2-person task. The tumble-folding rear seat makes it easy to expand the cargo area.

VALUE FOR THE MONEY: Toyota had fired a blank with its old Previa, but hit the bull's-eye with Sienna. Priced to compete with similarly equipped domestic rivals delivering better-than-expected power and economy, this highly refined new minivan is a formidable force and a must-consider on the used-minivan market.

TROUBLE SPOTS

Brake noise: Original brakes tend to groan and squeak. Replacement brake pads and rotors correct the problem. (1998)

Headlights: The headlight-aiming specifications are inadequate on dark roads, so they have been revised to allow aiming one-inch higher. (1998-99)

Windows: If the window switch on the passenger side quits working, an improved replacement switch may remedy the problem. (1998-99)

AVERAGE REPLACEMENT COSTS

A/C Compressor	$1,140	CV Joints	$890
Alternator	485	Exhaust System	315
Automatic Trans.	1,055	Radiator	475
Brakes	220	Shocks and/or Struts	630
Clutch	410	Timing Chain/Belt	610

NHTSA RECALL HISTORY

1998-99 w/lug nuts, Pt. No. 1207, supplied by Prime Wheel and distributed in TX, OK, LA, AR, and MS : Lug nuts are defective, causing loss of torque, fatigue fracture of wheel, and possible loss of wheel. **2001:** Front-subframe assembly was not adequately welded. This condition could cause failure of the assembly, increasing the risk of a crash.

PRICES

	Good	Average	Poor
1998 Sienna	$8,500-11,500	$7,700-10,400	$4,400-6,000
1999 Sienna	10,000-13,500	9,000-12,200	5,200-7,000
2000 Sienna	12,000-16,000	10,800-14,400	6,700-9,000
2001 Sienna	14,500-18,000	13,200-16,400	9,000-11,200
2002 Sienna	17,000-20,800	15,600-19,100	10,900-13,300
2003 Sienna	19,500-23,500	17,900-21,600	12,700-15,300

For detailed information on this vehicle visit
http://used.consumerguide.com and enter code **2318**

1995-03 TOYOTA TACOMA

CLASS: Compact pickup truck

BUILT IN: Japan, USA

PROS: Acceleration (V6) • Reliability

CONS: Engine noise • Step-in height (4WD) • Price • Ride

EVALUATION: Acceleration with the base engine feels brisk, particularly with the manual transmission. The 2.7-liter 4 cylinder in 4WD models has marginally more horsepower and torque, but feels more taxed in all driving situations. Tacomas with the 3.4-liter V6 have strong standing-start acceleration with either transmission. The 2001 test 2WD automatic V6 PreRunner Double Cab did 0-60 mph in a respectable 9.7 sec. And we averaged 16.1 mpg with 4WD and manual transmission, 19.4 with 2WD and automatic in our tests of V6 Xtracabs.

Ride quality is poor. Tacoma pounds over bumps and bounds over dips in the pavement. Handling is nothing special either, but at least the brakes work well.

Inside, the Tacoma feels rather spartan. There is enough room for two adults to stretch out in front, but the rear area, like in all compact pickups, is best left to cargo and not people. Controls are well-arranged, but are a bit on the small side—especially radio controls. Visibility is excellent and noise levels are only marginally higher than in comparable Ford or Chevy compact trucks.

Tacoma's payload ratings are competitive with anything in this class, but even with the 3.4-liter V6, towing limits fall short of the Ranger and S-Series by about 1000 pounds. Note also that Tacoma has only a single 6.2-foot cargo bed length; while nearly all competitors offer a regular-cab model with a cargo bed of 7 or 7.5 feet.

VALUE FOR THE MONEY: The only advantage a Tacoma might have over domestic compacts would be in reliability. This is one case where we would shop the competition despite Toyota's reputation.

TROUBLE SPOTS

Exhaust system: In compliance with emission-control regulations, the oxygen sensor will be replaced free at the 80,000-mile maintenance. (1995)

AVERAGE REPLACEMENT COSTS

A/C Compressor	$1,315	Exhaust System	$242
Alternator	360	Radiator	520
Automatic Trans.	1,457	Shocks and/or Struts	210
Brakes	190	Timing Chain/Belt	200
Clutch	915	Universal Joints	200

NHTSA RECALL HISTORY

1995: Battery may have defective weld inside positive or negative terminal, which can result in a no-start condition or explosion. **1995-96:** Under certain conditions, front suspension support can crack. **1998-99:** Some wheel lug nuts are defective, causing loss of torque, fatigue fracture of wheel, and possible loss of wheel. **1999-2000:** Trailer-towing wire harness may have deficient waterproofing and improper installation. An electrical short circuit will occur if water enters the converter housing. **2001-03 double cab:** If side impact occurs, the fuel inlet hose could be damaged, resulting in leakage and possible fire. Dealer will inspect and install a hose protector.

PRICES

	Good	Average	Poor
1995 Tacoma 2WD	$3,300-5,000	$2,600-4,000	$800-1,300
Tacoma 4WD	5,000-7,500	4,300-6,400	2,000-3,000
1996 Tacoma 2WD	3,800-6,000	3,100-4,900	1,100-1,800
Tacoma 4WD	5,800-8,800	5,000-7,700	2,400-3,700
1997 Tacoma 2WD	4,500-7,000	3,700-5,800	1,600-2,500
Tacoma 4WD	6,600-10,000	5,800-8,800	3,000-4,500
1998 Tacoma 2WD	5,400-9,000	4,600-7,700	2,200-3,700
Tacoma 4WD	7,800-12,000	7,000-10,800	4,000-6,100
1999 Tacoma 2WD	6,400-10,500	5,600-9,200	2,900-4,800
Tacoma 4WD	9,000-13,500	8,100-12,200	4,700-7,000
2000 Tacoma 2WD	7,500-12,500	6,800-11,300	3,800-6,300
Tacoma 4WD	10,300-15,000	9,300-13,500	5,500-8,000

2001 Tacoma 2WD	$8,500-15,000	$7,700-13,500	$4,400-7,800
Tacoma 4WD	11,500-17,500	10,400-15,800	6,300-9,600
2002 Tacoma 2WD	9,500-16,000	8,600-14,400	4,900-8,300
Tacoma 4WD	12,700-19,500	11,400-17,600	7,400-11,300
2003 Tacoma 2WD	10,500-18,000	9,500-16,200	5,600-9,500
Tacoma 4WD	14,000-21,000	12,700-19,100	8,500-12,800

For detailed information on this vehicle visit
http://used.consumerguide.com and enter code 2252

1995-98 TOYOTA TERCEL

CLASS: Subcompact car
BUILT IN: Japan
PROS: Fuel economy
• Maneuverability
CONS: Noise • Rear-seat room

EVALUATION: The latest engine is noisy, but its greater power shows up in quicker acceleration. Nevertheless, performance is still far from lively, even with a manual transmission. Automatic transmissions are rather slow to downshift to deliver suitable highway passing power. Fuel economy is exceptional: We averaged 30 mpg in a DX model with automatic.

Though refreshingly frugal, long rides in a Tercel aren't all pleasure, by any means. The suspension allows a lot of bouncing on wavy roads, and the ride becomes choppy on rough surfaces. In addition, there's still plenty of road noise. Handling ability is hampered by narrow tires, which run out of grip early in hard cornering.

Inside, the dashboard is simple, functional, and conveniently laid out, but the rear seat remains tight for anyone over 5-foot-10. Adults have ample room up front, but trunk space is on the skimpy side.

VALUE FOR THE MONEY: Far from exciting in concept or reality, Tercel's mission has been to be the least-expensive Toyota, and it shows against the plusher, more substantial Corolla and other subcompact leaders. On the other hand, Toyota's reputation for reliability makes the Tercel worth considering if you need basic transportation but are on a tight budget.

TROUBLE SPOTS

Audio system: A poor antenna ground causes static on the AM band of the radio. (1995-96)

Climate control: Poor heater performance may be due to a defective thermostat. (1995-96)

Dashboard lights: The check-engine light may come on when the car is driven at altitudes above 5900 feet, which may require a new computer. (1995-96)

Windows: The front windows may be hard to operate. (1995-96)

AVERAGE REPLACEMENT COSTS

A/C Compressor	$1,350	CV Joints	$1,045
Alternator	330	Exhaust System	355
Automatic Trans.	680	Radiator	305
Brakes	220	Shocks and/or Struts	1,100
Clutch	370	Timing Chain/Belt	190

NHTSA RECALL HISTORY

None to date.

PRICES

	Good	Average	Poor
1995 Tercel	$2,100-2,800	$1,500-2,000	$400-500
1996 Tercel	2,500-3,300	1,800-2,400	500-700
1997 Tercel	3,300-4,000	2,600-3,200	800-1,000
1998 Tercel	4,300-5,200	3,500-4,300	1,500-1,800

For detailed information on this vehicle visit
http://used.consumerguide.com and enter code 2242

2000-03 TOYOTA TUNDRA

CLASS: Full-size pickup truck

BUILT IN: USA

PROS: Acceleration (V8) • Build quality • Interior materials

CONS: Fuel economy (V8) • Rear-seat comfort (extended cab) • Rear-seat entry/exit (extended cab)

EVALUATION: For really heavy work or demanding towing, choose a ¾- ton domestic-brand pickup. But for refinement that's likely to appeal to light-duty users or first-time pickup buyers, Toyota has scored a winner.

Although V8 models don't leap ahead from a stop, power builds quickly and passing response is strong. Toyota claimed 0-60 mph acceleration in about 8 seconds for a 2WD regular-cab Tundra with the V8. A heavier Access Cab V8 model performed the same task in 8.8 seconds.

Gas mileage is comparable to the Tundra's bigger rivals. When new, a V8 4WD Access Cab truck averaged 13.9 mpg.

A Tundra rides more comfortably than competitors with similar wheelbase, though its stiff suspension triggers abrupt vertical motions on uneven surfaces. Handling comes with similar qualifiers. Specifically, a Tundra takes corners with above average balance and the tail resists skipping in bumpy turns. But as with any large pickup, it suffers a lot of body lean in corners, close-quarters maneuverability is subpar, and 4WD models are plagued by slow, numb steering.

Stopping power and brake modulation with optional ABS is excellent. Noise levels are nearly carlike, especially with the smooth V8.

Front-seat room and comfort for two is similar to any full-size pickup, though the cab doesn't feel quite as expansive as some. Positioning of the steering wheel; pedals; and clear, simple controls is first-rate. On the down side, the column automatic-transmission lever is close to the wiper stalk.

Both 2WD and 4WD models demand a bit of a jump to climb aboard. The Access Cab's back seat is more cramped than the competition and its seatback is uncomfortably upright. Leg room is sparse without moving the front seats well forward.

VALUE FOR THE MONEY: Simply put, Tundra is a fine truck, priced competitively and executed with typical Toyota thoroughness. Except for back-seat comfort, matches any comparably equipped domestic-brand model—and is built in Indiana.

TROUBLE SPOTS

Brakes: Front brake vibration requires resurfacing the rotors (2000); new rear brake pads are available to replace the originals that vibrated (1999-2000); and new starwheel parking-brake adjusters are available to eliminate vibrations. (2000-01)

Engine noise: Idler pulleys for the supercharger belt on 3.4L V6 engines may rattle because the bearings spin on the shaft requiring replacement with a revised pulley. (2000)

Engine temperature: Temperature gauge reads hot when actual engine temperature is normal. A revised gauge is available. (2000-01)

AVERAGE REPLACEMENT COSTS

A/C Compressor	$615	CV Joints	$835
Alternator	345	Exhaust System	350
Automatic Trans.	1,450	Radiator	310
Brakes	220	Shocks and/or Struts	890
Clutch	890	Timing Chain/Belt	190

NHTSA RECALL HISTORY

2000: The taillight socket may have been improperly molded, allowing the bulb to fall out.

PRICES

	Good	Average	Poor
2000 Tundra V6	$9,000-15,000	$8,100-13,500	$4,700-7,800
Tundra V8	14,000-18,500	12,700-16,800	8,500-11,300
2001 Tundra V6	10,500-17,000	9,500-15,300	5,600-9,000
Tundra V8	15,500-20,500	14,100-18,700	9,900-13,100
2002 Tundra V6	12,000-19,500	10,800-17,600	6,700-10,900
Tundra V8	17,200-22,500	15,800-20,700	11,000-14,400
2003 Tundra V6	14,000-23,000	12,700-20,900	8,500-14,000
Tundra V8	20,000-25,000	18,400-23,000	13,000-16,300

For detailed information on this vehicle visit
http://used.consumerguide.com and enter code **2468**

1994-98 VOLKSWAGEN GOLF/JETTA

CLASS: Subcompact car
BUILT IN: Mexico
PROS: Acceleration
• Antilock brakes (optional)
• Maneuverability
• Passenger and cargo room
• Steering/handling
CONS: Engine noise
• Road noise

EVALUATION: The 4-cylinder models have adequate acceleration from a standing start and lively passing power with either transmission. The 4-speed automatic downshifts promptly, providing adequate power for passing, but lacks smoothness. Naturally, acceleration is a bit friskier and fuel economy is better with the standard 5-speed manual. We averaged 23.8 mpg with the automatic and 26.5 mpg with the 5-speed. The GTI VR6 and GLX Jetta models with their 2.8-liter V6 deliver very impressive acceleration, but be prepared to pay extra. Unlike their predecessors, the current models don't suffer the constant thumping from the suspension and tires. Road noise is still prominent at highway speeds and the exhaust is too loud when cruising at 60-65 mph. Like the previous models, these third-generation Golf and Jetta models have sporty handling for family cars. The steering is firm, and the tires grip well when taking turns at high speeds. The dashboard has a functional layout, with all controls mounted high for easy operation while driving. Since they ride on the same 97.4-inch wheelbase as the preceding models, interior space is about the same. All body styles have ample cargo space and the Jetta's trunk is huge when compared to the car's compact size.

VALUE FOR THE MONEY: Our only reservation with these delightful subcompacts is Volkswagen reliability and high prices. Otherwise, they are an excellent choice that is a little out of the norm.

TROUBLE SPOTS

Engine stalling: If the engine occasionally loses power, stalls, or stumbles, the problem may be vibration of the mass airflow sensor. (1994-95)

Suspension noise: A dull clunking noise from the front end may be due to too much free play in the upper MacPherson strut bearings. (1994-95)

Tire wear: Cupping of the rear tires may be caused by too much positive rear toe, which is corrected by replacing the rear-axle stub shafts. (1993-96)

Water leak: Leaks at the bulkhead should have been corrected during pre-delivery inspection. (1994)

AVERAGE REPLACEMENT COSTS

A/C Compressor	$640	CV Joints	$845
Alternator	660	Exhaust System	485
Automatic Trans.	720	Radiator	585
Brakes	210	Shocks and/or Struts	410
Clutch	530	Timing Chain/Belt	110

NHTSA RECALL HISTORY

1994-95 w/V6 engine: Improper material was used in manufacturing radiator-fan motor shaft for VR6 engine, causing shaft to wear and become noisy; shaft could seize, rendering fan motor inoperative and eventually causing engine to overheat and stall. **1994-95:** Jack could collapse during use. **1994-95:** Misrouted rear brake line could be damaged , which may result in leakage and diminished braking in one circuit. **1994-96:** Bolts securing front hood latch can loosen, causing disengagement of hood striker from latch and possible unexpected opening of hood. **1997-98 Jetta:** If the vehicle is driven with a rear flat tire, the fuel-tank filler neck can wear, causing a fuel leak.

PRICES

	Good	Average	Poor
1994 Golf	$2,500-3,200	$1,800-2,300	$500-700
Jetta	2,800-3,700	2,100-2,800	600-800
Jetta GLX	4,200-5,000	3,400-4,100	1,400-1,700
1995 Golf	2,800-3,700	2,100-2,800	600-800
Golf GTI	5,000-5,800	4,300-4,900	2,000-2,300
Jetta	3,100-4,000	2,400-3,100	700-1,000
Jetta GLX	5,000-5,800	4,300-4,900	2,000-2,300
1996 Golf	3,400-4,200	2,700-3,300	900-1,100
Golf GTI	4,500-6,200	3,700-5,100	1,600-2,200
Jetta	3,700-4,600	3,000-3,700	1,100-1,300
Jetta GLX	5,700-6,500	4,900-5,600	2,300-2,700
1997 Golf	4,200-5,000	3,400-4,100	1,400-1,700
Golf GTI	5,400-7,500	4,600-6,500	2,200-3,100
Jetta	4,500-6,000	3,700-5,000	1,600-2,200
Jetta GLX	6,700-7,600	5,900-6,700	3,100-3,500
1998 Golf	5,000-5,800	4,300-4,900	2,000-2,300
Golf GTI	6,200-8,500	5,400-7,400	2,700-3,700
Jetta	5,400-7,000	4,600-6,000	2,200-2,900
Jetta GLX	8,000-9,000	7,200-8,100	4,100-4,600

For detailed information on this vehicle visit
http://used.consumerguide.com and enter code **2112**

1999-03 VOLKSWAGEN GOLF/JETTA

CG BEST BUY

CLASS: Subcompact car

BUILT IN: Germany, Mexico, Brazil

PROS: Acceleration (V6) • Build quality • Cargo room (Golf) • Fuel economy (4-cyl, TDI) • Ride/handling

CONS: Acceleration (4-cyl w/automatic transmission) • Automatic-transmission performance • Rear-seat entry/exit (Golf)

VOLKSWAGEN

EVALUATION: Sporty road manners lead the list of merits. The ride is firm but comfortable, cornering stable, steering linear with fine on-center feel. GTI and V6 cars handle best with only a modest sacrifice in ride comfort, though they suffer more body lean than expected. Braking is terrific.

With automatic, the 4-cylinder gas engine furnishes only modest acceleration for passing. A manual-shift Jetta GL took 10.8 seconds to reach 60 mph. V6 models have authoritative acceleration and spirited passing response, though the automatic transmission is reluctant to downshift at moderate speeds. A 5-speed GTI GLX did 0-60 in 7.6 seconds and averaged 23.5 mpg. Jettas with V6/automatic returned 18.9 to 21.6 mpg, and a Golf GL 4-cylinder with 5-speed got a pleasing 25 mpg. Even with automatic, a turbo Jetta 1.8T accelerated 0-60 mph in 8.9 seconds and averaged 26.1 mpg. TDI models are surprisingly sprightly around town and get terrific mileage. A 5-speed TDI Golf averaged 41.5 mpg. Noise levels are among the lowest in the class. All engines are quiet, though the TDIs are somewhat noisier at high speeds. Interior materials and workmanship excel. Front head and leg room are exceptional. Rear seats are more subcompact-snug. Modest leg room shrinks quickly as front seats move back, though Golfs feel more spacious, thanks to their straight-back roofline. No body style is wide enough for three adults. All seats are comfortably firm. Height-adjustable front buckets are supportive on long trips. Gauges and switches are simple, logically arranged, and nicely backlit. Low audio and climate controls are tricky to adjust while driving. Rear access in 2-door Golfs far surpasses most coupes. Narrow doors make rear entry/exit a squeeze in Jettas and 4-door Golfs. Jettas have large trunks, and all have folding rear seatbacks.

VALUE FOR THE MONEY: Though priced at the top of the subcompact class when new, even base models had plenty of features as well as solid build quality. No competitor offers a V6, and few provide as much driving satisfaction.

TROUBLE SPOTS

Audio system: The door speakers may rattle due to loose rivets or wiring harness contacting the speakers. Requires new fasteners and rerouting wires. (1999)

Clutch: Due to the return spring falling out of position, the clutch pedal may not fully return and the cruise may not disengage. (1999)

Engine noise: Due to the throttle cable contacting the engine cover, the throttle pedal vibrates and there is a rapping noise under the hood. (1999-2000)

Vehicle noise: A humming noise when cornering may be coming from the differential. Draining the automatic-transmission fluid and replacing it with synthetic may help. (1999)

AVERAGE REPLACEMENT COSTS

A/C Compressor	$495	CV Joints	$1,370
Alternator	360	Exhaust System	370
Automatic Trans.	1,100	Radiator	405
Brakes	360	Shocks and/or Struts	490
Clutch	470	Timing Chain/Belt	280

NHTSA RECALL HISTORY

1999 Jetta: If the vehicle is driven with a rear flat tire, the fuel-tank filler neck can wear, causing a fuel leak and possible fire. **1999 Jetta:** Some vehicles do not comply with head-injury criterion requirements. **1999:** Sound-absorbing mat attached to inside of B-pillar side-trim panel could ignite when exposed to exhaust gas of seatbelt pretensioner, if it's triggered during a crash. **2000-01 Golf:** Front-suspension control arm could gradually loosen and ultimately separate from its bracket in normal driving. **2001-02:** ABS Electrical Control Unit can short circuit, causing a fire.

PRICES

	Good	Average	Poor
1999 Golf	$6,500-8,500	$5,700-7,500	$2,900-3,800
Golf GTI	8,500-10,500	7,700-9,500	4,400-5,500
Jetta	8,000-11,000	7,200-9,900	4,100-5,600
Jetta GLX	11,000-12,000	9,900-10,800	5,900-6,500
2000 Golf	7,600-10,000	6,800-9,000	3,800-5,000
Golf GTI	9,800-10,800	8,800-10,800	5,100-6,200
Jetta	9,000-12,000	8,100-10,800	4,700-6,200
Jetta GLX	13,000-14,500	11,800-13,200	7,500-8,400
2001 Golf	9,000-11,500	8,100-10,400	4,700-6,000
Golf GTI	12,000-14,000	10,800-12,600	6,700-7,800
Jetta	10,400-14,500	9,400-13,100	5,500-7,700
Jetta GLX	15,000-16,500	13,700-15,000	9,500-10,400
2002 Golf	10,500-13,000	9,500-11,700	5,600-6,900
Golf GTI	14,000-16,000	12,700-14,600	8,500-9,800
Jetta	12,500-17,000	11,300-15,300	7,100-9,700
Jetta GLX	17,000-18,500	15,600-17,000	10,900-11,800
2003 Golf	13,000-16,200	11,800-14,700	7,500-9,400
Golf GTI	16,200-18,500	14,700-16,800	10,400-11,800
Jetta	14,800-19,000	13,500-17,300	9,300-12,000
Jetta GLX	19,500-22,500	17,900-20,700	12,700-14,600

For detailed information on this vehicle visit
http://used.consumerguide.com and enter code **2404**

1998-03 VOLKSWAGEN NEW BEETLE

CG BEST BUY

CLASS: Sporty coupe
BUILT IN: Mexico
PROS: Acceleration (Turbo) • Standard antilock brakes • Build quality • Fuel economy • Side airbags
CONS: Rear-seat room • Visibility

EVALUATION: The smooth-running base gas engine feels peppy with manual transmission, though it's short on power at speeds above 60 mph with either gearbox. VW's turbodiesel has no problem keeping up with traffic, but its passing power does not match that of the gas engine—and being

VOLKSWAGEN

a diesel, it suffers more vibration and noise. Although the turbocharged gasoline engine suffers a delay in power delivery below 3000 rpm, it accelerates strongly after that. The Turbo S, introduced in 2002, is faster than other Beetles—7.4 sec 0-60 in our test—but it further exaggerates the turbo-lag problem. The automatic transmission on one test car was slow to engage after being shifted from Park, but generally changed up and down smoothly and promptly. Our 2.0-liter test cars averaged 26.4 mpg with manual shift, 21.1 mpg with automatic. A GLS Turbo with automatic returned 22.7 mpg, while a stick-shift diesel got a super-frugal 42.1 mpg.

Thanks in part to unusual-for-the-class 16-inch tires, the ride is comfortable but firm, soaking up most bumps with ease. Steering and handling are a notch above the class norm, but the slab-sided New Beetle gets jostled by crosswinds. Braking is strong and sure. Above 70 mph, passengers have to raise their voices to carry on a conversation, though automatic-transmission models are somewhat quieter on the highway, due to their gearing.

Interiors brim with high-grade materials and expensive-looking touches, though it takes a few tries to become familiar with the unorthodox radio buttons. Power accessory switches mounted flat on the door panels are awkward to reach. Front seats are comfortable and supportive, and few cars of any size offer as much front head and leg room. In back, leg room is tight if the front seats are more than halfway back. More serious, passengers over 5-foot-6 will find their heads against the inner hatch lid. Front roof pillars are thick at their bases. Also, outside mirrors are mounted unusually high, cutting the driver's vision of some traffic. Interior storage space is skimpy. Luggage room under the rear hatch is modest, but the rear seats fold nearly flat to conveniently expand the cargo area. Paint quality and fit-and-finish have been excellent. Bodies have been solid and rattle-free on New Beetles tested.

VALUE FOR THE MONEY: As sport coupes go, this one is actually quite practical. The New Beetle's driving and emotional appeal are strong enough too, to overcome its skimpy rear seat and visibility blind spots. New Beetles were in short supply and shockingly high demand at first, but that began to taper off somewhat, so more are likely to be available on used-car lots.

TROUBLE SPOTS

Audio system: Poor AM radio reception when switches (brake, lights, locks, etc.) are operated is usually due to the radio-antenna cable being routed too close to the wiring harness. (1998-99)

Tire wear: To reduce tire wear and improve handling, the rear-wheel alignment specifications have been revised. (1998-2000)

Vehicle noise: The dashboard may whistle at speeds over 45 mph because of poor sealing of the HVAC plenum. (1998-99)

Vehicle noise: The speakers in the doors may rattle due to loose rivets. (1998-99)

AVERAGE REPLACEMENT COSTS

A/C Compressor	$630	CV Joints	$535
Alternator	455	Exhaust System	590
Automatic Trans.	1,005	Radiator	335
Brakes	370	Shocks and/or Struts	620
Clutch	570	Timing Chain/Belt	160

NHTSA RECALL HISTORY

1998-01: The brake-lamp switch may malfunction. Dealer will inspect and replace all affected parts. **2001-02:** ABS Electrical Control Unit can short circuit, causing a fire.

PRICES

	Good	Average	Poor
1998 New Beetle	$6,500-7,500	$5,700-6,600	$2,900-3,400
1999 New Beetle	7,500-8,800	6,800-7,900	3,800-4,400
New Beetle GLX	9,000-10,000	8,100-9,000	4,700-5,200
2000 New Beetle	8,700-10,500	7,800-9,500	4,500-5,500
New Beetle GLX	10,500-12,000	9,500-10,800	5,600-6,400
2001 New Beetle	10,000-12,000	9,000-10,800	5,200-6,200
New Beetle GLX	12,000-14,000	10,800-12,600	6,700-7,800
2002 New Beetle	11,700-14,700	10,500-13,200	6,400-8,100
New Beetle GLX	14,500-16,000	13,200-14,600	9,000-9,900
New Beetle Turbo S	15,200-16,500	13,800-15,000	9,600-10,400
2003 Beetle convertible	14,000-16,500	12,700-15,000	8,500-10,100
GLS 1.8T, GLX conv.	20,000-22,500	18,400-20,700	13,000-14,600
New Beetle	13,800-17,200	12,600-15,700	8,300-10,300
New Beetle GLX	17,000-19,000	15,600-17,500	10,900-12,200
New Beetle Turbo S	18,000-20,000	16,600-18,400	11,500-12,800

For detailed information on this vehicle visit
http://used.consumerguide.com and enter code **2321**

1995-97 VOLKSWAGEN PASSAT

CLASS: Midsize car
BUILT IN: Germany
PROS: Antilock brakes
• Fuel economy (TDI)
• Traction control (GLX)
• Passenger and cargo room
• Steering/handling
CONS: No glovebox
• Ride (GLX)

EVALUATION: Though not as strong or smooth as the engine in a Toyota Camry or Nissan Maxima, Passat's V6 delivers more than adequate power over a broad range of speeds. The manual shift's clutch and gearshift work smoothly. Passat's 4-speed automatic transmission does its job unobtrusively and downshifts promptly for passing. Naturally, the 4-cylinder GLS is slower in both standing-start acceleration and highway passing, but still adequate. For a real eye-opener, take a spin in the diesel-powered TDI edition. Our long-term test of a TDI revealed adequate power and a relatively high degree of refinement. You also get outstanding fuel economy. We've averaged 37.7 mpg, hitting 45 mpg during highway trips.

A softened suspension and stiffened body structure in this generation yield improved ride quality. A Passat GLX still offers sporty handling, but absorbs bumps with less harshness. The TDI's suspension is softer yet, thus trading some handling prowess for greater composure over bumps.

Controls for the radio and climate system are high in the center of the dashboard, easy to see and reach. The climate system is controlled by three clearly marked rotary knobs. Oddly, too, switches for front power windows are on door armrests, while those for rear windows are on the dashboard—a Volkswagen quirk. Because of the passenger-airbag mounting position, no glovebox is installed. Interior storage is nevertheless adequate.

Despite the Passat's compact 103.3-inch wheelbase, its interior is exceptionally roomy—especially in back, with ample leg room and enough head space for 6-footers. Both body styles have a split folding rear seat. The sedan has a large trunk, with a flat floor and bumper-height opening for easy loading/unloading. Wagons have a flat, wide cargo area that provides generous luggage space.

VALUE FOR THE MONEY: Roomy, sporty, well-equipped: All told, this is an interesting and competent alternative to Japanese-brand sedans.

TROUBLE SPOTS

Air conditioner: Models equipped with a variable-displacement A/C compressor may not cool properly due to restrictions in the system. (1995-96)

Automatic transmission: Automatic transmission may shift erratically due to an incorrect throttle angle setting. (1995-96)

Coolant leak: A low-coolant-level malfunction can be the result of the wrong concentration of antifreeze or a bad coolant sensor. (1995-96)

Manual transmission: The manual-transmission shift lever may knock or vibrate in forward gears requiring realignment of the selector shaft housing. (1995-96)

Wipers: The windshield wipers may chatter because of misalignment of the wiper arms. (1996)

AVERAGE REPLACEMENT COSTS

A/C Compressor	$620	CV Joints	$1,320
Alternator	640	Exhaust System	440
Automatic Trans.	795	Radiator	485
Brakes	390	Shocks and/or Struts	680
Clutch	585	Timing Chain/Belt	360

NHTSA RECALL HISTORY

1995 w/VR6 engine: Radiator-fan-motor shaft could wear, become noisy and seize, rendering fan motor inoperative and eventually causing engine to overheat and stall. **1996:** The ignition switch can fail causing the headlights and windshield wipers to become inoperative.

PRICES

	Good	Average	Poor
1995 Passat GLS	$3,300-4,100	$2,600-3,200	$800-1,000
Passat GLX	4,200-5,200	3,400-4,300	1,400-1,700
1996 Passat GLS	4,000-4,800	3,300-3,900	1,300-1,500
Passat TDI, GLX	4,800-6,000	4,000-5,000	1,800-2,300
1997 Passat	5,500-7,000	4,700-6,000	2,300-2,900

For detailed information on this vehicle visit
http://used.consumerguide.com and enter code **2246**

1998-03 VOLKSWAGEN PASSAT

CG BEST BUY

CLASS: Midsize car
BUILT IN: Germany
PROS: Standard antilock braking • Build quality • Cargo room • Side airbags • Passenger room • Ride
CONS: Acceleration (Turbo w/automatic) • Tire noise

EVALUATION: Passat's suspension smothers all but the worst bumps and dips, and a tangibly solid structure only adds to the sense of comfort. Braking is swift and undramatic from most any speed. Wind noise is low.

Turbo models are quiet enough and generally free of turbo-lag hesitation, but with automatic transmission, it just does not have the brawn for quick get-aways and easy high-gear climbing up long, steep grades. The Tiptronic's man-ual-shift capability helps somewhat, but the GLS Passat feels transformed with the standard 5-speed manual transmission, becoming lively, eager, and gen-uinely sporty. A Passat with Tiptronic averaged 22.2 mpg, but premium fuel is recommend. Near 2-ton W8 did 7.2 sec in our 0-60 mph runs vs. VW's claimed 6.5, but had ample midrange punch. It averaged 16.2 mpg. We'd recommend the V6 or W8 engine if you're not an ardent fan of manual transmissions.

Passat's ace in the hole has always been generous interior room, and the new one continues that tradition. Expect spacious comfort for four adults (even five on short hops), plus an almost cavernous trunk and easy entry/exit. Six-footers have only about a half-inch of head clearance beneath the available moonroof, but leg room is plentiful all around.

Combining readable gauges and simple controls, the dashboard also is Audi-like, except for simpler climate controls and different—but still very legible—gauges. Visibility is fine except to the rear, where the styling hides the car's cor-ners. Like Audi's A4, Passat feels impressively stout, even on the worst roads. Overall fit and finish are equally satisfying, but interior decor looks a bit drab. Nothing feels low-budget, however, and the GLS V6 and GLX flaunt real wood trim. Materials and workmanship rival those of more costly automobiles.

VALUE FOR THE MONEY: Turbo fours with automatic don't have much strength for a modern family 4 door. If possible, try the different engine/trans-mission combinations to see which one fits your needs. Otherwise, VW's largest car is suave, sporty, spacious, and solid. It's also strong on features per dollar and "European" personality. We'd give it a good long look.

TROUBLE SPOTS

Vehicle noise: The speakers in the doors may rattle due to loose rivets. (1998-99)
Windows: The windows suffer from stress cracks and distortion. (1999-2000)

AVERAGE REPLACEMENT COSTS

A/C Compressor	$595	CV Joints	$1,320
Alternator	640	Exhaust System	595
Automatic Trans.	790	Radiator	560
Brakes	390	Shocks and/or Struts	670
Clutch	585	Timing Chain/Belt	430

NHTSA RECALL HISTORY

1998: If engine backfires during cold-start, an air screen loosely seated in air-flow meter can become damaged; screen pieces could enter intake system and prevent the throttle plate from returning to its full idle position. **1998-00:** If the rear tire goes flat and the vehicle is driven too long afterwards, the fuel-tank filler neck can wear, causing a fuel leak and possible fire. **1998-99 w/automatic transmission:** Control valve may not open or close fully at temperatures below -4 degrees (F) under certain conditions, causing insufficient vacuum for the brake booster. **1998-99:** Some tie-rod seals may not seal properly; if moisture and/or dust particles enter the swivel bearing mechanism, the bearing could wear over time, diminishing steering control. **2000-01:** Sulfur in fuel could cause fuel gauge to read "full" when the tank is actually less than full.

PRICES

	Good	Average	Poor
1998 Passat 4-cylinder	$7,500-8,500	$6,800-7,700	$3,800-4,300
Passat V6	8,300-9,800	7,500-8,800	4,300-5,100
1999 Passat 4-cylinder	9,500-10,600	8,600-9,500	4,900-5,500
Passat V6	10,800-12,800	9,700-11,500	5,800-6,900
2000 Passat 4-cylinder	12,000-13,400	10,800-12,100	6,700-7,500
Passat V6	13,000-15,800	11,800-14,400	7,500-9,200
Passat V6 AWD	14,200-17,200	12,900-15,700	8,700-10,500
2001 Passat 4-cylinder	14,000-15,200	12,700-13,800	8,500-9,300
Passat V6	15,500-18,500	14,100-16,800	9,900-11,800
Passat V6 AWD	17,000-20,000	15,600-18,400	10,900-12,800
2002 Passat 4-cylinder	16,500-18,000	15,000-16,400	10,600-11,500
Passat V6	18,200-22,000	16,700-20,200	11,600-14,100
Passat V6 AWD	19,700-23,000	18,100-21,200	12,800-15,000
Passat W8	26,000-29,000	24,200-27,000	17,200-19,100
2003 Passat 4-cylinder	19,200-21,500	17,700-19,800	12,500-14,000
Passat V6	21,200-25,000	19,500-23,000	13,800-16,300
Passat V6 AWD	23,500-27,500	21,600-25,300	15,300-17,900
Passat W8	32,000-35,000	29,800-32,600	22,400-24,500

For detailed information on this vehicle visit
http://used.consumerguide.com and enter code 2322

2001-03 VOLVO S60

CLASS: Near-luxury car
BUILT IN: Sweden
PROS: Available AWD
• Front-seat comfort
CONS: Navigation-system controls • Rear visibility

EVALUATION: Solid and substantial, Volvo's stylish sedans perform pleasantly. All S60s hesitate somewhat off the line, but pick up speed impressively enough—especially the turbos. With manual shift, a T5 accelerated to 60 mph in 7.3 seconds, but manual-gearbox action feels crude. Turbo engines' throttle lag leaves you short of power at times, and mild "torque-steer" wander occurs on front-drive models in hard takeoffs.

An early 2.4T AWD model did 0-60 mph in 7.9 seconds. Volvo's AWD system is unique, in that it locates the power-transfer coupling for the rear wheels at the back of the car. Operating as smoothly as more conventional systems, it helps maintain outstanding grip on slippery surfaces.

A 2.4T averaged 21.7 mpg, while manual-shift T5s managed 21.5 mpg in a city/highway mix and 17.9 mpg with performance tests. Gas mileage with a 2.4 T AWD sedan averaged 23.5 mpg. Volvo recommends premium fuel for the turbo engines.

Structures are satisfyingly solid, but suspensions allow minor road imperfections to be felt more than in most class rivals. That's especially true in the T5, with its extra-firm damping and thumpy low-profile performance tires.

Road manners are confident in all models, with sharp steering, modest body lean, and good grip. The 2.4T AWD feels more secure than a front-drive 2.4T, and more supple than the T5. The T5 tries hard, but cannot match the moves of rear-drive sport sedans. Brakes are strong and easily modulated, though some drivers consider them touchy in urban driving.

Engines are muted at modest rpm, but these inline fives are never as smooth as rivals' V6s. The T5 grows awfully throaty at full throttle. Wind noise and tire slap are high for this class.

Gauges are well-marked, logical, and nicely lit. On the downside, the radio's 20 station presets are selected by scrolling with a single rotary dial rather than by individual buttons—a feature not everyone cares for. The dashboard-top navigation screen is difficult to read in daylight, and the system's controls are on the steering wheel, inaccessible to the passenger. Interior decor is stylish and modern, but some budget-grade plastic panels fall short of Audi/Lexus quality.

Comfortable, supportive front seats are wider and softer than the European norm. Leg and head room are outstanding. Rearward visibility is restricted by a high parcel shelf, bulky headrests, and sloped roofline.

The nicely shaped rear seat is comfortable for two medium-sized adults, but leg room is very tight if front seats are set more than halfway back. The wide, deep trunk isn't too tall and has a smallish opening. Cabin storage is adequate.

VALUE FOR THE MONEY: Arguably the most stylish Volvo ever, the S60 is the best-handling Volvo sedan yet. Even so, compromises in rear-seat room, ride quality, and powertrain smoothness are hard to overlook in the hotly contested near-luxury class. The all-season 2.4T AWD is an asset to this line, but not enough to threaten the Acura TL and Lexus ES 300 for overall value.

TROUBLE SPOTS

Clutch: On Turbo models, the clutch pedal may vibrate due to the hydraulic fluid transmitting pressures. A new hydraulic line with a loop that absorbs the shocks is available. (2001-02)

Oil leak: Oil may leak from the differential vent. There is a replacement vent valve available. (2001)

VOLVO

AVERAGE REPLACEMENT COSTS

A/C Compressor	$770	CV Joints	$1,235
Alternator	640	Exhaust System	895
Automatic Trans.	1,710	Radiator	650
Brakes	445	Shocks and/or Struts	1,320
Clutch	725	Timing Chain/Belt	415

NHTSA RECALL HISTORY

2001-03 S60: On certain passenger cars, the second ISOFIX guide was not installed and, in certain cases, the owner's manual ISOFIX information is incorrect.

PRICES

	Good	Average	Poor
2001 S60	$16,500-18,500	$15,000-16,800	$10,600-11,800
S60 T5	20,000-22,000	18,400-20,200	13,000-14,300
2002 S60	20,000-22,500	18,400-20,700	13,000-14,600
S60 AWD	23,500-25,000	21,600-23,000	15,300-16,300
S60 T5	24,000-26,000	22,300-24,200	15,600-16,900
2003 S60	24,000-27,500	22,300-25,600	15,600-17,900
S60 AWD	27,500-30,000	25,600-27,900	18,400-20,100
S60 R	32,000-34,000	29,800-31,600	22,400-23,800
S60 T5	28,500-31,000	26,500-28,800	19,400-21,100

For detailed information on this vehicle visit
http://used.consumerguide.com and enter code **4492**

1998-00 VOLVO S70/V70

CLASS: Near-luxury car
BUILT IN: Canada, Sweden, Belgium
PROS: Acceleration (turbo models) • Standard antilock brakes • Side airbags • Steering/handling

CONS: Ride (T5, R models) • Road noise

EVALUATION: Acceleration with the base engine is adequate. However, things pick up considerably in the turbocharged models. Their passing punch is outstanding, but "turbo lag" (a momentary delay in power delivery) is evident at low speeds. The turbo engines are well-suited to the automatic transmission, which shifts smoothly and downshifts promptly. Fuel economy has been better than expected. A T5 sedan returned 20.3 mpg, whereas an AWD wagon averaged 18.4 mpg. While those numbers aren't outstanding, they are very good for the near-luxury class. Wind noise is subdued, but the engines are vocal in hard acceleration and road noise can be prominent. All S/V70s handle well. Body lean is minimal, and the tires grip securely in turns. Ride quality varies greatly, depending on the model. Base and GLT models ride smoothly over broken pavement and skim over highway expansion joints. However, the T5 and R models have a stiffer suspension and tires, and thus ride harshly on rough pavement. The

AWD provides terrific traction in all conditions, without requiring any special effort from the driver. Standard antilock brakes have good stopping power.

Climate and radio controls are easier to use than in the past. Also, the switches for power windows and door locks are conveniently located on the door armrests instead of the center console. However, some other controls are hidden behind the steering wheel. Front and rear passenger room changed only slightly, compared to the 850, with the biggest additions coming in rear leg room. That translates into ample space for front-seat occupants, and adequate room for two passengers in back.

At 15.1 cubic feet for the sedan, cargo space is more than adequate. The sedan also has a 60/40 split folding rear seat, which expands cargo capacity. Wagons have a generous cargo hold, made more versatile by standard folding rear seat-backs. Visibility is excellent to all directions, thanks to large side and rear windows.

VALUE FOR THE MONEY: S70/V70 models have been competitively priced against other near-luxury sedans, such as the Cadillac Catera and Infiniti I30. They offer a wagon and AWD choices that the others ignore. GLT versions, with their strong turbo engine, are the best all-around values in this line of younger-feeling Volvos.

TROUBLE SPOTS

Dashboard lights: If liquids leak into the center console it can short the mode switch which illuminates the check-engine light. (2000)
Fuel economy: Due to contamination entering via the reference tub, oxygen sensors may fail prematurely. (1998)
Headlights: There were campaigns to replace the headlight-wiring assembly (with built-in resistor), headlight bulbs, and headlight-wiper stop lug. Turn-signal-bulb sockets are also covered because of poor contact with bulbs. (1998-2000)
Oil consumption: The screen in the oil filler can come loose inside the filler neck and often would've been replaced when the vehicle was in for other services. (2000)
Trunk latch: On some vehicles, the tailgate-latch mechanism that fails in cold weather. (2000)
Vehicle noise: Whining noise below 60 mph requires a damper on the four-wheel-drive viscous coupling. (2000)

AVERAGE REPLACEMENT COSTS

A/C Compressor	$575	CV Joints	$1,150
Alternator	410	Exhaust System	455
Automatic Trans.	920	Radiator	475
Brakes	310	Shocks and/or Struts	1,400
Clutch	650	Timing Chain/Belt	415

NHTSA RECALL HISTORY

1998: Front-passenger airbag may be overly sensitive to certain electrostatic discharges; could possibly cause inadvertent deployment. **1998:** Operation of headlight switch over extended period of time can result in inconsistent operation. **1999 S70:** Fuel-filter bracket configuration margins on some cars are insufficient; in the event of a crash, fuel leakage could occur. **2000:** Front turn signal may not operate as desired because there is inadequate contact between the bulb and the socket.

VOLVO

PRICES	Good	Average	Poor
1998 AWD, XC, R	$12,000-15,000	$10,800-13,500	$6,700-8,400
S/V 70 T5	10,500-12,500	9,500-11,300	5,600-6,600
S/V70, GLT	7,500-11,000	6,800-9,900	3,800-5,500
1999 S/V70 T5, AWD	13,000-14,700	11,800-13,400	7,500-8,500
S/V70, GLT	10,500-13,500	9,500-12,200	5,600-7,200
XC, R	15,500-18,500	14,100-16,800	9,900-11,800
2000 S/V70, GLT	13,500-16,700	12,300-15,200	8,000-9,900
T5, AWD, XC, R	16,500-22,000	15,000-20,000	10,600-14,100

> For detailed information on this vehicle visit
> http://used.consumerguide.com and enter code **2320**

1999-03 VOLVO S80

CLASS: Luxury car
BUILT IN: Sweden
PROS: Acceleration (T6)
• Build quality • Passenger
and cargo room
CONS: Navigation-system
controls • Rear visibility

EVALUATION: In base trim, the S80 has only adequate power, whereas the turbocharged T6 is downright stirring—quick by nearly any standard. Fuel economy is reasonably good, too. A base S80 averaged 19.2 mpg, while a T6 turned in a 20.7-mpg average. Shift action is smooth. Both versions offer sure-footed handling. Steering seems firm and precise, but some drivers might consider it numb or overassisted. Stable on the road, base sedans easily absorb bumps that register sharply in the stiffer-suspended T6. Best to try the T6 on a variety of surfaces, to make sure ride comfort is acceptable. Doors open wide for easy entry/exit and the S80 provides generous room, front and rear. The dashboard layout is clean and modern, but the radio's station-memory function uses a dial instead of buttons and is a chore to preset.

When activated, the optional navigation system's map screen rises from the middle of the upper dashboard. It's near eye level, and controls are on the steering wheel rather than on the dashboard. But like many such systems, this one demands study and patience to program and operate. In addition, the screen can be hard to see, especially in bright sunlight.

Rearward visibility isn't the greatest, for a full-size automobile. In addition, the S80's large trunk is tempered by its small opening.

VALUE FOR THE MONEY: A serious contender among luxury-class sedans, the S80 earns high marks for refinement, ergonomics, and trunk space. Volvo managed to pack a lot of safety and convenience features into its stylish, functional sedan. Fun to drive, the S80 is roomier than the rival BMW 5-Series, but handling and performance in the base 2.9 model are underwhelming.

TROUBLE SPOTS

Ball joints: Ball joints wear prematurely and should be replaced regardless of time or mileage. (1999-2000)

Oil consumption: The screen in the oil filler can get loose inside the filler neck and often would've been replaced when the vehicle was in for other services. (2000)

Poor transmission shift: On less than 10,000 vehicles, the transmission was receiving an announced software upgrade (2000-01) and those with a GM (model 4T65) transmission needed a replacement shift solenoid to correct a shudder between 2nd and 3rd gear. (1999-2000)

Vehicle noise: Whining noise below 60 mph requires a damper on the four-wheel-drive viscous coupling. (2000)

AVERAGE REPLACEMENT COSTS

A/C Compressor	$615	CV Joints	$740
Alternator	310	Exhaust System	380
Automatic Trans.	1,340	Radiator	350
Brakes	750	Shocks and/or Struts	450
Clutch	850	Timing Chain/Belt	245

NHTSA RECALL HISTORY

1999: Some electric cooling fans could be inadequate, allowing components to overheat and even melt. **1999-00:** The ball joint between the front wheel-king pin and the suspension link arm could be loose. **2001:** Rear-outboard seatbelt-anchorage bolts may be loose, leaving occupants improperly restrained in crash.

PRICES

	Good	Average	Poor
1999 S80 2.9	$13,500-15,000	$12,300-13,700	$8,000-8,900
S80 T6	15,500-17,000	14,100-15,500	9,900-10,900
2000 S80 2.9	16,000-17,500	14,600-15,900	10,200-11,200
S80 T6	18,500-20,000	17,000-18,400	11,800-12,800
2001 S80 2.9	20,000-21,500	18,400-19,800	13,000-14,000
S80 T6, Executive	22,500-24,500	20,700-22,500	14,600-15,900
2002 S80 2.9	24,000-26,000	22,300-24,200	15,600-16,900
S80 T6, Executive	26,500-28,500	24,600-26,500	17,500-18,800
2003 S80 2.9	29,000-31,000	27,000-28,800	20,000-21,400
S80 T6, Elite	32,000-37,000	29,800-34,400	22,400-25,900

For detailed information on this vehicle visit
http://used.consumerguide.com and enter code **2470**

2001-03 VOLVO V70/XC

CLASS: Near-luxury car
BUILT IN: Sweden
PROS: Acceleration (T5)
• Cargo room • Interior materials
CONS: Fuel economy (T5)
• Ride control (T5)

EVALUATION: For everyday use, Volvo's 2.4T wagon is a good choice. The XC ranks as a sensible SUV alternative, but the T5 tends to ride too stiffly for the unexceptional handling it provides. Acceleration is good once the turbocharger has an opportunity to begin delivering its boost. A test T5 wagon

VOLVO

accelerated to 60 mph in a respectable 8 seconds. Both engines suffer occasional turbo lag, but using manual-shift buttons with the Geartronic automatic transmission minimizes that lag somewhat. Engine aside, the automatic transmission is generally smooth and responsive. Both engines require premium gasoline. As for economy, a T5 averaged 16.5 mpg while an XC managed 18.7 mpg. Road manners are responsive, but unremarkable. All told, the 2.4T wagon provides the best ride/handling balance. All models offer good grip and steering that's satisfyingly weighty and precise. With 8.2 inches of ground clearance, the Cross Country wagon has more body lean in turns than its mates, but substantially less than any true SUV. Most pavement flaws will be felt by occupants, but only large, sharp bumps register harshly. Braking is terrific, but tire drone is noticeable on most surfaces. Inside, these wagons look and feel much like the S80 "flagship" sedan. Volvo's navigation system is hard to read in some light conditions. Visibility is generally, though rear headrests interfere. Back-seat foot space is decent, but cushions are too short for best thigh support. Cargo space is ample.

VALUE FOR THE MONEY: Roomy and contemporary, solid and versatile, Volvo's latest wagons are the best ones yet. The XC furnishes appealing all-weather security and delivers some SUV-style attributes.

TROUBLE SPOTS

Dashboard lights: If liquids leak into the center console it can short the mode switch which illuminates the check-engine light. (2000-01)

AVERAGE REPLACEMENT COSTS

A/C Compressor	$615	CV Joints	$1,410
Alternator	310	Exhaust System	410
Automatic Trans.	1,340	Radiator	345
Brakes	750	Shocks and/or Struts	450
Clutch	850	Timing Chain/Belt	245

NHTSA RECALL HISTORY

2001: Rear-outboard seatbelt-anchorage bolts may be loose, leaving occupants improperly restrained in crash. **2001:** The bolted joint that is part of the child-restraint hardware may have been incorrectly tightened, leaving occupant improperly restrained in a crash.

PRICES

	Good	Average	Poor
2001 V70 2.4, 2.4T	$20,000-22,000	$18,400-20,200	$13,000-14,300
V70 T5	22,500-24,000	20,700-22,100	14,600-15,600
V70 XC	23,000-24,500	21,200-22,500	15,000-15,900
2002 V70 2.4, 2.4T	23,000-26,000	21,200-23,900	15,000-16,900
V70 T5	25,500-27,500	23,700-25,600	16,600-17,900
V70 XC	26,000-28,000	24,200-26,000	17,200-18,500
2003 V70 2.4, 2.4T	26,000-29,500	24,200-27,400	17,200-19,500
V70 T5	29,000-31,000	27,000-28,800	20,000-21,400
V70 XC	29,500-31,500	27,400-29,300	20,400-21,700

For detailed information on this vehicle visit
http://used.consumerguide.com and enter code **2471**